한국의 토익 수험자 여러분께,

토익 시험은 세계적인 직무 영어능력 평가 시험으로, 지난 40여 년간 비즈니스 현장에서 필요한 영어능력 평가의 기준을 제시해 왔습니다. 토익 시험 및 토익스피킹, 토익라이팅 시험은 세계에서 가장 널리 통용되는 영어능력 검증 시험으로, 160여 개국 14,000여 기관이 토익 성적을 의사결정에 활용하고 있습니다.

YBM은 한국의 토익 시험을 주관하는 ETS 독점 계약사입니다.

ETS는 한국 수험자들의 효과적인 토익 학습을 돕고자 YBM을 통하여 'ETS 토익 공식 교재'를 독점 출간하고 있습니다. 또한 'ETS 토익 공식 교재' 시리즈에 기출문항을 제공해 한국의 다른 교재들에 수록된 기출을 복제하거나 변형한 문항으로 인하여 발생할 수 있는 수험자들의 혼동을 방지하고 있습니다.

복제 및 변형 문항들은 토익 시험의 출제의도를 벗어날 수 있기 때문에 기출문항을 수록한 'ETS 토익 공식 교재'만큼 시험에 잘 대비할 수 없습니다.

'ETS 토익 공식 교재'를 통하여 수험자 여러분의 영어 소통을 위한 노력에 큰 성취가 있기를 바랍니다.

감사합니다.

Dear TOEIC Test Takers in Korea,

The TOEIC program is the global leader in English-language assessment for the workplace. It has set the standard for assessing English-language skills needed in the workplace for more than 40 years. The TOEIC tests are the most widely used English language assessments around the world, with 14,000+ organizations across more than 160 countries trusting TOEIC scores to make decisions.

YBM is the ETS Country Master Distributor for the TOEIC program in Korea and so is the exclusive distributor for TOEIC Korea.

To support effective learning for TOEIC test-takers in Korea, ETS has authorized YBM to publish the only Official TOEIC prep books in Korea. These books contain actual TOEIC items to help prevent confusion among Korean test-takers that might be caused by other prep book publishers' use of reproduced or paraphrased items.

Reproduced or paraphrased items may fail to reflect the intent of actual TOEIC items and so will not prepare test-takers as well as the actual items contained in the ETS TOEIC Official prep books published by YBM.

We hope that these ETS TOEIC Official prep books enable you, as test-takers, to achieve great success in your efforts to communicate effectively in English.

Thank you.

입문부터 실전까지 수준별 학습을 통해 최단기 목표점수 달성!

ETS TOEIC® 공식수험서 스마트 학습 지원

www.ybmbooks.com에서도 무료 MP3를 다운로드 받을 수 있습니다.

ETS 토익 모바일 학습 플랫폼!
ETS 토익기출 수험서 앱

구글플레이 앱스토어

교재 학습 지원
- LC 음원 MP3
- 교재 해설 동영상 강의
- 교재/부록 모의고사 채점 분석
- 단어 암기장

부가 서비스
- 데일리 학습(토익 기출문제 풀이)
- 토익 최신 경향 무료 특강
- 토익 타이머

모의고사 결과 분석
- 파트별/문항별 정답률
- 파트별/유형별 취약점 리포트
- 전체 응시자 점수 분포도

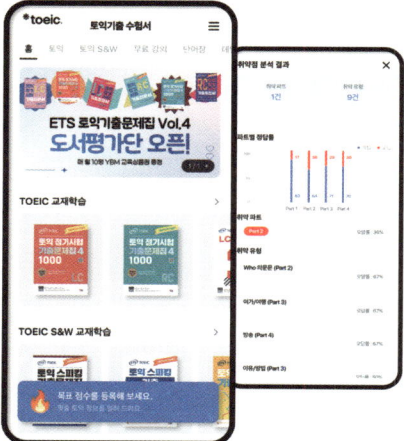

ETS 토익 학습 전용 온라인 커뮤니티!
ETS TOEIC® Book 공식카페

etstoeicbook.co.kr

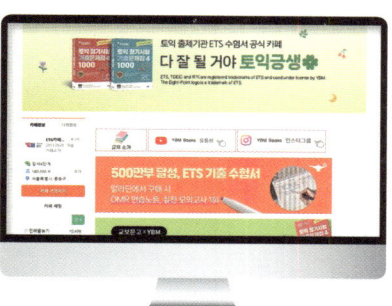

강사진의 학습 지원   토익 대표강사들의 학습 지원과 멘토링

교재 학습관 운영   교재별 학습게시판을 통해 무료 동영상 강의 등 학습 지원

학습 콘텐츠 제공   토익 학습 콘텐츠와 정기시험 예비특강 업데이트

*toeic®

ETS 토익® 정기시험
기출문제집 5
1000 RC

발행인	허문호
발행처	YBM

편집	이태경, 김혜윤, 이진열
디자인	김현경
마케팅	고영노, 김동진, 박찬경, 하재희, 문근호, 고은

초판발행	2025년 12월 15일
2쇄 발행	2025년 12월 26일

신고일자	1964년 3월 28일
신고번호	제 1964-000003호
주소	서울시 종로구 종로 104
전화	(02) 2000-0515 [구입문의] / (02) 2000-0388 [내용문의]
팩스	(02) 2285-1523
홈페이지	www.ybmbooks.com

ISBN	978-89-17-24380-2

ETS, TOEIC and 토익 are registered trademarks of Educational Testing Service, Princeton, New Jersey, U.S.A., used in the Republic of Korea under license. Copyright © 2025 by Educational Testing Service, Princeton, New Jersey, U.S.A. All rights reserved. Reproduced under license for limited use by YBM. These materials are protected by United States Laws, International Copyright Laws and International Treaties. In the event of any discrepancy between this translation and official ETS materials, the terms of the official ETS materials will prevail. All items were created or reviewed by ETS. All item annotations and test-taking tips were reviewed by ETS.

서면에 의한 저자와 출판사의 허락 없이 내용의 일부 혹은 전부를 인용 및 복제하거나 발췌하는 것을 금합니다.
낙장 및 파본은 교환해 드립니다.
구입철회는 구매처 규정에 따라 교환 및 환불처리 됩니다.

ETS 토익 정기시험 기출문제집 5
1000 RC

PREFACE

Dear test taker,

English-language proficiency has become a vital tool for success. It can help you excel in business, travel the world, and communicate effectively with friends and colleagues. The TOEIC® test measures your ability to function effectively in English in these types of situations. Because TOEIC scores are recognized around the world as evidence of your English-language proficiency, you will be able to confidently demonstrate your English skills to employers and begin your journey to success.

The test developers at ETS are excited to help you achieve your personal and professional goals through the use of the ETS TOEIC® 정기시험 기출문제집 1000 Vol. 5. This book contains test questions taken from actual, official TOEIC tests. These questions will help you become familiar with the content and the format of the TOEIC test. This book also contains detailed explanations of the question types and language points contained in the TOEIC test. These test questions and explanations have all been prepared by the same test specialists who develop the actual TOEIC test, so you can be confident that you will receive an authentic test-preparation experience.

Features of the ETS TOEIC® 정기시험 기출문제집 1000 Vol. 5 include the following.

- Ten full-length test forms all accompanied by answer keys and official scripts
- Specific and easy to understand explanations for learners
- The very same ETS voice actors that you will hear in an official TOEIC test

By using the ETS TOEIC® 정기시험 기출문제집 1000 Vol. 5 to prepare for the TOEIC test, you can be assured that you have a professionally prepared resource that will provide you with accurate guidance so that you are more familiar with the tasks, content, and format of the test and that will help you maximize your TOEIC test score. With your official TOEIC score certificate, you will be ready to show the world what you know!

We are delighted to assist you on your TOEIC journey with the ETS TOEIC® 정기시험 기출문제집 1000 Vol. 5 and wish you the best of success.

최신 기출문제 전격 공개!

유일무이

출제기관이 독점 제공한 기출문제가 담긴 유일한 교재!
이 책에는 정기시험 기출문제 10세트가 수록되어 있다. 시험에 나온 최신 기출문제로 실전 감각을 키워 시험에 확실하게 대비하자!

국내최고

기출 포인트를 꿰뚫는 명쾌한 해설!
최신 출제 경향을 가장 정확하게 알 수 있는 기출문제를 풀고 출제 포인트가 보이는 명쾌한 해설로 토익을 정복해 보자!

독점제공

ETS 제공 표준점수 환산표로 실력 진단!
출제기관 ETS가 독점 제공하는 표준점수 환산표를 수록했다. 채점 후 환산표를 통해 자신의 실력이 어느 정도인지 가늠해 보자!

스마트 학습

동영상 강의, 기출어휘 단어장, 채점서비스 무료 제공!
ETS 토익기출 수험서 앱 다운로드 및 실행 ▶ 토익 ▶ 실전서 ▶ ETS 토익 정기시험 기출문제집 1000 Vol. 5 RC를 클릭해 무료 제공하는 자료로 스마트하게 학습하자!

* ybmbooks.com에서도 단어장 MP3파일, 단어장 PDF, 정답 PDF, 토익 연습용 답안지 PDF 제공

TOEIC 소개

TOEIC Test of English for International Communication(국제적 의사소통을 위한 영어 시험)의 약자로, 영어가 모국어가 아닌 사람들이 일상생활 또는 비즈니스 현장에서 꼭 필요한 실용적 영어 구사 능력을 갖추었는가를 평가하는 시험이다.

시험 구성

구성	PART	유형		문항 수	시간	배점
Listening	Part 1	사진 묘사		6	45분	495점
	Part 2	질의 응답		25		
	Part 3	짧은 대화		39		
	Part 4	짧은 담화		30		
Reading	Part 5	단문 빈칸 채우기		30	75분	495점
	Part 6	장문 빈칸 채우기		16		
	Part 7	독해	단일 지문	29		
			이중 지문	10		
			삼중 지문	15		
Total		7 Parts		200문항	120분	990점

평가 항목

LC	RC
단문을 듣고 이해하는 능력	읽은 글을 통해 추론해 생각할 수 있는 능력
짧은 대화체 문장을 듣고 이해하는 능력	장문에서 특정한 정보를 찾을 수 있는 능력
비교적 긴 대화체에서 주고받은 내용을 파악할 수 있는 능력	글의 목적, 주제, 의도 등을 파악하는 능력
장문에서 핵심이 되는 정보를 파악할 수 있는 능력	뜻이 유사한 단어들의 정확한 용례를 파악하는 능력
구나 문장에서 화자의 목적이나 함축된 의미를 이해하는 능력	문장 구조를 제대로 파악하는지, 문장에서 필요한 품사, 어구 등을 찾는 능력

※ 성적표에는 전체 수험자의 평균과 해당 수험자가 받은 성적이 백분율로 표기되어 있다.

수험 정보

시험 접수

시험 약 2개월 전부터 아래와 같은 방법으로 접수할 수 있다.
인터넷 접수: TOEIC위원회 공식 홈페이지(https://exam.toeic.co.kr)를 통해 접수
모바일 접수: TOEIC위원회 공식 애플리케이션 또는 모바일 웹사이트
　　　　　　(https://m.exam.toeic.co.kr)를 통해 접수

시험장 준비물

신분증	규정 신분증만 가능 (주민등록증, 운전면허증, 기간 만료 전의 여권, 공무원증 등)
필기구	연필, 지우개 (볼펜이나 사인펜은 사용 금지)

시험 진행 시간

09:20	입실 (9:50 이후 입실 불가)
09:30 ~ 09:45	답안지 작성에 관한 오리엔테이션
09:45 ~ 09:50	휴식
09:50 ~ 10:05	신분증 확인
10:05 ~ 10:10	문제지 배부 및 파본 확인
10:10 ~ 10:55	듣기 평가 (LISTENING TEST)
10:55 ~ 12:10	독해 평가 (READING TEST)

성적 확인

성적은 TOEIC 홈페이지에 안내된 성적 발표일에 인터넷 홈페이지, 애플리케이션을 통해 확인 가능하다. 최초 성적표 발급은 우편 또는 온라인을 통해 수령 가능하며, 재발급은 성적 유효기간(시험 시행일로부터 2년) 내에만 가능하다. 단, 유효기간은 공공기관에 한하여 2023년 4월부터 5년으로 연장되었다.

토익 점수

TOEIC 점수는 듣기 영역(LC) 점수와 읽기 영역(RC) 점수, 그리고 두 영역을 합계한 전체 점수로 구성된다. 각 영역의 점수는 5점 단위로 5점에서 495점까지 주어지고, 두 영역을 합계한 전체 점수는 10점에서 990점까지 주어진다. TOEIC 성적은 각 문제 유형의 난이도에 따른 점수 환산표에 의해 결정된다.

토익 경향 분석

PART 1 사진 묘사 Photographs

총 6문제

1인 등장 사진
주어는 He/She, A man/woman 등이며 주로 앞부분에 나온다.

2인 이상 등장 사진
주어는 They, Some men/women/people, One of the men/women 등이며 주로 중간 부분에 나온다.

사물/배경 사진
주어는 A car, Some chairs 등이며 주로 뒷부분에 나온다.

사람 또는 사물 중심 사진
주어가 일부는 사람, 일부는 사물이며 주로 뒷부분에 나온다.

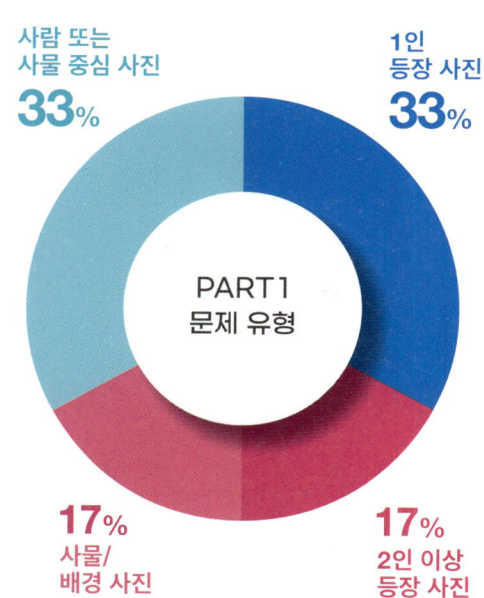

PART 1 문제 유형
- 1인 등장 사진 33%
- 사람 또는 사물 중심 사진 33%
- 2인 이상 등장 사진 17%
- 사물/배경 사진 17%

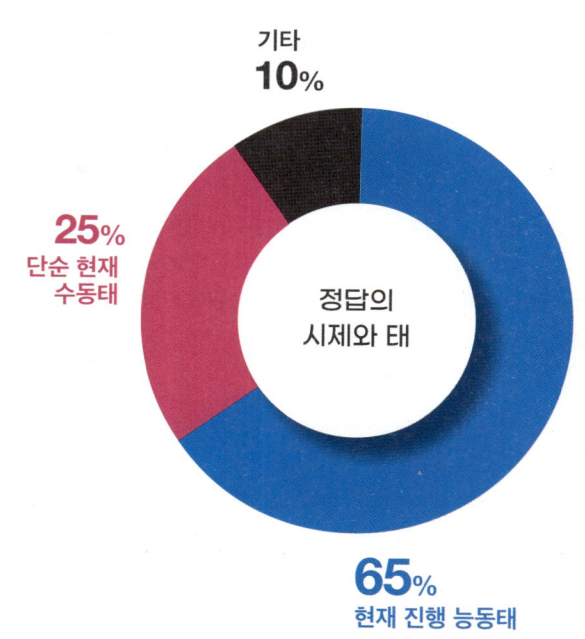

정답의 시제와 태
- 현재 진행 능동태 65%
- 단순 현재 수동태 25%
- 기타 10%

현재 진행 능동태
<is/are + 현재분사> 형태이며 주로 사람이 주어이다.

단순 현재 수동태
<is/are + 과거분사> 형태이며 주로 사물이 주어이다.

기타
<is/are + being + 과거분사> 형태의 현재 진행 수동태, <has/have + been + 과거분사> 형태의 현재 완료 수동태, '타동사 + 목적어' 형태의 단순 현재 능동태, There is/are와 같은 단순 현재도 나온다.

PART 2 질의 응답 Question-Response

총 25문제

평서문
질문이 아니라 객관적인 사실이나 화자의 의견 등을 나타내는 문장이다.

의문사 의문문
각 의문사마다 1~2개씩 나온다. 의문사가 단독으로 나오기도 하지만 What time ~?, How long ~?, Which room ~? 등과 같이 다른 명사나 형용사와 같이 나오기도 한다.

명령문
동사원형이나 Please 등으로 시작한다.

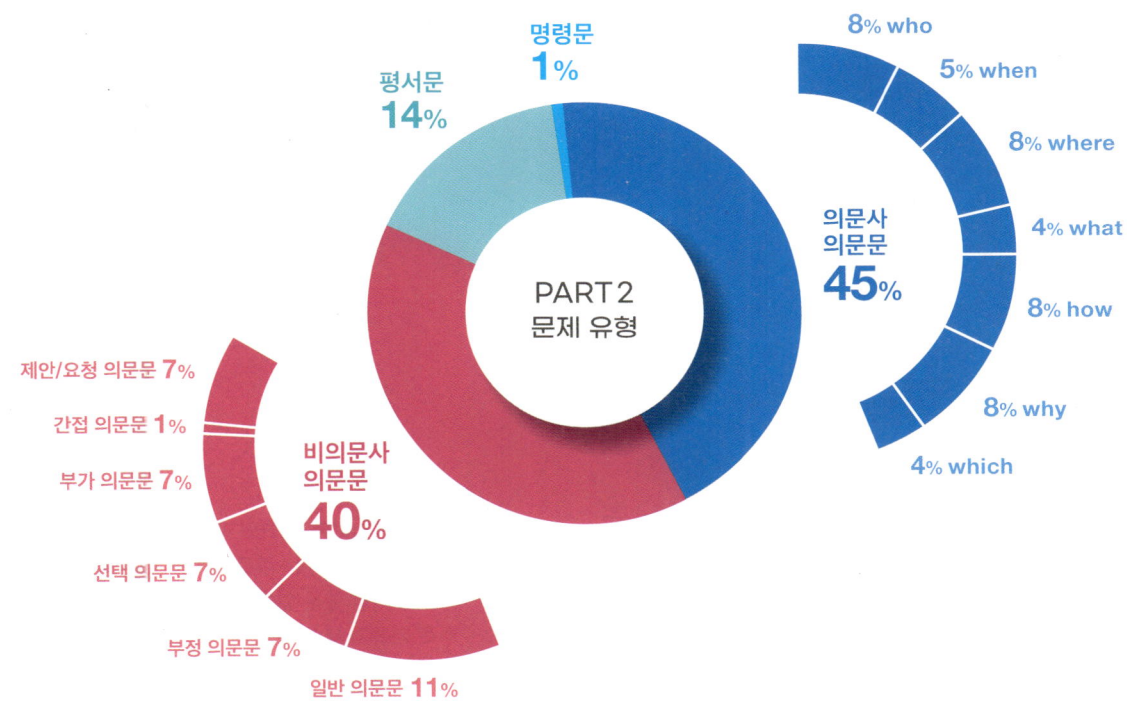

비의문사 의문문
일반 의문문 적게 나올 때는 1~2개, 많이 나올 때는 3~4개씩 나오는 편이다.
부정 의문문 Don't you ~?, Isn't he ~? 등으로 시작하는 문장이며 일반 긍정 의문문보다는 약간 더 적게 나온다.
선택 의문문 A or B 형태로 나오며 A와 B의 형태가 단어, 구, 절일 수 있다.
부가 의문문 ~ don't you?, ~ isn't he? 등으로 끝나는 문장이며, 일반 부정 의문문과 비슷하다고 볼 수 있다.
간접 의문문 의문사가 문장 앞이 아니라 문장 중간에 들어 있다.
제안/요청 의문문 정보를 얻기보다는 상대방의 도움이나 동의 등을 얻기 위한 목적이 일반적이다.

토익 경향 분석

PART 3 짧은 대화 Short Conversations

총 13대화문 39문제 (지문당 3문제)

- 3인 대화의 경우 남자 화자 두 명과 여자 화자 한 명 또는 남자 화자 한 명과 여자 화자 두 명이 나온다. 따라서 문제에서는 2인 대화에서와 달리 the man이나 the woman이 아니라 the men이나 the women 또는 특정한 이름이 언급될 수 있다.

- 대화 & 시각 정보는 항상 파트의 뒷부분에 나온다.

- 시각 정보의 유형으로는 chart, map, floor plan, schedule, table, weather forecast, directory, list, invoice, receipt, sign, packing slip 등 다양한 자료가 골고루 나온다.

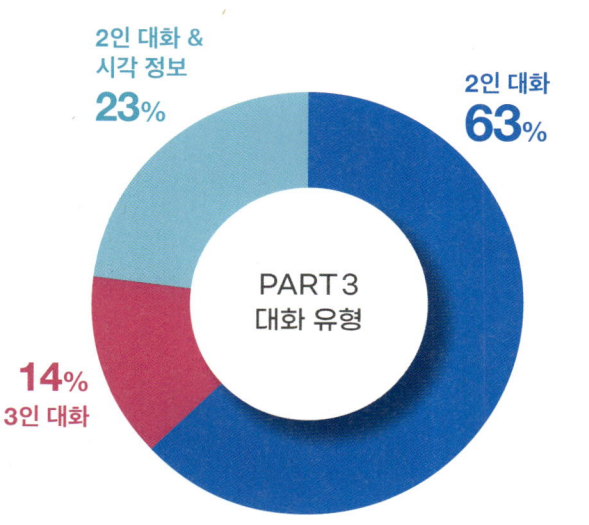

PART 3 대화 유형
- 2인 대화 63%
- 2인 대화 & 시각 정보 23%
- 3인 대화 14%

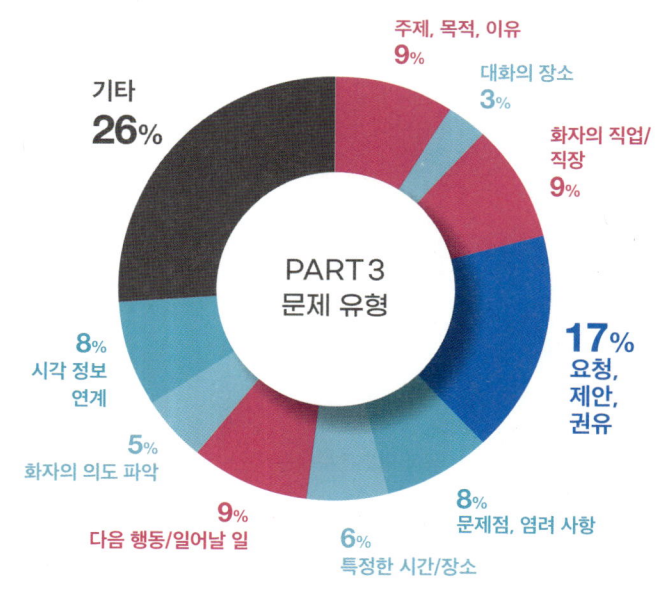

PART 3 문제 유형
- 요청, 제안, 권유 17%
- 주제, 목적, 이유 9%
- 대화의 장소 3%
- 화자의 직업/직장 9%
- 문제점, 염려 사항 8%
- 특정한 시간/장소 6%
- 다음 행동/일어날 일 9%
- 화자의 의도 파악 5%
- 시각 정보 연계 8%
- 기타 26%

- 주제, 목적, 이유, 대화의 장소, 화자의 직업/직장 등과 관련된 문제는 주로 대화의 첫 번째 문제로 나오며 다음 행동/일어날 일 등과 관련된 문제는 주로 대화의 세 번째 문제로 나온다.

- 화자의 의도 파악 문제는 주로 2인 대화에 나오지만, 가끔 3인 대화에 나오기도 한다. 시각 정보 연계 대화에는 나오지 않고 있다.

- Part 3에서 화자의 의도 파악 문제는 2개가 나오고 시각 정보 연계 문제는 3개가 나온다.

PART 4 짧은 담화 Short Talks

총 10담화문 30문제 (지문당 3문제)

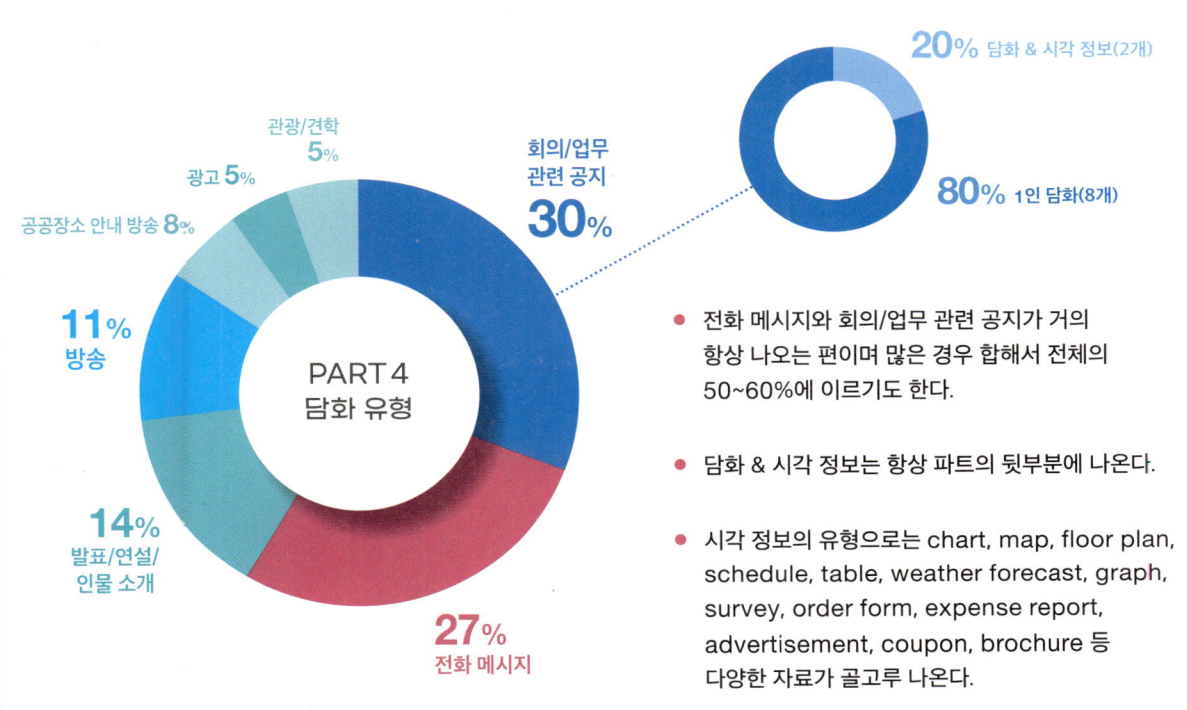

- 전화 메시지와 회의/업무 관련 공지가 거의 항상 나오는 편이며 많은 경우 합해서 전체의 50~60%에 이르기도 한다.

- 담화 & 시각 정보는 항상 파트의 뒷부분에 나온다.

- 시각 정보의 유형으로는 chart, map, floor plan, schedule, table, weather forecast, graph, survey, order form, expense report, advertisement, coupon, brochure 등 다양한 자료가 골고루 나온다.

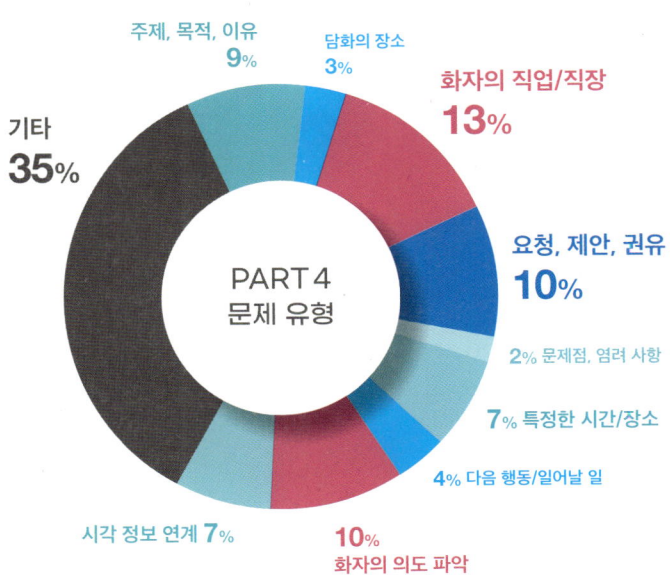

- 문제 유형은 기본적으로 Part 3과 거의 비슷하다.

- 주제, 목적, 이유, 담화의 장소, 화자의 직업/직장 등과 관련된 문제는 주로 담화의 첫 번째 문제로 나오며 다음 행동/일어날 일 등과 관련된 문제는 주로 담화의 세 번째 문제로 나온다.

- Part 4에서 화자의 의도 파악 문제는 3개가 나오고 시각 정보 연계 문제는 2개가 나온다.

토익 경향 분석

PART 5 단문 빈칸 채우기 Incomplete Sentences

총 30문제

문법 문제

시제와 대명사와 관련된 문법 문제가 2개씩, 한정사와 분사와 관련된 문법 문제가 1개씩 나온다. 시제 문제의 경우 능동태/수동태나 수의 일치와 연계되기도 한다. 그 밖에 한정사, 능동태/수동태, 부정사, 동명사 등과 관련된 문법 문제가 나온다.

어휘 문제

동사, 명사, 형용사, 부사와 관련된 어휘 문제가 각각 2~3개씩 골고루 나온다. 전치사 어휘 문제는 3개씩 꾸준히 나오지만, 접속사나 어구와 관련된 어휘 문제는 나오지 않을 때도 있고 3개가 나올 때도 있다.

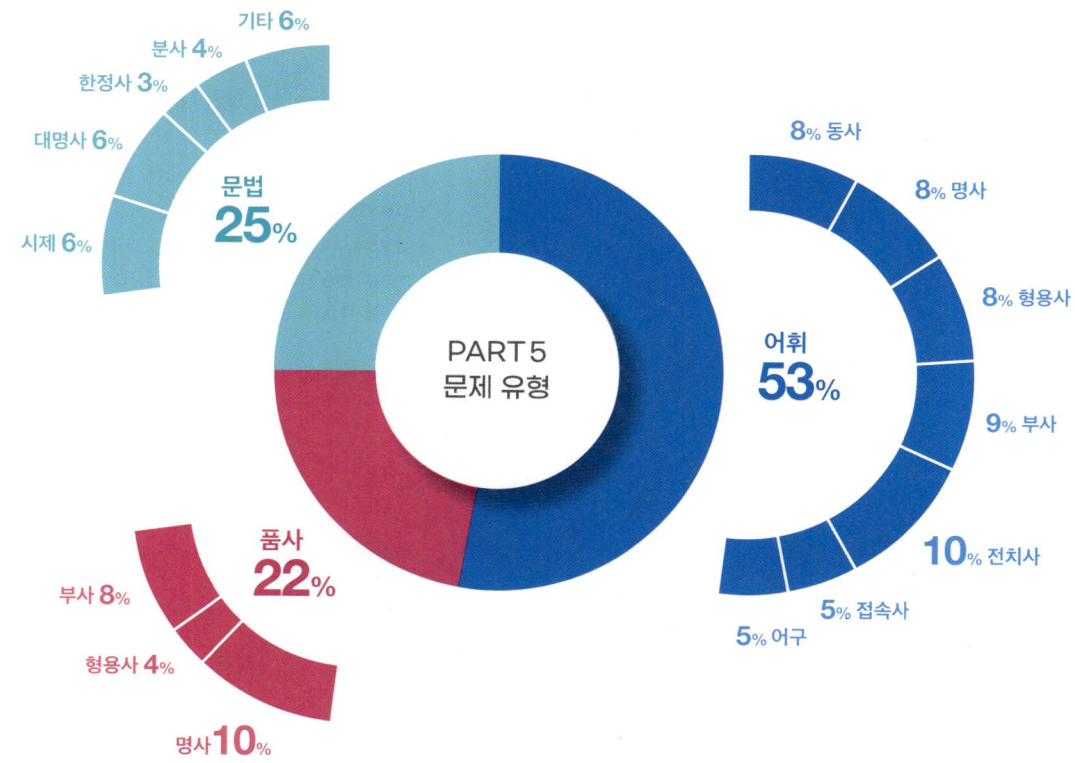

품사 문제

명사와 부사와 관련된 품사 문제가 2~3개씩 나오며, 형용사와 관련된 품사 문제가 상대적으로 적은 편이다.

PART 6 장문 빈칸 채우기 Text Completion

총 4지문 16문제 (지문당 4문제)

한 지문에 4문제가 나오며 평균적으로 어휘 문제가 2개, 품사나 문법 문제가 1개, 문맥에 맞는 문장 고르기 문제가 1개 들어간다. 문맥에 맞는 문장 고르기 문제를 제외하면 문제 유형은 기본적으로 파트 5와 거의 비슷하다.

문맥에 맞는 문장 고르기
문맥에 맞는 문장 고르기 문제는 지문당 한 문제씩 나오는데, 나오는 위치의 확률은 4문제 중 두 번째 문제, 세 번째 문제, 네 번째 문제, 첫 번째 문제 순으로 높다.

어휘 문제
동사, 명사, 부사, 어구와 관련된 어휘 문제는 매번 1~2개씩 나온다. 부사 어휘 문제의 경우 therefore(그러므로)나 however(하지만)처럼 문맥의 흐름을 자연스럽게 연결해 주는 부사가 자주 나온다.

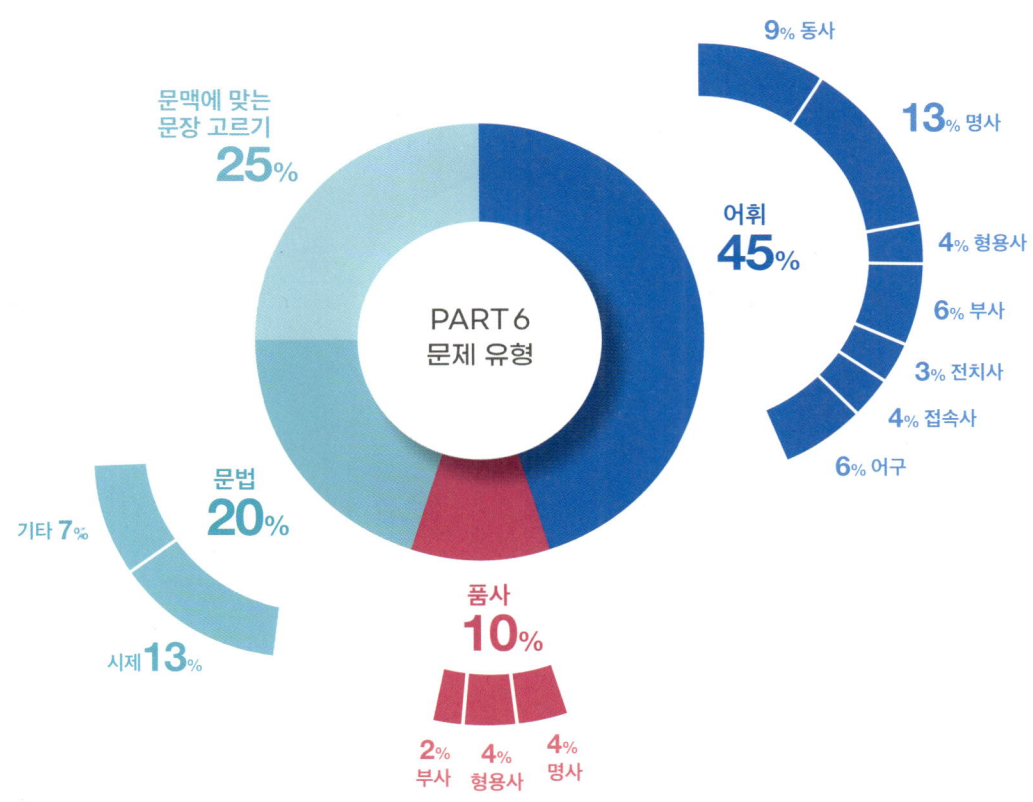

문법 문제
문맥의 흐름과 밀접하게 관련되어 있는 시제 문제가 2개 정도 나오며, 태나 수의 일치와 연계되기도 한다. 그 밖에 대명사, 능동태/수동태, 부정사, 접속사/전치사 등과 관련된 문법 문제가 나온다.

품사 문제
명사나 형용사 문제가 부사 문제보다 좀 더 자주 나온다.

토익 경향 분석

PART 7 독해 Reading Comprehension

지문 유형	지문당 문제 수	지문 개수	비중 %
단일 지문	2문항	4개	약 15%
	3문항	3개	약 16%
	4문항	3개	약 22%
이중 지문	5문항	2개	약 19%
삼중 지문	5문항	3개	약 28%

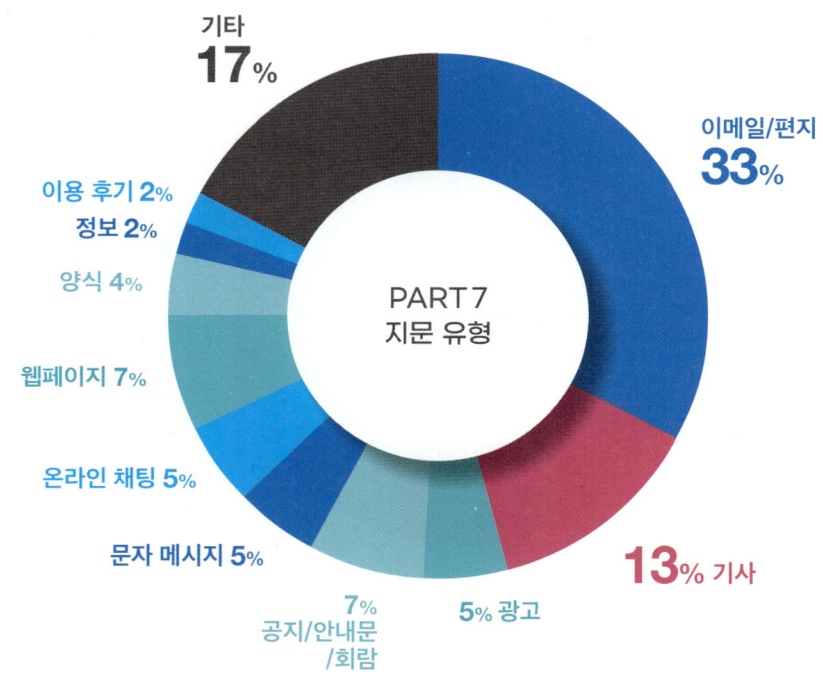

- 이메일/편지, 기사 유형 지문은 거의 항상 나오는 편이며 많은 경우 합해서 전체의 50~60%에 이르기도 한다.

- 기타 지문 유형으로 agenda, brochure, comment card, coupon, flyer, instructions, invitation, invoice, list, menu, page from a catalog, policy statement, report, schedule, survey, voucher 등 다양한 자료가 골고루 나온다.

(이중 지문과 삼중 지문 속의 지문들을 모두 낱개로 계산함 - 총 23지문)

총 15지문 54문제 (지문당 2~5문제)

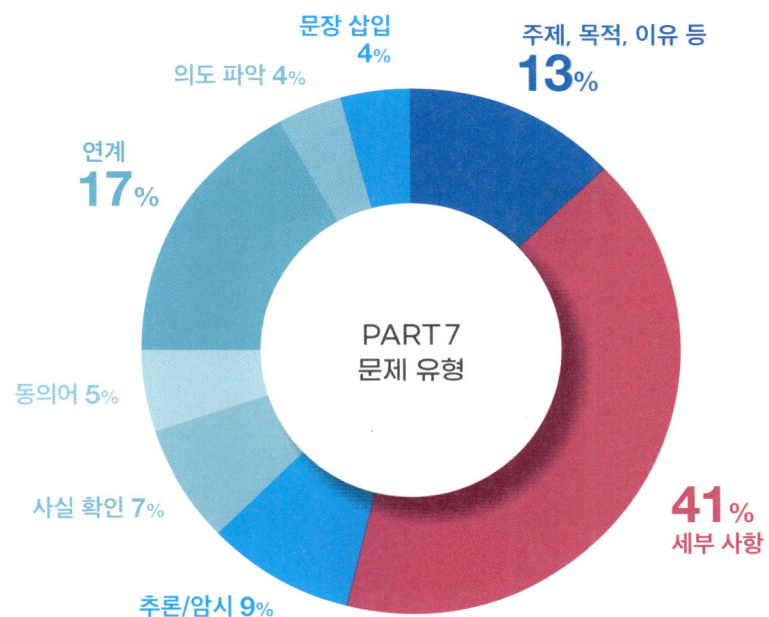

- 동의어 문제는 주로 이중 지문이나 삼중 지문에 나온다.
- 연계 문제는 일반적으로 이중 지문에서 한 문제, 삼중 지문에서 두 문제가 나온다.
- 의도 파악 문제는 문자 메시지(text-message chain)나 온라인 채팅(online chat discussion) 지문에서 출제되며 두 문제가 나온다.
- 문장 삽입 문제는 주로 기사, 이메일, 편지, 회람 지문에서 출제되며 두 문제가 나온다.

점수 환산표 및 산출법

점수 환산표 이 책에 수록된 각 TEST를 풀고 난 후, 맞은 개수를 세어 점수를 환산해 보자.

LISTENING Raw Score (맞은 개수)	LISTENING Scaled Score (환산 점수)	READING Raw Score (맞은 개수)	READING Scaled Score (환산 점수)
96-100	475-495	96-100	460-495
91-95	435-495	91-95	425-490
86-90	405-470	86-90	400-465
81-85	370-450	81-85	375-440
76-80	345-420	76-80	340-415
71-75	320-390	71-75	310-390
66-70	290-360	66-70	285-370
61-65	265-335	61-65	255-340
56-60	240-310	56-60	230-310
51-55	215-280	51-55	200-275
46-50	190-255	46-50	170-245
41-45	160-230	41-45	140-215
36-40	130-205	36-40	115-180
31-35	105-175	31-35	95-150
26-30	85-145	26-30	75-120
21-25	60-115	21-25	60-95
16-20	30-90	16-20	45-75
11-15	5-70	11-15	30-55
6-10	5-60	6-10	10-40
1-5	5-50	1-5	5-30
0	5-35	0	5-15

점수 산출 방법   아래의 방식으로 점수를 산출할 수 있다.

STEP 1

자신의 답안을 수록된 정답과 대조하여 채점한다. 각 Section의 맞은 개수가 본인의 Section별 '실제 점수(통계 처리하기 전의 점수, raw score)'이다. Listening Test와 Reading Test의 정답 수를 세어, 자신의 실제 점수를 아래의 해당란에 기록한다.

	맞은 개수	환산 점수대
LISTENING		
READING		
총점		

Section별 실제 점수가 그대로 Section별 TOEIC 점수가 되는 것은 아니다. TOEIC은 시행할 때마다 별도로 특정한 통계 처리 방법을 사용하며 이러한 실제 점수를 환산 점수(converted[scaled] score)로 전환하게 된다. 이렇게 전환함으로써, 매번 시행될 때마다 문제는 달라지지만 그 점수가 갖는 의미는 같아지게 된다. 예를 들어, 어느 한 시험에서 총점 550점의 성적을 받는 실력이라면 다른 시험에서도 거의 550점대의 성적을 받게 되는 것이다.

STEP 2

실제 점수를 의 표에 기록한 후 왼쪽 페이지의 점수 환산표를 보도록 한다. TOEIC이 시행될 때마다 대개 이와 비슷한 형태의 표가 작성되는데, 여기 제시된 환산표는 본 교재에 수록된 Test용으로 개발된 것이다. 이 표를 사용하여 자신의 실제 점수를 환산 점수로 전환하도록 한다. 즉, 예를 들어 Listening Test의 실제 정답 수가 61~65개이면 환산 점수는 265점에서 335점 사이가 된다. 여기서 실제 정답 수가 61개이면 환산 점수가 265점이고, 65개이면 환산 점수가 335점 임을 의미하는 것은 아니다. 본 책의 Test를 위해 작성된 이 점수 환산표가 자신의 영어 실력이 어느 정도인지 대략적으로 파악하는 데 도움이 되긴 하지만, 이 표가 실제 TOEIC 성적 산출에 그대로 사용된 적은 없다는 사실을 밝혀 둔다.

ETS 토익 정기시험 기출문제집 5
1000 RC

TEST 01
무료 동영상 강의

저자와 출판사의 사전 허락 없이 내용의 일부 혹은 전부를 인용 및 복제하거나 발췌하여 사용할 수 없습니다.

RC
기출 TEST 01

READING TEST

In the Reading test, you will read a variety of texts and answer several different types of reading comprehension questions. The entire Reading test will last 75 minutes. There are three parts, and directions are given for each part. You are encouraged to answer as many questions as possible within the time allowed.

You must mark your answers on the separate answer sheet. Do not write your answers in your test book.

PART 5

Directions: A word or phrase is missing in each of the sentences below. Four answer choices are given below each sentence. Select the best answer to complete the sentence. Then mark the letter (A), (B), (C), or (D) on your answer sheet.

101. The lecture will take place at 6:00 P.M., ------- which attendees may ask questions.

    (A) across
    (B) after
    (C) inside
    (D) among

102. The ------- antique shop in Pepper Valley will close down next month.

    (A) last
    (B) lasts
    (C) lasted
    (D) lasting

103. Merryville residents will receive an online status ------- about the ongoing bridge construction project.

    (A) update
    (B) change
    (C) payment
    (D) request

104. As a result of ------- many years leading media organizations, Ms. Ayo was selected for the Dowel Journalism Prize.

    (A) she
    (B) her
    (C) hers
    (D) herself

105. To stop the ------- of computer viruses, do not open suspicious e-mails.

    (A) break
    (B) spread
    (C) balance
    (D) surface

106. The hiring manager ------- considered each applicant's résumé and qualifications.

    (A) caring
    (B) careful
    (C) carefully
    (D) carefulness

107. In October, Mr. Sakamoto will leave for New Zealand ------- will oversee the opening of the new Auckland branch.

    (A) because
    (B) in addition
    (C) and
    (D) prior to

108. Tarateer Pharmaceuticals is varying its product ------- to include over-the-counter medications.

    (A) to line
    (B) lining
    (C) lined
    (D) line

109. Dynart, Inc., continuously ------- new ways to reduce its use of plastics.
(A) seeks
(B) seeker
(C) to seek
(D) seeking

110. The cash registers at Pirkle Books automatically ------- the remaining inventory of books available.
(A) calculate
(B) calculator
(C) calculating
(D) calculation

111. The product team is designing mapping software that can ------- locate underground minerals.
(A) infinitely
(B) sincerely
(C) precisely
(D) greatly

112. According to CEO Mayu Yamada, it would not be ------- responsible to expand the warehouse at this time.
(A) finance
(B) financials
(C) financially
(D) financing

113. Analysts cannot say with any ------- what the regional demand for electric trucks will be.
(A) certainty
(B) justice
(C) excellence
(D) denial

114. As part of its marketing campaign, Elegancia Dishware is ------- soliciting feedback from customers.
(A) lightly
(B) loyally
(C) actively
(D) cleanly

115. Rain gardens are intended to ------- water to prevent flooding of local roads.
(A) engage
(B) undergo
(C) absorb
(D) overwhelm

116. Theta Industries' training program aims to increase the ------- of its manufacturing systems.
(A) producer
(B) produced
(C) productive
(D) productivity

117. The board of directors has voted to award Mr. Mitrakos a bonus for his role ------- obtaining the international contract.
(A) in
(B) at
(C) except
(D) apart

118. The finance director gave his approval ------- the project can move forward.
(A) along
(B) furthermore
(C) cautiously
(D) so that

119. The newspaper article describes ways job seekers can ------- for having little workplace experience.
(A) reply
(B) capture
(C) compensate
(D) accumulate

120. Mr. Ellis and Ms. Barnes were both highly qualified, but ------- got the job.
(A) myself
(B) neither
(C) anybody
(D) whoever

121. Ennis Photography purchased all new lighting equipment ------- the high cost.
    (A) even though
    (B) however
    (C) until
    (D) despite

122. Marburton residents who wish to ------- a home should contact the award-winning team at Kwan Real Estate.
    (A) seller
    (B) sold
    (C) sell
    (D) selling

123. Maswa Bistro began a ------- agreement with local farmers to purchase a set amount of produce each week.
    (A) disruptive
    (B) cooperative
    (C) grateful
    (D) concerned

124. The City of Doyle's new downtown parking ------- have been met with opposition by residents and visitors.
    (A) restricts
    (B) restricted
    (C) restrictions
    (D) restricting

125. The plumbing position requires extensive training, even for those who studied ------- in technical school.
    (A) diligently
    (B) scientifically
    (C) objectively
    (D) decidedly

126. With its fixed price -------, Omega Cellular guarantees no phone bill increases for three years.
    (A) assurance
    (B) assuredly
    (C) assuring
    (D) assures

127. As chief analytics officer, Mr. Ko has worked at Lochston Ltd. with great ------- for more than twenty years.
    (A) deduction
    (B) duplication
    (C) declaration
    (D) dedication

128. Milltown Hospital's cafeteria serves lunch seven days a week ------- only on weekdays.
    (A) up to
    (B) as though
    (C) each time
    (D) rather than

129. The store's entire inventory of lumber comes from a nearby ------- supplier.
    (A) financial
    (B) promotional
    (C) chemical
    (D) commercial

130. For a $95 ------- fee, our mechanics will determine what repairs are needed.
    (A) diagnosed
    (B) diagnostic
    (C) diagnosable
    (D) diagnose

PART 6

Directions: Read the texts that follow. A word, phrase, or sentence is missing in parts of each text. Four answer choices for each question are given below the text. Select the best answer to complete the text. Then mark the letter (A), (B), (C), or (D) on your answer sheet.

Questions 131-134 refer to the following flyer.

Look to Riessler Landscaping for your Garden Needs

Riessler Landscaping has everything you need to create your dream garden. We will listen to your ideas and offer suggestions that match your gardening desires. ------- . The nursery here at
                                                                                                                        131.
Riessler Landscaping includes plants of many varieties and sizes that burst with eye-catching colors year-round. You are guaranteed to find something that will add ------- to your garden. We
                                                                                                                        132.
are ------- equipped to construct small ponds or other water features. And as our name suggests,
   133.
we can take on more ambitious landscaping projects—whatever you need! With more than 40 years in the landscape–design business, ------- expertise is unmatched.
                                                                 134.

---

131. (A) Staff members have written articles for the local newspaper.
     (B) Installing lights can enhance the effect of a well-designed garden.
     (C) Local competitors cannot beat the prices we charge.
     (D) Riessler Landscaping's goal is to make your vision a reality.

132. (A) years
     (B) space
     (C) beauty
     (D) moisture

133. (A) also
     (B) rarely
     (C) somehow
     (D) nevertheless

134. (A) its
     (B) our
     (C) others
     (D) their

Questions 135-138 refer to the following letter.

10 January

Cindy Mulligan
88 Manchester Road
HARROGATE
HG82 2MJ

Dear Ms. Mulligan,

We are delighted to celebrate your 30th anniversary with Brandrix Distribution Centre. ------- . Your
135.
dedication, loyalty, and hard work have contributed greatly to our success over the years. We appreciate your commitment to excellence. Over the years, you ------- great initiative, creativity,
136.
and leadership.

You will ------- be receiving a commemorative plaque by post. We hope this token of our gratitude
137.
reminds you how much you mean to us.

Congratulations on reaching this ------- . Thank you for being part of our Brandrix family.
138.

Sincerely,

Lance Powar, Vice President of Human Resources
Brandrix Distribution Centre

---

135. (A) We especially value our long-term customers.
(B) Please join our holiday celebration.
(C) Our annual report will be released soon.
(D) You have been a valuable member of our team.

136. (A) will show
(B) must show
(C) have shown
(D) are showing

137. (A) then
(B) soon
(C) instead
(D) likewise

138. (A) milestone
(B) consensus
(C) destination
(D) understanding

Questions 139-142 refer to the following e-mail.

To: Kay Berman <kberman@xmail.com>
From: Ali Chaleby <achaleby@ralenciadesign.com>
Date: August 21
Subject: Plans for living room
Attachment: Samples

Dear Ms. Berman,

My design team is in the process of ------- the plans for your living room. Based on our last
                                     139.
conversation, I have chosen different paints for the walls and borders. Please review the attached

file and decide whether you like those new ------- . If not, it is not too late to make a change.
                                            140.
------- . Your review will help us refine the design before we start.
141.

Please let ------- know if you have any questions. I look forward to hearing from you.
           142.

Kind regards,

Ali Chaleby, Ralencia Design

---

139. (A) finalizing
(B) finalize
(C) finalized
(D) finalizes

140. (A) organizations
(B) schedules
(C) colors
(D) times

141. (A) I have already begun drawing up plans for your kitchen.
(B) We are not planning to begin work for another two weeks.
(C) Your living room is particularly spacious and airy.
(D) We have not yet received your current payment.

142. (A) them
(B) ours
(C) his
(D) me

Questions 143-146 refer to the following e-mail.

To: Marsha Zalen <mzalen@mansfield.com>
From: Kaymar PCP <info@kaymarpcp.com>
Date: September 8
Subject: Your recent office visit

Dear Ms. Zalen,

Thank you for your recent visit to Kaymar Primary Care Practice. We hope you found our services ------- **143.**, and we welcome suggestions for improvement.

We have posted a ------- **144.** of your consultation on our portal. Please take a moment to go through it and let us know if you have any questions.

As a reminder, you can log in to the portal for various activities. ------- **145.**, you can make appointments and payments, view your medical history, review lab results, and request medication refills. ------- **146.**. Rest assured that your personal information is safe and secure.

We thank you for your business and look forward to serving you again.

Kaymar Primary Care Practice

---

143. (A) satisfied
(B) satisfaction
(C) satisfactory
(D) satisfactorily

144. (A) photo
(B) lecture
(C) summary
(D) schedule

145. (A) To repeat
(B) For instance
(C) Otherwise
(D) Consequently

146. (A) We hope you will use this resource to manage your health-care needs.
(B) The staff will close the office early on Friday afternoons.
(C) Please be sure to come to our office fifteen minutes in advance.
(D) We apologize for any confusion about your appointment time.

PART 7

Directions: In this part you will read a selection of texts, such as magazine and newspaper articles, e-mails, and instant messages. Each text or set of texts is followed by several questions. Select the best answer for each question and mark the letter (A), (B), (C), or (D) on your answer sheet.

Questions 147-148 refer to the following notice.

Dear High View Apartments Resident,

Riverside Paving Company is coming to High View Apartments on May 3 and 4 to resurface the parking area. All vehicles must be removed by 8 A.M. on May 3 for the work to commence. Residents may use the parking area again starting on May 5 at 8 A.M. We realize that trying to find another place to park is inconvenient, but it is necessary for the job to be completed in the two days scheduled. Note that all parking spaces will be widened, and some spaces could be moved during the work. You will receive an e-mail if your parking space is moved more than 20 meters from your previous one.

Thank you for your cooperation,
Judith Alvarez, Property Manager

147. What is the purpose of the notice?
(A) To invite residents to a meeting on May 3
(B) To request feedback about parking facilities
(C) To inform residents of an upcoming project
(D) To announce an increase in parking fees

148. What is suggested about High View Apartments?
(A) It charges residents a monthly maintenance fee.
(B) It recently hired a new property manager.
(C) It has the parking area repaved every year.
(D) It assigns tenants specific parking spots.

Questions 149-150 refer to the following text-message chain.

Carol Barger (10:45 A.M.)
Hello, Ms. Seang.

Leakhena Seang (10:55 A.M.)
Good morning!

Carol Barger (11:15 A.M.)
We have fifteen participants enrolled in your mosaic workshop tomorrow. That is five more than last summer. Your workshops get more popular every year! Do you have enough materials on hand for that many participants?

Leakhena Seang (11:23 A.M.)
I have plenty to go around. We'll be creating mosaic designs using bits of sea glass I collected on my vacation last summer. They are pieces of brown, green, and blue bottles that have washed up on the beach. The sand has smoothed all the sharp edges, so they're perfectly safe for everyone to use.

Carol Barger (11:30 A.M.)
Sounds good. See you tomorrow at breakfast.

149. What most likely is Ms. Seang's job?

(A) Glassmaker
(B) Art instructor
(C) Beach lifeguard
(D) Program administrator

150. At 11:23 A.M., what does Ms. Seang imply when she writes, "I have plenty to go around"?

(A) She intends to create an extra-large mosaic.
(B) She has been collecting sea glass for many years.
(C) She can share her sea glass with all the workshop participants.
(D) She does not think she will use much of her sea glass.

Questions 151-152 refer to the following e-mail.

E-mail

To: Sales Team
From: Laura Correa
Date: 5 October
Subject: Updates

Dear Team,

As announced in the Brighter Sails September newsletter, our performance has been consistently strong this year. This is an accomplishment we can all be proud of. Please take a moment to congratulate each other. We will continue to dream up new and exciting plans for the future!

In other news, Jasen Norton will transfer to our Kingston headquarters next month. We are sad to lose Mr. Norton, but we gratefully acknowledge his excellent work and wish him continued success in his new role.

There will be a farewell luncheon for Mr. Norton on 28 October at 1:00 P.M. in the second-floor conference room. Bring your good cheer and perhaps a story to share. The company will supply lunch, a cake, and decorations. Let me know by 12 October whether you will be able to attend.

Sincerely,

Laura Correa, Sales Manager
Brighter Sails Ltd.

---

151. What is mentioned about Mr. Norton?

(A) He will be attending a sales conference.
(B) He sent Ms. Correa an office supply request.
(C) He wrote an article in the September newsletter.
(D) He will be moving to another company location.

152. What does Ms. Correa ask members of the sales team to do?

(A) Send her stories for a newsletter
(B) Give her names of potential new hires
(C) Inform her of plans to attend an event
(D) Help her decorate the office

Questions 153-154 refer to the following article.

Refurbished Theater Gives Town a Boost

BEACHVILLE (February 24)—Beachville residents and tourists have a good reason to celebrate. The 40-year-old Crown Coastal Theater is scheduled to reopen in June. Many were saddened when the former theater owners decided to close the venue over a year ago, citing the cost of needed renovations. Fortunately, the theater has new owners who have spent the last year updating the interior and the projection system.

Christine Lafferty said that she and her childhood friend Morgan Flanagan spent plenty of time at the theater while growing up. "Going to the movies is the thing to do on a rainy day in a seaside town. We were sorry to see it close." The friends, who also own the popular Blue Bay Bistro, decided to buy the theater and make the necessary repairs to keep it a thriving business. For more information about the theater and its upcoming events, visit www.crowncoastaltheater.com.

153. What is the purpose of the article?

(A) To report on beach conditions
(B) To announce a business reopening
(C) To promote a movie premiere
(D) To advertise a new restaurant

154. Who is Ms. Flanagan?

(A) A town council member
(B) An event coordinator
(C) Ms. Lafferty's business partner
(D) The writer of the article

Questions 155-157 refer to the following e-mail.

E-mail

To:	Randi Longfellow <rlongfellow@sapphiremail.com.au>
From:	Deon Welman <deonwelman@skyviewscopes.com.au>
Date:	27 March
Subject:	Makatasi model METX-33948

Dear Ms. Longfellow,

Thank you for ordering the Makatasi ETX-Triple Refracting Telescope, model METX-33948. Unfortunately, the item you requested is on back order. — [1] —. If you would prefer not to wait, we have a similar telescope made by another manufacturer, Belter Telescopes. Like the Makatasi model you ordered, the Belter BTR-1483 has a 120 mm aperture and a retractable lens hood. — [2] —. In addition, all Belter telescopes include a padded carrying case. The Belter BTR-1483 costs $200 less than the Makatasi METX-33948.

If you wish to revise your order, simply reply to this e-mail within 48 hours or go to our Web site to chat with a representative at http://www.skyviewscopes.com.au. We will then change your order, refund $200 to your credit card, and ship your new telescope overnight at no extra charge. — [3] —. Otherwise, we will notify you when the Makatasi model METX-33948 is back in stock and provide delivery information at that point. — [4] —.

Best regards,

Deon Welman
Sales Representative, Skyview Scopes

---

155. What is the purpose of the e-mail?

(A) To request payment
(B) To provide operating instructions
(C) To advertise a new product
(D) To offer a substitute item

156. What is mentioned about the Belter BTR-1483 telescope?

(A) It can only be ordered online.
(B) It will ship directly from the manufacturer.
(C) It includes a protective case.
(D) It is the most expensive telescope of its type.

157. In which of the positions marked [1], [2], [3], and [4] does the following sentence best belong?

"You can see a full list of specifications on our Web site."

(A) [1]
(B) [2]
(C) [3]
(D) [4]

Questions 158-160 refer to the following e-mail.

To:	Sun-Hi Myo <shmyo@sunmail.co.nz>
From:	Jan Delpit <jdelpit@hamerkoptech.co.nz>
Date:	8 March
Subject:	RE: Inquiry about job opening

Hello,

Thank you for your e-mail. I am currently on holiday and will return to the office on 15 March. I will respond to your message as soon as possible after I return.

If you require general assistance during my absence or have questions about the open position in our sales department, please contact my assistant Sita Viswan at 04 555 0193 or sviswan@hamerkoptech.co.nz. For questions about specific Hamerkoptech software products, contact the customer service department at customerservice@hamerkoptech.co.nz.

Additionally, I am happy to announce that our new graphic design software program will be released on 2 April. You can read more about the program at Hamerkoptech's newly redesigned Web site, www.hamerkoptech.co.nz. There, you may also sign up to receive our weekly newsletter by following the instructions on the home page.

Sincerely,

Jan Delpit

158. What is one purpose of the e-mail?
(A) To explain how to use a software program
(B) To request Ms. Myo's assistance with a project
(C) To introduce a new staff member
(D) To indicate that Mr. Delpit is out of the office

159. What will happen on April 2 ?
(A) A job opening will be filled.
(B) A product will be launched.
(C) A client meeting will take place.
(D) A Web site redesign will begin.

160. How can people subscribe to a newsletter?
(A) By calling Ms. Viswan
(B) By replying to Mr. Delpit's e-mail
(C) By visiting Hamerkoptech's Web site
(D) By contacting the customer service department

Questions 161-163 refer to the following article.

Vimalo Brands Enters a New Era

By Yvette Maurer

VANCOUVER (2 August)—Vimalo Brands, the large consumer goods company that markets popular nutritional-support and personal-care products, including Powerburst breakfast drinks and Honeysoft soaps and lotions, will soon offer something new for its customers: frozen foods. "Our new Nutridinna line is not just about convenience," CEO Danitza Martens said during a press conference earlier today. "Frozen foods are not a new concept, but our method of flash-freezing fresh produce and meats ensures that our products retain their texture and flavour as well as their healthy vitamins and minerals. Now our customers can enjoy the convenience of frozen food without sacrificing quality."

Vimalo Brands has partnered with Vancouver-area farms to obtain produce and meat for the Nutridinna line. "By keeping our operations local, we avoid shipping delays and can flash-freeze freshly harvested vegetables at their peak of ripeness," Martens said. "Our customers benefit further, since our products can be kept in the freezer for up to six months." Nutridinna foods will be available in supermarkets beginning in November. Frozen fish and other seafood will be added early next year.

161. What is one purpose of the article?

(A) To discuss a cooking technique
(B) To report on a corporate merger
(C) To announce a new product line
(D) To introduce a recently hired executive

162. The word "just" in paragraph 1, line 8, is closest in meaning to

(A) recently
(B) exactly
(C) slightly
(D) only

163. What does Ms. Martens suggest about flash-frozen food?

(A) It is less expensive than fresh food.
(B) It is as nutritious as fresh food.
(C) It is as easy to ship as fresh food.
(D) It is less flavorful than fresh food.

Questions 164-167 refer to the following advertisement.

Are you ready to work hard as part of a team of like-minded individuals? Are you willing to put your education, your experience, and your imagination to great use? If so, then we have the job for you. Karning Creative Designs is expanding, and with our success comes your opportunity.

Karning Creative Designs began ten years ago as a two-person operation set up in the home of our current CEO and founder Shirin Navani. Now located in a beautiful loft in downtown Hollinson, our firm currently employs 25 full-time staff members. At Karning, we design paper-based brochures, catalogs, ads, and posters for our clients. We are currently seeking qualified designers and artists who will shine in a fast-paced, collaborative environment.

The ideal candidate
- Holds a degree in design, advertising, or graphic art—although several years of direct experience may substitute for a degree
- Demonstrates a strong ability to work closely with colleagues
- Maintains a critical eye for detail and precision
- Consistently meets deadlines and can flourish under pressure

Graphic design or related experience is a plus but not strictly necessary.

If you are ready to join our team, we want to meet you! Contact Salvador Tomassin at 608-555-0144 for further details. All applications must be received by March 31.

164. According to the advertisement, who most likely is Ms. Navani?

(A) A Karning Creative Designs client
(B) A business owner
(C) A photographer
(D) A real estate agent

165. What is indicated about Karning Creative Designs?

(A) Its primary focus is Web design.
(B) It initially employed two people.
(C) It was founded by Mr. Tomassin.
(D) Its staff are permitted to work from home.

166. What is required of job applicants?

(A) Skill in working with others
(B) Previous design experience
(C) A willingness to work on weekends
(D) An ability to use certain software applications

167. What will happen on March 31?

(A) A project will begin.
(B) A deadline will occur.
(C) A graphic designer will relocate.
(D) An application form will be made available.

Questions 168-171 refer to the following article.

NEW HAVEN (June 1)—Marco's Italian Restaurant on Frontage Road will be reopening in late June. It closed three months ago after a water leak caused extensive damage to the kitchen. A significant amount of work needed to be done in the kitchen and dining areas. — [1] —. The restaurant will accommodate larger parties when it reopens.

During the past three months, many of the restaurant's employees were able to work at Marco's Italian Market, which is located on the opposite side of the street. — [2] —. "The leak happened right before the market's busy season started," said Tom Marco, who owns both businesses. "We needed to add staff there temporarily, and I was happy to keep my restaurant crew employed." Most of those employees have now returned to work in the restaurant. — [3] —.

Mr. Marco has planned a grand reopening for June 25. Guests will enjoy live music and a new tasting menu. — [4] —. Reservations are required for the day of the celebration and can be made by calling 203-555-0124. "We are excited to be able to prepare our traditional dishes and welcome the community back again," stated Mr. Marco.

---

168. What does the article mention about Marco's Italian Restaurant?

(A) It is the oldest restaurant in New Haven.
(B) It is looking for a chef who can cook traditional dishes.
(C) It needed major renovations.
(D) It opened in a new location.

169. What is indicated about Marco's Italian Market?

(A) It supplies ingredients to Marco's Italian Restaurant.
(B) It occasionally hires temporary workers.
(C) It is scheduled to close in three months.
(D) It is located next door to Marco's Italian Restaurant.

170. What will happen during the event on June 25 ?

(A) The restaurant will reduce its menu prices.
(B) The restaurant will offer special menu items.
(C) Mr. Marco will celebrate his retirement.
(D) The New Haven business community will honor Mr. Marco.

171. In which of the positions marked [1], [2], [3], and [4] does the following sentence best belong?

"During repairs, some additional dining space was added."

(A) [1]
(B) [2]
(C) [3]
(D) [4]

Questions 172-175 refer to the following online chat discussion.

Marlys Barry (10:17 A.M.)
This is Ms. Barry from the data analysis department. I have included my colleague, Ms. Choi. We're contacting you about your data request for the e-mail addresses of all account holders, sorted by age.

Alexander Kubelski (10:17 A.M.)
Yes, how soon can you complete the request?

Marlys Barry (10:18 A.M.)
I have a question for you first. Do you really need the e-mail addresses of all account holders? That would be a huge file. Or do you need the e-mail addresses of account holders only within a certain age-group?

Alexander Kubelski (10:19 A.M.)
I see what you mean. I want to e-mail account holders aged 55 to 65 to invite them to meet with a retirement planning expert. Do I have to submit a new project request form?

Bora Choi (10:21 A.M.)
That's not necessary, Mr. Kubelski. We can update your current request form for you. You do not want to lose your place in the queue.

Alexander Kubelski (10:21 A.M.)
Great, thank you! Is it possible for you to get me that list right away?

Marlys Barry (10:22 A.M.)
There are several projects ahead of yours.

Alexander Kubelski (10:23 A.M.)
I was hoping to send out the e-mail invitations tomorrow.

Marlys Barry (10:24 A.M.)
We will get to it as soon as we can.

172. Why did Ms. Barry begin an online chat with Mr. Kubelski?

(A) To refer him to a different department
(B) To decline an invitation
(C) To issue an apology
(D) To ask for clarification about a request

173. Who will receive an e-mail from Mr. Kubelski?

(A) Account holders in one age-group
(B) Data analysis team members
(C) Financial planners
(D) All Mr. Kubelski's clients

174. What does Ms. Choi offer to do?

(A) Write an e-mail
(B) Make a change to a form
(C) Open an account
(D) Revise a policy

175. At 10:22 A.M., what does Ms. Barry most likely mean when she writes, "There are several projects ahead of yours"?

(A) Ms. Barry will move Mr. Kubelski's request to the end of the queue.
(B) Ms. Barry will not be able to send out the invitations for Mr. Kubelski.
(C) Mr. Kubelski's request will not be the first job Ms. Barry completes.
(D) Mr. Kubelski will need to assist with other projects first.

Questions 176-180 refer to the following article and e-mail.

Tips for designing a Web site for a food-truck business

Owners of food trucks move from place to place, within and between cities, as they carry out their business, so they often rely on word of mouth or social media to attract customers. As a result, they may not build a Web site of their own. But in fact, by the very nature of their business, it is crucial that food truck owners have a fixed place for the public to learn about them, order from them, contact them, etc. Furthermore, market research shows that a Web site can help build a loyal customer base. So, here are some tips for developing a great Web site for your food truck.

The Home page should have bold graphics with your food truck's name. The text must prominently display key information, such as your truck's locations and operating hours. Online forms with fields to fill out, such as reservation requests for special events or services, give new visitors too much visual information. They are better incorporated as links or pop-up windows.

The Food Menu page needs attractive, high-definition images along with vivid and precise text that describes each menu item in detail. Remember that your photos should be big enough to look appealing on larger computer monitors.

The About Us page should include some text explaining your food truck's theme and concept, and some biographical data detailing your background in the food industry.

The News page can include text informing visitors about seasonal food items and upcoming promotions or special events such as food festivals.

To:	Doug Abruzzo <dabruzzo@dzacreative.com>
From:	Ed Vale <evale@saffronmail.com>
Date:	March 29
Subject:	Feedback

Dear Mr. Abruzzo,

Thank you again for creating the prototype Web site for my food-truck business. I just wanted to reiterate that it has gotten positive feedback from customers who have tested it. I am so glad we followed the advice in that article you sent me about Web site design for food trucks!

As we discussed in our phone call yesterday, we will move forward with the prototype Web site and launch it as the official site on April 5. However, I still do not see the information I sent about our new promotion that will begin in mid-April, a free dessert with any sandwich purchase. Please be sure to add this important information before we launch the site.

Regards,

Ed

176. According to the article, what is one way that food truck owners traditionally attract customers?

    (A) By word of mouth
    (B) From highway billboards
    (C) Through newspaper advertisements
    (D) From signs at food festivals

177. According to the article, what information does not need to appear on the Home page?

    (A) Truck locations
    (B) Hours of operation
    (C) Company name
    (D) Seasonal food items

178. In what field does Mr. Abruzzo most likely work?

    (A) Market research
    (B) Catering
    (C) Web design
    (D) Package delivery

179. In which section of the Web site will information most likely be added?

    (A) The Home page
    (B) The Food Menu page
    (C) The About Us page
    (D) The News page

180. According to the e-mail, when will the Web site launch?

    (A) On March 28
    (B) On March 29
    (C) On April 5
    (D) On April 15

Questions 181-185 refer to the following e-mail and press release.

E-mail

To:	Manny Green <mgreen@rhba.com>
From:	John LaRose <jlarose@rilamore.edu>
Date:	May 18
Subject:	Drilling notice

Dear Mr. Green:

As a courtesy, I am writing to you at the Red Hills Business Association, asking you to help me get the word out to your membership. It was announced in last month's *Daily Gazette* that Rilamore University is moving forward with its Net Zero Initiative. Within three years, we expect to have geothermal wells installed and operational for the heating and cooling of our entire campus. Limiting the institution's reliance on fossil fuels has long been a goal, and the new system is a significant step toward achieving that goal.

Over the next month, we will conduct test drilling in several campus locations. If all goes according to schedule, the crew will be drilling adjacent to the Red Hills Business District and Oak Street Apartments starting Wednesday, June 5. We want to tell business owners and residents near the campus to expect a higher-than-usual noise level during the two weeks we estimate it will take to complete the work. The work hours for the drilling crew are 10 A.M. to 3 P.M. each day, Monday through Friday.

We apologize in advance for the inconvenience this may cause to our neighbors. Any questions or concerns should be directed to me at 813-555-0123.

John LaRose
Community Liaison, Rilamore University Office of Communications

---

FOR IMMEDIATE RELEASE

Contact: Manny Green, mgreen@rhba.com

RED HILLS (May 25)—The Red Hills Business Association is shifting the dates of its much-anticipated Lunch Hour Concert Series. Normally presented each Thursday in June, the four free concerts will instead take place each Thursday in July. The lineup of artists remains unchanged—the Jaystone Jazz Trio will open the series on July 4, followed on successive Thursdays by Joss and the Jaybirds, Ray Starform, and the Barklay Bass Quintet.

As usual, all three blocks of Oak Street will be closed to traffic, restaurants will serve lunch at outdoor tables, and local arts-and-crafts vendors will display their work on the lawn of the Cultural Center. It is a beautiful celebration in the heart of a popular Red Hills neighborhood. We hope to see you there!

181. What is indicated about the Net Zero Initiative?

(A) It is being funded by the Red Hills Business Association.
(B) It was inspired by similar initiatives in other cities.
(C) It will use geothermal energy to power a city.
(D) It will change the way an institution heats its buildings.

182. In the e-mail, the word "conduct" in paragraph 2, line 1, is closest in meaning to

(A) behave
(B) accompany
(C) transmit
(D) carry out

183. What can be concluded about the Red Hills Business District?

(A) It is located near a university campus.
(B) It hosts an arts festival every July.
(C) It includes the Oak Street Apartments.
(D) It is home to the offices of the *Daily Gazette*.

184. Why most likely did the Red Hills Business Association change the dates of its concert series?

(A) To take advantage of a new power source
(B) To accommodate students' schedules
(C) To avoid noise from nearby construction
(D) To prevent a conflict with a similar event

185. What is mentioned in the press release about the Cultural Center?

(A) It will provide lunch for musicians.
(B) It will have artwork for sale on its property.
(C) It will offer arts-and-crafts workshops.
(D) It will provide the stage for performers.

Questions 186-190 refer to the following advertisement, form, and review.

Lawal Home Service: Serving Southern California for over 40 years

Lawal Home Service provides roofing and solar solutions for Southern California residents in Inglewood and the surrounding areas. In addition to roof replacement, we offer a wide array of services, from attic insulation and gutter restoration to fixing leaks and installing solar panels.

Lawal Home Service prides itself on transparent communication and attention to detail. Our project supervisors are always on-site to answer client questions, provide updates, and ensure a safe and clean worksite. To request a free roofing diagnosis, visit www.lawalhomeservice.com or call our booking agent at 310-555-0108.

Lawal Home Service Contact Form

Trust the experts at Lawal Home Service to diagnose your roofing needs promptly and professionally. Please take a few minutes to complete the form with as much detail as possible. Remember, all roofs installed by Lawal have a 25-year warranty.

Name	Drew Gerson
Date	December 12
E-mail	dgerson95@onyxmail.com
Phone	310-555-0192
Address	820 North Acacia Street Inglewood, CA 90301
How may we help you?	During last week's windstorm, several roof shingles were torn loose and need replacing. I am considering replacing the entire roof as it is over 30 years old, and water has begun to drip through the section over the patio. I would appreciate talking to someone who could tell me my options and provide an estimate.

Neighborhood Reviews: Lawal Home Service

★★★★★

"I was very pleased with the thoroughness of their work."

I left a description of my problem with Lawal Home Service, and one of the company's estimators came to inspect my roof the very next day. After I decided to replace the roof, the Lawal Home Service crew was able to get to work the following week. Diana Perez was on-site for the whole job as promised and answered all my questions. Work was started on December 19, and it was finished on December 20. Once the roofing was finished, the crew did a great job cleaning up. They used two magnetic devices resembling lawnmowers and swept over my entire lawn to find any dropped roofing nails. I had never seen anything like that! I was very pleased with the thoroughness of their work.

— Drew Gerson, Inglewood, CA

---

186. According to the advertisement, what is one type of work performed by Lawal Home Service?

(A) Planting trees
(B) Repairing gutters
(C) Building home additions
(D) Replacing heating systems

187. What does Mr. Gerson indicate on the form about his roof?

(A) It has developed a leak.
(B) It was recently replaced.
(C) It was not expensive to install.
(D) It is under warranty for 30 years.

188. When did Lawal Home Service inspect Mr. Gerson's roof?

(A) On December 12
(B) On December 13
(C) On December 19
(D) On December 20

189. Who most likely is Ms. Perez?

(A) A project supervisor
(B) A roofing estimator
(C) An interior decorator
(D) A booking agent

190. According to the review, what surprised Mr. Gerson about the crew from Lawal Home Service?

(A) The price they charged
(B) The warranty they offered
(C) The quality of their materials
(D) The tools they used for a job

Questions 191-195 refer to the following e-mails and form.

To:	Omar Balaji <obalaji@darbourycompany.com>
From:	Juanita Pereira <jpereira@bunbunbooks.com>
Date:	May 10
Subject:	Notebook inquiry

Dear Mr. Balaji,

We are expanding our office supply section at Bun Bun Books and would like to offer a selection of blank notebooks with lined pages. We would like your help creating the following cover designs.

Cover Design Name	Central Image	Background Color
Great Thoughts	Lightbulb, lightning bolt, and star icons	Blue
World Suitcase	Suitcase with country name travel stickers	Black
Lavender Bouquet	Large bunch of lavender on tall, pale green stems	Yellow
Sail Away	Sun setting in the sky above a sailboat on a lake	White

We need to have notebooks in stock in time for our annual sale starting August 1. After approving the sample covers, when would we need to place our order?

Thank you,

Juanita Pereira

To:	Juanita Pereira <jpereira@bunbunbooks.com>
From:	Omar Balaji <obalaji@darbourycompany.com>
Date:	May 25
Subject:	Re: Notebook inquiry

Hello, Ms. Pereira,

I have shipped some sample notebook covers for your inspection. Unfortunately, I was not able to include one of the designs for your approval because it needed a late-stage change to the background color. The sticker art did not show up well against the original black background. We are testing a light-beige color, and I will send the updated sample cover to you after it has been approved internally.

I should have the last sample to you by the end of this week. As long as you send your approval of all covers by June 11, we will be able to ship your entire order of bound notebooks before July 20. You will have everything before your sale that begins on August 1. Please contact me if you have any questions.

Best regards,

Omar Balaji, Darboury Company

Darboury Company
Order Form

Customer: Bun Bun Books
Ship by: July 15
Shipping method: Standard
Requested delivery date: July 20

Item code	Product Description	Cover Design	Amount
N3-GT	Standard-size spiral notebook	Great Thoughts	200
N3-WS	Standard-size spiral notebook	World Suitcase	200
H3-LB	Small hardbound journal notebook	Lavender Bouquet	150
H3-SA	Small hardbound journal notebook	Sail Away	150
D1	Large metal display rack (holds standard-size spiral notebooks)	—	1

191. What is one service that Darboury Company most likely provides?

    (A) Travel booking
    (B) Textbook publishing
    (C) Flower delivery
    (D) Graphic design

192. What sample was delayed?

    (A) Great Thoughts
    (B) World Suitcase
    (C) Lavender Bouquet
    (D) Sail Away

193. When is the deadline for Ms. Pereira to approve samples?

    (A) May 25
    (B) June 11
    (C) July 20
    (D) August 1

194. What does the form indicate about the Bun Bun Books order?

    (A) It will include a display stand.
    (B) It will ship overnight.
    (C) It will be paid upon delivery.
    (D) It will arrive late.

195. What is the background color on the cover of item N3-GT?

    (A) Blue
    (B) Black
    (C) Yellow
    (D) White

Questions 196-200 refer to the following e-mail, review, and notice.

To:	Managers
From:	Charlotte Black
Date:	August 16
Subject:	Employee of the month

Dear Managers,

It is time to vote for the Wilson Autos Employee of the Month for September. Here are the nominees.

Erica Boyd has been with us for only a few months but has already shown great promise and is eager to learn new things.

Lauren Almahdi is very proactive. If something needs to be done, she will point it out to a manager and volunteer to take care of it herself.

Nick Salehi found a glitch in our computer system and stopped us from incorrectly ordering unnecessary inventory (thus saving us money).

Max Rhodes has been especially helpful with training new hires. He is calm and patient and explains our procedures well.

Please respond to this e-mail by Friday with your vote. The winner must receive at least three votes. The winner will be posted at our front desk and on our Web site next Monday.

Thanks,

Charlotte Black
General Manager, Wilson Autos

---

https://www.westchesterreviews.com

Wilson Autos (Westchester)

★★★★★

My wife and I just bought a new Excelera truck at the Wilson Autos Westchester location with the help of Erica Boyd. Even though she was new, she was very knowledgeable about all the trucks on the lot that we wanted to test drive. The few questions she was unable to answer were quickly addressed by her mentor, Max. We were very pleased with the customer service and even more delighted when the general manager agreed to sell us the Excelera for the same price that a competing dealership was advertising. I highly recommend Wilson Autos if you are in the market for a new vehicle!

—Henry Riggs, August 22

The employee of the month for September is ERICA BOYD!

In her three months at Wilson Autos, Erica has picked up new skills quickly and is always trying to learn more. She has become very knowledgeable about our inventory and is able to share her knowledge with customers to complete sales. She has also been instrumental in encouraging satisfied customers to post comments on our social media pages. We received more great reviews in the past month than we did in the four previous months combined!

Erica has received a $50 gift card to Alonzo's Restaurant as a thank-you for her excellent work. Congratulations, Erica!

196. What is the purpose of the e-mail?
  (A) To share a list of job candidates
  (B) To ask for opinions from managers
  (C) To summarize a managers' meeting
  (D) To nominate a manager for an award

197. According to the e-mail, who identified a technical problem?
  (A) Mr. Salehi
  (B) Ms. Almahdi
  (C) Mr. Rhodes
  (D) Ms. Black

198. What can be concluded about Mr. Riggs?
  (A) His previous vehicle was an Excelera truck.
  (B) He is a neighbor of Ms. Boyd's.
  (C) He has purchased a vehicle from Wilson Autos in the past.
  (D) He negotiated with Ms. Black for a lower price.

199. What is indicated in the notice about Ms. Boyd?
  (A) She eats regularly at Alonzo's Restaurant.
  (B) She manages social media sites for Wilson Autos.
  (C) She is responsible for an increase in customer feedback.
  (D) She recently completed a sales training course.

200. What is most likely true about Ms. Boyd?
  (A) She received votes from at least three managers.
  (B) She was the top salesperson in August.
  (C) She has years of experience in the auto industry.
  (D) She was hired by Wilson Autos in April.

Stop! This is the end of the test. If you finish before time is called, you may go back to Parts 5, 6, and 7 and check your work.

TEST 02
무료 동영상 강의

RC
기출 TEST 02

READING TEST

In the Reading test, you will read a variety of texts and answer several different types of reading comprehension questions. The entire Reading test will last 75 minutes. There are three parts, and directions are given for each part. You are encouraged to answer as many questions as possible within the time allowed.

You must mark your answers on the separate answer sheet. Do not write your answers in your test book.

PART 5

Directions: A word or phrase is missing in each of the sentences below. Four answer choices are given below each sentence. Select the best answer to complete the sentence. Then mark the letter (A), (B), (C), or (D) on your answer sheet.

101. The all-new Amore sports sedan is engineered for maximum reliability ------- gas mileage.
    (A) so
    (B) but
    (C) and
    (D) nor

102. The staff was grateful for the ------- that Mr. Schuller distributed at the meeting.
    (A) information
    (B) informed
    (C) informs
    (D) inform

103. The next meeting of the planning committee will be held ------- at 2 P.M.
    (A) barely
    (B) closely
    (C) evenly
    (D) promptly

104. Reimbursement for travel expenses will be included in ------- October 1 paycheck.
    (A) you
    (B) your
    (C) yours
    (D) yourself

105. The ------- design engineer on the drone camera project is Iseul Bae.
    (A) lead
    (B) each
    (C) front
    (D) most

106. After reading several reviews, Mr. Kim was able to decide which printer ------- for the office.
    (A) buying
    (B) had bought
    (C) buy
    (D) to buy

107. Please remove the boxes left in the staff lounge ------- 5 P.M.
    (A) of
    (B) to
    (C) as
    (D) by

108. The Southport ------- plant is expected to begin production in three days.
    (A) manufacture
    (B) manufactured
    (C) manufacturing
    (D) manufactures

109. After accepting a job offer, a candidate must ------- all onboarding tasks before the start date.
(A) complete
(B) proceed
(C) recover
(D) enlist

110. Although ------- training has just begun, Ms. Yu has already mastered the company's proprietary accounting software.
(A) her
(B) she
(C) hers
(D) herself

111. Ms. Clayton was ------- to find that none of her files had been lost during the power failure.
(A) easy
(B) delightful
(C) relieved
(D) absolute

112. During Mr. Nagahori's tenure as CEO at Unten Properties, the company has grown -------.
(A) signify
(B) significance
(C) significant
(D) significantly

113. Safety must always be the top ------- in each step of the glassblowing process.
(A) surface
(B) material
(C) priority
(D) position

114. Central Science Museum hosts online seminars by experts who ------- topics related to information technology.
(A) are covered
(B) covering
(C) to cover
(D) cover

115. Conradia Computers ------- changed the direction of its marketing strategy last week.
(A) thickly
(B) abruptly
(C) formerly
(D) frequently

116. Because of an abundance of ------- candidates, Xaniper Industries may take longer than expected to name a new CEO.
(A) qualify
(B) qualifier
(C) qualified
(D) qualifies

117. All of our tablet computers come with a one-year warranty ------- includes hardware repairs and replacements.
(A) that
(B) who
(C) what
(D) it

118. The Exprite Foundation Board of Directors is ------- of nine members who are elected annually by the public.
(A) expected
(B) described
(C) composed
(D) announced

119. Mortgage brokers generally prefer to review all the financial documents ------- meeting with a new client.
(A) toward
(B) further
(C) lately
(D) before

120. Management ------- candidates for promotion by the end of the month.
(A) identify
(B) identifying
(C) will identify
(D) to identify

121. While we typically charge $25 for missed appointments, we understand that ------- circumstances may arise.

(A) unforeseen
(B) excessive
(C) approximate
(D) acclaimed

122. At Blu Hedge, clients receive 1 percent interest, pay no account fees, and can make unlimited -------.

(A) transfer
(B) transfers
(C) transferred
(D) transferring

123. Farist Bakery, which specializes in dessert catering, is located ------- the Liverpool Convention Complex.

(A) near
(B) without
(C) since
(D) following

124. The presentations were ------- than we expected, so there was ample time left for questions.

(A) brief
(B) briefly
(C) briefer
(D) briefest

125. According to our -------, your order will arrive in three days or we will refund 50 percent of the cost.

(A) distribution
(B) guarantee
(C) exception
(D) discount

126. Several Seoul-based companies have ------- redesigned their workplaces to be more colorful and comfortable.

(A) note
(B) noted
(C) notable
(D) notably

127. The employee picnic will be postponed until next Friday because of the ------- cold temperatures this week.

(A) deceptively
(B) unnecessarily
(C) irresponsibly
(D) unseasonably

128. The accounting department is in first place in the office fund-raising challenge, ------- just two more days to go.

(A) against
(B) namely
(C) with
(D) else

129. Pink Geranium Coffee has struggled to ------- its new bottled espresso from similar beverages on the market.

(A) participate
(B) distinguish
(C) overturn
(D) revoke

130. ------- it is occasionally inconvenient, Mr. Ohtani expects all team members to attend his weekly meeting.

(A) Though
(B) As soon as
(C) Because
(D) When

PART 6

Directions: Read the texts that follow. A word, phrase, or sentence is missing in parts of each text. Four answer choices for each question are given below the text. Select the best answer to complete the text. Then mark the letter (A), (B), (C), or (D) on your answer sheet.

Questions 131-134 refer to the following advertisement.

Muffin Lady Muffins

One day nearly 160 years ago, Arianna Sweeney brought some of her homemade muffins to the local town square to give to her friends. Everyone loved them! ------- , Ms. Sweeney started
                                                                                                    131.
sharing muffins with anyone who wanted one. ------- . After a few months, she became known
                                              132.
around town as the Muffin Lady.

Today, Muffin Lady Muffins are made by hand ------- the same original recipes developed by
                                              133.
Arianna Sweeney. We are committed to baking Muffin Lady Muffins authentically with only the finest ingredients. We hope you enjoy our delicious ------- !
                                                                                         134.

131. (A) Now that
     (B) After all
     (C) Otherwise
     (D) Before long

132. (A) With many savory options, muffins are not just for breakfast anymore.
     (B) Every week, she baked a new variety to deliver to eager takers.
     (C) She would take daily walks with her friends.
     (D) Unfortunately, it took nearly three hours to prepare a batch.

133. (A) using
     (B) used
     (C) use
     (D) to use

134. (A) creates
     (B) created
     (C) creatively
     (D) creations

Questions 135-138 refer to the following product description.

Teksheen Supply >> Products >> Natural Hand Soap

Many brands of hand soap contain unnecessary chemicals. For those who ------- a soap with no
                                                                         135.
added artificial substances, Teksheen Supply's natural hand soap is the ideal choice. This unscented soap is packaged in a handy dispenser bottle. ------- patented formula is designed to
                                                                                           136.
keep your hands clean yet soft with a mix of natural vitamins and oils. ------- . Do you operate a
                                                                         137.
business and want a safe and effective hand soap manufactured through sustainable processes? If so, you may purchase this ------- in bulk at discounted prices. Visit our Ordering
                                                                    138.
page for details.

135. (A) prefer
     (B) preferring
     (C) preferable
     (D) preference

136. (A) Its
     (B) Such
     (C) Some
     (D) None

137. (A) Many soaps have a fragrance that is too strong for customers.
     (B) Handwashing is essential for workers in the food industry.
     (C) Several factors can influence the price of soap products.
     (D) All the ingredients are sourced from plants found in the wild.

138. (A) equipment
     (B) fabric
     (C) issue
     (D) item

Questions 139-142 refer to the following article.

Moortap Bistro Plans to Close Its Doors

When Rowena Ellison opened the Moortap Bistro in a remote village in the Downland Moors, she wanted to attract customers from larger towns. She ------- an unusual menu of local dishes
                                                                                                                                              139.
prepared with less familiar ingredients, all in a beautiful setting. Her plan worked.

The ------- became one of the area's most successful venues and remains so now. At this point,
     140.
though, Ellison says she is ready to close the bistro and retire.

"I've loved every minute of this adventure," says Ellison. "I've been in the restaurant business for almost 50 years. ------- . It's such a ------- environment. I'm finally ready to slow down."
                                                141.   **142.**

Ellison intends to spend more time in her garden. She is searching for a buyer for the bistro.

139. (A) offers
 (B) offered
 (C) will offer
 (D) is offering

140. (A) field
 (B) clinic
 (C) eatery
 (D) theater

141. (A) I update the menu quarterly based on diners' feedback.
 (B) Even so, business has not been good lately.
 (C) My parents managed the bistro before I was born.
 (D) But the time has come for something new.

142. (A) fast-paced
 (B) comforting
 (C) widespread
 (D) family-oriented

Questions 143-146 refer to the following e-mail.

To: Amelia Sanchez <amelia.sanchez@silvermail.co.uk>
From: Brooks Hunley <b.hunley@carltonamespaving.co.uk>
Date: 10 October
Subject: Follow-up on our recent meeting

Dear Ms. Sanchez,

I am following up on our recent site visit with recommendations for repairing your business's driveway.

As noted during the visit, the current driveway contains several low spots where water collects during heavy rains. We could address this drainage issue in ------- ways. The first would be to patch the low spots with filler. ------- , we could remove all of the old asphalt and replace it with a porous material such as crushed gravel. ------- . A gravel bed allows rainwater to pass into the underlying soil and be reabsorbed.

Please give me a call ------- it is convenient so that we can talk about next steps.

Brooks Hunley

Carlton Ames Paving

143. (A) any
(B) several
(C) much
(D) enough

144. (A) Likewise
(B) Therefore
(C) Regardless
(D) Alternatively

145. (A) We regularly repair both commercial and private driveways.
(B) This approach is the one we would recommend.
(C) Please consider posting a review on our Web site.
(D) We will provide you with an itemized receipt.

146. (A) yet
(B) whenever
(C) until
(D) besides

PART 7

Directions: In this part you will read a selection of texts, such as magazine and newspaper articles, e-mails, and instant messages. Each text or set of texts is followed by several questions. Select the best answer for each question and mark the letter (A), (B), (C), or (D) on your answer sheet.

Questions 147-148 refer to the following information.

Enjoy Radial Tunes on Us!

Congratulations on your purchase of a Gregerson Pro Phone 13. As a special gift, we are offering you a free three-month subscription to Radial Tunes, an extensive digital music library. As a Radial Tunes subscriber, you can access hundreds of songs, music videos, and playlists specially curated by other users. To subscribe, simply complete the following form. You will receive a coupon code via e-mail. To redeem it, visit www.radialtunes.com/signup and enter the code. The code is valid for one-time use only and expires 24 hours after being sent.

Name: Terrence Furuta

E-mail: tfuruta@silkmail.com

Where did you purchase your Gregerson product?
PNE Retailers, Winnipeg, Canada

---

147. What is NOT offered to Radial Tunes subscribers?

(A) Access to a large library of songs
(B) Music playlists posted by subscribers
(C) Music videos
(D) Audio interviews with popular musicians

148. What is indicated about Mr. Furuta?

(A) He recently moved to Canada.
(B) He could not activate a special service.
(C) He recently bought a Gregerson Pro Phone 13.
(D) He is employed by PNE Retailers.

Questions 149-150 refer to the following memo.

> # MEMO
>
> To: All Staff
> From: Jun Heo, Associate Director, Human Resources
> Date: March 31
> Re: New business cards
>
> As a result of our merger with Frantum Corporation, printed business cards for all Ketola Enterprises employees will be replaced. All employees should receive the new business cards by May 1. Please stop distributing the old business cards when the new cards are delivered. The new cards will feature the new corporate name (yet to be revealed) and our exciting new logo. The new cards will be printed on a higher-quality paper stock, as many of you requested.
>
> If your new business cards are not delivered to your desk by May 1, please contact me directly at extension 2933.

149. What prompted the need for the memo?

(A) A recent increase in remote work
(B) A change in a company's name
(C) A series of printing errors
(D) A complaint about paper quality

150. What is suggested about the new business cards?

(A) They will be issued only to full-time employees.
(B) They will be mailed to employees' homes.
(C) They will be printed during the month of April.
(D) They will include the original Frantum Corporation logo.

Questions 151-152 refer to the following online chat discussion.

Priya Begani [9:02 A.M.]
Hi, Jared. Could you tell me the date of the management skills workshop you're leading?

Jared Oxley [9:03 A.M.]
Thursday, September 4. It will take up most of the day. Are you still planning to come?

Priya Begani [9:05 A.M.]
I wouldn't miss it! I only asked because I'm trying to decide when to schedule an accounting department meeting during that week, and the only days I'll be in the office are September 2, 3, and 4. After that, I won't be back until September 15, which would be too late.

Jared Oxley [9:06 A.M.]
Don't forget that the office will be closed on the morning of September 2 for maintenance work. The crew is supposed to be finished by noon, but you never know.

Priya Begani [9:07 A.M.]
Oh, right. The last time they did maintenance work, the office ended up being closed all day. That leaves only one sure date for that accounting meeting then. Thanks for reminding me.

Jared Oxley [9:08 A.M.]
No problem. By the way, a few of us are getting together at Ayala's Bistro after work today. Would you like to join us?

Priya Begani [9:09 A.M.]
I can't—I have a doctor's appointment after work. I'll go next time!

---

151. At 9:05 A.M., what does Ms. Begani imply when she writes, "I wouldn't miss it"?

(A) She will be present at an upcoming workshop.
(B) The accounting meeting is extremely important.
(C) A social event after work promises to be fun.
(D) She does not expect Mr. Oxley to return a document he borrowed.

152. When most likely will Ms. Begani meet with the accounting department?

(A) On September 2
(B) On September 3
(C) On September 4
(D) On September 15

Questions 153-155 refer to the following e-mail.

To:	Kele Tso <k.tso@faeberelectric.com>
From:	Connie Watkins <c.watkins@faeberelectric.com>
Date:	May 13
Subject:	RE: Employee handbook

This e-mail is being sent to all employees who have not yet signed the *Faeber Electric Employee Handbook* acceptance page. Acceptance of the terms is required of all employees and was requested in an e-mail I sent on May 1. Failure to sign the form may result in delayed salary payments.

The *Faeber Electric Employee Handbook* and the signature page are available at faeberelectric.com/handbook. A chart summarizing the key points in the handbook is also available on that site.

If you have any questions, please contact your manager or reach out directly to me.

Best,

Connie Watkins
Human Resources Officer

153. What is the purpose of the e-mail?

(A) To notify Mr. Tso about a Web site address change
(B) To explain how to access an employee payment system
(C) To remind Mr. Tso of the requirement to sign a form
(D) To inform Mr. Tso about a change to his work schedule

154. What does the e-mail indicate about Ms. Watkins?

(A) She is a new employee at Faeber Electric.
(B) She wrote the *Faeber Electric Employee Handbook*.
(C) She sent an e-mail to employees on May 1.
(D) She is Mr. Tso's manager.

155. The word "points" in paragraph 2, line 2, is closest in meaning to

(A) details
(B) locations
(C) opinions
(D) stages

Questions 156-157 refer to the following Web page.

About Our Magazine

CVT Direct is an Australian trade magazine published by Lorne Transportation, the largest freight vehicle corporation in the country. The magazine is sent free upon request to mid- and upper-level managers of dealerships with fleets of 25 or more vehicles for transporting goods nationwide.

To receive a subscription to *CVT Direct*, send your company mailing address, e-mail, and phone number to cvtsubscription@lornetransportation.com.au. All personally identifiable information will be treated confidentially in accordance with the Lorne privacy statement, which can be found at lornetransportation.com.au. Your personally identifiable information may be used to provide you with additional information about Lorne's products and services.

156. Executives in what industry would most likely read *CVT Direct* magazine?

(A) Automotive repair
(B) Commercial trucking
(C) Mechanical engineering
(D) Warehouse construction

157. What is one topic the Web page addresses?

(A) Recent changes to a distribution strategy
(B) How subscriber information is used
(C) Requirements for ordering products
(D) Why demand for a publication has increased

Questions 158-160 refer to the following flyer.

Trust Gernack Home with Your Next Remodeling Project!

Gernack Home has proudly provided customized home-renovation solutions in the Nashville area for 30 years. We work with clients on projects of all kinds, no matter how large or small. Our specialties are renovating kitchens and bathrooms, converting basements and garages into recreation rooms or home offices, and building home additions.

We can assure you that Gernack Home installs only products of the highest quality. You will surely join our list of satisfied customers once you see the work done by our team of expert installers.

Call (615) 555-0118 to schedule a visit for a free consultation. Or visit the showroom on our Web site at www.gernackhome.com. While there, take advantage of our latest feature: a virtual home renovation assistant. Our online assistants can help you build a virtual room so that you can take a first look at the renovation of your dreams.

---

158. What is NOT indicated as a service provided by Gernack Home?

(A) Kitchen renovation
(B) Home-office creation
(C) Patio installation
(D) Home-addition building

159. The word "assure" in paragraph 2, line 1, is closest in meaning to

(A) advise
(B) promise
(C) comfort
(D) support

160. What is a new offering provided by Gernack Home?

(A) An online showroom
(B) A visualization tool
(C) A photo-sharing page
(D) A mobile app for scheduling visits

Questions 161-163 refer to the following e-mail.

To:	Lauri Woods <lauriwoods@coralmail.com>
From:	Customer Service <customerservice@honeycanyonapparel.com>
Date:	October 4
Subject:	Thank you

Dear Ms. Woods,

Thank you for your recent purchase! We hope you are enjoying your items. — [1] —.

We wanted to take the opportunity to suggest some other items you might like. — [2] —. Please visit honeycanyonapparel.com/wardrobe and enter code RN49X to see a list of suggestions curated especially for you. — [3] —. Among the selections, we have highlighted several sweaters that would look beautiful with the skirt you bought.

And, to thank you for being a Honey Canyon customer for so many years, we are also offering you a 20 percent discount on your next order. — [4] —. Simply place an order within one month to receive the discount.

We look forward to helping you fill your closet with our latest styles!

Sincerely,

Customer Service, Honey Canyon Apparel

161. What is one purpose of the e-mail?

(A) To announce that items have been restocked
(B) To process a returned item
(C) To announce a new line of business wear
(D) To share personalized clothing recommendations

162. What is indicated about Ms. Woods?

(A) She is applying for a job at Honey Canyon Apparel.
(B) She has shopped at Honey Canyon Apparel before.
(C) She prefers to wear casual clothing.
(D) She works as a fashion designer.

163. In which of the positions marked [1], [2], [3], and [4] does the following sentence best belong?

"This will be automatically applied to your shopping cart when you check out."

(A) [1]
(B) [2]
(C) [3]
(D) [4]

Questions 164-167 refer to the following advertisement.

Nibora XC-35 Sport Utility Vehicle (SUV)

Wherever you want to go, from the beach to the backwoods, the Nibora XC-35 can take you there! The XC-35's powerful engine provides up to 275 horsepower, while the redesigned body gives this SUV a sleek and sporty look. With significant clearance from the ground and strong stabilization to protect from bumps, the Nibora XC-35 offers a smooth ride even on the roughest terrain and will give you the confidence to take it on any wilderness adventure.

The Nibora XC-35 is available as a gas-powered vehicle or a hybrid. Customers may also choose between manual and automatic transmissions. All vehicles come standard with all-wheel drive and a navigation system with phone pairing.

Options available for the XC-35 include a sunroof, a Sonic Boom stereo system, cruise control, a roof rack, and more. To save on the options you love, visit your nearby Nibora dealer to see what kinds of value packages they offer.

And before you visit, go to www.nibora.com/build and customize the look of your new Nibora XC-35 by choosing exterior color, upholstery style, and graphic decals.

Buy your new Nibora XC-35 today!

164. What is suggested about the XC-35 ?

(A) It is Nibora's best-selling vehicle.
(B) It is good for parking in small spaces.
(C) It has received more positive reviews than other SUVs have received.
(D) It is good for driving on many types of surfaces.

165. What feature comes with all XC-35 SUVs?

(A) A hybrid engine
(B) All-wheel drive
(C) A sunroof
(D) Cruise control

166. What is mentioned in the advertisement about the options for the XC-35 ?

(A) They can be discounted if bought as a package.
(B) They are unavailable in some dealerships.
(C) Some will be discontinued soon.
(D) Some are available only if bought in a package.

167. According to the advertisement, how can customers choose the look of their XC-35 ?

(A) By making a telephone call
(B) By visiting a Web site
(C) By sending an e-mail
(D) By reviewing automobile magazines

Questions 168-171 refer to the following advertisement.

Koloa Music Education Collective

It's never too late to learn to play an instrument. A leader in children's music lessons for over 15 years, Koloa Music Education Collective is pleased to announce our private music education program for adults. — [1] —. Beginning on August 28, we will offer guitar and violin instruction for beginners.

All our instructors hold at least a bachelor's degree in music and have performance experience in orchestras or bands. Our instructors also have a record of success in music education. Instruction is available in several formats. We can schedule in-person instruction at our office or your residence. — [2] —.

Students must provide their instruments. — [3] —. To learn more and to find a list of recommended musical instrument stores, please visit our Web site at www.koloamusiceducationcollective.com.

If you are interested in scheduling our services, please fill out our online information form on our Web site. You can request the instructor of your choice, or we can match you with an instructor. — [4] —. An instructor will contact you within 48 hours. We are excited to help you become the musician you have always wanted to be!

168. Who most likely is the intended audience of the advertisement?

(A) Coordinators of after-school music programs
(B) Professional musicians
(C) Individuals with no music experience
(D) Music store owners

169. What is indicated about Koloa Music Education Collective?

(A) It offers group lessons for adults.
(B) It employs musicians who have university degrees.
(C) It operates a recording studio.
(D) It provides a complimentary musical instrument.

170. Who from Koloa Music Education Collective will first contact an interested customer?

(A) A manager
(B) A sales associate
(C) An office administrator
(D) An instructor

171. In which of the positions marked [1], [2], [3], and [4] does the following sentence best belong?

"Alternatively, we can provide online lessons to accommodate your schedule."

(A) [1]
(B) [2]
(C) [3]
(D) [4]

Questions 172-175 refer to the following online chat discussion.

Lynette Walter (4:45 P.M.)
Can the three of us get together for lunch tomorrow before the sales meeting?

Tripp Hines (4:46 P.M.)
Sure, Lynette. Is there something specific you would like to talk about?

Lynette Walter (4:47 P.M.)
I just want to make sure that we're on the same page about the new marketing campaign.

Tripp Hines (4:48 P.M.)
The one for the line of summer shoes?

Lynette Walter (4:49 P.M.)
Yes. I need to catch up on what I missed while I was away in Boston, both the text and the graphics being developed.

April Au (4:50 P.M.)
Sorry, when and where is the sales meeting? I checked my calendar, and I could not find that meeting.

Tripp Hines (4:51 P.M.)
It starts at 3:00 in the boardroom. You don't need to be there. It's only for people involved in the graphics.

April Au (4:52 P.M.)
What a relief! And yes, I can go to lunch with you, Lynette, and provide an update on the language being considered.

Lynette Walter (4:53 P.M.)
Wonderful. I'll see you both tomorrow at 1:30 in the lobby. We can decide where to eat then.

172. Why does Ms. Walter want to have lunch with Mr. Hines and Ms. Au?

(A) To share her experiences on a recent trip
(B) To debate pricing for a line of footwear
(C) To discuss a marketing campaign for a product
(D) To plan a summer retreat for the sales team

173. Who is expected to attend the meeting at 3:00 P.M.?

(A) Graphic designers
(B) Copy editors
(C) Only sales managers
(D) Only staff from the Boston office

174. At 4:52 P.M., what does Ms. Au most likely mean when she writes, "What a relief"?

(A) She is pleased that Ms. Walter agrees with her.
(B) She is grateful to be invited to an event.
(C) She is happy her calendar is correct.
(D) She is happy to meet with her friends.

175. Where will Ms. Au, Mr. Hines, and Ms. Walter meet tomorrow?

(A) In the boardroom
(B) In the lobby
(C) In Ms. Walter's office
(D) In the break room

Questions 176-180 refer to the following invoice and e-mail.

Greatford Curtains
137 Chapel Way, Birmingham B8 3HU
0121 496 0608

Thank you for your order and for supporting our family's small business. To show our appreciation, we are offering you 10 percent off your next order of £200 or more. Use coupon code NEWCURTAINS.

Customer Information
Nicolla Grant
17 Durst Place
Whitstable CT5 1AH

Date: 23 July

Order Number: 19842

Fabric Samples	Number	Price
Cambridge	x1	£ 8.00
Manchester	x1	£ 8.00
Oxford	x1	£ 8.00
Windsor	x1	£ 8.00
Shipping		£ 4.25
Subtotal		£36.25
VAT		£ 7.25
Total		**£43.50**

To:	Greatford Curtains <customerservice@greatfordcurtains.co.uk>
From:	Nicolla Grant <ngrant@sapphiremail.co.uk>
Date:	27 July
Subject:	Order #19842

Good afternoon,

I received my fabric samples today, and they are beautiful! I would like to get a quote for custom curtains for my dining room using the Manchester fabric. I need four panels, 117 cm x 228 cm each, made in your box pleat style. Please let me know how much that will cost and when I can expect to receive them. As a reminder, I have a coupon code for 10 percent off.

I am also interested in curtains for my living room, but the shades of blue in all the samples I received do not work well in that space. Could you please send me samples of your Edinburgh and Norwich fabrics? I understand that they come in shades of green. Feel free to charge the credit card I saved to my online profile during my last order on 23 July.

Thank you,

Nicolla Grant

176. What is indicated about Greatford Curtains?

(A) It is a family-owned business.
(B) It is having a clearance sale.
(C) It is located at 17 Durst Place.
(D) It offers free shipping.

177. What does Ms. Grant request?

(A) A refund of an overpayment
(B) An exchange of an item that is too small
(C) A price for a customized product
(D) Express shipping on an order

178. What is most likely true about the Cambridge fabric sample listed on the invoice?

(A) It is blue.
(B) It cost £43.50.
(C) It will be used in a custom order.
(D) It will be used in Ms. Grant's dining room.

179. What is suggested about order number 19842 ?

(A) It arrived later than expected.
(B) It was missing several items.
(C) It included a sample of Norwich fabric.
(D) It was placed online.

180. In the e-mail, the word "last" in paragraph 2, line 4, is closest in meaning to

(A) final
(B) previous
(C) remaining
(D) separate

Questions 181-185 refer to the following announcement and e-mail.

Join Us for the Portland Friends of the Wild
Fourteenth Annual Dinner and Fund-Raiser
Saturday, August 13, 5:00 to 9:00 P.M.
At Golden Owl Hall, 926 Hope Street, Portland, OR 97035

We have planned a fabulous night of food and fun in support of Portland Friends of the Wild, a nonprofit environmental organization working to preserve our city's parks and green spaces since 1981.

The evening will include a three-course vegetarian dinner prepared by Green Earth Provisions and an auction of pieces by local artists, followed by dancing to the musical stylings of DJ Shay Silverman.

Tickets for the event are $100 per person and are available for purchase until August 10 at www.portlandfriendsofthewild.org/fund-raiser. If you have questions about the event or would like to donate something for our auction, please contact Minna Nguyen at mnguyen@portlandfriendsofthewild.org.

To:	Daniella Atkins <datkins@silkmail.com>
From:	Minna Nguyen <mnguyen@portlandfriendsofthewild.org>
Date:	June 17
Subject:	Portland Friends of the Wild event

Dear Ms. Atkins,

I hope this e-mail finds you well. My name is Minna Nguyen, and I am the new head of fund-raising operations for Portland Friends of the Wild. I know you worked with Stefano Cleary, who was the head of fund-raising operations when you donated one of your beautiful sculptures last year. Stefano speaks so highly of you!

On that note, would you be open to donating another piece of sculpture to this year's fund-raiser, which is coming up in August? We would be thrilled to include your work again. And as a token of our appreciation, we would happily offer two free tickets to the event. We are working with a new catering company this year, and the food should be delicious.

Please let me know your thoughts by July 15. I can be reached at (503) 555-0145.

Sincerely,

Minna Nguyen

181. What is indicated about Portland Friends of the Wild?

(A) It has an office on Hope Street.
(B) It was founded by Mr. Silverman.
(C) It holds a fund-raising event every two years.
(D) It focuses on protecting the environment.

182. Where will Portland Friends of the Wild's event be held?

(A) In a park
(B) In a banquet hall
(C) In an artist's studio
(D) In Ms. Nguyen's home

183. What is one purpose of the e-mail?

(A) To request a payment
(B) To confirm a purchase
(C) To request a contribution
(D) To confirm the receipt of tickets

184. What can be concluded about Green Earth Provisions?

(A) It has been in business since 1981.
(B) It will prepare a chicken dish for the fund-raiser.
(C) It has several locations in downtown Portland.
(D) It will provide the food for the fund-raiser for the first time.

185. What is true about Mr. Cleary?

(A) He previously worked in the position Ms. Nguyen now holds.
(B) He has been offered free tickets to the fund-raiser.
(C) He owns one of Ms. Atkins' sculptures.
(D) He is an accomplished sculptor.

Questions 186-190 refer to the following Web page and e-mails.

https://www.deltacityartmuseum.org/exhibits

Delta City Art Museum—Current Exhibits

The Impressionists, May 1–June 30, Main Gallery
Paintings from this well-known nineteenth-century art movement will be on display, including works by both famous and lesser-known artists.

Native American Pottery, May 15–July 16, Shawe Memorial Gallery
Visitors to this exhibit will learn about the wide range of pottery-related techniques developed and utilized by Indigenous peoples across North America.

Classical Greece and Beyond, May 22–August 21, Techtmann Gallery
This exhibit features statues of human subjects from classical Greece, along with modern pieces influenced by the classical style.

Artists of Delta City, Permanent Exhibit, Zhang Atrium
This popular exhibit showcases contemporary works by local artists in various media, including oil and watercolor paintings, photographs, fiber art, and mixed-media works. Although the exhibit is ongoing, individual pieces are displayed on a rotating basis and are on view for a limited time only.

E-Mail Message

To: Delta City Art Museum <info@deltacityartmuseum.org>
From: Lorelei Desnoyers <lorelei.desnoyers@klarsenuniversity.edu>
Date: May 2
Subject: Inquiry

Good morning,

I am a new art instructor at Klarsen University. One of my colleagues told me that the Delta City Art Museum provides tours for local art students. I am interested in bringing my Art 103 class to view and sketch some of the pieces you have on display. Since Art 103 focuses on studying and drawing the human form, the statues will be getting most of our attention. However, I'm hoping that we could have a brief tour of the whole museum before we begin our work. Please let me know if this could be arranged.

Thank you in advance for your assistance!

Lorelei Desnoyers
School of Art & Design
Klarsen University
504-555-0177

To:	Lorelei Desnoyers <lorelei.desnoyers@klarsenuniversity.edu>
From:	Jocelyn Grady <jgrady@deltacityartmuseum.org>
Date:	May 3
Subject:	RE: Inquiry

Dear Ms. Desnoyers,

Thank you for your e-mail. Your colleague was correct: the museum does indeed provide that service. We would likely schedule you on a Tuesday, since that is typically our least busy day. I have forwarded your message to our office of public programs. A staff member will contact you by phone with more details.

Please note that the use of paints, including watercolors, is prohibited in all museum galleries. Pencils and charcoal are permitted, although visitors are asked to take care not to leave smudges on museum surfaces. We also allow photography and video recording as long as patrons are considerate of other visitors.

We are grateful for your interest in Delta City Art Museum and look forward to hosting your class.

Jocelyn Grady
Information and Community Outreach
Delta City Art Museum

---

186. What is indicated on the Web page about the *Artists of Delta City* exhibit?

(A) It includes pottery by Native American artists.
(B) It will be closed from May through August.
(C) The works of art on display are regularly changed.
(D) The paintings on view were created in the nineteenth century.

187. Where will Ms. Desnoyers' class most likely spend their time sketching?

(A) In the Main Gallery
(B) In the Shawe Memorial Gallery
(C) In the Techtmann Gallery
(D) In the Zhang Atrium

188. According to Ms. Grady, what did Ms. Desnoyers' colleague correctly state?

(A) That the museum gives class tours
(B) That the museum provides drawing lessons
(C) That the museum offers group discounts
(D) That the museum allows private events

189. What will Ms. Desnoyers most likely do as a result of the second e-mail?

(A) She will forward the e-mail.
(B) She will visit a museum office.
(C) She will consult a Web site.
(D) She will expect a telephone call.

190. What activity does Ms. Grady indicate is forbidden in the museum galleries?

(A) Taking photographs
(B) Recording videos
(C) Drawing with charcoal
(D) Painting with watercolors

Questions 191-195 refer to the following article, letter, and invoice.

BOSTON (January 3)–According to a recent survey by the National Dentifrice Council, the United States toothpaste packaging market is expected to grow by more than 3 percent over the next decade.

Collapsible toothpaste tubes continue to lead the market overall, but because they are composed of multiple layers, it is nearly impossible to recycle them. They are beginning to lose a small part of their market share to recyclable forms of packaging, including jars, bottles, and refillable pump dispensers.

Green Globe
550 Industrial Parkway
Silver Hills, KY 40502

March 7

Rohit Patel
Director of Operations
Macker Drugstores
536 Herald Street, Suite 202
Columbus, OH 43004

Dear Mr. Patel,

Thank you for allowing me to speak with you and your team about Green Globe All-Natural Toothpaste.

As I explained during our meeting, I founded Green Globe ten years ago to offer an alternative to the nonrecyclable packaging used by nearly every other toothpaste brand. Our toothpaste is packaged in 100-milliliter glass jars. It is currently sold in stores throughout the United States and Canada. I hope that shoppers will soon be able to buy the product in all the stores in the Macker Drugstores chain.

I understand that you would like to purchase two cases initially to test sales in a single store. Let me emphasize that, as soon as you are ready, we can immediately ship cases to all Macker Drugstores—and, of course, we will offer you a significant discount on all orders over ten cases.

Thank you again for taking the time to meet with me. I look forward to working with you.

Sincere regards,

Verna Brown

Verna Brown

INVOICE

Green Globe · 550 Industrial Parkway · Silver Hills, KY 40502

Order 673348
March 15

Ship to:
Macker Drugstores Distribution Center
4000 Highway 36
Logan, OH 43138

Item	Quantity	Price per unit	Amount
Green Globe All-Natural Toothpaste	2 cases	$145.00	$290.00
		Shipping	$26.00
		Subtotal	$316.00
		Tax	$19.00
		Discount	$0.00
		TOTAL	**$335.00**

191. What does the article state about collapsible toothpaste tubes?

    (A) They are difficult to recycle.
    (B) They are not very popular.
    (C) They were invented in the United States.
    (D) They were not included in a survey.

192. Why did Ms. Brown most likely send the letter?

    (A) To request a meeting
    (B) To recommend a job candidate
    (C) To follow up on a sales presentation
    (D) To place an order for a product

193. What is indicated about products sold in the type of packaging used by Green Globe?

    (A) They are recommended by the National Dentifrice Council.
    (B) They can be purchased only at Macker Drugstores.
    (C) Their manufacturing cost is higher than average.
    (D) Their share of the market is rising.

194. What does Ms. Brown indicate about Green Globe toothpaste?

    (A) It was originally packaged in tubes.
    (B) It was created by a dentist.
    (C) It is available in two countries.
    (D) It comes in multiple flavors.

195. What is most likely true about the order placed by Macker Drugstores?

    (A) The same order will be delivered every month.
    (B) The merchandise will be used in a market test.
    (C) The price was discounted significantly.
    (D) The shipping fee was refunded by Green Globe.

Questions 196-200 refer to the following e-mail, schedule, and review.

E-mail

To: Sleepy Time Hotel <information@sleepytimehotel.com>
From: Jongwoo Cho <jongwoo.cho@onyxmail.com>
Date: August 15
Subject: My hotel stay

Greetings!

I made an online booking for a two-night stay at your hotel for this upcoming Friday, August 19, but I cannot figure out how to get to the hotel once I'm in Charlesville. I downloaded the City Link Line app as suggested on your Web site, but I am finding it difficult to navigate. No options are coming up for the Dalton light-rail station, which you specifically mention as the station where hotel guests should disembark. Could you please clarify how best to get to the hotel? Judging from the pictures on the Web site, the hotel looks like a beautiful place to stay. I am looking forward to spending a couple of nights right by the beach.

Thank you,

Jongwoo Cho

City Link Line

Monday to Friday Schedule – Johnstown to Charlesville

Departs from Johnstown	Arrives in Charlesville
7:00 A.M.	8:36 A.M.
10:05 A.M.	11:41 A.M.
1:00 P.M.	2:36 P.M.
4:05 P.M.	5:41 P.M.
7:00 P.M.	8:36 P.M.

https://www.sleepytimehotel.com/reviews

My stay at the Sleepy Time Hotel was fantastic. Initially, I was worried I could not get to the hotel easily from Johnstown, where I had just finished an exhilarating three-day professional conference. The hotel Web site is not crystal clear about transportation options. Since I am not familiar with this part of the country, I e-mailed the hotel, and someone responded immediately. Ultimately, it was easy to get to Charlesville. First, I took the 4:05 P.M. train out of Johnstown. Once I arrived at Charlesville Central Station, I rode the elevator to the basement, where the light-rail train platforms are located. I then boarded a light-rail train and rode it to the station directly across the street from the hotel. Apparently, the Charlesville light-rail system is relatively new. Keep in mind that there are no restaurants near the hotel, but there is a small grocery store around the corner. So I was able to purchase some food and have a picnic on the beach. Overall, this small hotel with lovely, bright rooms is a perfect escape from city life. I felt so relaxed when I finally returned to my office and got back to work.

Jongwoo Cho, posted on August 26

196. What is the purpose of the e-mail?

(A) To cancel a hotel reservation
(B) To obtain clear directions to a hotel
(C) To request instructions for downloading an app
(D) To learn more about a hotel's social media account

197. What does the e-mail suggest about the Sleepy Time Hotel?

(A) It is near a body of water.
(B) It used to have a restaurant.
(C) It is part of a large hotel chain.
(D) It mainly serves business travelers.

198. What is most likely true about the Dalton light-rail station?

(A) It has a large parking area.
(B) It is connected to a conference center.
(C) It is across the street from the Sleepy Time Hotel.
(D) It is being renovated.

199. At what time did Mr. Cho's train most likely arrive in Charlesville?

(A) At 11:41 A.M.
(B) At 2:36 P.M.
(C) At 5:41 P.M.
(D) At 8:36 P.M.

200. What does Mr. Cho mention in the review?

(A) He ate at a restaurant in Charlesville.
(B) He travels to Johnstown regularly.
(C) He visited a grocery store on August 26.
(D) He recently completed a business trip.

Stop! This is the end of the test. If you finish before time is called, you may go back to Parts 5, 6, and 7 and check your work.

ETS 토익 정기시험
기출문제집 5
1000 RC

TEST 03
무료 동영상 강의

저자와 출판사의 사전 허락 없이 내용의 일부 혹은 전부를 인용 및 복제하거나 발췌하여 사용할 수 없습니다.

RC
기출 TEST 03

READING TEST

In the Reading test, you will read a variety of texts and answer several different types of reading comprehension questions. The entire Reading test will last 75 minutes. There are three parts, and directions are given for each part. You are encouraged to answer as many questions as possible within the time allowed.

You must mark your answers on the separate answer sheet. Do not write your answers in your test book.

PART 5

Directions: A word or phrase is missing in each of the sentences below. Four answer choices are given below each sentence. Select the best answer to complete the sentence. Then mark the letter (A), (B), (C), or (D) on your answer sheet.

101. Despite ------- youth, Ms. Cho is already quite popular on social media.
    (A) she
    (B) her
    (C) hers
    (D) herself

102. Most of the materials distributed at last month's accounting conference are now ------- online.
    (A) available
    (B) intended
    (C) comparable
    (D) decisive

103. A full-scale ------- will be conducted by the accounting department.
    (A) reviewer
    (B) review
    (C) reviewed
    (D) reviews

104. Poshy Shoes vice president Lucille Jeris has been ------- to president of the company.
    (A) provided
    (B) decorated
    (C) promoted
    (D) responded

105. The report found that employees who take regular breaks are more ------- than those who take no breaks.
    (A) production
    (B) productively
    (C) productivity
    (D) productive

106. Customers of Twins Photocopiers are encouraged to contact a ------- if their machines need repairs.
    (A) replacement
    (B) technician
    (C) renewal
    (D) structure

107. The heavy traffic on the way to the airport ------- caused Ms. Ikeda to miss her flight.
    (A) nearly
    (B) near
    (C) nears
    (D) nearness

108. A news source suggested that the merger will ------- take place next year.
    (A) originally
    (B) probably
    (C) regularly
    (D) thoughtfully

109. The Seaborne Inn has ------- beautiful guest rooms that can be booked on a monthly basis.

(A) various
(B) among
(C) throughout
(D) itself

110. Ahearn Accessories' retail shop is located ------- Gordon Avenue and Hutch Street.

(A) until
(B) against
(C) at
(D) aside from

111. A majority of the city's residents rated its transportation app as -------.

(A) acceptability
(B) acceptable
(C) acceptance
(D) accepting

112. Dr. Cheung ------- Silk Valley Hospital at next weekend's medical fair.

(A) represent
(B) did represent
(C) is representing
(D) had represented

113. Frankie's Boutique had a financially ------- quarter after taking measures to reduce costs.

(A) plain
(B) profitable
(C) full
(D) additional

114. Because it submitted the lowest bid, Deb's Gifting has been chosen as the ------- of this year's holiday cards.

(A) supply
(B) supplier
(C) supplies
(D) supplying

115. The Whitetail Institute is the only ------- that tracks deer populations in rapidly expanding suburban areas.

(A) leadership
(B) neighborhood
(C) official
(D) organization

116. The committee members ------- attended the meeting are listed in the appendix.

(A) who
(B) they
(C) when
(D) some

117. Our new app is ------- designed to provide data-driven insights to investment professionals.

(A) specify
(B) specific
(C) specificity
(D) specifically

118. The results of the study suggest that more people ------- with night driving than previously believed.

(A) struggles
(B) struggling
(C) to struggle
(D) struggle

119. Each department has been asked to develop an action plan in ------- to the budget cuts announced last week.

(A) response
(B) effect
(C) apology
(D) confirmation

120. Our popular online training materials have ------- been shown to improve job seekers' skills.

(A) consistently
(B) emotionally
(C) spaciously
(D) randomly

GO ON TO THE NEXT PAGE

121. Ms. Yamada, ------- director of the Midlands Chamber of Commerce, was recently appointed to the state trade commission.
    (A) formed
    (B) former
    (C) formalize
    (D) formality

122. The software uses computer memory efficiently, allowing users to open ------- five files simultaneously.
    (A) far from
    (B) as for
    (C) up to
    (D) out of

123. A monthly newsletter is an excellent way to ------- your group's activities and events.
    (A) realize
    (B) propose
    (C) observe
    (D) promote

124. ------- the hotel does not have a restaurant on site, there are many dining options nearby.
    (A) While
    (B) Such as
    (C) Unless
    (D) Without

125. ------- a slight decline in revenue from the previous quarter, Blakely Components is moving forward with its expansion plan.
    (A) Aside
    (B) Despite
    (C) Becoming
    (D) Often

126. Abelia Dairy Company has undergone several changes in leadership ------- the past ten years.
    (A) over
    (B) into
    (C) since
    (D) beside

127. Opal City's Community Theater is holding ------- for its spring production during the first week of December.
    (A) to audition
    (B) auditioned
    (C) auditions
    (D) audition

128. Mr. Kane said he packed so ------- this morning that he forgot to bring a suit and tie for tomorrow's dinner.
    (A) enormously
    (B) briefly
    (C) hastily
    (D) mysteriously

129. Long before the training program began, Ms. Morris ------- the schedule to allow her team to attend.
    (A) was revised
    (B) is revising
    (C) had revised
    (D) has to revise

130. Mr. Swan will return to the planning meeting ------- the interns have arrived.
    (A) once
    (B) unlike
    (C) whereas
    (D) regarding

PART 6

Directions: Read the texts that follow. A word, phrase, or sentence is missing in parts of each text. Four answer choices for each question are given below the text. Select the best answer to complete the text. Then mark the letter (A), (B), (C), or (D) on your answer sheet.

Questions 131-134 refer to the following bank advertisement.

Take advantage of double rewards for a limited time!

Stretch your holiday season's shopping spree into January, and we will reward you with $4 cash back on every ------- of $50 or more. Additionally, cashback rewards will be ------- deposited into a
          131.   132.
separate Avanti savings account and earn a 3% annual interest rate. Enroll in our double-rewards program on Avanti's mobile or desktop app. ------- , stop by an Avanti branch for assistance.
                                                                133.
------- . On February 1, cashback rewards will return to $2 per $50 transaction.
134.

131. (A) purchase
     (B) purchaser
     (C) purchased
     (D) purchasing

132. (A) automate
     (B) automatic
     (C) automation
     (D) automatically

133. (A) Alternatively
     (B) Likewise
     (C) Nevertheless
     (D) Frequently

134. (A) The use of double rewards is a common practice in the banking industry.
     (B) Don't wait—the double-rewards promotion ends on January 31.
     (C) Please make sure to check your credit card balance weekly.
     (D) Thank you for providing feedback on your recent transaction.

Questions 135-138 refer to the following e-mail.

To: Shipping Team
From: Martina West
Date: February 21
Subject: Exciting news

Dear Team,

I am excited to share the news that Winnie Liu, our longtime team captain, will be moving on. Fortunately, she will not be leaving the company. ------- , Winnie will serve as our new regional distribution manager. We are thrilled about her ------- .
              135.   136.

We would like to show our appreciation for everything Winnie has done for our department, especially for our team. We will be hosting a party for Winnie in the break room at 3:00 P.M. on February 28, her ------- day with us. ------- . We look forward to seeing you there.
                                   137.   138.

Best,

Martina West
Shipping Manager
Croce Company

135. (A) Originally
     (B) Instead
     (C) Regardless
     (D) Moreover

136. (A) availability
     (B) promotion
     (C) cooperation
     (D) generosity

137. (A) final
     (B) finalize
     (C) finalized
     (D) finally

138. (A) Our day will start at 8:00 A.M., as usual.
     (B) She was the best candidate for the job.
     (C) Please join us for coffee and cake.
     (D) The break room is currently closed for maintenance.

Questions 139-142 refer to the following blog post.

How to Pitch Your Start-up to a Potential Investor

When planning a presentation for potential investors, do not keep them in suspense.

------- . This has the added benefit of grabbing investors' attention. Your company's young,
139.
dynamic team may be its greatest asset. On the other hand, if your team has years of valuable

experience together and this is ------- to the product or service you offer, mention that early as
140.
well. Finally, if ------- sets your company apart is its unique vision, make it your leading statement.
141.

If you can convince your audience that your company's product or service is destined for success,

you will likely acquire the ------- you seek.
142.

---

139. (A) Investors often expect a share of ownership.
(B) Reveal your company's greatest strength from the outset.
(C) Make sure to cite any sources you quote during your presentation.
(D) An infusion of cash is often necessary for growth.

140. (A) capable
(B) progressive
(C) first
(D) relevant

141. (A) it
(B) that
(C) what
(D) anything

142. (A) funding
(B) property
(C) materials
(D) awards

Questions 143-146 refer to the following e-mail.

To: Botswana Mining Staff
From: Phildah Ramogapi, Human Resources Director
Date: 4 April
Subject: Payroll portal upgrade

Good morning,

Botswana Mining's online payroll portal will be unavailable between 8 and 12 April to allow for a software upgrade. Please refrain from accessing the ------- over these five days.
                                                                    143.

The updated site ------- users to perform advanced operations, including setting up and managing
                144.
direct deposit preferences and accessing tax documents. It will also feature a live-chat function so that users can directly contact a human resources team member when needed. ------- .
                                                                                              145.

If you need to access your payroll and benefits details ------- the period mentioned above, please
                                                        146.
send an e-mail to hr@botswanamining.co.bw or visit our office in room 107 of the Ujima Tower.

Regards,

Phildah Ramogapi
Human Resources Director

---

143. (A) course
(B) system
(C) account
(D) plan

144. (A) enabled
(B) enabling
(C) will enable
(D) would have enabled

145. (A) This gathering will promote innovation among our employees.
(B) Our shareholders will be pleased with this new product.
(C) Productivity reductions will likely occur next month.
(D) This function will optimize the services offered by the department.

146. (A) apart from
(B) along with
(C) during
(D) toward

PART 7

Directions: In this part you will read a selection of texts, such as magazine and newspaper articles, e-mails, and instant messages. Each text or set of texts is followed by several questions. Select the best answer for each question and mark the letter (A), (B), (C), or (D) on your answer sheet.

Questions 147-148 refer to the following advertisement.

**Sumner Auto Supply
Service Special**

$29.95

Service includes:

- Conventional oil change
- Premium oil filter change
- Complimentary car inspection

This offer is valid only at our Smithville and Parkertown locations through August 31. Customers must present this coupon at the time of service. Limit one coupon per customer.

---

147. What service is NOT included with the special?

(A) An oil change
(B) A filter change
(C) A car inspection
(D) A car wash

148. What is indicated about the coupon?

(A) It can be used at all Sumner Auto Supply locations.
(B) It is available only to first-time customers.
(C) It must be used before the end of August.
(D) It can be used multiple times.

Questions 149-150 refer to the following article.

Melbury Daily News Briefs

(2 February)—Commuters are relieved that the River Avenue Railway Station is finally going to be renovated. The 100-year-old station is one of the busiest in the city, and it is in desperate need of repair.

At its 31 January meeting, the city council gave final approval to renovation plans submitted by the municipal engineering department, including a new entrance and roof. Also planned are murals for the station's interior walls. Local artists have been commissioned to submit proposals in March.

Work will begin in two weeks and take approximately eight months to complete. The station will remain open throughout.

149. What is the main purpose of the article?

(A) To report on the closure of a railway station
(B) To publicize the start of a renovation project
(C) To describe the significance of a historic building
(D) To emphasize the important role of local artists

150. According to the article, what will happen in March?

(A) Service on a new railway line will begin.
(B) A railway station's roof will be replaced.
(C) The city council will vote on a parking plan for River Avenue.
(D) Artists will deliver wall decoration ideas.

Questions 151-152 refer to the following e-mail.

E-mail

To: Tom Sanchez <tsanchez65@mailcurrent.net>
From: Jun Osman <josman@oregonartmuseum.org>
Date: September 19
Subject: New museum wing opening

Dear Mr. Sanchez:

Your presence is requested at the official opening of the Oregon Art Museum's Prosner Wing. The ceremony will be held on November 3 at 6:00 P.M. Appetizers and drinks will be served. Our first featured artist, Taro Mifune, will be on hand to mingle with the crowd and discuss his exhibit, *Oregonian Reflections*.

This private celebration is limited to invaluable museum members like you. You may bring one guest to the event. To ensure we have an accurate count of attendees, please respond no later than October 20.

Sincerely,

Jun Osman
Director, Oregon Art Museum

---

151. What is the purpose of the e-mail?

(A) To request that Mr. Sanchez pay for a painting
(B) To recruit a celebrity to act as master of ceremonies
(C) To invite Mr. Sanchez to an event
(D) To announce the opening of a new museum

152. What is indicated about Mr. Sanchez?

(A) He will cater an event at a museum.
(B) He is employed at the Oregon Art Museum.
(C) He displays his art throughout Oregon.
(D) He has a membership at an art museum.

Questions 153-154 refer to the following text-message chain.

Avani Mehta (8:57 A.M.)
Hi, Ed. I'm on the bus on my way to the warehouse. Remember that mobile app I told you about—the one for finding available storage locations? I'm using it now, and I think I've found something for us at 10 Maple Street.

Ed Beiger (8:59 A.M.)
Great. Are you sure it's not just an event space?

Avani Mehta (9:01 A.M.)
The description says it's ideal for retailers needing storage space, and it offers temporary rental terms.

Ed Beiger (9:02 A.M.)
That could work. Let's check out the particulars together later today after we complete our inventory work.

Avani Mehta (9:04 A.M.)
Sure. Our van is already loaded with our overstocked items. You could drive it over. If the location turns out to be a good fit, we can use the app to book the space and unload the van right there and then.

Ed Beiger (9:05 A.M.)
That's exactly what I was thinking.

Avani Mehta (9:06 A.M.)
Wonderful. See you soon.

153. What are the writers mainly discussing?

(A) Renting a temporary space
(B) Hiring seasonal workers
(C) Planning a sales event
(D) Developing a mobile phone app

154. At 9:05 A.M., what does Mr. Beiger most likely mean when he writes, "That's exactly what I was thinking"?

(A) He will be at a warehouse by the time Ms. Mehta arrives.
(B) He will load a van with overstocked items.
(C) He is willing to drive a van to a location.
(D) He will download a mobile phone app.

Questions 155-157 refer to the following Web page.

---

https://www.dannlabrothers.com/about

| Home | **About Us** | Products | Testimonials |

Dannla Brothers can help you make the most of your screen time.

Computers are an important part of our lives, and laptops in particular have become the default type of computer in the workplace. They enable users to work not only from home or the office but virtually anywhere. No matter where you choose to work, Dannla Brothers has products to maximize your productivity in front of the screen. We manufacture ergonomic laptop stands, comfortable chairs, and adjustable standing desks, among other products.

Because you use our products all day every business day, we constantly strive to improve their design. Built to last, every item we sell is backed by a ten-year guarantee on construction and finish. We invite you to visit our Testimonials page to review independent assessments of our products by noted business and technology publications.

To view our offerings and their features, visit our Products page. Note that we offer free standard shipping on all orders over $150. Expedited delivery is available for an extra fee. If you represent a business organization seeking to provide ergonomic solutions to your entire staff, we can offer a substantial volume discount. To receive a free price quote for a bulk order, please e-mail us at info@dannlabrothers.com. We will respond to your inquiry within 24 hours.

---

155. What kind of business is Dannla Brothers?

(A) A maker of computer furniture
(B) A provider of Internet service
(C) A seller of used computer equipment
(D) A distributor of computer components

156. What are visitors to the Web page encouraged to do?

(A) Purchase an extended warranty
(B) Submit photos of their workspace
(C) Attend technology seminars
(D) Read product reviews

157. According to the Web page, why should someone send an e-mail?

(A) To schedule a tour of a facility
(B) To learn about faster delivery options
(C) To obtain a price quote for a large order
(D) To receive product assembly information

Questions 158-160 refer to the following memo.

> ## MEMO
>
> To: All Staff
> From: Joan Paulsen, CEO, Osmond Microtronics Ltd.
> Date: 19 May
> Subject: Follow-up
>
> It was a pleasure to see so many of you at our company-wide meeting last week. Let me congratulate you again on our sales increase as well as the launch of our newest products, which are already regaining significant market share from our competitors.
>
> I would like to announce that several executive positions have been filled. Frank Gruen will be our chief financial officer, Patricia Lesner will serve as vice president of research and development, Lana Avon will be our director of marketing, and product designer Lewis Sung will now oversee his department as director of product design.
>
> One position remains open: director of human resources. Although Marcus Bromley's executive assignment was intended to remain unchanged, he recently decided to retire. We shall miss his analytical skills and bright sense of humour. Mr. Bromley plans to settle permanently in his native Pretoria in June. We all wish him a well-deserved happy future.

158. What did Ms. Paulsen do at a recent meeting?

(A) She discussed the merger of some competitors.
(B) She shared upcoming plans for marketing new products.
(C) She congratulated staff on the latest sales figures.
(D) She introduced some newly hired executives.

159. Who received a job promotion from within Osmond Microtronics Ltd.?

(A) Mr. Gruen
(B) Ms. Lesner
(C) Ms. Avon
(D) Mr. Sung

160. Why does Ms. Paulsen mention Pretoria?

(A) A colleague is planning to move there.
(B) Osmond Microtronics Ltd. will be relocating there.
(C) Most competitors are headquartered there.
(D) The company's products are now available there.

Questions 161-163 refer to the following e-mail.

To:	Henry Able <henryable@bormaninstitute.edu>
From:	Martha McGrath <mmcgrath@delahuntgreene.com>
Date:	December 2
Subject:	Your presentation

Dear Dr. Able:

— [1] —. Thank you for leading a professional development seminar at Delahunt, Greene, and Associates (DGA) last week. We appreciate new perspectives, particularly from individuals who work in academia. Our public relations staff was impressed with your insights into effective cross-cultural communication. We were particularly intrigued by your study on the importance of word choice in international communication. — [2] —. Would you mind providing us with a copy of the article you referenced?

DGA would like to explore additional ways we could partner with you or other researchers at the Borman Institute. — [3] —. Please suggest a convenient time when I could call you to discuss how we can work together in the future. Until then, thanks again for sharing your time and thoughts with us. — [4] —.

All the best,

Martha McGrath, DGA Public Relations Director

---

161. What is most likely true about Dr. Able?

(A) He does consulting work for government agencies.
(B) He conducts research at an institution.
(C) He has spoken at DGA on other occasions in the past.
(D) He has vast experience as a corporate executive.

162. What does Ms. McGrath indicate that she would like to do in the future?

(A) Teach at the Borman Institute
(B) Give a presentation at a seminar
(C) Offer Dr. Able a position at DGA
(D) Collaborate with Dr. Able's team

163. In which of the positions marked [1], [2], [3], and [4] does the following sentence best belong?

"We would love to read your complete research report."

(A) [1]
(B) [2]
(C) [3]
(D) [4]

Questions 164-167 refer to the following job posting.

Report Reviewer

Neveck Associates is looking to hire a report reviewer to join our New York regional team. This is a work-from-home position that involves collaborating with engineers to review and revise their technical reports. The regular work hours for this full-time position are Monday through Friday, 9:00 A.M. to 5:00 P.M. Salary is commensurate with experience. — [1] —.

The job involves editing engineering reports to ensure they meet quality specifications and comply with industry standards. — [2] —. The report reviewer will also need to track edits and discuss feedback patterns with authors at internal weekly meetings. — [3] —. Strong interpersonal skills and the ability to communicate across company departments are essential.

— [4] —. Applicants must have a bachelor's degree and at least two years of work experience in a relevant area. Formal training in technical writing would be a plus. Interested applicants should send a cover letter and résumé to hiringmanager@neveckassociates.com.

164. What is indicated about the available position?

(A) It is a remote position.
(B) It is a managerial role.
(C) It is a part-time job.
(D) It is a trainee position.

165. What is listed as a job requirement?

(A) A background in engineering
(B) Three years of editorial experience
(C) Good communication skills
(D) Previous experience at Neveck Associates

166. What does the job posting NOT mention?

(A) The job responsibilities
(B) The work schedule
(C) The starting date
(D) The education requirements

167. In which of the positions marked [1], [2], [3], and [4] does the following sentence best belong?

"Health insurance and retirement benefits are included."

(A) [1]
(B) [2]
(C) [3]
(D) [4]

Questions 168-171 refer to the following article.

New Garden Coming Soon to Raxford Park

ELBART CITY (March 30)—Local community group Friends of Green Spaces (FGS) is raising funds to build a new garden in Raxford Park. The group, which relies entirely on donations, collaborates with the city parks department on restoration and enhancement. It also offers guided nature tours and other educational programs.

"The goal of the current project," said FGS director Carol Reynoso, "is to create an attractive space to draw in more of the region's abundant birdlife."

Ms. Reynoso, a 25-year member of the FGS, is a lifelong resident of Elbart City. She is especially enthusiastic about the project because the city's elementary school borders the park. This means that the schoolchildren will be able to enjoy the garden every day.

Ms. Reynoso said that enough funds have already been secured to enable the FGS to begin garden construction in mid-April. The selection of plants will be made by Elbart University faculty. FGS volunteers will do the planting after parks department crews have laid fresh topsoil on the area designated for the garden. An opening ceremony is planned for May.

168. What is mentioned about the FGS?

(A) It was established ten years ago.
(B) It has discontinued its guided walks.
(C) It offers nature-related courses.
(D) It is funded by the city government.

169. Why does the FGS want to build a garden in Raxford Park?

(A) To display flowers native to the region
(B) To grow vegetables for school lunches
(C) To create an outdoor nature laboratory
(D) To attract a wide variety of birds

170. Who will select the plants for the new garden?

(A) Ms. Reynoso
(B) Members of the local community
(C) University professors
(D) Schoolchildren and their teachers

171. What work will be done by Elbart City employees?

(A) Raising funds
(B) Organizing an opening ceremony
(C) Purchasing supplies
(D) Preparing the ground for planting

Questions 172-175 refer to the following online chat discussion.

Eva Parkin [3:00 P.M.] Hi, all. Thanks for meeting to discuss our presentation to the board of directors next Friday. We'll only have a few minutes to make our case, so we must be prepared.

Nijad Naifeh [3:01 P.M.] I heard there's a possibility that the board won't increase our budget. I thought they believed in aggressive marketing.

Eva Parkin [3:02 P.M.] They do, but they have questions about our product. They are concerned about our recent sales downturn.

Nijad Naifeh [3:03 P.M.] But this has been a trend in the industry as a whole. Sales usually slow down this time of year.

Eva Parkin [3:04 P.M.] That's a great point. Could you send me any related data?

Nijad Naifeh [3:05 P.M.] I have the details onscreen right now. Give me a minute.

Eva Parkin [3:06 P.M.] The board will also ask why our proposed marketing budget focuses on social media rather than newspapers or radio. Lili, can you help with that?

Lili Tuan [3:07 P.M.] Sure. What would you like me to talk about?

Eva Parkin [3:08 P.M.] They wonder whether we have enough experience in this kind of advertising. Since this was your specialty at your last job, could you talk about possible strategies we could use here?

Lili Tuan [3:09 P.M.] Yes, no problem. I can list a few at the meeting.

172. What does Ms. Parkin want the board of directors to do?

(A) Increase her team's marketing budget
(B) Adopt a more aggressive pay scale
(C) Approve a new organizational structure
(D) Support a product-development strategy

173. What do the writers indicate about their product?

(A) It needs to be updated.
(B) It is sold only in retail stores.
(C) It is not as popular as competitors' products.
(D) It does not sell well at a certain time of year.

174. At 3:05 P.M., what does Mr. Naifeh imply when he writes, "I have the details onscreen right now"?

(A) He can correct some data errors.
(B) He can fulfill Ms. Parkin's request.
(C) He has been taking thorough notes.
(D) He will share information on a competitor's product.

175. What kind of advertising did Ms. Tuan focus on at her previous job?

(A) Radio
(B) Television
(C) Newspaper
(D) Social media

Questions 176-180 refer to the following Web page and online review.

https://www.branxleycycles.com.my/about

| Home | **About** | Shop | Contact |

About Our Products

We make three-wheeled cargo bicycles for commercial and personal use. All our bicycles are made by hand in our production facility in Kuala Lumpur with parts made by local craftspeople. For more than 40 years, we have been building high-quality, eco-friendly bicycles that are good for the health of both people and the planet. We are proud of our products, and we invite our customers to take photos of their Branxley bicycles in action and share the images via social media.

Update—30 August

We have experienced a dramatic surge in orders. Even with our staff working overtime to catch up, it may take longer than usual for customers to receive their bicycles. Currently, we are expecting a delivery time of 10 to 12 weeks for all bicycles ordered on or after August 15. We appreciate your understanding in this matter.

---

https://www.consumerreviewsplus.com.my

Review of Branxley Cycles

I have been a cycling enthusiast most of my life. Recently, I decided I needed a bicycle to bring bulky items home from stores. I searched online and inquired at local shops, but no one had quite what I wanted. After talking with a coworker, I learned about Branxley Cycles. I contacted the company via e-mail, and all my questions were answered promptly and thoroughly. I ordered a three-wheeled cargo bicycle from them on August 20 that was delivered in only two weeks. Branxley Cycles cargo bicycles have become very popular with area businesses; I see them everywhere now. It is hard to believe the company can meet the demand, but they manage to do it. I am very happy with my Branxley Cycles purchase, and I recommend it to everybody that comments on it as I ride it around town.

—Jason Stewart, September 20

176. According to the Web page, what is true about Branxley Cycles?

(A) It is under new management.
(B) It has just opened a showroom.
(C) It makes its products with locally sourced parts.
(D) It has won several awards for its products.

177. What does Branxley Cycles encourage its customers to do?

(A) Participate in group rides
(B) Post photos online
(C) Visit a manufacturing facility
(D) Attend a sales event

178. According to the review, how did Mr. Stewart learn about Branxley Cycles?

(A) By talking to a colleague at work
(B) By visiting a local store
(C) By searching online
(D) By traveling around the country

179. What can be concluded about the reviewer?

(A) He works as a delivery person in his hometown.
(B) He likes to build bicycles as a hobby.
(C) He was given a personal tour of a bicycle factory.
(D) He received his order sooner than he expected.

180. In the review, the word "meet" in paragraph 1, line 8, is closest in meaning to

(A) reach
(B) satisfy
(C) encounter
(D) connect

Questions 181-185 refer to the following article and review.

EDINBURGH (2 July)—Jackson Milne says being part of a family business feels good. He jokes that he has a prime seat in his organisation—and, in a way, he does. The century-old company Milne Associates designs and supplies seats to theatres here in Edinburgh as well as in London and New York. It was founded by his great-grandfather Angus Milne. Jackson Milne has worked in every area of the business, from the factory floor to the executive suite. He became the company's director of design last year.

"Making these seats can be quite challenging, especially ones for older buildings," said Mr. Milne, who designed the seats for the 135-year-old Wolff Theatre. That is where the hit musical *Skyscraping* is now playing to packed houses most nights.

"Our priority is creating pieces that are functional and in harmony with their surroundings," he said. "We try to balance aesthetics, practicality, and convenience."

City Travel Review: Plenty to See and Do in Edinburgh

I had a delightful day in Edinburgh last week. I hadn't been to the city in quite a while—more than 25 years—and so much has changed! One day was not enough to see everything, so I'm already planning another trip for later in the summer.

My friend and I took the train there, and our first order of business was a guided tour of Old Town. It was marvellous! We had lunch at the Red Rose Café, which I highly recommend to anyone who appreciates delicious food at a reasonable price. The day's highlight was attending a performance of *Skyscraping*. It was wonderful! I enjoyed everything about it—the acting, the story, and the songs. The Wolff Theatre is a lovely historical venue. After our long day around town, we were grateful for the theatre's new, comfortable seating.

—Punam Nandi, 15 July

181. What is the purpose of the article?
(A) To report on the opening of a family-owned store
(B) To profile a successful local business
(C) To discuss changes in seating designs
(D) To promote a current theater production

182. What is indicated in the article about Angus Milne?
(A) He used to travel to New York every year.
(B) He moved his firm from London to Edinburgh.
(C) He created a company 100 years ago.
(D) He wrote a popular musical.

183. What does Ms. Nandi mention in her review?
(A) She went on a tour with her family in early July.
(B) She wants to return to Edinburgh.
(C) She has seen *Skyscraping* multiple times.
(D) She used to live in Edinburgh's Old Town.

184. In the review, the word "appreciates" in paragraph 2, line 3, is closest in meaning to
(A) values
(B) increases
(C) comprehends
(D) knows

185. What can be concluded about Ms. Nandi?
(A) She was not looking forward to her trip to Edinburgh.
(B) She thinks the Red Rose Café is overpriced.
(C) She frequently sees shows at the Wolff Theatre.
(D) She had a good experience with a product from Milne Associates.

Questions 186-190 refer to the following Web page and e-mails.

https://www.orvalenaturalhistorymuseum.org/upcomingevents

| Home | Exhibits | Upcoming Events | Contact Us |

The Orvale Natural History Museum's monthly lecture series will continue on October 18 with a lecture by resident archaeologist Dr. Maria Fiallo. The lecture, titled "Earthenware Relics from the Central Prairie," will take place at 7:00 P.M. in the Chovey Community Room near the north entrance of the museum. Dr. Fiallo will discuss last month's unearthing of several pottery pieces in the Central Prairie region, marking the first find of its kind in this area. "Surprisingly," said Dr. Fiallo, "the site was literally stumbled upon by a farmer digging a well on his land. Thankfully, he alerted our museum's research team as soon as he spotted the pieces."

Audiences will get to see some of the earthenware up close at the event, as well as other types of everyday objects. However, many of the pieces will be shown in photographs, as they are too delicate to be moved around. Dr. Fiallo says she is looking forward to sharing this latest discovery. "The findings give us a glimpse into how people went about their daily lives over 800 years ago," she said.

The lecture is free and open to the public.

E-Mail Message

To: Richard Choi
From: Deborah Voll
Date: October 11
Subject: Lecture series

Hi, Richard,

I was just contacted by Professor Allen Whitford from Orvale University's archaeology department. He would like to bring two of his classes to Dr. Fiallo's lecture on October 18. Both classes are studying how to identify and analyze historical artifacts, so he was very happy with the topic of our lecture this month. What's more, Professor Whitford is a former research colleague of Dr. Fiallo. I am inclined to indicate my support, but I just want to make sure we can accommodate the approximately 30 students he is planning to bring—in addition, of course, to members of the public who want to attend.

We will need more than 75 seats, so let's discuss moving the lecture to another location in the museum. There are a couple of alternative spaces, right? I would like to reply to Professor Whitford as soon as possible.

Thanks!

Deb

E-mail

To: Maria Fiallo <mfiallo@orvalenaturalhistorymuseum.org>
From: Allen Whitford <awhitford@orvaleuniversity.edu>
Date: October 19
Subject: Lecture

Dear Dr. Fiallo,

Thanks so much for your informative lecture yesterday evening. My students were thrilled to see some of the pottery up close on the display table. They were especially impressed by the stone tools included among the items. That these artifacts were so close by all this time was truly amazing for my students to contemplate. I am so glad the pieces are safe at the Orvale Natural History Museum, which I know to be a good steward of such treasures.

I hope you will consider my invitation to collaborate with my team and me here at Orvale University on some exciting research projects we have planned. Let me know if you are interested, and I will forward the details.

Sincerely,

Allen Whitford

---

186. According to the Web page, who made a recent discovery?

(A) A farmer
(B) An archaeologist
(C) A historian
(D) A photographer

187. Why are some objects unavailable to see in person during a lecture?

(A) They are being cleaned.
(B) They are too fragile.
(C) They are too large.
(D) They are at a different location.

188. What is suggested about the Chovey Community Room?

(A) It opens daily at 7:00 P.M.
(B) It requires a special pass to enter.
(C) It seats no more than 75 people.
(D) It is near the museum's south entrance.

189. According to the second e-mail, what does Professor Whitford want Dr. Fiallo to do?

(A) Set up a meeting with him at the museum
(B) Bring some artifacts to his classroom
(C) Repeat her lecture at a university
(D) Collaborate on research projects

190. What is suggested about the tools that Professor Whitford's students looked at?

(A) They will be donated to the university for research purposes.
(B) They were under glass in a display case.
(C) They are more than 800 years old.
(D) They are still in use.

Questions 191-195 refer to the following calendar and e-mails.

	JUNE				
	Monday 7	**Tuesday 8**	**Wednesday 9**	**Thursday 10**	**Friday 11**
9:00 A.M.	Out of office (traveling from eyewear seminar in Boston)		Data security training	Out of office (personal appointments)	Weekly planning and review
10:00 A.M.		Budget meeting	E-mail review and cleanup		
11:00 A.M.					
12:00 P.M.					
1:00 P.M.		Applicant interviews	Human resources meeting	Sales review meeting	
2:00 P.M.					Technology updates
3:00 P.M.					

E-mail

To:	Cindy Weaver
From:	Sarah Moreland
Date:	June 7, 6:31 A.M.
Subject:	Delayed return

Hi, Cindy,

My return flight has just been canceled, and the next available one is tomorrow morning. I expect to return to the office just in time for the data security training, but I need your help rearranging my calendar.

• The budget meeting needs to occur this week, so please contact the team to schedule another time. You can use my Friday morning planning time but not my personal time on Thursday morning.

• I'd like to interview our selected applicants later this week, maybe on Friday afternoon if the candidates are amenable; please call them to check. In connection with this, I need to meet with human resources staff only after all the interviews are done; please reschedule that meeting to sometime early next week.

• I have some important news for the marketing team about new eyewear promoted at the seminar. Could you see if they can meet on Wednesday afternoon?

Many thanks,

Sarah Moreland

E-mail

To: Sarah Moreland
From: Cindy Weaver
Date: June 7, 2:31 P.M.
Subject: Re: Delayed return

Good afternoon, Ms. Moreland,

I have been working on your calendar per your request. I have rescheduled your budget meeting for 10:00 A.M. on Friday. Eric Kim says that he has no critical new information to share with you at his 2:00 P.M. meeting with you on Friday, so I can postpone that. Fortunately, all job candidates have agreed to have their interviews on Friday afternoon, and I have moved your human resources meeting to 9:00 A.M. next Monday.

I have been unable to get through to every marketing team member to set up a meeting to discuss the new eyewear. I will keep trying.

Best regards,

Cindy

---

191. When will Ms. Moreland return to the office?

(A) On Tuesday
(B) On Wednesday
(C) On Thursday
(D) On Friday

192. Who most likely is Ms. Weaver?

(A) A travel agent
(B) An eyewear salesperson
(C) An accountant
(D) An executive assistant

193. According to the first e-mail, what will likely be discussed during the human resources meeting?

(A) The results of some interviews
(B) Revisions to a budget
(C) The need for new scheduling software
(D) New eyewear models

194. What is the subject of Ms. Moreland's meeting with Mr. Kim?

(A) Human resources policies
(B) Technology updates
(C) Weekly planning
(D) Marketing strategies

195. What does Ms. Weaver indicate she will do?

(A) Reserve an additional night at a hotel
(B) Attempt to contact some marketing team members
(C) Place a new eyewear order
(D) Check that Ms. Moreland's office has been cleaned

Questions 196-200 refer to the following Web pages and e-mail.

https://www.musiclinkplus.ie/home

| Home | Job Listings | Musician Profiles | Resources |

Music Link Plus (MLP) supports job seekers and recruiters in the music industry.

For Job Seekers: Start by creating a free MLP profile. You will then receive full access to employment opportunities on our Job Listings page. Our Resources page provides sheet music and singers' recordings to help you prepare for an audition. The page also features complete instructions on how to create and upload a video recording to our Web site if a recruiter requests a video sample from you.

For Recruiters: Begin by opening an account by paying an initial fee of €300, after which you will be charged €150 annually. Your account entitles you to list unlimited job postings. You will also be able to select the pieces you want your candidates to perform from a wide menu that we provide. Candidates will be able to upload their audition videos right on this Web site.

E-Mail Message

To: Janice Trapani, Choir Director
From: Kevin Ellis, General Manager
Date: 7 July
Subject: Planning for autumn

Hello, Janice,

I need to update you on a couple of issues affecting our autumn schedule.

• The arts commission has asked our Gradey City Choir to debut a special piece of music in November, the oratorio *By the Meadow* by Gradey City's own Jeffrey Stolartz. It is such an honour to be selected to perform this composition! This addition to our schedule completes our autumn lineup.

• Unfortunately, I learned late last week that two singers need to be replaced before rehearsals begin in August. Since we are already one week into July, I opened an account with Music Link Plus (MLP) this morning to expedite our search. Tomorrow, I plan to post our positions on their Job Listings page. Using this Web site will allow us to reach countless potential applicants. Additionally, MLP gives us the option of having candidates audition by providing video recordings. Given our time constraints, we should consider having auditions done this way. However, if you feel that in-person auditions are necessary, please let me know by the end of the day today.

Kevin

https://www.musiclinkplus.ie/joblistings

Home | Job Listings | Musician Profiles | Resources

Vocalist Positions (Gradey City Choir)

Posted on: 8 July

Application deadline: 21 July

Gradey City Choir seeks two singers for its autumn season: an alto and a tenor. Successful candidates will join our dynamic choir under the direction of Janice Trapani and will be expected to report to Neufried Auditorium on 11 August for autumn performance rehearsals.

Applicants must supply an audition video. Simply follow the instructions on the Resources page. We have selected a portion from Franka Berman's *Still Waters Cantata* for candidates to sing. Hiring decision notifications will be sent to your personal e-mail address on 4 August.

196. What is indicated about Mr. Stolartz?
    (A) He is originally from Gradey City.
    (B) He will lead choir performances.
    (C) He used to sing in the Gradey City Choir.
    (D) He is a former choir director.

197. According to the e-mail, what is Mr. Ellis concerned about?
    (A) Promoting autumn performances
    (B) Hiring singers at short notice
    (C) Learning parts of *By the Meadow*
    (D) Training a new choir director

198. What is one thing Mr. Ellis did on July 7?
    (A) He asked MLP for a discount.
    (B) He scheduled two auditions.
    (C) He paid MLP a €300 fee.
    (D) He contacted Mr. Stolartz.

199. When do practice sessions for the autumn performances begin?
    (A) On July 8
    (B) On July 21
    (C) On August 4
    (D) On August 11

200. What do applicants need to do to audition for the Gradey City Choir?
    (A) Sing a musical selection with a member of the Gradey City Choir
    (B) Request an interview appointment
    (C) Choose a piece of music they would like to perform
    (D) Visit the Resources page to upload a video recording

Stop! This is the end of the test. If you finish before time is called, you may go back to Parts 5, 6, and 7 and check your work.

TEST 04
무료 동영상 강의

RC
기출 TEST 04

READING TEST

In the Reading test, you will read a variety of texts and answer several different types of reading comprehension questions. The entire Reading test will last 75 minutes. There are three parts, and directions are given for each part. You are encouraged to answer as many questions as possible within the time allowed.

You must mark your answers on the separate answer sheet. Do not write your answers in your test book.

PART 5

Directions: A word or phrase is missing in each of the sentences below. Four answer choices are given below each sentence. Select the best answer to complete the sentence. Then mark the letter (A), (B), (C), or (D) on your answer sheet.

101. Ms. Chiu recently announced that ------- is planning to retire in September.
    (A) her
    (B) hers
    (C) herself
    (D) she

102. Mr. Kashnitz will interview the applicants ------- the holiday.
    (A) above
    (B) before
    (C) among
    (D) along

103. The real estate agent may ------- a buyer with a neighborhood analysis upon request.
    (A) providing
    (B) provide
    (C) provided
    (D) provides

104. The city's development committee is looking for a ------- to plant a community garden.
    (A) flower
    (B) topic
    (C) location
    (D) show

105. We hope our customer service team has answered your questions in a ------- manner.
    (A) satisfy
    (B) satisfactory
    (C) satisfaction
    (D) satisfactorily

106. Mr. Hanley expressed interest in the position ------- held by Ms. Akello.
    (A) previously
    (B) slowly
    (C) widely
    (D) loosely

107. Once Ms. Jeong ------- the contract, she will sign and return it to Allory Pharmaceuticals.
    (A) to receive
    (B) receives
    (C) was received
    (D) receiving

108. Ten board members plan to attend, which is just ------- to approve the proposal.
    (A) enough
    (B) several
    (C) most
    (D) those

109. Mr. Aziz is often alone in the shop while his partner is out making a -------.
    (A) deliver
    (B) delivery
    (C) delivered
    (D) delivering

110. The Pacific Coast Sunset Run has been ------- to August 31 because of bad weather.
    (A) canceled
    (B) combined
    (C) rescheduled
    (D) administered

111. Graber hair and nail growth supplements come in ------- pill and liquid form.
    (A) these
    (B) both
    (C) almost
    (D) likely

112. The posters must be completed soon ------- they can be put up in advance of the gala.
    (A) so that
    (B) despite
    (C) whenever
    (D) as if

113. Mr. Olivero praised the film in his review, even though he ------- disliked its aesthetic style.
    (A) personal
    (B) personally
    (C) personals
    (D) person

114. ------- weeks of record-setting rain, expect only blue skies this weekend.
    (A) After
    (B) Besides
    (C) Opposite
    (D) Alongside

115. The Serenica dining table comes with levelers ------- its stability on uneven surfaces.
    (A) ensure
    (B) ensures
    (C) to ensure
    (D) to be ensured

116. Applicants to any open position at Allcrest Engineering can expect a ------- within three business days.
    (A) degree
    (B) raise
    (C) change
    (D) response

117. ------- prepares the patient's medical records is required to maintain confidentiality.
    (A) Whoever
    (B) Who
    (C) Whose
    (D) What

118. Because of the high demand for our services, our office was ------- expanded last year.
    (A) significantly
    (B) tightly
    (C) remotely
    (D) identically

119. The Terry Hoig Prize for ------- architecture was awarded to Ms. Helblon on Tuesday.
    (A) sustain
    (B) sustainable
    (C) sustainer
    (D) sustains

120. We have been ------- problems with the thermostat in the western end of the warehouse.
    (A) experiencing
    (B) regarding
    (C) repurposing
    (D) establishing

121. Two students from Wrisley University worked ------- on the design of the new library in Lorth Park.

    (A) collaborate
    (B) collaborative
    (C) collaboratively
    (D) collaborated

122. The images displayed on our gallery's Web site may not reflect the ------- colors of the artwork for sale.

    (A) loyal
    (B) smart
    (C) close
    (D) exact

123. At Beautyvale Cosmetics, our representatives answer customers' ------- within 24 hours of receipt.

    (A) inquirers
    (B) inquired
    (C) to inquire
    (D) inquiries

124. We would like to attend the retreat, but ------- we are unavailable on that date.

    (A) regrettably
    (B) scarcely
    (C) exceptionally
    (D) annually

125. In celebration of Ms. Tseng's promotion, tea and cookies will be served ------- the meeting.

    (A) later
    (B) as soon as
    (C) following
    (D) in case of

126. Beginning next month, all employees at Sartson Analytics will have the ------- of working from home two days per week.

    (A) place
    (B) combination
    (C) range
    (D) option

127. The accounting department's new policy outlines the ------- process for the procurement of office equipment.

    (A) preferring
    (B) preferably
    (C) preferred
    (D) preferability

128. All documents ------- to the company merger will become available to the public within one year.

    (A) assigning
    (B) facilitating
    (C) pertaining
    (D) embarking

129. Granta Hospital has added several pediatric nurses to its staff as part of its new ------- with the Friel School of Nursing.

    (A) affiliation
    (B) affiliated
    (C) affiliating
    (D) affiliates

130. During checkout, cashiers must be able to scan purchased items accurately ------- field questions from customers.

    (A) but
    (B) for instance
    (C) although
    (D) as well as

PART 6

Directions: Read the texts that follow. A word, phrase, or sentence is missing in parts of each text. Four answer choices for each question are given below the text. Select the best answer to complete the text. Then mark the letter (A), (B), (C), or (D) on your answer sheet.

Questions 131-134 refer to the following article.

New Vietnamese Restaurant Opens

SAN FRANCISCO (November 5)—Celebrity chef Eric Hoang ------- his first restaurant, Ngon
                                                              131.
Mieng. It opened last week in the North Beach neighborhood. Ngon Mieng serves authentic

Vietnamese cuisine and some innovative dishes developed by Chef Hoang. The restaurant took

over the space once occupied by the restaurant Plantains, ------- closed last year.
                                                           132.

Chef Hoang won first place on the reality television show *Best Chefs in the U.S.* two years ago.

------- . "After receiving the award, opening a restaurant became my dream," he said. "I am excited
133.
to bring my culinary creations to the North Beach area."

At the grand opening, diners echoed Chef Hoang's enthusiasm for the ------- . "Without a doubt,
                                                                    134.
it was some of the best I've ever eaten," said customer Judy Blackburn.

131. (A) will launch
     (B) could launch
     (C) has launched
     (D) was launching

132. (A) they
     (B) this
     (C) where
     (D) which

133. (A) San Francisco has many popular Vietnamese restaurants.
     (B) The restaurant may expand to other California cities next year.
     (C) The show is entering its fifth season.
     (D) He was thrilled to win that competition.

134. (A) food
     (B) event
     (C) area
     (D) performance

Questions 135-138 refer to the following notice.

Connelly's Parking Garage

Parking is $10 per hour unless you get your parking validated at a ------- store. Stores that can
                                                                          135.
validate your parking include Raymond's Department Store, Lola's Fine Dining, Monique's

Boutique, and Gretsch Chocolatiers. Just bring your entrance ticket to ------- of these
                                                                        136.
establishments. ------- . You will get your first hour of parking at no charge. ------- , the fee will be
                 137.   **138.**
$5 per hour.

---

135. (A) participates
(B) participated
(C) participating
(D) participation

136. (A) any
(B) all
(C) each
(D) either

137. (A) Park only in specified spots.
(B) Make sure to lock your vehicle.
(C) We cannot accept cash at this time.
(D) A cashier will gladly stamp it for you.

138. (A) If not
(B) Then
(C) In that case
(D) Nevertheless

Questions 139-142 refer to the following announcement.

Lost Ocean Theater is thrilled to announce a unique offering coming to its downtown location next week. The talented comedian Maddy Chang ------- a one-person show based on her memoir, *That's All I Wanted*. Chang's book, filled with funny and engaging ------- , is brought to life through this performance. Fans will enjoy experiencing Chang's brilliance in person, while newcomers to her work will receive a ------- introduction to her entertaining world.

Show times are Thursday through Sunday at 7:00 P.M., with an additional matinee on Saturday at 1:00 P.M. ------- . Additional information can be found at www.lostoceantheater.com.

139. (A) will perform
 (B) to perform
 (C) performed
 (D) performing

140. (A) reasons
 (B) structures
 (C) characters
 (D) signs

141. (A) delight
 (B) delights
 (C) delighted
 (D) delightful

142. (A) The theater will close for renovations.
 (B) Call the theater at 704-555-0138 to reserve tickets.
 (C) Chang's memoir is available online and at local booksellers.
 (D) Chang was raised in Southern California and attended college in Minnesota.

Questions 143-146 refer to the following e-mail.

To: tvargas@sandelleinn.com
From: moira@petalsaplenty.com
Date: November 2
Subject: Floral arrangement

Dear Ms. Vargas,

I left a complimentary floral arrangement with your receptionist today, and she suggested that I contact you directly. I specialize in floral design. I created this bouquet for you, using bold colors that match the inn's lobby, to give you an idea of how I ------- my work.
                                                                                                143.

I was told that you do not currently have a budget for décor. ------- , perhaps we could still
                                                                144.
partner in some way. I see that you host small events, and your Web site has links to local DJs, caterers, and other service providers that you recommend. Would you consider including my company, Petals Aplenty, on your list of ------- ? I would be happy to reciprocate by promoting
                                                                145.
your inn on my own Web site. ------- .
                                  146.

I look forward to hearing from you.

Moira Voss, Owner, Petals Aplenty

143. (A) document
 (B) approach
 (C) schedule
 (D) verify

144. (A) Even so
 (B) For example
 (C) On the contrary
 (D) As you suggested

145. (A) refers
 (B) referred
 (C) referrals
 (D) referable

146. (A) I want to thank you again for the nomination.
 (B) I can certainly see the resemblance.
 (C) I think it was all just a misunderstanding.
 (D) I believe this arrangement can benefit us both.

PART 7

Directions: In this part you will read a selection of texts, such as magazine and newspaper articles, e-mails, and instant messages. Each text or set of texts is followed by several questions. Select the best answer for each question and mark the letter (A), (B), (C), or (D) on your answer sheet.

Questions 147-148 refer to the following job posting.

Help Wanted

Zestful Cuisine is looking for a server to join our restaurant's team! We specialize in French and Spanish food.

This is a full-time or part-time position. Days and nights are available.

Candidate must have a positive attitude, excellent customer service skills, and the ability to multitask in a fast-paced environment.

Zestful Cuisine offers competitive pay rates based on job experience. All servers receive one meal during each shift. We provide a career path with promotion and increased pay.

Applications are available on our Web site, www.zestfulcuisine.com.

147. What is suggested about Zestful Cuisine?
  (A) It offers shift flexibility to employees.
  (B) It pays all employees the same base salary.
  (C) It offers promotions after six months.
  (D) It requires staff to attend a training session.

148. According to the job posting, what is an essential quality for a candidate?
  (A) Knowledge of food safety regulations
  (B) Fluency in several languages
  (C) Previous experience at a restaurant
  (D) Ability to communicate with customers

Questions 149-151 refer to the following article.

WINNIPEG (10 May)—Manitoba-based satellite manufacturer Alita Technology has been awarded a $9 million grant to develop an airborne sensing instrument to be used in the collection of climate data. The device will be engineered to calculate the density and depth of snowpack throughout Canada.

Alita Technology is collaborating with the Microwave Engineering Lab at the University of Southam on the initiative. Dr. Hugh Jaris, director of the lab's Remote Sensing Unit, will lead the effort to test one or more prototypes by collecting and analysing data next winter.

Snowpack data is used to measure year-to-year snow trends and fluctuations as well as to help determine how much water from snowmelt will be available in key areas of the country.

149. According to the article, who is responsible for engineering the device?

(A) Dr. Jaris
(B) Alita Technology
(C) The University of Southam's Microwave Engineering Lab
(D) The government of Winnipeg

150. The word "initiative" in paragraph 2, line 3, is closest in meaning to

(A) motivation
(B) technique
(C) advantage
(D) project

151. What is indicated about Dr. Jaris?

(A) He is employed by a university laboratory.
(B) He has published a book on device design and development.
(C) He assembles prototypes of sensing instruments.
(D) He works as an engineer at Alita Technology.

Questions 152-153 refer to the following receipt.

Stub Master—Your Ticket Source for Concerts, Sports, and Theater

Hello, Mr. Sato,

Thanks for your purchase! Your mobile ticket is ready and available in the Stub Master account you created online. All Stub Master tickets contain a unique barcode and may not be printed, copied, or shared. Please use the Stub Master app on your phone to access your ticket so that it can be scanned electronically for entry to the event.

Confirmation #:	9035768
Date:	Saturday, June 25
Time:	7 P.M.
Event:	Monterrey Medallions at Mayville Dodgers
Venue:	Alonso Reyes Stadium
Order:	1 ticket; bleachers – uncovered; regular season baseball
Total:	$25 (price includes a $3 building fee)
Notes:	Participate in the burger and hot dog buffet for $15 on-site. For corporate ticket purchases, contact service@stubmaster.com.

152. What is mentioned about Stub Master tickets?

(A) They are mailed to customers.
(B) They include parking fees in the price.
(C) They are discounted for corporate purchases.
(D) They are saved electronically.

153. What is true about the event Mr. Sato will attend?

(A) It will take place on June 7.
(B) It is a baseball game.
(C) It will take place indoors.
(D) It includes a free buffet.

Questions 154-156 refer to the following press release.

FOR IMMEDIATE RELEASE

Contact: Nadia Khumalo, nadia_khumalo@gulfbrookcreations.co.za

CAPE TOWN (20 August)—Gulfbrook Creations today announced the appointment of Ms. Candace Masondo as the company's chief design officer (CDO), effective 1 September. — [1] —. Most recently, Ms. Masondo headed the materials development division at Deavora Dynamix, based in Durban. — [2] —. She was the driving force behind that company's mission to develop accessibility products to enhance independent living in South Africa's domestic market.

Mr. Jonathan Ngobeni, Gulfbrook's president, acknowledges Ms. Masondo's skills and resourcefulness. "In her three-decades-long design career, Ms. Masondo has designed numerous products that reflect inclusiveness and self-sufficiency. Throughout those years, she has emphasized and demonstrated the importance of collaboration between engineers, designers, and consumers. She has won several prestigious awards for her work. Her achievements demonstrate her commitment to colleagues and product users. We are excited that she will be joining our team." — [3] —.

"It is a tremendous honour and privilege to be appointed Gulfbrook's CDO," Ms. Masondo said. "I will do my best to advance the company's mission and strengthen its industry presence." — [4] —.

Gulfbrook Creations is headquartered in Johannesburg. For 45 years, the company has been manufacturing equipment that facilitates independent living, including ergonomic furniture, audio- and visual-enhancement devices, and motorized mobility aids. Its products are marketed mainly in Africa.

154. What is mentioned about Ms. Masondo?

(A) She received some awards in August.
(B) She regularly meets with consumers.
(C) She frequently travels abroad for business.
(D) She has been a product designer for 30 years.

155. What do Gulfbrook Creations and Deavora Dynamix have in common?

(A) Their export markets
(B) Their types of products
(C) Their years of operation
(D) Their headquarters location

156. In which of the positions marked [1], [2], [3], and [4] does the following sentence best belong?

"She served in that capacity for ten years, having joined Deavora Dynamix two years after it began operations."

(A) [1]
(B) [2]
(C) [3]
(D) [4]

Questions 157-158 refer to the following text-message chain.

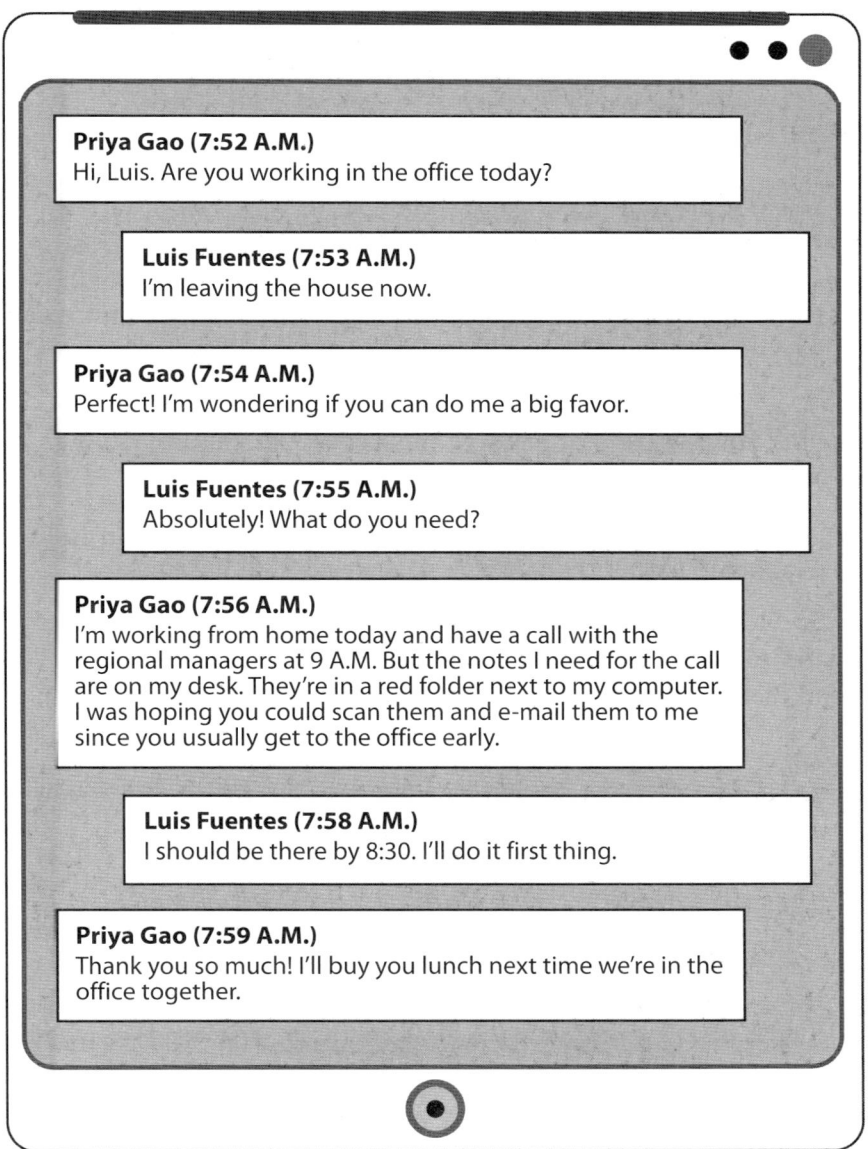

Priya Gao (7:52 A.M.)
Hi, Luis. Are you working in the office today?

Luis Fuentes (7:53 A.M.)
I'm leaving the house now.

Priya Gao (7:54 A.M.)
Perfect! I'm wondering if you can do me a big favor.

Luis Fuentes (7:55 A.M.)
Absolutely! What do you need?

Priya Gao (7:56 A.M.)
I'm working from home today and have a call with the regional managers at 9 A.M. But the notes I need for the call are on my desk. They're in a red folder next to my computer. I was hoping you could scan them and e-mail them to me since you usually get to the office early.

Luis Fuentes (7:58 A.M.)
I should be there by 8:30. I'll do it first thing.

Priya Gao (7:59 A.M.)
Thank you so much! I'll buy you lunch next time we're in the office together.

157. At 7:53 A.M., what does Mr. Fuentes imply when he writes, "I'm leaving the house now"?

   (A) He is late for work.
   (B) He will be home in time for lunch.
   (C) He is on his way to the office.
   (D) He already scanned a document.

158. What problem does Ms. Gao have?

   (A) She mislabeled a folder.
   (B) She left important information in her office.
   (C) She needs help fixing her computer.
   (D) She forgot the number for a conference call.

Questions 159-161 refer to the following Web page.

https://www.morrisville.gov.za/cityplanning/buildingpermits

Requesting a Building Permit

A city-issued building permit may be required before initiating construction work within Morrisville city limits. No city permit is required for work on a building's interior systems, such as plumbing, electrical, or heating and cooling. A permit will be needed for adding to or expanding the size of a building, for changing the exterior appearance of a building, or for any brand-new construction project. Below are the steps for obtaining a permit and for ensuring full compliance with city policies.

1. Check that the building is appropriately registered. See the Registration and Land Use page for more information.

2. Submit an application for a building permit. Please contact Ronald Abioye at the City Planning Office if you need assistance completing this application.

3. You will receive a letter, and if your application is approved, your official building permit will be enclosed. Work may commence once the permit is received and then posted in an easily visible location at the main entrance of the construction site.

159. What type of project would require a permit?

(A) Improving a building's plumbing system
(B) Installing an air-conditioning system
(C) Upgrading the wiring in a residence
(D) Enlarging an office building

160. According to the Web page, why should someone contact Mr. Abioye?

(A) To make changes to a plan
(B) To schedule building maintenance
(C) To receive help when filling out a form
(D) To check on the status of an application

161. What is indicated on the Web page as a step in the preconstruction process?

(A) A document is displayed.
(B) The worksite is inspected.
(C) A plan is signed by an engineer.
(D) The building owner receives an e-mail.

Questions 162-163 refer to the following schedule.

Millsberg Summer Festival
Millsberg's annual Summer Festival returns this June for its sixtieth year!

Opening Parade

June 20, 10:00 A.M.

This is the Summer Festival's oldest and best-known event. The parade marks the official start of the festival and features elaborate floats and marching bands.

Children's Fun Fair

June 20–26, noon–8:00 P.M.

Carnival rides and entertainment at Millsberg Park

Outdoor Concert Series

June 20–26, 7:00 P.M.

Live music, including folk, jazz, and classical, at Greenrow Park

Wood-fired pizza and other snacks will be available for purchase.

Open-Air Art Studio

June 26, 3:00 P.M.–9:00 P.M.

On the final day of the festival, local painters, photographers, and potters welcome the public to view their works at the park in front of the Riverside Art Complex.

---

162. What is indicated about the festival?
    (A) It takes place several times a year.
    (B) It has activities for all ages.
    (C) Its events are held indoors.
    (D) Its events are held at a single location.

163. At what event can visitors purchase food?
    (A) Opening Parade
    (B) Children's Fun Fair
    (C) Outdoor Concert Series
    (D) Open-Air Art Studio

Questions 164-167 refer to the following information.

Watch the game you love for the price that's right!

Stream exciting, insightful content from the Total Basketball Channel (TBC) on your smartphone, tablet, or smart TV by subscribing to a TBC Plan! Download the TBC app or visit www.totalbasketballchannel.com to sign up for one of the following subscription options.

TBC Platinum Plan All live games, commercial-free	TBC Gold Plan Most live games, commercial-free	TBC Silver Plan Most live games played by a team of your choice	TBC Copper Plan TBC game highlights
• Stream all games and commentary • Watch on up to three devices • Includes nationally televised games • $29/month or $149/year	• Stream games for any team • Watch on up to three devices • Excludes nationally televised games • $19/month or $99/year	• Stream games played by your favorite TBC team • Watch on up to two devices • Includes commercials • Excludes nationally televised games • $9/month or $49/year	• Weekly replays of game highlights • Watch or download commentary shows • Includes commercials • Watch on one device • $5/month or $29/year

164. Where would the information most likely be found?

    (A) In a journal for sports psychologists
    (B) In a manual of basketball rules
    (C) In a sports magazine
    (D) In a basketball player's biography

165. What is unique about the TBC Platinum Plan?

    (A) It has no advertisements.
    (B) It does not have a monthly payment option.
    (C) It allows streaming on up to three devices.
    (D) It includes nationally televised games.

166. What plan is designed for a subscriber who is only interested in a single team?

    (A) The TBC Platinum Plan
    (B) The TBC Gold Plan
    (C) The TBC Silver Plan
    (D) The TBC Copper Plan

167. How much is the TBC Gold Plan?

    (A) $9 per month
    (B) $19 per month
    (C) $29 per year
    (D) $49 per year

Questions 168-171 refer to the following blog post.

Regina's Art World Blog

As regular readers of my blog know, over the past few weeks, I have concentrated on the revitalization of the Brentler Heights waterfront district by developer and former architect David Greeley. — [1] —. By far, the most impressive result of this program is the renovation of a former industrial building on Paxton Street. The building's first floor now houses a popular coffee shop and bookstore, and its beautifully landscaped gardens include creative metal sculptures. — [2] —. I am pleased to report that the second floor will be occupied by the Brentler Heights Gallery.

The gallery will be run by Francine Skandar, a Brentler Heights artist I met years ago at a jewelry-making workshop. I always admired her work, and I obtained many of her creations to sell at my shop. I was delighted to learn that she will be managing this high-profile gallery. On a media tour, Ms. Skandar highlighted how Mr. Greeley retained nearly all of the Paxton Street building's original features to give it a vintage character. — [3] —. This makes it an ideal backdrop for all types of art.

The gallery's inaugural exhibit will showcase Ms. Skandar's work. — [4] —. The grand opening will occur on June 8 and 9 from 2:00 P.M. to 7:00 P.M. For more information, visit www.brentlerheightsgallery.org.

—Regina Nguyen, May 2

168. What topic is reported on in the blog post?

(A) The transformation of a city district
(B) The new publication released by a local architect
(C) An art class given at the Brentler Heights Gallery
(D) A grant given to Brentler Heights artists

169. What is indicated about Ms. Skandar?

(A) She teaches jewelry-making classes at a university.
(B) She was a supplier for Ms. Nguyen's business.
(C) She has lived in Brentler Heights for most of her life.
(D) She creates large metal sculptures for gardens.

170. What is true about the Brentler Heights Gallery?

(A) It opened five years ago in another location.
(B) It is located in an older, refurbished space.
(C) It occupies two floors of a building.
(D) It will be managed by Mr. Greeley.

171. In which of the positions marked [1], [2], [3], and [4] does the following sentence best belong?

"In the future, Ms. Skandar plans to feature collections from other local artists."

(A) [1]
(B) [2]
(C) [3]
(D) [4]

Questions 172-175 refer to the following online chat discussion.

Liz Yuen (8:58 A.M.)
Hi, all. Thank you for your prompt feedback on the Web site content I sent out in the group e-mail. Everyone agrees that the photos and the accompanying content do not seem to market the calendars strongly enough.

Helen Black (8:59 A.M.)
Right. But, to confirm that we're looking at the same material—there are several photos showing our desktop calendar each with the caption "The promise of a new year with a calendar from Stenmex Stationery."

Liz Yuen (9:01 A.M.)
That's correct. But the main problem is that the photos and the content that accompanies them need to be more engaging and interactive.

Jeff Spina (9:02 A.M.)
I agree. What if we ask customers to send us their written comments on how they use our calendars to help them organize their home offices? They could also send us a picture of their home office with our calendar in the image.

Helen Black (9:04 A.M.)
I'd be happy to share a photo of my own setup—from one of the days that I'm working from home. And I could write an explanation of how using the calendar helps me keep track of things. We could use that as an example for customers to follow.

Liz Yuen (9:05 A.M.)
Great idea. And what about the problems with the functionality of the Web site?

Jeff Spina (9:06 A.M.)
That would be great, Helen.

Helen Black (9:07 A.M.)
I saw those.

Jeff Spina (9:08 A.M.)
I'll speak with Ryeo Jee about that. Her team should be able to get the pop-up window and social media links working again soon.

Liz Yuen (9:09 A.M.)
Thanks, Jeff. Once the site is functional and we have our content finalized, her team can update the home page with what we have decided.

172. What are the chat participants discussing?

(A) Changes to a Web site
(B) Feedback from customers
(C) How to order new stationery
(D) What marketing firm to select

173. What is indicated about Ms. Black?

(A) She is a freelance photographer.
(B) She sometimes works from home.
(C) She designed a popular office calendar.
(D) She bought new office furniture recently.

174. At 9:07 A.M., what does Ms. Black imply when she writes, "I saw those"?

(A) She has selected some photographs.
(B) She accepted Ms. Yuen's meeting request.
(C) She received several e-mails from Mr. Spina.
(D) She knows that a Web site is not working correctly.

175. What does Ms. Yuen thank Mr. Spina for?

(A) Offering to contact a colleague
(B) Finalizing an employee contract
(C) Reviewing Ms. Jee's performance
(D) Taking photographs of a workspace

Questions 176-180 refer to the following article and e-mail.

Hillside House Is Ready for Business

AUCKLAND (2 April)—Hillside House, Auckland's newest and most spectacular event space, is now open. This unique venue is a secluded haven only minutes away from the city centre. Its glass walls give guests an enchanted view of green gardens and bright flowers, while multiple windows in the ceiling make the sky part of the interior decoration.

Hillside House is the perfect setting for weddings and other social gatherings, as well as corporate events. The kitchen is under the direction of Chef Bashu Malik, a two-time Franklin Heard Foundation winner. Chef Malik oversees Hillside House's menus, whether the event hosts choose eclectic small plates, a family-style dinner, or a buffet brunch.

"Choosing the right venue is the key to success," says Hillside House Managing Director Russell Isley. "We offer everything—a beautiful setting, an experienced staff, and great food. Our events coordinator will work with you to make your wedding or corporate function an occasion to remember."

To:	Hayley Colling <hcolling@kitchendesigns.co.nz>
From:	Reka Taimona <rtaimona@hillsidehouse.co.nz>
Date:	10 May
Subject:	Information
Attachment:	Hillside House options

Dear Ms. Colling:

Thank you for reaching out to Hillside House about your upcoming product launch! Yes, 16 June is available; your Kitchen Designs corporate celebration is now on our schedule.

In preparation for the event, please note that we offer several unique branding opportunities. For example, we can display your company's logo in neon lights and hang up banners. Chef Malik and his staff can also work with you to include logos on food items or a cake. I am attaching information about the menu options and pricing. We have a state-of-the-art sound system and audiovisual equipment for speeches and presentations. If you would like entertainment for your event, I can also supply you with a list of bands and musicians.

Please let me know if you have any other questions. We at Hillside House look forward to hosting your event.

Sincerely,

Reka Taimona, Events Coordinator
Hillside House

176. What is indicated in the article about Hillside House?
    (A) It is far from downtown Auckland.
    (B) It is located in a recently renovated building.
    (C) It features a view of the outdoors.
    (D) It will be purchased by Mr. Isley.

177. In the article, the word "function" in paragraph 3, line 7, is closest in meaning to
    (A) occupation
    (B) use
    (C) organization
    (D) gathering

178. What is one purpose of the e-mail?
    (A) To offer a discount on a service
    (B) To request feedback on a menu
    (C) To provide a reminder about a deadline
    (D) To confirm a reservation for a party

179. What did Ms. Taimona send with the e-mail?
    (A) Images of decorations
    (B) A list of musicians
    (C) Details about food and costs
    (D) Designs for a corporate logo

180. What can be concluded about Ms. Colling's corporate event?
    (A) It will feature food prepared by an award-winning chef.
    (B) It will be attended by more than 100 people.
    (C) It will conclude with a presentation of awards to Kitchen Designs staff.
    (D) It will include music performed by a live band.

Questions 181-185 refer to the following e-mails.

To:	Customer Service <customerservice@takembootcompany.com>
From:	Bella Meyers <b.meyers@leadmail.com>
Date:	15 August
Subject:	Order 13783

Hello,

I recently ordered a pair of your Western boots in style Erin, size 40, in the chocolate colour. The boots arrived yesterday, but unfortunately, their actual colour is different from the colour pictured on your Web site. I had been hoping to wear the boots to a special event next month, but they are much darker than expected and do not match my planned outfit.

I would like to exchange the boots for another pair of the same style and size but in the terracotta colour. Please let me know how to proceed. I have purchased several pairs of boots from your company in the past and have always been pleased with their durability and comfort.

Bella Meyers

To:	Bella Meyers <b.meyers@leadmail.com>
From:	Customer Service <customerservice@takembootcompany.com>
Date:	16 August
Subject:	RE: Order 13783

Dear Ms. Meyers,

Thank you for your e-mail. I am sorry you were disappointed with your order. We are happy to arrange an exchange as long as the boots you wish to return have not been worn.

At the moment, boots in the size, style, and colour you are requesting are out of stock. Because we are a small company, our inventory is not always fully available. Other than what you have purchased, we currently have the Erin boots of your size in the following colours: sand and forest. Since you are interested in a paler colour, I recommend sand. It is a warm shade and very versatile. Additionally, we have other styles available in your preferred colour, including Viola boots, our most popular style.

Please let me know if you would like to exchange your boots for any of the above options. If so, I can send you a postage-paid return label via e-mail for you to print at home.

Thank you for your business. If you have not signed up for our newsletter yet, I suggest you do. We offer discounts on discontinued styles.

Sincerely,

Brendan Stephens, Customer Service Representative
Takem Boot Company

181. What problem is explained in the first e-mail?

(A) An order was received later than expected.
(B) A product's color on a Web site is inaccurate.
(C) Some boots were not as comfortable as previous pairs were.
(D) An item was accidentally ordered in the wrong size.

182. What does Ms. Meyers indicate?

(A) She has been a frequent customer of Takem Boot Company.
(B) She still needs to buy an outfit for an event.
(C) She had difficulty navigating a Web site.
(D) She prefers dark-colored boots.

183. What color is currently NOT available for boots in the Erin style?

(A) Sand
(B) Forest
(C) Chocolate
(D) Terracotta

184. What does the second e-mail suggest about Takem Boot Company?

(A) It has stores in several locations.
(B) It charges a shipping fee for returns.
(C) It sells a lot of Viola boots.
(D) It is the most popular boot company in the region.

185. What does Mr. Stephens offer to do?

(A) Print a document
(B) E-mail a shipping label
(C) Send a product catalog
(D) Give a discount on new-style boots

Questions 186-190 refer to the following e-mail, article, and Web page.

To:	Jessica Marpone <jmarpone@halecityca.gov>
From:	Greg Tanner <gtanner@halecitynews.com>
Date:	July 1
Subject:	Community comments

Dear Ms. Marpone,

My last article about East Core Park attracted quite a few online comments. The comments were from residents complaining about overgrown weeds and fallen branches on the Blue Trail. They say the Red Trail is in good condition, but maintenance issues have persisted on the Blue Trail for quite some time.

As the newest member of the city council, you might not have heard many complaints yet. However, if you do get briefings regarding the situation, I would be grateful for any updates you can pass along. I reached out to parks commissioner Oscar Lunes for comments about this, but he hasn't responded. Someone mentioned he might be busy preparing for retirement.

Sincerely,

Greg Tanner
Hale City News

City Parks Department Launches Volunteer Initiative

By Greg Tanner

Hale City (July 12)—In response to residents' concerns about conditions on the hiking paths at East Core Park, the Hale City Parks Department offers an explanation and an outline of its plans for trail upkeep.

"Trail maintenance is transitioning from being performed by city employees to an all-volunteer model," said newly appointed parks commissioner Helen Yancey. "Before my predecessor stepped down after twenty years of service to the city, he began this shift. The result was a temporary suspension of maintenance on the Blue Trail."

Ms. Yancey added that the volunteer model will save money and allow residents greater involvement with the park system. Accordingly, the Hale City Parks Department has scheduled its first volunteer cleanup event, Trail Cleanup Day, on August 12, from 9:00 A.M. to 2:00 P.M. Those interested in volunteering may register online at www.halecityparks.org/events.

Hale City Parks Department

August Announcements

The Hale City Parks Department's inaugural Trail Cleanup Day, held on August 8, was a great success. An enthusiastic group of volunteers cleared debris and weeds from the Blue Trail at East Core Park and had the path clean and usable just before noon on the bright, warm day.

Special thanks go to the following participants.

- Amy Harris, for coordinating volunteer efforts and bringing beverages
- Jason Skoda, resident of the adjacent East Heights neighborhood, for lending his power trimmer, pruning shears, and rakes to our crew of volunteers

We encourage residents to visit this page often to learn about upcoming volunteer events.

---

186. Why did Mr. Tanner write the e-mail?

(A) To inform his supervisor of an upcoming event
(B) To ask for information about trail maintenance
(C) To discuss enlarging a city park
(D) To congratulate a new city council member

187. What is suggested about Ms. Yancey?

(A) She is a replacement for Mr. Lunes.
(B) She lives near East Core Park.
(C) She trains new park volunteers.
(D) She is a fund-raising specialist.

188. What interrupted the maintenance of the Blue Trail?

(A) An expansion of the Red Trail
(B) A departmental policy change
(C) A large gathering held at a park
(D) An extended period of wet weather

189. What most likely is true about Trail Cleanup Day?

(A) Mr. Tanner initially planned it.
(B) The work took two days to complete.
(C) Volunteers attended a training session before the event.
(D) The date of the trail cleanup was changed.

190. According to the Web page, what did one nearby resident provide volunteers with?

(A) Breakfast foods
(B) Advice on hiking for health
(C) Landscaping tools
(D) Transportation to a park

GO ON TO THE NEXT PAGE

Questions 191-195 refer to the following e-mails and chart.

E-Mail Message

To: All Staff
From: Miranda Noonan
Date: June 26
Subject: Art auction
Attachment: 📎 Donations

Dear Employees,

Ogunsanya and Bolden Law Firm is hosting our annual art auction, with all proceeds going to building a community garden. Many local artists plan to donate pieces for our auction, and as always, we encourage all amateur artists in our firm to donate work as well. Get out those paintbrushes and pencils and unleash your creativity. It is always a treat to see our colleagues' art hanging alongside pieces by professional artists!

This year's auction will be at Seven Gates Hotel and Restaurant on Friday, July 27, at 7:00 P.M. Our event will be held in the hotel restaurant, which has excellent lighting for our purposes.

I have attached a chart listing the professional art that has been donated so far. If you are interested in contributing this year, please e-mail me the details about your submission. Keep in mind that photographs, paintings, and drawings are the most popular mediums. However, one local artist donated a large sculpture, which will be the auction's centerpiece. Apart from that piece, we will only accept sculptures under 50 centimeters tall.

Best regards,

Miranda Noonan, Auction Chairperson

Ogunsanya and Bolden Art Auction: Local Artist Donations

Name	Name of piece and medium	Dimensions
Brian Healey	*Surface of the Moon* (photograph)	45 cm x 76 cm
Michaela Green	*Streetlight* (sculpture)	90 cm
Shinji Hasegawa	*Shuki—Artist's Dog* (drawing)	30 cm x 45 cm
Kim Cheung	*Cornfield Sunrise* (painting)	40 cm x 70 cm

═══ E-Mail Message ═══

To: Miranda Noonan
From: Omonuwa Orou
Date: June 29
Subject: Re: Art auction

Hello, Ms. Noonan,

I am planning to contribute a piece of art again this year, but I've noticed its subject is very similar to that of another piece listed in your e-mail attachment. I've painted an orchard near my parents' house as it looks just when the sun is rising above it. Could I ask that my painting be placed away from the similar artwork?

Thanks,

Omonuwa Orou

---

191. What is the purpose of the first e-mail?
    (A) To commission a work of art
    (B) To stress the importance of community gardens
    (C) To inform employees about an upcoming event
    (D) To share information about local artists

192. Why does Ms. Noonan comment on the event venue?
    (A) To reassure employees that the space will not be too crowded
    (B) To explain why the location is appropriate for the event
    (C) To ensure guests dress accordingly
    (D) To explain why the firm is donating money

193. What artist donated the centerpiece of the auction?
    (A) Brian Healey
    (B) Michaela Green
    (C) Shinji Hasegawa
    (D) Kim Cheung

194. What is indicated about Mr. Orou?
    (A) He has donated art in the past.
    (B) He wants his art to be hung near the entrance.
    (C) He usually paints every morning.
    (D) He has invited his parents to the event.

195. What piece of art is similar in subject to Mr. Orou's painting?
    (A) *Surface of the Moon*
    (B) *Streetlight*
    (C) *Shuki—Artist's Dog*
    (D) *Cornfield Sunrise*

Questions 196-200 refer to the following e-mails and sign.

E-mail

To:	Haruka Maeda <hmaeda@frantaexports.co.uk>
From:	Jerome Lennox <j.lennox@silkmail.co.uk>
Date:	7 May
Subject:	Job 3723
Attachment:	📎 lennox_résumé

Dear Ms. Maeda,

I am writing regarding the open office manager position (job 3723) at Franta Exports here in my hometown of Liverpool. With eight years of experience in office management and administration, I am confident that I have the skills and expertise required to excel in this role. In my current position as office manager at Wyler International, I am responsible for managing all aspects of office operations, including budgeting, scheduling, and staff management. My résumé is attached.

I am excited about the possibility of bringing my skills and experience to Franta Exports. I look forward to hearing from you soon.

Sincerely,

Jerome Lennox

To:	Jerome Lennox <j.lennox@silkmail.co.uk>
From:	Haruka Maeda <hmaeda@frantaexports.co.uk>
Date:	23 May
Subject:	Upcoming interview

Dear Mr. Lennox,

Please respond to this e-mail to verify your intention to participate in a telephone interview with Franta Exports. You are scheduled for an interview with Alisha Scott at 11 A.M. on 28 May for the office manager position.

Your initial interview is scheduled as an online telephone appointment. You may call from a smartphone or a computer. However, please ensure that you have a stable Internet connection. We will send you a text message 30 minutes before your scheduled interview with further instructions.

Within two days following your online interview, we will inform you whether we would like to schedule a follow-up in-person appointment at our headquarters in Portsmouth.

Sincerely,

Haruka Maeda, Human Resources Associate

Welcome to the Franta Exports Liverpool Office!

Office hours: Monday to Saturday from 8 A.M. to 4 P.M.

Office manager: Jerome Lennox

Franta Exports has eighteen offices worldwide, including five in the United Kingdom at the following convenient locations.

- 732 Park Avenue, Portsmouth PO5 3QQ (U.K. Headquarters)
- 10 Donegal Lane, Belfast BT1 3JF
- 660 Richmond Avenue, Cardiff CF24 2PX
- 42 Church Road, Edinburgh EH4 6DU
- 9233 Victoria Street, Liverpool CH44 6PX

196. What is the purpose of the first e-mail?
    (A) To express interest in an open position
    (B) To answer a question about an office job
    (C) To provide notice of a planned meeting
    (D) To request a transfer to another office

197. In the second e-mail, what does Ms. Maeda request of Mr. Lennox?
    (A) That he travel to Ms. Scott's office
    (B) That he reschedule a telephone conference call
    (C) That he complete an online survey
    (D) That he confirm an interview appointment

198. What is indicated on the sign?
    (A) The Franta Exports Liverpool office is open on Sundays until 4 P.M.
    (B) Franta Exports is currently hiring an office manager.
    (C) Franta Exports has offices in multiple countries.
    (D) Franta Exports has eighteen offices in the United Kingdom.

199. What can be concluded about Mr. Lennox?
    (A) He interviewed for a managerial position in Cardiff.
    (B) He was hired to work at an office in his hometown.
    (C) He is required to travel throughout the United Kingdom.
    (D) He works at the same location as Ms. Scott does.

200. Where was Mr. Lennox's follow-up meeting held?
    (A) At 732 Park Avenue
    (B) At 10 Donegal Lane
    (C) At 660 Richmond Avenue
    (D) At 42 Church Road

Stop! This is the end of the test. If you finish before time is called, you may go back to Parts 5, 6, and 7 and check your work.

ETS 토익 정기시험 기출문제집 5 1000 RC

TEST 05
무료 동영상 강의

저자와 출판사의 사전 허락 없이 내용의 일부 혹은 전부를 인용 및 복제하거나 발췌하여 사용할 수 없습니다.

RC
기출 TEST 05

READING TEST

In the Reading test, you will read a variety of texts and answer several different types of reading comprehension questions. The entire Reading test will last 75 minutes. There are three parts, and directions are given for each part. You are encouraged to answer as many questions as possible within the time allowed.

You must mark your answers on the separate answer sheet. Do not write your answers in your test book.

PART 5

Directions: A word or phrase is missing in each of the sentences below. Four answer choices are given below each sentence. Select the best answer to complete the sentence. Then mark the letter (A), (B), (C), or (D) on your answer sheet.

101. Mr. Choi, who recently joined the advisory board, is an experienced accountant ------- investor.

    (A) but
    (B) that
    (C) and
    (D) yet

102. The first 150 visitors to the new fitness park will each receive a complimentary water -------.

    (A) bottle
    (B) bottled
    (C) bottling
    (D) to bottle

103. Operating instructions for the printer will be e-mailed to employees -------.

    (A) short
    (B) shortly
    (C) shorter
    (D) shortening

104. Dozens of ------- customers have posted positive reviews of Stellenbosch Cycle Works.

    (A) satisfy
    (B) satisfied
    (C) satisfaction
    (D) satisfies

105. Ms. Lim's best-selling novel has been ------- praised.

    (A) respectively
    (B) tightly
    (C) unhappily
    (D) widely

106. The marketing manager, Ms. Abyola, plans to meet with the press following ------- meeting with the vice president.

    (A) her
    (B) she
    (C) hers
    (D) herself

107. Last weekend, Terriville Community Center held a ------- game night for neighborhood children.

    (A) removable
    (B) plentiful
    (C) lively
    (D) current

108. Mr. Lenthe will distribute ------- of the workshop agenda to all managers by Tuesday morning.

    (A) copies
    (B) copier
    (C) copy
    (D) copying

109. Employees are eligible for more vacation time ------- they have been employed for five years.
    (A) after
    (B) neither
    (C) so
    (D) thus

110. Managers at Afton Accounting are urged to provide ------- feedback to employees on a regular basis.
    (A) construct
    (B) constructor
    (C) constructive
    (D) construction

111. Many farmers markets operate on a seasonal -------, opening in spring and closing in late autumn.
    (A) topic
    (B) basis
    (C) root
    (D) sum

112. ------- in the housing market has continued to drag down real estate profits.
    (A) Weak
    (B) Weakly
    (C) Weakness
    (D) Weakened

113. The sudden merger of Alvy Brothers and Craford Enterprises ------- most financial analysts.
    (A) enabled
    (B) arranged
    (C) surprised
    (D) suspected

114. Of all the mistakes people make in the office, not proofreading their e-mails is one of the -------.
    (A) commoners
    (B) most common
    (C) in common
    (D) more commonly

115. Cayfair Global's ------- mission is to transport and deliver client goods in a timely manner.
    (A) prompt
    (B) primary
    (C) bright
    (D) nearest

116. The department supervisor is ------- for ensuring that all safety gear is stowed properly at the end of the shift.
    (A) responsibilities
    (B) responsibility
    (C) responsibly
    (D) responsible

117. A three-year project deepened the -------, allowing it to accommodate the largest cargo ships.
    (A) tide
    (B) boat
    (C) harbor
    (D) island

118. The experiment's initial results were ------- different from what was expected.
    (A) wild
    (B) wildest
    (C) wildly
    (D) wildness

119. ------- critical reviews, the movie was a great success at the box office.
    (A) During
    (B) About
    (C) Despite
    (D) Over

120. The spray-on sealant ------- as a protective layer that keeps your tiles from getting scratched.
    (A) acts
    (B) acting
    (C) action
    (D) actively

121. The contract for the renovation of the park will not be awarded ------- all bids have been submitted.

(A) nor
(B) next
(C) until
(D) because

122. A recent study showed that substituting refined sugars with maple syrup may have some important ------- benefits.

(A) only
(B) full
(C) legal
(D) health

123. Margie Fung was ------- the winners at Sternetz Institute's art competition.

(A) from
(B) upon
(C) among
(D) beyond

124. Posting updates too infrequently on social media can cause small businesses ------- by their customers.

(A) forgets
(B) to forget
(C) been forgotten
(D) to be forgotten

125. Ideal for conference rooms, our soundproof panels have been specially designed to ------- unwanted background noise.

(A) compete
(B) absorb
(C) surpass
(D) remain

126. Mr. Sato will call into the meeting ------- the hotel's wireless network.

(A) used
(B) using
(C) use
(D) had used

127. Not only has Mr. Ogbu ------- worked on the project, but he has also trained Ms. Jeong to continue the work.

(A) accessibly
(B) diligently
(C) eventfully
(D) completely

128. Belker Auto offers a ten-year warranty for ------- who want greater peace of mind.

(A) this
(B) those
(C) somebody
(D) everyone

129. After months of planning, the Lanton Bookstore school reading program will finally ------- in October.

(A) observe
(B) represent
(C) commence
(D) access

130. Independent consultants can be a valuable source of ------- advice to new entrepreneurs.

(A) unfulfilled
(B) indefinite
(C) obedient
(D) impartial

PART 6

Directions: Read the texts that follow. A word, phrase, or sentence is missing in parts of each text. Four answer choices for each question are given below the text. Select the best answer to complete the text. Then mark the letter (A), (B), (C), or (D) on your answer sheet.

Questions 131-134 refer to the following e-mail.

To: Creative Team
From: Camille Patel
Date: December 9
Re: Colleague departure

Dear Team Members,

As many of you have recently learned, Claudia Hoffman will end her tenure as art director on Monday, December 30. After ten years in this ------- , she will be taking on a new professional challenge in Paris. ------- , she will join the leadership team at a top advertising agency. Marcos Molina from Spencer Design will become our new art director. ------- .
131.   **132.**   **133.**

I would like to personally thank Ms. Hoffman for her tremendous leadership. She ------- a key factor in our agency's success. Please join me in celebrating her achievements at a farewell dinner after work hours on Friday, December 27. The details will be forthcoming.
134.

Sincerely,

Camille Patel
Human Resources Officer

---

131. (A) role
(B) school
(C) production
(D) warehouse

132. (A) There
(B) Instead
(C) Otherwise
(D) Afterward

133. (A) Let him know if you would like to apply.
(B) The salary levels are more competitive.
(C) He will be joining us on January 12.
(D) Spencer Design has lost revenue over the last two years.

134. (A) will be
(B) could be
(C) has been
(D) would have been

Questions 135-138 refer to the following booklet.

The Tominos Team Leadership Seminar

Your success ------- a team leader depends on your ability to consistently inspire your team
               135.
members to perform at the highest level. Good leaders know how to find viable solutions to

workplace problems and implement them accordingly. ------- . How can you gain these skills?
                                                         136.

In this seminar, you ------- how to better align your team members' performance with your
                   137.
organization's goals. ------- in the seminar acquire proven tools and techniques for successfully
               138.
directing a team in today's fast-paced business environment.

---

135. (A) where
     (B) therefore
     (C) for
     (D) as

136. (A) One common problem is employee tardiness.
     (B) Our seminars cost £120 per session.
     (C) They communicate with their team regularly to keep them informed.
     (D) Sign up now and receive a ten percent discount on the registration fee.

137. (A) learned
     (B) will learn
     (C) had learned
     (D) will have learned

138. (A) Authorities
     (B) Candidates
     (C) Participants
     (D) Subscribers

Questions 139-142 refer to the following e-mail.

To: Kana Inoue <kana.inoue@mymail.co.uk>
From: Brian Halstan <bhalstan@impressionise.co.uk>
Date: 9 May
Subject: Free consultation offer

Dear Ms. Inoue,

I am writing on behalf of Impressionise. We are a design firm specialising in medical facilities: waiting rooms, offices, and examination and therapy rooms. Our research indicates that you are planning to open a physiotherapy practice in Queen's Point ------- the next few months. No
                                                                                                139.
doubt, you want your facilities to be comfortable and calming while enhancing your professional practice and conforming to your brand image. ------- . We would love to work with you to create
                                                                                          140.
an inviting ------- that you can be proud of. You can view photographs of our ------- projects at
           141.   142.
www.impressionise.co.uk/portfolio. If interested, please reply to this e-mail to schedule a free consultation.

Sincerely,

Brian Halstan, Sales Manager
Impressionise

139. (A) either
     (B) perhaps
     (C) within
     (D) since

140. (A) Let us help you achieve these objectives.
     (B) Ask us about potential tax advantages.
     (C) Our software makes booking appointments easy.
     (D) A well-trained staff is all you need to succeed.

141. (A) space
     (B) event
     (C) signal
     (D) moment

142. (A) educational
     (B) residential
     (C) preventive
     (D) previous

Questions 143-146 refer to the following information.

Digital Chicory is a monthly magazine that provides resources and tutorials for Web designers. *Digital Chicory* accepts informative and well-written articles of 800 to 1,200 words. ------- . If you have an idea for an article, please send your pitch to writer@digitalchicory.org.
143.
------- , be sure to spend some time reading our publication so that you can develop an
144.
understanding of our audience and general writing style. ------- respond promptly to article
145.
proposals, which should be submitted as single-page outlines. Full-length ------- are typically
146.
discouraged at the proposal stage. However, if you are a new writer for our magazine, please include samples of previously published writing.

143. (A) Lengthier articles are sometimes considered as well.
(B) The editorial staff has won numerous awards.
(C) Subscribe now and receive a free tote bag.
(D) Please allow four to six weeks for delivery.

144. (A) In any event
(B) If you cannot
(C) Before you do
(D) On the contrary

145. (A) We
(B) They
(C) Some
(D) These

146. (A) forms
(B) drafts
(C) contracts
(D) schedules

PART 7

Directions: In this part you will read a selection of texts, such as magazine and newspaper articles, e-mails, and instant messages. Each text or set of texts is followed by several questions. Select the best answer for each question and mark the letter (A), (B), (C), or (D) on your answer sheet.

Questions 147-148 refer to the following information.

> ### Your Business Gets Noticed When You Advertise Here!
> Prime advertising space is available with sizes ranging from a quarter column to a full page. The *Clearpoint Times* reaches thousands of your neighbors each week. Use the *Clearpoint Times* to spread the word about your business. It works! For rates and additional information, call us at 515-555-0130.

147. What is the main purpose of the information?

(A) To announce the opening of a new business
(B) To publicize storage spaces available for rent
(C) To attract people who want to promote their businesses
(D) To encourage people to buy newspaper subscriptions

148. What is suggested about the *Clearpoint Times*?

(A) It is currently for sale.
(B) It is a real estate magazine.
(C) It is a local weekly publication.
(D) It is a national daily newspaper.

Questions 149-150 refer to the following e-mail.

To:	Donna Witt <d.witt@seemail.net>; Jack Witt <j.witt@seemail.net>
From:	David Paltz <dpaltz@emeraldglen.com>
Date:	August 5
Subject:	Barkley Drive patio project

Hello, Donna and Jack,

I am just checking in as I finalize my schedule for the upcoming months. I would like to schedule a time to revisit your property and discuss your landscaping project in more detail. To get started, it would be helpful if the two of you could brainstorm some of your design expectations and overall vision for the project. Your ideas will help me better determine the materials and time needed. I can then give a more accurate price estimate.

David Paltz
Emerald Glen Landscaping

149. What is the purpose of the e-mail?

(A) To request a meeting
(B) To confirm a recent price change
(C) To apologize for a scheduling delay
(D) To seek additional staff for some work

150. What does Mr. Paltz ask Mr. and Ms. Witt to do?

(A) Submit a payment
(B) Reschedule a work project
(C) Avoid parking near a job site
(D) Provide him with landscaping ideas

Questions 151-152 refer to the following advertisement.

Cavalina Hotel
Blue Globe Magazine's "Best Hotel" Award Winner!

Cavalina Hotel is a breathtaking sanctuary where guests can escape the hectic bustle of city life. Located 50 kilometers from the international airport in Jeel City, the hotel faces the beautiful Sea Mariner Bay. Windsurfing, paddleboarding, and several hiking and biking trails are all a short walk from our front door. Our knowledgeable staff are happy to arrange a kayaking excursion or a fishing trip to one of the nearby lakes. After a good night's sleep in one of our comfortable rooms, you'll be eager to explore the region right after breakfast!

Property Amenities: free parking, swimming pool, bicycle rental, fitness center, two restaurants

Room Types: single room, two-room suite with balcony, two-room suite with kitchen

---

151. For whom is the advertisement most likely intended?

(A) People who want to tour Jeel City
(B) People who enjoy outdoor activities
(C) Business conference organizers
(D) Hotel industry professionals

152. What is suggested about some of the rooms at Cavalina Hotel?

(A) They contain antique furniture.
(B) They have recently been updated.
(C) Guests can view them online.
(D) Guests can prepare food in them.

Questions 153-154 refer to the following text-message chain.

Paul Cho (9:47 A.M.)
Hi, Marisol. I wanted to let you know that I was talking to the director of Yadav Digital Marketing, Elise Mayer. There's an open position there, and I mentioned you. She says you should definitely apply.

Marisol Rosetti (9:49 A.M.)
That's wonderful to hear! Thanks for passing my name along.

Paul Cho (9:50 A.M.)
I know you'd be a great fit. You check all the boxes.

Marisol Rosetti (9:51 A.M.)
Do you think Ms. Mayer would want to see a cover letter in addition to my résumé?

Paul Cho (9:52 A.M.)
I wouldn't bother. Elise and I have been friends for years. Just make sure your résumé is up to date and reflects your relevant experience.

Marisol Rosetti (9:53 A.M.)
I'll do that. Thank you so much, Paul. I really appreciate it!

153. At 9:50 A.M., what does Mr. Cho most likely mean when he writes, "I know you'd be a great fit"?

(A) He would like to hire Ms. Rosetti.
(B) He has worked at Yadav Digital Marketing for a long time.
(C) He thinks Yadav Digital Marketing needs a new director.
(D) He thinks Ms. Rosetti is a good candidate for a job.

154. What is indicated about Mr. Cho?

(A) He has known Ms. Mayer for a long time.
(B) He works at the same company as Ms. Mayer.
(C) He will help Ms. Rosetti write a cover letter.
(D) He is a director at a marketing firm.

Questions 155-157 refer to the following article.

Product Launch Delayed

Covered Bridge Industries has delayed the launch of its new Balmy Breeze soft drink. The company had planned to release the product in June to take advantage of the higher sales demand during the summer months. The company said the delay was caused by a shortage of one of the drink's main components, mango extract, which led to the postponement of quality testing until August.

Covered Bridge now hopes to complete all quality testing by November so that it can launch the product the following month. While sales will likely be weaker than originally hoped, the company will promote Balmy Breeze as an excellent choice for winter holiday celebrations.

155. What kind of company most likely is Covered Bridge Industries?

(A) An ice cream producer
(B) An advertising agency
(C) A beverage manufacturer
(D) A maker of electric fans

156. Why did the leaders of Covered Bridge Industries not follow their original plan?

(A) They wanted to wait for more favorable market conditions.
(B) Quality tests revealed several problems.
(C) Their advertising campaign was not ready on time.
(D) An essential ingredient was unavailable.

157. During what month will Covered Bridge Industries most likely launch a new product?

(A) In June
(B) In August
(C) In November
(D) In December

GO ON TO THE NEXT PAGE

Questions 158-160 refer to the following memo.

MEMO

From: Leah Achen, Head of Technology Resources
To: All Employees
Date: June 28
Subject: Video-editing software change

Effective July 20, employees will no longer have access to the Zipvid app for creating animated videos. — [1] —. We will instead be using Curtain Call, which we trust will prove to be a more reliable program that is less likely to crash. — [2] —. Employees who need to convert their videos from the format Zipvid uses to a format compatible with Curtain Call should install the converter utility to their work computers. This utility can be found in our company's online software library. — [3] —. For assistance with this process, please contact Manuel Costa in Technology Support. — [4] —.

158. Why is the Zipvid app no longer being used?

(A) It is more expensive than similar programs.
(B) It was used by only a few employees.
(C) It malfunctioned too frequently.
(D) It is not compatible with new computers.

159. According to the memo, what can Mr. Costa help employees do?

(A) Convert videos
(B) Recover lost data
(C) Order software
(D) Complete a form

160. In which of the positions marked [1], [2], [3], and [4] does the following sentence best belong?

"It has already been installed on all work computers, so you can begin using it immediately."

(A) [1]
(B) [2]
(C) [3]
(D) [4]

Questions 161-164 refer to the following article.

Local Businesses Thriving

GREENWOOD (July 6)—Why a particular business succeeds is often a mystery, but a couple of local shops appear to have learned the secret. Two years after opening their doors, A Thousand Stories and Rosier's Garden Center are flourishing.

"There was a lot of trial and error at the outset, but we finally figured it out," said Liz Ohtani, who, together with Sandra Rivera, owns A Thousand Stories. "I manage the stock, and Sandra handles the public-facing part, including special events with authors."

Ms. Rivera added, "We make a fantastic team. But I think our strongest asset is our supportive neighborhood. People here love books and reading, and they visit us regularly. We also have an active social media presence, and that helps too."

Louie Rosier, owner of Rosier's Garden Center, agreed that getting a business up and running takes effort and patience.

Mr. Rosier, whose store specializes in native plants and flowers, admitted that his first year with the garden center was tough. He recalled, "It took a long time to turn a profit. Sometimes I considered shutting it all down and going back to my former job."

Despite the difficult start, Mr. Rosier persevered. Now that the business is doing well, he is exploring opening another store.

"I'd like to reach customers beyond the Greenwood area," he said. "I'm currently looking at Morganville to see if that would be the best location for a second store."

161. What type of business do Ms. Ohtani and Ms. Rivera most likely operate?

(A) A real estate office
(B) An event planning service
(C) A bookshop
(D) A media company

162. What is one similarity between A Thousand Stories and Rosier's Garden Center?

(A) Both are operated by co-owners.
(B) Both serve customers worldwide.
(C) Both advertise primarily online.
(D) Both struggled when they first opened.

163. The word "turn" in paragraph 5, line 4, is closest in meaning to

(A) join
(B) gain
(C) change
(D) reverse

164. According to the article, what will Mr. Rosier most likely do soon?

(A) He will write a book about his experience.
(B) He will move his home to Morganville.
(C) He will return to his previous career.
(D) He will open another garden center.

Questions 165-167 refer to the following notice.

Important Information Regarding Employee Safety

All employees are expected to follow the guidelines in the employee manual as well as posted safety rules. Certain jobs require employees to follow the additional safety guidelines provided by their supervisors. Because we take safety seriously, we urge any employee who becomes aware of a breach of these protocols to contact a supervisor or the safety coordinator. Further, any employee who has concerns about these protocols or would like to propose additional measures should contact the safety coordinator directly.

Additionally, contact information for employees who are trained in first aid can be found in the employee manual. Free first aid training and certification are available twice yearly to all employees. For more information about when trainings are held, please contact Lynn Schneider at lschneider@rinckindustry.com.

---

165. What responsibility of a supervisor is mentioned in the notice?

(A) Distributing employee manuals
(B) Overseeing the work of the safety coordinator
(C) Regularly updating the posted safety rules
(D) Providing safety guidelines for specific jobs

166. The word "measures" in paragraph 1, line 6, is closest in meaning to

(A) amounts
(B) procedures
(C) dimensions
(D) penalties

167. According to the notice, why should employees contact Ms. Schneider?

(A) To apply for a new position
(B) To update their contact information
(C) To suggest additional safety rules
(D) To request a training schedule

Questions 168-171 refer to the following job description.

**Dora County Department of Transportation
Division of Administrative Services**

HIGHWAY SUPERVISOR

The highway supervisor oversees all tasks related to the construction and maintenance of road-related structures throughout Dora County, including creating work objectives for all emergency program activities. Key responsibilities include the organization of all snow-removal operations and construction projects. — [1] —. Therefore, the supervisor must also be able to perform construction and maintenance work as needed and possess an appropriate level of skill in operating the relevant equipment.

— [2] —. The supervisor assists in the hiring and training of subordinates and works with division leaders to conduct evaluations and yearly performance reviews of crew members. Crucially, the supervisor instructs crew members in safety procedures and monitors the safety of works in progress. The supervisor informs the division director of major personnel problems; the director will recommend an appropriate course of action in all instances. — [3] —. Significant concerns raised by employees are brought to the attention of division leaders by the supervisor, who functions as a liaison between crew members and the Division of Administrative Services.

Managing the division's designated budget is a critical aspect of the position. The supervisor shows proficiency in the use of computers to keep track of the budget each month. — [4] —. The supervisor prepares expenditure reports and time sheets as well as statistical and narrative reports related to maintenance and repair activities, being sure to record the amount of time, number of employees, and materials used for each activity.

168. What is suggested about Dora County?

(A) It gets cold enough to snow there.
(B) It has a large population.
(C) It purchases equipment from local vendors.
(D) It has many four-lane highways.

169. According to the job description, what should the highway supervisor do if a serious problem with a crew member arises?

(A) Suggest a replacement worker.
(B) Restrict the crew member's activities.
(C) Notify the division director of the issue.
(D) Designate a liaison to explain the matter to management.

170. What is NOT a responsibility of the highway supervisor?

(A) Operating construction equipment
(B) Conducting yearly performance reviews
(C) Managing the monthly budget
(D) Negotiating crew member salaries

171. In which of the positions marked [1], [2], [3], and [4] does the following sentence best belong?

"The position features several duties related to staff management."

(A) [1]
(B) [2]
(C) [3]
(D) [4]

Questions 172-175 refer to the following text-message chain.

Marcus Gollancz (3:18 P.M.)
Jennifer, can you be at the Browns' house at 7:00 A.M. tomorrow to remove the furnace ductwork? Arthur's foundation-repair crew will need to access that area of the crawl space under the house.

Jennifer Kaluza (3:20 P.M.)
OK, it should take me about an hour. That's 210 Leon Drive, right?

Marcus Gollancz (3:20 P.M.)
That's right.

Arthur Gruyter (3:21 P.M.)
My crew will be there to start work shortly after 8:00 A.M. tomorrow. Our work patching and waterproofing the foundation will likely take three or four days. It's an unusually large job.

Jennifer Kaluza (3:22 P.M.)
So, when would you like me to come back to reinstall the ductwork?

Marcus Gollancz (3:23 P.M.)
The Browns are away on vacation, so I think Friday afternoon should be fine.

Jennifer Kaluza (3:23 P.M.)
I'm scheduled to work at Mr. Amadi's apartment on Friday—can the Browns' ductwork wait until Monday?

Marcus Gollancz (3:24 P.M.)
Sure. Early on Monday would work.

Jennifer Kaluza (3:25 P.M.)
You got it, Marcus.

172. What is the purpose of the conversation?

(A) To inform a homeowner about a construction project
(B) To explain why a repair cannot be completed on time
(C) To discuss the timing of a public event
(D) To coordinate a work schedule

173. What can be concluded about 210 Leon Drive?

(A) It is a private home.
(B) It is an office building.
(C) It is an apartment complex.
(D) It is an industrial warehouse.

174. What is suggested about the members of Mr. Gruyter's work crew?

(A) They have added Ms. Kaluza to their group.
(B) They are repairing Mr. Gollancz' office.
(C) They usually complete jobs in fewer than three days.
(D) They have already begun work on Mr. Amadi's apartment.

175. At 3:25 P.M., what does Ms. Kaluza most likely mean when she writes, "You got it"?

(A) She wants to confirm that Mr. Gollancz understands her.
(B) She will be at 210 Leon Drive early Monday morning.
(C) She will send Mr. Gruyter a bill for some work.
(D) She hopes Mr. Gollancz will contact the Brown family.

Questions 176-180 refer to the following Web page and e-mail.

https://www.jjshomeandgarden.com/cementmixers

JJ's Home and Garden Suppliers
Cement Mixers

Model	Name	Description	Price
HCC-TX	Easy Star	• 2 cubic feet, 1 hp • In-store pickup only	$189
CVY-XU	Mr. Buddy*	• 2 cubic feet, 5 hp • Delivery only, 1–2 weeks	$359
PIT-RX	Concretizer	• 4 cubic feet, 3 hp • In-store pickup and 5-day delivery	$499
HTK-LM	Big Mix	• 5 cubic feet, 5 hp • In-store pickup only	$629
PPP-HT	Max for Pros	• 6 cubic feet, 7 hp • Delivery only, 2–4 weeks	$949

*Out of stock until July 26

To:	Customer Service <customerservice@jjshomeandgarden.com>
From:	Marshall Weaver <mweaver01@gomail.net>
Date:	June 25
Subject:	Delayed order

Dear Customer Service Representative:

I received a confirmation e-mail on June 15 that my 4-cubic-foot cement mixer would be delivered one week ago from JJ's Home and Garden Suppliers. I have a small business and am dependent on my equipment. I have not yet received the product, and I have already left several unanswered phone messages. If the cement mixer is not at my business by the end of the day today, I can still pick it up at either the New Gralen or the Paloner store if I have to, as I need it for a job tomorrow afternoon. If one is not available by tomorrow, I ask that you cancel my order and provide me with a full refund. I will instead buy a Mr. Buddy from Alliance Hardware Store, a small, local store where it is currently in stock (and at your same price).

Please advise me on the status of my order immediately. I hope that my order with you will arrive today and that no further action will be needed by either of us.

Sincerely,

Marshall Weaver

176. What is indicated on the Web page?

    (A) Big Mix is currently not available.
    (B) Mr. Buddy is the best-selling item.
    (C) Some items cannot be delivered.
    (D) All cement mixers have been discounted.

177. What item did Mr. Weaver order from JJ's Home and Garden Suppliers?

    (A) Easy Star
    (B) Concretizer
    (C) Big Mix
    (D) Max for Pros

178. In the e-mail, the word "full" in paragraph 1, line 7, is closest in meaning to

    (A) supplied
    (B) occupied
    (C) complete
    (D) abundant

179. What is suggested about JJ's Home and Garden Suppliers?

    (A) It specializes in the sale of large construction equipment.
    (B) It sells most of its products online.
    (C) It offers free delivery on all products.
    (D) It has stores in more than one location.

180. What is the cost of a model CVY-XU cement mixer at Alliance Hardware Store?

    (A) $189
    (B) $359
    (C) $499
    (D) $629

GO ON TO THE NEXT PAGE

Questions 181-185 refer to the following Web page and e-mail.

---

https://www.collingswoodglobal.com/about

| Home | **About** | Services | Contact Us |

The international trade business can be complicated, especially if you are unfamiliar with the steps and documentation involved. Guidelines vary from country to country, and special licenses and permits may be needed.

Let the experienced consultants at Collingswood Global help! First, you will complete our short questionnaire about your business. Once we assess your needs, we will match you with one of our team members, listed below.

- Margaret Giordano: agricultural products

- Jonah Woodrow: household appliances

- Felicity Wong: precious stones

- Malik Fadel: automotive parts

We offer a single introductory session for $329 per hour. Your consultant will determine the rates for any subsequent sessions based on your needs. If you would like to receive guidance regularly, you would pay a monthly retainer at a cost to be negotiated during the introductory session.

E-Mail Message

To: contact@collingswoodglobal.com
From: Sanjeev Yadav <sanjeev.yadav@isvaraniltd.com>
Date: December 12
Subject: Preconsultation questionnaire follow-up

To Whom It May Concern:

I filled out the questionnaire on your Web page, but I am not sure that my form went through. I never got a confirmation e-mail. As I mentioned in the form, we are a five-year-old company specializing in high-end washers and dryers. We sell our machines to stores all along the East Coast of the United States and are well-informed about domestic cargo procedures. However, we want to venture into international trade, particularly throughout Europe, and we would like ongoing support in this endeavor. Please contact me to discuss Isvarani Ltd.'s needs in more detail.

Many thanks,

Sanjeev Yadav, Owner, Isvarani Ltd.

181. What does the Web page indicate about guidelines for international trade?

(A) They are different for each country.
(B) They often serve multiple purposes.
(C) They are updated on a regular basis.
(D) They are stricter than they once were.

182. What does the Web page mention about the cost of a monthly retainer?

(A) It cannot be negotiated.
(B) It costs $329 per month.
(C) It is set during an initial meeting.
(D) It may be waived based on client needs.

183. Why does Mr. Yadav provide information about his company in the e-mail?

(A) He is responding to a request from a prospective colleague.
(B) He forgot to include the information on a form.
(C) He is following an established process.
(D) He is unsure whether a questionnaire he completed was received.

184. Who will Mr. Yadav most likely work with?

(A) Ms. Giordano
(B) Mr. Woodrow
(C) Ms. Wong
(D) Mr. Fadel

185. What is mentioned in the e-mail about Isvarani Ltd.?

(A) It wants its suppliers to remain confidential.
(B) It violated an international policy by accident.
(C) It has plans to expand its operations.
(D) It needs more information about domestic cargo requirements.

Questions 186-190 refer to the following article, e-mail, and letter.

Customers' Corner

Customers' Corner is a recurring feature in *Atlas Financial Review* (*AFR*) about customer-centric trends in Africa's banking industry. This installment of the series discusses Sonfaya Mutual's business advantage savings account (BASA).

Sonfaya Mutual's BASA has an annual percentage yield of 2.2 percent, which is 1.6 percent higher than the yield of the business savings account offered by its nearest competitor. Moreover, it comes with a range of customer privileges, including yearly tax preparation with a certified tax accountant, one-on-one consultations with a dedicated account manager, and financial education programmes, both in-person and online. Except for the assistance with tax paperwork, these offerings are provided at no expense to BASA holders.

A minimum deposit of FRW 100,000 is required to open a BASA, while a monthly administration fee of FRW 1,500 is charged. For new BASA holders, the monthly cost is waived for the first six months. For more details, go to www.sonfayamutual.com/basa.

Sonfaya Mutual is headquartered in Kigali, Rwanda, with offices in the countries of Tanzania, Uganda, and Zambia. An in-depth article about Sonfaya Mutual's origins, growth, and milestones was published in *AFR*'s January issue. Previous issues are at www.atlasfinancialreview.com/archives. Send questions about archived matters to archivist@atlasfinancialreview.com.

To:	archivist@atlasfinancialreview.com
From:	ochabinga@mesuradobankofliberia.com.lr
Date:	1 November
Subject:	Missing AFR issue

To Whom It May Concern:

I read the article on Sonfaya Mutual's BASA in the most recent issue of *AFR* with interest. Subsequently, I visited your Web site, looking for the previous *AFR* issue referenced in the article. Unfortunately, I could not locate it on the archival page. Please advise on how I can obtain that back issue.

Sincerely,

Odette Chabinga
Vice President, Mesurado Bank of Liberia

23 November

Ms. Julienne Nirere
B.P. 2581
KIGALI

Dear Ms. Nirere,

Thank you for being a valued checking account holder with Sonfaya Mutual for fifteen years. We are, furthermore, pleased that you strengthened your relationship with us by opening a business advantage savings account (BASA).

Your checking and savings accounts are now joined, enabling you to transfer money from one account to the other online. Moreover, if you wish to withdraw funds from your BASA, you can use your debit card at any of our ATMs.

Finally, our recently launched online stock-trading platform, available to you at no charge, is excellent for allowing investors to manage their finances at their own pace. Contact our Wealth Management Department for details.

Sincerely,

Philbert Akamanzi

Philbert Akamanzi, Senior Accounts Manager

---

186. What is mentioned about Sonfaya Mutual's financial education programs?

(A) They are offered for free.
(B) They are held once a month.
(C) They are led by account managers.
(D) They are held in partnership with *AFR*.

187. What is indicated in the article about Sonfaya Mutual?

(A) It raised the amount for opening a BASA.
(B) It will continue to add customer privileges.
(C) It updated its Web site recently.
(D) It is an international company.

188. Why is Ms. Chabinga looking for a previous *AFR* issue?

(A) To learn about the offerings of Sonfaya Mutual's competitors
(B) To know more about current customer-centric trends
(C) To learn about the history of Sonfaya Mutual
(D) To know more about Sonfaya Mutual's BASA

189. What is suggested about Ms. Nirere?

(A) She will not have to pay the BASA monthly fee for six months.
(B) She did not receive her debit card in a timely fashion.
(C) She is a new Sonfaya Mutual customer.
(D) She met with Mr. Akamanzi recently.

190. What is a purpose of the letter?

(A) To explain the benefits of investing
(B) To describe the options for managing funds
(C) To explain how online stock trading works
(D) To provide a department's contact information

Questions 191-195 refer to the following e-mail, form, and receipt.

To:	Valley Road Bed and Breakfast <info@valleyroadbandb.com>
From:	Maya Rodriguez <m.rodriguez@intermountaingraphics.com>
Date:	March 30
Subject:	Breakfast schedule

Hello,

I have a reservation to stay at your bed and breakfast next week. I wanted to inquire about breakfast times. I need to leave before 7 A.M. on Saturday morning, April 11, for my conference at the Ivor Hotel and Conference Center. Will breakfast be available before then? If not, what restaurants near the conference would you recommend that would be open at that time?

Sincerely,

Maya Rodriguez

Intermountain Graphics Travel Expense Reimbursement Form

All Intermountain Graphics employees who travel on official company business must fill out a Travel Expense Reimbursement Form and upload their receipts within 30 days of travel in TravelNow, our electronic travel reimbursement system. All forms must be approved and signed by the employee's department manager.

Employee: Maya Rodriguez   **Date:** April 28

Purpose of Trip: To attend the Digital Graphic Designers Conference

Date	Category	Description	Total
April 10	Transportation	Flight to/from San Jose International Airport	$230.00
April 10	Transportation	Taxi to Valley Road Bed and Breakfast	$31.00
April 11	Transportation	Taxi to the Ivor Hotel and Conference Center	$22.50
April 11	Meals	Breakfast at Eileen's Diner	$23.85
April 11	Other	Conference Registration	$175.00
April 11	Meals	Dinner at Antonio's	$48.67
April 12	Lodging	Valley Road Bed and Breakfast, two nights	$299.00
April 12	Transportation	Taxi to the San Jose International Airport	$31.00
		Total amount to be reimbursed	**$861.02**

Approved by _Eun Park_   **Signature** _Eun Park_

Eileen's Diner
Located in the Ivor Hotel and
Conference Center

Family-owned and operated for
over two decades!
1000 Mission Rico Blvd.
Santa Clara, CA 95054
(408) 555-0126

Saturday, April 11, 6:46 A.M.

Breakfast Sandwich	$14.99
Coffee	$3.50
Subtotal	$18.49
Tax	$1.11
Total owed:	$19.60
Tip	$4.25
Total paid:	**$23.85**

Credit Card: XXXXXXXXXXX5348
Customer Name: Maya Rodriguez

Customer Copy

---

191. What can be concluded about Valley Road Bed and Breakfast?
    (A) It does not serve breakfast before 7:00 A.M.
    (B) It provides a shuttle service to the airport.
    (C) It is located next to the Ivor Hotel and Conference Center.
    (D) It is no longer accepting reservations for April.

192. According to the form, what are employees expected to do?
    (A) Seek permission to travel from the finance department
    (B) Present their work at a conference
    (C) E-mail expense reports to a manager
    (D) Submit receipts within 30 days of travel

193. What is most likely true about the Digital Graphic Designers Conference?
    (A) It lasted three days.
    (B) It began on April 28.
    (C) It was held in Santa Clara.
    (D) It provided meals to participants.

194. Based on the form, what is true about Ms. Park?
    (A) She is a financial analyst.
    (B) She organizes conferences.
    (C) She is a department manager.
    (D) She owns a bed-and-breakfast.

195. What is indicated on the receipt about Eileen's Diner?
    (A) It is open 24 hours a day.
    (B) It offers daily breakfast specials.
    (C) It has locations around the country.
    (D) It has been in business for more than twenty years.

Questions 196-200 refer to the following e-mails and report.

To:	Jae-Jun Nahm
From:	Stacy Landon
Date:	May 4
Subject:	Quinar 5000

Jae-Jun,

The Quinar 5000 in Building F is not working properly. It does not run at a steady speed and requires constant attention from line workers. It was checked at the monthly inspection and received an acceptable rating. However, it is now slowing production throughout Building F. I believe it may fail completely unless it is looked at very soon.

Please send a technician to check it as soon as possible, since the production schedule will likely need to be adapted because of downtime during the service visit.

Thank you.

Stacy Landon
Production Manager

To:	Stacy Landon
Cc:	Alex Nadiner
From:	Jae-Jun Nahm
Date:	May 4
Subject:	RE: Quinar 5000

Stacy,

Unfortunately, our internal equipment repair schedule is beyond capacity, so I am bringing on some new technicians next week. Meanwhile, I have authorized Konner Services to send one of their technicians to inspect the machine and make any necessary repairs. We have used this company before, and they are excellent. They will send someone tomorrow between 1:00 and 2:00 P.M. They informed me that the equipment may be down for up to two hours because of testing. Since I know there is a large shipment of product due to Altran Motors next week, I took the liberty of copying Alex Nadiner, who may need to assign some line workers to put in overtime to make up for the delay.

Jae-Jun Nahm
Director of Maintenance

Konner Services Inspection and Repair Report

Machine:	Quinar 5000
Location:	Haverford Industries, 837 West Lorrie Street, Building F
Date of inspection:	May 5
Labor charges:	2.5 hours
Results:	
Test 102:	Acceptable
Test 393:	Cleaning needed
Test 477:	Faulty Baum X33 main switch
Test 488:	Worn belts and hoses
Fluid levels:	Good
Gauges:	Good

Comments: The technician cleaned the machinery and replaced the malfunctioning switch. However, the belts and hoses should be replaced soon, which will require shutting down the line for about four hours. The line manager has been advised of this situation so that personnel can be reassigned accordingly during this repair.

---

196. What is the purpose of the first e-mail?
 (A) To verify an equipment order
 (B) To request machinery repair
 (C) To report on a monthly inspection
 (D) To encourage increased production

197. What has Mr. Nahm decided to do to solve the problem in Building F?
 (A) Employ additional workers
 (B) Hire an outside company
 (C) Lease a new building
 (D) Purchase a new machine

198. Who most likely is Mr. Nadiner?
 (A) The director of maintenance
 (B) The lead technician
 (C) A line worker
 (D) A line manager

199. What company does Ms. Landon most likely work for?
 (A) Quinar Machines
 (B) Altran Motors
 (C) Konner Services
 (D) Haverford Industries

200. Based on the report, what test resulted in the replacement of a machine part?
 (A) 102
 (B) 393
 (C) 477
 (D) 488

Stop! This is the end of the test. If you finish before time is called, you may go back to Parts 5, 6, and 7 and check your work.

TEST 06
무료 동영상 강의

RC

기출 TEST 06

READING TEST

In the Reading test, you will read a variety of texts and answer several different types of reading comprehension questions. The entire Reading test will last 75 minutes. There are three parts, and directions are given for each part. You are encouraged to answer as many questions as possible within the time allowed.

You must mark your answers on the separate answer sheet. Do not write your answers in your test book.

PART 5

Directions: A word or phrase is missing in each of the sentences below. Four answer choices are given below each sentence. Select the best answer to complete the sentence. Then mark the letter (A), (B), (C), or (D) on your answer sheet.

101. On Saturday, the Edbridge Orchestra will ------- a new work by local composer Nina Borstein.

    (A) make
    (B) operate
    (C) perform
    (D) fulfill

102. It is important to be especially ------- when in the company of new clients.

    (A) polite
    (B) politely
    (C) politest
    (D) politeness

103. Although Ms. Endou was not chosen for an award, ------- achievements were praised.

    (A) she
    (B) her
    (C) hers
    (D) herself

104. At the end of the year, organizations face pressure to achieve their financial -------.

    (A) procedure
    (B) goals
    (C) season
    (D) bills

105. Online ordering is ------- on Naito Café's Web site.

    (A) called
    (B) printed
    (C) capable
    (D) available

106. Mayor Park plans to meet with his campaign staff ------- the televised debate.

    (A) following
    (B) beside
    (C) from
    (D) under

107. Mr. Suh has requested that a more ------- copy machine be purchased for the finance department.

    (A) reliably
    (B) relying
    (C) relied
    (D) reliable

108. Mr. Aponte's photograph of the autumn foliage will be featured on the front ------- of *Outward Expansion Magazine*.

    (A) cover
    (B) coverage
    (C) covered
    (D) coverable

109. Handi Office Supplies' new desk organizers serve ------- practical and stylish additions to any office workstation.

(A) of
(B) as
(C) out
(D) until

110. The efficient redesign of the airline terminal led to ------- flight delays.

(A) friendlier
(B) accurate
(C) previous
(D) fewer

111. Mr. Ogbu's editor appreciated his ability to approach the subject matter -------.

(A) objects
(B) objectivity
(C) objectively
(D) objected

112. Mr. Nakayama was named Employee of the Year, ------- being new to the company.

(A) despite
(B) unless
(C) prior to
(D) whether

113. For the ------- selection of premium paints and art-making supplies anywhere, visit your nearest Painters' Best store.

(A) widen
(B) widening
(C) widest
(D) widely

114. The Stallmain Corporation's latest survey was intended to ------- employee satisfaction in several key categories.

(A) overcome
(B) prolong
(C) deserve
(D) determine

115. Garza's Restaurant is ------- decorated with paintings and photographs of southern Mexico.

(A) elaborately
(B) elaborating
(C) elaborates
(D) elaboration

116. Mr. Brighton's first ------- at Glynn Engineering was in the materials testing group.

(A) assign
(B) assigned
(C) assigning
(D) assignment

117. The installation of new benches throughout Haverford Park will cost ------- €5,000.

(A) briefly
(B) roughly
(C) correctly
(D) generously

118. ------- who is unable to attend the quarterly stakeholder meeting is welcome to appoint a representative.

(A) Such
(B) Whichever
(C) Anyone
(D) Those

119. Singer Maria Stanley ------- today that she is scheduling a world tour.

(A) reveal
(B) revealed
(C) to reveal
(D) revealing

120. Biographer Amber Bowen has been recognized for her distinctive writing -------.

(A) styleless
(B) styled
(C) stylish
(D) style

121. The award-winning stationery created by the artists at Paperi Designs is of ------- quality.
    (A) comfortable
    (B) exceptional
    (C) hospitable
    (D) ambitious

122. During the past quarter, ------- all of Renafy Technology's sales came from one region.
    (A) between
    (B) nearly
    (C) somewhat
    (D) next to

123. Commercial property insurance covers the ------- associated with repairing or rebuilding a business property after certain events.
    (A) expenses
    (B) symptoms
    (C) challenges
    (D) opportunities

124. The first-aid class usually fills up quickly, so prompt ------- is recommended.
    (A) registration
    (B) detection
    (C) information
    (D) certification

125. Manufacturing all its products in-house allows Long Bridge Steel Corp. to ------- every aspect of the production process.
    (A) expect
    (B) impress
    (C) remain
    (D) control

126. ------- its use on home-cooking shows, consumer demand for Silvershine Cookware has doubled.
    (A) Moreover
    (B) For example
    (C) Even though
    (D) Because of

127. Artists at Cavin Graphics work ------- with clients through all stages of the design process to ensure satisfaction.
    (A) collaborative
    (B) collaboratively
    (C) collaborates
    (D) collaborators

128. Brile Construction's contract for the mall development project has finally been ------- by the city supervisor.
    (A) verifying
    (B) verifiably
    (C) verified
    (D) verification

129. ------- 4,000 Urlvac trash removal systems are in use in the eastern region.
    (A) Always
    (B) Quite
    (C) Almost
    (D) Closely

130. The conference schedule will be posted online ------- mailed to attendees.
    (A) in order that
    (B) as soon as
    (C) in case
    (D) rather than

PART 6

Directions: Read the texts that follow. A word, phrase, or sentence is missing in parts of each text. Four answer choices for each question are given below the text. Select the best answer to complete the text. Then mark the letter (A), (B), (C), or (D) on your answer sheet.

Questions 131-134 refer to the following notice.

Bicycles on Buses Program

All Travelbee buses are now outfitted with exterior bicycle racks. This ------- has been installed
                                                                         131.
to encourage our passengers to incorporate bicycle riding into their lives for transportation,

exercise, and pleasure. ------- . Please note, however, that electric bicycles are not
                        132.

------- . For more information on our complimentary Bicycles on Buses program, please visit
133.

www.travelbee.com/bicyclesonbuses. There you can also learn about great bicycle trails that

------- accessed from our bus routes.
134.

131. (A) furniture
     (B) exhibition
     (C) equipment
     (D) application

132. (A) No additional fee will be charged for bringing a bicycle.
     (B) Always make sure to exit at the correct bus stop.
     (C) Special lanes for bicycles are now found on most highways.
     (D) Some passengers qualify for reduced bus fare.

133. (A) efficient
     (B) common
     (C) flexible
     (D) permitted

134. (A) were
     (B) can be
     (C) had to be
     (D) will have been

GO ON TO THE NEXT PAGE

Questions 135-138 refer to the following article.

Corporate Training News

Multinational appliance manufacturer Crystal Technologies recently ------- an innovative training program for workers. The program uses what are called "escape rooms" to build teamwork and creative problem-solving skills. A special facility has been built for this purpose within the company's headquarters in Inverness, Scotland. The facility consists of four rooms, ------- of which is designed to represent a different geographic area that is part of Crystal's global operations. Working in teams of five, employees must solve a business problem particular to that area to be able to unlock the door and enter the next room. ------- . Crystal plans to install escape rooms in its main production facilities outside of Europe ------- .

135. (A) exported
(B) changed
(C) considered
(D) implemented

136. (A) each
(B) either
(C) theirs
(D) another

137. (A) Constructing an escape room is surprisingly expensive.
(B) Poor training can be a problem in manufacturing operations.
(C) The course must be completed within a half hour.
(D) The company produces electronics and major home appliances.

138. (A) as well
(B) again
(C) after all
(D) at that time

Questions 139-142 refer to the following e-mail.

To: allclients@yardleyriverdentalgroup.com
From: tliu@yardleyriverdentalgroup.com
Date: 7 January
Subject: Parking area

Dear Clients,

Yardley River Dental Group will be closing our client parking area next week in order to ------- some needed repairs. -------. During this time, we request that you park your vehicles in the staff parking area, which is to the left of your usual area. (Staff members will park at a specially arranged off-site location while the repairs are being conducted.) From the staff parking area, you will find a walkway that ------- around the side of the building to our front entrance. We apologize for the ------- and thank you for your patience.

Tina Liu, Office Manager

139. (A) carry out
(B) communicate
(C) bring up
(D) label

140. (A) Clients will comment on the uneven pavement in the parking area.
(B) We are located along the bus 11 and bus 27 routes.
(C) It will be closed from Tuesday morning through Friday.
(D) The group recently welcomed several new dentists and hygienists.

141. (A) to lead
(B) leads
(C) leader
(D) was leading

142. (A) inconvenience
(B) addition
(C) error
(D) damage

Questions 143-146 refer to the following notice.

Attention: All Randall-Humboldt Employees

Randall-Humboldt recently experienced a reduction in mail-room staffing. ------- , starting on
                                                                            143.
October 7, mail will no longer be delivered to employees' desks. Departments will be responsible

for picking up and distributing their own mail. Each department ------- one employee to handle mail
                                                                 144.
duties. It is up to the department head to determine how best to assign this responsibility. Mail will

be available for pickup by 10:00 A.M. each morning.

It is strongly recommended ------- employees contact senders of unwanted or junk mail and ask to
                            145.
be removed from those mailing lists. ------- . It will also benefit the environment by reducing waste.
                                       146.

---

143. (A) As a result
     (B) Instead
     (C) Nevertheless
     (D) If so

144. (A) designated
     (B) would have designated
     (C) should designate
     (D) was to designate

145. (A) since
     (B) that
     (C) such as
     (D) whoever

146. (A) Doing so will help streamline mail distribution.
     (B) Mail is sometimes damaged while in transit.
     (C) The mail room can hold no more than four employees at one time.
     (D) Direct mail marketing can be an effective way to sell products.

PART 7

Directions: In this part you will read a selection of texts, such as magazine and newspaper articles, e-mails, and instant messages. Each text or set of texts is followed by several questions. Select the best answer for each question and mark the letter (A), (B), (C), or (D) on your answer sheet.

Questions 147-148 refer to the following advertisement.

Bumbleberry Farm
8715 71st Street NW, Stanfurt, Oregon 97074
(971) 555-0144

Pick your own blueberries!

Bumbleberry Farm is known for its sweet, juicy blueberries. Come and enjoy an afternoon in our blueberry fields picking your own. We cater to families, but everyone is welcome!

Enjoy fresh blueberries as a healthy snack, or use them in homemade jams and baked goods. They are also great for adding to your favorite cereal in the morning.

Picking season this year is set to run from July 1 to September 15. Our fields are open Tuesday through Sunday from 10:00 a.m. to 3:00 p.m.

Admission to the fields is $2.00 per person, with a cost of $2.50 for each half liter of berries picked. Groups of up to 8 persons are welcome. Limit 1 liter per person.

For more information, visit our Web site at www.bumbleberryfarm.com.

---

147. What is indicated about Bumbleberry Farm?

(A) It is open seven days a week.
(B) It is family-friendly.
(C) It operates a bakery.
(D) It offers group discounts.

148. What is NOT mentioned as a way to enjoy blueberries?

(A) In jams
(B) In baked goods
(C) On breakfast cereal
(D) On ice cream

Questions 149-151 refer to the following news article.

Tin Prices May Improve

LONDON (12 September)—Prices for tin rose to a record high in August. International inventories are unusually low at this time, and problems with availability persist. The price increases are driven by reduced supply in countries that produce the metal, coupled with increasing worldwide demand for and manufacturing of electronics, whose components are joined together with tin compounds.

Chilean Smelting, Inc., a major producer, has invested in improved equipment and aims to increase production. As a result, tin traders predict some moderation in prices as supplies rise.

149. According to the article, what is contributing to the demand for tin?

(A) Government regulations on tin production
(B) Increased production of electronic goods
(C) Improvements in mining technology
(D) A global rise in the sale of canned foods

150. The word "driven" in paragraph 1, line 5, is closest in meaning to

(A) urged
(B) chased
(C) transported
(D) caused

151. What is indicated about Chilean Smelting, Inc.?

(A) It is a leading supplier of tin.
(B) It recently hired more workers.
(C) It is looking for new investors.
(D) It regularly offers discounted pricing.

Questions 152-153 refer to the following letter.

Langdale Exterior Solutions • 39 Alderson Road • Highfield, Sheffield S2 4UA

17 September

Mr. Atharv Chatterjee
7 Croft Road
Brinsworth, Rotherham S60 5AP

Hello, Mr. Chatterjee,

Congratulations on the purchase of your new home! I'd like to introduce Langdale Exterior Solutions. We have worked with clients in the Sheffield area for over 30 years. Our team of experienced professionals makes us the most trusted landscape company in the area.

We can assist you in finding optimal solutions for your outdoor spaces at reasonable prices. We perform services from lawn maintenance to tree and shrub care. If you are interested in hardscape features such as brick pathways or rustic stone walls, we will provide recommendations on materials and styles that suit your tastes. We will even bring samples directly to you to help you make your design selections.

Call us today at 0114 496 0101 to schedule a free initial consultation.

Sincerely,

Tabatha Meyers

Tabatha Meyers, Owner, Langdale Exterior Solutions

---

152. What is the main purpose of the letter?

(A) To offer real estate sales services
(B) To promote a landscaping business
(C) To advertise a line of gardening products
(D) To advise on local construction regulations

153. What is NOT indicated about Langdale Exterior Solutions?

(A) They bring product samples to customers' homes.
(B) They do not charge for a first meeting.
(C) They work with clients on design decisions.
(D) They specialize in the construction of houses.

Questions 154-157 refer to the following letter.

Katsunori Sanu
860 Cottonwood Avenue, Apartment 5A
Walkerton, ON N0G 2V0

January 3

Gisel Valdez
3758 Fallon Drive
Ottawa, ON K1Z 7B5

Dear Ms. Valdez,

Per my lease agreement, this letter constitutes written notice that I will be moving out of my apartment on February 28, the day my lease expires. — [1] —. I have accepted a job offer in Toronto and will be relocating. Please let me know when I can expect the return of my security deposit.

— [2] —. I have enjoyed my three years living here. I will gladly recommend the Cottonwood Apartments to anyone looking to rent in the area. One thing I have really liked is that I have never had to wait long to use a washer or dryer in the laundry room since there are plenty of machines available. — [3] —. Most impressive, though, is your maintenance service. The crew members quickly addressed all issues, replacing smoke detectors, changing filters in my furnace, and weatherproofing windows before the cold season set in.

I will let you know my new address as soon as I have one. — [4] —. You can always reach me on my mobile phone, 613-555-0129.

Sincerely,

Katsunori Sanu
Katsunori Sanu

---

154. Who most likely is Ms. Valdez?

(A) Mr. Sanu's lawyer
(B) Mr. Sanu's employer
(C) A financial adviser
(D) A property manager

155. What does the letter indicate about the laundry room at Cottonwood Apartments?

(A) It has several washers and dryers.
(B) It contains an oversized washer.
(C) It is unavailable in the morning hours.
(D) It is available to nonresidents for a fee.

156. What is NOT mentioned about the maintenance crew?

(A) They repaired kitchen appliances.
(B) They installed smoke detectors.
(C) They put clean filters in the furnaces.
(D) They took extra steps to keep the apartments warm.

157. In which of the positions marked [1], [2], [3], and [4] does the following sentence best belong?

"I also appreciate that the landscaping is always well maintained."

(A) [1]
(B) [2]
(C) [3]
(D) [4]

Questions 158-159 refer to the following e-mail.

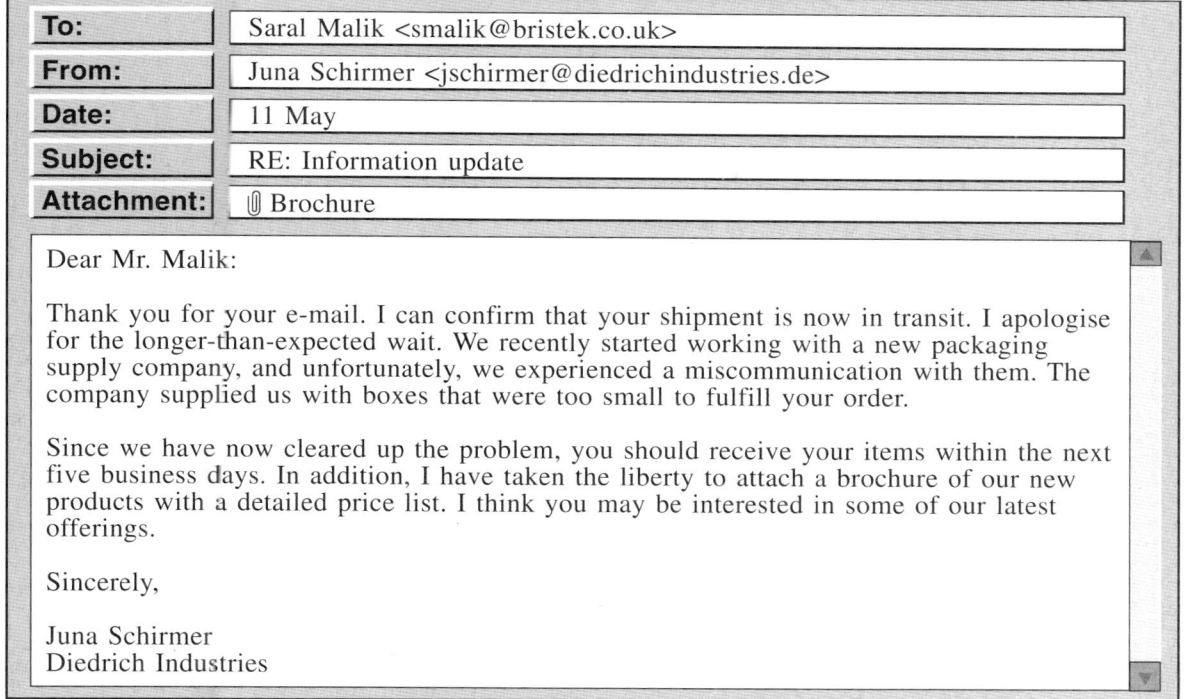

158. What is the purpose of the e-mail?

(A) To explain the cause of a delay
(B) To ask a question about a delivery
(C) To confirm that payment was received
(D) To request information about a product

159. What did Ms. Schirmer provide with the e-mail?

(A) A checklist for packaging items correctly
(B) A list of new items for purchase
(C) Revised box specifications
(D) Information about a shipping warehouse

Questions 160-161 refer to the following text-message chain.

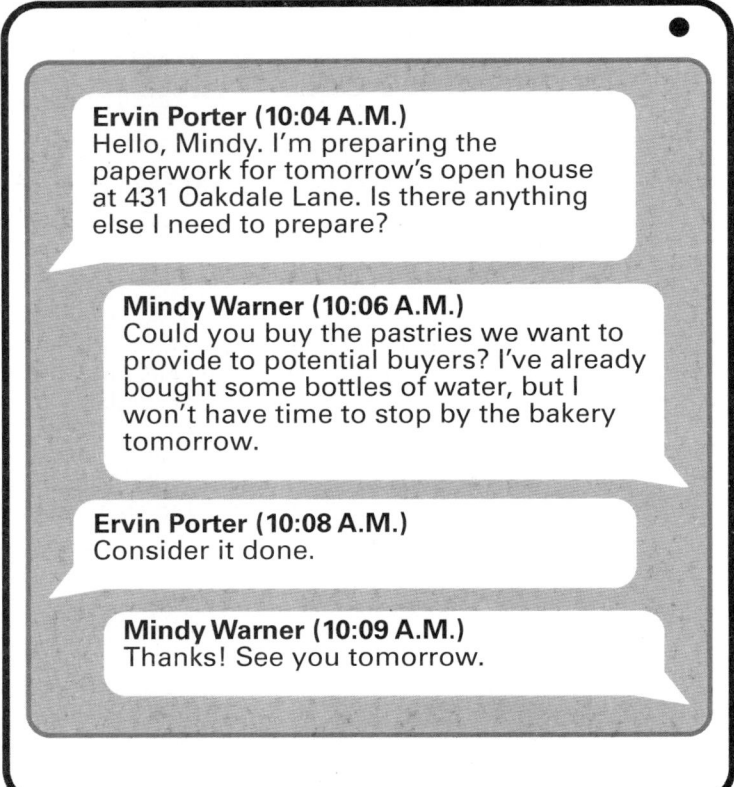

Ervin Porter (10:04 A.M.)
Hello, Mindy. I'm preparing the paperwork for tomorrow's open house at 431 Oakdale Lane. Is there anything else I need to prepare?

Mindy Warner (10:06 A.M.)
Could you buy the pastries we want to provide to potential buyers? I've already bought some bottles of water, but I won't have time to stop by the bakery tomorrow.

Ervin Porter (10:08 A.M.)
Consider it done.

Mindy Warner (10:09 A.M.)
Thanks! See you tomorrow.

160. In what industry do Mr. Porter and Ms. Warner most likely work?

    (A) Finance
    (B) Real estate
    (C) Home security
    (D) Food distribution

161. At 10:08 A.M., what does Mr. Porter most likely mean when he writes, "Consider it done"?

    (A) He has already met the buyers.
    (B) He has already delivered the bottles of water.
    (C) He will purchase some baked goods.
    (D) He will help complete some paperwork.

Questions 162-164 refer to the following blog post.

Games Now Blog

A reader recently asked whether any innovations in 3-D printing are pertinent to the board game industry. — [1] —. In this month's post, I am happy to report that some of the latest advances do indeed offer exciting possibilities for board game production. Customization is a key benefit. — [2] —. This allows components with intricate designs to be tailored to specific themes. Innovations in materials that can be loaded into a 3-D printer offer an unprecedented range of textures for game pieces, enhancing players' tactile experiences. — [3] —.

3-D printers are also getting faster. This is particularly relevant to small-batch production of board games. — [4] —. Small batches are ideal for limited-edition games and new versions of existing games. Companies that exploit these advancements can give themselves an edge in a highly competitive market.

—Salvador Torres, June 1

---

162. What is most likely true about Mr. Torres?

(A) He works for a company that makes 3-D printers.
(B) He writes a weekly blog about video game technology.
(C) He began his career as a graphic artist.
(D) He researched the answer to a question about 3-D printing.

163. What is indicated about the small-batch production of games?

(A) It is more common than mass production.
(B) It costs the same with or without 3-D printing.
(C) It is most often used to make children's games.
(D) It is useful in making multiple versions of a game.

164. In which of the positions marked [1], [2], [3], and [4] does the following sentence best belong?

"Companies can even select materials that are biodegradable."

(A) [1]
(B) [2]
(C) [3]
(D) [4]

Questions 165-168 refer to the following notice.

Stay in Style!

QRN Airport invites travelers to experience our new Repose Lounge. Just like Repose Lounges in other airports, it offers a peaceful, comfortable space where you can unwind if you have a long layover between flights, have arrived early for a flight, or are dealing with an unexpected delay. The Repose Lounge is open daily between 5:00 A.M. and 8:30 P.M. and features the following amenities.

✓ A private conference room for meetings and calls

✓ Printing and copying services

✓ Wi-Fi and charging stations

✓ Beverages, baked goods, and snacks

✓ A selection of current newspapers and magazines

Repose Lounge passes are available for $180 and are valid for one year from the date of purchase. To access a Repose Lounge, guests must present a government-issued photo ID and a same-day boarding pass.

To celebrate the grand opening at QRN Airport, we are offering Repose Lounge passes at half price between March 15 and March 30. To obtain a pass or make a reservation, go to www.qrnairport.com/repose or visit the service desk just outside the lounge in terminal B.

---

165. The word "space" in paragraph 1, line 2, is closest in meaning to

(A) distance
(B) area
(C) condition
(D) vacancy

166. What is indicated about the Repose Lounge at QRN Airport?

(A) It is open 24 hours a day.
(B) It is located in an airport hotel.
(C) It is only for travelers flying internationally.
(D) It has printers available.

167. What is offered to Repose Lounge visitors?

(A) Refreshments
(B) Books
(C) Movies
(D) Computers

168. According to the notice, what will happen between March 15 and March 30 ?

(A) Renovations will be completed.
(B) A service-desk representative will be hired.
(C) Terminal B will be closed.
(D) A discount will be offered.

Questions 169-171 refer to the following article.

Be Green Aware in Misford

March 26—The village of Misford will celebrate its annual Green Awareness Week in April. This event is coordinated by the village's Green Earth Committee and is part of a long-term effort to keep Misford green and clean.

The activities will start on Sunday, April 1, with a cleanup of the Misford Stream trails. Two teams of volunteers will work on either side of the stream to pick up any rubbish and clear the paths of fallen branches.

On Monday, residents are encouraged to walk along the trails and take photographs. The Green Earth Committee is accepting digital images and will select the ten best to post to the village Web site.

On Tuesday and Wednesday, residents who come to the village hall can pick up cloth bags to replace single-use plastic shopping bags, the sale of which will be banned in our county starting next month.

On Thursday, the Misford Library will host a panel on ways to conserve energy and reduce and recycle waste. These are fundamental goals of the village and its Green Earth Committee. Children are welcome to attend with an adult.

Finally, on Saturday, 500 tree saplings will be offered to residents free of charge. The trees are native to the region and can be planted in private gardens or in some public areas.

---

169. What will be posted to Misford's Web site?

(A) An event registration page
(B) Maps of Misford's hiking trails
(C) Photographs of a specified area
(D) A new-resident welcome packet

170. What is one goal of the Green Earth Committee?

(A) To supervise children
(B) To eliminate regulations
(C) To encourage waste reduction
(D) To advise village council members

171. What is NOT mentioned as a planned activity during Green Awareness Week?

(A) Planting native trees
(B) Riding bicycles on a trail
(C) Participating in a cleanup effort
(D) Distributing cloth bags

GO ON TO THE NEXT PAGE

Questions 172-175 refer to the following online chat discussion.

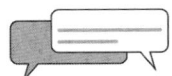

Catherine Radiss [9:12 A.M.]
Good morning, Gina and Jay. Do you have a moment?

Gina Karp [9:13 A.M.]
Sure.

Catherine Radiss [9:14 A.M.]
The department bulletin is going out tomorrow by e-mail. Do you have anything that you would like to add to it? We don't have a lot of news this month.

Gina Karp [9:15 A.M.]
How soon do you need it?

Jay Nusaputra [9:16 A.M.]
I do have something, Catherine. It's a quick reminder summarizing the process for requesting vacation time. Nothing else at the moment.

Catherine Radiss [9:17 A.M.]
I'll need anything you have by the end of the day today.

Gina Karp [9:18 A.M.]
I'm afraid there's nothing I can get to you that quickly. I'm preparing for a full afternoon of interviews. I'll be sure to have a report on current projects ready for the next bulletin.

Jay Nusaputra [9:19 A.M.]
I'll just need an hour or so to finish it up, as I have no client meetings this morning. I can send you the reminder before lunch.

172. What are the writers discussing?

(A) An interview request
(B) An office newsletter
(C) A project evaluation
(D) A vacation itinerary

173. At 9:16 A.M., what does Mr. Nusaputra most likely mean when he writes, "I do have something"?

(A) He has received a colleague's reminder.
(B) He must take time off from work.
(C) He can make a contribution.
(D) He has finished an assignment.

174. When will Ms. Karp's report most likely be sent to the staff?

(A) In an hour
(B) In a day
(C) In a week
(D) In a month

175. What will Mr. Nusaputra probably do next?

(A) Take a lunch break
(B) Meet with a client
(C) Write to Ms. Karp
(D) Finish drafting a reminder

Questions 176-180 refer to the following e-mails.

To:	All Staff
From:	Liza Pacurar
Subject:	Special issue
Date:	November 12

Dear All,

Once again, I'd like to express my gratitude for the great efforts you have made to help us meet the publication deadline for our annual special issue of *Best Design Insights* magazine. What follows is a summary of the main points we discussed at today's meeting.

• Karine Xu reported that advertisers have expressed heightened interest in the issue, so the deadline for submitting advertisements will be extended one week.

• For this issue, we will use our alternate printing service, Sklarr Press, to meet our tight delivery deadline.

• We've gotten approval to increase the budget so that Mark Janskee's team can work overtime to review the pages with special layout components, in particular multiple photographs arranged in a photomontage. Mark will then submit a custom design request to the printer.

• The draft of the special issue is longer than we want. So, we reduced the page total by condensing the text of our interview with animation artist Bret Lusk.

Liza Pacurar, Editor
Best Design Publications

To:	Liza Pacurar
From:	Karine Xu
Subject:	RE: Special issue
Date:	November 14

Hi Liza,

I'm happy with the plan to use Sklarr Press to print our magazine's special issue, just as we did last year. I'm confident they can meet our publication deadline. Our customization request will probably incur an extra fee, but any added expense should be offset by the expected boost in advertising revenue.

Next on my agenda is to remind our subscribers that they have this extra issue to look forward to. I'll let them know via e-mail.

Karine Xu, Marketing Coordinator
Best Design Publications

176. What is the purpose of the first e-mail?

(A) To introduce a new staff member
(B) To provide a summary of a meeting
(C) To propose that a project be delayed
(D) To request work samples from an artist

177. In the first e-mail, what is indicated about the magazine's special issue?

(A) It will include an interview with an animator.
(B) It will only be available online.
(C) It will reprint articles from previous issues.
(D) It will contain fewer advertisements than expected.

178. In the second e-mail, what is mentioned about Sklarr Press?

(A) It specializes in large orders.
(B) It used to be owned by Ms. Xu.
(C) It has printed issues of *Best Design Insights* in the past.
(D) It is the oldest print service in the region.

179. What most likely will add to the cost of printing this year's special issue?

(A) A shortened deadline
(B) An increase in advertisements
(C) The large number of printed pages
(D) The placement of photographs on pages

180. What will Ms. Xu probably do next?

(A) Send subscribers a reminder
(B) Reduce the length of some articles
(C) Survey staff about preferences for the cover design
(D) Meet with a team of graphic designers

Questions 181-185 refer to the following e-mails.

E-Mail Message

To: Shaan Iqbal
From: Maggie Rosen
Date: July 12
Subject: Office celebration

Dear Shaan,

As you know, we have planned an office party in honor of Walter Weber for July 28. I was pleased to learn from my assistant that you will be attending, and I was wondering if you would be willing to say a few words about Walter during the event. He founded this firm 25 years ago and has always been an integral part of it. Since you work closely with him in the finance department, I thought you might be well positioned to talk about him as a mentor, worker, and leader. The party will begin at 6 P.M. The speeches will start at 7:30 P.M. and continue for about an hour. I am sure everyone, not just Walter, would love to hear from you! Please let me know as soon as possible.

Many thanks,

Maggie Rosen
Director of Human Resources
Weber Richter Associates

E-Mail Message

To: Maggie Rosen
From: Shaan Iqbal
Date: July 12
Subject: Re: Office celebration

Dear Maggie,

Thanks for thinking of me! I have really been looking forward to Walter's party, and it would be a tremendous honor for me to speak about him. Walter actually interviewed me when I first applied for a job with the company fifteen years ago. His guidance over the years has been invaluable.

Please note that I have a meeting with the sales team scheduled for 5 P.M. that day, so I should arrive at the party just as the speeches begin. If you schedule me to deliver one of the later speeches, there should be no problem.

Sincerely,

Shaan Iqbal
Weber Richter Associates

181. Why did Ms. Rosen send an e-mail to Mr. Iqbal?

(A) To invite him to a celebration
(B) To ask for help organizing a party
(C) To inform him about a colleague's accomplishments
(D) To ask him to give a speech at an event

182. What is indicated about Mr. Iqbal?

(A) He regularly gives presentations.
(B) He will reschedule a meeting with the sales team.
(C) He has been with the company for 25 years.
(D) He works in the finance department.

183. What is indicated about Mr. Weber?

(A) He recently opened a new branch office.
(B) He is planning to sell the company.
(C) He was directly involved with Mr. Iqbal's hiring.
(D) He will arrive late to the party on July 28.

184. In the second e-mail, the word "note" in paragraph 2, line 1, is closest in meaning to

(A) spread out
(B) be aware
(C) show
(D) mention

185. At approximately what time does Mr. Iqbal plan to arrive at the party?

(A) 5:00 P.M.
(B) 6:00 P.M.
(C) 7:30 P.M.
(D) 8:30 P.M.

Questions 186-190 refer to the following announcement, e-mail, and Web page.

Alamito Botanical Society

Submit your home garden to be one of several stops on this year's Gorgeous Gardens Tour, scheduled for July 3!

This year's tour theme is Winged Paradise, with a focus on flowering plants favored by regional birds and butterflies, including the lesser goldfinch and the ringlet butterfly. All proceeds from ticket sales for this year's tour will go toward replanting the cottonwood forest in Presidio County Park.

Hosting a tour garden is free for members of the Alamito Botanical Society. Simply complete the form at www.alamitobotanicalsociety.org/gorgeousgardens and submit it with digital photos of your garden by May 20. Gardens selected to participate in the tour must be within Presidio County and include only plants native to the region. If you have questions regarding participating as a tour stop, please send an e-mail to info@alamitobotanicalsociety.org.

E-mail

To:	info@alamitobotanicalsociety.org
From:	rebeccaolton@mailhost.com
Date:	May 1
Subject:	Question about garden tour

Hello,

I became a member of the Alamito Botanical Society last year shortly after moving to Presidio County. The society's Web site, resources, and educational lectures have been helpful regarding my ambitious project: to cover five acres of my land with various native plants that will attract birds and other animals. About one and a half acres of soil have been cultivated so far.

It would be a privilege to show my work to the public and to meet more people who value gardens as we members of the society do. Thus, I am writing to ask if I may participate in the Gorgeous Gardens Tour. I must admit that beautiful lavender bushes that are not native to the area were already growing on the property before I purchased it. However, lavender is not on the invasive-species list, and I continue to let them grow because the butterflies, bees, and other wildlife love the blooms.

Thank you,

Rebecca Olton

https://www.alamitobotanicalsociety.org/education/lectures

The leaders and members of the Alamito Botanical Society cordially invite the public to attend its educational lectures, held at the horticultural department of Marfa Community College. All lectures occur on the third Wednesday of the month at 7:00 P.M. Advance registration is not required.

February: Schedule Your Salad – Get tips for establishing a planting timetable and for selecting delicious vegetables to grow.
March: Nourish the Neighbors – Understand how to use plants native to our region to create landscapes that are inviting to wildlife.
April: Pest Deterrence – Learn natural, pesticide-free techniques that can prevent harmful insects from eating your fruits and vegetables.
May: Pollen Transportation – No butterflies or bees visiting your garden? No worries. Humans can pollinate certain plants using simple techniques.

186. In the announcement, what is mentioned about the Gorgeous Gardens Tour?

    (A) Its focus will be on gardens that have a pond.
    (B) Profits from ticket sales will go toward planting trees.
    (C) One of the featured stops will be in a county park.
    (D) It will take place in May.

187. What does Ms. Olton mention in her e-mail?

    (A) She would like to join the Alamito Botanical Society.
    (B) She plans to donate the land needed for a recreation area.
    (C) She wants to meet people who share her interest in plants.
    (D) She knows people who want to buy tickets for a tour.

188. What most likely will prevent Ms. Olton's garden from being selected as a tour stop?

    (A) It includes a plant that comes from another region.
    (B) It does not meet the size requirement.
    (C) It features trees rather than flowers.
    (D) It is located outside the tour area.

189. On the Web page, what is suggested about the lectures?

    (A) They are for Alamito Botanical Society members only.
    (B) They require a printed invitation.
    (C) They take place every month.
    (D) They are given at various locations.

190. What lecture is Ms. Olton most likely to be interested in?

    (A) Schedule Your Salad
    (B) Nourish the Neighbors
    (C) Pest Deterrence
    (D) Pollen Transportation

GO ON TO THE NEXT PAGE

Questions 191-195 refer to the following advertisement and e-mails.

Opportunity for Landowners

Terra Jaunts organizes nature hikes, farm stays, camping trips, athletic competitions, and other activities for company retreats. We are seeking farmers, ranchers, and other landowners who can help us expand our list of destinations. Terra Jaunts pays up to $300 per day to our partners for the daytime use of their property and provides all or most needed equipment.

Our required criteria are as follows.

1. The site is located within 100 kilometers of a medium to large city.
2. The site is able to host a retreat one or two days per month.
3. The site has adequate parking space for 50 cars or two buses.
4. The site can accommodate up to 75 people.

To:	Celia Newsom <cnewsom@pinkridgeranch.com>
From:	Oliver Jeong <ojeong@terrajaunts.com>
Date:	April 19
Subject:	Your application

Dear Ms. Newsom,

Thank you for applying to be a host. Even though you have less space for vehicles than we normally require, Pink Ridge Ranch might be suitable for our smaller events with fewer than 25 people. We appreciate your having created an illustrated list of all the native flowers and trees growing wild on your property; none of our other hosts offers anything like this. Your list of plants would be a real asset for groups engaged in activities involving the identification of species.

I would like to arrange a site visit with my associate Peter Cumberland either this week or next. After 1 P.M. on a Thursday or Friday would work best for us, but we will try to accommodate your schedule if you prefer a morning or a different day.

Sincerely,

Oliver Jeong
Montana Site Coordinator

E-mail

To: Oliver Jeong <ojeong@terrajaunts.com>
From: Celia Newsom <cnewsom@pinkridgeranch.com>
Date: May 1
Subject: RE: Your application

Dear Mr. Jeong:

Thank you for touring my ranch on Thursday. I am glad you were able to follow my complicated written directions for driving to and from the ranch after your GPS app stopped working. It was wonderful to meet you both and have a chance to show you around.

I received your follow-up voicemail yesterday. After further consideration, I have decided not to pursue this opportunity after all. The hiking paths on my property are quite overgrown, as your partner pointed out. Unfortunately, I do not have the time or staff to ensure that everything is properly groomed throughout the year. If this situation changes, I will reapply.

Kind regards,

Celia Newsom, Owner, Pink Ridge Ranch

---

191. What does the advertisement mention about Terra Jaunts?

(A) It employs 75 people.
(B) It arranges team-building trips for corporate clients.
(C) It hosts monthly retreats for its staff.
(D) It has a service contract with two bus companies.

192. What can be concluded about Pink Ridge Ranch?

(A) It has a reliable wireless network.
(B) It has several large greenhouses.
(C) It earned $300 for hosting a group of hikers.
(D) It is located within 100 kilometers of an urban area.

193. According to Mr. Jeong, what distinguishes Ms. Newsom from other property owners?

(A) The information that she provides about plants
(B) The variety of flowers she is able to grow
(C) Her flexible schedule
(D) Her interest in art

194. What is suggested about Pink Ridge Ranch?

(A) It requires an access code to enter.
(B) It recently changed ownership.
(C) It can be difficult to find.
(D) It is a popular hiking destination.

195. What is most likely true about Mr. Cumberland?

(A) He does not work on Fridays.
(B) He expressed concern about a set of trails.
(C) He owns an organic farm in Montana.
(D) He left a voicemail for Ms. Newsom on April 22.

Questions 196-200 refer to the following e-mails and schedule.

To:	Department Managers <managementteam@a-qualityelectronics.com>
From:	Eileen Wrenn <ewrenn@a-qualityelectronics.com>
Date:	October 7
Subject:	Upcoming visit with Kenji Tanaka
Attachment:	Draft schedule

Good morning,

Mr. Harlington has asked me to let all department managers know that Kenji Tanaka, the chief operating officer of our Japanese subsidiary Kanazawa Electronics, will be visiting our corporate headquarters next week. Please let me know as soon as possible whether you will be able to attend the afternoon meeting and dinner on October 14 so I can make the appropriate arrangements.

A draft schedule is attached to this e-mail. Mr. Tanaka will take the distinguished visitor slot, which Mr. Harlington created last quarter in an effort to reinvigorate our corporate culture.

Departmental reports will begin promptly at 3:00 P.M., following the presentations by Mr. Harlington and Mr. Tanaka, respectively. Details will be announced soon regarding the information that department managers will present in their status reports.

Best,

Eileen Wrenn, Executive Assistant

DRAFT SCHEDULE
A-Quality Electronics Quarterly Meeting
Monday, October 14

12:00–1:00 P.M.	All staff	Catered lunch
1:00–2:00 P.M.	President	Discussion of company goals and performance objectives; status of joint projects
2:00–3:00 P.M.	Distinguished visitor	Update on Kanazawa Electronics: operational successes and challenges faced by the subsidiary in the third quarter
3:00–5:00 P.M.	Department managers	Departmental reports: agenda to be determined
6:00–9:00 P.M.	All staff	Dinner at Mapleton Grill, downtown Mapleton

To:	Eileen Wrenn <ewrenn@a-qualityelectronics.com>
From:	Deborah Powell <dpowell@a-qualityelectronics.com>
Date:	October 7
Subject:	Re: Upcoming visit with Kenji Tanaka

Hi Eileen,

I'm confirming my availability for the meeting with Kenji Tanaka. I plan to update the executives on the marketing team's activities for the third quarter.

Question: do you think Mr. Tanaka might like to go to a baseball game after dinner? He enjoyed seeing the Mapleton Ospreys play after he attended the second quarter meeting in July.

The only problem is that all games in October begin at 8:00 P.M., so we would need to begin dinner at around 5:00 P.M. That would give us enough time to get to the stadium before the game starts. I know this is a lot to ask for, but I think it is worth considering, knowing how much our distinguished visitor enjoyed the Ospreys game and how important he is to the company.

Let me know what you think so I can secure tickets before his visit. Thanks!

Deborah Powell

196. Who most likely is Mr. Harlington?
    (A) The founder of Kanazawa Electronics
    (B) The president of A-Quality Electronics
    (C) A department manager
    (D) An executive assistant

197. According to the first e-mail, what should managers do as soon as possible?
    (A) Provide feedback on a schedule
    (B) Prepare presentations for a meeting
    (C) Save a date for lunch
    (D) Indicate their availability for a meeting

198. According to the schedule, what happened in the third quarter?
    (A) New projects were profitable.
    (B) Corporate objectives changed.
    (C) A subsidiary faced some difficulties.
    (D) New operational staff were hired.

199. What will Ms. Powell most likely do on October 14?
    (A) She will join other managers in delivering reports.
    (B) She will discuss the marketing department's goals.
    (C) She will purchase some baseball tickets.
    (D) She will take Mr. Tanaka out to lunch.

200. What does Ms. Powell request?
    (A) Moving a meeting date
    (B) Asking Mr. Tanaka to speak last
    (C) Rescheduling a meal
    (D) Arranging transportation to a stadium

Stop! This is the end of the test. If you finish before time is called, you may go back to Parts 5, 6, and 7 and check your work.

ETS 토익 정기시험 기출문제집 5
1000 RC

TEST 07
무료 동영상 강의

RC
기출 TEST 07

READING TEST

In the Reading test, you will read a variety of texts and answer several different types of reading comprehension questions. The entire Reading test will last 75 minutes. There are three parts, and directions are given for each part. You are encouraged to answer as many questions as possible within the time allowed.

You must mark your answers on the separate answer sheet. Do not write your answers in your test book.

PART 5

Directions: A word or phrase is missing in each of the sentences below. Four answer choices are given below each sentence. Select the best answer to complete the sentence. Then mark the letter (A), (B), (C), or (D) on your answer sheet.

101. After Ms. Takido finishes ------- presentation, the audience will be permitted to ask questions.
    (A) her
    (B) she
    (C) hers
    (D) herself

102. Mike's Café offers a free ------- with every meal on Tuesdays from 11 A.M. to 7 P.M.
    (A) table
    (B) drink
    (C) price
    (D) menu

103. Mr. Ozawa generally prefers ------- to work by train instead of by car.
    (A) commute
    (B) to commute
    (C) having commuted
    (D) is commuting

104. ------- the new branch office was understaffed, more workers were hired.
    (A) Because
    (B) Having
    (C) Usually
    (D) Following

105. Dumbbells, also known as free weights, are ------- for keeping fit at home.
    (A) use
    (B) using
    (C) to use
    (D) useful

106. The scheduled completion date was September 4, but the job was ------- finished two weeks ahead of schedule.
    (A) additionally
    (B) rarely
    (C) extremely
    (D) actually

107. Please click on the ------- below to subscribe to our monthly newsletter.
    (A) link
    (B) linker
    (C) linking
    (D) linkage

108. Candidates for the entry-level marketing position need to have a ------- understanding of consumer behavior.
    (A) proud
    (B) basic
    (C) short
    (D) considerate

109. Ms. Persson was able to respond ------- to government leaders about their concerns regarding the funding plan.
(A) directly
(B) direct
(C) directions
(D) directed

110. Leigh Ainsley, the featured soloist in tonight's performance, began taking violin lessons ------- the age of five.
(A) on
(B) at
(C) with
(D) along

111. From among the seven candidates for the management position, the hiring committee must choose only -------.
(A) one
(B) either
(C) such
(D) other

112. GT International Foods sells unique products that are difficult to find -------.
(A) aside
(B) instead
(C) likewise
(D) elsewhere

113. Contact the hotel's main office ------- you wish to receive daily linen service.
(A) moreover
(B) besides
(C) if
(D) also

114. Please ------- yourself with the company's tuition-reimbursement policy before enrolling in any classes.
(A) organize
(B) identify
(C) consider
(D) familiarize

115. The proposed purchase agreement is ------- being evaluated by officials at Corlan Tech.
(A) active
(B) actively
(C) activity
(D) activate

116. Another ------- option for getting to the airport will be available once the subway station at the international terminal is completed.
(A) convenient
(B) receptive
(C) fortunate
(D) traditional

117. Given the forecast for rain on Saturday, the ceremony ------- indoors at the Raheen Gallery.
(A) is held
(B) was held
(C) will be held
(D) had been held

118. As Mr. Rzayev requested, the extra wood pallets have been stacked ------- the old warehouse.
(A) between
(B) across
(C) over
(D) behind

119. Professor McNamara has published books on a ------- range of topics.
(A) diversion
(B) diversely
(C) diverse
(D) diversify

120. A ------- of clearly defined milestones was likely why the software development project failed.
(A) consent
(B) break
(C) lack
(D) complex

GO ON TO THE NEXT PAGE

121. Rosemont Department Store employees are said to be very well-informed, -------, and responsive.
    (A) person
    (B) personably
    (C) personify
    (D) personable

122. The security officer at the front gate will ------- delivery drivers as to where to drop off packages.
    (A) invite
    (B) instruct
    (C) provide
    (D) present

123. ------- some tickets to the concert are still available, all the best seats have already been taken.
    (A) Although
    (B) Except
    (C) Notice
    (D) After

124. Visitors must park in the designated parking area ------- risk having their vehicle towed.
    (A) or
    (B) but
    (C) yet
    (D) and

125. When Ms. Liu was hired, the ------- was to train her to work in the chemistry lab.
    (A) intend
    (B) intention
    (C) intended
    (D) intentional

126. A ------- effect of increased tourism in our city has been rapid growth in the number of hospitality-related jobs.
    (A) tentative
    (B) negotiable
    (C) favorable
    (D) perceptive

127. The new payroll system will send an e-mail to employees ------- a manager edits their time sheet.
    (A) now that
    (B) or else
    (C) despite
    (D) whenever

128. The order of the speakers has been changed ------- Mr. Chen arrives late.
    (A) so
    (B) as of
    (C) during
    (D) in case

129. Even though the fuel container can hold up to a ------- of ten liters, the manufacturer recommends putting in only nine.
    (A) maximum
    (B) potential
    (C) greatness
    (D) collection

130. Ever since the Unicycle Café opened for business last May, it ------- weekly live music events.
    (A) to have hosted
    (B) has been hosting
    (C) was hosted
    (D) will be hosting

PART 6

Directions: Read the texts that follow. A word, phrase, or sentence is missing in parts of each text. Four answer choices for each question are given below the text. Select the best answer to complete the text. Then mark the letter (A), (B), (C), or (D) on your answer sheet.

Questions 131-134 refer to the following advertisement.

Do you fancy playing games with your mates? Do you enjoy tasty tea and snacks? If so, you won't want to miss Game Night at Chez Tournoi. Each Friday from 6 to 10 P.M., Chez Tournoi welcomes you to its 44 Broad Avenue, Kingston, location for some fun and ------- . Choose from
131.
our collection of board games, card games, trivia games, and more. ------- . While you play, you
132.
can savour our freshly brewed tea, coffee, and hot chocolate ------- our mouthwatering pastries.
133.
Game Night at Chez Tournoi is the perfect opportunity ------- and socialise. Reserve your spot by
134.
ringing 01555-672212 or visiting www.cheztournoi.co.uk/gamenight.

131. (A) cash
 (B) exercise
 (C) laughter
 (D) lessons

132. (A) Or bring your own if you prefer.
 (B) Vote for your favorite comedian.
 (C) The most popular drink is our caramel latte.
 (D) We also have several openings for servers.

133. (A) in contrast to
 (B) furthermore
 (C) so that
 (D) as well as

134. (A) is relaxing
 (B) to relax
 (C) relaxes
 (D) relaxation

Questions 135-138 refer to the following e-mail.

To: Patton Henry <p.henry@xmail.com>
From: Joanna Kanarak <jkanarak@kanarakrealty.com>
Date: December 29
Subject: Lease renewal

Dear Mr. Henry,

My records indicate that your lease is due to expire on March 31. If you wish to renew your ------- 135. , please let me know before January 31. If you do not reply to this e-mail, ------- 136. will assume that you do not wish to continue living in the 22 Fister Road property. ------- 137. , it will be listed as a rental available to a new tenant on April 1. If you want to move to an apartment larger or smaller than your current one, just let me know. ------- 138. .

Sincerely,

Joanna Kanarak, Kanarak Realty

135. (A) license
(B) contract
(C) subscription
(D) membership

136. (A) I
(B) they
(C) some
(D) everyone

137. (A) In any event
(B) As expected
(C) In that case
(D) For instance

138. (A) This business was started 22 years ago.
(B) Kanarak Realty is happy to help you however we can.
(C) You have occupied the current property for nearly two years.
(D) Your apartment has three bedrooms and two bathrooms.

Questions 139-142 refer to the following brochure.

Where to Stay in Devegas

The Devegas Peninsula features a wide range of ------- options. More than twenty luxury hotels
                                                    139.
------- found along Devegas Beach, along with several moderately priced hotels in the Devegas
140.
Park neighborhood. ------- , a range of small inns and short-term apartment rentals are scattered
                    141.
throughout the area. ------- . Several inexpensive campsites and youth hostels are available
                     142.
throughout the year. For a detailed listing of vacation properties and hotels on the peninsula, see the back cover of this brochure.

139. (A) dining
     (B) investment
     (C) entertainment
     (D) accommodation

140. (A) were
     (B) can be
     (C) would be
     (D) have been

141. (A) After all
     (B) In addition
     (C) Fortunately
     (D) Nevertheless

142. (A) Tourists flock to the peninsula during the summer months.
     (B) Plan your vacation while space remains available.
     (C) Travelers on a budget also have options.
     (D) The Devegas Peninsula is more than ten kilometers long.

Questions 143-146 refer to the following notice.

Nelsign

Your signature has been captured.

The document is waiting for four more signatures.

Once all parties have signed the Nelsign document, you will ------- by e-mail. At that time, the sender will also receive an alert that all necessary signatures on the contract have been acquired.
143.

Upon ------- , all signers may access and save the document. If you have a Nelsign account, this contract and any other documents you have previously signed electronically with Nelsign will be
144.

saved in your profile. ------- . For any questions ------- the signing process, contact our customer support center at inquiries@nelsign.com.
145.   146.

---

143. (A) notify
 (B) be notified
 (C) notifying
 (D) have notified

144. (A) complete
 (B) completed
 (C) completely
 (D) completion

145. (A) For those who need to create an account, simply visit our Web site.
 (B) The contract's effective date appears at the top of the document.
 (C) The privacy terms are attached to the contract.
 (D) Our company is located in Utah.

146. (A) around
 (B) through
 (C) regarding
 (D) assuming

PART 7

Directions: In this part you will read a selection of texts, such as magazine and newspaper articles, e-mails, and instant messages. Each text or set of texts is followed by several questions. Select the best answer for each question and mark the letter (A), (B), (C), or (D) on your answer sheet.

Questions 147-148 refer to the following coupon.

COUPON

If you love the delicious cheese and crackers served at Truli Cafés, you can now enjoy this popular snack at home! Truli crackers and cheese are now available at major supermarkets.

Save $2.00 on the purchase of ONE box of Truli crackers (any size) when you buy any TWO packages of Truli cheese.

Limit one coupon per customer. This coupon may not be combined with other special offers.

Expires July 31.

---

147. What is indicated about boxes of Truli crackers?

(A) They come in various sizes.
(B) They are available in several flavors.
(C) They are sold exclusively at Truli Cafés.
(D) They cost $2.00 more than a package of Truli cheese.

148. What is indicated about the coupon?

(A) It can be used more than once.
(B) It requires the purchase of another product.
(C) It can be used for buying hot drinks.
(D) It must be used before July 1.

Questions 149-150 refer to the following text message.

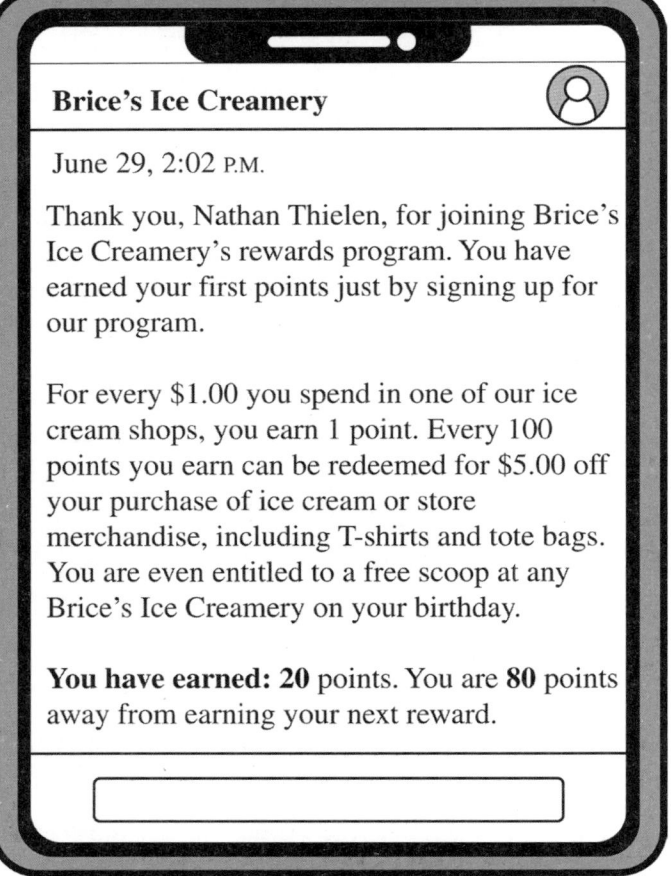

Brice's Ice Creamery

June 29, 2:02 P.M.

Thank you, Nathan Thielen, for joining Brice's Ice Creamery's rewards program. You have earned your first points just by signing up for our program.

For every $1.00 you spend in one of our ice cream shops, you earn 1 point. Every 100 points you earn can be redeemed for $5.00 off your purchase of ice cream or store merchandise, including T-shirts and tote bags. You are even entitled to a free scoop at any Brice's Ice Creamery on your birthday.

You have earned: 20 points. You are **80** points away from earning your next reward.

149. What does the text message indicate about Brice's Ice Creamery?

(A) It has more than one location.
(B) It rents space for birthday parties.
(C) It sells ice cream cones for $5.00 each.
(D) It rewards customers for referring friends.

150. What did Mr. Thielen receive for signing up for the rewards program?

(A) 1 point
(B) 20 points
(C) 80 points
(D) 100 points

Questions 151-152 refer to the following e-mail.

E-mail

To: Charlie Tran <Charlie.Tran@mailcrate.com>
From: Grace Drance <GDrance@hoppersmedicalcenter.org>
Date: January 10
Subject: Missed appointment

Dear Mr. Tran,

I am contacting you because you did not appear for your 1:00 p.m. appointment for your annual physical exam at Hopper's Medical Center (HMC) today. As you know, it is our policy to charge the full appointment fee for missed appointments unless the patient notifies us at least 24 hours in advance of the scheduled visit.

However, we are waiving the fee because this is your first missed appointment in fifteen years of being a patient at the center. Please contact the office as soon as possible to reschedule your appointment. Your physician, Dr. Ramanathan, has created additional appointment times this month because he will be on vacation in February.

Sincerely,

Grace Drance, Scheduling Assistant

---

151. What is one purpose of the e-mail?

(A) To remind a patient of an upcoming appointment
(B) To recommend that an appointment be rescheduled
(C) To inform a patient that a fee has been charged
(D) To provide a patient with the results of a recent physical exam

152. What is indicated about Dr. Ramanathan?

(A) He will be taking time off soon.
(B) He is a longtime friend of Mr. Tran.
(C) He earned his medical degree 24 years ago.
(D) He is relocating his practice in February.

Questions 153-154 refer to the following text-message chain.

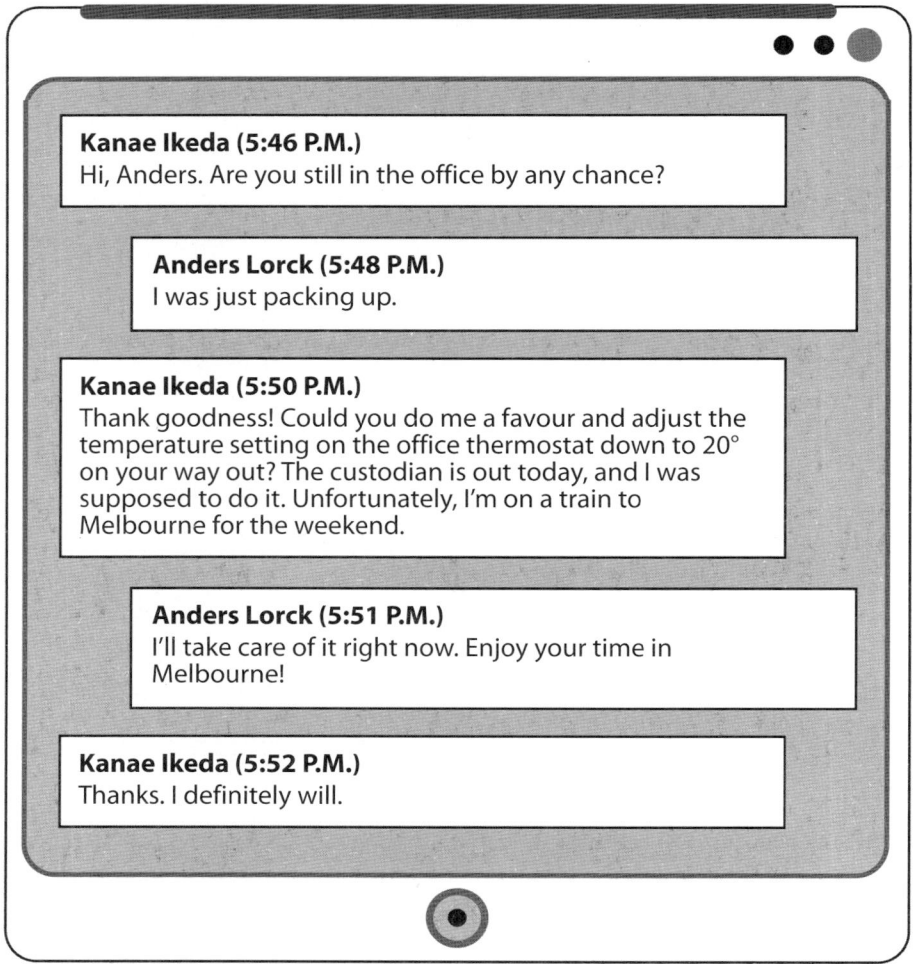

Kanae Ikeda (5:46 P.M.)
Hi, Anders. Are you still in the office by any chance?

Anders Lorck (5:48 P.M.)
I was just packing up.

Kanae Ikeda (5:50 P.M.)
Thank goodness! Could you do me a favour and adjust the temperature setting on the office thermostat down to 20° on your way out? The custodian is out today, and I was supposed to do it. Unfortunately, I'm on a train to Melbourne for the weekend.

Anders Lorck (5:51 P.M.)
I'll take care of it right now. Enjoy your time in Melbourne!

Kanae Ikeda (5:52 P.M.)
Thanks. I definitely will.

153. At 5:48 P.M., what does Mr. Lorck imply when he writes, "I was just packing up"?

(A) He is preparing for a trip.
(B) He has not yet left the office.
(C) He must return some important documents.
(D) He plans to work late this evening.

154. What is most likely true about Ms. Ikeda?

(A) She forgot to perform a task.
(B) She usually works from home.
(C) She regularly travels to Melbourne.
(D) She thinks the office is too cold.

Questions 155-157 refer to the following Web page.

---

https://www.qualitekkresearch.com/aboutus

| Home | **About Us** | Register | Testimonials |

Thousands of large companies use surveys to measure customer satisfaction with the goal of improving their business. Qualitekk Research serves its client companies by analyzing survey results and producing detailed reports containing insights about customers' preferences. — [1] —. Over twelve years of operation, Qualitekk Research has built a strong reputation for providing valuable data.

Every day, consumers complete more than 20,000 online surveys that provide feedback on hundreds of different products. — [2] —. We connect consumers with surveys about products that may interest them. Participants who submit a survey that we facilitate will earn reward points from us. After as few as five surveys, points can be redeemed for a gift card usable at many stores. — [3] —.

If you would like to join, visit our Register page and complete the member profile questionnaire. This information will help us identify surveys that match your interests. We will then send you links to those surveys to complete at your leisure. If your interests change, simply update your profile. — [4] —. All responses in Qualitekk Research surveys are confidential, and you will never be personally identified with survey data.

---

155. What is indicated about Qualitekk Research?

(A) It recently revised its Web site.
(B) It has won awards for its services.
(C) It produces reports for companies.
(D) It has been in business for twenty years.

156. What are Qualitekk Research's participants encouraged to do?

(A) Write their own survey questions
(B) Persuade their friends to register
(C) Submit photos of preferred products
(D) Update their member profiles if necessary

157. In which of the positions marked [1], [2], [3], and [4] does the following sentence best belong?

"These numbers continue to grow as online commerce increases."

(A) [1]
(B) [2]
(C) [3]
(D) [4]

Questions 158-160 refer to the following memo.

> # MEMO
>
> To: Swansea Spotlight Theatre staff
> From: Rhian Griffud, Chief Executive
> Date: 7 September
> Subject: What's happening
>
> Dear Staff:
>
> I am thrilled about the imminent reopening of our theatre, and I hope you are too. It has been a long process, and audiences will undoubtedly appreciate all the renovations, including the newly upholstered seats and the updated heating and air-conditioning system. I believe that all of us who work in the theatre will enjoy the changes as well. I know you must be eager to rehearse in the newly refurbished building next week.
>
> One of the more visible updates to the space is the Swansea Spotlight Bistro, a new restaurant with a large seating area that replaces our previous concession stand. The bistro faces the street and will be open to the public even when no performances are scheduled. The menu will feature a wide selection of beverages, snacks, and meals, and it will change with the seasons to highlight locally available products.
>
> On 2 October, we will celebrate the theatre's grand reopening with a one-night musical showcase starring some of the best actors and singers in Wales. One week later, we will begin the run of *Blake's River*. I appreciate all your hard work and patience as we start this new chapter in the history of Swansea Spotlight Theatre, and I look forward to our exciting future together.

158. What is the purpose of the memo?

(A) To announce a collaboration with another theater group
(B) To update employees about the completion of a project
(C) To schedule some rehearsal spaces
(D) To report on problems with a heating and cooling system

159. What is indicated about the Swansea Spotlight Bistro?

(A) It will feature a fixed menu.
(B) It will be open only during performances.
(C) It replaces a concession stand.
(D) It needs more tables and chairs.

160. What is mentioned about October 2 ?

(A) A single performance of a show will take place.
(B) Town officials will attend an event.
(C) *Blake's River* will begin its run.
(D) New costumes will be delivered for an upcoming play.

Questions 161-163 refer to the following company Web page.

Join the Building Blocks Team

Building Blocks is the newest employee-led volunteer group at Milos Tek Corporation. Unlike other company groups that organize charity fund-raisers or clean up local parks, Building Blocks asks its members to share their professional expertise with others. We offer free seminars on management, public relations, grant writing, and various types of application software to nonprofit organizations in Lalortown. These organizations include youth clubs, community sports leagues, the Lalortown Nature Center, and Lalortown's public radio station!

Participation in Building Blocks generally involves more time than what is encouraged by other volunteer groups at Milos Tek. While each seminar is typically one hour long, planning and preparation are also part of our activities. Those who choose to volunteer with us can expect to dedicate about two hours each week to our work.

We will hold a 30-minute information session on Friday, May 3, at 12:30 P.M., in conference room B-2. In the meantime, if you have questions, please contact Min-Gyu Byun at byun003@milostek.com.

---

161. For whom is the information most likely intended?

(A) Lalortown residents who work for nonprofit organizations
(B) Lalortown residents who are changing careers
(C) Milos Tek employees who want to help the local community
(D) Milos Tek employees who want to mentor newly hired staff members

162. What is the main activity performed by Building Blocks?

(A) Developing radio programming
(B) Planning fund-raisers
(C) Presenting informational sessions
(D) Organizing job fairs

163. What is required of Building Blocks members?

(A) They must be residents of Lalortown.
(B) They must give a fairly large amount of time.
(C) They must hold advanced academic degrees.
(D) They must attend a day-long seminar each month.

Questions 164-167 refer to the following article.

Mehan Motors Appoints New CEO

By Jonas Schulz

DETROIT (January 2)—This will be a year of firsts at Mehan Motors. For the first time in its 35-year history, the company is changing its top leadership; Mehan will soon welcome the first American and the first woman to hold the title of CEO. — [1] —.

Dana Loeb will begin her tenure at Mehan Motors on February 1, the company announced yesterday. Ms. Loeb graduated with top honors from Clover University of Technology in Boston, where she completed a degree in electrical engineering. — [2] —. She eventually rose to lead the electric vehicle (EV) division at Tafts Motors in Detroit. Within two years, the company promoted her to the position of chief operating officer.

Ms. Loeb eventually left her position at Tafts Motors to become CEO of the British car company Norana, where she spearheaded the introduction of its popular subcompact EV, the Radar. Within its category, this vehicle achieved a stunning 20% higher range on a single charge than its nearest EV competitor. — [3] —.

Ms. Loeb summarized her vision for Mehan Motors in a recent interview. — [4] —. "I look forward to leveraging the company's abundant talent to build EVs that are affordable to a mass market. The vehicles must be offered at a price that is reasonable for the average consumer."

164. What is the purpose of the article?

    (A) To describe the future of electric vehicles
    (B) To profile a company's incoming leader
    (C) To analyze trends in the sales prices of automobiles
    (D) To explain how a company decision was made

165. Where was Ms. Loeb's first experience working on electric vehicles?

    (A) At Mehan Motors
    (B) At Clover University of Technology
    (C) At Norana
    (D) At Tafts Motors

166. What is special about the Radar?

    (A) Its large size
    (B) Its attractive body design
    (C) Its long battery life
    (D) Its low price

167. In which of the positions marked [1], [2], [3], and [4] does the following sentence best belong?

    "She also earned a certificate in corporate management."

    (A) [1]
    (B) [2]
    (C) [3]
    (D) [4]

Questions 168-171 refer to the following advertisement.

Dan's Specialty Bicycles
60 Everett Way, London, SW11 1AH
Hours: Monday–Sunday 10 A.M.–6 P.M.

Tenth Annual Sale of Secondhand Bicycles!

We are known for our stock of high-end racing bicycles, but for a limited time every year, we offer a wide selection of secondhand mountain, road, and hybrid bicycles for all ages and abilities. Each bicycle has been refurbished by a certified technician to ensure a smooth, safe ride. Prices range from £15 to £50.

The sale runs from 9 May to 22 May. Show or mention this advertisement to receive ten percent off the price of any secondhand or new bicycle. For more information, visit www.dansspecialtybicycles.co.uk.

---

168. What is the main purpose of the advertisement?

(A) To announce a store's grand opening
(B) To encourage bicyclists to compete in a race
(C) To generate interest in an annual event
(D) To invite people to attend a bicycle repair workshop

169. What is indicated about Dan's Specialty Bicycles?

(A) It will increase the price of most bicycles by ten percent next year.
(B) It has several locations in London.
(C) It is open seven days a week.
(D) It will host a party in May.

170. What is suggested about the secondhand bicycles?

(A) They will be available for sale all year.
(B) Each comes with a bicycle helmet.
(C) Some are designed for children.
(D) Some need to be repaired.

171. What information is NOT included in the advertisement?

(A) The type of bicycle regularly sold at Dan's Specialty Bicycles
(B) The credentials of those who serviced some bicycles
(C) How to save money on a purchase at Dan's Specialty Bicycles
(D) Where to find bicycle trails in the London area

Questions 172-175 refer to the following online chat discussion.

Morton Talbert (7:32 P.M.)
Has anyone used the Internet device Bam Booster?

Chaya Leven (7:37 P.M.)
I have used other brands in the past, but now I have the Bam Booster 10, and I love it.

Laria Jones (7:38 P.M.)
I have a poor connection to the Internet in my basement. I have tried several Internet boosters, but they haven't helped at all. They're just not worth the money.

Morton Talbert (7:40 P.M.)
I am looking for a reliable booster that's easy to set up.

Chaya Leven (7:41 P.M.)
That one is the best.

Leonard Keff (7:48 P.M.)
I have the Bam Booster 7. It works fine and was easy to set up, but I've heard their newer Bam Booster 10 model is better.

Danyelle Walken (7:52 P.M.)
I have the Zeertox Signal Booster and it's somewhat big and unsightly. On the positive side, it's inexpensive and it works.

Chaya Leven (7:58 P.M.)
The Bam Booster 10 is much smaller. It does cost more than other brands, though.

Morton Talbert (8:02 P.M.)
I didn't realize there was more than one Bam Booster model. Thanks, everybody! Now I know what to get.

172. Why did Mr. Talbert initiate the online chat discussion?

(A) To solicit advice about purchasing a product
(B) To provide a review of an appliance
(C) To offer a specialized tool for sale
(D) To ask how to install equipment in a basement

173. Who reported a negative experience with multiple products?

(A) Mr. Talbert
(B) Ms. Jones
(C) Mr. Keff
(D) Ms. Walken

174. At 7:41 P.M., what does Ms. Leven imply when she writes, "That one is the best"?

(A) She appreciated a prior online chat discussion.
(B) She has been eager to try a new product.
(C) She finds Mr. Talbert's question helpful.
(D) She is pleased with the device she uses.

175. What is indicated about the Zeertox Signal Booster?

(A) It is too expensive.
(B) It is unreliable.
(C) It is better than the older version.
(D) It is comparatively large.

Questions 176-180 refer to the following e-mail and advertisement.

E-Mail Message

To: Mark Schroeder
From: Ashley Nguyen
Date: May 5
Subject: Seasonal hiring

Hi, Mark,

I hope you can take care of our summer hiring this year. Last year, Nancy Adams put an advertisement in the *Shoreline Observer*, and we had applicants right away. I suggest using that paper again. We should hire the same number of workers as last year, but this time, all four should be full-time. Please write a new advertisement, and we can look at it together next week before sending it out.

And by the way, thanks for your work getting the Gravel Road store ready to open. I know you will be a great store manager when it is operational next month. One of your first responsibilities will be to put together a terrific staff.

Best,

Ashley Nguyen, General Manager
Surf Bird Beachwear

Surf Bird Beachwear is Hiring for the Summer!

Surf Bird Beachwear, Jaxon Shore's best shop for casual clothing and beach supplies, has openings for four full-time workers. These seasonal positions will be available from the beginning of June until the end of August. Duties include handling sales, stocking shelves, assisting customers, and setting up displays. Some early morning and weekend work is required. We offer a competitive salary and excellent working conditions.

Surf Bird Beachwear has two locations in Jaxon Shore: the original Pelican Inlet store and, opening in June, our new Gravel Road location. All interviews will be conducted at the Gravel Road store. Go to www.surfbirdbeachwear.com/jobs to apply.

176. Why did Ms. Nguyen write the e-mail?

(A) To make a job offer to an applicant
(B) To assign a task to an employee
(C) To announce opening hours at a store
(D) To ask a question about newspaper advertising

177. What is suggested about the workers who were hired last year?

(A) They will be rehired this year.
(B) They will begin working in May.
(C) They lived near Jaxon Shore.
(D) They did not all work full-time.

178. What is NOT mentioned as a job duty in the advertisement?

(A) Placing items on shelves
(B) Displaying merchandise
(C) Unloading deliveries
(D) Helping shoppers

179. What is most likely true about the job interviews?

(A) They will take place in July.
(B) They will be held at the Pelican Inlet location.
(C) They will be led by Mr. Schroeder.
(D) They will be conducted online.

180. In the advertisement, the word "original" in paragraph 2, line 1, is closest in meaning to

(A) first
(B) unique
(C) imaginative
(D) best

Questions 181-185 refer to the following e-mail and blog post.

To:	Executive Team
From:	Kota Adachi
Date:	October 11
Subject:	Trak-4 jets

Dear Team:

In late December, we will take possession of the first six of the twelve Trak-4 jets we ordered last year. The remaining jets will be delivered throughout the coming year. I believe these narrow-body jets represent the future of our airline. In addition to being the quietest jets on the market today, they are 20 percent more fuel efficient than the DB90s that we currently fly. They also have a smaller passenger capacity of 76 seats, making them ideally suited to underserved regional markets.

In anticipation of the upcoming delivery, we must decide what routes to fly the new aircraft on. Perhaps we need to rethink our entire hub system. We currently have seven regional urban hubs where our flights connect. Passengers flying between smaller cities must change planes at one of these hubs. Landing fees at these larger airports tend to be very high. We could drastically reduce our operating expenses by flying narrow-body craft directly to and from airports located away from these major urban centers.

I am setting up a meeting one week from today to discuss this issue. We will analyze the profitability of each of our current routes in order to reach an informed decision.

Kota Adachi
CEO, Ventana Airlines

Travelaider: A Blog about Where, Why, and How to Travel

By Ken Ogawa

Springfield (January 20)—I recently flew nonstop from Silver City to Centerville on Ventana Airlines. That's right, I said "nonstop." Ventana now offers direct flights between these two small cities with no need for travelers to change planes at Midwest National Airport, our only regional hub. I surely will not miss hurrying between terminals at Midwest through a sea of fellow passengers.

As for the flight itself, Ventana's new jets are a vast improvement over the old ones. The possibility of being stuck in the middle seat is no longer a concern. The new aircraft have only two seats on each side of the aisle, so everyone gets an aisle or window seat. The seats are also more comfortable than most airplane seats. The legroom was a little tight for a person my size, but someone of average height should have plenty of room to stretch out.

181. According to the e-mail, what will happen over the next twelve months?

(A) Travel to smaller cities will decrease.
(B) Landing fees at airports will increase.
(C) Ventana Airlines will receive new aircraft.
(D) Ventana Airlines will hire 76 additional staff.

182. How does the Trak-4 jet compare with the DB90 aircraft?

(A) It has more legroom.
(B) It has larger windows.
(C) It can accommodate more passengers per flight.
(D) It has no middle seats in its cabin.

183. What can be concluded about the Ventana Airlines executive team?

(A) It is no longer interested in using the Trak-4 jet.
(B) Its next meeting will be held on January 20.
(C) It decided to add routes that bypass urban hubs.
(D) It received an award for achieving its profitability goals.

184. What does Mr. Ogawa dislike about connecting at a hub?

(A) Waiting in line at security checkpoints
(B) Rushing from one terminal to another
(C) Having to eat quickly at the airport
(D) Boarding and deboarding the aircraft

185. What is most likely true about Mr. Ogawa?

(A) He is relatively tall.
(B) He is a commercial pilot.
(C) He lives in Centerville.
(D) He prefers a window seat.

Questions 186-190 refer to the following notice, e-mail, and schedule.

Attention: Oxton Science Museum Visitors

The Gartner Wing of the museum is currently closed. We apologize for the inconvenience.

Please be patient as we prepare the space for our next exhibit, *The Power of Light*. Designed by curator Sachiko Morishita, it explores innovations that will affect the future, particularly in the world of lasers and optics. The exhibit will be open to members and private group tours starting August 15 and to the general public starting September 2.

To:	Summer Interns <interns@renmarksolutions.com>
From:	Tae-Ho Mun <thmun@renmarksolutions.com>
Date:	July 7
Subject:	August trip

Good morning, team,

Interns and their mentors are invited to take a trip to the Oxton Science Museum on Friday, August 19. Many of you have been on previous Renmark Solutions trips, so you know they are always educational and exciting. Participants will get a look at the science and technology that drives our company and customers.

We will see *The Power of Light* exhibit as part of our group tour. Vouchers will be handed out for lunch at the museum's restaurant.

Our schedule is as follows.

9:00 A.M.	Meet in the company lobby (The bus departs at 9:15 A.M.)
10:00 A.M. to noon	Private group tour
Noon to 1:00 P.M.	Lunch in the museum restaurant
1:45 to 2:00 P.M.	Meet in room 203
3:15 P.M.	Bus leaves for the return to Renmark Solutions offices

Yours,

Tae-Ho Mun
Research and Development Manager

Oxton Science Museum
Viewing Room Schedule (Room 203)—August 19

Time	Event Title	Event Description
9:45 A.M.	"Optical Systems and Applied Observation"	Lecture by Professor Kaori Okada of Oxton University
10:30 A.M.	"Quantum Optics"	Presentation by Oxton Science Museum curator Wallace McCabe
1:00 P.M.	"Increasing the Use of Lasers"	Presentation by Jee-Min Hahm of Solfis University
1:45 P.M.	*Mirrors, Lenses, and Prisms*	Short film by FK Institute of Technology
2:45 P.M.	"New Platforms, New Products"	Product demonstrations by Bigham Industries

186. What is one purpose of the notice?
    (A) To direct people to a different entrance
    (B) To warn visitors about a temporary closure
    (C) To announce the grand opening of an institution
    (D) To explain a change in operating hours

187. What is indicated about some of Renmark Solutions' interns?
    (A) They have volunteered at the Oxton Science Museum before.
    (B) They installed some audiovisual equipment for Mr. Mun.
    (C) They have joined Renmark Solutions trips in the past.
    (D) They assisted with the setup of an educational display.

188. What is suggested about the trip on August 19 ?
    (A) It will be led by Mr. Mun.
    (B) Its participants will travel by train.
    (C) It includes a tour of Ms. Morishita's exhibit.
    (D) It must be paid for in advance by attendees.

189. Why will the interns go to room 203 ?
    (A) To attend a lecture by Ms. Okada
    (B) To see a presentation by Mr. McCabe
    (C) To view a presentation by Solfis University
    (D) To watch a film by FK Institute of Technology

190. According to the schedule, when will a company give a presentation about its merchandise?
    (A) At 9:45 A.M.
    (B) At 10:30 A.M.
    (C) At 1:00 P.M.
    (D) At 2:45 P.M.

Questions 191-195 refer to the following advertisement, price list, and review.

Protecto Umbrella Wrapping Machines

Visitors entering and walking through a building with wet umbrellas unintentionally create wet and slippery floors. The Protecto Umbrella Wrapping machine (PUW machine) provides a simple and convenient way to address this problem. The machine is best placed in the entryway of your building. Upon entry, visitors insert their wet umbrellas into the machine. It automatically wraps the umbrella in a clear plastic bag, after which visitors can take their umbrellas. Upon leaving, they can discard the used bags in any nearby trash can.

PUW machines are available with one or two umbrella-wrapping devices and come in stainless steel or black. The machine wraps umbrellas in 1.5 seconds. The stand is mobile and thus can be rolled around to different locations. Purchase a PUW machine throughout November and receive a lightweight umbrella featuring our company logo.

Protecto Products Price List

Product Number	Description	Price per Unit
143	PUW machine with two umbrella-wrapping devices. Price includes 2,000 bags. Perfect for large, high-foot-traffic areas. Available in stainless steel or black.	$450
144	PUW machine with one umbrella-wrapping device. Price includes 1,000 bags. Available in stainless steel or black.	$350
192	Box of 3,000 plastic bags for refilling any of our units. Available online only.	$100
194	Box of 1,000 plastic bags for refilling any of our units. Available online only.	$35

https://www.setterlyproductreviews.com/officeequipment

Office Equipment Review: Protecto Umbrella Wrapping Machines

I love our new PUW machine! As the facilities manager of a medium-sized office building, I often have to deal with the inconvenience of wet floors caused by visitors entering with umbrellas. We used to have a large umbrella stand in the lobby where visitors could leave umbrellas, but only a few people used it. Then we tried an umbrella stand that included disposable plastic bags that visitors could tear off and put their umbrellas in. However, this method was ineffective because the bags were rather flimsy, thus failing to prevent water leakage.

So, in November, we decided to try a PUW machine. Because we have many visitors, we purchased the PUW machine with two devices and ordered it in stainless steel to match our modern-looking lobby.

Since then, the entranceway has been safer and cleaner. Visitors love that it is automatic, and everyone is grateful that the lobby is no longer wet and slippery because of umbrellas dripping with water!

—Andrew Barr

---

191. What does the advertisement suggest about PUW machines?
(A) Their material makes them cost-efficient.
(B) They can wrap an umbrella in less than one second.
(C) Their wheels allow them to be moved around.
(D) They contain a receptacle for used bags.

192. What does the price list indicate about bags?
(A) They are available to buy in different quantities.
(B) They fit in all brands of umbrella-wrapping machines.
(C) They are not included in the price of PUW machines.
(D) They are sold in retail stores.

193. What is suggested about Mr. Barr?
(A) He is a longtime customer of Protecto.
(B) He received an umbrella with his order.
(C) He works in a quiet office building.
(D) He recently changed jobs.

194. What is the cost of the product that Mr. Barr reviewed?
(A) $35
(B) $100
(C) $350
(D) $450

195. What problem does Mr. Barr describe?
(A) Protecto products are not modern-looking.
(B) Visitors were not using an umbrella stand.
(C) The lobby of his building is not clean.
(D) Some disposable umbrella bags were too small.

Questions 196-200 refer to the following Web page and e-mails.

---

https://www.croydonconstruction.co.nz/news

| Home | News | Jobs | Contact Us |

In December, Croydon Construction will mark 25 years in business on the South Island of New Zealand. We take great pride in the many buildings we have built here in Christchurch, where our headquarters are located, and in other locations along the South Island's east coast.

We have been busy recently with some exciting projects. In Christchurch, we are building the Willoughby Medical Clinic on Grove Road, with a grand opening date of 1 November, and we are expanding the Blakefield Community Centre on Springdale Avenue. In Ashburton, we have nearly finished a 107-unit apartment complex on Passerine Way and have just broken ground on the new wing of the Dismus School on Sixth Street. Steve Kogler is our new chief site engineer.

Are you interested in employment with Croydon Construction? We're hiring for both office and jobsite positions. Go to our Jobs page to view open positions and to apply.

E-mail

To:	Sanaa Rahija <srahija@wilmawindows.co.nz>
From:	Zack Makoare <zmakoare@croydonconstruction.co.nz>
Date:	15 August
Subject:	Shipment overdue

Dear Ms. Rahija:

I am writing to check on the status of order 47992, which should have arrived here by 31 July and is now two weeks overdue. We are extremely concerned. The building's completion date cannot be postponed. Please let me know when we can expect our windows to arrive. We shall withhold the balance of payment until the items have been received. Wilma Windows has been our supplier for many years, and this is the first time a problem like this has occurred.

Thank you for your prompt attention to this matter.

Sincerely,

Zack Makoare
Construction Manager, Croydon Construction

E-Mail Message

To: Zack Makoare <zmakoare@croydonconstruction.co.nz>
From: Sanaa Rahija <srahija@wilmawindows.co.nz>
Date: 16 August
Subject: RE: Shipment overdue

Dear Mr. Makoare:

Please accept my apologies for the lateness of order 47992. A machine in our factory malfunctioned, creating flaws in the window glass. The machine has been repaired, and the factory is back to its usual production schedule. We are expediting your order and will ship it tomorrow. It will arrive at your medical clinic construction site on 20 August. As a goodwill gesture, we will refund your entire shipping fee.

Sincerely,

Sanaa Rahija

---

196. What is suggested on the Web page about Croydon Construction?

(A) It recently hired Mr. Kogler.
(B) It has been in business for only a short time.
(C) It is planning to move its headquarters to Christchurch.
(D) It completes projects in countries outside of New Zealand.

197. According to the Web page, what should job applicants do?

(A) Visit the company headquarters in person
(B) Attend a career fair
(C) Contact the hiring manager by e-mail
(D) Submit an application online

198. In the second e-mail, what problem does Ms. Rahija describe?

(A) The wrong product was manufactured.
(B) The factory was understaffed.
(C) Some equipment did not operate properly.
(D) Some items in an order broke during transport.

199. Where most likely will order 47992 be delivered?

(A) To Grove Road
(B) To Springdale Avenue
(C) To Passerine Way
(D) To Sixth Street

200. What can be concluded about Mr. Makoare?

(A) He plans to retire on November 1.
(B) He wants to change his order to a better type of window glass.
(C) He will probably have to postpone a building's completion date.
(D) He will soon pay a supplier in full.

Stop! This is the end of the test. If you finish before time is called, you may go back to Parts 5, 6, and 7 and check your work.

ETS 토익 정기시험 기출문제집 5 1000 RC

TEST 08
무료 동영상 강의

RC
기출 TEST 08

READING TEST

In the Reading test, you will read a variety of texts and answer several different types of reading comprehension questions. The entire Reading test will last 75 minutes. There are three parts, and directions are given for each part. You are encouraged to answer as many questions as possible within the time allowed.

You must mark your answers on the separate answer sheet. Do not write your answers in your test book.

PART 5

Directions: A word or phrase is missing in each of the sentences below. Four answer choices are given below each sentence. Select the best answer to complete the sentence. Then mark the letter (A), (B), (C), or (D) on your answer sheet.

101. Sydney Fashion Week drew thousands of ------- visitors to the city last week.
    (A) excite
    (B) excited
    (C) excites
    (D) excitement

102. Ms. Choi was pleased to learn that ------- is a finalist in the technology competition.
    (A) she
    (B) her
    (C) hers
    (D) herself

103. All visitors to the factory should use the ------- on the north side of the building.
    (A) enter
    (B) entrance
    (C) entering
    (D) entered

104. Unfortunately, we cannot provide an ------- time for the delivery of the new laptops.
    (A) exact
    (B) obvious
    (C) absent
    (D) inspirational

105. Tourists visiting Star Island are asked ------- the privacy of residents.
    (A) respects
    (B) have respected
    (C) to respect
    (D) will respect

106. Rivlyn, Inc., has recycled ------- 11 million kilograms of paper waste over the past decade.
    (A) firmly
    (B) nearly
    (C) closely
    (D) freely

107. The new Dorvale 500 exercise machine is significantly heavier and sturdier than the previous -------.
    (A) time
    (B) model
    (C) weight
    (D) class

108. Beachside Inn is the perfect place to ------- an event for your corporate clients.
    (A) entertain
    (B) gather
    (C) host
    (D) stay

109. ------- in cloud computing have transformed the gaming industry in many ways.
   (A) Advance
   (B) Advancing
   (C) Advancement
   (D) Advancements

110. To provide feedback ------- your recent dental appointment, please respond to this brief survey.
   (A) about
   (B) below
   (C) near
   (D) onto

111. If your company computer is not ------- functional, please call the IT Department at extension 12.
   (A) complete
   (B) completed
   (C) completely
   (D) completing

112. The ------- of electric buses to our current fleet has made commuting much more pleasant.
   (A) replacement
   (B) addition
   (C) substitution
   (D) building

113. The Zwick Air Wave generates a powerful blast to cool your workspace -------.
   (A) quickness
   (B) quicken
   (C) quickens
   (D) quickly

114. The Oak Hill Art Museum offers several ------- exhibits and a series of limited-time exhibits.
   (A) previous
   (B) permanent
   (C) inevitable
   (D) entire

115. Any remote employees wanting an additional computer monitor should ------- Ms. Suzuki.
   (A) participate
   (B) activate
   (C) convene
   (D) notify

116. Customer loyalty programs are ------- for many retail businesses.
   (A) profited
   (B) profitable
   (C) profitably
   (D) profitability

117. Prompt submission of travel vouchers ------- the accounts department will expedite refunds.
   (A) to
   (B) as
   (C) on
   (D) up

118. After extensively ------- our hiring policies, the consultant recommended a simpler process.
   (A) be reviewing
   (B) reviewed
   (C) reviewing
   (D) reviews

119. Under the ------- of Ms. Kenu, the historical society's fund-raiser went very well this year.
   (A) cover
   (B) field
   (C) direction
   (D) summary

120. The company decided to proceed ------- with plans to expand into new sales territories.
   (A) caution
   (B) cautionary
   (C) cautious
   (D) cautiously

GO ON TO THE NEXT PAGE

121. ------- access the building, enter the code listed on the tenant directory.
(A) In order to
(B) For instance
(C) Due to
(D) As a result of

122. Mr. Davis ------- the marketing department will attend Monday's meeting with the client.
(A) when
(B) into
(C) so
(D) from

123. Several ------- reviews helped make the debut novel a best seller.
(A) pending
(B) resolved
(C) outstanding
(D) equivalent

124. Please ------- us in welcoming Dr. Sito, who brings ten years of experience in the aerospace industry to his new position.
(A) join
(B) joins
(C) joining
(D) joined

125. A survey of new car buyers asked them to ------- features in order from most to least important.
(A) opt
(B) turn
(C) rank
(D) guide

126. As head of the Poels Museum, Mr. Ahuja oversaw the ------- of several significant works of art.
(A) acquires
(B) acquired
(C) acquisition
(D) acquisitional

127. Later today, we will hold a meeting to discuss changes to protocols ------- they go into effect next month.
(A) rather than
(B) as well as
(C) despite
(D) before

128. Customer service representatives can be reached ------- calling 800-555-0121 between 8:00 A.M. and 4:00 P.M.
(A) by
(B) because
(C) ever
(D) at

129. Collaboration between multiple agencies is ------- challenging, but our project-based consulting can simplify the process for you.
(A) well
(B) often
(C) deliberately
(D) finally

130. The desserts we had at Giovanni's Bistro were not as delicious as ------- we enjoyed at Monteverdi's Taverna.
(A) whose
(B) those
(C) which
(D) them

PART 6

Directions: Read the texts that follow. A word, phrase, or sentence is missing in parts of each text. Four answer choices for each question are given below the text. Select the best answer to complete the text. Then mark the letter (A), (B), (C), or (D) on your answer sheet.

Questions 131-134 refer to the following directions.

Directions to the Carrill Laboratory

Enter through the main door at 3017 Bowman Street and sign in with the ------- guard. Take the
                                                                            131.
elevator to the second floor. ------- , you may use the stairs to the left of the elevator. Once you
                               132.
reach the second floor, turn left ------- , then continue straight until you reach the double doors.
                                  133.
Proceed through the doors and pass the visitors' lounge. ------- .
                                                          134.

---

131. (A) secure
     (B) security
     (C) securely
     (D) securing

132. (A) Alternatively
     (B) Consequently
     (C) Furthermore
     (D) Nevertheless

133. (A) temporarily
     (B) responsibly
     (C) patiently
     (D) immediately

134. (A) The laboratory is the next door on the right.
     (B) The visitors' parking area is usually full on weekdays.
     (C) The laboratory's speaker series is open to the public.
     (D) This year marks the laboratory's thirty-fifth anniversary.

GO ON TO THE NEXT PAGE

Questions 135-138 refer to the following notice.

Mapleglen University

Master of Business Administration

At Mapleglen University, we understand that December is a ------- time of year for
                                                              135.
undergraduates. That is why we are giving you extra time to submit your application for our

Master of Business Administration (MBA) program. We have extended our initial deadline to

December 31. ------- for admission to the March semester, please ensure that we receive your
             136.
official undergraduate transcripts by the same date. Please contact our admissions department at

apply@mapleglen.edu if you have any questions ------- the MBA program requirements.
                                              137.
------- .
138.

---

135. (A) cold
(B) long
(C) busy
(D) sure

136. (A) Being considered
(B) To be considered
(C) Having been considered
(D) Considering

137. (A) between
(B) after
(C) except
(D) regarding

138. (A) We look forward to reading your application.
(B) Undergraduate programs frequently require personal statements.
(C) We have added a course in public health.
(D) A record number of prospective students have applied.

Questions 139-142 refer to the following e-mail.

To: Senior executive staff
From: Seok Kang
Date: 15 September
Subject: App update
Attachment: App_specs; Press_release

As you all know, to coincide with the upcoming launch of the restaurant's new menu, we have made several changes to our mobile app. ------- , we have corrected several issues with the previous version. ------- . I am delighted to report that our focus group members gave the redesigned app great reviews. In particular, ------- commented on how simple it is to use the different features. I have attached the app's specifications and a draft of the press release to this e-mail. If you have any questions or suggestions, please let me know by 17 September. The official launch for the app and menu ------- on Thursday, 25 September.

139. (A) After all
    (B) In any case
    (C) On the contrary
    (D) Most significantly

140. (A) I hope to have an update soon concerning the new location.
    (B) Among these problems was a tendency for the screen to freeze.
    (C) Many restaurant apps now include online ordering.
    (D) The new items will be added to the menu next month.

141. (A) we
    (B) you
    (C) they
    (D) none

142. (A) has been announced
    (B) will be announced
    (C) announcing
    (D) announces

Questions 143-146 refer to the following product review.

Let me disclose up front that I received a free Tipti PX200 digital camera in exchange for this post. ------- , I never hesitate to share my candid opinion, even when I receive free cameras and equipment. ------- . The Tipti PX200 is intended for video bloggers and online content creators, but it is unsuitable for filmmakers needing a greater range of features. This is an important ------- . If you are looking for a compact camera that makes it ------- to post short videos online, this is an excellent option for the price.

—Sonja Stanberry

143. (A) In fact
(B) However
(C) Therefore
(D) To the contrary

144. (A) I am always honest when I review a product.
(B) I am curious about other similarly sized cameras.
(C) Many people take photographs with their phones.
(D) Publishers also regularly offer free books to reviewers.

145. (A) event
(B) policy
(C) credential
(D) distinction

146. (A) easy
(B) ease
(C) easing
(D) to ease

PART 7

Directions: In this part you will read a selection of texts, such as magazine and newspaper articles, e-mails, and instant messages. Each text or set of texts is followed by several questions. Select the best answer for each question and mark the letter (A), (B), (C), or (D) on your answer sheet.

Questions 147-148 refer to the following e-mail.

> To: All Staff
> From: Karina Rybak, Marketing Dept.
> Date: 2 February
> Subject: Information
>
> As some of you know, Sun-Yi Pak is transferring to our Seoul office. Her going-away party will take place at 3:00 P.M. on 21 February in the second-floor conference room. Please reply to this e-mail by 16 February to let me know if you plan to attend. The company will provide pizza and cake, and we want to make sure that there is enough food for everyone. I hope to see you there to celebrate Sun-Yi!

147. What is the purpose of the e-mail?
 (A) To ask for help in planning a conference
 (B) To introduce a new employee
 (C) To invite staff to a social event
 (D) To announce the opening of the Seoul office

148. According to the e-mail, what should staff members do by February 16?
 (A) Make transfer requests
 (B) E-mail Ms. Rybak
 (C) Sign a card
 (D) Submit catering orders

Questions 149-150 refer to the following flyer.

Johan's Power Washing
Serving the Meadowbrook community for over 25 years!

Power washing beautifies your home and
helps maintain the integrity of your structure!

The services we offer include:

- Power washing of siding, porches, decks, and more
- Gutter cleaning and brightening
- Concrete scrubbing and sealing
- Window washing

Johan G. Matey
506-555-0193
www.johanspowerwashing.ca

Call now for a free estimate or to schedule a cleaning.

---

149. What is the purpose of the flyer?
 (A) To advertise a local business
 (B) To announce a community meeting
 (C) To request feedback on a company's services
 (D) To notify residents about home maintenance regulations

150. What information is NOT included in the flyer?
 (A) A Web address
 (B) A list of services
 (C) A phone number
 (D) A mailing address

Questions 151-152 refer to the following text-message chain.

Mei Kim (10:02 A.M.)
Hi, Stan. Do you have lunch plans?

Stan Snyder (10:05 A.M.)
I was just going to grab a sandwich from the company café and eat at my desk. Why do you ask?

Mei Kim (10:06 A.M.)
How about joining me at the Sunny Owl Restaurant? I'd love to talk to you about the McMillan project before we meet with the client this afternoon.

Stan Snyder (10:09 A.M.)
That's a good idea. I have some questions too—about the project's budget. Maybe we should ask Maria Trujillo to join us as well?

Mei Kim (10:10 A.M.)
I'll handle it. Shall we meet in the lobby at 11:45?

Stan Snyder (10:11 A.M.)
That's perfect. I'll see you then.

---

151. What is most likely true about Ms. Trujillo?

(A) She is Mr. Snyder's and Ms. Kim's supervisor.
(B) She eats lunch regularly at the company café.
(C) She has information about a project's budget.
(D) She is unable to meet with the client in the afternoon.

152. At 10:10 A.M., what does Ms. Kim most likely mean when she writes, "I'll handle it"?

(A) She is on her way to the client's office.
(B) She will invite a colleague to lunch.
(C) She will ask the Sunny Owl Restaurant to deliver some food.
(D) She remembered something she should bring to the client meeting.

Questions 153-154 refer to the following notice.

Welcome to the Westover Zoo!

- Admission tickets are required for all visitors, including infants. Tickets may be printed or presented electronically.
- Your ticket is good only on the date indicated. Exchanges may be requested up to 24 hours before the date on your ticket. For exchanges and other information, visit our Web site, westoverzoo.org.
- Our parking area is free but fills quickly. We encourage visitors to take public transportation. Buses on both the orange and the blue routes stop at the zoo entrance. During the summer months, extra buses run on these routes to accommodate visitors.

153. What is NOT indicated about the Westover Zoo?

(A) Children visiting the zoo are required to have tickets.
(B) The zoo is open only in the summer months.
(C) The zoo has a Web site.
(D) Visitors to the zoo may use paper or electronic tickets.

154. What is mentioned about transportation in the notice?

(A) Visitors must pay an additional fee to park at the zoo.
(B) Visitors may ride public buses for free.
(C) There is limited parking available for visitors.
(D) There is a taxi stand for visitors at the zoo entrance.

Questions 155-157 refer to the following article.

Construction Projects Planned

HILLSDALE (July 7)—To accommodate Hillsdale's ever-growing population, the town council announced on Thursday that two major construction projects are planned.

The first project is the construction of a new commercial area at the south end of town, since the downtown commercial district has no room to expand. — [1] —. One section of the area will be dedicated exclusively to restaurants and small stores, while the other will be reserved for office space. — [2] —.

The second project will build residential housing on a large empty lot at the south end. — [3] —. The new residential area and the new commercial area will be connected by a park with paved pathways.

City planners hope both projects will begin within the next month, with businesses and residents moving in late next year. — [4] —.

155. What is suggested about the town of Hillsdale?

    (A) It has no restaurants downtown.
    (B) It is bordered by a large park on its south side.
    (C) It needs more housing.
    (D) It has undergone much construction in recent years.

156. What is indicated about the proposed commercial area?

    (A) It will be within walking distance of the new homes.
    (B) It will cost less to build than the new residential area.
    (C) It will be built after the new housing is finished.
    (D) It will be built on land currently used as a park.

157. In which of the positions marked [1], [2], [3], and [4] does the following sentence best belong?

    "This area will include apartments as well as single-family homes."

    (A) [1]
    (B) [2]
    (C) [3]
    (D) [4]

Questions 158-160 refer to the following information.

Mirei Hair Care

a Japanese subsidiary of
Khalinde Global Cosmetics, Inc.

Investment Options for Mirei Hair Care

Option	Estimated Cost	Main Benefit
1. Construct bigger manufacturing facility	¥418 million	Larger production capacity
2. Increase advertising budget	¥210 million	Better brand awareness
3. Buy out leading competitor	¥180 million	Reduced competition
4. Expand distribution	¥148 million	Increased sales
5. Redesign packaging	¥129 million	Lower per-item cost

158. For whom is the information most likely intended?

(A) Individuals who invest in the hair-care industry
(B) Researchers who develop cosmetics products
(C) The executives who lead an international company
(D) The customers who buy Mirei Hair Care products

159. What strategy is proposed to make the company more widely known by the public?

(A) Option 2
(B) Option 3
(C) Option 4
(D) Option 5

160. What is NOT listed as a potential benefit?

(A) Increased production capability
(B) Fewer job vacancies
(C) Lower costs
(D) Higher sales

Questions 161-163 refer to the following policy.

https://www.barbadosairlines.com/baggage

Barbados Airlines Baggage Policies

All Barbados Airlines passengers may bring one personal item (for example, a handbag or laptop bag) into the cabin with them. — [1] —. Personal items must fit under the seat; therefore, they cannot be larger than 45 × 35 × 20 centimetres. Child safety seats do not count toward a passenger's personal item allowance. — [2] —.

For a fee of €20, a passenger may take on board a carry-on item such as a suitcase or duffel bag. To fit in the overhead storage compartment, carry-on items must not exceed 56 × 36 × 23 centimetres, including handles, straps, and wheels. Any carry-on item larger than these dimensions will be checked into the baggage hold and will incur a fee of €50.

— [3] —. With special permission, oversized items like sporting equipment and musical instruments can be taken into the cabin as carry-on items. — [4] —.

161. According to the policy, what is considered a personal item?

(A) A purse
(B) A guitar
(C) A large suitcase
(D) A child seat

162. What is indicated about carry-on items?

(A) They are free for all passengers.
(B) They have a maximum allowable size.
(C) They cannot have wheels.
(D) They do not include sporting equipment.

163. In which of the positions marked [1], [2], [3], and [4] does the following sentence best belong?

"Before bringing large items like these on board, please contact a customer service representative."

(A) [1]
(B) [2]
(C) [3]
(D) [4]

GO ON TO THE NEXT PAGE

Questions 164-167 refer to the following invitation.

Madson Industrial Supply Virtual Staff Event

11 April, 7 to 10 P.M.

Calling all Madson Industrial Supply employees! This year's staff gathering features a new twist: an online trivia competition to test your knowledge of popular culture, sports, and entertainment. To foster company-wide collaboration, employees based in the London and Glasgow offices will sign into the Z-Hype room from their homes and be combined into virtual teams for this friendly competition.

Our virtual trivia night will last roughly two hours. Day passes to Good Stuff Theme Park in Manchester will be awarded to the winning team. Once the trivia competition has finished, we will keep the Z-Hype room open for another hour so that employees can mingle.

In addition to the trivia competition, we are excited to feature two contests that are old favourites: an award for the employee wearing the finest festive attire and an award for the most creative Z-Hype virtual background. We've seen many people work from a virtual beach, but how about from a famous World Heritage site or an extraterrestrial universe? Remember last year when Gerard Baxter sported a white tuxedo while phoning in from the rings of Saturn? Use your imagination to come up with something unexpected! Each prize winner will receive a gift card for a meal at Sondra's Grill.

If you plan to join the fun, please complete the questionnaire on the company Web site by 28 March. Friends and family are welcome to participate. We look forward to seeing you there!

164. What is indicated about the staff event?

(A) It will last for one hour.
(B) It will be held in the London office.
(C) It will be open only to employees.
(D) It will take place on April 11.

165. What do the event's three competitions have in common?

(A) They require participants to join a team.
(B) They award prizes to the winners.
(C) They involve responding to trivia questions.
(D) They have been featured at previous staff events.

166. Why does the invitation mention Mr. Baxter?

(A) To introduce a new leader
(B) To address an attendee's concerns
(C) To give an example of how people have participated in the past
(D) To announce a longtime employee's promotion

167. What most likely is Z-Hype?

(A) A video conferencing platform
(B) An amusement park
(C) An e-mail service
(D) An online survey company

Questions 168-171 refer to the following contract.

Grotel Corporation

EVENT SPEAKER AGREEMENT

This agreement is between Grotel Corporation and __Jack Kolman__ (Event Speaker). The parties agree that the Event Speaker shall deliver a speech lasting __60 minutes__ for the following:

Name: Annual Employee Recognition and Honors
Date and Time: September 12, 7:00–8:00 P.M.
Location: Millar Conference Hall

1. Compensation and Expenses. Upon fulfillment of the agreement, Grotel Corporation agrees to pay the Event Speaker a fee of $1,250. Grotel Corporation will reimburse the Event Speaker for lodging and transportation up to $500, provided that original receipts are submitted.

2. Equipment. Grotel Corporation will provide the Event Speaker with the following equipment: projector, large screen, Internet connection, microphone. (Please see accompanying document for specific information.)

3. Cancellation. Either party may cancel the agreement without obligation to the other as long as written notice of intent to cancel is provided at least 30 days before the date of the event.

Event Speaker Signature: *Jack Kolman*   **Grotel Corporation Representative:** *Ezra Tan*
Date: June 2   **Date:** June 4

---

168. For what type of event has Mr. Kolman most likely been hired?

(A) An academic conference
(B) An industry trade show
(C) An awards ceremony
(D) A corporate training workshop

169. What is indicated about the payment Mr. Kolman will receive?

(A) It will be deposited directly to his bank.
(B) It will be issued to him in advance.
(C) It may be increased if the event takes longer than an hour.
(D) It may include transportation costs.

170. What information is included with the contract?

(A) Details about equipment that will be provided
(B) Instructions for submitting original receipts
(C) Driving directions to the venue
(D) An agenda for the event

171. What is indicated about an event cancellation?

(A) It may incur an administrative fee.
(B) It may be announced by phone.
(C) It will not be accepted unless a valid reason is provided.
(D) It will not be permitted if the event is two weeks away.

Questions 172-175 refer to the following online chat discussion.

Brett Tennison (8:16 A.M.)
Hi, Lianne and Shruthi. Did you two get the e-mail I sent yesterday?

Lianne Gammon (8:17 A.M.)
About the company video you want to make?

Brett Tennison (8:18 A.M.)
Yes. People want to feel a personal connection to the companies they work with. A video could help potential clients relate better to our team and generate business.

Shruthi Mehta (8:19 A.M.)
I drafted an e-mail in response, but I haven't sent it yet. I wanted to go over it in my mind before sharing.

Lianne Gammon (8:20 A.M.)
I like the idea. We'll have to be creative to get people interested, though.

Shruthi Mehta (8:21 A.M.)
I'm not convinced that a video about us is a good idea. I just work at my computer all day. Who would want to watch that?

Brett Tennison (8:22 A.M.)
That's why I asked for input. We'll want the video to show our personalities as well as what it is that we do. We can hire professionals to edit it. But let's first decide how we want it to be structured and then record it ourselves.

Lianne Gammon (8:23 A.M.)
Why don't we make a few—so that we can reach different audiences? How about a short one to use as a paid ad and a longer one to post on our Web site?

172. Why does Mr. Tennison want to make a video?

(A) To generate new business
(B) To highlight an innovative product
(C) To train employees in a new process
(D) To announce a change in leadership

173. Why did Ms. Mehta not respond to an e-mail?

(A) She needed more time to think about it.
(B) She was too busy with other work.
(C) She believed her input was not needed.
(D) She misunderstood the contents of the e-mail.

174. At 8:21 A.M., what does Ms. Mehta imply when she writes, "I just work at my computer all day"?

(A) She is not satisfied with her job.
(B) She is not qualified to assist potential clients.
(C) She has very few work responsibilities.
(D) She thinks a video about her job would be boring.

175. What does Ms. Gammon suggest the writers do with a video?

(A) Edit it in the office
(B) Add original music to it
(C) Make multiple versions of it
(D) Include a company history in it

Questions 176-180 refer to the following advertisement and review.

Coming soon from Meridian Press!
A Life in the Spotlight: The True Story of Ibra Maalim
by Helena Mackay

A Life in the Spotlight is the first biography of Ibra Maalim, who created some of the most memorable characters on the big screen. The son of a politician and a newspaper reporter, Mr. Maalim had originally planned to be an archaeologist. While he was a university student, he had a chance encounter with the director Nina Chen, who cast Mr. Maalim in a small role in her film *The Winds of Sorrento*. He quickly rose to fame. Over the next 30 years, Mr. Maalim became a household name, regularly appearing in motion pictures in Britain and the United States.

Ms. Mackay is known for giving balanced, objective views of her numerous biographical subjects, and *A Life in the Spotlight* is no exception. She sheds light on previously unknown details of Mr. Maalim's life, gathered from extensive interviews with his longtime agent. Written in straightforward and accessible prose by an award-winning author, this book explores Mr. Maalim's life beginning with his childhood in India. It is sure to inform and entertain all of his fans.

★★★★☆ A must-read for Maalim fans!

As a longtime fan of Ibra Maalim, I was looking forward to reading *A Life in the Spotlight*. I was not disappointed. Mackay paints a fascinating portrait of this enigmatic figure. There are dozens of interesting anecdotes about his life on and off set, most of which were told to Mackay in interviews with Alidia Lugo, who knew Maalim well. Mackay reveals Maalim's strengths and shortcomings, making the book more credible. I only have two complaints. The book says almost nothing about his childhood years or his relationships with his fellow University of Leeds students. I also wish there were more than two photographs, especially considering how much Maalim's reputation was based on his photogenic qualities.

—Salvador Guerrero

176. What is Mr. Maalim most famous for doing?

    (A) Making archaeological discoveries
    (B) Writing fictional books
    (C) Being a politician
    (D) Acting in films

177. What does the advertisement indicate about Ms. Mackay?

    (A) She interviewed Mr. Maalim several times.
    (B) She has written many biographies.
    (C) She worked as a newspaper reporter.
    (D) She has collaborated on projects with Ms. Chen.

178. In the advertisement, the word "accessible" in paragraph 2, line 4, is closest in meaning to

    (A) understandable
    (B) open
    (C) popular
    (D) fashionable

179. How most likely did Ms. Lugo know Mr. Maalim?

    (A) She was his university classmate.
    (B) She was his childhood friend.
    (C) She was his agent.
    (D) She was his favorite director.

180. According to the review, what is one problem with *A Life in the Spotlight* ?

    (A) It does not have enough photographs.
    (B) It has not won any awards.
    (C) It is too expensive.
    (D) It repeats too many well-known anecdotes.

Questions 181-185 refer to the following advertisement and review.

Big Strike Lanes
20 Fortune Way, Glasgow, G41 4LM
(0141) 496 0184

The excitement is all around you at Big Strike Lanes! Bring your family and friends to bowl, play video games, try out our unique virtual-reality station, and savour delicious meals at our own restaurant. With 18 bowling lanes, state-of-the-art gaming consoles, and award-winning food, Big Strike Lanes has something for everyone.

Visit us for one of our deals today; they will not be available after 31 May!

Gold Deal	Platinum Deal
Enjoy one hour of bowling and a £25 gaming credit. A £40 value for only £30!	Enjoy two hours of bowling and two virtual-reality experiences. A £50 value for only £40!

Big Strike Lanes: Plenty To Enjoy

16 May

I was very sad when Freeside Bowling shut its doors last year. Rustic, quaint, and run by the same family for three generations, it had the type of charm that only an old establishment can provide. I have many happy memories of good times there.

Then Big Strike Lanes opened a few months ago, and I wondered how it would compare. A few friends and I decided to visit and take advantage of a promotional offer, and I'm happy to say that our experience was better than expected. The bowling was great, and I really enjoyed the virtual reality, which I had never tried before.

At the restaurant, our servers were friendly, and the food was delicious. My only criticism of the place is the location. Big Strike Lanes is situated in a large shopping centre next to a busy motorway, so the surroundings are not exactly inviting.

—Sophie Shaw

181. What can customers do at Big Strike Lanes?

(A) Purchase movies
(B) Eat on-site
(C) Take bowling lessons
(D) Reserve the site for parties

182. According to the advertisement, what will happen on May 31 ?

(A) A price reduction will end.
(B) A review will be posted online.
(C) A special menu will become available.
(D) A game arcade will open.

183. What does Ms. Shaw suggest in her review?

(A) She has participated in virtual reality experiences before.
(B) She prefers modern buildings to older ones.
(C) She regrets that an entertainment business closed.
(D) She used to work in a restaurant as a server.

184. How much did Ms. Shaw pay for entertainment activities?

(A) £25
(B) £30
(C) £40
(D) £50

185. In the review, the word "situated" in paragraph 3, line 2, is closest in meaning to

(A) established
(B) arranged
(C) parked
(D) positioned

Questions 186-190 refer to the following meeting minutes, article, and e-mail.

Minutes of the Special Meeting of the Arlford City Council
14 January

1. Call to Order
Mayor Tremblay called the meeting to order at 6:30 P.M. All members were present.

2. Vote Taken on Resolution No. 2023-167B
The council approved a resolution to earmark $1.5 million for costs related to establishing Winglite Airlines service at the Arlford Regional Airport. The resolution, authorising an adjustment to the Airport Operating Fund, was passed by a vote of 7–0. Winglite Airlines and the city will bear some costs equally. Costs to be split include recruitment and training of additional security and emergency services workers. Other expenses will be covered 100 percent by the city of Arlford. Chief among these is the construction of another lane on Aviation Boulevard to accommodate the expected increase in airport traffic. Work on the boulevard will start immediately so that it will be finished before the airline begins its service.

3. Adjournment
The meeting was adjourned at 7:25 P.M.

Winglite Airlines to Begin Service from Arlford Regional Airport

ARLFORD (18 March)—Darwin-based carrier Winglite Airlines has announced plans to begin nonstop daily flights between Arlford Regional Airport and Cranton. Winglite Airlines is one of several recent start-ups specialising in flying to smaller markets in Australia that are not served by the main airlines. "We look forward to providing the region's residents with affordable, convenient service to Cranton," stated Savita Grewal, public relations director at Winglite Airlines.

According to Ms. Grewal, the airline has scheduled its inaugural flight from Arlford Regional Airport for 1 August. Initially, Winglite will offer two daily flights to Cranton. Additional destinations are being considered for the future, including Eider Bay and West Linport. A decision regarding added routes is expected by 31 December.

To:	oliverp01@roommateroundup.com
From:	sgirard@emailcloud.com
Date:	15 July
Subject:	Room in downtown Arlford

Hello, Oliver,

I am interested in sharing the apartment you listed on the Roommate Roundup Web site. I'm looking for a fully furnished space with a private bathroom, and I see that yours has all that plus the bonus of reserved parking. At $850, including utilities, the monthly rent is just within my budget. I agree to give you the required security deposit of one month's rent in advance.

I am quiet, easygoing, and reasonably neat. I work as a flight attendant with Winglite Airlines. I have been assigned to the airline's new route out of Arlford that begins next month. I will be in Arlford only half the time and will stay in a hotel near my destination airport for the rest of the week. That means you would have the apartment to yourself much of the time.

I'm currently in Eider Bay but will be back next week. Could we set a time when I can meet you and look at the apartment?

Many thanks,

Stuart Girard

186. For what activity will Winglite Airlines and the city of Arlford share expenses?

   (A) Extending a runway
   (B) Collecting data about airport usage
   (C) Improving roads near the airport
   (D) Paying for more security personnel

187. What does the article indicate about Winglite Airlines?

   (A) It is headed by Ms. Grewal.
   (B) It flies to less popular airports.
   (C) It has been in operation for many decades.
   (D) It currently offers flights from Arlford to several destinations.

188. When should the Aviation Boulevard project be completed?

   (A) By January 14
   (B) By March 18
   (C) By August 1
   (D) By December 31

189. According to the e-mail, what will Mr. Girard do if he moves into the apartment?

   (A) Park his car on the street
   (B) Provide his own furniture
   (C) Pay a deposit of $850
   (D) Share a bathroom

190. Where will Mr. Girard usually stay when he is not in Arlford?

   (A) In Darwin
   (B) In Cranton
   (C) In Eider Bay
   (D) In West Linport

Questions 191-195 refer to the following Web pages and online review.

---

https://forklifttrainingacademy.com/certification

| About | **Certification** | Registration | Student Log-in | Contact |

Forklift Operation Training and Certifications

The Forklift Training Academy's one-day courses satisfy all requirements for certification in Canada and the United States. We offer courses for first timers needing initial certification and for experienced operators needing recertification. A passing score on a final examination is required for certification. Certification is valid for three years.

We have recently transitioned from in-person to online courses only, available on mobile devices, tablets, or computers.

Visit our registration page for more information or to sign up. All reservations must be booked and paid for at least three days in advance of the selected course date.

---

https://forklifttrainingacademy.com/registration

| About | Certification | **Registration** | Student Log-in | Contact |

Registration Form

Name: Philippe Durand
E-mail: philippe.durand@silkmail.com

Select your preferred course date:

- Certification—Instructor: Mr. Harris / April 4, 8:00 A.M.–4:00 P.M. ☐
- Recertification—Instructor: Ms. Gogh / April 7, 8:30 A.M.–2:30 P.M. ☐
- Certification—Instructor: Ms. Baldwin / April 10, 8:00 A.M.–4:00 P.M. ☒
- Recertification—Instructor: Ms. Baldwin / April 14, 8:30 A.M.–2:30 P.M. ☐
- Certification—Instructor: Mr. Minors / April 21, 8:00 A.M.–4:00 P.M. ☐

Review: Forklift Training Classes

By Julie Dye

May 18

I took the forklift training class for recertification for my job at Able Industries last month. I was concerned about taking the course online; however, it covered all the material from the on-site training that I had for my original certification—and more. It was also great that I did not have to travel to take the course and that I received my recertification that very same day! The trainer, Ms. Gogh, was excellent. She answered all my questions and was attuned to the challenges that forklift operators face. My only recommendation for the Forklift Training Academy is that they offer more variety in course days and times.

191. What is indicated about Forklift Training Academy courses?

    (A) They are conducted online.
    (B) They take longer than one day.
    (C) They require an in-person examination.
    (D) They are difficult to pass.

192. What is suggested about Mr. Durand?

    (A) He took his course to get a promotion.
    (B) He paid for his course at least three days in advance.
    (C) His exam scores were posted online.
    (D) His certification was about to expire.

193. Who taught the course on April 14 ?

    (A) Mr. Harris
    (B) Ms. Gogh
    (C) Ms. Baldwin
    (D) Mr. Minors

194. When did Ms. Dye take her course?

    (A) On April 4
    (B) On April 7
    (C) On April 10
    (D) On April 21

195. What can be concluded about Ms. Dye?

    (A) She was unhappy with her training.
    (B) She taught an online course.
    (C) She writes reviews for a living.
    (D) She is an experienced forklift operator.

Questions 196-200 refer to the following e-mails and chart.

To:	Janice Bledstone <jbledstone@nickbeatsband.com>
From:	Michael Cheung <mcheung@stickersbeyours.com>
Date:	June 13
Subject:	Nick Beats promotional stickers

Dear Ms. Bledstone:

Congratulations on your remarkable success managing the Nick Beats band. I have a proposal for you. Why not have your group's logo made into bumper stickers, roll stickers, paper stickers, or vinyl stickers?

Stickers, or decals, are a great way to promote your band. They are a very affordable product that you can sell to your audiences. You could also give them away after a show. Whether you want to use stickers as giveaways or to make extra cash, Stickers Be Yours has you covered. Our stickers are waterproof and resist fading. They last a long time and will adhere to any surface. You can choose from hundreds of templates or upload your own artwork. For more information, please call me at 863-555-0128 or visit our Web site at stickersbeyours.com.

By the way, I am a personal fan of Matt Grimm. In fact, I play in a band myself, and I try to model my style of playing after his. Please send him my regards, whether or not we do business together.

Sincerely,

Michael Cheung

Nick Beats Vinyl Stickers

Item Number	Sticker Name	Description	Retail Price
1022	Signed Drum Set	Matt Grimm's drum set and signature	$1.99
1028	Portrait Shots	Collage showing all five musicians	$2.25
1035	Tour Bus	The group's famous striped bus	$2.99
1042	Album Cover	Cover art from *Laurel in Love*	$3.45
1056	Nick Beats Band	The group's logo and name in flaming colors	$4.99

```
                    E-Mail Message
    To:       Michael Cheung <mcheung@stickersbeyours.com>
    From:     Janice Bledstone <jbledstone@nickbeatsband.com>
    Date:     August 4
    Subject:  Reorder
```

Dear Mr. Cheung,

Thank you again for the outstanding work you did for Nick Beats. Matt Grimm and the other band members love the stickers, which are selling very well. They received the most comments on the group collage. It really came out beautifully, and we appreciate your help with it. Lorraine Farina, who did the original photography, thinks you could have a second career in graphic art!

We still have plenty of them left from our first order, but I do need 500 more of item 1056.

Gratefully,

Janice Bledstone

196. What is suggested in the first e-mail about products made by Stickers Be Yours?

(A) They appeal mainly to children.
(B) They cannot be used on surfaces made of brick or concrete.
(C) They are intended solely for advertising purposes.
(D) They remain sticky even in wet weather.

197. What is most likely true about Mr. Cheung?

(A) He plays the drums.
(B) He manages a band.
(C) He and Mr. Grimm attended the same school.
(D) He met Ms. Bledstone at a Nick Beats performance.

198. How much does a sticker that features a vehicle cost?

(A) $2.25
(B) $2.99
(C) $3.45
(D) $4.99

199. What can be concluded about Nick Beats' most popular sticker?

(A) It is given out for free to the audience at Nick Beats concerts.
(B) It will be changed to make Mr. Grimm's portrait bigger.
(C) It was designed with the help of Mr. Cheung.
(D) It features Ms. Farina's signature.

200. What is indicated about the sticker ordered by Ms. Bledstone?

(A) It is smaller than the other stickers.
(B) It was based on an album cover.
(C) It has been reordered before.
(D) It is the most expensive sticker sold.

Stop! This is the end of the test. If you finish before time is called, you may go back to Parts 5, 6, and 7 and check your work.

ETS 토익 정기시험 기출문제집 5 1000 RC

TEST 09
무료 동영상 강의

RC
기출 TEST 09

READING TEST

In the Reading test, you will read a variety of texts and answer several different types of reading comprehension questions. The entire Reading test will last 75 minutes. There are three parts, and directions are given for each part. You are encouraged to answer as many questions as possible within the time allowed.

You must mark your answers on the separate answer sheet. Do not write your answers in your test book.

PART 5

Directions: A word or phrase is missing in each of the sentences below. Four answer choices are given below each sentence. Select the best answer to complete the sentence. Then mark the letter (A), (B), (C), or (D) on your answer sheet.

101. Our ------- indicate that your company car is due for regular service next month.
    (A) records
    (B) recording
    (C) recorded
    (D) recordable

102. The ------- entrance to our office building will be closed on Tuesday because of construction.
    (A) next
    (B) main
    (C) sure
    (D) early

103. Any document marked "Confidential" must be handled and stored -------.
    (A) careful
    (B) carefully
    (C) carefulness
    (D) more careful

104. The new technology ------- trains to switch quickly between electric and diesel modes.
    (A) rides
    (B) forms
    (C) allows
    (D) conducts

105. The Chocobonne Corporation says it plans to open 28 new ------- in the next three years.
    (A) stores
    (B) storing
    (C) store
    (D) storage

106. The Lofstrom Shopping Center is ------- new tenants to rent vacant retail space.
    (A) seeking
    (B) growing
    (C) facing
    (D) relating

107. The painter Marion Settimi developed ------- distinctive style during the years she lived in Indonesia.
    (A) herself
    (B) hers
    (C) her
    (D) she

108. The company picnic at Floral Park will begin at noon on Saturday and end ------- 4:00 P.M.
    (A) around
    (B) until
    (C) outside
    (D) within

109. Last Monday, the department ------- Mr. Okada's recent promotion to manager.
(A) will be celebrating
(B) celebrated
(C) is celebrating
(D) celebrates

110. Ms. Xuan's ------- for reducing the company's energy consumption is worth considering.
(A) revision
(B) attention
(C) meaning
(D) proposal

111. Dr. Grayston ------- accepted the position of school superintendent.
(A) enthusiast
(B) enthusiastic
(C) enthusiastically
(D) enthusiasm

112. Austina Gallery is located at the northern end of Arch Street, ------- the Verdigris Bistro.
(A) opposite
(B) except
(C) across
(D) plus

113. Mr. Garcia promised ------- a mentor to Ms. Winston after he retired.
(A) became
(B) becoming
(C) to become
(D) had become

114. Once considered a specialty product, shoes made from recycled materials are now ------- available.
(A) upward
(B) widely
(C) enough
(D) closely

115. Yuping University has formed ------- with local businesses to create internship opportunities for its students.
(A) partner
(B) partners
(C) partnering
(D) partnerships

116. Our market research shows that buyers with limited ------- of a product often look for information from expert sources.
(A) knowledge
(B) approval
(C) perception
(D) consideration

117. ------- is preventing the graphic artists from accessing the image files in the main database.
(A) Many
(B) Other
(C) Something
(D) Whoever

118. ------- a delay, Thaintech completed the renovation of its warehouse before the target date of April 7.
(A) Although
(B) Despite
(C) According to
(D) However

119. While its credit card system is offline, the Lexler Department Store is ------- closed for business.
(A) effect
(B) effecting
(C) effective
(D) effectively

120. Nearly half of the toy manufacturers surveyed reported increased sales ------- the last two years.
(A) onto
(B) under
(C) against
(D) over

121. Nonprofit groups ------- up to three applications for funding consideration during any given calendar year.
    (A) be submitted
    (B) submitting
    (C) submits
    (D) may submit

122. Critics reacted ------- to the new musical, praising the exciting design and impressive choreography.
    (A) intentionally
    (B) favorably
    (C) uncertainly
    (D) continuously

123. *Clausen's Notes* is well-known ------- writers and publishers for its in-depth reviews of books.
    (A) owed to
    (B) because
    (C) among
    (D) in between

124. The ongoing shortage of hardwood has caused the price of certain furniture items to -------.
    (A) drain
    (B) loop
    (C) soar
    (D) fling

125. Attach the ------- tray to any flat steel surface for easy storage of and access to household or automotive tools.
    (A) magnetic
    (B) magnetize
    (C) magnets
    (D) magnetically

126. The customer ------- to buy an extended warranty on the dishwasher, so it is not eligible for a free repair.
    (A) rejected
    (B) neglected
    (C) omitted
    (D) dismissed

127. Although much of the material was technical in nature, the audience appeared to remain ------- throughout Ms. Sharma's presentation.
    (A) engage
    (B) engaged
    (C) engagingly
    (D) engagement

128. ------- fresh fruit and vegetables, vendors at the Wattville Farm Market also sell various handmade goods.
    (A) Compared with
    (B) In addition to
    (C) Rather than
    (D) As a result of

129. ------- route they choose, it should take the management team approximately four hours to drive to the hotel in Antibes.
    (A) What
    (B) Some
    (C) Somewhere
    (D) Whichever

130. All Baraantec Ltd. hand tools undergo ------- inspections to ensure they are free of defects.
    (A) rigorous
    (B) negotiated
    (C) returnable
    (D) portable

PART 6

Directions: Read the texts that follow. A word, phrase, or sentence is missing in parts of each text. Four answer choices for each question are given below the text. Select the best answer to complete the text. Then mark the letter (A), (B), (C), or (D) on your answer sheet.

Questions 131-134 refer to the following advertisement.

Retro Crafters focuses on furniture designs from the 1950s through the 1970s. Our products are crafted to highlight the beauty of natural ------- . To us, small knots, tiny nicks, and color variations
131.
are not imperfections. ------- . Our latest collection features a wall-mounted oak shelving system
132.
with narrow rails. The rails can support shelves, cabinets, drawers, and even a desktop to create
a customizable system. ------- , the wall-mounted design frees up floor space. Our products are
133.
carried by furniture ------- in many urban centers around the country. Furniture stores interested in
134.
offering our products should contact Nya Fernaut, sales director.

131. (A) textiles
 (B) wood
 (C) environment
 (D) light

132. (A) They can easily be covered by paint.
 (B) They are the result of poor maintenance.
 (C) They can reduce the value of an item.
 (D) They are what makes each piece unique.

133. (A) Moreover
 (B) Nevertheless
 (C) On the contrary
 (D) Regardless

134. (A) retail
 (B) retailing
 (C) retailers
 (D) retailed

Questions 135-138 refer to the following instructions.

Caring for Your Rice Cooker

Before cleaning your rice cooker, detach the power cord from the electrical outlet. Make sure all ------- are completely cooled down. Next, remove the detachable pot and hand-wash it in warm, soapy water, along with the lid and rice paddle. Note that the pot is not dishwasher safe. Note also that its nonstick surface ------- damaged by abrasive cleaners. Rather than scrape off any tough residue, soak the pot in warm, soapy water for ten minutes. ------- . The exterior of the rice cooker should never be submerged in water. ------- , gently wipe it down with a damp cloth.

135. (A) vehicles
(B) appliances
(C) ingredients
(D) components

136. (A) was
(B) can be
(C) is being
(D) has been

137. (A) Then, use a soft brush or sponge to finish cleaning.
(B) Cleaning utensils must be purchased separately.
(C) Finally, place the cooker back in its box.
(D) A light will go on when the rice is cooked.

138. (A) If not
(B) Instead
(C) Meanwhile
(D) In that case

Questions 139-142 refer to the following e-mail.

To: Britta Gehring <bgehring@gehringaccounting.com>
From: Mikel Zubiondo <mikel@zubiondodesign.com>
Date: December 12
Subject: Logo sketches
Attachment: Gehring_sketches

Dear Ms. Gehring,

Thank you for entrusting me with the design of the logo for your business. I took ------- notes during our meeting last week, and I feel that I understand the business values you want the logo to convey. I have attached five sketches for you. ------- represents your business in a slightly different way. Two have a classic, timeless look, while the others are minimalist and modern. ------- .

Once you review the sketches, let me know which you like and what changes I should make, if any. I look forward to ------- the design with you.

Best regards,

Mikel Zubiondo
Zubiondo Design

---

139. (A) extents
     (B) extending
     (C) extensive
     (D) extensively

140. (A) Someone
     (B) Mine
     (C) Theirs
     (D) Each

141. (A) Nonetheless, they all give an impression of trustworthiness and precision.
     (B) Those companies have logos that are very memorable.
     (C) Even so, designing a logo can be a costly process.
     (D) I recommend using fewer colors than were initially requested.

142. (A) researching
     (B) publicizing
     (C) demonstrating
     (D) finalizing

Questions 143-146 refer to the following article.

LONDON (2 June)—Locke and Jeeves, the owner of Fernsby Shoes and Athletic Footwear, announced today the acquisition of Shipley Designs for an ------- amount. The ------- comes as no
143.   144.
surprise to shoe industry insiders, who have speculated for some time about Shipley's financial challenges. Five of the six Shipley stores will be part of the Locke and Jeeves deal, including the flagship store here in London. ------- .
145.

Locke and Jeeves CEO Zachary Thayne has expressed enthusiasm about the deal. "Shipley is an iconic design house that ------- much to the Locke and Jeeves portfolio in the area of reliably
146.
traditional footwear," said Mr. Thayne.

143. (A) external
(B) arbitrary
(C) indivisible
(D) undisclosed

144. (A) trade
(B) closure
(C) purchase
(D) appointment

145. (A) The fate of the shop in Leeds is still unknown.
(B) Shipley Designs was founded almost 90 years ago.
(C) Customers can now take advantage of a great deal.
(D) All London locations are open seven days a week.

146. (A) will be adding
(B) had been adding
(C) must have added
(D) would have added

PART 7

Directions: In this part you will read a selection of texts, such as magazine and newspaper articles, e-mails, and instant messages. Each text or set of texts is followed by several questions. Select the best answer for each question and mark the letter (A), (B), (C), or (D) on your answer sheet.

Questions 147-148 refer to the following invitation.

147. What is the purpose of the event?

(A) To interview candidates for a management position
(B) To celebrate the retirement of an employee
(C) To allow conference participants to network with one another
(D) To introduce a new company executive to employees

148. According to the invitation, what will happen at the event?

(A) Refreshments will be served.
(B) The president will give a speech.
(C) Financial reports will be distributed.
(D) The chief financial officer will receive an award.

Questions 149-150 refer to the following e-mail.

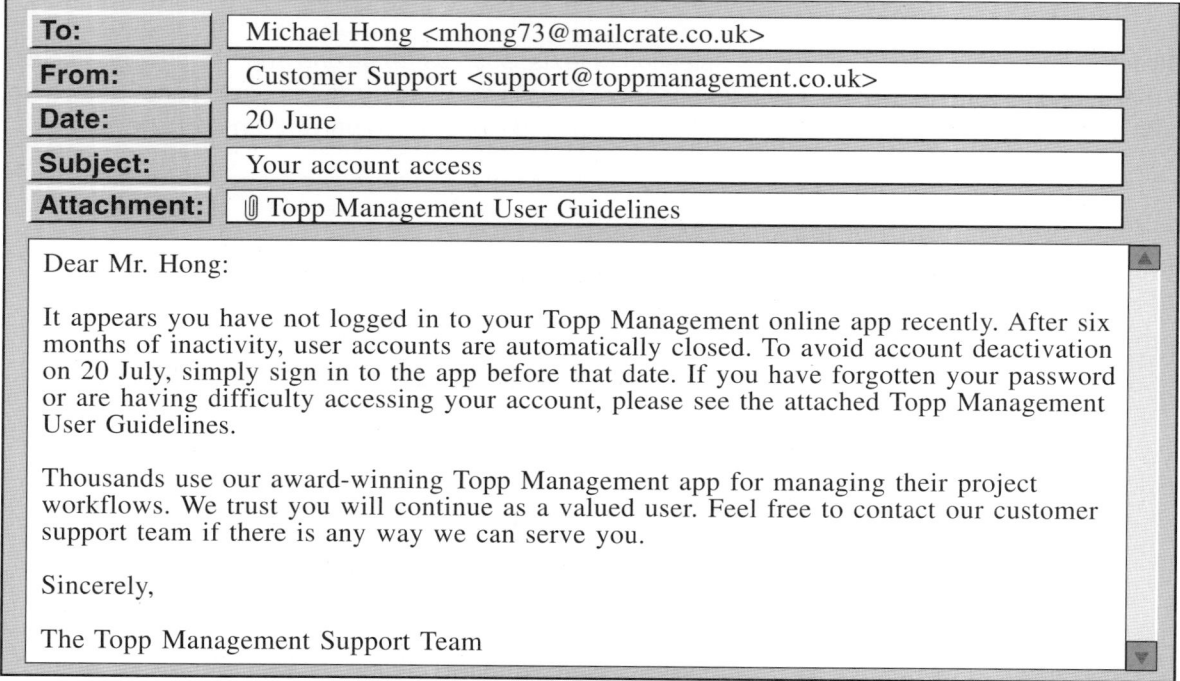

To:	Michael Hong <mhong73@mailcrate.co.uk>
From:	Customer Support <support@toppmanagement.co.uk>
Date:	20 June
Subject:	Your account access
Attachment:	📎 Topp Management User Guidelines

Dear Mr. Hong:

It appears you have not logged in to your Topp Management online app recently. After six months of inactivity, user accounts are automatically closed. To avoid account deactivation on 20 July, simply sign in to the app before that date. If you have forgotten your password or are having difficulty accessing your account, please see the attached Topp Management User Guidelines.

Thousands use our award-winning Topp Management app for managing their project workflows. We trust you will continue as a valued user. Feel free to contact our customer support team if there is any way we can serve you.

Sincerely,

The Topp Management Support Team

149. What is most likely true about Mr. Hong's account?

(A) It requires a new password.
(B) It was created on June 20.
(C) It was updated by a colleague of his.
(D) It has not been used in a few months.

150. What must Mr. Hong do to maintain access to his account?

(A) Reply to the e-mail
(B) Sign in before July 20
(C) Renew his annual membership
(D) Speak with a customer service agent

Questions 151-152 refer to the following online chat discussion.

John Dakers [9:30 A.M.]
Hello. I have a furnace service appointment scheduled this morning. Is a technician on the way to my house yet?

HVAC Customer Service [9:31 A.M.]
Let me check.

HVAC Customer Service [9:32 A.M.]
Our system shows that someone will be there today between 3:00 P.M. and 5:00 P.M.

John Dakers [9:33 A.M.]
My notes say 9:00 to 11:00 A.M. today. I took time off from work.

HVAC Customer Service [9:34 A.M.]
I am sorry for any miscommunication. A technician will be there later today.

John Dakers [9:36 A.M.]
But I need to get to the office soon.

HVAC Customer Service [9:37 A.M.]
Our apologies, Mr. Dakers. I will see if we can make some schedule changes.

HVAC Customer Service [9:42 A.M.]
Good news. I reached your technician. She is finishing a job now and can be there within the hour.

John Dakers [9:43 A.M.]
Thank you very much. I appreciate it.

151. Why does Mr. Dakers contact HVAC Customer Service?

(A) To express displeasure over the quality of work
(B) To confirm that he will be available to work
(C) To ensure that a service will be provided as planned
(D) To cancel a service he no longer needs

152. At 9:36 A.M., what does Mr. Dakers most likely mean when he writes, "But I need to get to the office soon"?

(A) He has a question for his supervisor.
(B) He lives far away from his office.
(C) A technician should go to Mr. Dakers' workplace.
(D) An afternoon appointment is unacceptable.

Questions 153-155 refer to the following memo.

> **MEMO**
>
> To: All employees
> From: Loretta Hirano, Human Resources Director
> Date: Friday, April 7, 9:03 A.M.
> Subject: Summer work arrangements
>
> Dear colleagues,
>
> As you know, the period from June 1 through August 31 is ordinarily our busiest time. This summer promises to be even busier than usual, as business has increased by 15% since this time last year.
>
> Management is also well aware that summer is the time when many of our employees like to take time off from work. Still, we must have sufficient staff on hand to deliver service of the highest quality, a policy for which Bellerson Financial is highly regarded by its customers.
>
> Therefore, if you are planning to take a vacation between June 1 and August 31, kindly submit your request by Friday, April 28. You will receive a response as soon as possible but no later than Monday, May 8.
>
> Thank you for your assistance.

153. The word "ordinarily" in paragraph 1, line 1, is closest in meaning to

(A) dully
(B) typically
(C) acceptably
(D) minimally

154. What is indicated about Bellerson Financial?

(A) It recently promoted Ms. Hirano to Human Resources Director.
(B) It experienced some financial difficulties in recent months.
(C) It offers extended service hours between June and August.
(D) It has built a reputation among customers for its excellent service.

155. What is the deadline for requesting vacation time?

(A) April 28
(B) May 8
(C) June 1
(D) August 31

Questions 156-158 refer to the following article.

Teleteknic Unveils New Phone Models

SYDNEY (21 March)—Electronics giant Teleteknic announced that it is launching three new models of its popular smartphone: the Strato, the Alto, and the Cirro. In terms of physical dimensions and data storage, the Strato is the smallest model, the Alto is in the middle, and the Cirro is the largest. The Cirro model also includes an electronic stylus for writing or drawing on the screen.

Most of the changes from Teleteknic's previous phone models are minor. However, users will be impressed by a significant improvement to the camera. All new models include an upgraded camera with advanced zoom features and automatic focus. It also allows users to take better photos in lower light conditions. Another advancement is in the batteries: the latest phones have a longer battery life and charge faster.

Consumers can get a glimpse of the phones in a promotional video posted on the company's Web site at www.teleteknic.com.au, or they can see the models in person at next month's technical trade show. Preorders are now being accepted at Teleteknic's online shop. The new phones are expected to be on store shelves in November.

156. How does the Cirro model differ from the other new phone models?

(A) It took the longest time to develop.
(B) It comes with an additional tool.
(C) It includes expandable memory.
(D) It has a screen on the front and the back.

157. What feature of the phones has had the greatest improvement?

(A) The operating system
(B) The camera
(C) The screen
(D) The speaker

158. Where can customers currently order the new phones?

(A) In electronics shops
(B) In department stores
(C) At technical trade shows
(D) At the company's online shop

Questions 159-160 refer to the following online post.

Tottenton Community Online Message Board > General

Posted by Thalia Finley on Thursday, 14 September, at 11:41 A.M.:

I am a documentary filmmaker working to tell the story of how Tottenton evolved from a decaying industrial town into a hub for environmentally responsible building initiatives and sustainable architectural design. I am seeking Tottenton residents at least 50 years of age who lived here during the period of transition and can tell me what it was like. If you are interested in participating, please call me at 020 7946 0532. I'll then send you a personal release form to fill out, and we can arrange to meet for a 30- to 45-minute interview.

159. What is Ms. Finley's film project about?
(A) The life of a public figure
(B) The restoration of a historic landmark
(C) A town's transformation over a period of time
(D) A manufacturing company's innovative policies

160. What does Ms. Finley want people to do?
(A) Attend a film screening
(B) Share their memories
(C) Provide constructive criticism
(D) Avoid entering an area during filming

Questions 161-164 refer to the following instructions.

> ### Personal Statements
>
> Personal statements are brief pieces of writing that showcase a job applicant's most notable talents, accomplishments, and qualities. Personal statements are evaluated both for the facts and details they offer and for the way the writer conveys this information. — [1] —. Therefore, when you are composing a personal statement, it is important to be thoughtful about issues such as word choice and tone.
>
> Though there is no set length for personal statements, employers sometimes offer guidelines. — [2] —. If the employer does not provide a word count, aim for between 300 and 500 words. One page is generally considered the maximum length.
>
> When crafting a personal statement, provide concrete examples of times when you had to rely on your unique qualities. This can be an effective way of demonstrating to a prospective employer your ability to overcome challenges. It is also a good idea to give examples of how you work with or learn from others. — [3] —.
>
> Do not forget to mention the specific job you are applying for and explain why you would be a good fit. Your final paragraph is an ideal place for this information, as you can create a separate version of this paragraph for each position you apply for. Finally, ensure that you have carefully proofread your statement before submitting it. — [4] —.

161. For whom are the instructions most likely intended?

(A) Job applicants
(B) Management team members
(C) Professional writers
(D) Human resources staff

162. What is NOT mentioned as something to be considered when writing a personal statement?

(A) The total number of words
(B) The quality of the writing
(C) Details about the writer's education
(D) Examples of past challenges

163. What can be concluded about the final paragraph of a personal statement?

(A) It is the ideal place for a summary of facts and details.
(B) It is the only paragraph that does not need careful proofreading.
(C) It should appear on the second page.
(D) It should be easily customizable.

164. In which of the positions marked [1], [2], [3], and [4] does the following sentence best belong?

"You might explain, for instance, how a person you respect had a positive impact on your life."

(A) [1]
(B) [2]
(C) [3]
(D) [4]

Questions 165-168 refer to the following text-message chain.

Ji-Min Jeon (8:04 A.M.)
Karl, I am on-site at the Crosley Bridge now.

Karl Scholz (8:06 A.M.)
What do you think?

Ji-Min Jeon (8:08 A.M.)
It definitely needs routine maintenance, and we may have to plan some additional work.

Karl Scholz (8:09 A.M.)
Is it something our crews can do, or do we need to contract it out?

Ji-Min Jeon (8:13 A.M.)
Not sure yet. I still need to take pictures and finish the routine inspection. Nothing appears to be critical, but given its age, I expect some preventive work may be required. In any case, I suggest you consider moving up the date of the next in-depth inspection.

Ana Vega (8:14 A.M.)
Hi, Ji-Min. Would it be possible for you to be back here for a 12:30 lunch meeting? I know it's short notice, but I have some questions about the Ninth Street Bridge inspection I'm conducting this afternoon. Your previous in-depth report that led to the repair work on that bridge was excellent.

Karl Scholz (8:15 A.M.)
Ji-Min, I know I asked you to go to Lentox County to check out another bridge, but you can do that later this afternoon.

Ji-Min Jeon (8:18 A.M.)
Thank you, Ana. I'll be there by 12:30, after I finish up here.

Ana Vega (8:19 A.M.)
Perfect.

165. What is the main purpose of the text-message chain?

(A) To determine an employee's current availability
(B) To provide an update about a bridge
(C) To discuss whether an outside contractor is needed
(D) To thank a coworker for an in-depth report

166. Where is Ms. Jeon at the time of the text-message chain?

(A) At a cafeteria
(B) At her office
(C) At the Crosley Bridge
(D) At a site in Lentox County

167. What can be concluded about Mr. Scholz?

(A) He is Ms. Vega's assistant.
(B) He plans to have lunch with Ms. Vega.
(C) He recently hired Ms. Jeon.
(D) He directs Ms. Jeon's work.

168. At 8:18 A.M., what does Ms. Jeon most likely mean when she writes, "I'll be there by 12:30"?

(A) She is leaving a site now.
(B) She has to inspect another bridge.
(C) She intends to be at a meeting.
(D) She will arrive after her lunch break.

Questions 169-171 refer to the following e-mail.

E-mail

To:	John Fukiyama <john.fukiyama6775@xmail.ca>
From:	Stephanie Acro <sacro@salvadorfashionassociates.ca>
Date:	18 November
Subject:	Search committee
Attachment:	📎 Confidentiality Agreement

Dear Mr. Fukiyama:

I am writing to gauge your interest in becoming a part of a search committee for the newly vacated Senior Director of Graphic Design position here at Salvador Fashion Associates. As you may have heard, Jake Harris left our company last month to start his own business, leaving us without anyone to head our Graphic Design department. As someone who held this role prior to your retirement four years ago, you know exactly what knowledge and skills are needed for this position, making you an ideal candidate for our search committee. Sheila Mendez, our Executive Director of Marketing, and I will also be part of the committee conducting this search.

If you agree to be a part of the committee, please sign and return the attached confidentiality agreement. At that point, I will send you the applications with their respective résumés and a timeline for the hiring process. For your time and effort, we will compensate you at the standard rate for external consultants. Please let me know your answer as soon as possible. It would be great to work with you again.

Best regards,

Stephanie Acro
Director of Human Resources
Salvador Fashion Associates, Toronto

---

169. What is the purpose of the e-mail?

(A) To present a consulting opportunity
(B) To schedule a departmental meeting
(C) To announce an upcoming job opening
(D) To welcome a recently hired employee

170. What is indicated about Mr. Fukiyama?

(A) He meets regularly with Ms. Acro.
(B) He used to be a senior executive.
(C) He operates his own fashion business.
(D) He often serves on search committees.

171. What does Ms. Acro offer to send to Mr. Fukiyama?

(A) A payment schedule
(B) A list of required skills
(C) A collection of résumés
(D) A revised meeting agenda

Questions 172-175 refer to the following article.

Local Museum Goes Interactive

DERRY (April 7)—The Regional History Museum (RHM) has upgraded many of its exhibits to include interactive technologies. The enhanced exhibitions opened on Monday, one week before the scheduled completion date. The museum remained open during the installation, although some offerings were unavailable during the process of upgrading. — [1] —. The enhancements were funded by Arnsby Metal Manufacturing, a major industrial firm in the area.

— [2] —. According to RHM director Ann Wert, interactive technology allows exhibits to present information and engage users through various audio and visual media. "Visitors can now learn the region's history in an immersive way," said Ms. Wert.

The director's persistent efforts helped to determine the priorities for the project. — [3] —. "Every week in the museum lobby, I interview patrons and record their opinions," said Ms. Wert. "The changes reflect their wishes and ideas."

The improved RHM exhibits also give the user control over the experience. — [4] —. A touchscreen allows visitors to communicate electronically with an exhibit's unique database and target their interests. The museum now features 26 interactive exhibits that play audio narratives and informative videos.

Ms. Wert suggests that guests stroll around the city's adjoining heritage district and admire its vintage architecture after they visit the museum. Guide maps of the district are available in the museum's lobby.

172. What is indicated in the article about the upgrades to exhibits?

    (A) They were completed ahead of schedule.
    (B) They were designed by Arnsby Metal Manufacturing.
    (C) They were demonstrated at a press conference.
    (D) They led to an increase in ticket prices.

173. What is suggested about Ms. Wert?

    (A) She was recently named museum director.
    (B) She meets with museum visitors in person.
    (C) She designed some of the museum's original displays.
    (D) She previously worked for a technology company.

174. What does Ms. Wert encourage museum visitors to do?

    (A) Purchase items in the gift shop
    (B) Sign up for a museum membership
    (C) Visit a nearby historic neighborhood
    (D) Post photos of their visit on social media

175. In which of the positions marked [1], [2], [3], and [4] does the following sentence best belong?

    "Visitors will now be able to choose topics they want to learn more about."

    (A) [1]
    (B) [2]
    (C) [3]
    (D) [4]

Questions 176-180 refer to the following chart and e-mail.

Sixth Annual Arts and Crafts Festival
Somerville Park, Broad Avenue, Springdale

Vendor	Booth	Description
Great Woods Crafts	101	Elegant salad bowls, serving utensils, cutting boards, and related items lovingly carved from salvaged, purified wood
Folding Designs	102	Stunning paper art items, such as jewelry, greeting cards, bookmarks, and wall hangings
Fairy Dust Pottery	103	Whimsical but functional ceramic mugs, bowls, plates, and water pitchers
Franny's Sensational Scents	104	Natural, organic soaps in different colors, scents, and textures, all infused with herbs and flowers harvested from our own garden
Charmed Glass	105	Unique handmade earrings, necklaces, pins, and other wearable art created from glass

To:	cho@mailcurrent.com
From:	k.mcfarlan@magentamail.com
Date:	July 14
Subject:	Question for you
Attachment:	Photo

Hello, Mr. Cho,

It was a pleasure to speak with you at last month's crafts festival in Somerville Park. Anytime I wear the beautiful pendant you sold me, admirers are stunned when I tell them it is an artistically folded page from a book.

Unfortunately, a piece of the item has broken, and I do not have the tools to repair it. When you gave me your business card, you told me to contact you if I had any problems. I have attached a photo of the item to this e-mail. I work in Springdale, just 3 kilometers north of Somerville Park, on the same street where the festival took place, in fact. I could bring the item to you if you live in the area, or I could mail it to you. Please let me know how to proceed in having the item repaired.

Warm regards,

Kelly McFarlan

176. What do the vendors in booths 101 and 103 have in common?

(A) They use recycled materials exclusively.
(B) They have retail stores in Springdale.
(C) They make wall hangings.
(D) They sell items for the kitchen.

177. What is mentioned about Franny's Sensational Scents?

(A) It sells scented candles.
(B) It has a booth at the craft festival every year.
(C) Its items are also sold online.
(D) Its items contain parts of plants.

178. Why did Ms. McFarlan e-mail Mr. Cho?

(A) To follow up on an offered service
(B) To place an order
(C) To outline a marketing strategy
(D) To propose a partnership

179. Where did Ms. McFarlan most likely purchase an item at the festival?

(A) At booth 101
(B) At booth 102
(C) At booth 104
(D) At booth 105

180. What is suggested about Ms. McFarlan's workplace?

(A) It is an arts and crafts studio.
(B) It is near Mr. Cho's home.
(C) It is on Broad Avenue.
(D) It is a publishing company.

Questions 181-185 refer to the following Web page and online review.

https://www.superracleaning.com/specialservices

Superra Cleaning—Special Services

Superra Cleaning is the leading provider of residential cleaning services in the Elmwood Valley region. We have built our reputation on our thorough weekly, biweekly, and monthly house cleaning packages. However, customers may not be familiar with our intensive special cleaning services. These services require no long-term contract and are priced affordably. Here is a list of our offerings and a new feature all customers may enjoy.

- **Post-event cleaning**: A two-person cleaning crew, plus a supervisor, will clean up after a special event so the space looks the way it did before you arrived.

- **One-time house cleaning**: The ideal service for anyone who hosts guests but does not have time to tidy up beforehand. A supervisor will oversee a three-person cleaning team to ensure your home is sparkling clean.

- **Move-out cleaning**: Perfect for tenants vacating apartments or homes, this service allows you to focus on moving while we do the cleaning. Under the guidance of a supervisor, a two-person team will handle all the necessary dusting and scrubbing.

- **Free cleaning tips**: Over the past two months, we have posted video tutorials featuring clever cleaning tips. We hope you will find them useful.

Prices for each special service vary based on the size of the space. Contact us at (616) 555-0189 to request a price quote.

Posted on May 24 by Kenneth Singh

I found myself in a situation recently that required one of Superra Cleaning's special services. At the last minute, a friend informed me that he would be visiting the next day, and I had fallen behind on my house cleaning. It was the first time that I had to use a professional cleaning service, and I am glad I chose Superra. The crew arrived on time and worked hard throughout the afternoon. They did not mind the late notice. The crew even swept off my front porch after cleaning my home's interior.

Note that Superra can be quite busy during the summer season. As it turned out, I managed to contact them at just the right time. Luckily, another customer had canceled a cleaning an hour or so before my call, but otherwise, Superra was booked up for the entire week.

181. What is suggested about Superra Cleaning?

(A) It uses environmentally friendly cleaning materials.
(B) It merged with a competing business.
(C) It is best known for its regular service packages.
(D) It has lowered the prices of its services.

182. According to the Web page, what do the special services have in common?

(A) Supervised work teams
(B) Affordable long-term contracts
(C) Options for weekend service
(D) Discounts for first-time clients

183. What did Superra Cleaning do recently?

(A) It released the results of a customer survey.
(B) It celebrated a business anniversary.
(C) It hired additional staff members.
(D) It published instructional content.

184. What is most likely true about Mr. Singh?

(A) He provided a team with his own cleaning materials.
(B) He had to cancel a cleaning service appointment.
(C) He was visited by a three-person cleaning team.
(D) He is a regular client of Superra Cleaning.

185. In the online review, the word "just" in paragraph 2, line 2, is closest in meaning to

(A) directly
(B) exactly
(C) simply
(D) possibly

Questions 186-190 refer to the following Web page, e-mail, and sign.

https://www.beachsideusedbooks.co.uk

| Home | About Us | Our Selection | **Book Exchange** |

Beachside Used Books will give you store credit for your old books!

We welcome secondhand hardback books in exchange for shop credit. Books published twenty or more years ago and first editions are favoured. Our standards for accepting a book for resale are as follows.

- No stains or water damage on any pages
- No creased, torn, or missing pages
- No textbooks, encyclopaedias, or other reference books
- No cookbooks except those by a celebrity chef such as Ian Wu
- No children's picture books

To:	info@beachsideusedbooks.co.uk
From:	rhys.townsend@walemail.com
Date:	Thursday, 3 January, 11:03 A.M.
Subject:	Enquiry

Hello,

I am new to the area, and a neighbour mentioned your shop. I would like to bring in some of my old books and use the shop credit to buy books for my six-year-old son. In addition to the picture books he has outgrown, I also have some newer science fiction paperbacks in good condition, two first-edition classic novels inherited from my great-grandmother, and three cookbooks filled with recipes submitted by members of a charity I run. May I stop in next Tuesday or Wednesday? If that's not possible, I could come on Saturday or Sunday before 9:00 A.M.

Sincerely,

Rhys Townsend

Beachside Used Books
Hours of Operation

Monday: CLOSED
Tuesday: CLOSED
Wednesday: 9:00 A.M. to 8:00 P.M.
Thursday: 9:00 A.M. to 8:00 P.M.
Friday: 9:00 A.M. to 8:00 P.M.
Saturday: 10:00 A.M. to 5:00 P.M.
Sunday: Noon to 5:00 P.M.

186. What is the purpose of the Web page?
   (A) To announce a store's sales event
   (B) To explain a store's policy
   (C) To invite people to join a book club
   (D) To collect used books for donation

187. What does the Web page suggest about Mr. Wu?
   (A) He is a famous person.
   (B) He owns a restaurant.
   (C) He repairs damaged books.
   (D) He is a regular customer of Beachside Used Books.

188. What items offered by Mr. Townsend will Beachside Used Books most likely accept?
   (A) The picture books
   (B) The science fiction books
   (C) The classic novels
   (D) The cookbooks

189. What does Mr. Townsend indicate in the e-mail?
   (A) He learned how to cook from his grandmother.
   (B) He recommended Beachside Used Books to a friend.
   (C) He often takes his son to the library.
   (D) He oversees a charity organization.

190. When most likely will Mr. Townsend visit Beachside Used Books?
   (A) On Tuesday
   (B) On Wednesday
   (C) On Saturday
   (D) On Sunday

Questions 191-195 refer to the following e-mail, contact list, and schedule.

E-Mail Message

To: Max Aurinen <maurinen@edwildurables.com>
From: Jessica Seung <jseung@edwildurables.com>
Date: April 21
Subject: Shadowing appointments

Hello, Max,

On May 6, we will welcome Mr. David Rein for his first day as a new employee. Mr. Rein is a graduate of Northburg University and has worked at Zelehost, Inc., and Dorfax Industries. Mr. Rein will fulfill the role of an assistant manufacturing supervisor in our Large Appliance Division. Please prepare his initial onboarding paperwork and arrange a schedule for his first two weeks with Edwil Durables, Inc.

As part of his training for his new position, let's have him shadow our team leaders in several areas for a couple of days. This will allow him to learn more about the various departments he will eventually be interacting with. Also, assuming Amos Hillman returns on the expected date from his vacation in Thailand, please schedule a day for Mr. Rein to learn how prototypes are developed in the product labs.

Thank you,

Jessica Seung, Human Resources Director

Edwil Durables, Inc.
Contact List of Department Leaders

Name	Title and Division	Building and Office	Phone Extension
Shane Faraci	Director, Information Systems	Ardmore, Room 210	022
Margery Gazda	Sr. Director, Retail Department	Ardmore, Room 323	023
Patricia Nesbit	Director, Small Appliance Division	Winston West, Room 07	333
Latisha Lake	Director, Large Appliance Division	Winston East, Room 102	145
Orville Martin	Sr. Director, Electronics Division	Meisner, Room 410	254

Onboarding Schedule for David Rein

Paper Work and Orientation

May 6	9 A.M. to noon	Complete documentation, benefits presentation, and enrollment
	Noon to 1 P.M.	Lunch
	1 P.M. to 3 P.M.	Meet with assigned department head
	3 P.M. to 5 P.M.	Meet with Information Systems staff for laptop and profile setup

Shadowing

May 7	9 A.M. to 5 P.M.	Latisha Lake
May 8	9 A.M. to 5 P.M.	Orville Martin
May 9	9 A.M. to 5 P.M.	Amos Hillman
May 10	9 A.M. to 5 P.M.	Margery Gazda

191. Why did Ms. Seung write the e-mail?

(A) To recommend a job applicant
(B) To respond to a customer inquiry
(C) To outline a plan for a new staff member
(D) To approve an employee's vacation time

192. Who most likely is Mr. Aurinen?

(A) A student at Northburg University
(B) A sales agent from Zelehost, Inc.
(C) A client of Dorfax Industries
(D) An administrative assistant at Edwil Durables, Inc.

193. Who will be Mr. Rein's director?

(A) Mr. Faraci
(B) Ms. Gazda
(C) Ms. Lake
(D) Mr. Martin

194. What is suggested by the contact list?

(A) The company has several buildings.
(B) An operator directs each incoming call.
(C) One director leads two divisions.
(D) Some directors share an office.

195. What is suggested about Mr. Hillman?

(A) He is a new team member.
(B) He returned from a trip in time to meet Mr. Rein.
(C) He was recently promoted.
(D) He works in the human resources department.

Questions 196-200 refer to the following article, Web page, and work order.

Video Firm Reaches New Heights

PRETORIA (22 March)—Blue Lapis, a producer of industrial videos, announced today that it is now contracting with two drone pilots to provide the company's clients with aerial videography.

"We have always excelled at capturing breathtaking video imagery for a wide range of industries, but we can now do so from new perspectives," said Yunus Maseko, the CEO of Blue Lapis. "Whether for marketing, progress reporting, training, or something else, we offer our clients high-resolution videos from the sky. In fact, we just completed the first aerial videos for Kwanduma Realty Ltd., and everyone is very pleased with the results."

Prices for aerial videography range from R15,000 to R45,000 per session. The prices include basic editing in the Blue Lapis studio. An additional hourly fee is charged if extensive editing or special effects are required. Visit www.bluelapis.co.za for more information.

---

https://www.rfa.web.za/certification

| About | News | **Certification** | Resources |

The Remote Flight Association (RFA) provides training leading to certification for the operation of unmanned aircraft.

Piloting a drone for commercial use requires certification as a precondition of employment. Obtaining a certification card involves:

- completing a course in unmanned aircraft flight regulations
- filing an online application
- registering your equipment with the appropriate civil aviation authority
- completing an interview with a flight examiner to demonstrate knowledge of airspace regulations

After you have successfully completed all required steps, your flight examiner will submit your results for processing. You should receive your certification card within ten business days.

Download our manual for a complete outline of the certification process.

Blue Lapis
Work Order for Drone Video

Client: Lunsklip Construction

Office address: 220 Sand River Street, Pretoria, 0048

Contact person: Tokozile Shabangu, Phone 012 555 0175

Requested date for work: Friday, 12 April

Drone contractor: Olivia Rowley, Card No. 01562

Videography: The client wants a video to show investors. The client requests a drone flight over the entire length of the highway demonstrating the scale of the project, hovering over the section currently under construction, and zooming in to capture action shots of the work. The objective is to present how the highway project is proceeding and highlight what has been completed thus far. Contact Ms. Shabangu to review the flight plan and discuss other areas of focus along the highway.

Notes: No special effects or extra editing is wanted. Include in the title credits the client company's name, project name, and the date the flyover video was taken. Lunsklip Construction is a long-time customer with high expectations. Please consult with Ms. Shabangu throughout the filming and editing process.

---

196. What is mentioned in the article about Blue Lapis?

(A) Its work can serve many business purposes.
(B) Its pricing is lower than that of its competitors.
(C) It has a new chief executive officer.
(D) It is hiring several video editors.

197. According to the Web page, what is one thing people wishing to become drone pilots must do?

(A) Call the association's office
(B) Take a test online
(C) Participate in an interview
(D) Submit professional references

198. According to the work order, why did Lunsklip Construction request a video?

(A) To show progress on a project
(B) To conduct a safety inspection
(C) To find an ideal route for a highway
(D) To map the land features in an area

199. What can be concluded about Ms. Rowley?

(A) She has worked with Ms. Shabangu for many years.
(B) She is a construction supervisor with Lunsklip Construction.
(C) She registered some equipment with an aviation authority.
(D) She is a flight examiner.

200. What is most likely true about Lunsklip Construction?

(A) It did not suggest plans for the video.
(B) It will not need to pay an additional hourly fee.
(C) It is in a partnership with Kwanduma Realty Ltd.
(D) It is a new client of Blue Lapis.

Stop! This is the end of the test. If you finish before time is called, you may go back to Parts 5, 6, and 7 and check your work.

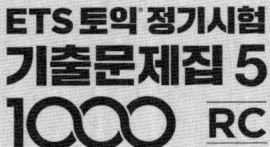

TEST 10
무료 동영상 강의

저자와 출판사의 사전 허락 없이 내용의 일부 혹은 전부를 인용 및 복제하거나 발췌하여 사용할 수 없습니다.

RC
기출 TEST 10

READING TEST

In the Reading test, you will read a variety of texts and answer several different types of reading comprehension questions. The entire Reading test will last 75 minutes. There are three parts, and directions are given for each part. You are encouraged to answer as many questions as possible within the time allowed.

You must mark your answers on the separate answer sheet. Do not write your answers in your test book.

PART 5

Directions: A word or phrase is missing in each of the sentences below. Four answer choices are given below each sentence. Select the best answer to complete the sentence. Then mark the letter (A), (B), (C), or (D) on your answer sheet.

101. Sophia Hollinger was commended for ------- work on the Kala account.

    (A) her
    (B) she
    (C) hers
    (D) herself

102. Last summer, jazz musician Jay Deswani ------- on the main concert stage at Waterfront Park.

    (A) located
    (B) requested
    (C) supplied
    (D) performed

103. The purchasing department ordered six ------- cases of ink toner.

    (A) add
    (B) additional
    (C) additionally
    (D) adding

104. Please complete the questionnaire to help our team ------- understand the financial services you are interested in.

    (A) better
    (B) more
    (C) very
    (D) surely

105. ------- of the garments will begin two weeks after the contract is signed.

    (A) Product
    (B) Produce
    (C) Produced
    (D) Production

106. The minutes of last week's board meeting had only three ------- errors.

    (A) junior
    (B) minor
    (C) soft
    (D) light

107. Patrons are asked to silence their phones ------- the show begins.

    (A) when
    (B) which
    (C) what
    (D) why

108. The majority of the company's employees commute to work ------- train.

    (A) on
    (B) by
    (C) in
    (D) from

109. Line 73 is the oldest ------- operating bus line in Raymo City's history.
    (A) continues
    (B) continued
    (C) continuous
    (D) continuously

110. This message is a ------- to pick up your package at your local post office as soon as possible.
    (A) promotion
    (B) reminder
    (C) process
    (D) report

111. Pet Orbit customers ------- want receipts delivered by e-mail can opt for this service.
    (A) whose
    (B) who
    (C) those
    (D) whoever

112. Mr. Takajian may be an entry-level employee, ------- he does not hesitate to take initiative.
    (A) but
    (B) or
    (C) equally
    (D) accordingly

113. Carter Department Store allows customers ------- items on hold for up to 24 hours.
    (A) place
    (B) to place
    (C) placing
    (D) to be placed

114. Using unique colors and styles, the decor experts at Mamie's Interiors bring a ------- look to homes.
    (A) brief
    (B) dependent
    (C) motivational
    (D) fashionable

115. ------- efficient project management, Sparksware's latest software program was released on time.
    (A) Along with
    (B) Regarding
    (C) Because of
    (D) Subsequent

116. The summer line of outdoor furniture will be available ------- select stores as early as February.
    (A) until
    (B) at
    (C) over
    (D) before

117. There has been a ------- decrease in requests for customer support this quarter.
    (A) notice
    (B) noticing
    (C) noticeable
    (D) noticeably

118. Bina Dal always wanted to become a diplomat, ------- she studied international relations at university.
    (A) so
    (B) once
    (C) overall
    (D) whereas

119. Thank you for responding ------- with information about the T-Max 400 printer and scanner.
    (A) prompt
    (B) promptly
    (C) prompted
    (D) prompts

120. Owing to the weather, we need to ------- your appointment for tree removal service.
    (A) reschedule
    (B) borrow
    (C) contain
    (D) reconstruct

GO ON TO THE NEXT PAGE

121. It will require a ------- effort between the two countries to complete the railway line.
    (A) coordinate
    (B) coordinates
    (C) coordinated
    (D) coordination

122. According to the restaurant's -------, guests must wait to be seated by the front-of-house staff.
    (A) offerings
    (B) funds
    (C) bill
    (D) policy

123. Tickets for Saturday's football game sold out on Thursday, much sooner than organizers -------.
    (A) will anticipate
    (B) had anticipated
    (C) anticipating
    (D) to anticipate

124. Renewing your auto registration online ------- at the motor vehicle office will save you time.
    (A) just
    (B) neither
    (C) at any rate
    (D) rather than

125. ------- Latoya Model Management's sound reputation, aspiring models can expect a flourishing career.
    (A) Given
    (B) Ahead of
    (C) Preferably
    (D) Provided that

126. Employees are asked to update their contact information ------- the staff directory can be finalized.
    (A) so that
    (B) as though
    (C) namely
    (D) likewise

127. Glistonford Manufacturing cautions consumers not to buy inferior ------- of its adjustable desks.
    (A) imitates
    (B) imitative
    (C) imitated
    (D) imitations

128. ------- the fact that the use of social media is widespread, many people still rely on newspapers for fact-checked information.
    (A) Opposite
    (B) Without
    (C) Unlike
    (D) Despite

129. Citing energy efficiency and cost reductions, the presenter made several ------- arguments for installing solar panels.
    (A) absent
    (B) affordable
    (C) convincing
    (D) intrigued

130. After leaving his official government role, Dr. Beasly was ------- Director of the Nanboro Youth Farming Program.
    (A) hired
    (B) named
    (C) admitted
    (D) established

PART 6

Directions: Read the texts that follow. A word, phrase, or sentence is missing in parts of each text. Four answer choices for each question are given below the text. Select the best answer to complete the text. Then mark the letter (A), (B), (C), or (D) on your answer sheet.

Questions 131-134 refer to the following memo.

To: All Warehouse Employees
From: Paul Wandayi, Warehouse Manager
Date: 15 March
Re: New crates coming

Beginning 1 April, Windquest Farms will use Flexmerge crates to transport our fruits and vegetables. These ------- will simplify work and shrink operational costs.
     131.

Flexmerge crates are collapsible, which means they are easy to stack and they save space. ------- . They are also highly durable. This feature minimizes the need ------- frequent
132.   133.
replacement of crates. Finally, they are designed with ergonomic features, thereby

------- the risk of injuries. Safety is our top priority here at Windquest Farms.
134.

131. (A) desks
 (B) programs
 (C) agencies
 (D) containers

132. (A) We will need more of them in the months ahead.
 (B) More of them were bought by farmers and wholesalers.
 (C) Accordingly, more of them can be loaded onto trucks when empty.
 (D) Soon more of them will be available on our Web site.

133. (A) to
 (B) for
 (C) among
 (D) besides

134. (A) reducing
 (B) reduces
 (C) reduced
 (D) reducer

Questions 135-138 refer to the following article.

Popular TV Show Returns for Third Season

Sunday marks the start of the third season of the award-winning TV series *King of the Meer*. This political thriller ------- on the book *Whispered Illusions* by Noriaki Arishima.
135.

Some reviewers of the television series believe that the third season might be even better than the previous ones. ------- , other reviewers argue that the series might lose its appeal with the introduction of so many new characters, resulting in a complicated and confusing plotline.
136.

Director Amber Randolph has responded to that ------- . "The abundance of new characters
137.
can make the story challenging to follow," she said. "------- . We'll see what the fans of the
138.
show think."

135. (A) basing
(B) will be based
(C) was based
(D) is based

136. (A) From here on
(B) In contrast
(C) To be specific
(D) To sum up

137. (A) advertisement
(B) treatment
(C) criticism
(D) need

138. (A) But they succeeded despite many difficulties.
(B) But they bring greater depth to the narrative.
(C) But it will be a useful learning experience.
(D) But it brought them closer together.

Questions 139-142 refer to the following e-mail.

To: Jee-Wah Cho <cho8876@sunmail.com>
From: Ken Belfant <kenbelfant@fluffytimeindustries.com>
Date: 6 April
Subject: Recipe contest

Dear Ms. Cho,

Thank you for ------- your interesting recipe that uses our low-fat, sugar-free Fluffy Time Whipped
                139.
Topping. ------- has been entered into our upcoming contest. The winning recipes will appear on
        140.
our product's packaging. ------- . In the meantime, I will be sending you a coupon for 25 percent
                           141.
off your next purchase of any Fluffy Time product via a separate e-mail that you should receive

------- .
142.

We are so glad you enjoy our products. Best of luck in the contest!

With gratitude,

Ken Belfant, Promotions Coordinator
Fluffy Time Industries

---

139. (A) share
     (B) shared
     (C) sharing
     (D) shares

140. (A) It
     (B) One
     (C) Each
     (D) Theirs

141. (A) Fluffy Time is a favorite of children everywhere.
     (B) Contest winners will be notified in June.
     (C) We are sorry that you were disappointed.
     (D) You may want to try our chocolate cream recipe.

142. (A) briefly
     (B) concisely
     (C) temporarily
     (D) shortly

Questions 143-146 refer to the following brochure.

Bingo Imprint creates designs for promotional products such as notebooks, refrigerator magnets, and apparel. We allow our clients to determine their level of involvement in the design process. ------- (143.), some submit a detailed sketch of the design. Others are ------- (144.) content to leave the development and creation of the design up to our graphic artists. Once the invention has been finalized, it will be shared with the client for approval. ------- (145.) . We guarantee that all work will be completed within five business days from when the order is placed.

You can count ------- (146.) Bingo Imprint for unique designs, competitive pricing, and timely delivery.

143. (A) Similarly
 (B) However
 (C) As a result
 (D) In the meantime

144. (A) perfect
 (B) perfected
 (C) perfection
 (D) perfectly

145. (A) This step facilitates communication among employees.
 (B) This step ensures that the product satisfies expectations.
 (C) Customers appreciate the company's suggested alternative.
 (D) Customers have greeted this measure with great concern.

146. (A) along
 (B) down
 (C) off
 (D) on

PART 7

Directions: In this part you will read a selection of texts, such as magazine and newspaper articles, e-mails, and instant messages. Each text or set of texts is followed by several questions. Select the best answer for each question and mark the letter (A), (B), (C), or (D) on your answer sheet.

Questions 147-148 refer to the following form.

Crystal Brothers
Satisfaction Survey

Thank you for hiring Crystal Brothers to clean your building. Please circle the appropriate numbers, ranging from 5, "Excellent," to 1, "Poor." Circle "NP" for a type of room that is not present in the location that was cleaned.

Customer: Geraldine Hwang   Date: February 22

Cleaning Services						
Living room	5	④	3	2	1	NP
Kitchen	⑤	4	3	2	1	NP
Dining room	5	④	3	2	1	NP
Bedroom(s)	⑤	4	3	2	1	NP
Lobby	5	4	3	2	1	ⓃP
Conference room(s)	5	4	3	2	1	ⓃP
Other Information						
Was it easy to make an appointment?	5	4	3	2	①	
Did our staff follow your specific instructions?	⑤	4	3	2	1	
Did our staff provide information before the visit?	5	④	3	2	1	
Was the cost of the service what you expected?	⑤	4	3	2	1	

147. What type of building did Crystal Brothers clean?

    (A) A hotel
    (B) A warehouse
    (C) An office building
    (D) A home

148. What part of the cleaning service was Ms. Hwang least satisfied with?

    (A) The price
    (B) The scheduling
    (C) The customizing
    (D) The staffs punctuality

Questions 149-150 refer to the following Web page.

https://www.hamptonlandscaping.com/productdelivery

Product Delivery

Hampton Landscaping offers customers the option of having landscaping products delivered to their residences or businesses. This includes topsoil, compost, gravel, bark dust, firewood, and planting mixes. For your convenience, we offer large- and small-volume deliveries Monday through Saturday. Delivery rates vary based on volume, product, and location. Please call us at 904-555-0132 for detailed pricing. You do not need to be home for delivery. Please note that the requested delivery area must be accessible for our trucks. In the event that this requirement is not met, a $50 restocking fee will be charged.

149. What is true about Hampton Landscaping?

(A) It serves only private residences.
(B) It delivers orders of varying sizes.
(C) It charges one standard delivery fee.
(D) It makes deliveries seven days a week.

150. In what situation would a customer be billed $50 ?

(A) When the products to be delivered exceed a specific weight
(B) When the customer is not present to receive an order
(C) When the delivery address is not within the metro area
(D) When a delivery driver cannot access a drop-off location

Questions 151-152 refer to the following text-message chain.

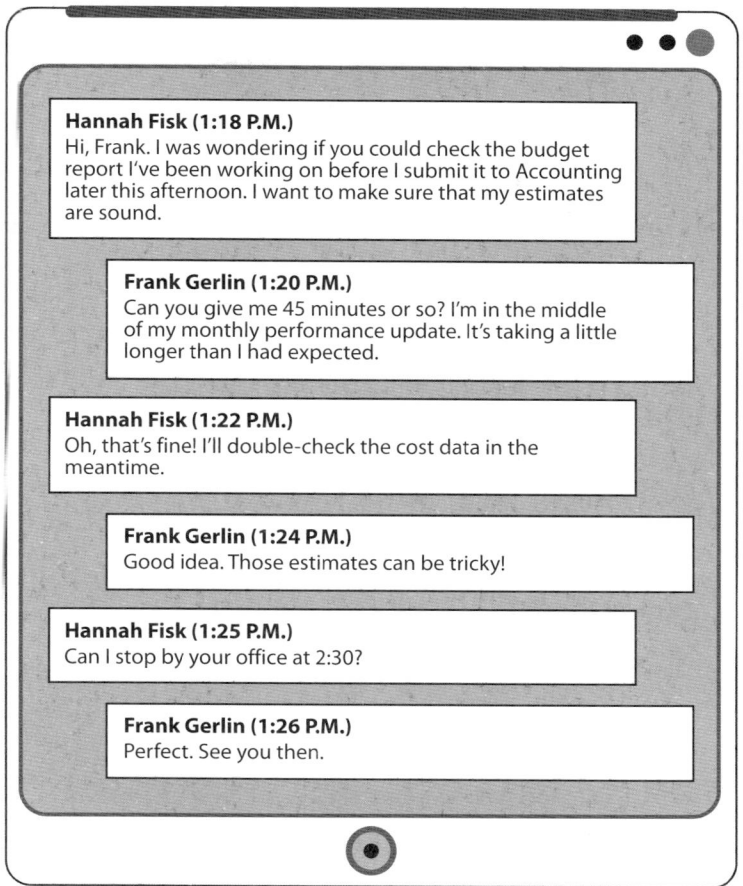

151. At 1:20 P.M., what does Mr. Gerlin imply when he writes, "Can you give me 45 minutes or so"?

(A) He is willing to assist Ms. Fisk later.
(B) His performance update was due yesterday.
(C) Compiling cost estimates should take less than an hour.
(D) He will complete the budget report himself.

152. What will Ms. Fisk most likely do next?

(A) She will work on her monthly performance update.
(B) She will ask Accounting to extend a deadline.
(C) She will contact another colleague for advice.
(D) She will review a portion of the budget report.

GO ON TO THE NEXT PAGE

Questions 153-154 refer to the following e-mail.

To:	Seo-Yun Jang <s_jang@lazulinamail.com>
From:	Travel Today <team@traveltoday.com>
Date:	March 18
Subject:	Price alert

Hello, Travel Today Subscriber,

You recently signed up for airfare notifications. Please see the information below for price cuts on your preferred trips. Remember that airlines usually offer a limited number of the lowest fares, so you may want to make a reservation soon to take advantage of these prices.

If you have questions or need assistance making reservations, please contact us at 210-555-0137.

Thank you,

Your Travel Today Team

Trip 1: Seattle to Chicago July 28 One way, 1 adult, economy seat		Trip 2: Los Angeles to New York August 15 One way, 1 adult, comfort-plus seat	
Nomata Airlines 1 stop (Denver) 2:42 P.M.–11:05 P.M.	Average price: $401 Current price: $315	Nomata Airlines 1 stop (Houston) 6:00 A.M.–5:32 P.M.	Average price: $465 Current price: $385
Blue Range Airways Nonstop 4:40 P.M.–10:40 P.M.	Average price: $439 Current price: $376	Blue Range Airways Nonstop 11:30 A.M.–8:00 P.M.	Average price: $518 Current price: $436

153. What is the purpose of the e-mail?

(A) To confirm a purchase
(B) To provide cost information
(C) To request a seat upgrade
(D) To cancel a reservation

154. What do both trips have in common?

(A) The departure date
(B) The destination city
(C) The choice of airlines
(D) The type of seating

Questions 155-157 refer to the following e-mail.

To:	rogelio.garza@gerimail.net
From:	sasha_lombardo@onyxmail.com
Date:	January 18
Subject:	My cookbook
Attachment:	📎 Draft manuscript

Rogelio,

Here is the latest draft of the cookbook I will be self-publishing. Thank you for reviewing my recipes to ensure they are easy to follow. Your input is much appreciated. — [1] —. This project has taken a lot of my energy over the past few years, and I am thrilled it is finally coming together. — [2] —.

I already received feedback from a few others and was told that the instructions in some places were confusingly worded. — [3] —. I am interested to know if you think so as well. I do have one request—when you respond, can you please include your comments in the margins so they are all in this one document? — [4] —.

You'll also notice that some pages have special boxes marked with a big red X. You can ignore those. I did not take great pictures of certain steps, so the Xs are reminders to take better ones to insert later.

Thanks again!

Sasha

155. What does Ms. Lombardo ask Mr. Garza to do?

(A) Make sure her recipes are clear
(B) Create an index of all her ingredients
(C) Suggest possible publishers for her book
(D) Help her format a final manuscript

156. What do boxes marked with a red X indicate?

(A) Ideas for formatting modifications
(B) Suggestions for inserting page breaks
(C) Images that need to be replaced
(D) Terms that should be defined

157. In which of the positions marked [1], [2], [3], and [4] does the following sentence best belong?

"Otherwise it is hard to keep track of all the changes."

(A) [1]
(B) [2]
(C) [3]
(D) [4]

Questions 158-160 refer to the following letter.

Priscilla Yamaguchi
Falkenweg 19
10719 Berlin

23 March

Dear Ms. Yamaguchi,

I am writing to you to share the exciting news that Aqua Voyage Cruise Lines will be expanding its fleet next July. As part of our plan, we would welcome the opportunity to form a partnership with you.

You have established a solid reputation regarding your restaurant chain, Saffron Moon. Your commitment to offering your customers across Europe unique and delicious menu items aligns with our vision for providing cruise-ship passengers with distinct restaurant options.

There are several benefits of entering into a partnership with us. Since our cruise excursions attract a diverse group of people, an even more extensive group will become familiar with your restaurant chain. Aqua Voyage Cruise Lines will mention your top-rated chain in our brochures and feature it on our Web site. Through our network of suppliers, we can help negotiate exceptionally low rates for recipe ingredients and restaurant equipment, thereby reducing your expenses.

If you are interested in pursuing this proposition and wish to discuss the details, you can reach me at kbasrawi@aquavoyagecruiselines.de or by phone at 30-23125 032.

Sincerely,

Khalid Basrawi

Khalid Basrawi, Vice President of Corporate Development
Aqua Voyage Cruise Lines

---

158. What is suggested about Ms. Yamaguchi?

(A) She has won several business awards.
(B) She has scheduled a cruise vacation in July.
(C) She operates restaurants in multiple European locations.
(D) She is planning to revise her restaurant chain's menu.

159. The word "solid" in paragraph 2, line 1, is closest in meaning to

(A) precise
(B) reliable
(C) compact
(D) thorough

160. What is NOT mentioned as a benefit of the proposed partnership?

(A) Increased advertising opportunities
(B) Lower cost for food preparation supplies
(C) Exposure to a new customer base
(D) Quality training programs

Questions 161-163 refer to the following article.

KMC Scores Major Triumph

WESTERN AUSTRALIA (21 June)—On 19 June, Western Australia's Karinya Medical Centre (KMC) was awarded the Valorcare Foundation's Stellar Service Merit, regarded as one of the highest honours an Australian hospital can receive. To qualify for the award, hospitals must meet a set of criteria, including timely access to care, superior medical outcomes, extensive staff training, and exceptional patient satisfaction.

"Congratulations to KMC's board of directors, management, and staff," said Lee Cinder, president of the Valorcare Foundation. "The centre has consistently demonstrated dedication to high-quality care; therefore, we are pleased to recognise it this year as one of the nation's outstanding medical facilities."

Dr. Linh Nguyen, who became CEO of KMC last March, said, "We are extremely proud that KMC is among the seven hospitals in the country recognised by the Valorcare Foundation. This award reflects our commitment to putting patient well-being at the forefront of everything we do. Since KMC opened its doors, we have set high patient care standards and strive to maintain this goal every year. For 47 years now, I believe we have been quite successful in this endeavour."

161. What is one purpose of the article?

(A) To announce a hospital merger
(B) To offer praise to an organization
(C) To explain the reasons for a leadership change
(D) To emphasize the need for high-quality care

162. What is NOT indicated about KMC?

(A) It has been in operation for more than four decades.
(B) It has high patient-satisfaction ratings.
(C) It recently appointed a new leader.
(D) It has received many honors over the years.

163. The word "reflects" in paragraph 3, line 5, is closest in meaning to

(A) shows
(B) notices
(C) imitates
(D) recommends

Questions 164-167 refer to the following online chat discussion.

Alexa Balog (4:02 P.M.) I'm on lifeguard duty today at Rosemoor Park. Jamie Kerr asked me to fill in for him. Just letting you know that I've had to close the pool several times because of the bad weather.

Maxwell Diego (4:03 P.M.) Is the weather bad right now?

Alexa Balog (4:03 P.M.) No, but it was raining heavily about 20 minutes ago.

Maxwell Diego (4:04 P.M.) Then you'll have to wait ten more minutes before reopening. As you know, the rule for Pool Guardian lifeguards is to wait for 30 minutes after bad weather passes.

Alexa Balog (4:06 P.M.) Yes, I understand. But no one has been here since 2:30. Can I close the pool now?

Maxwell Diego (4:07 P.M.) That would make sense. What's our policy on that, Mr. Nolan?

Wade Nolan (4:08 P.M.) Sorry, but we can't. Our contract says we must supply Rosemoor Park with a lifeguard until 5 P.M. on Thursdays. So Alexa needs to stay.

Alexa Balog (4:09 P.M.) OK. I'm in the equipment shed. I've been cleaning it up and straightening up the pool supplies here.

Wade Nolan (4:10 P.M.) But if there's heavy rain again after 4:30, just go ahead and close things up, Alexa.

Maxwell Diego (4:10 P.M.) It must be spotless now.

Alexa Balog (4:11 P.M.) It has never looked so good. And thanks, Mr. Nolan.

---

164. What can be concluded about Ms. Balog?

(A) She is afraid of heavy rain.
(B) She was hired to clean the pool.
(C) She is an employee of Pool Guardian.
(D) She works at Rosemoor Park every Thursday.

165. Why does Ms. Balog want to close the pool early?

(A) Because she has completed all her duties
(B) Because Mr. Kerr has not arrived
(C) Because she is not allowed to swim
(D) Because no guests are currently using the pool

166. What is implied about Rosemoor Park?

(A) It has a contract with a company that provides lifeguards.
(B) Its pool has been closed all week.
(C) Its pool has been poorly maintained.
(D) It would like to hire Ms. Balog to work full-time.

167. At 4:11 P.M., what does Ms. Balog most likely mean when she writes, "It has never looked so good"?

(A) She washed the pool deck.
(B) She did a good job organizing the equipment shed.
(C) The rain has finally stopped.
(D) The water in the pool is extremely clear.

Questions 168-171 refer to the following Web page.

---

https://www.sagemontservices.com

| Home | **About Us** | IT Services | Client Testimonials |

At Sagemont Services, we offer custom-tailored information technology solutions to clients in various industries. Founded over twenty years ago, Sagemont Services began as a start-up competing with larger businesses in a crowded field. — [1] —. Subsequently, we have become a leader in the industry. Our expert staff members are cross-trained in every aspect of our services.

We have helped several businesses complete technology projects on tight deadlines in the past few months. — [2] —. For example, with the online retailer Clothing Discounters rapidly expanding, we assisted the company in increasing its call-center capability. Specifically, in just two days, we provided the company with all the equipment and connections needed for newly hired customer-service agents to handle calls from home. — [3] —.

To learn more about how we meet the needs of our customers, please visit the Client Testimonials page. — [4] —.

---

168. What kind of business is Sagemont Services?

(A) A technology consulting firm
(B) A telephone service provider
(C) A computer software supplier
(D) An executive recruiting service

169. According to the Web page, what has Sagemont Services done recently?

(A) It has developed a series of online workshops.
(B) It has hired additional staff members.
(C) It has updated some space in its main office.
(D) It has completed projects within a short time period.

170. What is indicated about Clothing Discounters?

(A) It has won awards.
(B) It is growing quickly.
(C) It is less than one year old.
(D) It plans to open physical stores.

171. In which of the positions marked [1], [2], [3], and [4] does the following sentence best belong?

"This solution eliminated the possibility of business disruption."

(A) [1]
(B) [2]
(C) [3]
(D) [4]

Questions 172-175 refer to the following article.

MCAC to Exhibit Alonso's Works

MAURELY CITY (August 29)—Using recycled materials has become popular with artists, and local sculptor Ida Alonso has happily embraced this trend. Her new exhibition, *Throwaways into Treasure*, runs from today until November 4 at the Maurely City Art Center (MCAC). Ms. Alonso had the idea for the project while reading about recycled plastic being made into park benches in the *Journal for Professional Landscape Architects*. She then began to collect old plastic bottles and cardboard shipping boxes and innovatively combined them with commercially made, recyclable building materials.

For the exhibition, Ms. Alonso has created a life-size imitation of commercial offices, with cubicles and partitions made from recovered materials. "By means of my synthetic office space, I am hoping to highlight the idea that old, unwanted objects can take on a new purpose," Ms. Alonso said. Guests who attend the art show will have the opportunity to bring in their own recyclable plastic items and place them in large collection bags set up around the perimeter of the exhibition room. Ms. Alonso also plans to add more recyclable material to her installation as the show progresses.

Although MCAC will be the only venue for Ms. Alonso's show, the exhibition is expected to travel in a different sense. On the exhibition's final day, the works will be dismantled, and all the recyclable materials, including the items brought by visitors, will be transported to a Flyner Industries facility, where they will be shredded and transformed into material for waterproof curtains.

MCAC is open daily from 10:00 A.M. to 5:00 P.M. Admission to the art center is free. In addition to Ms. Alonso's show, works by several local art students will be on view in MCAC's main gallery.

172. What is indicated about Ms. Alonso?

(A) She manages her own art gallery.
(B) She previously worked for a shipping company.
(C) She was inspired by an article in a trade publication.
(D) She works part-time as an interior designer.

173. According to the article, what will visitors to Ms. Alonso's exhibition be able to do?

(A) Meet local artists in person
(B) Drop off recyclable plastics
(C) Operate specialized office equipment
(D) Purchase repurposed paper products

174. What will happen on November 4 ?

(A) Parts of an exhibition will be taken to an industrial plant.
(B) Some films about recycling will be shown.
(C) Winners of a slogan contest will be announced.
(D) An art center will close for renovations.

175. What is indicated about MCAC?

(A) It requires reservations to visit.
(B) It charges an entrance fee.
(C) It displays works by art students.
(D) It sponsors its own art workshops.

GO ON TO THE NEXT PAGE

Questions 176-180 refer to the following table and article.

Superb Hotels—Lisbon Customer Survey Results / June		
Feature	Satisfaction Level	Change from May
Guest room	91%	+8% ↑
Breakfast	82%	+10% ↑
Reception	80%	–5% ↓
Overall experience	87%	+7% ↑
Collected and analysed by Naomi Akdemir, Customer Solutions, Exelrate		

Exelrate Relocates Main Office

TORONTO (3 July)—Consumer analysis giant Exelrate will soon begin construction of its new headquarters in Toronto. Many well-known businesses use Exelrate's services to obtain an accurate understanding of their customers' experiences. The company's entry into North American markets is a promising sign of expected growth in the coming years. The recently promoted vice president of development, Rosa Martin, will be directing this expansion once she wraps up her work running the Customer Solutions Team at Exelrate's current headquarters in Frankfurt at the end of this month.

The new office building was designed by Frank Tsudama, whose latest project involved Seoul's futurist Global Trade Centre. Exelrate's building will feature a ground-level courtyard with seating areas for public use, symbolising its insertion into the community. The establishment of companies like Exelrate will help cement Toronto's fame as a centre for data and management consulting.

176. What does the table indicate about customers' satisfaction with their overall experience?

(A) It is mentioned in marketing materials.
(B) It is better than it was the previous month.
(C) It is reported on a quarterly basis.
(D) It decreased by five percent in June.

177. What is suggested about Exelrate?

(A) It both collects and analyzes data.
(B) It is a hotel chain.
(C) It renovates industrial buildings.
(D) It was founded in Toronto.

178. In the article, the word "directing" in paragraph 1, line 10, is closest in meaning to

(A) aiming
(B) leading
(C) financing
(D) addressing

179. Where was Ms. Akdemir's supervisor based in July?

(A) In Toronto
(B) In Lisbon
(C) In Frankfurt
(D) In Seoul

180. What is Mr. Tsudama's area of expertise?

(A) Management consulting
(B) Tourism
(C) Architecture
(D) Hospitality

Questions 181-185 refer to the following notice and review.

WELCOME TO RICHMOND SUPERMARKET!
DID YOU KNOW?

Richmond Supermarket is now offering cooking classes in our own state-of-the-art kitchen, the same kitchen where we create flavourful soups, salads, and entrées for our prepared foods department. Every Monday evening from 7:00 P.M. to 8:30 P.M. we turn our kitchen over to a guest chef from one of Richmond's many fine restaurants. Participants learn to prepare a different dish each week. Learn new techniques you can bring home to delight your friends and family! All classes use ingredients you can find right here in the store.

This month's classes are as follows:

2 August	Butter Chicken (India)
9 August	Pad Thai (Thailand)
16 August	Fish Tacos (Mexico)
23 August	Roast Vegetable Lasagna (Italy)

The fee for each class is $55.00. To register, please call us at 604-555-0175 or visit www.richmondsupermarket.ca. There is a limit of 15 students per class. Classes sell out quickly, so reserve your spot today.

---

https://www.richmondsupermarket.ca/reviews

| Online Shopping | Contact Us | **Reviews** | Cooking Classes |

Thanks to Richmond Supermarket's new cooking classes, community members can take lessons from some of the best chefs in the area. Last week I learned how to prepare fish tacos with Mateo Bernal, head chef at Bernal's Restaurant. We made every component of the tacos from scratch, including the corn tortillas, grilled tilapia, and tomatillo salsa. Before leaving, each attendee received a small notebook containing the recipe we made that day as well as a few of Mr. Bernal's other favourite recipes. I'm going to clear my Monday evenings so I can go back again and again!

—Astrid Klein

181. For whom is the notice most likely intended?
 (A) Kitchen workers
 (B) Store customers
 (C) Restaurant chefs
 (D) Cookbook authors

182. What is indicated in the notice about August's cooking classes at Richmond Supermarket?
 (A) They feature dishes from different countries.
 (B) They are held on different days of the week.
 (C) They are taught by supermarket employees.
 (D) They require students to register in person.

183. When most likely did Ms. Klein participate in a Richmond Supermarket cooking class?
 (A) On August 2
 (B) On August 9
 (C) On August 16
 (D) On August 23

184. What ingredient is NOT mentioned in the review?
 (A) Corn tortillas
 (B) Grilled tilapia
 (C) Tomatillo salsa
 (D) Shredded cabbage

185. What does Ms. Klein say she intends to do?
 (A) Take a trip to Mexico
 (B) Eat at Bernal's Restaurant
 (C) Attend more cooking classes
 (D) Collect recipes in a notebook

Questions 186-190 refer to the following article, schedule, and e-mail.

New Dean Appointed at Institute

YORK (17 January)—The Callard Eye Institute announced on Tuesday that Jennifer Robbins, M.D., has accepted the position of dean, effective immediately.

Dr. Robbins, who grew up in York, earned her medical degree at Labato School of Medicine and completed a postdoctoral residency at Petersen Medical Center. Before she arrived at the institute, Dr. Robbins was the founder and director of the ophthalmology clinic at Morseville Hospital. Her innovations in treating eye diseases have benefited thousands of patients worldwide.

On April 17, Dr. Robbins will be in Berlin to receive the Kramer Medal for Medical Excellence at this year's conference of the International Center for Vision Advancement.

International Center for Vision Advancement (ICVA) Conference
JT Pepper Convention Hall (17–19 April)
Rosenthaler Strasse 65, Berlin, Germany 25627

Day 1 Schedule: Monday, 17 April

8:00–10:00 A.M.	Breakfast	Maiwald Lounge
10:00–11:00 A.M.	Welcome and keynote address	Jahn Conference Hall
11:15 A.M.–1:15 P.M.	Session 1: New Technologies	Breakout rooms, as assigned
1:30–3:30 P.M.	Lunch group seminar	Edwards Room
3:45–5:45 P.M.	Session 2: Quality Eye Care	Breakout rooms, as assigned
6:00–7:30 P.M.	Free period	---
7:30–9:00 P.M.	Dinner	Regal Ballroom
9:00–9:30 P.M.	Dessert and awards ceremony	Regal Ballroom

```
                        *E-mail*
    To:       Dae-Ho Sohn
    From:     Paulina Raskin
    Subject:  Your presentation
    Date:     22 April
```

Dear Dr. Sohn,

I just wanted to thank you again for speaking at the ICVA conference in Berlin last week. I am sure I am not alone in saying that the highlight of the conference was your keynote address. Your insights into recent advancements in eye-surgery techniques captured the attention of everyone in the room. We were grateful that you could join us and even more appreciative of all the help and guidance you have provided in the past as an active member of the ICVA Board of Directors.

Sincerely,

Paulina Raskin
President, International Center for Vision Advancement

---

186. What is indicated about Dr. Robbins in the article?

(A) She is starting a new job.
(B) She owns a house in York.
(C) She specializes in designing eyeglasses.
(D) She has taught classes in Berlin.

187. Where did Dr. Robbins complete her postdoctoral residency?

(A) At the Callard Eye Institute
(B) At Labato School of Medicine
(C) At Petersen Medical Center
(D) At Morseville Hospital

188. Where most likely did Dr. Robbins receive the Kramer Medal?

(A) In the Maiwald Lounge
(B) In the Jahn Conference Hall
(C) In the Edwards Room
(D) In the Regal Ballroom

189. Why did Ms. Raskin send the e-mail to Dr. Sohn?

(A) To ask him to join the board of the ICVA
(B) To invite him to speak at a conference
(C) To request information about his surgical techniques
(D) To express gratitude for his participation in an event

190. When did Dr. Sohn most likely make a speech on April 17?

(A) At 8:00 A.M.
(B) At 10:00 A.M.
(C) At 11:15 A.M.
(D) At 3:45 P.M.

Questions 191-195 refer to the following Web page and e-mails.

---

https://www.freewheeloasis.com/trade-in-and-consignment

| Home | Service and Repair | **Trade-in and Consignment** | Accessories |

Freewheel Oasis offers two programs that make selling your bicycle easier: trade-in and consignment. If you select our trade-in program, you give us your bicycle, and, in exchange, we give you credit toward the purchase of a new one. If you opt for our consignment program, we will sell your bicycle for you.

To take advantage of either option, e-mail us at programs@freewheeloasis.com to schedule an appointment. In your e-mail, you should also indicate whether you wish to trade in your bicycle or place it on consignment. You will receive a response from our customer service manager. We take appointments during regular business hours, Monday through Saturday from 9:00 A.M. to 5:00 P.M.

When you come in for your appointment, a technician will assess the condition of your bicycle, and a sales associate will determine its current value. If the value specified is acceptable to you and you wish to trade in your bicycle, we deduct that amount from the purchase price of your new bicycle. If you prefer a consignment arrangement, we will sell your bicycle for the agreed-upon amount. Note that we will withhold a service fee equal to 15 percent of this amount at the time your bicycle is sold, while the rest of the earnings will be sent to you.

E-mail

To:	programs@freewheeloasis.com
From:	Nicola Johnson <njohnson92@rapidonet.com>
Date:	November 2
Subject:	Appointment request

Hello,

I have a mountain bicycle that is now six years old. However, I only used it for the first three years. I have tried to sell it myself but was not successful, so I would like to place it on consignment with you. Therefore, I would like to schedule an appointment.

Also, I recently accepted a job in Kuwait and will be leaving on November 30. Do you expect that the bicycle will be sold by then? If not, how can I receive my portion of the selling price?

Best regards,

Nicola Johnson

E-Mail Message

To: Nicola Johnson <njohnson92@rapidonet.com>
From: programs@freewheeloasis.com
Date: November 2
Subject: RE: Appointment request

Hi, Nicola,

Thanks for your interest in placing your bicycle on consignment with Freewheel Oasis. Your appointment is scheduled for Friday, November 4, at 3:00 P.M. Let me know if this arrangement works for you.

Our consignment policy stipulates that once the sale of a bicycle has been finalized, the money owed to the customer must be paid into the person's bank account. Please note that Freewheel Oasis cannot guarantee the sale of a bicycle by a date specified by the bicycle owner.

Best of luck with your new endeavor!

Sincerely,

Peter Moran

---

191. According to the Web page, what is suggested about Freewheel Oasis?

(A) It is currently having a sale on used bicycles.
(B) It performs inspections on certain bicycles.
(C) It has recently increased in popularity.
(D) It is open daily.

192. What does Ms. Johnson indicate in her e-mail?

(A) She regularly travels abroad.
(B) She got her bicycle six years ago.
(C) She prefers an appointment on November 30.
(D) She has made repairs to the bicycle by herself.

193. What can be concluded about Ms. Johnson?

(A) She is currently working in Kuwait.
(B) She has done business with Freewheel Oasis before.
(C) She has agreed to let Freewheel Oasis charge her a service fee.
(D) She plans to buy a bicycle from Freewheel Oasis.

194. What is one purpose of Mr. Moran's e-mail?

(A) To ask for additional information about a service request
(B) To request the rescheduling of an appointment
(C) To indicate the completion date of a service
(D) To state a company rule

195. Who most likely is Mr. Moran?

(A) A customer service manager
(B) A bank accountant
(C) A sales associate
(D) A bicycle repair technician

Questions 196-200 refer to the following e-mails and checklist.

To:	y.kuroda@coralmail.com
From:	simoncady@techsolve.com
Date:	May 12, 1:30 P.M.
Subject:	Paperwork
Attachment:	📎 Checklist

Dear Ms. Kuroda,

We still need a few things for your personnel file. At the training for new hires this morning, we provided you with a checklist of the documents that we need to have on file. For your reference, I've attached a scanned copy of your checklist to this e-mail.

First, our security office requires proof of your identity. Employees usually submit a copy of their driver's license (front and back) or the personal information page from their passport, but any official government identification is acceptable. We also require your banking information to set up the electronic transfer of your salary to your account.

The final item on the list will only be needed if you join the company softball team. Do you play? Our company team participates in a league, and it's a great way to build rapport with the people you will be working alongside. The season is just beginning. I can send you details if you're interested.

Finally, I want to encourage you to attend the company picnic, which is always held on the third Friday in May at Briarwood Park. It's an opportunity to interact with your coworkers in an informal, nonworking environment. It's always well attended.

If you have any questions, contact me and we can schedule a chat.

Simon Cady, Human Resources Division
Techsolve, Inc.

New Employee Forms Checklist

Name: Yumiko Kuroda
Department: Data entry
Start Date: May 15

_____ 1. Proof of identity (copy of driver's license, passport, or other official ID)
✓ 2. Personal data form
✓ 3. Tax withholding form
_____ 4. Bank account information form
✓ 5. Insurance selection form
_____ 6. Release of liability form (if required)

```
E-Mail Message
```

To: simoncady@techsolve.com
From: y.kuroda@coralmail.com
Date: May 12, 3:21 P.M.
Subject: Re: Paperwork

Hello Mr. Cady,

Thank you for your e-mail. I am excited about starting work. And thanks, too, for sending a copy of the checklist I received in the orientation session. I don't drive, so I don't have a driver's license, but I can provide a copy of the page from my passport. I am about to gather the necessary information for the fourth item on the list. I will bring everything to the office on Monday.

I'll have to think about whether I want to join the company softball team. How much of a time commitment is it? I played softball in college. I wasn't very good, but I did enjoy playing.

The company picnic sounds like fun. I love Briarwood Park and look forward to the opportunity to get to know my coworkers better. If employees bring dishes for the picnic, I'd be happy to make something. Or is the food being provided by a caterer?

Thanks again for your support.

Yumiko Kuroda

---

196. What is the main purpose of the first e-mail?
(A) To offer Ms. Kuroda a job
(B) To request some documents
(C) To invite Ms. Kuroda to watch a ball game
(D) To schedule an appointment

197. Where most likely was Ms. Kuroda on the morning of May 12?
(A) At a training for new hires
(B) At a job interview
(C) At a security office
(D) At a college reunion

198. Why might Ms. Kuroda need to submit a release form?
(A) If she borrows some money
(B) If she plays on a sports team
(C) If she attends a social event
(D) If she gets a promotion

199. What does Ms. Kuroda indicate about a company picnic?
(A) She does not know where it will take place.
(B) She does not know whether she can go to it.
(C) She is eager to meet her coworkers there.
(D) She would be happy to organize the catering for it.

200. What will Ms. Kuroda most likely do next?
(A) Eat lunch with her coworkers
(B) Look for details of her bank account
(C) E-mail a list to Mr. Cady
(D) Ask Mr. Cady about applying for a passport

Stop! This is the end of the test. If you finish before time is called, you may go back to Parts 5, 6, and 7 and check your work.

RC

ANSWERS

TEST 1
TEST 2
TEST 3
TEST 4
TEST 5
TEST 6
TEST 7
TEST 8
TEST 9
TEST 10

기출 TEST 1

101 (B)	102 (A)	103 (A)	104 (B)	105 (B)
106 (C)	107 (C)	108 (D)	109 (A)	110 (A)
111 (C)	112 (C)	113 (A)	114 (C)	115 (C)
116 (D)	117 (A)	118 (D)	119 (C)	120 (B)
121 (D)	122 (C)	123 (B)	124 (C)	125 (A)
126 (A)	127 (D)	128 (D)	129 (D)	130 (B)
131 (D)	132 (C)	133 (A)	134 (B)	135 (D)
136 (C)	137 (B)	138 (A)	139 (A)	140 (C)
141 (B)	142 (D)	143 (C)	144 (C)	145 (B)
146 (A)	147 (C)	148 (D)	149 (B)	150 (C)
151 (D)	152 (C)	153 (B)	154 (C)	155 (D)
156 (C)	157 (B)	158 (D)	159 (B)	160 (C)
161 (C)	162 (D)	163 (B)	164 (B)	165 (B)
166 (A)	167 (B)	168 (C)	169 (B)	170 (B)
171 (A)	172 (D)	173 (A)	174 (B)	175 (C)
176 (A)	177 (D)	178 (C)	179 (D)	180 (C)
181 (D)	182 (D)	183 (A)	184 (C)	185 (B)
186 (B)	187 (A)	188 (B)	189 (A)	190 (D)
191 (D)	192 (B)	193 (B)	194 (A)	195 (A)
196 (B)	197 (A)	198 (D)	199 (C)	200 (A)

기출 TEST 2

101 (C)	102 (A)	103 (D)	104 (B)	105 (A)
106 (D)	107 (D)	108 (C)	109 (A)	110 (A)
111 (C)	112 (D)	113 (C)	114 (D)	115 (B)
116 (C)	117 (A)	118 (C)	119 (D)	120 (C)
121 (A)	122 (B)	123 (A)	124 (C)	125 (B)
126 (D)	127 (D)	128 (C)	129 (B)	130 (A)
131 (D)	132 (B)	133 (A)	134 (D)	135 (A)
136 (A)	137 (D)	138 (D)	139 (B)	140 (C)
141 (D)	142 (A)	143 (B)	144 (D)	145 (B)
146 (B)	147 (D)	148 (C)	149 (B)	150 (C)
151 (A)	152 (B)	153 (C)	154 (C)	155 (A)
156 (B)	157 (B)	158 (C)	159 (B)	160 (B)
161 (D)	162 (B)	163 (D)	164 (C)	165 (B)
166 (A)	167 (B)	168 (C)	169 (B)	170 (D)
171 (B)	172 (C)	173 (A)	174 (C)	175 (B)
176 (A)	177 (C)	178 (B)	179 (D)	180 (C)
181 (D)	182 (B)	183 (C)	184 (D)	185 (A)
186 (C)	187 (C)	188 (A)	189 (D)	190 (D)
191 (A)	192 (C)	193 (D)	194 (C)	195 (B)
196 (B)	197 (A)	198 (C)	199 (C)	200 (D)

기출 TEST 3

101 (B)	102 (A)	103 (B)	104 (C)	105 (D)
106 (B)	107 (A)	108 (B)	109 (A)	110 (C)
111 (B)	112 (C)	113 (B)	114 (B)	115 (D)
116 (A)	117 (D)	118 (D)	119 (A)	120 (A)
121 (B)	122 (C)	123 (D)	124 (A)	125 (B)
126 (A)	127 (C)	128 (C)	129 (C)	130 (A)
131 (A)	132 (D)	133 (A)	134 (B)	135 (B)
136 (B)	137 (A)	138 (C)	139 (B)	140 (D)
141 (C)	142 (A)	143 (B)	144 (C)	145 (D)
146 (C)	147 (D)	148 (C)	149 (B)	150 (D)
151 (C)	152 (D)	153 (A)	154 (C)	155 (A)
156 (D)	157 (C)	158 (C)	159 (D)	160 (A)
161 (B)	162 (D)	163 (B)	164 (A)	165 (C)
166 (C)	167 (A)	168 (C)	169 (D)	170 (C)
171 (D)	172 (A)	173 (D)	174 (B)	175 (D)
176 (C)	177 (B)	178 (A)	179 (D)	180 (B)
181 (B)	182 (C)	183 (B)	184 (A)	185 (D)
186 (A)	187 (B)	188 (C)	189 (D)	190 (C)
191 (B)	192 (D)	193 (A)	194 (B)	195 (B)
196 (A)	197 (B)	198 (C)	199 (D)	200 (D)

기출 TEST 4

101 (D)	102 (B)	103 (B)	104 (C)	105 (B)
106 (A)	107 (B)	108 (A)	109 (B)	110 (C)
111 (B)	112 (A)	113 (B)	114 (A)	115 (C)
116 (D)	117 (A)	118 (A)	119 (B)	120 (A)
121 (C)	122 (A)	123 (D)	124 (A)	125 (C)
126 (D)	127 (C)	128 (C)	129 (A)	130 (D)
131 (C)	132 (D)	133 (D)	134 (A)	135 (C)
136 (A)	137 (D)	138 (B)	139 (A)	140 (C)
141 (D)	142 (B)	143 (B)	144 (A)	145 (C)
146 (D)	147 (A)	148 (D)	149 (B)	150 (D)
151 (A)	152 (D)	153 (B)	154 (D)	155 (B)
156 (B)	157 (C)	158 (B)	159 (D)	160 (C)
161 (A)	162 (B)	163 (C)	164 (C)	165 (D)
166 (C)	167 (B)	168 (A)	169 (B)	170 (B)
171 (D)	172 (A)	173 (B)	174 (D)	175 (A)
176 (C)	177 (D)	178 (D)	179 (C)	180 (A)
181 (B)	182 (A)	183 (D)	184 (C)	185 (B)
186 (B)	187 (A)	188 (B)	189 (D)	190 (C)
191 (C)	192 (B)	193 (B)	194 (A)	195 (D)
196 (A)	197 (D)	198 (C)	199 (B)	200 (A)

기출 TEST 5

101 (C)	102 (A)	103 (B)	104 (B)	105 (D)
106 (A)	107 (C)	108 (A)	109 (A)	110 (C)
111 (B)	112 (C)	113 (C)	114 (B)	115 (B)
116 (D)	117 (C)	118 (C)	119 (C)	120 (A)
121 (C)	122 (D)	123 (C)	124 (D)	125 (B)
126 (B)	127 (B)	128 (B)	129 (C)	130 (D)
131 (A)	132 (A)	133 (C)	134 (C)	135 (D)
136 (C)	137 (B)	138 (C)	139 (C)	140 (A)
141 (A)	142 (D)	143 (A)	144 (C)	145 (A)
146 (B)	147 (C)	148 (C)	149 (A)	150 (D)
151 (B)	152 (D)	153 (D)	154 (A)	155 (C)
156 (D)	157 (D)	158 (C)	159 (A)	160 (B)
161 (C)	162 (D)	163 (B)	164 (D)	165 (D)
166 (B)	167 (D)	168 (A)	169 (C)	170 (D)
171 (B)	172 (D)	173 (A)	174 (C)	175 (B)
176 (C)	177 (B)	178 (C)	179 (D)	180 (B)
181 (A)	182 (C)	183 (D)	184 (B)	185 (C)
186 (A)	187 (D)	188 (C)	189 (A)	190 (B)
191 (A)	192 (D)	193 (C)	194 (C)	195 (D)
196 (B)	197 (B)	198 (D)	199 (D)	200 (C)

기출 TEST 6

101 (C)	102 (A)	103 (B)	104 (B)	105 (D)
106 (A)	107 (D)	108 (A)	109 (B)	110 (D)
111 (C)	112 (A)	113 (C)	114 (D)	115 (A)
116 (D)	117 (B)	118 (C)	119 (B)	120 (C)
121 (B)	122 (B)	123 (A)	124 (A)	125 (D)
126 (D)	127 (B)	128 (C)	129 (C)	130 (D)
131 (C)	132 (A)	133 (D)	134 (B)	135 (D)
136 (A)	137 (C)	138 (A)	139 (A)	140 (C)
141 (B)	142 (A)	143 (A)	144 (C)	145 (B)
146 (A)	147 (B)	148 (D)	149 (B)	150 (D)
151 (A)	152 (B)	153 (D)	154 (D)	155 (A)
156 (C)	157 (C)	158 (A)	159 (B)	160 (B)
161 (C)	162 (D)	163 (D)	164 (C)	165 (B)
166 (D)	167 (A)	168 (C)	169 (C)	170 (C)
171 (B)	172 (B)	173 (C)	174 (D)	175 (D)
176 (B)	177 (A)	178 (C)	179 (D)	180 (A)
181 (D)	182 (D)	183 (C)	184 (B)	185 (C)
186 (B)	187 (C)	188 (A)	189 (C)	190 (B)
191 (B)	192 (A)	193 (A)	194 (C)	195 (B)
196 (B)	197 (D)	198 (C)	199 (A)	200 (C)

기출 TEST 7

101 (A)	102 (B)	103 (B)	104 (A)	105 (D)
106 (D)	107 (A)	108 (B)	109 (A)	110 (B)
111 (A)	112 (D)	113 (C)	114 (D)	115 (B)
116 (A)	117 (C)	118 (D)	119 (C)	120 (C)
121 (D)	122 (B)	123 (A)	124 (A)	125 (B)
126 (C)	127 (D)	128 (D)	129 (A)	130 (B)
131 (C)	132 (A)	133 (D)	134 (B)	135 (B)
136 (A)	137 (C)	138 (B)	139 (D)	140 (B)
141 (B)	142 (C)	143 (B)	144 (D)	145 (A)
146 (C)	147 (A)	148 (B)	149 (A)	150 (B)
151 (B)	152 (A)	153 (B)	154 (A)	155 (C)
156 (D)	157 (B)	158 (B)	159 (C)	160 (A)
161 (C)	162 (C)	163 (B)	164 (B)	165 (D)
166 (C)	167 (B)	168 (C)	169 (C)	170 (C)
171 (D)	172 (A)	173 (B)	174 (D)	175 (D)
176 (B)	177 (D)	178 (C)	179 (C)	180 (A)
181 (C)	182 (D)	183 (D)	184 (B)	185 (A)
186 (B)	187 (C)	188 (C)	189 (D)	190 (D)
191 (C)	192 (A)	193 (B)	194 (D)	195 (B)
196 (A)	197 (D)	198 (C)	199 (A)	200 (D)

기출 TEST 8

101 (B)	102 (A)	103 (B)	104 (A)	105 (C)
106 (B)	107 (B)	108 (C)	109 (D)	110 (A)
111 (C)	112 (B)	113 (D)	114 (B)	115 (D)
116 (B)	117 (A)	118 (C)	119 (C)	120 (D)
121 (A)	122 (D)	123 (C)	124 (A)	125 (C)
126 (C)	127 (D)	128 (A)	129 (B)	130 (B)
131 (B)	132 (A)	133 (D)	134 (A)	135 (C)
136 (B)	137 (D)	138 (A)	139 (D)	140 (B)
141 (C)	142 (B)	143 (B)	144 (A)	145 (D)
146 (A)	147 (C)	148 (B)	149 (A)	150 (D)
151 (C)	152 (B)	153 (B)	154 (C)	155 (C)
156 (A)	157 (C)	158 (C)	159 (A)	160 (B)
161 (A)	162 (B)	163 (D)	164 (D)	165 (B)
166 (C)	167 (A)	168 (C)	169 (D)	170 (A)
171 (D)	172 (A)	173 (A)	174 (D)	175 (C)
176 (D)	177 (B)	178 (A)	179 (C)	180 (A)
181 (B)	182 (A)	183 (C)	184 (C)	185 (D)
186 (D)	187 (B)	188 (C)	189 (C)	190 (B)
191 (A)	192 (B)	193 (C)	194 (B)	195 (D)
196 (D)	197 (B)	198 (B)	199 (C)	200 (D)

기출 TEST 9

101 (A)	102 (B)	103 (B)	104 (C)	105 (A)
106 (A)	107 (C)	108 (A)	109 (B)	110 (D)
111 (C)	112 (A)	113 (C)	114 (B)	115 (D)
116 (A)	117 (C)	118 (B)	119 (D)	120 (D)
121 (D)	122 (B)	123 (C)	124 (C)	125 (A)
126 (B)	127 (B)	128 (B)	129 (D)	130 (A)
131 (B)	132 (D)	133 (A)	134 (C)	135 (D)
136 (B)	137 (A)	138 (B)	139 (C)	140 (D)
141 (A)	142 (D)	143 (D)	144 (C)	145 (A)
146 (A)	147 (D)	148 (A)	149 (D)	150 (B)
151 (C)	152 (D)	153 (B)	154 (D)	155 (A)
156 (B)	157 (B)	158 (D)	159 (C)	160 (B)
161 (A)	162 (C)	163 (D)	164 (C)	165 (B)
166 (C)	167 (D)	168 (C)	169 (A)	170 (B)
171 (C)	172 (A)	173 (B)	174 (C)	175 (D)
176 (D)	177 (D)	178 (A)	179 (B)	180 (C)
181 (C)	182 (A)	183 (D)	184 (C)	185 (B)
186 (B)	187 (A)	188 (C)	189 (D)	190 (B)
191 (C)	192 (D)	193 (C)	194 (A)	195 (B)
196 (A)	197 (C)	198 (A)	199 (C)	200 (B)

기출 TEST 10

101 (A)	102 (D)	103 (B)	104 (A)	105 (D)
106 (B)	107 (A)	108 (B)	109 (D)	110 (B)
111 (B)	112 (A)	113 (B)	114 (D)	115 (C)
116 (B)	117 (C)	118 (A)	119 (B)	120 (A)
121 (C)	122 (D)	123 (B)	124 (D)	125 (A)
126 (A)	127 (D)	128 (D)	129 (C)	130 (B)
131 (D)	132 (C)	133 (B)	134 (A)	135 (D)
136 (B)	137 (C)	138 (B)	139 (C)	140 (A)
141 (B)	142 (D)	143 (C)	144 (D)	145 (B)
146 (D)	147 (D)	148 (B)	149 (B)	150 (D)
151 (A)	152 (D)	153 (B)	154 (C)	155 (A)
156 (C)	157 (C)	158 (C)	159 (B)	160 (D)
161 (B)	162 (D)	163 (A)	164 (C)	165 (D)
166 (A)	167 (B)	168 (A)	169 (D)	170 (B)
171 (C)	172 (C)	173 (B)	174 (A)	175 (C)
176 (B)	177 (A)	178 (B)	179 (C)	180 (C)
181 (B)	182 (A)	183 (C)	184 (D)	185 (C)
186 (A)	187 (C)	188 (D)	189 (D)	190 (B)
191 (B)	192 (B)	193 (C)	194 (D)	195 (A)
196 (B)	197 (A)	198 (B)	199 (C)	200 (B)

ANSWER SHEET

ETS 토익 정기시험 기출문제집

성명 (한글/한자/영자)

수험번호

응시일자 : 20   년   월   일

Test 01 (Part 5~7)

101–200

Test 02 (Part 5~7)

101–200

ANSWER SHEET

ETS 토익 정기시험 기출문제집

수험번호

응시일자 : 20   년   월   일

성명
- 한글
- 한자
- 영자

Test 03 (Part 5~7)

번호	답	번호	답	번호	답	번호	답
101	ⓐⓑⓒⓓ	121	ⓐⓑⓒⓓ	141	ⓐⓑⓒⓓ	161	ⓐⓑⓒⓓ	181	ⓐⓑⓒⓓ
102	ⓐⓑⓒⓓ	122	ⓐⓑⓒⓓ	142	ⓐⓑⓒⓓ	162	ⓐⓑⓒⓓ	182	ⓐⓑⓒⓓ
103	ⓐⓑⓒⓓ	123	ⓐⓑⓒⓓ	143	ⓐⓑⓒⓓ	163	ⓐⓑⓒⓓ	183	ⓐⓑⓒⓓ
104	ⓐⓑⓒⓓ	124	ⓐⓑⓒⓓ	144	ⓐⓑⓒⓓ	164	ⓐⓑⓒⓓ	184	ⓐⓑⓒⓓ
105	ⓐⓑⓒⓓ	125	ⓐⓑⓒⓓ	145	ⓐⓑⓒⓓ	165	ⓐⓑⓒⓓ	185	ⓐⓑⓒⓓ
106	ⓐⓑⓒⓓ	126	ⓐⓑⓒⓓ	146	ⓐⓑⓒⓓ	166	ⓐⓑⓒⓓ	186	ⓐⓑⓒⓓ
107	ⓐⓑⓒⓓ	127	ⓐⓑⓒⓓ	147	ⓐⓑⓒⓓ	167	ⓐⓑⓒⓓ	187	ⓐⓑⓒⓓ
108	ⓐⓑⓒⓓ	128	ⓐⓑⓒⓓ	148	ⓐⓑⓒⓓ	168	ⓐⓑⓒⓓ	188	ⓐⓑⓒⓓ
109	ⓐⓑⓒⓓ	129	ⓐⓑⓒⓓ	149	ⓐⓑⓒⓓ	169	ⓐⓑⓒⓓ	189	ⓐⓑⓒⓓ
110	ⓐⓑⓒⓓ	130	ⓐⓑⓒⓓ	150	ⓐⓑⓒⓓ	170	ⓐⓑⓒⓓ	190	ⓐⓑⓒⓓ
111	ⓐⓑⓒⓓ	131	ⓐⓑⓒⓓ	151	ⓐⓑⓒⓓ	171	ⓐⓑⓒⓓ	191	ⓐⓑⓒⓓ
112	ⓐⓑⓒⓓ	132	ⓐⓑⓒⓓ	152	ⓐⓑⓒⓓ	172	ⓐⓑⓒⓓ	192	ⓐⓑⓒⓓ
113	ⓐⓑⓒⓓ	133	ⓐⓑⓒⓓ	153	ⓐⓑⓒⓓ	173	ⓐⓑⓒⓓ	193	ⓐⓑⓒⓓ
114	ⓐⓑⓒⓓ	134	ⓐⓑⓒⓓ	154	ⓐⓑⓒⓓ	174	ⓐⓑⓒⓓ	194	ⓐⓑⓒⓓ
115	ⓐⓑⓒⓓ	135	ⓐⓑⓒⓓ	155	ⓐⓑⓒⓓ	175	ⓐⓑⓒⓓ	195	ⓐⓑⓒⓓ
116	ⓐⓑⓒⓓ	136	ⓐⓑⓒⓓ	156	ⓐⓑⓒⓓ	176	ⓐⓑⓒⓓ	196	ⓐⓑⓒⓓ
117	ⓐⓑⓒⓓ	137	ⓐⓑⓒⓓ	157	ⓐⓑⓒⓓ	177	ⓐⓑⓒⓓ	197	ⓐⓑⓒⓓ
118	ⓐⓑⓒⓓ	138	ⓐⓑⓒⓓ	158	ⓐⓑⓒⓓ	178	ⓐⓑⓒⓓ	198	ⓐⓑⓒⓓ
119	ⓐⓑⓒⓓ	139	ⓐⓑⓒⓓ	159	ⓐⓑⓒⓓ	179	ⓐⓑⓒⓓ	199	ⓐⓑⓒⓓ
120	ⓐⓑⓒⓓ	140	ⓐⓑⓒⓓ	160	ⓐⓑⓒⓓ	180	ⓐⓑⓒⓓ	200	ⓐⓑⓒⓓ

Test 04 (Part 5~7)

번호	답	번호	답	번호	답	번호	답	번호	답
101	ⓐⓑⓒⓓ	121	ⓐⓑⓒⓓ	141	ⓐⓑⓒⓓ	161	ⓐⓑⓒⓓ	181	ⓐⓑⓒⓓ
102	ⓐⓑⓒⓓ	122	ⓐⓑⓒⓓ	142	ⓐⓑⓒⓓ	162	ⓐⓑⓒⓓ	182	ⓐⓑⓒⓓ
103	ⓐⓑⓒⓓ	123	ⓐⓑⓒⓓ	143	ⓐⓑⓒⓓ	163	ⓐⓑⓒⓓ	183	ⓐⓑⓒⓓ
104	ⓐⓑⓒⓓ	124	ⓐⓑⓒⓓ	144	ⓐⓑⓒⓓ	164	ⓐⓑⓒⓓ	184	ⓐⓑⓒⓓ
105	ⓐⓑⓒⓓ	125	ⓐⓑⓒⓓ	145	ⓐⓑⓒⓓ	165	ⓐⓑⓒⓓ	185	ⓐⓑⓒⓓ
106	ⓐⓑⓒⓓ	126	ⓐⓑⓒⓓ	146	ⓐⓑⓒⓓ	166	ⓐⓑⓒⓓ	186	ⓐⓑⓒⓓ
107	ⓐⓑⓒⓓ	127	ⓐⓑⓒⓓ	147	ⓐⓑⓒⓓ	167	ⓐⓑⓒⓓ	187	ⓐⓑⓒⓓ
108	ⓐⓑⓒⓓ	128	ⓐⓑⓒⓓ	148	ⓐⓑⓒⓓ	168	ⓐⓑⓒⓓ	188	ⓐⓑⓒⓓ
109	ⓐⓑⓒⓓ	129	ⓐⓑⓒⓓ	149	ⓐⓑⓒⓓ	169	ⓐⓑⓒⓓ	189	ⓐⓑⓒⓓ
110	ⓐⓑⓒⓓ	130	ⓐⓑⓒⓓ	150	ⓐⓑⓒⓓ	170	ⓐⓑⓒⓓ	190	ⓐⓑⓒⓓ
111	ⓐⓑⓒⓓ	131	ⓐⓑⓒⓓ	151	ⓐⓑⓒⓓ	171	ⓐⓑⓒⓓ	191	ⓐⓑⓒⓓ
112	ⓐⓑⓒⓓ	132	ⓐⓑⓒⓓ	152	ⓐⓑⓒⓓ	172	ⓐⓑⓒⓓ	192	ⓐⓑⓒⓓ
113	ⓐⓑⓒⓓ	133	ⓐⓑⓒⓓ	153	ⓐⓑⓒⓓ	173	ⓐⓑⓒⓓ	193	ⓐⓑⓒⓓ
114	ⓐⓑⓒⓓ	134	ⓐⓑⓒⓓ	154	ⓐⓑⓒⓓ	174	ⓐⓑⓒⓓ	194	ⓐⓑⓒⓓ
115	ⓐⓑⓒⓓ	135	ⓐⓑⓒⓓ	155	ⓐⓑⓒⓓ	175	ⓐⓑⓒⓓ	195	ⓐⓑⓒⓓ
116	ⓐⓑⓒⓓ	136	ⓐⓑⓒⓓ	156	ⓐⓑⓒⓓ	176	ⓐⓑⓒⓓ	196	ⓐⓑⓒⓓ
117	ⓐⓑⓒⓓ	137	ⓐⓑⓒⓓ	157	ⓐⓑⓒⓓ	177	ⓐⓑⓒⓓ	197	ⓐⓑⓒⓓ
118	ⓐⓑⓒⓓ	138	ⓐⓑⓒⓓ	158	ⓐⓑⓒⓓ	178	ⓐⓑⓒⓓ	198	ⓐⓑⓒⓓ
119	ⓐⓑⓒⓓ	139	ⓐⓑⓒⓓ	159	ⓐⓑⓒⓓ	179	ⓐⓑⓒⓓ	199	ⓐⓑⓒⓓ
120	ⓐⓑⓒⓓ	140	ⓐⓑⓒⓓ	160	ⓐⓑⓒⓓ	180	ⓐⓑⓒⓓ	200	ⓐⓑⓒⓓ

ANSWER SHEET

ETS 토익 정기시험 기출문제집

성명
- 한글
- 한자
- 영자

수험번호

응시일자 : 20   년   월   일

Test 05 (Part 5~7)

Test 06 (Part 5~7)

ANSWER SHEET

ETS 토익 정기시험 기출문제집

Test 07 (Part 5~7)

Test 08 (Part 5~7)

ANSWER SHEET

ETS 토익 정기시험 기출문제집

성명: 한글 / 한자 / 영자

수험번호

응시일자: 20   년   월   일

Test 09 (Part 5~7)

101	ⓐⓑⓒⓓ	121	ⓐⓑⓒⓓ	141	ⓐⓑⓒⓓ	161	ⓐⓑⓒⓓ	181	ⓐⓑⓒⓓ
102	ⓐⓑⓒⓓ	122	ⓐⓑⓒⓓ	142	ⓐⓑⓒⓓ	162	ⓐⓑⓒⓓ	182	ⓐⓑⓒⓓ
103	ⓐⓑⓒⓓ	123	ⓐⓑⓒⓓ	143	ⓐⓑⓒⓓ	163	ⓐⓑⓒⓓ	183	ⓐⓑⓒⓓ
104	ⓐⓑⓒⓓ	124	ⓐⓑⓒⓓ	144	ⓐⓑⓒⓓ	164	ⓐⓑⓒⓓ	184	ⓐⓑⓒⓓ
105	ⓐⓑⓒⓓ	125	ⓐⓑⓒⓓ	145	ⓐⓑⓒⓓ	165	ⓐⓑⓒⓓ	185	ⓐⓑⓒⓓ
106	ⓐⓑⓒⓓ	126	ⓐⓑⓒⓓ	146	ⓐⓑⓒⓓ	166	ⓐⓑⓒⓓ	186	ⓐⓑⓒⓓ
107	ⓐⓑⓒⓓ	127	ⓐⓑⓒⓓ	147	ⓐⓑⓒⓓ	167	ⓐⓑⓒⓓ	187	ⓐⓑⓒⓓ
108	ⓐⓑⓒⓓ	128	ⓐⓑⓒⓓ	148	ⓐⓑⓒⓓ	168	ⓐⓑⓒⓓ	188	ⓐⓑⓒⓓ
109	ⓐⓑⓒⓓ	129	ⓐⓑⓒⓓ	149	ⓐⓑⓒⓓ	169	ⓐⓑⓒⓓ	189	ⓐⓑⓒⓓ
110	ⓐⓑⓒⓓ	130	ⓐⓑⓒⓓ	150	ⓐⓑⓒⓓ	170	ⓐⓑⓒⓓ	190	ⓐⓑⓒⓓ
111	ⓐⓑⓒⓓ	131	ⓐⓑⓒⓓ	151	ⓐⓑⓒⓓ	171	ⓐⓑⓒⓓ	191	ⓐⓑⓒⓓ
112	ⓐⓑⓒⓓ	132	ⓐⓑⓒⓓ	152	ⓐⓑⓒⓓ	172	ⓐⓑⓒⓓ	192	ⓐⓑⓒⓓ
113	ⓐⓑⓒⓓ	133	ⓐⓑⓒⓓ	153	ⓐⓑⓒⓓ	173	ⓐⓑⓒⓓ	193	ⓐⓑⓒⓓ
114	ⓐⓑⓒⓓ	134	ⓐⓑⓒⓓ	154	ⓐⓑⓒⓓ	174	ⓐⓑⓒⓓ	194	ⓐⓑⓒⓓ
115	ⓐⓑⓒⓓ	135	ⓐⓑⓒⓓ	155	ⓐⓑⓒⓓ	175	ⓐⓑⓒⓓ	195	ⓐⓑⓒⓓ
116	ⓐⓑⓒⓓ	136	ⓐⓑⓒⓓ	156	ⓐⓑⓒⓓ	176	ⓐⓑⓒⓓ	196	ⓐⓑⓒⓓ
117	ⓐⓑⓒⓓ	137	ⓐⓑⓒⓓ	157	ⓐⓑⓒⓓ	177	ⓐⓑⓒⓓ	197	ⓐⓑⓒⓓ
118	ⓐⓑⓒⓓ	138	ⓐⓑⓒⓓ	158	ⓐⓑⓒⓓ	178	ⓐⓑⓒⓓ	198	ⓐⓑⓒⓓ
119	ⓐⓑⓒⓓ	139	ⓐⓑⓒⓓ	159	ⓐⓑⓒⓓ	179	ⓐⓑⓒⓓ	199	ⓐⓑⓒⓓ
120	ⓐⓑⓒⓓ	140	ⓐⓑⓒⓓ	160	ⓐⓑⓒⓓ	180	ⓐⓑⓒⓓ	200	ⓐⓑⓒⓓ

Test 10 (Part 5~7)

101	ⓐⓑⓒⓓ	121	ⓐⓑⓒⓓ	141	ⓐⓑⓒⓓ	161	ⓐⓑⓒⓓ	181	ⓐⓑⓒⓓ
102	ⓐⓑⓒⓓ	122	ⓐⓑⓒⓓ	142	ⓐⓑⓒⓓ	162	ⓐⓑⓒⓓ	182	ⓐⓑⓒⓓ
103	ⓐⓑⓒⓓ	123	ⓐⓑⓒⓓ	143	ⓐⓑⓒⓓ	163	ⓐⓑⓒⓓ	183	ⓐⓑⓒⓓ
104	ⓐⓑⓒⓓ	124	ⓐⓑⓒⓓ	144	ⓐⓑⓒⓓ	164	ⓐⓑⓒⓓ	184	ⓐⓑⓒⓓ
105	ⓐⓑⓒⓓ	125	ⓐⓑⓒⓓ	145	ⓐⓑⓒⓓ	165	ⓐⓑⓒⓓ	185	ⓐⓑⓒⓓ
106	ⓐⓑⓒⓓ	126	ⓐⓑⓒⓓ	146	ⓐⓑⓒⓓ	166	ⓐⓑⓒⓓ	186	ⓐⓑⓒⓓ
107	ⓐⓑⓒⓓ	127	ⓐⓑⓒⓓ	147	ⓐⓑⓒⓓ	167	ⓐⓑⓒⓓ	187	ⓐⓑⓒⓓ
108	ⓐⓑⓒⓓ	128	ⓐⓑⓒⓓ	148	ⓐⓑⓒⓓ	168	ⓐⓑⓒⓓ	188	ⓐⓑⓒⓓ
109	ⓐⓑⓒⓓ	129	ⓐⓑⓒⓓ	149	ⓐⓑⓒⓓ	169	ⓐⓑⓒⓓ	189	ⓐⓑⓒⓓ
110	ⓐⓑⓒⓓ	130	ⓐⓑⓒⓓ	150	ⓐⓑⓒⓓ	170	ⓐⓑⓒⓓ	190	ⓐⓑⓒⓓ
111	ⓐⓑⓒⓓ	131	ⓐⓑⓒⓓ	151	ⓐⓑⓒⓓ	171	ⓐⓑⓒⓓ	191	ⓐⓑⓒⓓ
112	ⓐⓑⓒⓓ	132	ⓐⓑⓒⓓ	152	ⓐⓑⓒⓓ	172	ⓐⓑⓒⓓ	192	ⓐⓑⓒⓓ
113	ⓐⓑⓒⓓ	133	ⓐⓑⓒⓓ	153	ⓐⓑⓒⓓ	173	ⓐⓑⓒⓓ	193	ⓐⓑⓒⓓ
114	ⓐⓑⓒⓓ	134	ⓐⓑⓒⓓ	154	ⓐⓑⓒⓓ	174	ⓐⓑⓒⓓ	194	ⓐⓑⓒⓓ
115	ⓐⓑⓒⓓ	135	ⓐⓑⓒⓓ	155	ⓐⓑⓒⓓ	175	ⓐⓑⓒⓓ	195	ⓐⓑⓒⓓ
116	ⓐⓑⓒⓓ	136	ⓐⓑⓒⓓ	156	ⓐⓑⓒⓓ	176	ⓐⓑⓒⓓ	196	ⓐⓑⓒⓓ
117	ⓐⓑⓒⓓ	137	ⓐⓑⓒⓓ	157	ⓐⓑⓒⓓ	177	ⓐⓑⓒⓓ	197	ⓐⓑⓒⓓ
118	ⓐⓑⓒⓓ	138	ⓐⓑⓒⓓ	158	ⓐⓑⓒⓓ	178	ⓐⓑⓒⓓ	198	ⓐⓑⓒⓓ
119	ⓐⓑⓒⓓ	139	ⓐⓑⓒⓓ	159	ⓐⓑⓒⓓ	179	ⓐⓑⓒⓓ	199	ⓐⓑⓒⓓ
120	ⓐⓑⓒⓓ	140	ⓐⓑⓒⓓ	160	ⓐⓑⓒⓓ	180	ⓐⓑⓒⓓ	200	ⓐⓑⓒⓓ

*toeic.
ETS 토익 정기시험
기출문제집 5
1000 RC

정답 및 해설

기출 TEST 1

101 (B)	102 (A)	103 (A)	104 (B)	105 (B)
106 (C)	107 (C)	108 (D)	109 (A)	110 (A)
111 (C)	112 (C)	113 (C)	114 (C)	115 (C)
116 (D)	117 (A)	118 (D)	119 (C)	120 (B)
121 (D)	122 (C)	123 (B)	124 (C)	125 (A)
126 (A)	127 (D)	128 (D)	129 (D)	130 (B)
131 (D)	132 (C)	133 (A)	134 (B)	135 (D)
136 (C)	137 (B)	138 (D)	139 (A)	140 (C)
141 (B)	142 (D)	143 (C)	144 (C)	145 (B)
146 (A)	147 (C)	148 (D)	149 (B)	150 (C)
151 (D)	152 (C)	153 (B)	154 (C)	155 (D)
156 (C)	157 (B)	158 (D)	159 (B)	160 (C)
161 (C)	162 (D)	163 (B)	164 (B)	165 (B)
166 (A)	167 (B)	168 (C)	169 (B)	170 (B)
171 (A)	172 (D)	173 (A)	174 (B)	175 (C)
176 (A)	177 (A)	178 (C)	179 (D)	180 (C)
181 (D)	182 (D)	183 (A)	184 (C)	185 (B)
186 (B)	187 (A)	188 (B)	189 (A)	190 (D)
191 (D)	192 (C)	193 (B)	194 (A)	195 (A)
196 (B)	197 (A)	198 (D)	199 (C)	200 (A)

PART 5

101 전치사 어휘

해설 빈칸 뒤는 시간 표현인 6:00 P.M.을 수식하는 관계사절로, 관계대명사 which와 결합하여 적절한 의미를 완성하는 전치사를 고르는 문제이다. 선행사 6:00 P.M.을 대신하는 관계대명사 which를 목적어로 취해 '그 이후에 참석자들은 질문할 수 있다'는 문맥이 되어야 하므로 '~ 후에'를 뜻하는 (B) after가 정답이다. (A) across는 '~을 가로질러', (C) inside는 '~ 안에', (D) among은 '~ 사이에'라는 의미이다.

번역 강연은 오후 6시에 열리며, 그 후 참석자들은 질문을 할 수 있습니다.

어휘 take place 열리다   attendee 참석자

102 형용사 자리 _ 명사 수식

해설 빈칸 앞에 정관사 the가 있고, 뒤에 명사구 antique shop이 있으므로 빈칸은 명사를 수식하는 형용사 자리이다. '마지막 골동품 가게'라는 의미가 되어야 자연스러우므로 '마지막의'를 뜻하는 형용사 (A) last가 정답이다. (B) lasts는 동사이므로 빈칸에 들어갈 수 없고, (C) lasted는 자동사 last의 과거분사로 수동의 의미로 명사를 수식할 수 없으며, (D) lasting(지속적인)은 형용사이지만 의미상 적합하지 않다.

번역 페퍼 밸리에 있는 마지막 골동품 가게가 다음 달에 문을 닫을 예정이다.

어휘 antique 골동품   close down 문을 닫다, 폐점하다

103 명사 어휘 _ 복합명사

해설 빈칸에는 형용사 online의 수식을 받으면서 명사 status와 함께 복합명사를 만들어 적절한 문맥을 완성하는 명사가 들어가야 한다. '주민들은 프로젝트에 대해 온라인 현황 업데이트를 받을 것'이라는 내용이 되어야 자연스러우므로 '업데이트, 최신 정보'를 뜻하는 (A) update가 정답이다. (B) change는 '변화', (C) payment는 '지불', (D) request는 '요청'이라는 의미이다.

번역 메리빌 주민들은 진행 중인 다리 건설 프로젝트에 대해 온라인 현황 업데이트를 받을 것이다.

어휘 resident 주민   status 현황   ongoing 진행 중인

104 인칭대명사의 격 _ 소유격

해설 빈칸에는 뒤에 온 명사구 many years를 수식하는 인칭대명사가 들어가야 한다. 따라서 명사 앞에 쓰여 한정사 역할을 할 수 있는 소유격 인칭대명사 (B) her가 정답이다.

번역 다년간 언론 단체를 이끌어 온 결과, 아요 씨는 도웰 언론상의 수상자로 선정되었다.

어휘 media 언론   organization 단체   select 선정하다

105 명사 어휘

해설 빈칸은 to부정사 To stop의 목적어 역할을 하는 명사 자리로, '컴퓨터 바이러스의 확산을 막기 위해'라는 의미가 되어야 적절하므로 '확산'을 뜻하는 (B) spread가 정답이다. (A) break는 '중단', (C) balance는 '균형', (D) surface는 '표면'이라는 의미이다.

번역 컴퓨터 바이러스의 확산을 막기 위해 의심스러운 이메일은 열지 마십시오.

어휘 suspicious 의심스러운

106 부사 자리 _ 동사 수식

해설 빈칸은 주어 The hiring manager와 동사 considered 사이에서 동사를 수식하는 부사 자리이므로 '면밀히'를 뜻하는 부사 (C) carefully가 정답이다. (A) caring은 형용사/명사, (B) careful은 형용사, (D) carefulness는 명사이므로 빈칸에 들어갈 수 없다.

번역 채용 관리자는 각 지원자의 이력서와 자격을 면밀히 검토했다.

어휘 applicant 지원자   résumé 이력서   qualification 자격

107 접속사 자리 _ 등위접속사

해설 빈칸 앞에 완전한 절이 있고, 빈칸 뒤에 주어가 생략된 채 동사 will oversee로 시작하는 절이 왔으므로 빈칸에는 등위접속사가 들어가야 한다. 따라서 등위접속사 (C) and가 정답이다. (A) because는

부사절 접속사로 완전한 절을 이끌고, (B) in addition은 부사구, (D) prior to는 전치사로 절을 연결할 수 없다.

번역 10월에 사카모토 씨는 뉴질랜드로 떠날 예정이며 새로운 오클랜드 지점 개점을 감독할 것이다.

어휘 leave for ~으로 떠나다 oversee 감독하다 branch 지점

108 명사 자리 _ 복합명사 ▶동영상 강의

해설 빈칸은 동사 is varying의 목적어 자리로, 앞에 있는 product와 함께 복합명사를 만들 수 있는 명사가 들어가야 한다. '제품군을 다양화하고 있다'는 내용이 되어야 하므로 '(상품의) 종류'를 뜻하는 명사 (D) line이 정답이다. to부정사 (A) to line은 품사상 부적합하고, 명사 (B) lining은 '안감'이라는 의미로 product와 복합명사를 이루기에 적절하지 않으며, 과거분사 (C) lined는 product를 뒤에서 수식할 수는 있지만 의미상 적절하지 않다.

번역 타라티어 제약 회사는 일반 의약품을 포함할 수 있도록 제품군을 다양화하고 있다.

어휘 pharmaceuticals 제약 회사 vary 다양화하다 over-the-counter 처방전 없이 살 수 있는 medication 약

109 동사 자리

해설 문장에 동사가 보이지 않으므로 빈칸은 동사 자리이다. 따라서 '찾다, 구하다'를 뜻하는 동사 (A) seeks가 정답이다. (B) seeker는 명사, (C) to seek은 to부정사, (D) seeking은 동명사/현재분사이므로 동사 자리에 들어갈 수 없다.

번역 다이네트 사는 플라스틱 사용을 줄이기 위한 새로운 방법을 지속적으로 찾고 있다.

어휘 continuously 지속적으로 reduce 줄이다

110 동사 자리

해설 문장에 동사가 보이지 않으므로 빈칸은 동사 자리이다. 따라서 '산출하다, 계산하다'를 뜻하는 동사 (A) calculate가 정답이다. (B) calculator와 (D) calculation은 명사, (C) calculating은 동명사/현재분사이므로 빈칸에 들어갈 수 없다.

번역 퍼클 북스의 계산대는 구매 가능한 남은 도서 재고를 자동으로 산출한다.

어휘 cash register 계산대 remaining 남은 inventory 재고

111 부사 어휘

해설 빈칸은 조동사 can과 동사원형 locate 사이에서 동사를 수식하는 부사 자리로, '지하 광물을 정확하게 찾아낼 수 있는 소프트웨어'라는 내용이 되어야 적절하므로 '정확하게'를 뜻하는 (C) precisely가 정답이다. (A) infinitely는 '무한히', (B) sincerely는 '진심으로', (D) greatly는 '대단히'라는 의미로 문맥상 적합하지 않다.

번역 제품 팀은 지하 광물의 위치를 정확하게 찾아낼 수 있는 지도 소프트웨어를 설계 중이다.

어휘 locate ~의 위치를 찾아내다 underground 지하의 mineral 광물

112 부사 자리 _ 형용사 수식

해설 빈칸은 형용사 responsible을 수식하는 부사 자리로, '재정적으로 책임 있는 일이 아닐 것이다'라는 내용이 되어야 하므로 '재정적으로'를 뜻하는 부사 (C) financially가 정답이다. (A) finance는 명사/동사, (B) financials는 명사, (D) financing은 명사/동명사/현재분사이므로 빈칸에 들어갈 수 없다.

번역 마유 야마다 CEO에 따르면, 현시점에 창고를 확장하는 것은 재정적으로 무책임한 일일 것이다.

어휘 expand 확장하다 warehouse 창고

113 명사 어휘 ▶동영상 강의

해설 빈칸 앞의 with any와 결합하여 '어떠한 확신도 가지고 말할 수 없다'라며 수요를 정확히 예측할 수 없다는 문맥을 나타내야 적절하므로 '확신, 확실성'을 뜻하는 (A) certainty가 정답이다. (B) justice는 '공정성', (C) excellence는 '뛰어남', (D) denial은 '부정'이라는 의미이다.

번역 분석가들은 전기 트럭에 대한 지역별 수요가 얼마나 될지 확실하게 말할 수 없다.

어휘 analyst 분석가 regional 지역의 demand 수요 electric 전기의

114 부사 어휘

해설 동사 is soliciting을 수식하여 '의견을 적극적으로 요청하고 있다'는 내용이 되어야 자연스러우므로 '적극적으로, 활발하게'를 뜻하는 (C) actively가 정답이다. (A) lightly는 '가볍게', (B) loyally는 '충성스럽게', (D) cleanly는 '깨끗하게'라는 의미이다.

번역 엘레강시아 식기는 마케팅 캠페인의 일환으로 고객으로부터 의견을 적극적으로 요청하고 있다.

어휘 dishware 식기류 solicit 요청하다

115 동사 어휘

해설 '~하도록 의도되다'라는 뜻의 「be intended + to부정사」에서 to부정사 자리에 들어갈 동사 어휘를 고르는 문제이다. water를 목적어로 취해 '침수 예방을 위해 물을 흡수하도록 설계되었다'는 내용이 되어야 자연스러우므로 '흡수하다'를 뜻하는 (C) absorb가 정답이다. (A) engage는 '종사하다', (B) undergo는 '겪다', (D) overwhelm은 '압도하다'라는 의미이다.

번역 빗물 정원은 지역 도로의 침수를 예방하기 위해 물을 흡수하도록 설계되었다.

어휘 intend 의도하다 prevent 예방하다 flooding 침수

116 명사 자리 _ to부정사의 목적어

해설 빈칸은 to부정사 to increase의 목적어 자리로, 앞에 정관사 the가 있고 뒤에 전치사 of가 있으므로 빈칸에는 명사가 들어가야 한다. 향상 또는 증가시킬(increase) 수 있는 대상이어야 하고, '시스템의 생산성을 향상시키는 것을 목표로 한다'는 내용이 되어야 적절하므로 '생산성'을 뜻하는 명사 (D) productivity가 정답이다. (A) producer는 '생산자'를 뜻하는 명사로 의미상 부적절하고, (B) produced는 동사/과거분사, (C) productive는 형용사로 빈칸에 들어갈 수 없다.

번역 세타 산업의 교육 프로그램은 제조 시스템의 생산성을 향상시키는 것을 목표로 한다.

어휘 aim 목표하다 increase 향상시키다 manufacturing 제조

117 전치사 자리 / 어휘 ▶동영상 강의

해설 빈칸 앞의 role, 뒤의 동명사 obtaining과 결합하여 '획득하는 데 있어서의 역할'이라는 의미를 나타내야 적절하므로 전치사 (A) in이 정답이다. (B) at은 '~에서'라는 의미로 장소나 시점 앞에 쓰이고 (C) except는 '~을 제외하고'라는 의미로 문맥과 어울리지 않으며, (D) apart는 '떨어져'를 뜻하는 부사로 빈칸에 적합하지 않다.

번역 이사회는 미트라코스 씨에게 국제 계약을 따내는 데 있어서 그가 한 역할에 대해 보너스를 지급하기로 의결했다.

어휘 board of directors 이사회 award 주다, 수여하다 obtain 획득하다

118 접속사 자리 _ 부사절 접속사

해설 빈칸은 두 개의 완전한 절을 이어주는 접속사 자리이다. 따라서 보기 중에 유일한 접속사로 '~할 수 있도록'이라는 의미를 나타내는 부사절 접속사 (D) so that이 정답이다. (A) along은 전치사/부사, (B) furthermore와 (C) cautiously는 부사이므로 절을 연결할 수 없다.

번역 재무 이사는 프로젝트가 진행될 수 있도록 승인해 주었다.

어휘 approval 승인 move forward (앞으로) 나아가다

119 동사 어휘 ▶동영상 강의

해설 빈칸은 명사 ways를 수식하는 관계사절(job seekers ~ workplace experience)의 동사 자리이다. 뒤에 목적어 없이 전치사 for로 이어지므로 for와 자연스럽게 연결될 수 있는 자동사가 들어가야 한다. 문맥상 '구직자들이 부족한 경력을 보완할 수 있는'이라는 내용이 되어야 자연스러우므로 for와 함께 쓰여 '~을 보완하다'를 뜻하는 (C) compensate가 정답이다. (A) reply는 '대답하다'라는 의미의 자동사로 주로 전치사 to와 함께 쓰이고, (B) capture는 '포착하다', (D) accumulate는 '축적하다'라는 의미이다.

번역 그 신문 기사는 구직자들이 직장 경력이 부족한 것을 보완할 수 있는 방법을 설명한다.

어휘 describe 설명하다 job seeker 구직자

120 부정대명사

해설 빈칸은 등위접속사 but이 이끄는 절에서 동사 got의 주어 자리이다. 문맥상 '두 사람 모두 자격은 충분히 있지만 둘 다 일자리를 얻지 못했다'는 내용이 되어야 자연스러우므로 '둘 중 누구도 아니다'를 뜻하는 부정대명사 (B) neither가 정답이다. 재귀대명사 (A) myself는 주어 역할을 할 수 없고, 부정대명사 (C) anybody는 '누구라도'라는 뜻으로 의미상 적합하지 않으며, 접속사인 (D) whoever는 절을 연결해야 하므로 빈칸에 들어갈 수 없다.

번역 엘리스 씨와 반즈 씨 모두 자격이 충분히 있었지만 둘 다 일자리를 얻지는 못했다.

어휘 qualified 자격이 있는

121 전치사 자리 / 어휘

해설 빈칸 앞에 Ennis Photography가 주어, purchased가 동사, all new lighting equipment가 목적어인 완전한 절이 있고, 뒤에 명사구 the high cost가 있으므로 빈칸은 전치사 자리이다. '높은 비용에도 불구하고'라는 의미가 되어야 자연스러우므로 '~에도 불구하고'를 뜻하는 전치사 (D) despite가 정답이다. (A) even though는 접속사, (B) however는 부사/복합관계부사로 빈칸에 들어갈 수 없고, (C) until은 전치사이지만 '~까지'라는 뜻으로 시간적 조건을 나타내므로 문맥상 적절하지 않다.

번역 에니스 사진은 높은 비용에도 불구하고 모든 새로운 조명 장비를 구입했다.

122 to부정사 _ 동사의 목적어

해설 빈칸은 동사 wish의 목적어 역할을 하는 to부정사의 동사원형 자리이다. 따라서 동사원형 (C) sell이 정답이다. (A) seller는 명사, (B) sold는 동사/과거분사, (D) selling은 동명사/현재분사이므로 빈칸에 들어갈 수 없다.

번역 주택을 판매하고자 하는 마버턴 주민은 콴 부동산의 수상 경력이 있는 팀에 연락해야 한다.

어휘 resident 주민 real estate 부동산

123 형용사 어휘

해설 빈칸 뒤의 명사 agreement를 수식하여 '지역 농민들과 협력적인 계약을 시작했다'는 내용이 되어야 자연스러우므로 '협력하는'을 뜻하는 (B) cooperative가 정답이다. (A) disruptive는 '지장을 주는', (C) grateful은 '감사하는', (D) concerned는 '걱정하는'이라는 의미이다.

번역 마스와 비스트로는 지역 농민들과 매주 일정량의 농산물을 구매하는 협력적인 계약을 시작했다.

어휘 agreement 계약 set 일정한, 정해진 produce 농산물

124 명사 자리 _ 복합명사

해설 빈칸은 동사 have been met의 주어 자리로, 빈칸 앞의 명사 parking과 함께 복합명사를 만들 수 있는 복수 명사가 들어가야 한다. '주차 제한은 반대에 맞닥뜨렸다'는 의미가 되어야 하므로 '제한, 규제'라는 뜻의 명사 (C) restrictions가 정답이다. (A) restricts는 동사, (B) restricted는 동사/과거분사, (D) restricting은 동명사/현재분사로 빈칸에 들어갈 수 없다.

번역 도일 시의 새로운 시내 주차 제한은 주민과 방문객들의 반대에 맞닥뜨렸다.

어휘 opposition 반대   resident 주민

125 부사 어휘

해설 관계사절(who studied ~ school)의 동사 studied를 수식하여 '성실하게 공부한 사람들조차 훈련이 필요하다'라는 내용이 되어야 자연스러우므로 '성실하게'를 뜻하는 (A) diligently가 정답이다. (B) scientifically는 '과학적으로', (C) objectively는 '객관적으로', (D) decidedly는 '단호하게'라는 의미이다.

번역 배관직은 기술 학교에서 성실하게 공부한 사람들조차 광범위한 훈련을 필요로 한다.

어휘 plumbing 배관   position 직책   extensive 광범위한

126 명사 자리 _ 복합명사

해설 빈칸은 전치사 With의 목적어 자리로, 빈칸 앞의 명사 price와 함께 복합명사를 만들 수 있는 명사가 들어가야 한다. '고정된 가격 보장으로'라는 내용이 되어야 하므로 '보장'을 뜻하는 명사 (A) assurance가 정답이다. (B) assuredly는 부사, (C) assuring은 동명사/현재분사, (D) assures는 동사이므로 빈칸에 들어갈 수 없다.

번역 오메가 셀룰러는 고정 가격 보장으로 3년 동안 전화 요금 인상이 없음을 보장합니다.

어휘 fixed 고정된   guarantee 보장하다   bill 고지서

127 명사 어휘

해설 전치사 with, 형용사 great와 결합하여 '크게 헌신하며 일해 왔다'는 의미가 되어야 하므로 '헌신, 전념'이라는 뜻의 (D) dedication이 정답이다. (A) deduction은 '공제', (B) duplication은 '이중', (C) declaration은 '선언'이라는 의미로 문맥과 어울리지 않는다.

번역 최고 분석 책임자인 고 씨는 20년 넘게 로크스턴 사에 크게 헌신하며 근무해 왔다.

어휘 chief 최고위자인   analytics 분석

128 접속사 자리   ▶동영상 강의

해설 빈칸은 동사 serves를 수식하는 부사구 seven days a week와 only on weekdays를 연결하는 자리이며, 두 대상을 비교하여 '평일에만 하는 대신 일주일 내내'라는 의미를 나타내야 적절하므로 '~보다는, ~ 대신에'를 뜻하며 등위접속사처럼 동등한 요소를 연결하는 접속사 (D) rather than이 정답이다. 전치사 (A) up to (~까지는)는 의미상 어울리지 않고, (B) as though(마치 ~처럼)와 (C) each time(~할 때마다)은 부사절 접속사로 뒤에 완전한 절이 와야 한다.

번역 밀타운 병원 구내식당은 평일에만 하는 대신 일주일 내내 점심 식사를 제공한다.

129 형용사 어휘

해설 빈칸 앞의 형용사 nearby와 함께 명사 supplier를 수식하여 적절한 문맥을 완성하는 형용사를 골라야 한다. 상점에 목재를 제공해 주는 공급업체의 특성을 나타낼 수 있어야 하므로 '인근의 상업적인 공급업체'라는 의미가 되어야 적절하다. 따라서 '상업적인'을 뜻하는 (D) commercial이 정답이다. (A) financial은 '재정의', (B) promotional은 '홍보의', (C) chemical은 '화학의'라는 의미이다.

번역 그 상점의 전체 목재 재고는 인근의 상업적인 공급업체로부터 온다.

어휘 entire 전체의   inventory 재고   lumber 목재   nearby 인근의   supplier 공급업체

130 형용사 자리 _ 명사 수식   ▶동영상 강의

해설 빈칸은 숫자 표현 $95와 함께 명사 fee를 수식하는 형용사 자리이다. '95달러의 진단 수수료'라는 의미가 되어야 적절하므로 '진단의'를 뜻하는 형용사 (B) diagnostic이 정답이다. 과거분사 (A) diagnosed(진단된)와 형용사 (C) diagnosable(진단 가능한)은 빈칸에 들어갈 수는 있지만 의미상 부적합하고, (D) diagnose는 동사이므로 빈칸에 들어갈 수 없다.

번역 진단 수수료 95달러를 내면 우리 정비사들이 어떤 수리가 필요한지를 파악합니다.

어휘 mechanic 정비사   determine 알아내다

PART 6

131-134 전단

정원 관리를 위해 리슬러 조경을 찾아주세요.

리슬러 조경에는 귀하가 꿈꾸는 정원을 조성하는 데 필요한 모든 것이 있습니다. 귀하의 아이디어를 경청하고 귀하께서 원하는 정원 가꾸기에 알맞은 제안을 드립니다. **131 리슬러 조경의 목표는 귀하의 상상을 현실로 만드는 것입니다.** 여기 리슬러 조경의 묘목장에는 일 년 내내 눈길을 사로잡을 색으로 가득 찬 다양한 품종과 크기의 식물을 보유하고 있습니다. 귀하의 정원에 132 **아름다움**을 더해 줄 무언가를 반드시 찾게 되실 겁니다. 저희는 133 **또한** 작은 연못이나 다른 수경 시설을 시공할 수 있는 장비도 갖추고 있습니다. 그리고 저희 이름에서 알 수 있듯이, 저희는 귀하께서 무엇이 필요하시든 더 야심찬 조경 프로젝트도 수행할 수 있습니다! 조경 디자인 사업에 40년 넘는 경력을 가진 134 **저희의** 전문성은 타의 추종을 불허합니다.

어휘 landscaping 조경 suggestion 제안 match 맞추다 desire 바람 nursery 묘목장 variety 품종 burst (~에 가득) 차 있다 eye-catching 눈길을 끄는 year-round 일 년 내내 guarantee 보장하다 equip 장비를 갖추다 pond 연못 water feature 수경 시설 take on (일 등을) 맡다 ambitious 야심적인 expertise 전문성 unmatched 타의 추종을 불허하는

131 문맥에 맞는 문장 고르기

번역 (A) 직원들이 지역 신문을 위해 기사를 작성했습니다.
(B) 조명을 설치하면 설계가 잘 된 정원의 효과를 높일 수 있습니다.
(C) 지역 경쟁업체들은 저희가 청구하는 가격을 이길 수 없습니다.
(D) 리슬러 조경의 목표는 귀하의 상상을 현실로 만드는 것입니다.

해설 빈칸 앞에는 귀하의 아이디어를 경청하고 원하는 정원을 가꾸는 데 알맞은 제안을 해준다(We will listen to your ideas and offer suggestions that match your gardening desires)고 했고, 빈칸 뒤에는 다양한 식물 보유, 수경 시설 조성 등 고객이 꿈꾸는 정원을 실현하기 위해 리슬러 조경에서 제공하는 구체적인 서비스를 안내하고 있으므로, 빈칸에는 이 꿈의 실현이라는 두 내용을 자연스럽게 연결해 주는 문장이 필요하다. 따라서 리슬러 조경의 목표는 고객의 상상을 현실로 만드는 것이라고 언급하고 있는 (D)가 정답이다.

어휘 install 설치하다 enhance 높이다 effect 효과 competitor 경쟁자 beat 이기다 charge 청구하다 vision 상상 reality 현실

132 명사 어휘

해설 앞 문장에서 묘목장에는 눈길을 사로잡는 색으로 가득 찬 다양한 품종과 크기의 식물을 보유하고 있다(The nursery here at Riessler Landscaping includes plants of many varieties and sizes that burst with eye-catching colors)고 했으므로, '정원에 아름다움을 더해 줄 식물을 찾을 수 있다'는 내용이 되어야 자연스럽다. 따라서 '아름다움'을 뜻하는 (C) beauty가 정답이다. (A)의 year는 '해, 년', (B) space는 '공간', (D) moisture는 '수분'을 의미한다.

133 부사 어휘

해설 앞에서 리슬러 조경의 묘목장은 다양한 품종과 크기의 식물을 제공한다고 했는데, 빈칸이 있는 문장에서 작은 연못이나 다른 수경 시설을 시공할 수 있는 장비도 갖추고 있다며 식물 판매 외에 제공하고 있는 서비스를 추가로 소개하고 있으므로 '또한'이라는 뜻의 (A) also가 정답이다. (B) rarely는 '드물게', (C) somehow는 '어떻게든', (D) nevertheless는 '그럼에도 불구하고'라는 의미이다.

134 대명사 어휘

해설 빈칸은 명사 expertise를 한정 수식하는 자리이므로 소유격 대명사가 들어가야 한다. 해당 글은 리슬러 조경(Riessler Landscaping)을 홍보하는 전단의 지문이고, 지문 전체에 걸쳐 홍보의 주체인 리슬러 조경을 'We' 또는 'our'로 지칭하고 있으므로 빈칸이 있는 문장에서도 '저희의 전문성'이라고 하는 것이 적합하다. 따라서 (B) our가 정답이다.

135-138 편지

1월 10일

신디 멀리건
맨체스터 로드 88번지
헤러게이트
HG82 2MJ

멀리건 씨께,

브랜드릭스 유통 센터와 함께한 귀하의 30주년을 기념하게 되어 아주 기쁩니다. **135 당신은 우리 팀의 소중한 구성원이었습니다.** 귀하의 헌신, 충성심, 그리고 노고는 수년간 우리의 성공에 크게 기여했습니다. 우리는 탁월함을 향한 귀하의 헌신에 감사드립니다. 여러 해 동안 귀하는 뛰어난 진취성, 창의성, 그리고 리더십을 **136 보여주었습니다.**

137 곧 우편으로 기념패를 받게 되실 겁니다. 이 감사의 징표가 귀하가 우리에게 얼마나 큰 의미를 가지는지를 표현해 주기를 바랍니다.

이 **138 이정표에** 도달하신 것을 축하드립니다. 우리 브랜드릭스 가족의 일원이 되어 주셔서 감사합니다.

랜스 포워, 인사 부사장
브랜드릭스 유통 센터

어휘 delighted 아주 기뻐하는 anniversary (주년) 기념일 distribution 유통 dedication 헌신 loyalty 충성심 contribute 기여하다 appreciate 감사하다 commitment 헌신 excellence 탁월함 initiative 진취성 creativity 창의성 commemorative 기념하는 plaque 명패 post 우편 token 징표 gratitude 감사

135 문맥에 맞는 문장 고르기

번역 (A) 우리는 특히 장기 고객들을 소중히 여깁니다.
(B) 우리의 휴일 축하 행사에 함께해 주세요.
(C) 우리의 연례 보고서가 곧 발표될 예정입니다.
(D) 당신은 우리 팀의 소중한 구성원이었습니다.

해설 빈칸 앞에서 브랜드릭스 유통 센터와 함께한 귀하의 30주년을 기념하게 되어 아주 기쁘다(We are delighted to celebrate your 30th anniversary with Brandrix Distribution Centre)고 했고 빈칸 뒤에서 귀하의 헌신, 충성심, 그리고 노고는 수년간 우리의 성공에 크게 기여했다(Your dedication, loyalty, and hard work have contributed greatly to our success over the years)고 했으므로, 빈칸에는 함께 근무해 온 동료로서 가치를 인정하는 찬사가 이어져야 일관성 있는 문맥이 완성된다. 따라서 당신은 우리 팀의 소중한 구성원이었다고 언급하고 있는 (D)가 정답이다.

어휘 value 소중히 여기다 long-term 장기의 annual 연례의 release 발표하다 valuable 소중한

136 동사 어형 _ 시제

해설 적절한 시제를 선택하는 문제로, over the years가 문제 해결의 단서이다. '여러 해 동안 귀하는 뛰어난 진취성, 창의성, 리더십을 보여주었다'는 의미로, 과거부터 현재까지 계속된 행위에 대해 이야기할 때는 현재완료 시제를 써야 하므로 (C) have shown이 정답이다.

137 부사 어휘

해설 빈칸에는 미래 시제를 나타내는 조동사 will과 어울려 쓰이는 시간 부사가 들어가야 한다. 뒤 문장에서도 이 기념패를 통해 감사의 뜻이 잘 전달되기를 바란다고 했으므로 문맥상 '곧 기념패를 받게 될 것'이라는 내용이 되어야 하므로, '곧'을 뜻하는 (B) soon이 정답이다. (A) then은 '그때, 그러고 나서', (C) instead는 '대신에', (D) likewise는 '마찬가지로'라는 의미이다.

138 명사 어휘

해설 지문의 첫 문장에서 브랜드릭스 유통 센터와 함께한 귀하의 30주년을 기념하게 되어 매우 기쁘다(We are delighted to celebrate your 30th anniversary with Brandrix Distribution Centre)고 했으므로, 멀리건 씨가 회사에서 근무한지 30년이 되는 날을 축하하고 있음을 알 수 있다. 따라서 '30년이라는 이정표에 도달한 것을 축하한다-'는 내용이 되어야 적절하므로 '이정표'를 뜻하는 (A) milestone이 정답이다. (B) consensus는 '합의', (C) destination은 '목적지', (D) understanding은 '이해'라는 의미이다.

139-142 이메일

수신: 케이 버먼 〈kberman@xmail.com〉
발신: 알리 샬레비 〈achaleby@ralenciadesign.com〉
날짜: 8월 21일
제목: 거실 설계도
첨부: 샘플

버먼 씨께,

저의 디자인 팀은 귀하의 거실 설계도를 139 **마무리하는** 과정에 있습니다. 지난번 대화를 바탕으로, 벽과 테두리에 다른 페인트를 선택했습니다. 첨부된 파일을 검토하시고 이 새로운 140 **색상이** 마음에 드시는지 결정해 주세요. 마음에 들지 않는다면, 변경해도 늦지 않습니다. 141 **앞으로 2주간은 공사를 시작할 계획이 없습니다.** 검토해 주시면 저희가 시작하기 전에 디자인을 다듬는 데 도움이 될 것입니다.

문의 사항이 있으시면 142 **저에게** 알려 주세요. 귀하의 답변을 기다리겠습니다.

알리 샬레비, 랄렌시아 디자인

어휘 process 과정 border 테두리 attached 첨부된
refine 다듬다, 정제하다

139 동명사 _ 전치사의 목적어

해설 빈칸에는 전치사 of의 목적어 역할을 하며 빈칸 뒤에 오는 명사 the plans를 목적어로 취할 수 있는 동명사가 들어가야 한다. 따라서 동명사 (A) finalizing이 정답이다. (B) finalize와 (D) finalizes는 동사, (C) finalized는 동사/과거분사이므로 품사상 빈칸에 들어갈 수 없다.

140 명사 어휘

해설 앞 문장에서 지난번 대화를 바탕으로 벽과 테두리에 다른 페인트를 선택했다(Based on our last conversation, I have chosen different paints for the walls and borders)고 했으므로, 벽과 테두리에 바를 페인트의 색상을 바꿨다는 것을 알 수 있다. 따라서 '이 새로운 색상이 마음에 드는지 결정해 달라'는 내용이 되어야 하므로 '색상'을 뜻하는 (C) colors가 정답이다. (A)의 organization은 '단체', (B)의 schedule은 '시간표', (D)의 time은 '시간'이라는 의미이다.

141 문맥에 맞는 문장 고르기

번역 (A) 이미 귀하의 주방을 위한 설계도를 만들기 시작했습니다.
(B) 앞으로 2주간은 공사를 시작할 계획이 없습니다.
(C) 귀하의 거실은 특히 넓고 바람이 잘 통합니다.
(D) 저희는 아직 귀하의 현재 결제 금액을 받지 못했습니다.

해설 앞 문장에서 마음에 들지 않으면 변경해도 늦지 않다(If not, it is not too late to make a change)고 했고 뒤 문장에서 검토해 주면 일을 시작하기 전에 디자인을 다듬는 데 도움이 될 것(Your review will help us refine the design before we start)이라고 했으므로, 공사를 시작하기까지 아직 시간이 남아 있음을 알려주는 내용이 들어가야 자연스럽다. 따라서 앞으로 2주간 공사를 시작하지 않을 것임을 언급하는 (B)가 정답이다.

어휘 draw up ~을 만들다, 작성하다 particularly 특히
spacious 넓은 airy 바람이 잘 통하는 current 현재의

142 대명사 어휘

해설 뒤 문장에서 저는 귀하의 답변을 기다리겠다(I look forward to hearing from you)고 했으므로, '문의 사항이 있으시면 저에게 알려 달라'는 내용이 되어야 적절하다. 따라서 (D) me가 정답이다.

143-146 이메일

수신: 마샤 제일런 〈mzalen@mansfield.com〉
발신: 케이마르 PCP 〈info@kaymarpcp.com〉
날짜: 9월 8일
제목: 귀하의 최근 진료 방문

제일런 씨께,

케이마르 1차 진료소를 최근에 방문해 주셔서 감사합니다. 귀하께서 저희 서비스에 143 **만족하셨기를** 바라며 개선을 위한 제안을 환영합니다.

귀하의 진료 144 **요약**을 저희 포털에 게시해 두었습니다. 시간을 내셔서 검토해 주시고 질문이 있으시면 알려 주십시오.

참고로 알려드리자면, 다양한 활동을 위해 포털에 로그인하실 수 있습니다. 145 **예를 들어**, 예약 및 결제를 하고, 의료 기록을 조회하고, 검사 결과를 확인하고 약 재처방을 요청할 수 있습니다. 146 **귀하의 건강 관리에 필요한 사항들을 관리하시는 데 이 방편을 활용하시기 바랍니다.** 귀하의 개인정보는 안전하게 보호되고 있으니 안심하십시오.

저희를 이용해 주셔서 감사드리며 다시 모시기를 기대합니다.

케이마르 1차 진료소

> **어휘** primary care 1차 진료 practice (의사 등의) 사무실 suggestion 제안 improvement 개선 post 게시하다 consultation 진찰, 상담 portal 포털 (사이트) go through ~을 검토하다 reminder 상기시켜 주는 것 various 다양한 appointment 약속 lab 실험실 medication 약 refill 재처방 secure 안전한, 확실한 rest assured 안심하다

143 형용사 자리 _ 목적격 보어 / 형용사 vs. 과거분사

해설 빈칸은 동사 hope의 목적어 역할을 하는 명사절에서 5형식 동사 found의 목적격 보어 자리이다. 목적어 our services를 수식하여 '우리 서비스를 만족스럽게 여기기를 바란다'는 내용이 되어야 하므로 '만족스러운'을 뜻하는 (C) satisfactory가 정답이다. 과거분사 (A) satisfied는 '만족하는'이라는 의미로 수식 받는 명사 services가 감정을 느끼는 주체가 될 수 없으므로 답이 될 수 없고, 명사 (B) satisfaction은 services와 동격이 아니며, (D) satisfactorily는 부사이므로 품사상 목적격 보어 자리에 들어갈 수 없다.

144 명사 어휘

해설 앞에서 케이마르 1차 진료소를 최근에 방문해 주셔서 감사하다(Thank you for your recent visit to Kaymar Primary Care Practice)고 했고, 빈칸 뒤 문장에서 검토하고 질문이 있으면 알려달라(go through it and let us know if you have any questions)고 했다. 따라서 빈칸이 있는 문장에서 포털에 게시했다는 것은 제일런 씨가 병원에서 진료를 본 뒤 제공받아 검토할 자료, 즉 진료 요약 서류임을 알 수 있으므로 '요약'을 뜻하는 (C) summary가 정답이다. (A) photo는 '사진', (B) lecture는 '강의', (D) schedule은 '시간표'라는 의미이다.

145 접속부사

해설 앞 문장에서 다양한 활동을 위해 포털에 로그인할 수 있다(you can log in to the portal for various activities)고 했고, 빈칸 뒤에서 예약 및 결제, 의료 기록 조회, 검사 결과 확인, 약 처방 요청을 할 수 있다(you can make appointments and payments, view your medical history, review lab results, and request medication refills)며 포털에서 할 수 있는 활동의 예시를 구체적으로 나열하고 있다. 따라서 '예를 들어'를 뜻하는 (B) For instance가 정답이다. (A) To repeat는 '반복하자면', (C) Otherwise는 '그렇지 않으면', (D) Consequently는 '결과적으로'라는 의미이다.

146 문맥에 맞는 문장 고르기

번역 (A) 귀하의 건강 관리에 필요한 사항들을 관리하는 데 이 방편을 활용하시기 바랍니다.
(B) 직원들은 금요일 오후에 일찍 진료소를 닫을 예정입니다.
(C) 반드시 진료소에 15분 일찍 도착해 주십시오.
(D) 귀하의 예약 시간에 혼선이 있었던 점 사과드립니다.

해설 빈칸 앞에서 포털에 로그인하면(you can log in to the portal) 예약 및 결제, 의료 기록 조회, 검사 결과 확인, 약 재처방 요청 등의 다양한 활동을 할 수 있다(you can make appointments and payments, view your medical history, review lab results, and request medication refills)고 포털의 용도와 편리함을 소개하고 있으므로, 빈칸에는 포털 사용을 장려하는 내용이 들어가야 자연스럽다. 따라서 건강 관리를 하는 데 이 방편을 활용하라고 권장하고 있는 (A)가 정답이다.

어휘 resource 방편, 자원 in advance 미리 confusion 혼란

PART 7

147-148 공지

> 하이 뷰 아파트 주민 여러분께,
>
> 147 **리버사이드 포장 회사가 5월 3일과 4일에 하이 뷰 아파트로 와서 주차 구역을 재포장합니다.** 모든 차량은 작업이 시작될 수 있도록 5월 3일 오전 8시까지 이동되어야 합니다. 주민들은 5월 5일 오전 8시부터 주차 구역을 다시 이용할 수 있습니다. 다른 주차 공간을 찾는 것이 불편하다는 점은 알지만, 예정된 이틀 안에 작업이 완료되는 데 필요한 조치입니다. 모든 주차 공간이 넓어질 예정이며 일부 공간은 작업하는 동안 이동될 수 있다는 점에 유의해 주세요. 148 **귀하의 주차 공간이 기존 위치에서 20미터 이상 이동될 경우, 이메일을 받으시게 됩니다.**
>
> 협조해 주셔서 감사합니다.
> 주디스 알바레즈, 아파트 관리소장

> **어휘** resident 주민 paving (도로 등의) 포장 resurface 재포장하다 remove 이동시키다 commence 시작하다 realize 인식하다 inconvenient 불편한 widen 넓히다 previous 이전의 cooperation 협조 property 건물

147 주제 / 목적

번역 공지의 목적은?
(A) 5월 3일 회의에 주민들을 초대하려고
(B) 주차 시설에 대한 의견을 요청하려고
(C) 다가오는 공사에 대해 주민들에게 알리려고
(D) 주차 요금 인상을 발표하려고

해설 첫 문장에서 아파트 주민들에게 리버사이드 포장 회사가 5월 3일과 4일에 하이 뷰 아파트로 와서 주차 구역을 재포장한다(Riverside Paving Company is coming to High View Apartments on May 3 and 4 to resurface the parking area)고 알리고 있으므로, 주민들에게 주차장 공사를 공지하기 위한

글임을 알 수 있다. 따라서 (C)가 정답이다.

어휘 facility 시설 upcoming 다가오는 fee 요금, 수수료

> **Paraphrasing**
> 지문의 to resurface the parking area → 정답의 project

148 추론 / 암시

번역 하이 뷰 아파트에 대해 암시된 것은?
(A) 주민들에게 매월 관리비를 부과한다.
(B) 최근에 새로운 건물 관리소장을 채용했다.
(C) 매년 주차 구역을 재포장한다.
(D) 세입자들에게 특정 주차 공간을 배정해 준다.

해설 마지막 문장에서 아파트 주민에게 주차 공간이 기존 위치에서 20미터 이상 이동될 경우 이메일을 받게 된다(You will receive an e-mail if your parking space is moved more than 20 meters from your previous one)고 한 것으로 보아, 하이 뷰 아파트 주민들은 지정된 주차 공간이 있음을 유추할 수 있다. 따라서 (D)가 정답이다.

어휘 charge 부과하다 maintenance fee 관리비 repave 재포장하다 assign 배정하다 tenant 세입자 specific 특정한 spot 자리

> **Paraphrasing**
> 지문의 parking space → 정답의 parking spots

149-150 문자 메시지

캐롤 바거 (오전 10시 45분)
안녕하세요, 쌩 씨.

리케나 쌩 (오전 10시 55분)
좋은 아침입니다!

캐롤 바거 (오전 11시 15분)
149 내일 열리는 당신의 모자이크 워크숍에 등록한 참가자가 15명이에요. 지난 여름보다 다섯 명 더 많네요. 당신의 워크숍이 매년 더 인기를 얻고 있어요! 150 그 많은 참가자를 위한 재료가 충분히 준비되어 있나요?

리케나 쌩 (오전 11시 23분)
모두에게 나눠줄 만큼 충분히 있어요. 150 지난 여름휴가 때 제가 모아둔 바다 유리 조각을 활용해서 모자이크 디자인을 만들 거예요. 그것들은 해변에 떠밀려온 갈색, 초록색, 파란색 병 조각들이에요. 모래가 날카로운 가장자리를 전부 부드럽게 해줘서 모두가 사용하기에 완벽하게 안전해요.

캐롤 바거 (오전 11시 30분)
좋을 것 같네요. 내일 아침 식사 때 봐요.

어휘 participant 참가자 enroll 등록하다 material 재료 on hand 준비된 plenty 충분한 양 go around (몫이) 돌아가다 bit 조각 wash up 떠밀려오다 smooth 부드럽게 하다 edge 가장자리

149 추론 / 암시

번역 쌩 씨의 직업은 무엇일 것 같은가?
(A) 유리 공예가
(B) 미술 강사
(C) 해변 안전 요원
(D) 프로그램 관리자

해설 11시 15분에 바거 씨가 쌩 씨에게 내일 열리는 당신의 모자이크 워크숍에 등록한 참가자가 15명(We have fifteen participants enrolled in your mosaic workshop tomorrow)이라고 알려주고 있는 것을 통해, 쌩 씨는 미술 워크숍을 진행하는 강사임을 알 수 있다. 따라서 (B)가 정답이다.

어휘 instructor 강사 lifeguard (수영장의) 안전 요원 administrator 관리자

150 의도 파악

번역 오전 11시 23분에 쌩 씨가 "모두에게 나눠줄 만큼 충분히 있어요"라고 쓴 의도는?
(A) 초대형 모자이크를 만들 작정이다.
(B) 수년간 바다 유리를 모아왔다.
(C) 워크숍 참가자 전원에게 바다 유리를 나눠줄 수 있다.
(D) 바다 유리를 많이 사용하지 않을 생각이다.

해설 11시 15분에 바거 씨가 그 많은 참가자를 위한 재료가 충분히 준비되어 있는지(Do you have enough materials on hand for that many participants?)를 묻자, 11시 23분에 쌩 씨가 모두에게 나눠줄 만큼 충분히 있다(I have plenty to go around)고 답하면서 지난 여름휴가 때 모아둔 바다 유리 조각을 활용해서 모자이크 디자인을 만들 것(We'll be creating mosaic designs using bits of sea glass I collected on my vacation last summer)이라고 덧붙였다. 따라서 쌩 씨는 워크숍 참가자 모두에게 제공할 수 있을 만큼 바다 유리 조각이 충분히 있다는 의도로 한 말임을 알 수 있으므로 (C)가 정답이다.

어휘 intend 작정하다

151-152 이메일

수신: 영업팀
발신: 로라 코레아
날짜: 10월 5일
제목: 업데이트

팀 여러분께,

브라이터 세일즈 9월 소식지에 발표된 대로 올해 우리의 실적은 꾸준히 좋았습니다. 이는 우리 모두 자랑스러워할 만한 성취입니다. 시간을 내어 서로를 축하해 주세요. 우리는 계속해서 미래를 위한 새롭고 흥미로운 계획들을 구상할 것입니다!

다른 소식으로는, 151 제이슨 노턴 씨가 다음 달에 우리 킹스턴 본사로 전근할 예정입니다. 노턴 씨를 보내는 것은 슬프지만 그의 뛰어난 업무 성과에 감사드리며 새로운 역할에서도 지속적인 성공을 기원합니다.

10월 28일 오후 1시에 2층 회의실에서 노턴 씨를 위한 송별 오찬이 있을 예정입니다. 따뜻한 격려와 가능하다면 함께 나눌 이야기를 준비해 오세요. 회사에서 점심 식사, 케이크, 장식을 제공할 예정입니다. **152 10월 12일까지 참석 가능 여부를 저에게 알려주세요.**

로라 코레아, 영업 관리자
브라이터 세일즈 사

어휘 performance 실적 consistently 꾸준히, 일관되게 accomplishment 성취 dream up ~을 생각해 내다 gratefully 감사히 acknowledge 감사를 표하다 farewell 송별 luncheon 오찬 cheer 격려, 응원 supply 제공하다 decoration 장식

151 Not / True

번역 노턴 씨에 대해 언급된 것은?
(A) 영업 회의에 참석할 예정이다.
(B) 코레아 씨에게 사무용품 요청서를 보냈다.
(C) 9월 소식지에 글을 썼다.
(D) 회사의 다른 지점으로 옮길 예정이다.

해설 두 번째 단락 첫 문장에서 제이슨 노턴 씨가 다음 달에 킹스턴 본사로 전근할 예정(Jasen Norton will transfer to our Kingston headquarters next month)이라고 했으므로 (D)가 정답이다.

어휘 office supplies 사무용품

> **Paraphrasing**
> 지문의 transfer to our Kingston headquarters
> → 정답의 be moving to another company location

152 세부 사항

번역 코레아 씨가 영업팀원들에게 요청하는 것은?
(A) 소식지를 위한 이야기를 보내기
(B) 신입사원 후보자들의 이름을 알리기
(C) 행사 참석 계획을 알리기
(D) 사무실 장식을 돕기

해설 마지막 단락의 마지막 문장에서 코레아 씨가 영업팀원들에게 10월 12일까지 참석 가능 여부를 알려달라(Let me know by 12 October whether you will be able to attend)고 요청하고 있으므로 (C)가 정답이다.

어휘 potential ~이 될 가능성이 있는, 잠재적인 new hire 신입 사원 decorate 장식하다

> **Paraphrasing**
> 지문의 Let me know → 정답의 Inform her

153-154 기사

새롭게 단장한 극장이 마을에 활력을 불어넣다

비치빌 (2월 24일) — 비치빌 주민과 관광객들은 축하할 만한 충분한 이유가 있다. **153 40년 된 크라운 코스탈 극장이 6월에 다시 개관할 예정이다.** 1년여 전 극장의 이전 소유주들이 필요한 보수 공사 비용을 이유로 극장을 닫기로 결정했을 때 많은 이들이 슬퍼했다. 다행스럽게도 극장은 새로운 소유주들을 갖게 되어 내부와 영사 시스템을 업데이트하는 데 지난 1년을 보냈다.

154 크리스틴 래퍼티는 어린 시절 친구인 모건 플래너건과 자라면서 극장에서 많은 시간을 보냈다고 말했다. "영화를 보러 가는 것이 해안가 마을에서 비 오는 날 할 수 있는 일입니다. 우리는 극장이 문을 닫는 걸 보는 게 슬펐습니다." **154 이 친구들은 인기 식당인 블루 베이 비스트로도 소유하고 있으며, 극장을 인수하기로 결정하고 번창하는 사업으로 유지시키기 위해 필요한 수리를 했다.** 극장과 곧 있을 행사에 대한 자세한 정보는 www.crowncoastaltheater.com을 방문하면 된다.

어휘 refurbish 새로 꾸미다 boost 힘, 상승 sadden 슬프게 하다 former 이전의 venue 장소 cite (이유를) 들다 renovation 보수 interior 내부 projection 영사 plenty of 많은 thriving 번창하는

153 주제 / 목적

번역 기사의 목적은?
(A) 해변 상태에 대해 보도하려고
(B) 영업 재개를 알리려고
(C) 영화 시사회를 홍보하려고
(D) 새로운 식당을 광고하려고

해설 첫 단락 두 번째 문장에서 40년 된 크라운 코스탈 극장이 6월에 다시 개관할 예정(The 40-year-old Crown Coastal Theater is scheduled to reopen in June)이라고 했으므로 극장의 재개관을 알리는 기사임을 알 수 있다. 따라서 (B)가 정답이다.

어휘 condition 상태 promote 홍보하다 premiere 시사회 advertise 광고하다

154 세부 사항

번역 플래너건 씨는 누구인가?
(A) 마을 의회 회원
(B) 행사 진행자
(C) 래퍼티 씨의 동업자
(D) 기사 작성자

해설 두 번째 단락의 첫 문장에서 크리스틴 래퍼티는 어린 시절 친구인 모건 플래너건과 자라면서 극장에서 많은 시간을 보냈다(Christine Lafferty said that she and her childhood friend Morgan Flanagan spent plenty of time at the theater while growing up)고 했고, 같은 단락의 네 번째 문장에서 이 친구들은 인기 식당인 블루 베이 비스트로도 소유하고 있으며, 극장을 인수하기로 결정하고 번창하는 사업으로 유지시키기 위해 필요한 수리를 했다(The friends, who also own the popular Blue Bay Bistro, decided to buy the theater and make the necessary repairs to keep it a thriving business)고 했다. 이를 통해 플래너건 씨는 래퍼티 씨의 친구이자 사업 파트너임을 알 수 있으므로 (C)가 정답이다.

어휘 council 의회 coordinator 진행자, 조정자

155-157 이메일

수신: 랜디 롱펠로우 <rlongfellow@sapphiremail.com.au>
발신: 디온 웰먼 <deonwelman@skyviewscopes.com.au>
날짜: 3월 27일
제목: 마카타시 모델 METX-33948

롱펠로우 씨께,

마카타시 ETX 삼중 굴절 망원경, 모델 METX-33948을 주문해 주셔서 감사합니다. **155 안타깝게도 고객님께서 요청하신 제품은 현재 주문이 밀려 있습니다.** 기다리고 싶지 않으시다면 저희에게 다른 제조업체인 벨터 망원경에서 만든 유사한 망원경이 있습니다. **157 고객님께서 주문하신 마카타시 모델처럼 벨터 BTR-1483도 120mm 조리개와 접이식 렌즈 후드로 구성되어 있습니다. 저희 웹사이트에서 전체 사양 목록을 확인하실 수 있습니다.** 또한, **156 모든 벨터 망원경에는 패딩 처리된 휴대용 케이스가 포함되어 있습니다.** 벨터 BTR-1483은 마카타시 METX-33948보다 200달러 저렴합니다.

주문을 변경하기를 원하시면 48시간 이내에 이 이메일에 회신하시거나 저희 웹사이트 http://www.skyviewscopes.com.au를 방문하셔서 직원에게 문의해 주세요. 그러면 고객님의 주문을 변경하고, 고객님의 신용카드로 200달러를 환불해 드리며 추가 요금 없이 새로운 망원경을 익일 배송해 드리겠습니다. 그렇지 않으면, 마카타시 모델 METX-33948이 재입고될 때 알려드리고 그때 배송 정보를 보내드리겠습니다.

디온 웰먼
스카이뷰 스코프스 영업 사원

어휘 refracting 굴절 telescope 망원경 back 밀린 manufacturer 제조업체 aperture 조리개 retractable 접어 넣을 수 있는 padded 속을 채워 넣은 revise 변경하다 representative 직원 overnight 하룻밤 사이에 charge 요금 otherwise 그렇지 않으면 in stock 재고가 있는

155 주제 / 목적

번역 이메일의 목적은?
(A) 지불을 요청하려고
(B) 작동 설명서를 제공하려고
(C) 신제품을 광고하려고
(D) 대체 제품을 제안하려고

해설 첫 단락 두 번째 문장에서 안타깝게도 고객이 요청한 제품은 현재 주문이 밀려 있다(Unfortunately, the item you requested is on back order)고 했고, 기다리고 싶지 않으면 다른 제조업체인 벨터 망원경에서 만든 유사한 망원경이 있다(If you would prefer not to wait, we have a similar telescope made by another manufacturer, Belter Telescopes)고 했다. 따라서 이 이메일은 고객에게 재고가 바닥난 주문 제품 대신 바로 받아 볼 수 있는 다른 제품을 제안하기 위해 발송된 것임을 알 수 있으므로 (D)가 정답이다.

어휘 operating 조작상의 instruction 설명(서) substitute 대체의

156 Not / True

번역 벨터 BTR-1483 망원경에 대해 언급된 것은?
(A) 온라인으로만 주문할 수 있다.
(B) 제조업체로부터 직접 배송될 것이다.
(C) 보호용 케이스가 들어 있다.
(D) 이 종류의 망원경 중 가장 비싸다.

해설 첫 단락 여섯 번째 문장에서 모든 벨터 망원경에는 패딩 처리된 휴대용 케이스가 포함되어 있다(all Belter telescopes include a padded carrying case)고 했으므로, 벨터 BTR-1483 망원경에도 케이스가 제공된다는 것을 알 수 있다. 따라서 (C)가 정답이다.

어휘 protective 보호용의

> **Paraphrasing**
> 지문의 a padded carrying case → 정답의 a protective case

157 문장 삽입

번역 [1], [2], [3], [4]로 표시된 위치 중에서 다음 문장이 들어가기에 가장 적합한 곳은?

"저희 웹사이트에서 전체 사양 목록을 확인하실 수 있습니다."
(A) [1]
(B) [2]
(C) [3]
(D) [4]

해설 주어진 문장에서 '웹사이트에서 전체 사양 목록을 확인할 수 있다'며 제품의 사양을 전체적으로 확인할 수 있는 경로를 안내하고 있으므로, 그 앞에는 제품의 일부 사양을 소개하는 내용이 있어야 한다. 따라서 벨터 BTR-1483도 120mm 조리개와 접이식 렌즈 후드로 구성되어 있다(the Belter BTR-1483 has a 120 mm aperture and a retractable lens hood)며 대체 제품의 기본 사양 일부를 언급하고 있는 문장 뒤인 [2]에 들어가는 것이 글의 흐름상 자연스러우므로 (B)가 정답이다.

어휘 specification 사양

158-160 이메일

수신: 묘선희 <shmyo@sunmail.co.nz>
발신: 잰 델핏 <jdelpit@hamerkoptech.co.nz>
날짜: 3월 8일
제목: 회신: 채용 공고 관련 문의

안녕하세요,

이메일을 보내주셔서 감사합니다. **158 저는 현재 휴가 중으로, 3월 15일에 사무실로 복귀할 예정입니다.** 복귀하는 대로 최대한 빨리 메시지에 답해드리겠습니다.

제가 자리를 비운 동안 일반적인 도움이 필요하시거나 저희 영업 부서의 채용직에 대해 질문이 있으실 경우, 제 비서인 시타 비스완에게 04 555 0193 또는 sviswan@hamerkoptech.co.nz로 연락 주십시오. 특정 하머콥테크 소프트웨어 제품에 대한 질문은 customer service@hamerkoptech.co.nz로 고객 서비스 부서에 문의해 주십시오.

또한, **159** 저희의 새로운 그래픽 디자인 소프트웨어 프로그램이 4월 2일에 출시 예정이라는 소식을 전하게 되어 기쁩니다. **160** 하머콥테크의 새로 개편된 웹사이트 www.hamerkoptech.co.nz에서 이 프로그램에 대해 더 자세히 확인하실 수 있습니다. **160** 그곳에서 홈페이지의 안내를 따라 저희 주간 소식지 수령을 신청하실 수도 있습니다.

잰 델핏

어휘 inquiry 문의 job opening 채용 공고 currently 현재 general 일반적인 assistance 도움 absence 부재 specific 특정한 release 출시하다 sign up 신청하다 instruction 설명

158 주제 / 목적

번역 이메일의 목적 중 하나는?
(A) 소프트웨어 프로그램 이용 방법을 설명하려고
(B) 프로젝트에 묘 씨의 지원을 요청하려고
(C) 새로운 직원을 소개하려고
(D) 델핏 씨가 사무실에 없다는 것을 알리려고

해설 첫 단락 두 번째 문장에서 이메일의 작성자인 델핏 씨가 자신은 현재 휴가 중으로 3월 15일에 사무실로 복귀할 예정(I am currently on holiday and will return to the office on 15 March)이라면서 복귀하는 대로 최대한 빨리 메시지에 답하겠다(I will respond to your message as soon as possible after I return)고 했으므로, 델핏 씨는 현재 휴가 중으로 사무실을 비운 상태라서 바로 답변을 줄 수 없음을 알리기 위한 이메일임을 알 수 있다. 따라서 (D)가 정답이다.

어휘 indicate 나타내다

> **Paraphrasing**
> 지문의 on holiday → 정답의 out of the office

159 세부 사항

번역 4월 2일에 일어날 일은?
(A) 일자리가 충원된다.
(B) 제품이 출시된다.
(C) 고객 미팅이 열린다.
(D) 웹사이트 개편이 시작된다.

해설 세 번째 단락의 첫 문장에서 새로운 그래픽 디자인 소프트웨어 프로그램이 4월 2일에 출시 예정이라는 소식을 전하게 되어 기쁘다(I am happy to announce that our new graphic design software program will be released on 2 April)고 했으므로 (B)가 정답이다.

어휘 fill 채우다 launch 출시하다 take place 열리다

> **Paraphrasing**
> 지문의 released → 정답의 launched

160 세부 사항

번역 사람들은 어떻게 소식지를 구독할 수 있는가?
(A) 비스완 씨에게 전화함으로써
(B) 델핏 씨의 이메일에 회신함으로써
(C) 하머콥테크의 웹사이트를 방문함으로써
(D) 고객 서비스 부서에 연락함으로써

해설 세 번째 단락 두 번째 문장에서 하머콥테크의 새로 개편된 웹사이트(Hamerkoptech's newly redesigned Web site, www.hamerkoptech.co.nz)를 언급하며 그곳에서 홈페이지의 안내를 따라 주간 소식지 수령을 신청할 수도 있다(There, you may also sign up to receive our weekly newsletter by following the instructions on the home page)고 했으므로 (C)가 정답이다.

> **Paraphrasing**
> 지문의 sign up to receive our weekly newsletter → 질문의 subscribe to a newsletter

161-163 기사

비말로 브랜즈, 새로운 시대 진입

이벳 모러 작성

밴쿠버 (8월 2일) — **161** 파워버스트 아침 식사용 음료와 허니소프트 비누와 로션 등의 인기 있는 영양 보조 식품 및 개인 관리 제품을 판매하는 대형 소비재 기업인 비말로 브랜즈에서 조만간 고객들을 위해 새로운 제품인 냉동식품을 선보일 예정이다. "새로운 뉴트리디나 라인은 **162** 단지 편리한 것뿐만이 아닙니다."라고 오늘 오전 기자 회견에서 CEO인 다니차 마르텐스가 말했다. "냉동식품은 새로운 개념은 아니지만 **163** 신선한 농산물과 육류를 급속 냉동시키는 당사의 방식은 우리 제품이 식감과 맛뿐 아니라 건강에 유익한 비타민과 미네랄을 유지하도록 보장해 줍니다. 이제 우리 고객들은 품질을 희생하지 않고도 냉동식품의 편리함을 즐길 수 있습니다."

비말로 브랜즈는 뉴트리디나 제품 라인에 필요한 농산물과 육류를 확보하기 위해 밴쿠버 지역 농장들과 협력해 왔다. "사업을 현지화함으로써 저희는 배송 지연을 피하고 가장 잘 익었을 때 갓 수확된 채소를 급속 냉동할 수 있습니다."라고 마르텐스는 말했다. "우리 제품은 냉동실에 최대 6개월까지 보관할 수 있으므로 고객들은 더 많은 혜택을 누리게 됩니다." 뉴트리디나 식품은 11월부터 슈퍼마켓에서 이용 가능하다. 냉동 생선과 기타 해산물은 내년 초에 추가될 예정이다.

어휘 era 시대 consumer goods 소비재 market (상품을) 내놓다 nutritional 영양상의 support 보조, 지원 frozen 냉동된 convenience 편리 press conference 기자 회견 method 방법 flash-freeze 급속 냉동하다 produce 농산물 retain 유지하다 texture 질감 flavour 맛 sacrifice 희생하다 partner 협력하다 obtain 확보하다, 얻다 operation 사업

delay 지연 harvest 수확하다 peak 정점 ripeness 익음, 원숙 benefit 이익을 보다 freezer 냉동실

161 주제 / 목적

번역 기사의 목적 중 하나는?
(A) 요리 기법을 논의하려고
(B) 기업 합병에 대한 보도를 하려고
(C) 신제품 라인을 발표하려고
(D) 최근 채용된 임원을 소개하려고

해설 첫 단락 첫 번째 문장에서 비말로 브랜즈에서 조만간 고객들을 위해 새로운 제품인 냉동식품을 선보일 예정(Vimalo Brands ~ will soon offer something new for its customers: frozen foods)이라고 했으므로, 특정 기업의 새로운 제품군 출시를 알리기 위한 기사임을 알 수 있다. 따라서 (C)가 정답이다.

어휘 corporate 기업의 merger 합병 executive 임원

162 동의어 찾기

번역 첫 번째 단락 8행의 "just"와 의미가 가장 가까운 것은?
(A) 최근에
(B) 정확히
(C) 약간
(D) 오로지

해설 의미상 새로운 제품 라인이 '단지' 편리한 것뿐만은 아니라는 뜻으로 쓰였으므로, '단지, 오로지'를 뜻하는 (D) only가 정답이다.

163 추론 / 암시

번역 마르텐스 씨가 급속 냉동식품에 대해 암시하는 것은?
(A) 신선 식품보다 덜 비싸다.
(B) 신선 식품만큼 영양가가 있다.
(C) 신선 식품만큼 배송하기 쉽다.
(D) 신선 식품보다 덜 맛있다.

해설 첫 단락 세 번째 문장에서 마르텐스 씨가 신선한 농산물과 육류를 급속 냉동시키는 당사의 방식은 우리 제품이 식감과 맛뿐 아니라 건강에 유익한 비타민과 미네랄을 유지하도록 보장해 준다(our method of flash-freezing fresh produce and meats ensures that our products retain their texture and flavour as well as their healthy vitamins and minerals)고 했다. 따라서 마르텐스 씨에 따르면 급속 냉동 방식을 통해 냉동한 식품도 신선 식품 못지않게 영양이 보장된다는 것이므로 (B)가 정답이다.

어휘 nutritious 영양가 있는 flavorful 맛있는

> **Paraphrasing**
> 지문의 retain ~ their healthy vitamins and minerals
> → 정답의 nutritious

164-167 광고

마음이 통하는 사람들로 구성된 팀에서 열심히 일할 준비가 되었나요? 당신의 교육, 경험, 그리고 상상력을 크게 활용할 마음이 있나요? 그렇다면 당신을 위한 일이 여기 있습니다. 카닝 크리에이티브 디자인즈는 성장하고 있으며 우리의 성공과 함께 여러분에게도 기회가 주어집니다.

164, 165 카닝 크리에이티브 디자인즈는 현 CEO이자 창립자인 시린 나바니의 집에서 설립된 2인 기업으로 10년 전 시작했습니다. 현재 홀린슨 도심의 아름다운 로프트형 공간에 위치한 우리 회사는 25명의 정규직 직원을 고용하고 있습니다. 카닝에서는 고객을 위해 지면 안내 책자, 카탈로그, 광고, 포스터를 디자인합니다. 우리는 현재 빠르게 변화하는 협업이 요구되는 환경에서 빛을 발할, 자격 있는 디자이너와 아티스트를 찾고 있습니다.

이상적인 지원자
- 디자인, 광고, 또는 그래픽 아트 분야 학위 보유(단, 다년간의 직접적인 경력으로 학위 대체 가능)
- **166** 동료들과 밀접하게 협업할 수 있는 강한 능력 입증
- 세부 사항 및 정확성에 대한 비판적인 시각 유지
- 일관적인 마감 엄수와 압박감 속에서의 활약 가능성

그래픽 디자인 또는 관련 경험은 우대 사항이지만 반드시 필수는 아닙니다.

우리 팀과 함께 할 준비가 되셨다면 당신과 만나고 싶습니다! 자세한 사항은 살바도르 토마신에게 608-555-0144로 연락 주세요. **167** 모든 지원서는 3월 31일까지 접수되어야 합니다.

어휘 like-minded 마음이 맞는 individual 구성원, 개인 be willing to 기꺼이 ~하다 put ~ to use ~을 사용하다 expand 성장하다, 확장하다 opportunity 기회 operation 기업, 사업체 founder 창립자 loft 로프트 (천장이 높은 개방형 공간) paper-based 종이 기반의 qualified 자격이 있는 fast-paced 빠르게 진행되는 collaborative 협업하는 degree 학위 substitute 대체하다 demonstrate 입증하다 critical 비판적인 precision 정확성 consistently 일관되게 flourish 활약하다, 번창하다 pressure 압박 strictly 정확히 further 추가의

164 추론 / 암시

번역 광고에 따르면, 나바니 씨는 누구인 것 같은가?
(A) 카닝 크리에이티브 디자인즈의 고객
(B) 사업체 소유주
(C) 사진작가
(D) 부동산 중개인

해설 두 번째 단락 첫 문장에서 카닝 크리에이티브 디자인즈는 현 CEO이자 창립자인 시린 나바니의 집에서 설립된 2인 기업으로 10년 전 시작했다(Karning Creative Designs began ~ in the home of our current CEO and founder Shirin Navani)고 했으므로 나바니 씨는 카닝 크리에이티브 디자인즈의 소유주임을 알 수 있다. 따라서 (B)가 정답이다.

> **Paraphrasing**
> 지문의 current CEO and founder → 정답의 business owner

165 Not / True

번역 카닝 크리에이티브 디자인즈에 대해 명시된 것은?
(A) 주요 초점은 웹 디자인이다.
(B) 처음에 두 명이 근무했다.
(C) 토마신 씨가 설립했다.
(D) 직원들은 재택근무가 허용된다.

해설 두 번째 단락 첫 문장에서 카닝 크리에이티브 디자인즈는 현 CEO이자 창립자인 시린 나바니의 집에서 설립된 2인 기업으로 10년 전 시작했다(Karning Creative Designs began ten years ago as a two-person operation set up in the home of our current CEO and founder Shirin Navani)고 했으므로 카닝 크리에이티브 디자인즈는 창립 당시 직원이 두 명이었음을 알 수 있다. 따라서 (B)가 정답이다.

어휘 primary 주요한 initially 처음에 permit 허용하다

Paraphrasing
지문의 began ~ as a two-person operation
→ 정답의 initially employed two people

166 세부 사항

번역 취업 지원자에게 요구되는 것은?
(A) 다른 사람들과 함께 일하는 능력
(B) 이전의 디자인 경력
(C) 주말에 근무할 의지
(D) 특정 소프트웨어 사용 능력

해설 세 번째 단락의 두 번째 항목에서 동료들과 밀접하게 협업할 수 있는 강한 능력 입증(Demonstrates a strong ability to work closely with colleagues)을 이상적인 지원자의 요건 중 하나로 꼽고 있으므로 (A)가 정답이다.

어휘 willingness 의향, 기꺼이 하는 마음 certain 특정한

Paraphrasing
지문의 ability to work closely with colleagues
→ 정답의 Skill in working with others

167 세부 사항

번역 3월 31일에 일어날 일은?
(A) 프로젝트가 시작된다.
(B) 마감일이 된다.
(C) 그래픽 디자이너가 자리를 옮긴다.
(D) 지원서가 제공된다.

해설 마지막 단락의 마지막 문장에서 모든 지원서는 3월 31일까지 접수되어야 한다(All applications must be received by March 31)고 명시하고 있으므로 3월 31일이 입사 지원 마감일임을 알 수 있다. 따라서 (B)가 정답이다.

어휘 occur 발생하다 relocate 이동하다 form 양식

168-171 기사

뉴 헤이븐 (6월 1일) — 프론티지 로에 있는 마르코즈 이탈리안 레스토랑이 6월 말 다시 문을 연다. **168 이 레스토랑은 3개월 전에 누수로 인해 주방에 막대한 피해가 발생한 뒤 문을 닫았다. 주방과 식사 공간에 상당한 규모의 작업이 필요했다.** 보수 공사 중에 추가적인 식사 공간이 더해졌다. **171 레스토랑은 재개점하면 더 큰 단체 손님을 수용할 수 있을 것이다.**

지난 3개월 동안 레스토랑의 많은 직원들이 길 건너편에 위치한 마르코즈 이탈리안 마켓에서 일할 수 있었다. "누수는 시장의 성수기가 시작되기 직전에 발생했습니다."라고 두 사업체를 소유하고 있는 톰 마르코는 말했다. **169 "우리는 그곳에 일시적으로 직원을 늘릴 필요가 있었고, 레스토랑 직원들이 계속 근무할 수 있게 되어 기뻤습니다."** 그 직원들 대부분은 현재 레스토랑 근무에 복귀했다.

170 마르코 씨는 6월 25일 성대한 재개점을 계획하고 있다. 손님들은 라이브 음악과 새로운 시식 메뉴를 즐길 것이다. 축하 행사 당일에는 예약이 필수이며 203-555-0124로 전화하면 예약할 수 있다. "우리 식당의 전통 요리들을 준비하고 지역 주민들을 다시 맞이할 수 있어 기쁩니다."라고 마르코 씨는 말했다.

어휘 water leak 누수 extensive 막대한, 대규모의 significant 상당한 dining 식사 accommodate 수용하다 party 단체 opposite 건너편의 temporarily 일시적으로 tasting 시식 community 주민, 공동체 state 말하다

168 Not / True

번역 기사에서 마르코즈 이탈리안 레스토랑에 대해 언급하는 것은?
(A) 뉴 헤이븐에서 가장 오래된 식당이다.
(B) 전통 요리를 할 수 있는 요리사를 구하고 있다.
(C) 대대적인 보수 공사가 필요했다.
(D) 새로운 위치에 문을 열었다.

해설 첫 단락 두 번째 문장에서 마르코즈 이탈리안 레스토랑에 대해 3개월 전에 누수로 인해 주방에 막대한 피해가 발생한 뒤 문을 닫았다(It closed three months ago after a water leak caused extensive damage to the kitchen)고 했고, 주방과 식사 공간에 상당한 규모의 작업이 필요했다(A significant amount of work needed to be done in the kitchen and dining areas)고 했으므로 대대적인 보수 공사가 필요했음을 알 수 있다. 따라서 (C)가 정답이다.

Paraphrasing
지문의 A significant amount of work
→ 정답의 major renovations

169 Not / True

번역 마르코즈 이탈리안 마켓에 대해 명시된 것은?
(A) 마르코즈 이탈리안 레스토랑에 재료를 공급한다.
(B) 가끔 임시 직원을 고용한다.
(C) 3개월 후에 문을 닫을 예정이다.
(D) 마르코즈 이탈리안 레스토랑 옆에 위치해 있다.

해설 두 번째 단락 세 번째 문장에서 우리는 그곳(마르코즈 이탈리안 마켓)에 일시적으로 직원을 늘릴 필요가 있었고, 레스토랑 직원들이 계속 근무할 수 있게 되어 기뻤다(We needed to add staff there temporarily, and I was happy to keep my restaurant crew employed)고 했으므로, 마르코즈 이탈리안 마켓은 일시적으로 직원을 고용하기도 한다는 점을 알 수 있다. 따라서 (B)가 정답이다.

어휘 supply 공급하다   ingredient 재료   occasionally 가끔   temporary 임시의

170 세부 사항

번역 6월 25일 행사 중에 일어날 일은?
(A) 식당은 메뉴 가격을 낮출 것이다.
(B) 식당은 특별 메뉴를 제공할 것이다.
(C) 마르코 씨가 은퇴를 기념할 것이다.
(D) 뉴 헤이븐의 사업 공동체가 마르코 씨에게 훈장을 줄 것이다.

해설 세 번째 단락 첫 문장에서 마르코 씨는 6월 25일 성대한 재개점을 계획하고 있다(Mr. Marco has planned a grand reopening for June 25)면서, 손님들은 라이브 음악과 새로운 시식 메뉴를 즐길 것(Guests will enjoy live music and a new tasting menu)이라고 했다. 따라서 식당은 6월 25일 재개점 행사에서 특별 메뉴를 선보일 예정이므로 (B)가 정답이다.

어휘 reduce 줄이다   retirement 은퇴   honor 명예[훈장]를 주다

Paraphrasing
지문의 a new tasting menu → 정답의 special menu items

171 문장 삽입

번역 [1], [2], [3], [4]로 표시된 위치 중에서 다음 문장이 들어가기에 가장 적합한 곳은?

"보수 공사 중에 추가적인 식사 공간이 더해졌다."
(A) [1]
(B) [2]
(C) [3]
(D) [4]

해설 주어진 문장에서 보수 공사 중 추가적인 식사 공간(additional dining space)이 추가되었다고 설명하고 있으므로, 재개점하면 더 큰 단체 손님을 수용할 수 있을 것(The restaurant will accommodate larger parties when it reopens)이라고 언급한 문장 앞인 [1]에 들어가는 것이 글의 흐름상 자연스러우므로 (A)가 정답이다.

172-175 온라인 채팅

말리스 배리 (오전 10시 17분)
데이터 분석 부서의 배리입니다. 제 동료인 최 씨를 초대했어요. 172 모든 계정 보유자의 이메일 주소를 연령별로 정리한 데이터 요청과 관련해 연락드려요.

알렉산더 쿠벨스키 (오전 10시 17분)
네, 해당 요청을 얼마나 빨리해 주실 수 있을까요?

말리스 배리 (오전 10시 18분)
먼저 질문이 한 가지 있어요. 정말로 모든 계정 보유자의 이메일 주소가 필요하신 건가요? 엄청 큰 파일이 될 거예요. 아니면 특정 연령대 내의 계정 보유자의 이메일 주소만 필요하신가요?

알렉산더 쿠벨스키 (오전 10시 19분)
무슨 뜻인지 알겠어요. 173 55세에서 65세 사이의 계정 보유자들에게 은퇴 설계 전문가와의 만남에 초대하는 이메일을 보내려고 해요. 새 프로젝트 요청서를 제출해야 하나요?

최보라 (오전 10시 21분)
그러실 필요 없어요, 쿠벨스키 씨. 174 현재 요청서를 저희가 대신 수정해 드릴 수 있어요. 대기 순서를 놓치고 싶지 않잖아요.

알렉산더 쿠벨스키 (오전 10시 21분)
좋네요, 감사합니다! 175 그 목록을 바로 주실 수 있을까요?

말리스 배리 (오전 10시 22분)
요청하신 건보다 먼저 해야 할 프로젝트가 몇 개 있어요.

알렉산더 쿠벨스키 (오전 10시 23분)
내일 이메일 초대장을 발송하면 좋겠거든요.

말리스 배리 (오전 10시 24분)
가능한 한 빨리 시작할게요.

어휘 colleague 동료   sort 분류하다   complete 완료하다   certain 특정한   retirement 은퇴   expert 전문가   form 양식   queue (대기) 줄   ahead of ~보다 앞선   get to ~에 착수하다

172 주제 / 목적

번역 배리 씨가 쿠벨스키 씨와 온라인 채팅을 시작한 이유는?
(A) 그를 다른 부서에 보내기 위해서
(B) 초대를 거절하기 위해서
(C) 사과하기 위해서
(D) 요청 건에 대한 설명을 요구하기 위해서

해설 10시 17분에 배리 씨가 쿠벨스키 씨에게 모든 계정 보유자의 이메일 주소를 연령별로 정리한 데이터 요청과 관련해 연락한다(We're contacting you about your data request for the e-mail addresses of all account holders, sorted by age)고 했으므로, 쿠벨스키 씨가 요청한 데이터의 세부 사항을 확인하기 위해 메시지를 보냈음을 알 수 있다. 따라서 (D)가 정답이다.

어휘 refer A to B A를 B에게 보내다   decline 거절하다   issue 발표하다   apology 사과   clarification 설명, 해명

173 세부 사항

번역 쿠벨스키 씨로부터 누가 이메일을 받게 될 것인가?
(A) 한 연령대에 속한 계정 보유자들
(B) 데이터 분석 팀원들
(C) 재무 설계사들
(D) 쿠벨스키 씨의 모든 고객들

해설 10시 19분에 쿠벨스키 씨가 55세에서 65세 사이의 계정 보유자들에게 은퇴 설계 전문가와의 만남에 초대하는 이메일을 보내려고 한다(I want to e-mail account holders aged 55 to 65 to invite them to meet with a retirement planning expert)고 했으므로, 55~65세 사이의 계정 보유자들이 쿠벨스키 씨로부터 이메일을 받게 될 것임을 알 수 있다. 따라서 (A)가 정답이다.

174 세부 사항

번역 최 씨는 무엇을 하겠다고 제안하는가?
(A) 이메일 작성
(B) 양식 수정
(C) 계정 개설
(D) 정책 변경

해설 10시 21분에 최 씨가 현재 요청서를 대신 수정해 줄 수 있다(We can update your current request form for you)고 제안하고 있으므로 (B)가 정답이다.

어휘 revise 변경하다

Paraphrasing
지문의 update → 정답의 Make a change

175 의도 파악

번역 오전 10시 22분에 배리 씨가 "요청하신 건보다 먼저 해야 할 프로젝트가 몇 개 있어요"라고 쓴 의도는?
(A) 배리 씨는 쿠벨스키 씨의 요청을 맨 뒤 순서로 옮길 것이다.
(B) 배리 씨는 쿠벨스키 씨를 위한 초대장을 보낼 수 없을 것이다.
(C) 쿠벨스키 씨의 요청은 배리 씨가 먼저 완료할 작업이 아니다.
(D) 쿠벨스키 씨는 먼저 다른 프로젝트를 도와야 할 것이다.

해설 10시 21분에 쿠벨스키 씨가 그 목록을 바로 줄 수 있는지(Is it possible for you to get me that list right away?) 묻자 10시 22분에 배리 씨가 요청하신 건보다 먼저 해야 할 프로젝트가 몇 개 있다(There are several projects ahead of yours)고 대답한 것이므로, 배리 씨는 먼저 해야 할 작업이 있어서 쿠벨스키 씨가 요청한 목록을 바로 줄 수 없다는 의도로 한 말임을 알 수 있다. 따라서 (C)가 정답이다.

176-180 기사 + 이메일

푸드트럭 사업을 위한 웹사이트 디자인 팁

176 푸드트럭 소유주들은 사업을 하면서 도시 안팎을 이곳저곳 옮겨 다니므로 고객을 끌기 위해 종종 입소문이나 소셜 미디어에 의존한다. 그 결과, 이들은 자체 웹사이트를 만들지 않을 수도 있다. 하지만 사실 이들의 사업 특성상, 대중들이 푸드트럭에 대해 알아보고, 주문하고, 연락할 수 있는 고정된 장소를 갖는 것은 푸드트럭 소유주에게 대단히 중요하다. 뿐만 아니라, 시장 조사는 웹사이트가 충성 고객 기반을 구축하는 데 도움이 될 수 있음을 보여준다. 그래서 여러분의 푸드트럭을 위한 훌륭한 웹사이트를 개발하는 데 몇 가지 팁을 소개한다.

177(C) 메인 페이지에는 푸드트럭의 이름이 들어간 굵은 그래픽이 있어야 한다. 177(A), 177(B) 글에는 트럭의 위치와 운영 시간과 같은 핵심 정보가 눈에 띄게 표시되어야 한다. 특별 행사나 서비스 예약 요청처럼 입력란이 있는 온라인 양식은 새로운 방문자에게 과도한 시각 정보를 준다. 이것들은 링크나 팝업 창으로 포함시키는 것이 더 낫다.

음식 메뉴 페이지에는 각각의 메뉴를 상세하게 설명하는 생생하고 정확한 문구와 함께 매력적인 고화질 이미지가 필요하다. 사진은 큰 컴퓨터 모니터에서도 매력적으로 보일 수 있을 만큼 충분히 커야 한다는 점을 기억하라.

업체 소개 페이지에는 푸드트럭의 테마와 콘셉트를 설명하는 문구와 식품 업계에서의 경력을 설명하는 약력이 들어가야 한다.

177(D), 179 소식 페이지에는 방문자에게 계절 음식 메뉴와 다가오는 판촉 행사나 푸드 페스티벌 같은 특별 행사에 대해 알리는 글이 들어갈 수 있다.

어휘 carry out ~을 수행하다 rely on ~에 의존하다 word of mouth 입소문 attract 끌다 nature 특성, 본질 crucial 중대한 fixed 고정된 bold 굵은 text 글 prominently 눈에 띄게 operating 운영상의 field 란, 항목 visual 시각의 incorporate 포함하다 high-definition 고화질의 vivid 생생한 precise 정확한 in detail 상세하게 appealing 매력적인 biographical data 약력 background 경력, 배경 promotion 판촉 (활동)

수신: 더그 아브루쪼 〈dabruzzo@dzacreative.com〉
발신: 에드 베일 〈evale@saffronmail.com〉
날짜: 3월 29일
제목: 피드백

아브루쪼 씨께,

178 제 푸드트럭 사업을 위한 웹사이트 견본을 제작해 주셔서 다시 한번 감사드립니다. 웹사이트를 테스트해 본 고객들로부터 긍정적인 피드백을 받았다는 것을 거듭 말씀드리고 싶습니다. 푸드트럭 웹사이트 디자인에 관해 보내주신 기사 속 조언을 따르길 정말 다행입니다!

어제 전화 통화에서 논의한 대로, 180 웹사이트 견본을 진행시켜서 4월 5일에 공식 웹사이트로 개시할 예정입니다. 하지만 179 샌드위치 구매 시 무료 디저트를 주는 4월 중순에 시작하는 새 판촉 행사에 대해 제가 보내드린 정보는 아직 보이지 않네요. 사이트를 개시하기 전에 이 중요한 정보를 반드시 추가해 주세요.

에드

어휘 prototype 견본 reiterate 반복하다 move forward 진행하다 launch 개시하다 official 공식적인

176 세부 사항

번역 기사에 따르면, 푸드트럭 소유주들이 전통적으로 고객을 유치하는 한 가지 방법은?
(A) 입소문
(B) 고속도로 광고판
(C) 신문 광고
(D) 푸드 페스티벌의 표지판

해설 기사의 첫 단락 첫 문장에서 푸드트럭 소유주들은 고객을 끌기 위해 종종 입소문이나 소셜 미디어에 의존한다(Owners of food trucks ~ often rely on word of mouth or social media to attract customers)고 했으므로 (A)가 정답이다.

어휘 billboard 광고판

177 Not / True

번역 기사에 따르면, 메인 페이지에 게시될 필요가 없는 정보는?
(A) 트럭 위치
(B) 운영 시간
(C) 회사 이름
(D) 계절 음식 메뉴

해설 기사의 두 번째 단락 첫 문장에서 메인 페이지에는 푸드트럭의 이름이 들어간 굵은 그래픽이 있어야 한다(The Home page should have bold graphics with your food truck's name)고 했으므로 (C), 같은 단락 두 번째 문장에서 글에는 트럭의 위치와 운영 시간과 같은 핵심 정보가 눈에 띄게 표시되어야 한다(The text must prominently display key information, such as your truck's locations and operating hours)고 했으므로 (A)와 (B)가 메인 페이지에 명시되어야 할 정보로 언급되었다. 하지만 기사의 마지막 문장에서 소식 페이지에는 방문자에게 계절 음식 메뉴와 다가오는 판촉 행사나 푸드 페스티벌 같은 특별 행사에 대해 알리는 글이 들어갈 수 있다(The News page can include text informing visitors about seasonal food items and upcoming promotions or special events such as food festivals)고 했다. 따라서 계절 음식 메뉴는 메인 페이지가 아닌 소식 페이지에 들어갈 정보이므로 (D)가 정답이다.

178 추론 / 암시

번역 아브루쪼 씨는 어떤 분야에서 일할 것 같은가?
(A) 시장 조사
(B) 출장 요리
(C) 웹디자인
(D) 택배 배송

해설 이메일의 첫 단락 첫 문장에서 베일 씨가 아브루쪼 씨에게 자신의 푸드트럭 사업을 위한 웹사이트 견본을 제작해 줘서 다시 한번 감사드린다(Thank you again for creating the prototype Web site for my food-truck business)고 한 것으로 보아 아브루쪼 씨는 웹사이트를 디자인하는 일을 하고 있음을 짐작할 수 있다. 따라서 (C)가 정답이다.

> **Paraphrasing**
> 지문의 creating the prototype Web site
> → 정답의 Web design

179 연계

번역 정보는 웹사이트의 어느 섹션에 추가될 것 같은가?
(A) 메인 페이지
(B) 음식 메뉴 페이지
(C) 업체 소개 페이지
(D) 소식 페이지

해설 이메일의 두 번째 단락 두 번째 문장에서 샌드위치 구매 시 무료 디저트를 주는 4월 중순에 시작하는 새 판촉 행사에 대해 보낸 정보는 아직 보이지 않는다(I still do not see the information I sent about our new promotion that will begin in mid-April, a free dessert with any sandwich purchase)고 했고, 기사의 마지막 문장에서 소식 페이지에는 방문자에게 계절 음식 메뉴와 다가오는 판촉 행사나 푸드 페스티벌 같은 특별 행사에 대해 알리는 글이 들어갈 수 있다(The News page can include text informing visitors about seasonal food items and upcoming promotions or special events such as food festivals)고 했다. 따라서 판촉 행사에 관한 정보는 소식 페이지에 들어가야 하므로 (D)가 정답이다.

180 세부 사항

번역 이메일에 따르면, 웹사이트는 언제 개시될 예정인가?
(A) 3월 28일
(B) 3월 29일
(C) 4월 5일
(D) 4월 15일

해설 이메일의 두 번째 단락 첫 문장에서 웹사이트 견본을 진행시켜서 4월 5일에 공식 웹사이트로 개시할 예정(we will move forward with the prototype Web site and launch it as the official site on April 5)이라고 했다. 따라서 (C)가 정답이다.

181-185 이메일 + 보도 자료

수신: 매니 그린 〈mgreen@rhba.com〉
발신: 존 라로즈 〈jlarose@rilamore.edu〉
날짜: 5월 18일
제목: 시추 공사 공지

그린 씨께:

예를 갖추어 레드 힐스 비즈니스 협회에 계신 귀하께 글을 쓰고 있으며, 제가 귀하의 회원들에게 이 소식을 전하도록 도와주시기를 요청드립니다. **181** 지난달 〈데일리 가제트〉에 릴라모어 대학교가 넷 제로 이니셔티브를 진행한다는 계획이 발표되었습니다. 3년 이내에 저희는 캠퍼스 전체의 냉난방을 위해 지열 우물을 설치해 운영할 것으로 예상합니다. 기관의 화석 연료 의존도를 제한하는 것은 오랜 목표였으며, 새로운 시스템은 그 목표를 달성하기 위한 중요한 단계입니다.

183 다음 한 달 동안 저희는 캠퍼스 내 여러 위치에서 시추 테스트를 **182** 수행할 예정입니다. 모든 것이 일정에 따라 진행된다면 **183, 184** 작업팀은 6월 5일 수요일부터 레드 힐스 비즈니스 지구와 오크 가 아파트 인근에서 시추를 하게 됩니다. **184** 캠퍼스 주변의 업주 및 주민분들께 공사가 완료되는 데 걸릴 것으로 예상되는 2주 동안 평소보다 높은 수준의 소음이 발생할 수 있음을 말씀드리고자 합니다. 시추 작업팀의 작업 시간은 월요일부터 금요일까지 매일 오전 10시부터 오후 3시까지입니다.

이로 인해 이웃분들께 불편을 드리게 된 점 미리 사과드립니다. 질문 또는 우려 사항은 813-555-0123으로 저에게 보내 주십시오.

존 라로즈
릴라모어 대학교 커뮤니케이션 부서, 커뮤니티 연락 담당

어휘 drilling 시추 courtesy 예의 association 협회 get the word out 말을 퍼뜨리다 membership 회원 move forward 진행하다 initiative (목적 달성을 위한) 계획 geothermal 지열의 well 우물 install 설치하다 operational 운영의 entire 전체의 limit 제한하다 institution 기관 reliance 의존 fossil fuel 화석 연료 significant 중요한 achieve 달성하다 conduct 수행하다 adjacent to ~에 인접한 district 지구, 구역 estimate 추정하다 in advance 미리 inconvenience 불편 direct (편지 등을) ~에게 보내다 liaison 연락 담당자

즉각 보도용

연락 담당: 매니 그린, mgreen@rhba.com

레드 힐스 (5월 25일) — **184** 레드 힐스 비즈니스 협회는 많은 기대를 받고 있는 점심 콘서트 시리즈의 일정을 변경합니다. 보통 6월 매주 목요일에 열리던 이 네 번의 무료 콘서트는 대신 7월 매주 목요일에 개최됩니다. 출연진 명단은 변함없으며 7월 4일에 제이스톤 재즈 트리오가 시리즈를 시작하고, 목요일마다 연이어 조즈 앤 더 제이버즈, 레이 스타폼, 바클레이 베이스 퀸텟이 뒤따릅니다.

평년과 같이, 오크 가의 세 블록 전체에 교통이 통제되며 레스토랑에서는 야외 테이블에서 점심을 제공하고, **185** 지역 미술품 및 공예품 상인들은 문화센터 잔디밭에 작품을 전시할 예정입니다. 이 행사는 인기 있는 레드 힐스 지역의 심장부에서 열리는 아름다운 행사입니다. 그곳에서 여러분을 뵙기를 바랍니다!

어휘 immediate 즉각적인 release (뉴스 등의) 발표, 공개 shift 옮기다 anticipated 기대하던 normally 보통 present 공연하다 instead 대신에 take place 열리다 lineup (행사) 참석 예정자들 successive 연이은 craft 공예품 vendor 행상인

181 Not / True

번역 넷 제로 이니셔티브에 대해 명시된 것은?
(A) 레드 힐스 비즈니스 협회로부터 자금 지원을 받고 있다.
(B) 다른 도시의 유사한 이니셔티브에서 영감을 받았다.
(C) 도시에 전력을 공급하기 위해 지열 에너지를 사용할 것이다.
(D) 기관이 건물을 난방하는 방식을 바꿀 것이다.

해설 이메일의 첫 단락 두 번째 문장에서 지난달 〈데일리 가제트〉에 릴라모어 대학교의 넷 제로 이니셔티브 진행 계획이 발표되었다(It was announced in last month's *Daily Gazette* that Rilamore University is moving forward with its Net Zero Initiative)고 했고, 3년 이내에 캠퍼스 전체의 냉난방을 위해 지열 우물을 설치해 운영할 것으로 예상한다(Within three years, we expect to have geothermal wells installed and operational for the heating and cooling of our entire campus)면서 기관의 화석 연료 의존도 제한은 오랜 목표였으며 새로운 시스템은 그 목표를 달성하기 위한 중요한 단계(Limiting the institution's reliance on fossil fuels has long been a goal, and the new system is a significant step toward achieving that goal)라고 했다. 따라서 넷 제로 이니셔티브는 릴라모어 대학교의 냉난방 방식을 화석 연료가 아닌 지열 에너지를 활용하는 방식으로 바꾸는 사업 계획임을 알 수 있으므로 (D)가 정답이다.

어휘 fund 자금을 대다 inspire 영감을 주다

> **Paraphrasing**
> 지문의 Rilamore University → 정답의 institution

182 동의어 찾기

번역 이메일의 두 번째 단락 1행의 "conduct"와 의미가 가장 가까운 것은?
(A) 행동하다
(B) 동행하다
(C) 전송하다
(D) 수행하다

해설 의미상 다음 달에 시추 테스트를 '수행할 것'이라는 뜻으로 쓰였으므로 '수행하다, 실행하다'를 뜻하는 (D) carry out이 정답이다.

183 추론 / 암시

번역 레드 힐스 비즈니스 지구에 대해 결론지을 수 있는 것은?
(A) 대학교 캠퍼스 근처에 있다.
(B) 7월마다 예술 축제를 주최한다.
(C) 오크 가 아파트를 포함한다.
(D) 〈데일리 가제트〉의 사무실이 있는 곳이다.

해설 이메일의 두 번째 단락 첫 문장에서 다음 한 달 동안 캠퍼스 내 여러 위치에서 시추 테스트를 수행한다(Over the next month, we will conduct test drilling in several campus locations)고 했고, 그 다음 문장에서 작업팀은 6월 5일 수요일부터 레드 힐스 비즈니스 지구와 오크 가 아파트 인근에서 시추를 하게 된다(the crew will be drilling adjacent to the Red Hills Business District and Oak Street Apartments starting Wednesday, June 5)고 했다. 이를 통해 레드 힐스 비즈니스 지구는 대학 캠퍼스와 인접해 있음을 알 수 있으므로 (A)가 정답이다.

184 연계

번역 레드 힐스 비즈니스 협회는 왜 콘서트 시리즈의 날짜를 변경한 것 같은가?
(A) 새로운 전력원을 활용하기 위해서
(B) 학생들의 일정에 맞추기 위해서
(C) 근처 공사 소음을 피하기 위해서
(D) 비슷한 행사와 겹치는 것을 막기 위해서

해설 이메일의 두 번째 단락 두 번째 문장에서 작업팀은 6월 5일 수요일부터 레드 힐스 비즈니스 지구와 오크 가 아파트 인근에서 시추를 하게 된다(the crew will be drilling adjacent to the Red Hills Business District and Oak Street Apartments starting Wednesday, June 5)면서 캠퍼스 주변의 업주 및

주민분들께 공사가 완료되는 데 걸릴 것으로 예상되는 2주 동안 평소보다 높은 수준의 소음이 발생할 수 있음을 말씀드린다(We want to tell business owners and residents near the campus to expect a higher-than-usual noise level during the two weeks we estimate it will take to complete the work)고 했고, 보도 자료의 첫 단락 첫 문장에서 레드 힐스 비즈니스 협회는 많은 기대를 받고 있는 점심 콘서트 시리즈의 일정을 변경한다(The Red Hills Business Association is shifting the dates of its much-anticipated Lunch Hour Concert Series)면서 보통 6월 매주 목요일에 열리는 이 네 번의 무료 콘서트는 대신 7월 매주 목요일에 개최된다(Normally presented each Thursday in June, the four free concerts will instead take place each Thursday in July)고 했다. 따라서 레드 힐스 협회는 6월 5일부터 2주간 발생될 수 있는 공사 소음을 피하고자 콘서트 일정을 7월로 미뤘다는 것을 알 수 있으므로 (C)가 정답이다.

어휘 take advantage of ~을 활용하다   power source 전력원   accommodate 수용하다   prevent 막다   conflict 충돌

185 Not / True

번역 문화 센터에 대해 보도 자료에 언급된 것은?
(A) 음악가들을 위해 점심을 제공할 것이다.
(B) 건물 부지에 판매용 미술품을 놓을 것이다.
(C) 미술품과 공예품 워크숍을 제공할 것이다.
(D) 공연자들에게 무대를 제공할 것이다.

해설 보도 자료의 두 번째 단락 첫 문장에서 지역 미술품 및 공예품 상인들은 문화센터 잔디밭에 작품을 전시할 예정(local arts-and-crafts vendors will display their work on the lawn of the Cultural Center)이라고 했으므로 (B)가 정답이다.

어휘 property 건물 (구내)   performer 공연자

> **Paraphrasing**
> 지문의 arts-and-crafts vendors will display their work
> → 정답의 artwork for sale

186-190 광고 + 양식 + 후기

로얄 홈 서비스: 40년 이상 남부 캘리포니아에 서비스를 제공하고 있습니다.

로얄 홈 서비스는 잉글우드와 그 주변 지역의 남부 캘리포니아 주민들에게 지붕 공사 및 태양광 서비스를 제공합니다. 지붕 교체 외에도, 186 저희는 다락방 단열 및 홈통 복구에서 누수 보수와 태양광 패널 설치까지 다양한 서비스를 제공합니다.

로얄 홈 서비스는 투명한 소통과 세부 사항에 주의를 기울이는 것을 자랑으로 여깁니다. 189 저희 프로젝트 감독관들은 항상 현장에서 고객의 질문에 답하고 업데이트를 제공하며 안전하고 청결한 작업 현장을 보장합니다. 무료 지붕 공사 진단을 신청하려면 www.lawalhomeservice.com을 방문하시거나 310-555-0108로 예약 담당자에게 전화 주십시오.

어휘 southern 남부의   roofing 지붕 공사   solar 태양의   surrounding 주변의   replacement 교체   a wide array of 다수의   attic 다락방   insulation 단열   gutter (지붕의) 홈통   restoration 복구   leak 누수   install 설치하다   pride oneself on ~을 자랑하다   transparent 투명한   attention 주의   supervisor 감독관   on-site 현장의   worksite 작업장   diagnosis 진단   booking 예약

로얄 홈 서비스 연락 양식

로얄 홈 서비스의 전문가들을 믿고 지붕 공사에 필요한 것들을 신속하고 전문적으로 진단받으세요. 몇 분만 시간을 내셔서 가능한 한 많은 세부정보를 양식에 기입해 주세요. 로얄이 설치하는 모든 지붕은 25년 보증이 제공된다는 점을 기억하세요.

이름	드루 거슨
날짜	188 12월 12일
이메일	dgerson95@onyxmail.com
전화번호	310-555-0192
주소	노스 아카시아 로 820번지 잉글우드, 캘리포니아 90301
무엇을 도와드릴까요?	지난 주 강풍이 부는 동안 지붕널 몇 개가 떨어져 나가서 교체가 필요합니다. 187 지붕이 30년이 넘었고, 파티오 위쪽 부분에서 물이 떨어지기 시작해서 전체 지붕 교체를 고민 중입니다. 제가 선택할 수 있는 옵션을 알려주시고 견적을 내주실 분과 상담할 수 있으면 감사하겠습니다.

어휘 form 양식   expert 전문가   diagnose 진단하다   promptly 신속하게   complete (서식을 빠짐없이) 기입하다   warranty 보증   windstorm 강풍   shingle 지붕널   tear 뜯어 내다   loose 헐거워진   replace 교체하다   entire 전체의   drip 떨어지다   section 부분   appreciate 감사하다   estimate 견적

이웃 평가 : 로얄 홈 서비스
★★★★★

"그들이 철저히 작업하는 데 아주 만족했습니다."

188 저는 제 문제에 대한 설명을 로얄 홈 서비스에 남겼고, 이 회사의 견적 담당자 중 한 명이 바로 다음 날 지붕을 점검하러 왔습니다. 지붕을 교체하기로 결정하고 나서, 로얄 홈 서비스 작업팀이 그 다음 주에 작업에 착수할 수 있었습니다. 189 다이애나 페레즈는 약속한 대로 작업하는 내내 현장에 있었고 저의 모든 질문에 답해주었습니다. 작업은 12월 19일에 시작해서 12월 20일에 끝났습니다. 지붕 공사가 끝나자마자 작업팀은 청소를 훌륭하게 해 주셨습니다. 190 그들은 잔디 깎는 기계처럼 생긴 자기 장치 두 대를 이용해 잔디 전체를 쓸며 떨어진 지붕 못을 찾아냈습니다. 그런 건 여태 본 적이 없었습니다! 저는 그들이 철저하게 작업하는 데에 아주 만족합니다.

– 드루 거슨, 잉글우드, 캘리포니아

어휘 thoroughness 철저함 description 설명 estimator 견적인 inspect 점검하다 get to ~에 착수하다 magnetic 자기(자성)의 device 장치 resemble 닮다 lawnmower 잔디 깎는 기계 sweep 쓸다 nail 못

186 세부 사항

번역 광고에 따르면, 로얄 홈 서비스가 수행하는 종류의 작업 중 하나는?
(A) 나무 심기
(B) 홈통 수리
(C) 주택 증축 공사
(D) 난방 시스템 교체

해설 광고의 첫 단락 두 번째 문장에서 다락방 단열 및 홈통 복구에서 누수 보수와 태양광 패널 설치까지 다양한 서비스를 제공한다(we offer a wide array of services, from attic insulation and gutter restoration to fixing leaks and installing solar panels)고 했으므로 (B)가 정답이다.

Paraphrasing
지문의 restoration → 정답의 Repairing

187 Not / True

번역 거슨 씨가 양식에서 자신의 지붕에 대해 명시한 것은?
(A) 누수가 발생했다.
(B) 최근에 교체되었다.
(C) 설치 비용이 높지 않았다.
(D) 30년 보증을 받고 있다.

해설 양식의 마지막 항목 두 번째 문장에서 거슨 씨가 지붕이 30년이 넘었고 파티오 위쪽 부분에서 물이 떨어지기 시작해서 전체 지붕 교체를 고민 중(I am considering replacing the entire roof as it is over 30 years old, and water has begun to drip through the section over the patio)이라고 했다. 따라서 거슨 씨의 지붕에 누수가 있음을 언급하고 있으므로 (A)가 정답이다.

Paraphrasing
지문의 water has begun to drip → 정답의 leak

188 연계

번역 로얄 홈 서비스는 언제 거슨 씨의 지붕을 점검했는가?
(A) 12월 12일
(B) 12월 13일
(C) 12월 19일
(D) 12월 20일

해설 후기의 본문 첫 번째 문장에서 거슨 씨가 문제에 대한 설명을 로얄 홈 서비스에 남겼고 이 회사의 견적 담당자 중 한 명이 바로 다음 날 지붕을 점검하러 왔다(I left a description of my problem with Lawal Home Service, and one of the company's estimators came to inspect my roof the very next day)고 했으며, 양식의 중반부 날짜 항목에서 거슨 씨는 12월 12일(December 12)에 양식을 작성했다는 것을 알 수 있다. 따라서 로얄 홈 서비스는 거슨 씨가 양식을 작성한 다음 날인 12월 13일에 지붕을 점검하러 왔음을 알 수 있으므로 (B)가 정답이다.

189 연계

번역 페레즈 씨는 누구인 것 같은가?
(A) 프로젝트 감독관
(B) 지붕 공사 견적 담당자
(C) 실내 장식가
(D) 예약 담당자

해설 후기의 본문 세 번째 문장에서 다이애나 페레즈는 약속한 대로 작업하는 내내 현장에 있었고 모든 질문에 답해주었다(Diana Perez was on-site for the whole job as promised and answered all my questions)고 했고, 광고의 두 번째 단락 두 번째 문장에서 프로젝트 감독관들은 항상 현장에서 고객의 질문에 답한다(Our project supervisors are always on-site to answer client questions)고 했다. 따라서 페레즈 씨는 로얄 홈 서비스의 프로젝트 감독관임을 알 수 있으므로 (A)가 정답이다.

어휘 decorator 장식가

190 세부 사항

번역 후기에 따르면, 거슨 씨는 로얄 홈 서비스 작업팀의 어떤 점에 놀랐는가?
(A) 그들이 청구한 가격
(B) 그들이 제공한 보증
(C) 그들이 사용하는 자재의 품질
(D) 그들이 작업에 사용한 도구

해설 후기의 본문 여섯 번째 문장에서 거슨 씨가 그들은 잔디 깎는 기계처럼 생긴 자기 장치 두 대를 이용해 잔디 전체를 쓸어 떨어진 지붕 못을 찾아냈다(They used two magnetic devices resembling lawnmowers and swept over my entire lawn to find any dropped roofing nails)면서 그런 건 여태 본 적이 없었다(I had never seen anything like that!)고 감탄하고 있다. 따라서 거슨 씨는 로얄 홈 서비스의 작업팀에서 사용하는 기계에 대해 놀라워하는 것이므로 (D)가 정답이다.

어휘 charge 청구하다 material 자재 tool 도구

Paraphrasing
지문의 devices → 정답의 tools

191-195 이메일 + 이메일 + 양식

191 수신: 오마르 발라지 〈obalaji@darbourycompany.com〉
발신: 후아니타 페레이라 〈jpereira@bunbunbooks.com〉
날짜: 5월 10일
제목: 공책 문의

발라지 씨께,

저희 번번 북스에서는 사무용품 부문을 확장하고 있으며, 줄이 그어진 페이지가 있는 다양한 백지 공책들을 선보이고자 합니다. **191** 다음의 표지 디자인을 만드는 데 귀사의 도움을 받고 싶습니다.

표지 디자인 이름	중심 이미지	배경 색상
195 위대한 생각들	전구, 번개, 별 아이콘들	**195** 파랑
192 세계 여행 가방	나라 이름 여행 스티커가 붙어 있는 여행 가방	**192** 검정
라벤더 꽃다발	긴 연두색 줄기들 위에 있는 큰 라벤더 꽃다발	노랑
항해 떠나기	호수 위 조각배 위로 하늘에는 해가 지는 장면	하양

8월 1일에 시작하는 저희 연례 세일에 맞춰 공책을 입고해 두어야 합니다. 샘플 표지를 승인한 다음 언제 주문을 해야 하나요?

후아니타 페레이라

어휘 expand 확장하다 office supply 사무용품 a selection of 다양한 blank (글자가 없는) 빈 cover 표지 background 배경 lightbulb 전구 lightning bolt 번개 bouquet 꽃다발 bunch 다발 pale 연한 stem 줄기 in stock 재고로 있는 in time for ~에 맞춰서 approve 승인하다

수신: 후아니타 페레이라 〈jpereira@bunbunbooks.com〉
발신: 오마르 발라지 〈obalaji@darbourycompany.com〉
날짜: 5월 25일
제목: 회신: 공책 문의

안녕하세요, 페레이라 씨,

귀하께서 검토하실 수 있도록 공책 표지 샘플을 몇 개 보냈습니다. **192** 아쉽게도 배경 색상에 막판 수정이 필요해서 귀하의 승인이 필요한 디자인 중 하나를 포함시키지 못했습니다. 스티커 아트가 원래의 검정 바탕에서는 잘 보이지 않았습니다. 현재 밝은 베이지 색상을 테스트 중이며 내부 승인을 받은 뒤 업데이트된 표지 샘플을 보내드리겠습니다.

이번 주 말까지 마지막 샘플을 보내드릴 수 있을 것입니다. **193** 6월 11일까지 모든 표지에 대한 승인을 보내주신다면 7월 20일 이전에 제본된 공책의 전체 주문을 발송할 수 있을 것입니다. 8월 1일에 시작하는 귀하의 세일 이전에 모두 받아 보시게 될 것입니다. 질문이 있으시면 저에게 연락 주십시오.

오마르 발라지, 다버리 컴퍼니

어휘 inspection 검토, 점검 approval 승인 stage 단계 original 원래의 internally 내부적으로 entire 전체의 bound 제본하다(bind의 과거분사)

**다버리 컴퍼니
주문서**

194 고객: 번번 북스
발송 기한: 7월 15일
발송 방식: 표준
요청 배송일: 7월 20일

항목 코드	제품 설명	표지 디자인	수량
195 N3-GT	표준 크기 스프링 공책	**195** 위대한 생각들	200
N3-WS	표준 크기 스프링 공책	세계 여행 가방	200
H3-LB	소형 하드커버 일기장	라벤더 꽃다발	150
H3-SA	소형 하드커버 일기장	항해 떠나기	150
D1	**194** 대형 금속 진열대 (표준 크기 스프링 공책 배치용)	–	1

어휘 form 양식 description 설명 spiral 스프링 제본된 hardbound 딱딱한 표지를 씌운 journal 일기 rack 진열대, 선반

---

191 세부 사항

번역 다버리 컴퍼니에서 제공할 가능성이 높은 서비스 하나는?
(A) 여행 예약
(B) 교과서 출판
(C) 꽃 배달
(D) 그래픽 디자인

해설 첫 번째 이메일의 수신인인 오마르 발라지 씨(To: Omar Balaji)의 이메일 주소가 〈obalaji@darbourycompany.com〉이고, 첫 단락의 두 번째 문장에서 발라지 씨에게 표지 디자인을 만드는 데 도움을 받고 싶다(We would like your help creating the following cover designs)고 한 것으로 보아, 발라지 씨가 근무하는 다버리 컴퍼니는 문구 등을 위한 그래픽 디자인 서비스를 제공하는 회사임을 유추할 수 있다. 따라서 (D)가 정답이다.

192 연계

번역 어떤 샘플이 지연되었는가?
(A) 위대한 생각들
(B) 세계 여행 가방
(C) 라벤더 꽃다발
(D) 항해 떠나기

해설 두 번째 이메일의 첫 단락 두 번째 문장에서 아쉽게도 배경 색상에 막판 수정이 필요해서 승인이 필요한 디자인 중 하나를 포함시키지 못했다(Unfortunately, I was not able to include one of the designs for your approval because it needed a late-stage change to the background color)면서 스티커 아트가 원래의 검정 바탕에서는 잘 보이지 않았다(The sticker art did not show up well against the original black background)고 했고, 첫 번째 이메일의 표 중반부에 세계 여행 가방(World Suitcase)의 배경 색상이 검정(Black)이라고 나와 있다. 따라서 배경이 검정색인 세계 여행 가방의 샘플 제작이 지연되고 있음을 알 수 있으므로 (B)가 정답이다.

193 세부 사항

번역 페레이라 씨가 샘플을 승인해야 하는 마감일은 언제인가?
(A) 5월 25일
(B) 6월 11일
(C) 7월 20일
(D) 8월 1일

해설 두 번째 이메일의 두 번째 단락 두 번째 문장에서 페레이라 씨에게 6월 11일까지 모든 표지에 대한 승인을 보내준다면 7월 20일 이전에 제본된 공책의 전체 주문을 발송할 수 있을 것(As long as you send your approval of all covers by June 11, we will be able to ship your entire order of bound notebooks before July 20)이라고 했으므로, (B)가 정답이다.

194 Not / True

번역 양식에서 번번 북스 주문에 대해 명시하는 것은?
(A) 진열대가 포함될 것이다.
(B) 익일 배송될 것이다.
(C) 배송 시 결제될 것이다.
(D) 늦게 도착할 것이다.

해설 양식의 상단에 고객 이름은 번번 북스(Customer: Bun Bun Books), 하단의 제품 설명란에 대형 금속 진열대(Large metal display rack)가 표기되어 있으므로, 번번 북스의 주문 목록 중 진열대가 포함되어 있음을 알 수 있다. 따라서 (A)가 정답이다.

어휘 overnight 하룻밤 사이에

195 연계

번역 항목 N3-GT의 표지 배경 색상은?
(A) 파랑
(B) 검정
(C) 노랑
(D) 하양

해설 양식의 표 첫 항목에서 N3-GT는 위대한 생각들(Great Thoughts)의 표지 디자인임을 알 수 있고, 첫 번째 이메일의 표 첫 항목에서 위대한 생각들(Great Thoughts)의 배경 색상이 파랑(Blue)임을 알 수 있다. 따라서 N3-GT, 즉 위대한 생각들의 표지 배경 색상은 파랑이므로 (A)가 정답이다.

196-200 이메일 + 후기 + 공지

수신: 관리자들
발신: 샬럿 블랙
날짜: 8월 16일
제목: 이달의 직원

관리자 여러분께,

196, 200 9월 윌슨 오토의 이달의 직원에 투표할 시간입니다. 다음은 후보자들입니다.

에리카 보이드는 불과 몇 개월간 우리와 함께 했지만 이미 큰 가능성을 보여주었고 새로운 것을 배우는 데 열심입니다.

로렌 알마흐디는 매우 주도적입니다. 무언가 해야 할 일이 생기면 그녀는 그 일을 관리자에게 알리고 자원해서 직접 처리하려 합니다.

197 닉 살레히는 우리 컴퓨터 시스템에서 오류를 발견했고 불필요한 재고를 잘못 주문하는 것을 멈춰 주었습니다(그래서 비용을 절약해 주었습니다).

맥스 로즈는 신입 사원 교육에 특히 도움을 주었습니다. 그는 침착하고 인내심이 있으며 당사 절차를 잘 설명합니다.

196 금요일까지 여러분의 투표를 이 이메일로 회신해 주세요. **200** 수상자는 최소 3표 이상을 받아야 합니다. 수상자는 다음 주 월요일에 프론트 데스크와 웹사이트에 게시될 예정입니다.

198 샬럿 블랙
윌슨 오토 총괄 관리자

어휘 vote for ~에 투표하다 nominee 후보 promise 가능성 proactive 주도적인 point out ~을 지적하다 glitch 오류 incorrectly 잘못, 부정확하게 inventory 재고 hire 신입 사원 procedure 절차 post 게시하다

---

https://www.westchesterreviews.com

윌슨 오토 (웨스트체스터)
★★★★★

제 아내와 저는 최근 윌슨 오토 웨스트체스터 지점에서 에리카 보이드의 도움을 받아 신형 엑셀레라 트럭을 구입했습니다. 그녀는 신입이었지만 우리가 시승하기를 원했던 매장 내 모든 트럭에 대해 매우 잘 알고 있었습니다. 그녀가 답을 주지 못했던 몇몇 질문은 그녀의 멘토인 맥스 씨가 빠르게 해결해 주었습니다. 우리는 고객 서비스에 몹시 만족했으며 **198** 총괄 관리자가 경쟁 대리점에서 광고하는 동일가에 엑셀레라를 판매하기로 동의했을 때는 더욱 기뻤습니다. 신차 구입에 관심이 있으시다면 윌슨 오토를 강력히 추천합니다!

— 헨리 릭스, 8월 22일

어휘 knowledgeable 잘 아는 lot 부지 address 해결하다 delighted 매우 기쁜 compete 경쟁하다 dealership 대리점 in the market for ~ 구입에 관심이 있는

---

200 9월의 이달의 직원은 에리카 보이드입니다!

에리카는 윌슨 오토에서 3개월을 지내면서 새로운 기술을 빠르게 익혔고 항상 더 배우려고 노력하고 있습니다. 그녀는 우리 재고에 대해 매우 많이 알게 되었으며 고객들과 그녀의 지식을 공유하여 판매를 성사시킬 수 있습니다. **199** 그녀는 또한 만족한 고객들이 우리 소셜 미디어 페이지에 의견을 남기도록 하는 데 중요한 역할을 했습니다. 우리는 지난 한 달 동안 이전 4개월을 합한 것보다 더 많은 훌륭한 후기를 받았습니다.

에리카는 탁월한 업무에 대한 감사의 뜻으로 알론조 레스토랑의 50달러 상품권을 받았습니다. 축하합니다, 에리카!

어휘 pick up ~을 배우다 knowledge 지식 complete 완료하다 instrumental 중요한 comment 의견 review 후기 previous 이전의 combine 결합하다

196 주제 / 목적

번역 이메일의 목적은?
(A) 입사 후보자 명단을 공유하려고
(B) 관리자들로부터 의견을 요청하려고
(C) 관리자 회의를 요약하려고
(D) 수상할 관리자를 추천하려고

해설 이메일의 첫 단락 첫 문장에서 관리자들에게 9월 윌슨 오토의 이달의 직원에 투표할 시간(It is time to vote for the Wilson Autos Employee of the Month for September)이라고 알리면서, 마지막 단락 첫 문장에서 금요일까지 투표를 이 이메일로 회신해 달라(Please respond to this e-mail by Friday with your vote)고 요청하고 있다. 따라서 이 이메일은 9월 이달의 직원을 뽑기 위해 관리자들의 의견을 요청하는 글이므로 (B)가 정답이다.

어휘 candidate 후보자 summarize 요약하다 nominate 추천하다

197 세부 사항

번역 이메일에 따르면, 기술적 문제를 발견한 사람은 누구인가?
(A) 살레히 씨
(B) 알마흐디 씨
(C) 로즈 씨
(D) 블랙 씨

해설 이메일의 네 번째 단락에서 닉 살레히는 컴퓨터 시스템에서 오류를 발견했고 불필요한 재고를 잘못 주문하는 것을 멈춰 주었다(Nick Salehi found a glitch in our computer system and stopped us from incorrectly ordering unnecessary inventory)고 했다. 따라서 기술적 문제를 발견한 사람은 살레히 씨이므로 (A)가 정답이다.

어휘 identify 찾다

> **Paraphrasing**
> 지문의 a glitch in our computer system
> → 질문의 a technical problem

198 연계

번역 릭스 씨에 대해 결론지을 수 있는 것은?
(A) 그의 이전 차량이 엑셀레라 트럭이었다.
(B) 보이드 씨의 이웃이다.
(C) 과거에 윌슨 오토에서 차를 구입한 적이 있다.
(D) 가격을 낮추기 위해 블랙 씨와 협상했다.

해설 이메일의 하단에 샬럿 블랙(Charlotte Black)이 윌슨 오토 총괄 관리자(General Manager, Wilson Autos)라고 나와 있고, 릭스 씨가 작성한 후기의 네 번째 문장에서 총괄 관리자가 경쟁 대리점에서 광고하는 동일가에 엑셀레라를 판매하기로 동의했을 때 는 더욱 기뻤다(even more delighted when the general manager agreed to sell us the Excelera for the same price that a competing dealership was advertising)고 했다. 따라서 릭스 씨는 트럭을 할인받기 위해 윌슨 오토의 총괄 관리자인 블랙 씨와 협상했다는 것을 알 수 있으므로 (D)가 정답이다.

199 Not / True

번역 보이드 씨에 대해 공지에 명시된 것은?
(A) 알론조 레스토랑에서 정기적으로 식사를 한다.
(B) 윌슨 오토의 소셜 미디어 사이트를 관리한다.
(C) 고객 피드백 증가에 공이 있다.
(D) 최근에 판매 교육 과정을 수료했다.

해설 공지의 첫 단락 세 번째 문장에서 보이드 씨는 만족한 고객들이 소셜 미디어 페이지에 의견을 남기도록 하는 데 중요한 역할을 했다(She has also been instrumental in encouraging satisfied customers to post comments on our social media pages)고 했고, 지난 한 달 동안 이전 4개월을 합한 것보다 더 많은 훌륭한 후기를 받았다(We received more great reviews in the past month than we did in the four previous months combined!)고 했다. 따라서 고객 피드백이 증가하는 데 보이드 씨가 큰 공을 세웠음을 알 수 있으므로 (C)가 정답이다.

200 연계

번역 보이드 씨에 대해 사실일 것 같은 것은?
(A) 최소 3명의 관리자로부터 투표를 받았다.
(B) 8월에 최고 판매사원이었다.
(C) 자동차 업계에서 수년의 경력이 있다.
(D) 4월에 윌슨 오토에 채용되었다.

해설 이메일의 첫 단락 첫 문장에서 관리자들에게 9월 윌슨 오토의 이달의 직원에 투표할 시간(It is time to vote for the Wilson Autos Employee of the Month for September)이라고 했고 마지막 단락 두 번째 문장에서 수상자는 최소 3표 이상을 받아야 한다(The winner must receive at least three votes)고 했으며, 공지의 제목에서 9월의 이달의 직원은 에리카 보이드(The employee of the month for September is ERICA BOYD!)라고 발표했다. 보이드 씨는 9월 이달의 직원에 선정되었으므로 투표에서 관리자들로부터 최소 3표 이상을 받았다는 것을 알 수 있다. 따라서 (A)가 정답이다.

기출 TEST 2

101 (C)	102 (A)	103 (D)	104 (B)	105 (A)
106 (D)	107 (D)	108 (C)	109 (A)	110 (A)
111 (C)	112 (D)	113 (C)	114 (D)	115 (B)
116 (C)	117 (A)	118 (C)	119 (D)	120 (C)
121 (A)	122 (B)	123 (A)	124 (C)	125 (B)
126 (D)	127 (D)	128 (C)	129 (B)	130 (D)
131 (D)	132 (B)	133 (A)	134 (D)	135 (A)
136 (A)	137 (D)	138 (D)	139 (B)	140 (C)
141 (D)	142 (A)	143 (B)	144 (D)	145 (B)
146 (B)	147 (D)	148 (C)	149 (B)	150 (C)
151 (A)	152 (B)	153 (C)	154 (C)	155 (A)
156 (B)	157 (B)	158 (C)	159 (B)	160 (B)
161 (D)	162 (B)	163 (B)	164 (D)	165 (B)
166 (A)	167 (B)	168 (C)	169 (B)	170 (B)
171 (B)	172 (C)	173 (A)	174 (C)	175 (B)
176 (A)	177 (C)	178 (A)	179 (D)	180 (B)
181 (D)	182 (B)	183 (C)	184 (D)	185 (A)
186 (C)	187 (C)	188 (A)	189 (D)	190 (C)
191 (A)	192 (C)	193 (C)	194 (C)	195 (B)
196 (B)	197 (A)	198 (C)	199 (C)	200 (D)

PART 5

101 접속사 자리 _ 등위접속사

해설 전치사 for의 목적어 역할을 하는 명사구 maximum reliability와 gas mileage를 연결해 줄 등위접속사가 필요하다. '최고의 신뢰성과 연비를 목표로 설계 제작되었다'는 내용이므로 '~와'를 뜻하는 등위접속사 (C) and가 정답이다. (A) so는 '그래서'라는 뜻으로 뒤에 절이 와야 하고, (B) but은 '그러나'라는 의미로 적합하지 않고, (D) nor(~도 아니다)는 neither와 함께 상관접속사를 이룬다.

번역 최신 아모레 스포츠 세단은 최고의 신뢰성과 연비를 목표로 설계 제작되었다.

어휘 engineer (설계해서) 제작하다 maximum 최고의 reliability 신뢰성 gas mileage 연비

102 명사 자리 _ 전치사의 목적어

해설 빈칸은 전치사 for의 목적어 자리로, 앞에 정관사 the가 있고 뒤의 관계대명사 that절의 수식을 받고 있으므로 명사가 들어가야 한다. 따라서 명사 (A) information이 정답이다. (B) informed는 동사/과거분사, (C) informs와 (D) inform은 동사로 답이 될 수 없다.

번역 직원들은 술러 씨가 회의에서 배포한 정보에 감사했다.

어휘 grateful 감사하는 distribute 배포하다

103 부사 어휘

해설 빈칸 뒤의 시간 표현 at 2 P.M.과 함께 동사 will be held를 수식하여 '오후 2시 정각에 열릴 것이다'라는 내용이 되어야 자연스러우므로 '정확히 제시간에'를 뜻하는 (D) promptly가 정답이다. (A) barely는 '거의 ~않다', (B) closely는 '주의 깊게', (C) evenly는 '균등하게'라는 의미이다.

번역 기획 위원회의 다음 회의는 오후 2시 정각에 열릴 것이다.

어휘 committee 위원회

104 인칭대명사의 격 _ 소유격

해설 빈칸은 전치사 in의 목적어 역할을 하는 명사구 October 1 paycheck을 수식하는 자리이다. 따라서 소유격 인칭대명사인 (B) your가 정답이다.

번역 출장 경비 환급은 당신의 10월 1일 급여에 포함될 것입니다.

어휘 reimbursement 환급 expense 경비 paycheck 급여

105 형용사 어휘

해설 빈칸 뒤의 복합명사 design engineer를 수식하여 '수석 설계 엔지니어'라는 의미가 되어야 자연스러우므로 '수석의, 선임의'를 뜻하는 (A) lead가 정답이다. (B) each는 '각각의', (C) front는 '(위치상) 앞의', (D) most는 '대부분의'라는 의미이다.

번역 드론 카메라 프로젝트의 수석 설계 엔지니어는 배이슬이다.

어휘 design 설계 drone 드론

106 to부정사 _ 의문사 + to부정사

해설 to부정사 to decide의 목적어 자리에 명사절 접속사인 의문형용사 which와 명사 printer가 보이고 '어떤 프린터를 사야 할지를 결정하다'라는 의미가 되어야 적절하므로, 의문사와 결합하여 명사구를 이룰 수 있는 to부정사 (D) to buy가 정답이다. (A) buying은 동명사/현재분사로 명사절 축약 구조를 이루지 못하며, 동사인 (B) had bought와 (C) buy가 빈칸에 들어가면 주어가 없는 불완전한 절이 되므로 답이 될 수 없다.

번역 몇몇 후기를 읽은 뒤, 김 씨는 사무실에 어떤 프린터를 사야 할지 결정할 수 있었다.

107 전치사 어휘

해설 빈칸 뒤의 시간 명사구 5 P.M.을 목적어로 취해 '오후 5시까지 상자들을 치우라'는 의미가 되어야 자연스러우므로 '~까지'를 뜻하는 (D) by가 정답이다.

번역 오후 5시까지 직원 라운지에 남겨진 상자들을 치워 주세요.

108 명사 자리 _ 복합명사

해설 빈칸 뒤 명사 plant와 함께 쓰여 주어 역할을 하는 명사 자리로, '제조 공장'이라는 의미의 복합명사를 만드는 '제조(업)'을 뜻하는 명사 (C) manufacturing이 정답이다. (A) manufacture와 (D) manufactures는 주로 단독 명사로 쓰여 복합명사를 이루지 않고, (B) manufactured는 동사/과거분사로 빈칸에 적합하지 않다.

번역 사우스포트 제조 공장은 3일 후 생산을 시작할 것으로 예상된다.

어휘 plant 공장

109 동사 어휘 ▶동영상 강의

해설 주어 a candidate의 동사 자리로, all onboarding tasks를 목적어로 취해 '모든 신입사원 교육 과제를 마치다'라는 의미가 되어야 자연스러우므로 '마치다, 완료하다'를 뜻하는 (A) complete가 정답이다. (B) proceed는 '진행되다'라는 의미의 자동사로 목적어를 취할 수 없고, (C) recover는 '만회하다', (D) enlist는 '요청하다'라는 의미로 문맥상 적합하지 않다.

번역 일자리 제안을 수락한 후, 지원자는 시작일 전에 모든 신입사원 교육 과제를 마쳐야 한다.

어휘 accept 수락하다 candidate 지원자 onboarding 신입사원 교육 과정 task 과제, 과업

110 인칭대명사의 격 _ 소유격

해설 빈칸에는 Although가 이끄는 부사절의 주어인 명사 training을 수식하는 인칭대명사가 들어가야 한다. 따라서 명사 앞에 쓰여 한정사 역할을 할 수 있는 소유격 인칭대명사 (A) her가 정답이다.

번역 유 씨는 그녀의 교육이 이제 막 시작되었음에도 불구하고, 이미 회사의 전용 회계 소프트웨어에 통달했다.

어휘 master 통달하다 proprietary 전용의, 독점의

111 형용사 어휘 ▶동영상 강의

해설 문맥상 '클레이턴 씨는 파일이 손실되지 않았다는 것을 알고 안도했다'는 내용이 되어야 자연스러우므로 '안도하는, 다행으로 여기는'을 뜻하는 (C) relieved가 정답이다. (A) easy는 '쉬운', (B) delightful은 '기쁨을 주는', (D) absolute는 '완전한'이라는 의미이다.

번역 클레이턴 씨는 정전 중에 그녀의 파일이 하나도 손실되지 않았다는 것을 알고 안도했다.

어휘 power failure 정전

112 부사 자리 _ 동사 수식

해설 빈칸은 동사구 has grown을 수식하는 부사 자리이므로 '크게, 상당히'를 의미하는 (D) significantly가 정답이다. (A) signify는 동사, (B) significance는 명사, (C) significant는 형용사이므로 품사상 빈칸에 들어갈 수 없다.

번역 나가호리 씨가 언텐 프로퍼티즈에 CEO로 재임하는 동안 회사는 크게 성장했다.

어휘 tenure 재임 property 부동산

113 명사 어휘

해설 유리 세공에 있어 안전을 강조하는 내용의 문장이므로, 빈칸 앞의 형용사 top의 수식을 받아 '안전이 항상 최우선 사항이어야 한다'는 의미가 되어야 적절하다. 따라서 '우선 사항'을 뜻하는 (C) priority가 정답이다. (A) surface는 '표면', (B) material은 '재료', (D) position은 '위치'라는 의미이다.

번역 안전은 유리 세공 과정의 각 단계에서 항상 최우선 사항이어야 한다.

어휘 glassblowing 유리 세공 process 과정

114 동사 자리 _ 태

해설 빈칸은 선행사 experts를 수식하는 관계사절(who ~ information technology)의 동사 자리이고, 빈칸 뒤에 목적어 topics가 있으므로 '다루다'를 뜻하는 능동태 동사 (D) cover가 정답이다. (A) are covered는 수동태이므로 목적어를 취할 수 없고, (B) covering은 동명사/현재분사, (C) to cover는 to부정사이므로 품사상 빈칸에 들어갈 수 없다.

번역 센트럴 과학 박물관은 정보 기술과 관련된 주제를 다루는 전문가들에 의한 온라인 세미나를 주최한다.

어휘 expert 전문가 related 관련된

115 부사 어휘 ▶동영상 강의

해설 동사 changed를 수식하여 '회사에서 갑자기 전략을 바꿨다'는 내용이 되어야 자연스러우므로 '갑자기'를 뜻하는 (B) abruptly가 정답이다. (A) thickly는 '두껍게', (C) formerly는 '이전에', (D) frequently는 '자주'라는 의미이다.

번역 콘라디아 컴퓨터는 지난주에 마케팅 전략의 방향을 갑자기 바꿨다.

어휘 strategy 전략

116 형용사 자리 _ 명사 수식

해설 빈칸은 전치사 of의 목적어 역할을 하는 명사 candidates를 수식하는 형용사 자리이다. 따라서 '자격을 갖춘 지원자들이 많다'는 의미가 되도록 '자격을 갖춘'을 뜻하는 형용사 (C) qualified가 정답이다. (A) qualify와 (D) qualifies는 동사이므로 품사상 적절하지 않고, 명사 (B) qualifier(예선 통과자)는 candidates와 복합명사를 이루기에 적절하지 않다.

번역 자격을 갖춘 지원자들이 많아 자니퍼 인더스트리즈는 새 CEO를 임명하는 데 예상보다 더 오래 걸릴 수도 있다.

어휘 an abundance of 많은, 풍부한 candidate 지원자 name 임명하다

117 관계대명사 _ 주격

해설 빈칸 이하는 사물 선행사인 a one-year warranty를 수식하는 관계사절로, 빈칸 뒤에 동사 includes가 나오므로 주격 관계대명사가 와야 한다. 따라서 (A) that이 정답이다. (B) who는 사람 선행사를 수식하고, 명사절 접속사 (C) what은 선행사를 수식할 수 없으며, 인칭대명사 (D) it은 절을 연결할 수 없다.

번역 저희의 모든 태블릿 컴퓨터에는 하드웨어 수리 및 교체가 포함된 1년 보증이 딸려 옵니다.

어휘 warranty 보증   replacement 교체

118 동사 어휘

해설 주어 The Exprite Foundation Board of Directors의 동사 자리로, 빈칸 앞의 is와 함께 수동태를 이루어 전치사 of와 자연스럽게 연결될 수 있는 동사가 들어가야 한다. '엑스프라이트 재단 이사회는 9명의 이사들로 구성된다'는 의미가 되어야 자연스러우므로 be composed of의 형태로 '~으로 구성되다'를 의미하는 (C) composed가 정답이다. (A)의 expect는 '기대하다', (B)의 describe는 '묘사하다', (D)의 announce는 '발표하다'라는 의미이다.

번역 엑스프라이트 재단 이사회는 매년 대중에 의해 선출되는 9명의 이사들로 구성된다.

어휘 foundation 재단   elect 선출하다   annually 매년

119 전치사 자리 / 어휘

해설 주어 Mortgage brokers, 동사 prefer, 목적어 to review all the financial documents가 있는 완전한 절 뒤에 동명사 meeting을 연결하는 자리이므로 전치사가 들어가야 한다. meeting with a new client와 함께 쓰여 '새로운 고객과 만나기 전에'라는 의미가 되어야 자연스러우므로 (D) before가 정답이다. 전치사 (A) toward는 '~ 쪽으로'라는 의미로 적합하지 않고, (B) further는 형용사/부사, (C) lately는 부사이므로 품사상 답이 될 수 없다.

번역 주택담보대출 중개인들은 일반적으로 새로운 고객과 만나기 전에 모든 금융 서류를 검토하기를 선호한다.

어휘 mortgage 주택담보대출   broker 중개인   generally 일반적으로

120 동사 자리 _ 시제

해설 빈칸은 주어 Management의 동사 자리로, 미래를 나타내는 부사구 by the end of the month가 있으므로 미래 시제인 (C) will identify가 정답이다. 주어 Management가 3인칭 단수이므로 (A) identify는 답이 될 수 없고, (B) identifying은 동명사/현재분사, (D) to identify는 to부정사이므로 품사상 부적합하다.

번역 경영진은 이달 말까지 승진 후보자를 선정할 것이다.

어휘 candidate 후보자   identify 찾아내다, 파악하다

121 형용사 어휘

해설 빈칸은 that절의 주어 circumstances를 수식하는 형용사 자리로, '예기치 못한 상황이 발생한다는 점을 이해한다'는 내용이 되어야 자연스러우므로 '예기치 못한'을 뜻하는 (A) unforeseen이 정답이다. (B) excessive는 '과도한', (C) approximate는 '대략적인', (D) acclaimed는 '호평 받는'이라는 의미이다.

번역 우리는 예약을 지키지 못했을 경우 일반적으로 25달러를 청구하지만, 예기치 못한 상황이 발생할 수도 있다는 점을 이해합니다.

어휘 typically 일반적으로   charge 청구하다   circumstance 상황   arise 발생하다

122 명사 자리 _ 동사의 목적어   ▶ 동영상 강의

해설 빈칸은 동사 can make의 목적어 역할을 하는 명사 자리로, unlimited의 수식을 받아 '무제한으로 제공되는 여러 건의 이체들'이라는 의미가 되어야 적절하므로 복수 명사 (B) transfers가 정답이다. 가산/불가산명사가 모두 가능한 (A) transfer는 단수 명사일 경우 앞에 한정사가 필요하고, 불가산명사일 경우 이체 행위나 과정 자체를 뜻하므로 문맥상 어울리지 않는다. (C) transferred는 동사/과거분사, (D) transferring은 동명사/현재분사로 품사상 답이 될 수 없다.

번역 블루 헤지에서, 고객은 1퍼센트의 이자를 받고, 계좌 수수료를 지불하지 않으며, 무제한 이체를 할 수 있습니다.

어휘 interest 이자   fee 수수료   unlimited 무제한의

123 전치사 어휘

해설 빈칸 뒤에 장소를 나타내는 명사구 the Liverpool Convention Complex가 있고, 문맥상 '리버풀 컨벤션 단지 근처에 있다'는 의미가 되어야 자연스러우므로 '~ 근처에'를 뜻하는 (A) near가 정답이다. (B) without은 '~ 없이', (C) since는 '~ 이래로', (D) following은 '~ 후에'라는 의미이다.

번역 디저트 공급을 전문으로 하는 페어리스트 베이커리는 리버풀 컨벤션 단지 근처에 위치해 있다.

어휘 specialize in ~을 전문으로 하다   catering 음식 공급   complex (건물) 단지

124 형용사 자리 _ 주격 보어 / 비교급

해설 빈칸은 주어 The presentations를 보충 설명하는 주격 보어 자리이고, 뒤에 than이 있으므로 비교급 형용사 (C) briefer가 정답이다. (A) brief는 원급 형용사, (D) briefest는 최상급 형용사, (B) briefly는 부사이므로 빈칸에 들어갈 수 없다.

번역 발표는 우리가 예상했던 것보다 더 짧아서, 질문 시간이 충분히 남았다.

어휘 ample 충분한

125 명사 어휘

해설 주문이 3일 내로 도착하지 않을 시 일정 금액을 환불해 주겠다고 고객에게 약속하는 내용이므로 '당사의 보장에 따르면'이라는 내용이 되어야 적절하다. 따라서 '보장'을 뜻하는 (B) guarantee가 정답이다. (A) distribution은 '유통', (C) exception은 '예외', (D) discount는 '할인'이라는 의미이다.

번역 당사의 보장에 따르면, 귀하께서 주문하신 제품이 3일 내에 도착하지 않을 경우 비용의 50퍼센트를 환불해 드립니다.

126 부사 자리 _ 동사 수식

해설 빈칸은 동사구 have redesigned 사이에서 동사를 수식하는 부사 자리이므로, '눈에 뜨게, 현저히'라는 의미의 부사 (D) notably가 정답이다. (A) note는 동사/명사, (B) noted는 동사/과거분사, (C) notable은 형용사이므로 빈칸에 들어갈 수 없다.

번역 서울에 본사를 둔 몇몇 회사들은 눈에 띄게 업무 공간을 더 화사하고 편안하게 재설계했다.

어휘 redesign 재설계하다   workplace 작업 공간, 직장

127 부사 어휘

해설 행사가 연기된 이유를 설명하려면 '계절에 맞지 않게 추운 기온 탓'이라는 내용이 되어야 적절하므로, '계절에 맞지 않게'를 뜻하는 (D) unseasonably가 정답이다. (A) deceptively는 '속이는 듯이', (B) unnecessarily는 '불필요하게', (C) irresponsibly는 '무책임하게'라는 의미이다.

번역 이번 주의 계절에 맞지 않게 추운 기온 탓에 직원 야유회가 다음 주 금요일로 연기될 것이다.

어휘 postpone 연기하다   temperature 기온

128 전치사 자리 / 어휘

해설 콤마 앞에 완전한 절이 있고, 빈칸 뒤에 남아 있는 명사구 just two more days를 연결해 주는 자리이므로 전치사가 들어가야 한다. '단 이틀만을 남겨두고'라는 의미가 되어야 자연스러우므로 '~한 상태로, ~와 함께'를 뜻하는 (C) with가 정답이다. 전치사 (A) against(~에 반대하여)는 의미상 적절하지 않고, (B) namely는 부사, (D) else는 형용사/부사로 품사상 적합하지 않다.

번역 사내 모금 챌린지에서 단 이틀만을 남겨두고 회계 부서가 1위 자리에 있다.

어휘 fund-raising 모금

129 동사 어휘

해설 빈칸은 동사 has struggled의 목적어 역할을 하는 to부정사 자리에 들어갈 동사 어휘를 고르는 문제이다. its new bottled espresso를 목적어로 취해 '자사의 신상 병 에스프레소를 차별화하려고 애쓰고 있다'는 내용이 되어야 자연스러우므로 '차별화하다, 구별 짓다'를 뜻하는 (B) distinguish가 정답이다. (A) participate는 '참여하다'라는 뜻의 자동사로 목적어를 취할 수 없고, (C) overturn은 '뒤집다', (D) revoke는 '취소하다'라는 의미이므로 문맥상 적합하지 않다.

번역 핑크 제라늄 커피는 자사의 신상 병 에스프레소를 시장의 유사 음료들과 차별화하려고 애쓰고 있다.

어휘 struggle 애쓰다   bottled 병에 든

130 부사절 접속사 어휘

해설 빈칸은 두 개의 완전한 절을 이어주는 부사절 접속사 자리로, '불편하더라도 전원 참석을 기대한다'라고 상반되는 내용을 양보의 의미로 연결해야 자연스러우므로, '비록 ~일지라도'를 뜻하는 (A) Though가 정답이다. (B) As soon as는 '~하자마자', (C) Because는 '~ 때문에', (D) When은 '~할 때'라는 의미이다.

번역 간혹 불편하더라도, 오타니 씨는 모든 팀원이 그의 주간 회의에 참석하기를 기대한다.

어휘 occasionally 가끔   inconvenient 불편한

PART 6

131-134 광고

머핀 레이디 머핀즈

약 160년 전 어느 날, 아리아나 스위니는 집에서 만든 머핀 몇 개를 친구들에게 나눠주려고 동네의 마을 광장으로 가져갔습니다. 모두가 머핀을 좋아했습니다! **131 머지않아**, 스위니 씨는 머핀을 원하는 누구에게나 머핀을 나눠주기 시작했습니다. **132 매주 그녀는 새로운 종류를 구워 간절히 바라는 사람들에게 가져다주었습니다.** 몇 달 후, 그녀는 마을에서 머핀 레이디로 알려지게 되었습니다.

오늘날, 머핀 레이디 머핀즈는 아리아나 스위니가 개발한 오리지널 조리법을 똑같이 **133 사용하여** 수작업으로 만들어집니다. 저희는 최상의 재료로만 진정성 있게 머핀 레이디 머핀즈를 굽는 데 전념하고 있습니다. 여러분이 저희의 맛있는 **134 제품**을 즐기시기를 바랍니다!

어휘 square 광장   be committed to ~에 전념하다   authentically 진정으로   ingredient 재료

131 접속부사

해설 빈칸 앞 부분에 친구들에게 주려고 머핀을 광장으로 가져왔는데 모두가 머핀을 좋아했다는 내용이 이어지다가, 빈칸 뒤에서는 머핀을 원하는 사람들에게 나눠주기 시작했다는 문장이 왔다. 따라서 빈칸에는 시간의 경과에 따라 사건이 전개되는 과정을 나타내는 말이 들어가야 적합하므로, '머지않아, 곧'이라는 뜻의 (D) Before long이 정답이다. (A) Now that은 '~이므로', (B) After all은 '결국', (C) Otherwise는 '그렇지 않으면'이라는 의미이다.

132 문맥에 맞는 문장 고르기

번역 (A) 여러 맛있는 종류가 생기면서, 머핀은 더 이상 아침 식사용으로만 먹는 것이 아닙니다.
(B) 매주 그녀는 새로운 종류를 구워 간절히 바라는 사람들에게 가져다주었습니다.
(C) 그녀는 매일 친구들과 산책을 하곤 했습니다.
(D) 안타깝게도, 한 번 구워 낼 것을 준비하는 데 거의 세 시간이 걸렸습니다.

해설 빈칸 앞에서 사람들이 좋아하자 스위니 씨는 원하는 모두에게 머핀을 나눠 주기 시작했다(Ms. Sweeney started sharing muffins with anyone who wanted one)고 했고, 빈칸 뒤에서 몇 달 후 머핀 레이디로 알려졌다(After a few months, she became known around town as the Muffin Lady)고 했으므로, 빈칸에는 계속 머핀을 나눠 준 과정이 들어가는 것이 자연스럽다. 따라서 매주 새로운 종류의 머핀을 구워 사람들에게 가져다주었다고 언급하는 (B)가 정답이다.

어휘 savory 맛있는 variety 종류 eager 간절히 바라는 taker 받는 사람 batch 한 번 굽는 양

133 분사구문

해설 빈칸 앞에 완전한 절(Muffin Lady Muffins are made by hand)이 있으므로, 빈칸에는 뒤에 남아 있는 명사구(the same original recipes)를 연결하여 앞 절의 내용을 수식할 수 있는 준동사가 들어가야 한다. 문맥상 '오리지널 조리법을 똑같이 사용하여'라는 의미가 되어야 자연스러우므로 능동의 의미를 나타내는 현재분사 (A) using이 정답이다. 과거분사 (B) used는 목적어를 취할 수 없고, (C) use는 동사/명사로 빈칸에 들어갈 수 없으며, (D) to use는 '~하기 위해서'라는 뜻으로 목적이나 의도를 나타내므로 의미상 부적합하다.

134 명사 자리 _ 동사의 목적어

해설 빈칸은 명사절의 동사 enjoy의 목적어 역할을 하며, 소유격 대명사 our와 형용사 delicious의 수식을 받는 명사 자리이다. 따라서 명사 (D) creations가 정답이다. (A) creates는 동사, (B) created는 동사/과거분사, (C) creatively는 부사이므로 답이 될 수 없다.

135-138 제품 설명

텍신 서플라이 〉〉 제품 〉〉 천연 손 세정제

많은 브랜드의 손 세정제에는 불필요한 화학 물질이 들어있습니다. 인공 재료가 첨가되지 않은 비누를 135 **선호하는** 사람들에게, 텍신 서플라이의 천연 손 세정제는 이상적인 선택입니다. 이 무향 비누는 편리한 디스펜서 병에 담겨 있습니다. 136 **이 비누의** 특허 받은 제조법은 천연 비타민과 오일의 혼합물로 손을 깨끗하면서도 부드럽게 유지할 수 있게 설계되었습니다. 137 **모든 성분은 자연에서 발견되는 식물에서 추출합니다.** 사업체를 운영하면서 지속 가능한 공정으로 제조된 안전하고 효과적인 손 세정제를 원하십니까? 그렇다면, 이 138 **제품을** 할인된 가격에 대량으로 구매하실 수 있습니다. 자세한 내용은 저희 주문 페이지를 방문해 주세요.

어휘 chemical 화학 물질 artificial 인공의 substance 재료, 물질 unscented 향이 없는 handy 편리한 dispenser 디스펜서(누르면 내용물이 나오는 용기) patented 특허 받은 formula 제조법 effective 효과적인 sustainable 지속 가능한 in bulk 대량으로

135 동사 자리

해설 빈칸은 선행사 those를 수식하는 관계사절(who ~ artificial substances)의 동사 자리이므로 동사 (A) prefer가 정답이다. (B) preferring은 현재분사/동명사, (C) preferable은 형용사, (D) preference는 명사이므로 품사상 답이 될 수 없다.

136 대명사 어휘

해설 빈칸 뒤에 명사구 patented formula가 있으므로 빈칸에는 소유격 대명사 또는 한정사가 들어가야 한다. 또한 앞 문장에서 언급된 This unscented soap을 이어받아 '이 비누의 특허 받은 제조법'이라는 내용이 되어야 자연스러우므로 단수 명사 This unscented soap을 소유격 대명사로 나타낸 (A) Its가 정답이다. (B) Such (그러한)는 문법적으로는 가능하지만 의미상 어울리지 않고, (C) Some은 가산 단수 명사와 쓸 수 없으며, (D) None은 명사구를 수식할 수 없으므로 답이 될 수 없다.

137 문맥에 맞는 문장 고르기

번역 (A) 많은 비누가 고객들이 느끼기에 너무 강한 향을 지니고 있습니다.
(B) 손 세정은 식품업 종사자들에게 필수적입니다.
(C) 몇몇 요인은 비누 제품 가격에 영향을 미칠 수 있습니다.
(D) 모든 성분은 자연에서 발견되는 식물에서 추출합니다.

해설 앞에서 천연 비누가 천연 비타민과 오일의 혼합물(a mix of natural vitamins and oils)로 제조되었다고 비누의 성분을 제시하고 있으므로, 빈칸에는 천연 비누의 특징을 더욱 강조할 수 있는 성분의 출처를 밝히는 내용이 들어가야 자연스럽다. 따라서 모든 성분은 자연 식물에서 추출한다고 언급하는 (D)가 정답이다.

어휘 fragrance 향 essential 필수적인 factor 요인 influence 영향을 미치다 ingredient 성분 plant 식물

138 명사 어휘

해설 앞 내용 전반에 걸쳐 천연 손 세정제(Natural Hand Soap) 즉, 비누(soap) 제품에 대해 설명하고 있으므로, 빈칸이 있는 문장 또한 비누 제품을 지칭하여 '이 제품을 할인된 가격에 대량 구매할 수 있다'는 내용이 되어야 자연스럽다. 따라서 '제품, 품목'을 뜻하는 (D) item이 정답이다. (A) equipment는 '장비', (B) fabric은 '직물', (C) issue는 '문제'라는 의미이다.

139-142 기사

무어탭 비스트로, 폐업 계획

로웨나 엘리슨이 다운랜드 무어스의 외딴 마을에 무어탭 비스트로를 열었을 때, 그녀는 더 큰 도시로부터 손님들을 끌어오기를 바랐다. 그녀는 낯선 재료들로 준비한 로컬 요리로 구성된 색다른 메뉴를 아름다운 장소에서 **139 제공했다**. 그녀의 계획은 효과적이었다. **140 식당**은 지역에서 가장 성공적인 장소 중 하나가 되었고 지금도 여전히 그렇다. 하지만 이제 엘리슨은 비스트로를 닫고 은퇴할 준비가 되었다고 말한다.

"저는 이 모험의 모든 순간을 사랑했어요."라고 엘리슨은 말한다. "저는 거의 50년 동안 외식업을 해 왔습니다. **141 하지만 새로운 무언가를 위한 때가 되었어요.** 여긴 정말 **142 빠르게 돌아가는** 환경이에요. 전 마침내 속도를 늦출 준비가 되었습니다."

엘리슨은 정원에서 더 많은 시간을 보낼 작정이다. 그녀는 비스트로를 인수할 사람을 찾고 있다.

어휘 remote 외딴 unusual 색다른 familiar 익숙한 ingredient 재료 setting 장소 venue 장소 retire 은퇴하다

139 동사 어형_시제

해설 앞뒤 문맥에서 로웨나 엘리슨이 무어탭 비스트로를 개업했던 당시의 일을 과거 시제로 설명하고 있으므로, 빈칸이 있는 문장도 과거 시제로 '그녀는 색다른 메뉴를 제공했다'는 내용이 되어야 자연스럽다. 따라서 (B) offered가 정답이다.

140 명사 어휘

해설 앞 부분에서 로웨나 젤리슨이 무어탭 비스트로를 열었다(Rowena Ellison opened the Moortap Bistro)고 하며 식당에 대한 설명을 이어가고 있고, 빈칸 뒤 문장에서도 엘리슨이 비스트로를 닫을 준비가 되었다고 한다(Ellison says she is ready to close the bistro)고 했으므로, 빈칸이 있는 문장 또한 '식당은 지역에서 가장 성공적인 장소 중 하나가 되었다'며 식당에 대한 내용이 되어야 자연스럽다. 따라서 '식당'을 뜻하는 (C) eatery가 정답이다. (A) field는 '분야', (B) clinic은 '병원', (D) theater는 '극장'이라는 의미이다.

141 문맥에 맞는 문장 고르기

번역 (A) 식사 손님들의 피드백을 토대로 분기마다 메뉴를 업데이트했어요.
(B) 그렇다 하더라도, 최근 들어 장사가 잘되지 않았어요.
(C) 제 부모님은 제가 태어나기 전에 이 비스트로를 운영하셨어요.
(D) 하지만 새로운 무언가를 위한 때가 되었어요.

해설 빈칸 앞에서 엘리슨 씨가 거의 50년간 외식업을 해 왔다(I've been in the restaurant business for almost 50 years)고 했고, 빈칸 뒤에서 여긴 정말 빠르게 돌아가는 환경(such a fast-paced environment)이라며 마침내 속도를 늦출 준비가 되었다(ready to slow down)고 했다. 오랜 시간 해온 일에 대한 회고와 변화를 선언하는 문장 사이에 빈칸이 있으므로 새로운 시작에 대한 내용이 들어가야 적절하다. 따라서 새로운 무언가를 위한 때가 되었다고 언급하는 (D)가 정답이다.

어휘 quarterly 분기별로 diner 식사하는 사람 even so 그렇다 해도

142 형용사 어휘

해설 빈칸 뒤 문장에서 마침내 속도를 늦출 준비가 되었다고 한 것으로 보아 '여기는 정말 빠르게 돌아가는 환경이다'라는 내용이 되어야 적절하다. 따라서 '빠르게 전개되는'을 뜻하는 (A) fast-paced가 정답이다. (B) comforting은 '위로가 되는', (C) widespread는 '널리 퍼진', (D) family-oriented는 '가족지향의'라는 의미이다.

143-146 이메일

수신: 아멜리아 산체스 〈amelia.sanchez@silvermail.co.uk〉
발신: 브룩스 헌리 〈b.hunley@carltonamespaving.co.uk〉
날짜: 10월 10일
제목: 최근 회의에 대한 후속 조치

산체스 씨께,

최근 저희의 현장 방문에 관한 후속 조치로 귀사의 진입로 보수를 위한 권고안을 드립니다.

방문 중에 말씀드렸듯이, 현재 진입로에는 폭우 시 물이 고이는 낮은 지점이 몇 군데 있습니다. 이 배수 문제는 **143 몇** 가지 방식으로 해결할 수 있습니다. 첫 번째 방법은 낮은 지점을 충전재로 메우는 것입니다. **144 그렇지 않으면**, 기존의 아스팔트를 전부 제거하고 파쇄된 자갈과 같은 투수성 자재로 교체할 수도 있습니다. **145 이 방식이 저희가 추천하는 방법입니다.** 자갈층은 빗물이 아래에 있는 흙으로 스며들고 재흡수되도록 해 줍니다.

다음 단계에 대해 논의할 수 있도록 편하실 **146 때 언제든지** 전화 주십시오.

브룩스 헌리
칼튼 에임스 포장

어휘 follow-up 후속 조치 site 현장 driveway 진입로 address 해결하다 drainage 배수 patch 메우다 filler 충전재 porous 투수성의 crushed 파쇄된 gravel 자갈 bed 지층 underlying 밑에 있는 soil 흙 reabsorb 재흡수하다 paving 포장(재)

143 형용사 어휘

해설 빈칸이 있는 문장에서 배수 문제를 언급한 뒤, 빈칸 뒤로 배수 문제를 해결할 수 있는 두 가지 방법을 제시하고 있다. 따라서 '배수 문제는 몇 가지 방식으로 해결할 수 있다'는 내용이 되어야 자연스러우므로 복수 명사와 함께 쓰여 '몇몇의'를 뜻하는 (B) several이 정답이다. (A) any는 긍정문에서 '모든, 어떠한 ~이든'이라는 의미이고, (D) enough는 '충분한'이라는 의미로 문맥상 적합하지 않고, (C) much는 복수 명사와 함께 쓸 수 없다.

144 접속부사

해설 앞 문장에서 도로의 낮은 지점을 메우는 방법을 제시하고 있고, 빈칸 뒤에는 아스팔트를 제거하고 새로운 자재로 다시 포장하는 다른 방법을 소개하고 있다. 따라서 대안이 되는 선택지를 제시할 때 사용하는 '그렇지 않으면, 그 대신에'를 뜻하는 (D) Alternatively가 정답이다. (A) Likewise는 '마찬가지로', (B) Therefore는 '그러므로', (C) Regardless는 '그럼에도 불구하고'라는 의미이다.

145 문맥에 맞는 문장 고르기

번역 (A) 저희는 상업용과 개인용 진입로 모두 정기적으로 보수합니다.
(B) 이 방식이 저희가 추천하는 방법입니다.
(C) 저희 웹사이트에 후기를 올리는 것을 고려해 주십시오.
(D) 항목별로 구분된 영수증을 제공해 드릴 것입니다.

해설 앞 문장에서 배수 문제를 해결하기 위한 두 번째 방법으로 파쇄된 자갈과 같은 투수성 자재로 아스팔트를 교체하는 것(replace it with a porous material such as crushed gravel)을 안내하고 있고, 뒤 문장에서 자갈층은 빗물이 아래로 스며들고 다시 흡수되도록 해준다(A gravel bed allows rainwater to pass into the underlying soil and be reabsorbed)는 장점을 설명하고 있다. 따라서, 빈칸에는 이 두 번째 방식을 권한다는 내용이 들어가야 자연스러우므로 (B)가 정답이다.

어휘 regularly 정기적으로 commercial 상업의 approach 방법, 접근법 post 게시하다 itemized 항목별로 구분한

146 접속사 자리 _ 부사절 접속사

해설 동사 give로 시작하는 명령문 형태의 완전한 절 뒤에 주어 it, 동사 is, 보어 convenient를 갖춘 완전한 절이 왔으므로 빈칸에는 부사절 접속사가 들어가야 한다. '편할 때 언제든지 전화 주세요'라는 의미가 되어야 자연스러우므로 '~할 때 언제든지, ~할 때마다'를 뜻하는 부사절 접속사 (B) whenever가 정답이다. (A) yet(하지만)과 (C) until(~할 때까지)은 문맥상 어울리지 않고, (D) besides는 부사/전치사이므로 품사상 답이 될 수 없다.

PART 7

147-148 정보

저희 기기로 레디얼 튠즈를 즐겨보세요!

148 그레거슨 프로 폰 13을 구매하신 것을 축하드립니다. 특별 선물로 고객님께 방대한 디지털 음악 저장소인 레디얼 튠즈의 3개월 무료 구독권을 드립니다. **147** 레디얼 튠즈의 구독자로서 고객님은 수백 곡의 노래, 뮤직비디오, 다른 사용자들이 특별히 선별한 재생목록을 이용하실 수 있습니다. 구독하시려면 아래 양식을 간단히 작성해 주세요. 이메일을 통해 쿠폰 코드를 받게 됩니다. 코드를 사용하시려면 www.radialtunes.com/signup을 방문하셔서 코드를 입력하세요. 코드는 1회 사용만 유효하며 발송 후 24시간이 지나면 만료됩니다.

148 이름: 테런스 후루타
이메일: tfuruta@silkmail.com
고객님의 그레거슨 제품을 어디에서 구입하셨나요?
PNE 리테일러스, 캐나다 위니펙

어휘 subscription 구독 extensive 방대한, 광범위한 subscriber 구독자 access 이용하다 curate 선택하고 구성하다 redeem (상품권을) 현금이나 상품으로 교환하다 valid 유효한 expire 만료되다

147 Not / True

번역 레디얼 튠즈 구독자에게 제공되는 것이 아닌 것은?
(A) 방대한 노래 저장소 이용
(B) 구독자들이 게시한 음악 재생목록
(C) 뮤직비디오
(D) 인기 있는 음악가들과의 오디오 인터뷰

해설 세 번째 문장에서 레디얼 튠즈의 구독자로서 고객님은 수백 곡의 노래, 뮤직비디오, 다른 사용자들이 특별히 선별한 재생목록을 이용할 수 있다(As a Radial Tunes subscriber, you can access hundreds of songs, music videos, and playlists specially curated by other users)고 했으므로 (A), (B), (C)에 해당하는 서비스는 구독자에게 제공된다는 것을 확인할 수 있으나, 음악가들과의 인터뷰에 대한 언급은 없으므로 (D)가 정답이다.

148 Not / True

번역 후루타 씨에 대해 명시된 것은?
(A) 최근에 캐나다로 이사했다.
(B) 특별 서비스를 작동할 수 없었다.
(C) 최근에 그레거슨 프로 폰 13을 구입했다.
(D) PNE 리테일러스에 고용되었다.

해설 첫 문장에서 그레거슨 프로 폰 13을 구매한 것을 축하한다(Congratulations on your purchase of a Gregerson Pro Phone 13)고 했고, 하단의 성명란에 고객명이 테런스 후루타(Name: Terrence Furuta)라고 기재되어 있으므로, 후루타 씨는 최근에 그레거슨 프로 폰 13을 구입했다는 것을 알 수 있다. 따라서 (C)가 정답이다.

어휘 activate 작동시키다

Paraphrasing
지문의 purchase → 정답의 bought

149-150 회람

수신: 전 직원
발신: 허준, 인사부 부이사
150 날짜: 3월 31일
제목: 새 명함

149 프랜텀 코퍼레이션과의 합병 결과, 모든 케톨라 엔터프라이즈 직원들의 인쇄된 명함이 교체됩니다. 150 모든 직원들은 5월 1일까지 새로운 명함을 받게 될 것입니다. 새 명함을 받으시면 기존 명함을 배포하는 것을 중단해 주세요. 149 새 명함에는 새로운 회사명(아직 공개되지 않음)과 활기찬 새 로고가 포함될 것입니다. 새 명함은 여러분 중 다수가 요청한 대로 더 고급 재질의 종이에 인쇄될 예정입니다.

5월 1일까지 새 명함이 자리로 전달되지 않으면, 내선번호 2933번으로 저에게 직접 연락 주세요.

어휘 merger 합병 distribute 배포하다 feature 포함하다 reveal 드러내다 paper stock 제지 원료 directly 직접 extension 내선번호

149 주제 / 목적

번역 무엇이 회람을 작성하게 만들었는가?
(A) 최근 재택근무의 증가
(B) 회사명의 변경
(C) 일련의 인쇄 오류
(D) 종이 품질에 대한 불만

해설 첫 단락 첫 문장에서 프랜텀 코퍼레이션과의 합병 결과로 모든 케톨라 엔터프라이즈 직원들의 인쇄된 명함이 교체된다(As a result of our merger with Frantum Corporation, printed business cards for all Ketola Enterprises employees will be replaced)고 했고, 같은 단락 네 번째 문장에서 새 명함에는 새로운 회사명과 활기찬 새 로고가 포함될 것(The new cards will feature the new corporate name (yet to be revealed) and our exciting new logo)이라고 알리고 있다. 따라서 회람은 회사 합병으로 인해 회사명이 바뀜에 따라 명함이 교체될 예정임을 알리기 위한 것이므로 (B)가 정답이다.

어휘 a series of 일련의 complaint 불만

> **Paraphrasing**
> 지문의 the new corporate name
> → 정답의 change in a company's name

150 추론 / 암시

번역 새 명함에 대해 암시된 것은?
(A) 정규직 직원에게단 발급될 것이다.
(B) 직원들의 집으로 발송될 것이다.
(C) 4월 중에 인쇄될 것이다.
(D) 프랜텀 코퍼레이션의 원래 로고가 들어갈 것이다.

해설 상단에 회람이 작성된 날짜가 3월 31일(Date: March 31)로 되어 있고, 첫 단락 두 번째 문장에서 모든 직원들은 5월 1일까지 새로운 명함을 받게 될 것(All employees should receive the new business cards by May 1)이라고 했다. 따라서 새로운 명함은 4월에 인쇄되어 직원들에게 전달될 것임을 유추할 수 있으므로 (C)가 정답이다.

어휘 issue 발급하다 original 원래의

151-152 온라인 채팅

프리야 베가니 (오전 9시 2분)
안녕하세요, 자레드. 151 당신이 진행하는 관리 기술 워크숍 날짜를 알려 주시겠어요?

자레드 옥슬리 (오전 9시 3분)
152 9월 4일 목요일이요. 거의 하루 종일 진행될 거예요. 151 여전히 참석할 계획인가요?

프리야 베가니 (오전 9시 5분)
놓치지 않을 거예요! 152 그 주에 회계부 회의를 언제로 잡을지 정하는 중이라 물어봤을 뿐인데, 제가 사무실에 있을 날은 9월 2일, 3일, 4일뿐이에요. 그 후로는 9월 15일이 되어야 돌아올 텐데 그건 너무 늦어요.

자레드 옥슬리 (오전 9시 6분)
152 9월 2일 오전에는 유지 보수 작업으로 사무실을 닫을 거라는 점 잊지 마세요. 작업팀이 정오까지 작업을 완료할 예정이기는 하지만 모를 일이죠.

프리야 베가니 (오전 9시 7분)
아, 그러네요. 지난번 유지 보수 작업 때 사무실이 결국 하루 종일 닫혔죠. 그럼 152 회계부 회의를 할 수 있는 확실한 날짜가 딱 하루만 남네요. 상기시켜줘서 고마워요.

자레드 옥슬리 (오전 9시 8분)
천만에요. 그나저나 우리 중 몇 명이 오늘 퇴근 후 아알라즈 비스트로에서 모이기로 했어요. 함께 할래요?

프리야 베가니 (오전 9시 9분)
전 못 가요. 퇴근 후에 진료 예약이 있거든요. 다음에 갈게요!

어휘 take up (시간·공간을) 차지하다 maintenance 유지 보수 crew 작업팀 be supposed to ~하기로 되어 있다 end up -ing 결국 ~하게 되다 by the way 그런데 appointment 약속

151 의도 파악

번역 오전 9시 5분에 베가니 씨가 "놓치지 않을 거예요!"라고 쓴 의도는?
(A) 다가오는 워크숍에 참석할 것이다.
(B) 회계부 회의는 매우 중요하다.
(C) 퇴근 후 사교 행사가 재미있을 것 같다.
(D) 옥슬리 씨가 빌려 간 문서를 돌려주기를 기대하지 않는다.

해설 9시 2분에 베가니 씨가 당신이 진행하는 관리 기술 워크숍 날짜를 알려달라(Could you tell me the date of the management skills workshop you're leading?)고 물었고, 9시 3분에 옥슬리 씨가 날짜를 알려주며 여전히 참석할 계획인지(Are you still planning to come?)를 확인하자, 9시 5분에 베가니 씨가 놓치지 않을 것(I wouldn't miss it!)이라고 답했다. 따라서 베가니 씨는 옥슬리 씨가 진행하는 워크숍에 꼭 참석하겠다는 의도로 한 말임을 알 수 있으므로 (A)가 정답이다.

어휘 social 사교상의 promise ~일 것 같다 borrow 빌리다

152 추론 / 암시

번역 베가니 씨는 언제 회계부와 회의를 할 것 같은가?
(A) 9월 2일
(B) 9월 3일
(C) 9월 4일
(D) 9월 15일

해설 9시 3분에 옥슬리 씨가 9월 4일 목요일(Thursday, September 4)이라고 워크숍 날짜를 알려주고 있고, 9시 5분에 베가니 씨가 그 주에 회계부 회의를 언제로 잡을지 정하는 중이라 물어본 건데, 자신이 사무실에 있을 날은 9월 2일, 3일, 4일뿐(I only asked because I'm trying to decide when to schedule an accounting department meeting during that week, and the only days I'll be in the office are September 2, 3, and 4)이라고 했으며, 9시 6분에 옥슬리 씨가 9월 2일 오전에는 유지 보수 작업으로 사무실을 닫을 거라는 점을 잊지 말라(Don't forget that the office will be closed on the morning of September 2 for maintenance work)고 하자, 9시 7분에 베가니 씨가 회계부 회의를 할 수 있는 확실한 날짜가 딱 하루만 남는다(That leaves only one sure date for that accounting meeting then)고 했다. 따라서 워크숍 날짜와 보수 작업 날짜를 제외한 하루는 9월 3일이고, 베가니 씨는 이 날 회의를 할 것임을 짐작할 수 있으므로 (B)가 정답이다.

153-155 이메일

수신: 켈레 초 〈k.tso@faeberelectric.com〉
발신: 코니 왓킨스 〈c.watkins@faeberelectric.com〉
날짜: 5월 13일
제목: 회신: 직원 안내서

153 이 이메일은 〈페이버 일렉트릭 직원 안내서〉의 수락 페이지에 아직 서명하지 않은 모든 직원에게 발송됩니다. 모든 직원은 조건을 수락해야 하며 **154** 제가 5월 1일에 보낸 이메일에서 요청드렸습니다. 양식에 서명하지 않을 경우 급여 지급이 늦어질 수 있습니다.

〈페이버 일렉트릭 직원 안내서〉와 서명 페이지는 faeberelectric.com/handbook에서 확인하실 수 있습니다. 안내서의 주요 **155** 사항을 요약한 도표도 해당 사이트에서 확인하실 수 있습니다.

질문이 있으실 경우 관리자에게 문의하시거나 저에게 직접 연락 주세요.

코니 왓킨스
인사 담당자

어휘 handbook 안내서 acceptance 수락 terms 조건 failure 불이행 salary 급여 summarize 요약하다 reach out 연락하다 directly 직접

153 주제 / 목적

번역 이메일의 목적은?
(A) 초 씨에게 웹사이트 주소 변경을 알리려고
(B) 직원 급여 시스템 이용 방법을 설명하려고
(C) 초 씨에게 양식에 서명해야 함을 상기시키려고
(D) 초 씨에게 근무 일정 변경에 대해 알리려고

해설 첫 단락의 첫 문장에서 이 이메일은 〈페이버 일렉트릭 직원 안내서〉의 수락 페이지에 아직 서명하지 않은 모든 직원에게 발송된다(This e-mail is being sent to all employees who have not yet signed the *Faeber Electric Employee Handbook* acceptance page)고 했고, 모든 직원은 조건을 수락해야 한다(Acceptance of the terms is required of all employees)고 했다. 따라서 초 씨에게 양식에 반드시 서명해야 한다는 사실을 알려주기 위한 이메일임을 알 수 있으므로 (C)가 정답이다.

어휘 notify 알리다 access 이용하다 requirement 필요, 요건

154 Not / True

번역 이메일에서 왓킨스 씨에 대해 명시하는 것은?
(A) 페이버 일렉트릭의 신입 직원이다.
(B) 〈페이버 일렉트릭 직원 안내서〉를 작성했다.
(C) 5월 1일에 직원들에게 이메일을 보냈다.
(D) 초 씨의 관리자이다.

해설 첫 단락의 두 번째 문장에서 왓킨스 씨가 자신이 5월 1일에 보낸 이메일(an e-mail I sent on May 1)을 언급했으므로 (C)가 정답이다.

155 동의어 찾기

번역 두 번째 단락 2행의 "points"와 의미가 가장 가까운 단어는?
(A) 세부 사항
(B) 위치
(C) 의견
(D) 단계

해설 의미상 안내서의 주요 '사항'이라는 뜻으로 쓰였으므로 '세부 사항'을 의미하는 (A) details가 정답이다.

156-157 웹페이지

우리 잡지에 대하여

〈CVT 다이렉트〉는 국내 최대 화물 차량 기업인 론 트랜스포테이션에서 발행하는 호주의 무역 잡지입니다. **156** 이 잡지는 전국적으로 상품을 운송하기 위한 차량을 25대 이상 보유한 대리점의 중간 및 상급 관리자가 신청하면 무료로 발송됩니다.

〈CVT 다이렉트〉를 구독하시려면, 귀하의 회사 우편주소, 이메일, 전화번호를 cvtsubscription@lornetransportation.com.au로 보내주세요. **157** 모든 개인 식별 정보는 론 사의 개인정보 보호 정책에 따라 기밀로 취급되며, 이는 lornetransportation.com.au에서 확인하실 수 있습니다. **157** 귀하의 개인 식별 정보는 론 사의 제품 및 서비스에 대한 추가 정보를 제공하기 위해 사용될 수 있습니다.

어휘 freight 화물 vehicle 차량 upper 상위의 dealership 대리점 fleet 무리 transport 운송하다 goods 상품 nationwide 전국적으로 subscription 구독 identifiable 식별 가능한 treat 취급하다 confidentially 기밀로 in accordance with ~에 따라 privacy statement 개인정보 보호 정책

156 추론 / 암시

번역 어떤 업계의 경영진이 〈CVT 다이렉트〉 잡지를 읽을 것 같은가?
(A) 자동차 수리
(B) 상업용 트럭 운송
(C) 기계 엔지니어링
(D) 창고 건설

해설 첫 단락 두 번째 문장에서 이 잡지는 전국적으로 상품을 운송하기 위한 차량을 25대 이상 보유한 대리점의 중간 및 상급 관리자가 신청하면 무료로 발송된다(The magazine is sent free upon request to mid- and upper-level managers of dealerships with fleets of 25 or more vehicles for transporting goods nationwide)고 한 것을 통해, 〈CVT 다이렉트〉는 상업용 차량 운송 업체의 운영진들을 대상으로 하는 잡지임을 알 수 있다. 따라서 (B)가 정답이다.

어휘 executive 경영진 commercial 상업의 trucking 트럭 운송

157 주제 / 목적

번역 웹페이지에서 다루는 한 가지 주제는?
(A) 유통 전략의 최근 변화
(B) 구독자 정보가 사용되는 방식
(C) 제품 주문을 위한 요건
(D) 출판물의 수요가 증가한 이유

해설 두 번째 단락의 두 번째 문장에서 모든 개인 식별 정보는 론 사의 개인정보 보호 정책에 따라 기밀로 취급된다(All personally identifiable information will be treated confidentially in accordance with the Lorne privacy statement)고 했고, 같은 단락 세 번째 문장에서 귀하의 개인 식별 정보는 론 사의 제품 및 서비스에 대한 추가 정보를 제공하기 위해 사용될 수 있다(Your personally identifiable information may be used to provide you with additional information about Lorne's products and services)며 개인 정보 취급법에 대해 안내하고 있다. 따라서 (B)가 정답이다.

어휘 strategy 전략 subscriber 구독자 demand 수요

158-160 전단

다음 리모델링 프로젝트에는 거낙 홈을 믿어주세요!

거낙 홈은 내슈빌 지역에서 30년간 맞춤형 주택 수리 솔루션을 훌륭하게 제공해 왔습니다. 얼마나 크고 작은지에 상관없이, 저희는 모든 종류의 프로젝트에서 고객과 함께 일합니다. **158** 저희의 전문 분야는 주방과 욕실 개조, 지하실과 차고를 놀이공간이나 홈오피스로 바꾸는 작업, 그리고 주택 증축입니다.

저희는 거낙 홈이 최고 품질의 제품만을 설치한다고 **159** 보장 드릴 수 있습니다. 저희 전문 설치팀의 작업을 한 번 보신다면, 여러분은 분명 저희에게 만족한 고객 명단에 합류하게 될 겁니다.

(615) 555-0118번으로 전화하셔서 무료 상담 방문 일정을 예약하세요. 또는 저희 웹사이트 www.gernackhome.com에 있는 전시장을 방문하세요. 그곳에서 **160** 저희의 최신 기능인 가상 주택 개조 도우미를 활용해 보세요. 저희 온라인 도우미는 여러분이 꿈꾸는 개조 모습을 가장 먼저 확인해 보실 수 있도록 가상 공간을 만드는 일을 도와드립니다.

어휘 customized 맞춤형의 renovation 수리, 보수 solution 해결책 specialty 전문 분야 convert 전환하다 basement 지하실 garage 차고 assure 보장하다 expert 전문적인 installer 설치자 showroom 전시실 feature 기능 virtual 가상의

158 Not / True

번역 거낙 홈이 제공하는 서비스로 명시되지 않은 것은?
(A) 주방 개조
(B) 홈오피스 조성
(C) 파티오 설치
(D) 주택 증축

해설 첫 단락의 마지막 문장에서 거낙 홈의 전문 분야는 주방과 욕실 개조, 지하실과 차고를 놀이공간이나 홈오피스로 바꾸는 작업, 그리고 주택 증축(Our specialties are renovating kitchens and bathrooms, converting basements and garages into recreation rooms or home offices, and building home additions)이라고 했으므로 (A)와 (B), (D)는 거낙 홈의 서비스에 포함되어 있음을 확인할 수 있다. 파티오 설치는 언급되지 않았으므로 (C)가 정답이다.

어휘 installation 설치

159 동의어 찾기

번역 두 번째 단락 1행의 "assure"와 의미가 가장 가까운 단어는?
(A) 충고하다
(B) 약속하다
(C) 위로하다
(D) 지원하다

해설 의미상 최고 품질의 제품만을 설치함을 '보장한다'는 뜻으로 쓰였으므로 '약속하다'를 뜻하는 (B) promise가 정답이다.

160 세부 사항

번역 거낙 홈이 새롭게 제공하는 것은?
(A) 온라인 전시장
(B) 시각화 도구
(C) 사진 공유 페이지
(D) 방문 예약용 모바일 앱

해설 세 번째 단락 세 번째 문장에서 최신 기능인 가상 주택 개조 도우미를 활용해 보라(take advantage of our latest feature: a virtual home renovation assistant)면서, 이 온라인 도우미는 여러분이 꿈꾸는 개조 모습을 가장 먼저 확인할 수 있도록 가상 공간을 만드는 일을 돕는다(Our online assistants can help you build a virtual room so that you can take a first look at the renovation of your dreams)고 했다. 따라서 거낙 홈에서 가상 공간을 만들고 어떤 모습일지 미리 볼 수 있는 새로운 서비스를 제공하고 있음을 알 수 있으므로 (B)가 정답이다.

어휘 visualization 시각화 tool 도구

161-163 이메일

수신: 로리 우즈 〈lauriwoods@coralmail.com〉
발신: 고객 서비스 부서
　　　〈customerservice@honeycanyonapparel.com〉
날짜: 10월 4일
제목: 감사합니다

우즈 씨께,

최근 구매에 감사드립니다! 제품이 고객님 마음에 드시기를 바랍니다.

161 이번 기회에 고객님께서 좋아하실 만한 몇몇 다른 제품들을 추천하고자 합니다. honeycanyonapparel.com/wardrobe를 방문하시고 코드번호 RN49X를 입력하셔서 고객님을 위해 특별히 선별된 추천 상품 목록을 확인하세요. 추천 품목 중에서 고객님께서 구입하신 스커트와 잘 어울릴 만한 스웨터 몇 벌에 강조 표시를 해 두었습니다.

그리고 **162** 오랫동안 허니 캐니언의 고객이 되어 주신 점에 감사드리고자 **163** 다음 주문 시 20퍼센트 할인도 제공해 드립니다. 이는 결제 시 고객님의 장바구니에 자동으로 적용됩니다. 할인을 받으시려면 한 달 이내에 주문하기만 하면 됩니다.

고객님의 옷장을 저희의 최신 스타일로 가득 채워드리게 되기를 기대합니다!

허니 캐니언 의류 고객 서비스 부서

어휘 opportunity 기회　suggest 추천하다　curate 선별하다　highlight 강조하다　fill 채우다　apparel 의류

161 주제 / 목적

번역 이메일의 한 가지 목적은?
(A) 제품이 다시 들어왔음을 알리려고
(B) 반품된 제품을 처리하려고
(C) 신상 정장 라인을 알리려고
(D) 개인 맞춤 의류 추천을 공유하려고

해설 두 번째 단락의 첫 문장에서 이번 기회에 고객님이 좋아할 만한 몇 몇 다른 제품들을 추천하고자 한다(We wanted to take the opportunity to suggest some other items you might like)고 했으므로, 고객에게 의류 품목을 추천하기 위해 이메일을 보냈다는 것을 알 수 있다. 따라서 (D)가 정답이다.

어휘 restock 다시 채우다　process 처리하다　personalized 개인 맞춤형의　recommendation 추천

> **Paraphrasing**
> 지문의 suggest → 정답의 recommendations

162 Not / True

번역 우즈 씨에 대해 명시된 것은?
(A) 허니 캐니언 의류의 일자리에 지원하고 있다.
(B) 허니 캐니언 의류에서 이전에 쇼핑한 적이 있다.
(C) 캐주얼 의류 착용을 선호한다.
(D) 패션 디자이너로 일한다.

해설 세 번째 단락 첫 문장에서 우즈 씨에게 오랫동안 허니 캐니언의 고객이 되어 준 점에 감사하고자 다음 주문 시 20퍼센트 할인도 제공한다 (to thank you for being a Honey Canyon customer for so many years, we are also offering you a 20 percent discount on your next order)고 했으므로 우즈 씨는 허니 캐니언에서 오랫동안 쇼핑을 해 온 고객임을 알 수 있다. 따라서 (B)가 정답이다.

> **Paraphrasing**
> 지문의 being a Honey Canyon customer for so many years → 정답의 has shopped at Honey Canyon Apparel before

163 문장 삽입

번역 [1], [2], [3], [4]로 표시된 위치 중에서 다음 문장이 들어가기에 가장 적합한 곳은?
"이는 결제 시 고객님의 장바구니에 자동으로 적용됩니다."
(A) [1]
(B) [2]
(C) [3]
(D) [4]

해설 주어진 문장에서 이는 결제 시 자동으로 적용된다고 했으므로 결제 단계에서 적용 받을 수 있는 이것(This)에 관한 내용이 앞에 있어야 한다. 따라서 다음 주문 시 20퍼센트 할인을 제공해 준다(offering you a 20 percent discount on your next order)고 할인 혜택을 언급하는 내용 뒤인 [4]에 들어가는 것이 글의 흐름상 자연스러우므로 (D)가 정답이다.

어휘 automatically 자동으로　check out 결제하다, 계산하다

164-167 광고

니보라 XC-35 스포츠 유틸리티 차량(SUV)

당신이 가고 싶은 곳은 어디든, 해변에서 오지까지 니보라 XC-35가 그곳으로 데려가 줄 겁니다! XC-35의 강력한 엔진은 최대 275마력까지 제공하며, 새롭게 디자인된 차체는 이 SUV에 매끈하고 스포티한 외관을 부여합니다. **164** 지면으로부터의 상당한 간격과 충격으로부터 보호해 주는 강력한 안정성으로, 니보라 XC-35는 아주 거친 지형에서조차 부드러운 주행을 제공하며 어떠한 야생 모험에도 도전할 수 있는 자신감을 줄 것입니다.

니보라 XC-35는 가솔린 차량 또는 하이브리드 차량으로 구입할 수 있습니다. 고객들은 또한 수동 변속기와 자동 변속기 중에서 선택할 수 있습니다. **165** 모든 차량에 사륜구동과 휴대폰 연결이 가능한 내비게이션 시스템이 기본으로 제공됩니다.

XC-35에서 이용 가능한 옵션에는 선루프, 소닉 붐 스테레오 시스템, 크루즈 컨트롤, 루프랙 등이 있습니다. **166** 원하는 옵션에 비용을 아끼시려면 가까운 니보라 대리점을 방문하셔서 어떤 종류의 혜택 패키지를 제공하는지 확인하세요.

그리고 **167** 매장 방문 전에 www.nibora.com/build를 방문하셔서 외장 색상, 실내 시트 스타일, 그래픽 데칼을 선택하여 새로운 니보라 XC-35의 외관을 직접 꾸며보세요.

오늘 신형 니보라 XC-35를 구입하세요!

> 어휘 backwoods 오지 horsepower 마력 sleek 매끈한
> significant 상당한 clearance 간격 stabilization 안정성
> bump 충격 smooth 부드러운 rough 거친 terrain 지형
> manual 수동의 transmission 변속기 all-wheel drive
> 사륜구동 pairing 연동 roof rack 루프랙(지붕 위의 짐칸)
> dealer 대리점 exterior 외장의 upholstery (의자 등의) 덮개
> graphic decal 그래픽 데칼(차량 장식 스티커)

164 추론 / 암시

번역 XC-35에 대해 암시된 것은?
(A) 니보라에서 가장 많이 팔리는 차량이다.
(B) 좁은 공간에서 주차하기 좋다.
(C) 다른 SUV들보다 더 긍정적인 평가를 받았다.
(D) 다양한 종류의 지면에서 주행하기 좋다.

해설 첫 단락의 세 번째 문장에서 지면으로부터의 상당한 간격과 충격으로부터 보호해 주는 강력한 안정성으로, 니보라 XC-35는 아주 거친 지형에서조차 부드러운 주행을 제공하며 어떠한 야생 모험에도 도전할 수 있는 자신감을 줄 것(With significant clearance from the ground and strong stabilization to protect from bumps, the Nibora XC-35 offers a smooth ride even on the roughest terrain and will give you the confidence to take it on any wilderness adventure)이라고 했다. 이를 통해 XC-35는 다양한 조건의 지면에서 주행 능력이 뛰어나다는 것을 알 수 있으므로 (D)가 정답이다.

어휘 review 평가 surface 지면

> **Paraphrasing**
> 지문의 terrain → 정답의 surfaces

165 세부 사항

번역 모든 XC-35 SUV에 제공되는 기능은?
(A) 하이브리드 엔진
(B) 사륜구동
(C) 선루프
(D) 크루즈 컨트롤

해설 두 번째 단락의 세 번째 문장에서 모든 차량에 사륜구동과 휴대폰 연결이 가능한 내비게이션 시스템이 기본으로 제공된다(All vehicles come standard with all-wheel drive and a navigation system with phone pairing)고 했으므로 (B)가 정답이다.

166 Not / True

번역 XC-35의 옵션에 대해 광고에서 언급된 것은?
(A) 패키지로 구입할 경우 할인 받을 수 있다.
(B) 일부 대리점에서는 구입할 수 없다.
(C) 일부는 곧 없어질 예정이다.
(D) 일부는 패키지로 구입할 경우에만 이용 가능하다.

해설 세 번째 단락의 마지막 문장에서 원하는 옵션에 비용을 아끼려면 가까운 니보라 대리점을 방문하여 어떤 종류의 혜택 패키지를 제공하는지 확인하라(To save on the options you love, visit your nearby Nibora dealer to see what kinds of value packages they offer)고 했으므로 패키지로 구입할 경우 금액이 절감될 수 있음을 알 수 있다. 따라서 (A)가 정답이다.

어휘 discontinue 중단하다

167 세부 사항

번역 광고에 따르면, 고객들은 어떻게 XC-35의 외관을 선택할 수 있는가?
(A) 전화 통화를 함으로써
(B) 웹사이트를 방문함으로써
(C) 이메일을 보냄으로써
(D) 자동차 잡지를 살펴봄으로써

해설 네 번째 단락에서 매장 방문 전에 www.nibora.com/build를 방문하여 외장 색상, 실내 시트 스타일, 그래픽 데칼을 선택해 새로운 니보라 XC-35의 외관을 직접 꾸며보라(before you visit, go to www.nibora.com/build and customize the look of your new Nibora XC-35 by choosing exterior color, upholstery style, and graphic decals)고 했으므로 (B)가 정답이다.

어휘 automobile 자동차

> **Paraphrasing**
> 지문의 go to www.nibora.com/build
> → 정답의 visiting a Web site

168-171 광고

> **콜로아 음악 학원**
>
> **168** 악기 연주를 배우기에 너무 늦은 때는 없습니다. 15년 넘게 어린이 음악 수업을 선도해 온 콜로아 음악 학원은 성인을 위한 개인 음악 교육 프로그램을 발표하게 되어 기쁩니다. **168** 8월 28일부터 저희는 입문자를 위한 기타와 바이올린 강습을 제공합니다.
>
> **169** 저희의 모든 강사는 최소한 음악 학사 학위를 소지하고 있으며 오케스트라나 밴드에서 연주 경험이 있습니다. 저희 강사들은 또한 음악 교육에서 성공적인 경력을 갖고 있습니다. **171** 강습은 여러 형식으로 제공됩니다. 저희 교습소나 귀하의 거주지에서 대면 수업 일정을 잡아드릴 수 있습니다. 또는, 여러분의 일정에 맞춰 온라인 수업을 제공해 드릴 수 있습니다.
>
> 학생은 자신의 악기를 준비해야 합니다. 자세한 내용을 알아보고 추천 악기 상점 목록을 확인하시려면 저희 웹사이트 www.koloamusiceducationcollective.com을 방문해 주세요.
>
> **170** 저희 서비스를 예약하고 싶으시면, 웹사이트에서 온라인 정보 양식을 작성해 주세요. 선택하신 강사를 요청하실 수 있으며, 저희가 강사를 배정해 드릴 수도 있습니다. **170** 강사가 48시간 이내에 연락드릴 것입니다. 항상 바랐던 음악가가 되시는 데 도움을 드리게 되어 기쁩니다!

어휘	education 교육 collective 집단 instrument 악기 instruction 강습, 지도 bachelor's degree 학사 학위 performance 연주 format 형식 in-person 대면의 residence 거주지 fill out ~을 작성하다

168 추론 / 암시

번역 누가 광고의 대상으로 의도되는 것 같은가?
(A) 방과 후 음악 프로그램 책임자
(B) 전문 음악가
(C) 음악 경험이 없는 사람
(D) 악기 상점 주인

해설 첫 단락의 첫 번째 문장에서 악기 연주를 배우기에 너무 늦은 때는 없다(It's never too late to learn to play an instrument)고 했고, 같은 단락의 세 번째 문장에서 8월 28일부터 입문자를 위한 기타와 바이올린 강습을 제공한다(Beginning on August 28, we will offer guitar and violin instruction for beginners)고 한 것으로 보아, 악기 연주를 처음 배우려는 사람들을 대상으로 하는 광고임을 알 수 있다. 따라서 (C)가 정답이다.

어휘 coordinator 책임자, 조정자

169 Not / True

번역 콜로아 음악 학원에 대해 명시된 것은?
(A) 성인을 위한 그룹 수업을 제공한다.
(B) 대학교 학위를 가진 음악가들을 고용한다.
(C) 녹음 스튜디오를 운영한다.
(D) 무료 악기를 제공한다.

해설 두 번째 단락 첫 문장에서 모든 강사는 최소한 음악 학사 학위를 소지하고 있다(All our instructors hold at least a bachelor's degree in music)고 했으므로 (B)가 정답이다.

어휘 complimentary 무료의

> **Paraphrasing**
> 지문의 bachelor's degree → 정답의 university degrees

170 세부 사항

번역 콜로아 음악 학원에서 누가 관심 있는 고객에게 먼저 연락할 것인가?
(A) 관리자
(B) 영업 사원
(C) 사무 관리자
(D) 강사

해설 마지막 단락의 첫 문장에서 서비스를 예약하고 싶으면 웹사이트에서 온라인 정보 양식을 작성해 달라(If you are interested in scheduling our services, please fill out our online information form on our Web site)고 한 뒤, 같은 단락의 세 번째 문장에서 강사가 48시간 이내에 연락할 것(An instructor will contact you within 48 hours)이라고 했다. 따라서 (D)가 정답이다.

어휘 administrator 관리자

171 문장 삽입

번역 [1], [2], [3], [4]로 표시된 위치 중에서 다음 문장이 들어가기에 가장 적합한 곳은?

"또는, 여러분의 일정에 맞춰 온라인 수업을 제공해 드릴 수 있습니다."
(A) [1]
(B) [2]
(C) [3]
(D) [4]

해설 주어진 문장에서 또는(Alternatively) 일정에 맞춰 온라인 수업을 제공할 수 있다고 했으므로, 주어진 문장 앞에는 온라인 수업 외에 제공되는 다른 방식의 수업에 대한 내용이 있어야 한다. 따라서 강습은 여러 형식으로 제공된다(available in several formats)면서, 교습소나 거주지에서 진행하는 대면 수업(in-person instruction at our office or your residence)을 안내하는 내용 뒤인 [2]에 들어가는 것이 자연스러우므로 (B)가 정답이다.

어휘 accommodate (환경 등에) 맞추다

172-175 온라인 채팅

> **리넷 월터 (오후 4시 45분)**
> 우리 셋이 내일 영업 회의 전에 점심을 함께할 수 있을까요?
>
> **트립 하인즈 (오후 4시 46분)**
> 물론이죠, 리넷. 구체적으로 이야기하고 싶은 거라도 있나요?
>
> **리넷 월터 (오후 4시 47분)**
> 172 그냥 우리가 새로운 마케팅 캠페인과 관련해 같은 내용으로 이해하고 있는 게 맞는지 확인하고 싶어요.
>
> **트립 하인즈 (오후 4시 48분)**
> 여름 신발 라인 건이요?
>
> **리넷 월터 (오후 4시 49분)**
> 네. 개발 중인 문구와 그래픽 둘 다 제가 보스턴에 나가 있는 동안 놓친 부분을 따라잡아야 하거든요.
>
> **에이프릴 아우 (오후 4시 50분)**
> 죄송하지만 174 영업 회의는 언제 어디서 하는 건가요? 제 일정표를 확인했는데 그 회의를 찾을 수가 없어서요.
>
> **트립 하인즈 (오후 4시 51분)**
> 173 이사회실에서 3시에 시작해요. 174 당신은 올 필요 없어요. 173 그래픽과 관련된 사람들만 해당되거든요.
>
> **에이프릴 아우 (오후 4시 52분)**
> 안심이네요! 그리고 네, 리넷, 당신과 점심을 먹으러 갈 수 있고 고려 중인 문구에 대한 업데이트도 해 줄게요.
>
> **리넷 월터 (오후 4시 53분)**
> 좋아요. 175 두 분 모두 내일 1시 30분에 로비에서 만나요. 그때 어디서 먹을지 정하면 되겠네요.

어휘 specific 구체적인 be on the same page 이해하고 있는 내용이 같다 catch up 따라잡다 boardroom 이사회실 involved 관련된 relief 안심

172 세부 사항

번역 월터 씨는 왜 하인즈 씨 및 아우 씨와 함께 점심을 먹고 싶어 하는가?
(A) 최근 여행에 대한 경험담을 나누려고
(B) 신발 라인의 가격에 대해 토론하려고
(C) 제품의 마케팅 캠페인에 대해 논의하려고
(D) 영업팀을 위한 여름 수련회를 계획하려고

해설 4시 47분에 월터 씨가 우리가 새로운 마케팅 캠페인과 관련해 같은 내용으로 이해하고 있는 게 맞는지 확인하고 싶다(I just want to make sure that we're on the same page about the new marketing campaign)며 동료들과 점심을 함께 하고 싶은 이유를 말하고 있으므로 (C)가 정답이다.

어휘 debate 토론하다 retreat 수련회

173 세부 사항

번역 누가 오후 3시 회의에 참석할 것으로 예상되는가?
(A) 그래픽 디자이너
(B) 원고 편집자
(C) 영업 관리자들만
(D) 보스턴 사무소의 직원들만

해설 4시 51분에 하인즈 씨가 회의는 이사회실에서 3시에 시작한다(It starts at 3:00 in the boardroom)면서 그래픽과 관련된 사람들만 해당된다(It's only for people involved in the graphics)고 했으므로 (A)가 정답이다.

174 의도 파악

번역 오후 4시 52분에 아우 씨가 "안심이네요"라고 쓴 의도는?
(A) 월터 씨가 자신에게 동의해서 기쁘다.
(B) 행사에 초대받아 감사하다.
(C) 자신의 일정표가 맞아서 기쁘다.
(D) 친구들과 만나 기쁘다.

해설 4시 50분에 아우 씨가 영업 회의는 언제 어디서 하는 건지(when and where is the sales meeting?)를 물으며 자신의 일정표에서 그 회의를 찾을 수가 없다(I checked my calendar, and I could not find that meeting)고 걱정하자, 4시 51분에 하인즈 씨가 당신은 올 필요 없다(You don't need to be there)고 확인해 준 것에 대해 4시 52분에 아우 씨가 안심이다(What a relief!)라고 대답한 것이므로, 아우 씨는 자신의 일정표가 틀리지 않았다는 점에 안도하는 의도로 한 말임을 알 수 있다. 따라서 (C)가 정답이다.

175 세부 사항

번역 아우 씨와 하인즈 씨, 월터 씨는 내일 어디에서 만날 것인가?
(A) 이사회실
(B) 로비
(C) 월터 씨의 사무실
(D) 휴게실

해설 4시 53분에 월터 씨가 아우 씨와 하인즈 씨에게 내일 1시 30분에 로비에서 만나자(I'll see you both tomorrow at 1:30 in the lobby)고 했으므로 (B)가 정답이다.

176-180 송장 + 이메일

그레이트포드 커튼
채플 로 137번지, 버밍엄 B8 3HU
0121 496 0608

176 주문해 주시고 저희 가족의 작은 가게를 지원해 주셔서 감사합니다. 감사의 표시로 고객님께 200파운드 이상의 다음 주문 시 10퍼센트 할인을 제공해 드립니다. 할인 코드 NEWCURTAINS를 사용하세요.

고객 정보
니콜라 그랜트
더스트 플레이스 17번지
휘트스터블 CT5 1AH

179 날짜: 7월 23일

179 주문 번호: 19842

원단 샘플	수량	가격
178 케임브리지	1	8파운드
맨체스터	1	8파운드
옥스포드	1	8파운드
윈저	1	8파운드
배송		4.25파운드
소계		36.25파운드
부가가치세		7.25파운드
총액		43.50파운드

어휘 appreciation 감사 fabric 원단 subtotal 소계 VAT 부가가치세(Valued Added Tax의 약자)

수신: 그레이트포드 커튼
〈customerservice@greatfordcurtains.co.uk〉
발신: 니콜라 그랜트 〈ngrant@sapphiremail.co.uk〉
날짜: 7월 27일
제목: 주문번호 19842

안녕하세요,

오늘 원단 샘플을 받았는데 정말 아름답습니다! **177** 저의 식사 공간을 위해 맨체스터 원단을 사용한 맞춤 커튼 견적을 받고 싶습니다. 박스 플리트 스타일로 제작된 117cm x 228cm 크기의 패널 4개가 필요합니다. 이렇게 하면 비용이 얼마나 들지와 언제 받을 수 있는지를 알려 주세요. 참고로, 10퍼센트 할인 코드를 갖고 있습니다.

거실용 커튼에도 관심이 있지만 **178** 제가 받은 모든 샘플들의 파란 색감이 그 공간에는 잘 어울리지 않습니다. 에든버러와 노리치 원단 샘플을 보내주실 수 있을까요? 이 원단들은 녹색 색감으로 나오는 것으로 알고 있습니다. **179** 7월 23일에 한 **180** 지난 주문 때 제 온라인 프로필에 저장한 신용카드로 청구해 주세요.

감사합니다.

니콜라 그랜트

> **어휘** quote 견적(액) custom 맞춤의 dining 식사 pleat 플리트(상자형 겹주름) shade 색조 charge 청구하다

176 Not / True

번역 그레이트포드 커튼에 대해 명시된 것은?
(A) 가족 소유의 업체이다.
(B) 재고 정리 세일을 하고 있다.
(C) 더스트 플레이스 17번지에 위치해 있다.
(D) 무료 배송을 제공한다.

해설 송장의 첫 문장에서 주문해 주시고 가족의 작은 업체를 지원해 주셔서 감사하다(Thank you for your order and for supporting our family's small business)고 했으므로, 그레이트포드 커튼은 가족이 운영하는 업체라는 것을 알 수 있다. 따라서 (A)가 정답이다.

어휘 clearance (불필요한 것) 정리

> **Paraphrasing**
> 지문의 family's small business
> → 정답의 family-owned business

177 세부 사항

번역 그랜트 씨가 요청한 것은?
(A) 초과 지불금의 환불
(B) 너무 작은 제품의 교환
(C) 맞춤형 제품의 가격
(D) 주문품의 신속한 배송

해설 이메일의 첫 단락 두 번째 문장에서 그랜트 씨가 식사 공간을 위해 맨체스터 원단을 사용한 맞춤 커튼 견적을 받고 싶다(I would like to get a quote for custom curtains for my dining room using the Manchester fabric)고 했으므로 (C)가 정답이다.

어휘 overpayment 초과 지불(금) customized 맞춤의 express 신속한, 급행의

> **Paraphrasing**
> 지문의 a quote for custom curtains
> → 정답의 A price for a customized product

178 연계

번역 송장에 기재된 케임브리지 원단 샘플에 대해 사실일 것 같은 것은?
(A) 파란색이다.
(B) 43.50파운드다.
(C) 맞춤 주문에 사용될 것이다.
(D) 그랜트 씨의 식사 공간에 사용될 것이다.

해설 이메일의 두 번째 단락 첫 번째 문장에서 그랜트 씨가 받은 모든 샘플이 파란 색감(the shades of blue in all the samples I received)이라고 했고, 송장 하단의 주문 가격표에 케임브리지(Cambridge)원단이 포함되어 있다. 따라서 그랜트 씨가 받은 샘플 중 하나인 케임브리지 원단도 파란색이라는 것을 알 수 있으므로 (A)가 정답이다.

179 연계

번역 주문 번호 19842에 대해 암시된 것은?
(A) 예상보다 늦게 도착했다.
(B) 몇몇 제품이 누락되었다.
(C) 노리치 원단 샘플이 들어 있었다.
(D) 온라인으로 주문되었다.

해설 이메일의 두 번째 단락의 마지막 문장에서 그랜트 씨가 7월 23일에 한 지난 주문 때 자신이 온라인 프로필에 저장한 신용카드로 청구해 달라(Feel free to charge the credit card I saved to my online profile during my last order on 23 July)고 했고, 송장의 중반부에 7월 23일(Date: 23 July)에 그랜트 씨의 주문 번호가 19842(Order Number: 19842)라고 나와 있다. 따라서 주문 번호 19842는 온라인으로 주문되었음을 유추할 수 있으므로 (D)가 정답이다.

180 동의어 찾기

번역 이메일의 두 번째 단락 4행의 "last"와 의미가 가장 가까운 단어는?
(A) 최종의
(B) 이전의
(C) 남아 있는
(D) 별개의

해설 의미상 7월 23일에 한 '지난' 주문이라는 뜻으로 쓰였으므로 '이전의'를 뜻하는 (B) previous가 정답이다.

181-185 공지 + 이메일

> 포틀랜드 프렌즈 오브 더 와일드와 함께 해 주세요.
> **제14회 연례 만찬 및 기금 모금 행사**
> 8월 13일 토요일, 오후 5시부터 9시까지
> **182 골든 아울 홀**, 포틀랜드 호프 가 926번지, 오리건 주 97035
>
> 우리는 1981년부터 **181 우리 시의 공원과 녹지를 보존하기 위해 활동하고 있는 비영리 환경 단체인 포틀랜드 프렌즈 오브 더 와일드**를 지원하기 위해 음식과 즐거움이 있는 멋진 밤을 계획해 왔습니다.
>
> **184 이날 저녁에는 그린 어스 프로비전스가 준비한 3코스 채식 만찬과 지역 예술가들의 작품 경매가 포함되며**, DJ 셰이 실버만이 준비한 음악에 맞춰 춤 추는 시간이 뒤따를 예정입니다.
>
> 행사 티켓은 1인당 100달러이며 8월 10일까지 www.portlandfriendsofthewild.org/fund-raiser에서 구매 가능합니다. 행사에 대해 문의사항이 있거나 경매에 물건을 기부하고 싶으실 경우 mnguyen@portlandfriendsofthewild.org로 민 응우옌에게 연락해 주세요.

어휘 fund-raiser 기금 모금 행사 fabulous 멋진 nonprofit 비영리의 organization 단체 preserve 보존하다 auction 경매 donate 기부하다

수신: 다니엘라 앳킨스 〈datkins@silkmail.com〉
발신: 민나 응우옌 〈mnguyen@portlandfriendsofthewild.org〉
날짜: 6월 17일
제목: 포틀랜드 프렌즈 오브 더 와일드 행사

앳킨스 씨께,

이 이메일이 귀하께 잘 전달되기를 바랍니다. **185** 제 이름은 민나 응우옌이고 포틀랜드 프렌즈 오브 더 와일드의 새로운 기금 모금 운영 책임자입니다. 귀하께서 작년에 아름다운 조각품을 기부하셨을 당시, 기금 모금 운영 책임자였던 스테파노 클리어리와 작업하셨다고 알고 있습니다. 스테파노가 귀하에 대해 극찬을 했습니다!

그런 의미에서, **183** 8월에 열릴 올해의 기금 모금 행사에 또 다른 조각품을 기부해 주실 의향이 있으신가요? 귀하의 작품을 다시 포함시킬 수 있다면 정말 기쁠 것 같습니다. 그리고 감사의 표시로, 무료 행사 티켓 2장을 기쁜 마음으로 드리겠습니다. **184** 올해에는 저희가 새로운 음식 조달 업체와 협력하고 있어서 음식이 매우 맛있을 것으로 기대합니다.

7월 15일까지 귀하의 생각을 알려 주십시오. 저에게 (503) 555-0145로 연락하시면 됩니다.

민나 응우옌

어휘 head 책임자 operation 운영 sculpture 조각품 on that note 그런 의미로 thrilled 아주 신이 난 token 표시

181 Not / True

번역 포틀랜드 프렌즈 오브 더 와일드에 대해 명시된 것은?
(A) 호프 가에 사무실이 있다.
(B) 실버만 씨에 의해 설립되었다.
(C) 2년마다 기금 모금 행사를 주최한다.
(D) 환경 보호에 집중한다.

해설 공지의 첫 단락에서 우리 시의 공원과 녹지를 보존하기 위해 활동하고 있는 비영리 환경 단체인 포틀랜드 프렌즈 오브 더 와일드(Portland Friends of the Wild, a nonprofit environmental organization working to preserve our city's parks and green spaces)라고 단체를 소개하고 있으므로 (D)가 정답이다.

어휘 found 설립하다

Paraphrasing
지문의 preserve our city's parks and green spaces
→ 정답의 protecting the environment

182 세부 사항

번역 포틀랜드 프렌즈 오브 더 와일드의 행사는 어디에서 열릴 예정인가?
(A) 공원
(B) 연회장
(C) 예술가의 작업실
(D) 응우옌 씨의 집

해설 공지의 상단에 행사 장소가 골든 아울 홀(Golden Owl Hall)이라고 표기되어 있고, Hall은 일반적으로 연회장(banquet hall)을 나타내므로 (B)가 정답이다.

183 주제 / 목적

번역 이메일의 한 가지 목적은?
(A) 지불을 요청하려고
(B) 구매를 확인하려고
(C) 기부를 요청하려고
(D) 티켓 수령을 확인하려고

해설 이메일의 두 번째 단락 첫 문장에서 응우옌 씨가 앳킨스 씨에게 8월에 열릴 올해의 기금 모금 행사에 또 다른 조각품을 기부할 의향이 있는지(would you be open to donating another piece of sculpture to this year's fund-raiser, which is coming up in August?)를 묻고 있는 것으로 보아, 작품을 기부해 달라고 요청하기 위해 이메일을 보냈음을 알 수 있다. 따라서 (C)가 정답이다.

어휘 contribution 기부 receipt 수령

Paraphrasing
지문의 donating → 정답의 contribution

184 연계

번역 그린 어스 프로비전스에 대해 결론지을 수 있는 것은?
(A) 1981년부터 영업해 오고 있다.
(B) 기금 모금 행사를 위해 닭 요리를 준비할 것이다.
(C) 포틀랜드 시내에 여러 지점이 있다.
(D) 기금 모금 행사에 처음으로 음식을 제공할 것이다.

해설 공지의 두 번째 단락 첫 문장에서 이날 저녁에는 그린 어스 프로비전스가 준비한 3코스 채식 만찬과 지역 예술가들의 작품 경매가 포함된다(The evening will include a three-course vegetarian dinner prepared by Green Earth Provisions and an auction of pieces by local artists)고 했고, 이메일의 두 번째 단락 마지막 문장에서 올해에는 새로운 음식 조달 업체와 협력하고 있다(We are working with a new catering company this year)고 했다. 따라서 그린 어스 프로비전스가 이 모금 행사에 처음으로 음식을 납품한다는 것을 알 수 있으므로 (D)가 정답이다.

Paraphrasing
지문의 catering → 정답의 provide the food

185 Not / True

번역 클리어리 씨에 대해 사실인 것은?
(A) 현재 응우옌 씨가 맡고 있는 직책에서 예전에 근무했다.
(B) 기금 모금 행사에 무료 티켓을 제공받아 왔다.
(C) 앳킨스 씨의 조각품 중 하나를 갖고 있다.
(D) 뛰어난 조각가이다.

해설 이메일의 첫 단락 두 번째 문장에서 자신은 민나 응우옌이고 포틀랜드 프렌즈 오브 더 와일드의 새로운 기금 모금 운영 책임자(My name is Minna Nguyen, and I am the new head of fund-raising operations for Portland Friends of the Wild)라고 했고, 앳킨스 씨가 작년에 아름다운 조각품을 기부했을 당시 기금 모금 운영 책임자였던 스테파노 클리어리와 작업했다고 알고 있다(I know you worked with Stefano Cleary, who was the head of fund-raising operations when you donated one of your beautiful sculptures last year)고 했으므로, 클리어리 씨는 응우옌 씨의 전임자라는 것을 알 수 있다. 따라서 (A)가 정답이다.

어휘 previously 이전에 accomplished 뛰어난

186-190 웹페이지 + 이메일 + 이메일

---

https://www.deltacityartmuseum.org/exhibits

델타 시티 미술관 — 진행중인 전시

〈인상파 화가들〉, 5월 1일 ~ 6월 30일, 메인 갤러리
이 잘 알려진 19세기 예술 사조의 그림들이 전시될 예정으로, 유명 화가와 덜 알려진 화가들의 작품이 모두 포함됩니다.

〈아메리카 원주민 도자기〉, 5월 15일 ~ 7월 16일, 쇼 메모리얼 갤러리
이 전시회의 방문객들은 북미 전역의 토착민들에 의해 개발되고 활용된 광범위한 도자기 관련 기법에 대해 배우게 됩니다.

〈고대 그리스와 그 너머〉, 5월 22일 ~ 8월 21일, 187 텍트만 갤러리
이 전시회는 187 고대 그리스의 인물 조각상들과 고전 양식의 영향을 받은 현대 작품들을 함께 선보입니다.

〈델타 시티의 예술가들〉, 상설 전시, 장 아트리움
이 인기 있는 전시는 지역 예술가들의 현대 작품들을 다양한 매체로 선보이며, 유화와 수채화, 사진, 섬유 예술, 혼합 매체 작품이 포함됩니다. 비록 전시회는 계속되지만, 186 각각의 작품들은 돌아가면서 전시되며 한정된 기간 동안만 전시됩니다.

어휘 impressionist 인상파 화가 pottery 도자기 range 범위 utilize 활용하다 indigenous 토착의 beyond 그 너머 feature 포함하다 statue 조각상 influence 영향을 주다 permanent 영구적인 showcase 전시하다 contemporary 현대의 media 매체 fiber 섬유 ongoing 계속되는

수신: 델타 시티 미술관 〈info@deltacityartmuseum.org〉
발신: 로렐라이 데스노이어스
　　　〈lorelei.desnoyers@klarsenuniversity.edu〉
날짜: 5월 2일
제목: 문의

좋은 아침입니다,

저는 클라슨 대학교의 새로운 미술 강사입니다. 188 제 동료들 중 한 명이 저에게 델타 시티 미술관에서 지역 미술 전공 학생들을 위한 투어를 제공한다고 알려줬습니다. 저는 저의 미술 103 수업 학생들을 데리고 가서 몇몇 작품들을 감상하고 스케치하는 데 관심이 있습니다. 187 미술 103 수업은 인체 형상을 관찰하고 그리는 데 중점을 두고 있어서, 조각상들이 저희의 주된 관심을 받을 것입니다. 하지만 작업을 시작하기 전에 미술관 전체를 짧게 투어할 수 있기를 바랍니다. 이 투어가 준비될 수 있는지 알려주십시오.

도움 주시는 데 대해 미리 감사드립니다!

로렐라이 데스노이어스
미술 디자인 학부
클라슨 대학교
504-555-0177

어휘 inquiry 문의 study 관찰하다, 살피다 form 형체 attention 관심 arrange 준비하다 in advance 미리

수신: 로렐라이 데스노이어스
　　　〈lorelei.desnoyers@klarsenuniversity.edu〉
발신: 조슬린 그레이디 〈jgrady@deltacityartmuseum.org〉
날짜: 5월 3일
제목: 회신: 문의

데스노이어스 씨께,

이메일을 보내주셔서 감사합니다. 188 동료분 말씀이 맞으며, 미술관은 실제 해당 서비스를 제공하고 있습니다. 보통 화요일이 가장 덜 바쁜 날이라서 그날 일정을 잡아드리고자 합니다. 귀하의 메시지를 저희 공공 프로그램 담당 사무실로 전달했습니다. 189 직원이 더 자세한 내용을 가지고 전화 연락을 드릴 것입니다.

190 수채물감을 포함한 물감의 사용은 모든 미술관 갤러리에서 금지되어 있다는 점에 유의해 주십시오. 연필과 목탄은 허용되지만, 방문객들은 미술관 표면에 얼룩을 남기지 않도록 주의해야 합니다. 이용객들이 다른 방문객들을 배려하는 한 사진 촬영과 영상 녹화도 허용됩니다.

델타 시티 미술관에 대한 관심에 감사드리며 귀하의 수업을 맞이하게 되기를 기대합니다.

조슬린 그레이디
정보 및 커뮤니티 지원 부서
델타 시티 미술관

어휘 indeed 실제로 typically 보통 forward 전달하다 paint 그림물감 watercolor 수채물감 prohibit 금지하다 charcoal 목탄 permit 허용하다 smudge 얼룩 patron 이용객 considerate 배려하는 grateful 감사하는 outreach (지역 주민에 대한) 지원 활동

186 Not / True

번역 〈델타 시티의 예술가들〉 전시에 대해 웹페이지에 명시된 것은?
(A) 미국 원주민 예술가들의 도자기가 포함된다.
(B) 5월부터 8월까지 문을 닫는다.
(C) 전시되는 예술 작품이 정기적으로 바뀐다.
(D) 전시 중인 그림들은 19세기에 제작된 것이다.

해설 웹페이지의 네 번째 단락 마지막 문장에서 각각의 작품들은 돌아가면서 전시되며 한정된 기간 동안만 전시된다(individual pieces are displayed on a rotating basis and are on view for a limited time only)고 했으므로, 〈델타 시티의 예술가들〉의 전시품은 일정 주기에 따라 바뀐다는 것을 알 수 있다. 따라서 (C)가 정답이다.

> **Paraphrasing**
> 지문의 pieces are displayed on a rotating basis → 정답의 The works of art on display are regularly changed.

187 연계

번역 데스노이어스 씨의 학생들은 어디에서 스케치 시간을 보낼 것 같은가?
(A) 메인 갤러리
(B) 쇼 메모리얼 갤러리
(C) 텍트만 갤러리
(D) 장 아트리움

해설 첫 번째 이메일의 네 번째 문장에서 데스노이어스 씨가 미술 103 수업은 인체 형상을 관찰하고 그리는 데 중점을 두고 있어서 조각상들이 주된 관심을 받을 것(Since Art 103 focuses on studying and drawing the human form, the statues will be getting most of our attention)이라고 했고, 웹페이지의 세 번째 단락에서 텍트만 갤러리(Techtmann Gallery)에 고대 그리스의 인물 조각상들(statues of human subjects from classical Greece)이 전시된다고 했다. 따라서 데스노이어스 씨의 학생들은 인물 조각상이 있는 텍트만 갤러리에서 스케치 시간을 보낼 예정임을 짐작할 수 있으므로 (C)가 정답이다.

188 연계

번역 그레이디 씨에 따르면, 데스노이어스 씨의 동료가 맞게 말한 것은?
(A) 미술관이 수업 투어를 제공한다는 것
(B) 미술관에서 드로잉 수업을 제공한다는 것
(C) 미술관에서 단체 할인을 제공한다는 것
(D) 미술관이 개인 행사를 허용한다는 것

해설 두 번째 이메일의 첫 단락 두 번째 문장에서 그레이디 씨가 데스노이어스 씨에게 동료분 말이 맞으며 미술관은 실제 해당 서비스를 제공하고 있다(Your colleague was correct: the museum does indeed provide that service)고 했고, 첫 번째 이메일의 두 번째 문장에서 데스노이어스 씨가 자신의 동료들 중 한 명이 델타 시티 미술관에서 지역 미술 전공 학생들을 위한 투어를 제공한다고 알려줬다(One of my colleagues told me that the Delta City Art Museum provides tours for local art students)고 했다. 따라서 그레이디 씨는 데스노이어스 씨의 동료가 델타 시티 미술관에서 학생들을 위한 투어를 제공한다고 한 말이 맞다고 한 것임을 알 수 있으므로 (A)가 정답이다.

> **Paraphrasing**
> 지문의 provides tours for local art students
> → 정답의 gives class tours

189 추론 / 암시

번역 데스노이어스 씨는 두 번째 이메일의 결과로 무엇을 할 것 같은가?
(A) 이메일을 전달한다.
(B) 미술관 사무실을 방문한다.
(C) 웹사이트를 참고한다.
(D) 전화 연락을 기다린다.

해설 두 번째 이메일의 첫 단락 마지막 문장에서 데스노이어스 씨에게 직원이 더 자세한 내용을 가지고 전화 연락할 것(A staff member will contact you by phone with more details)이라고 안내하였으므로, 데스노이어스 씨는 미술관 직원으로부터 연락이 오기를 기다릴 것임을 알 수 있다. 따라서 (D)가 정답이다.

어휘 consult 참고하다

190 세부 사항

번역 그레이디 씨가 미술관 갤러리에서 금지되어 있다고 명시한 활동은?
(A) 사진 촬영
(B) 영상 녹화
(C) 목탄으로 그림 그리기
(D) 수채물감으로 색칠하기

해설 두 번째 이메일의 두 번째 단락 첫 문장에서 그레이디 씨가 수채물감을 포함한 물감의 사용은 모든 미술관 갤러리에서 금지되어 있다는 점에 유의해 달라(Please note that the use of paints, including watercolors, is prohibited in all museum galleries)고 했으므로 (D)가 정답이다.

191-195 기사 + 편지 + 송장 ▶동영상 강의

보스턴 (1월 3일) — 전국 치약 협회의 최근 조사에 따르면, 미국의 치약 포장 시장은 향후 10년 동안 3퍼센트 이상 성장할 것으로 예상된다.

191 눌러서 짜는 치약 튜브가 전반적으로 시장을 계속 주도하고는 있으나, 여러 겹으로 구성되어 있어서 재활용이 거의 불가능하다. 193 이것들은 단지, 병, 리필 가능한 펌프 디스펜서 등의 재활용이 가능한 포장 형태에 시장 점유율의 작은 부분을 잃기 시작하고 있다.

어휘 dentifrice 치약 collapsible 압출하는, 접을 수 있는 overall 전반적으로 compose 구성하다 layer 층 form 형태 jar 단지, 병 refillable 리필 가능한

그린 글로브
인더스트리얼 파크웨이 550번지
실버 힐스, 켄터키 주 40502

3월 7일

로힛 파텔
운영 이사
매커 드럭스토어
헤럴드 가 536번지, 202호
콜럼버스, 오하이오 주 43004

파텔 씨께,

192 그린 글로브 천연 치약에 대해 귀하 및 귀하의 팀과 이야기할 수 있게 허락해 주신 점 감사드립니다.

192 회의 도중 설명한 대로, 저는 거의 모든 다른 치약 브랜드에서 사용하는 재활용 불가능한 포장에 대안을 제공하기 위해, 10년 전에 그린 글로브를 설립했습니다. **193** 저희 치약은 100mm 유리단지에 포장됩니다. **194** 이 제품은 현재 미국과 캐나다 전역의 상점에서 판매되고 있습니다. 저는 쇼핑객들이 매커 드럭스토어 체인의 모든 매장에서 조만간 이 제품을 구입할 수 있기를 바랍니다.

195 단일 매장에서 판매를 테스트해 보기 위해 일단 두 상자를 구매하고자 하신다는 점 이해합니다. 준비가 되시는 대로 즉시, 모든 매커 드럭스토어 매장으로 상자를 발송해 드릴 수 있음을 강조 드리며, 당연히 10상자 이상의 모든 주문에는 상당한 할인을 제공해 드릴 것입니다.

시간을 내어 저와 만나 주셔서 다시 한번 감사드립니다. 귀하와 함께 일하게 되기를 기대합니다.

버나 브라운

어휘 found 설립하다 alternative 대안 nonrecyclable 재활용 불가능한 emphasize 강조하다 immediately 즉시 significant 상당한

송장
그린 글로브 · 인더스트리얼 파크웨이 550번지 · 실버 힐스, 켄터키 주 40502

주문번호 673348
3월 15일

195 배송지:
매커 드럭스토어 유통센터
36번 고속도로 4000번지
로건, 오하이오 주 43138

항목	수량	단가	금액
195 그린 글로브 천연 치약	**195** 2상자	145달러	290달러
		배송	26달러
		소계	316달러
		세금	19달러
		할인	0달러
		총계	335달러

어휘 quantity 수량 unit (상품의) 한 개, 구성 단위

191 Not / True

번역 기사에서 눌러서 짜는 치약 튜브에 대해 언급하는 것은?
(A) 재활용하기 어렵다.
(B) 그다지 인기가 없다.
(C) 미국에서 발명되었다.
(D) 조사에 포함되지 않았다.

해설 기사의 두 번째 단락 첫 문장에서 눌러서 짜는 치약 튜브가 전반적으로 시장을 계속 주도하고는 있으나, 여러 겹으로 구성되어 있어서 재활용이 거의 불가능하다(Collapsible toothpaste tubes continue to lead the market overall, but because they are composed of multiple layers, it is nearly impossible to recycle them)고 했으므로 (A)가 정답이다.

어휘 invent 발명하다

> **Paraphrasing**
> 지문의 nearly impossible to recycle
> → 정답의 difficult to recycle

192 주제 / 목적

번역 브라운 씨는 왜 편지를 보냈을 것 같은가?
(A) 회의를 요청하려고
(B) 채용 후보자를 추천하려고
(C) 영업 프레젠테이션에 대해 후속 조치를 취하려고
(D) 제품을 주문하려고

해설 편지의 첫 단락에서 브라운 씨가 그린 글로브 천연 치약에 대해 귀하 및 귀하의 팀과 이야기할 수 있게 허락한 점 감사드린다(Thank you for allowing me to speak with you and your team about Green Globe All-Natural Toothpaste)고 했고, 뒤이어 회의 도중 설명한 대로(As I explained during our meeting)라고 말을 이어나가는 것으로 보아, 잠재적 거래처에 영업 프레젠테이션을 하고 나서 그에 따른 업무를 이어가기 위해 편지를 작성했음을 알 수 있다. 따라서 (C)가 정답이다.

어휘 candidate 후보자 follow up 후속 조치하다

193 연계

번역 그린 글로브가 사용하는 포장 유형으로 판매되는 제품에 대해 명시된 것은?
(A) 전국 치약 협회에서 추천한다.
(B) 매커 드럭스토어에서만 구입할 수 있다.
(C) 제조 비용이 평균보다 높다.
(D) 시장 점유율이 증가하고 있다.

해설 편지의 두 번째 단락의 두 번째 문장에서 브라운 씨가 그린 글로브의 치약은 100mm 유리단지에 포장된다(Our toothpaste is packaged in 100-milliliter glass jars)고 했고, 기사의 두 번째 단락 마지막 문장에서 이것들(눌러서 짜는 치약 튜브)은 단지, 병, 리필 가능한 펌프 디스펜서 등의 재활용이 가능한 포장 형태에 시장 점유율의 작은 부분을 잃기 시작하고 있다(They are beginning to lose a small part of their market share to recyclable forms of packaging, including jars, bottles, and refillable pump dispensers)고 했다. 따라서 그린 글로브가 사용하는 유리단지 포장의 시장 점유율이 조금씩 높아지기 시작했다는 것을 알 수 있으므로 (D)가 정답이다.

어휘 average 평균

194 Not / True

번역 브라운 씨가 그린 글로브 치약에 대해 언급하는 것은?

(A) 원래 튜브에 포장되었다.
(B) 치과의사가 만들었다.
(C) 두 나라에서 구입할 수 있다.
(D) 다양한 맛으로 나온다.

해설 편지의 두 번째 단락 세 번째 문장에서 브라운 씨는 이 제품(그린 글로브 치약)은 현재 미국과 캐나다 전역의 상점에서 판매되고 있다(It is currently sold in stores throughout the United States and Canada)고 했으므로 (C)가 정답이다.

어휘 originally 원래 multiple 다양한, 여럿의 flavor 맛

Paraphrasing
지문의 sold in stores throughout the United States and Canada → 정답의 available in two countries

195 연계

번역 매커 드럭스토어가 한 주문에 대해 사실인 것 같은 것은?
(A) 같은 주문품이 매달 배송될 예정이다.
(B) 상품이 시장 테스트에 사용될 것이다.
(C) 가격이 상당히 할인되었다.
(D) 배송비는 그린 글로브가 환불해 주었다.

해설 송장의 배송지가 매커 드럭스토어 유통센터(Ship to: Macker Drugstores Distribution Center), 주문 제품은 그린 글로브 천연 치약(Green Globe All-Natural Toothpaste) 2상자(2 cases)이다. 편지의 세 번째 단락 첫 문장에서 그린 글로브의 브라운 씨가 매커 드럭스토어의 파텔 씨에게 단일 매장에서 판매를 테스트해 보기 위해 일단 두 상자를 구매하고자 하는 점을 이해한다(I understand that you would like to purchase two cases initially to test sales in a single store)고 했다. 따라서 매커 드럭스토어는 그린 글로브 치약 두 상자를 판매를 위한 테스트용으로 구입했다는 것을 알 수 있으므로 (B)가 정답이다.

어휘 merchandise 상품

196-200 이메일 + 시간표 + 후기

수신: 슬리피 타임 호텔 〈information@sleepytimehotel.com〉
발신: 조종우 〈jongwoo.cho@onyxmail.com〉
날짜: 8월 15일
제목: 호텔 숙박

안녕하세요!

저는 8월 19일 다가오는 금요일에 귀하의 호텔에서 2박을 지내기 위해 온라인 예약을 했는데, 찰스빌에 도착하고 나서 호텔로 가는 방법을 잘 모르겠습니다. 호텔의 웹사이트에서 추천한 대로 시티 링크 라인 앱을 다운로드했지만, 길을 찾기가 어렵습니다. **198 다른 경전철역에 대한 옵션도 전혀 제시되지 않는데, 이곳은 호텔 투숙객들이 하차해야 하는 역이라고 귀하께서 분명히 언급한 곳입니다. 196 호텔에 가기에 가장 좋은 방법을 명확히 알려주실 수 있을까요?** 웹사이트의 사진으로 미루어 보아, 호텔은 지내기에 아름다운 장소처럼 보입니다. **197 해변 바로 옆에서 이틀 밤을 보내게 되기를 기다리고 있습니다.**

조종우

어휘 figure out ~을 이해하다 navigate 길을 찾다
light-rail 경전철 specifically 분명히 disembark 내리다
clarify 명확히 하다 judge 판단하다

시티 링크 라인

월요일 ~ 금요일 시간표 — 존스타운에서 찰스빌까지

199 존스타운 출발	찰스빌 도착
오전 7시	오전 8시 36분
오전 10시 5분	오전 11시 41분
오후 1시	오후 2시 36분
199 오후 4시 5분	오후 5시 41분
오후 7시	오후 8시 36분

https://www.sleepytimehotel.com/reviews

슬리피 타임 호텔에서의 숙박은 환상적이었습니다. 처음에는 존스타운에서 호텔로 쉽게 갈 수 없을까봐 걱정했는데, **200 존스타운에서 저는 막 3일간의 즐거운 전문 컨퍼런스를 마친 상태였습니다.** 호텔 웹사이트에는 교통수단 옵션에 대해 명확하게 나와있지 않더군요. 저는 이 지역에 익숙하지 않아, 호텔에 이메일을 보냈고 누군가 즉시 답장을 보내주었습니다. 결과적으로, 찰스빌로 가는 것은 쉬웠습니다. 먼저, **199 저는 오후 4시 5분 존스타운발 기차를 탔습니다.** 찰스빌 중앙역에 도착하자마자, 엘리베이터를 타고 지하로 내려갔고, 거기에 경전철 플랫폼이 있었습니다. **198 그러고는 경전철을 타고 호텔 바로 길 건너에 있는 역까지 갔습니다.** 보아하니, 찰스빌 경전철 시스템은 비교적 새로 들어온 것이더라구요. 호텔 근처에 식당은 없지만 모퉁이에 작은 식료품점이 있다는 점을 기억하세요. 그래서 저는 음식을 좀 사서 해변으로 소풍을 갈 수 있었습니다. 전반적으로, 사랑스럽고 밝은 객실을 갖춘 이 소규모 호텔은 도시 생활로부터의 완벽한 도피처입니다. 마침내 사무실로 돌아가 업무에 복귀했을 때, 저는 충분히 재충전된 기분이었습니다.

조종우, 8월 26일 게시

어휘 initially 처음에 exhilarating 신나는 crystal clear 아주 명확한 transportation 교통 familiar 익숙한
immediately 즉시 ultimately 결과적으로, 궁극적으로
basement 지하 directly 바로 apparently 보아 하니
relatively 비교적 escape 도피

196 주제 / 목적

번역 이메일의 목적은?
(A) 호텔 예약을 취소하려고
(B) 호텔로 가는 명확한 길 안내를 받으려고
(C) 앱 다운로드를 위한 설명을 요청하려고
(D) 소셜 미디어 계정에 대해 더 알아보는 것

해설 이메일의 네 번째 문장에서 조 씨가 호텔에 가기에 가장 좋은 방법을 명확히 알려줄 수 있을지(Could you please clarify how best to get to the hotel?)를 묻고 있는 것으로 보아, 호텔로 가는 길 안내를 받고자 이메일을 작성했다는 것을 알 수 있다. 따라서 (B)가 정답이다.

어휘 obtain 얻다 directions 길 안내 instructions 설명, 사용법

Paraphrasing
지문의 how best to get to the hotel
→ 정답의 directions to a hotel

197 추론 / 암시

번역 이메일에서 슬리피 타임 호텔에 대해 암시하는 것은?
(A) 물가에 있다.
(B) 예전에는 식당이 있었다.
(C) 대형 호텔 체인에 속해 있다.
(D) 주로 출장객들에게 서비스를 제공한다.

해설 이메일의 마지막 문장에서 해변 바로 옆에서 이틀 밤을 보내게 되기를 기대하고 있다(I am looking forward to spending a couple of nights right by the beach)고 한 것을 통해 슬리피 타임 호텔은 해변과 아주 인접해 있음을 짐작할 수 있다. 따라서 (A)가 정답이다.

Paraphrasing
지문의 right by the beach → 정답의 near a body of water

198 연계

번역 달튼 경전철역에 대해 사실인 것 같은 것은?
(A) 넓은 주차장이 있다.
(B) 컨퍼런스 센터와 연결되어 있다.
(C) 슬리피 타임 호텔 길 건너에 있다.
(D) 보수 공사 중이다.

해설 이메일의 세 번째 문장에서 달튼 경전철역에 대한 옵션도 전혀 제시되지 않는데, 이곳은 호텔 투숙객들이 하차해야 하는 역이라고 호텔측에서 언급한 곳(No options are coming up for the Dalton light-rail station, which you specifically mention as the station where hotel guests should disembark)이라고 했고, 후기의 여덟 번째 문장에서 경전철을 타고 호텔 바로 길 건너에 있는 역까지 갔다(I then boarded a light-rail train and rode it to the station directly across the street from the hotel)고 했다. 따라서 호텔에 가기 위해 하차해야 하는 역인 달튼 경전철역은 호텔 바로 길 건너에 있다는 것을 알 수 있으므로 (C)가 정답이다.

199 연계

번역 조 씨의 기차는 찰스빌에 몇 시에 도착했을 것 같은가?
(A) 오전 11시 41분
(B) 오후 2시 36분
(C) 오후 5시 41분
(D) 오후 8시 36분

해설 후기의 여섯 번째 문장에서 조씨가 오후 4시 5분 존스타운발 기차를 탔다(I took the 4:05 P.M. train out of Johnstown)고 했고, 시간표의 하단에 오후 4시 5분 존스타운발 기차(Departs from Johnstown, 4:05 P.M.)는 찰스빌에 오후 5시 41분에 도착한다(Arrives in Charlesville, 5:41 P.M.)고 나와 있다. 따라서 (C)가 정답이다.

200 Not / True

번역 후기에서 조 씨가 언급하는 것은?
(A) 찰스빌에 있는 식당에서 식사했다.
(B) 존스타운에 정기적으로 여행을 간다.
(C) 8월 26일에 식료품점을 방문했다.
(D) 최근에 출장을 마쳤다.

해설 후기의 두 번째 문장에서 조 씨가 존스타운에서 막 3일간의 즐거운 전문 컨퍼런스를 마친 상태였다(Johnstown, where I had just finished an exhilarating three-day professional conference)고 했으므로, 최근에 존스타운에서 출장을 마쳤다는 것을 알 수 있다. 따라서 (D)가 정답이다.

기출 TEST 3

101 (B)	102 (A)	103 (B)	104 (C)	105 (D)
106 (B)	107 (A)	108 (B)	109 (A)	110 (C)
111 (B)	112 (C)	113 (B)	114 (B)	115 (D)
116 (A)	117 (D)	118 (D)	119 (A)	120 (A)
121 (B)	122 (C)	123 (D)	124 (A)	125 (B)
126 (A)	127 (C)	128 (C)	129 (C)	130 (A)
131 (A)	132 (D)	133 (A)	134 (B)	135 (B)
136 (B)	137 (A)	138 (C)	139 (B)	140 (D)
141 (C)	142 (A)	143 (B)	144 (A)	145 (C)
146 (C)	147 (D)	148 (C)	149 (B)	150 (D)
151 (C)	152 (D)	153 (A)	154 (C)	155 (A)
156 (D)	157 (C)	158 (C)	159 (D)	160 (A)
161 (B)	162 (C)	163 (B)	164 (C)	165 (C)
166 (C)	167 (A)	168 (C)	169 (D)	170 (C)
171 (D)	172 (A)	173 (D)	174 (B)	175 (D)
176 (C)	177 (B)	178 (D)	179 (D)	180 (B)
181 (B)	182 (C)	183 (B)	184 (C)	185 (B)
186 (A)	187 (B)	188 (D)	189 (D)	190 (C)
191 (B)	192 (D)	193 (A)	194 (B)	195 (B)
196 (A)	197 (B)	198 (C)	199 (D)	200 (D)

PART 5

101 인칭대명사의 격 _ 소유격

해설 빈칸에는 뒤에 온 명사 youth를 수식하는 말이 들어가야 한다. 따라서 명사 앞에 쓰여 한정사 역할을 할 수 있는 소유격 인칭대명사 (B) her가 정답이다.

번역 어린 나이에도 불구하고, 조 씨는 소셜 미디어에서 이미 꽤 인기가 많다.

어휘 youth 젊음 quite 꽤

102 형용사 어휘

해설 주어인 Most of the materials를 보충 설명하여 '대부분의 자료는 온라인에서 이용할 수 있다'는 내용이 되어야 적절하므로, '이용할 수 있는'을 뜻하는 (A) available이 정답이다. (B) intended는 '의도된', (C) comparable은 '비교할 만한', (D) decisive는 '결정적인'이라는 의미다.

번역 지난달 회계 컨퍼런스에서 배포된 대부분의 자료는 현재 온라인에서 이용할 수 있다.

어휘 material 자료 distribute 배포하다

103 명사 자리 _ 동사의 주어 / 수 일치

해설 빈칸은 동사 will be conducted의 주어 자리이고, 앞에 부정관사 A가 있으므로 단수 명사가 들어가야 한다. 또한 주어는 수행되는 대상으로 '전면적인 검토가 수행될 것이다'라는 내용이 되어야 적절하므로 '검토'를 뜻하는 단수 명사인 (B) review가 정답이다. (A) reviewer(검토자)는 단수 명사이지만 문맥상 어울리지 않고, (C) reviewed는 동사/과거분사로 빈칸에 들어갈 수 없으며, (D) reviews는 복수 명사이므로 답이 될 수 없다.

번역 전면적인 검토는 회계 부서에서 수행할 것이다.

어휘 full-scale 전면적인 conduct 수행하다 accounting 회계

104 동사 어휘

해설 주어 Poshy Shoes vice president Lucille Jeris의 동사 자리로, has been과 함께 수동태를 이루어 '제리스 부사장은 사장으로 승진되었다'는 의미를 나타내야 적절하므로 '승진시키다'라는 뜻의 동사 promote의 과거분사인 (C) promoted가 정답이다. (A)의 provide는 '공급하다', (B)의 decorate는 '장식하다'라는 뜻으로 문맥상 어울리지 않고, (D)의 respond는 '응답하다'라는 뜻의 자동사로 수동태가 불가능하다.

번역 포쉬 슈즈의 루실 제리스 부사장은 회사의 사장으로 승진했다.

어휘 vice president 부사장

105 형용사 자리 _ 주격 보어

해설 빈칸은 that절의 주어 employees (who take regular breaks)를 보충 설명하는 주격 보어 자리이고, 비교급을 만드는 부사 more와 함께 '규칙적으로 휴식을 취하는 직원들이 더 생산적이다'라는 내용이 되어야 하므로 '생산적인'을 뜻하는 형용사 (D) productive가 정답이다. (A) production(생산)과 (C) productivity(생산성)는 명사로 주어인 employees와 동격이 아니며, (B) productively는 부사이므로 빈칸에 들어갈 수 없다.

번역 보고서에 따르면 규칙적으로 휴식을 취하는 직원들이 휴식을 취하지 않는 직원들보다 더 생산적인 것으로 나타났다.

어휘 regular 규칙적인

106 명사 어휘

해설 빈칸은 to contact의 목적어 자리이므로 연락할 수 있는 대상이 들어가야 적절하다. '수리가 필요할 경우 기술자에게 문의해야 한다'는 내용이 되어야 하므로 '기술자'를 뜻하는 (B) technician이 정답이다. (A) replacement는 '교체', (C) renewal은 '갱신', (D) structure는 '구조'라는 의미로 연락의 대상이 될 수 없다.

번역 트윈스 복사기 고객들은 복사기에 수리가 필요한 경우 기술자에게 문의하도록 권고된다.

어휘 photocopier 복사기

107 부사 자리 _ 동사 수식

해설 빈칸은 동사 caused를 수식하는 부사 자리이고, '교통 체증으로 비행기를 거의 놓칠 뻔했다'는 내용이 되어야 하므로 '거의'를 뜻하는 부사 (A) nearly가 정답이다. (B) near도 '가까이'라는 위치 부사로 쓰일 수 있으나 주로 동사 뒤나 문장 끝에 위치하고 동사 앞에서 동사를 수식하지 않으며 문맥에도 어울리지 않는다. (C) nears는 동사, (D) nearness는 명사이므로 빈칸에 들어갈 수 없다.

번역 공항으로 가는 길에 심한 교통 체증으로 이케다 씨는 비행기를 거의 놓칠 뻔했다.

어휘 cause 야기하다 miss 놓치다

108 부사 어휘 ▶동영상 강의

해설 동사구 will take place를 수식하여 적절한 문맥을 완성하는 부사를 고르는 문제이다. next year와 함께 미래의 가능성을 나타내어 '합병이 아마도 내년에 성사될 것'이라는 내용이 되어야 자연스러우므로 '아마'를 뜻하는 (B) probably가 정답이다. (A) originally는 '원래', (C) regularly는 '정기적으로', (D) thoughtfully는 '사려 깊게'라는 의미이다.

번역 한 뉴스 소식통은 합병이 아마도 내년에 성사될 것임을 시사했다.

어휘 news source 소식통 merger 합병 take place 일어나다

109 형용사 자리

해설 뒤에 '형용사(beautiful)+명사(guest rooms)'가 있으므로 빈칸에는 형용사를 수식하는 부사 또는 명사를 수식하는 형용사가 들어갈 수 있다. 문맥상 '다양한 아름다운 객실'이라는 의미가 되어야 하므로 '다양한'을 뜻하는 형용사 (A) various가 정답이다. beautiful guest rooms는 동사 has의 목적어이므로, 전치사인 (B) among과 (C) throughout, 재귀대명사인 (D) itself는 빈칸에 들어갈 수 없다.

번역 시본 인은 월 단위로 예약 가능한 다양한 아름다운 객실을 보유하고 있다.

어휘 inn (작은) 호텔 basis 기준

110 전치사 어휘 ▶동영상 강의

해설 빈칸 앞에 위치를 나타내는 동사 is located, 뒤에 장소를 나타내는 명사구 Gordon Avenue and Hutch Street이 있다. '고든 가와 허치 가가 만나는 지점에 있다'는 내용이 되어야 적절하므로, '~에'라는 뜻으로 위치나 지점을 나타내는 전치사 (C) at이 정답이다. 참고로, 길 이름 두 개가 and로 연결되면 '(해당 길들이) 교차하는 지점'을 의미한다. (A) until은 '(시간) ~까지', (B) against는 '~에 반대하여', (D) aside from은 '~ 외에는'이라는 의미로 문맥상 어울리지 않는다.

번역 예언 액세서리의 소매점은 고든 가와 허치 가의 교차점에 있다.

어휘 retail shop 소매점

111 형용사 자리

해설 빈칸은 'rate A as B(A를 B하다고 평가하다)' 구문에서 전치사 as 뒤의 보어 자리로 형용사나 명사가 들어갈 수 있다. 일반적으로 전치사 뒤에는 형용사가 올 수 없지만 이 구문에서는 형용사가 올 수 있다. its transportation app의 상태나 특성을 보충 설명하는 말이 들어가 '교통 앱이 쓸만하다고 평가했다'라는 의미가 되어야 자연스러우므로, '수용 가능한, 괜찮은'을 뜻하는 형용사 (B) acceptable이 정답이다. (A) acceptability(수용 가능성)와 (C) acceptance(수용)는 명사, (D) accepting(솔직한)은 현재분사로서 보어 자리에 들어갈 수는 있으나 의미상 부적절하다.

번역 대다수의 시 주민들은 시의 교통 앱을 쓸만하다고 평가했다.

어휘 a majority of 대다수의 transportation 교통

112 동사 어형 _ 시제

해설 빈칸은 주어 Dr. Cheung의 동사 자리이다. 미래의 시점을 나타내는 at next weekend's medical fair라는 표현이 있으므로, 가까운 미래의 계획된 일정을 나타낼 수 있는 현재진행 시제 (C) is representing이 정답이다.

번역 정 박사는 다음 주말의 의료 박람회에서 실크 밸리 병원을 대표할 예정이다.

어휘 fair 박람회 represent 대표하다

113 형용사 어휘

해설 부사 financially와 함께 명사 quarter를 수식하여 적절한 문맥을 만드는 형용사를 골라야 한다. '비용 절감 조치를 취한 후 재정적으로 수익성 있는 분기를 보냈다'는 내용이 되어야 자연스러우므로 '수익성 있는'을 뜻하는 (B) profitable이 정답이다. (A) plain은 '평범한', (C) full은 '가득 찬', (D) additional은 '추가의'라는 의미이다.

번역 프랭키즈 부티크는 비용 절감 조치를 취한 후 재정적으로 수익성 있는 분기를 보냈다.

어휘 financially 재정적으로 quarter 분기 measure 조치 reduce 줄이다

114 명사 자리 _ 전치사의 목적어

해설 빈칸은 앞의 정관사 the와 함께 전치사 as의 목적어 역할을 하는 명사 자리로, '올해의 연하장 공급업체로 선정되었다'는 내용이 되어야 자연스러우므로 '공급업체'를 뜻하는 명사 (B) supplier가 정답이다. (A) supply는 '공급', (C) supplies는 '물품, 보급품'이라는 뜻으로 의미상 적합하지 않고, (D) supplying은 동명사/현재분사로 빈칸에 들어갈 수 없다.

번역 가장 낮은 입찰가를 제출한 덕분에 뎁스 기프팅은 올해의 연하장 공급업체로 선정되었다.

어휘 submit 제출하다 bid 입찰(가) holiday card 연하장

115 명사 어휘

해설 빈칸은 주어 The Whitetail Institute의 보어 자리로, 주어와 동격을 이루면서 형용사 only와 관계사절(that tracks ~ suburban areas)의 수식을 받기에 어울리는 명사를 고르면 된다. '화이트테일 연구소는 사슴 개체 수를 추적하는 유일한 기관'이라는 내용이 되어야 자연스러우므로 '기관'을 뜻하는 (D) organization이 정답이다. (A) leadership은 '지도력', (B) neighborhood는 '이웃', (C) official은 '(고위) 공무원'이라는 의미이다.

번역 화이트테일 연구소는 급격하게 팽창하는 교외 지역에서 사슴 개체 수를 추적하는 유일한 기관이다.

어휘 institute 연구소   track 추적하다   deer 사슴
population 개체 수   rapidly 급격히, 빠르게
expand 팽창되다   suburban 교외의

116 관계대명사 _ 주격

해설 주어는 The committee members, 동사는 are listed이며 빈칸부터 the meeting까지는 주어이자 선행사인 The committee members를 꾸미는 관계사절이다. 빈칸 뒤에 동사 attended가 있으므로 주격 관계대명사인 (A) who가 정답이다. (B) they와 (D) some은 대명사이므로 절을 연결할 수 없고, (C) when은 관계부사 / 부사절 접속사로 뒤에 완전한 절이 와야 한다.

번역 회의에 참석한 위원회 위원들은 부록에 나열되어 있다.

어휘 committee 위원회   appendix 부록

117 부사 자리 _ 동사 수식

해설 수동태 동사구 be동사 is와 과거분사 designed 사이에서 동사를 수식하는 부사 자리이므로, '특별히'를 뜻하는 부사 (D) specifically가 정답이다. (A) specify는 동사, (B) specific은 형용사, (C) specificity는 명사이므로 빈칸에 들어갈 수 없다.

번역 우리의 새로운 앱은 투자 전문가들에게 데이터를 기반으로 한 통찰을 제공하도록 특별히 개발되었다.

어휘 data-driven 데이터 기반의   insight 통찰(력)
investment 투자

118 동사 자리 _ 수 일치

해설 빈칸은 주절의 동사 suggest의 목적어 역할을 하는 that절의 동사 자리이고, 주어가 more people로 복수이므로 복수 동사인 (D) struggle(애쓰다, 분투하다)이 정답이다. (A) struggles는 수가 일치하지 않고, (B) struggling은 명사/현재분사, (C) to struggle은 to부정사이므로 빈칸에 들어갈 수 없다.

번역 연구 결과는 이전에 생각했던 것보다 더 많은 사람들이 야간 운전에 어려움을 겪고 있음을 시사한다.

어휘 result 결과   previously 이전에   struggle 애쓰다, 분투하다

119 명사 어휘

해설 전치사 in과 to 사이에 들어가 적절한 문맥을 이루는 명사를 골라야 한다. in response to는 '~에 대응하여'를 뜻하는 관용어구로, '예산 삭감에 대응하여'라는 의미로 문장을 자연스럽게 완성하는 (A) response(대응)가 정답이다. (B) effect(효과), (C) apology(사과), (D) confirmation(확인)은 'in ____ to' 구문으로 쓰이지 않는다.

번역 각 부서는 지난주에 발표된 예산 삭감에 대응하여 실행 계획을 마련하라는 요청을 받았다.

어휘 budget cut 예산 삭감

120 부사 어휘

해설 동사 have been shown을 수식하여 '구직자들의 기술을 향상시킨 것으로 일관되게 입증되어 왔다'는 내용이 되어야 자연스러우므로 '일관되게'를 뜻하는 (A) consistently가 정답이다. (B) emotionally는 '감정적으로', (C) spaciously는 '넓게', (D) randomly는 '무작위로'라는 의미로 문맥에 어울리지 않는다.

번역 우리의 인기 있는 온라인 교육 자료는 구직자들의 기술을 향상시킨 것으로 일관되게 입증되어 왔다.

어휘 material 자료   improve 향상시키다   job seeker 구직자

121 형용사 자리 _ 명사 수식

해설 빈칸은 주어 Ms. Yamada와 동격을 이루는 명사 director를 앞에서 수식하는 자리로, 형용사 또는 director와 복합명사를 이루는 명사가 들어갈 수 있다. of the Midlands Chamber of Commerce와 결합하여 '미들랜즈 상공 회의소의 전 이사'라는 의미가 되어야 하므로 '이전의'를 뜻하는 형용사 (B) former가 정답이다. (A) formed(형성된)는 과거분사로 빈칸에 들어갈 수는 있지만 의미상 적합하지 않고, (C) formalize는 동사로 빈칸에 들어갈 수 없으며, 명사 (D) formality(형식적인 일)는 director와 복합명사를 이루기에 적절하지 않다.

번역 미들랜즈 상공 회의소의 전 이사였던 야마다 씨는 최근 주 무역 위원회에 임명되었다.

어휘 Chamber of Commerce 상공 회의소   appoint 임명하다
commission 위원회

122 전치사 어휘

해설 문맥상 '최대 다섯 개의 파일을 동시에 열도록 해준다'는 의미가 되어야 자연스러우므로, '최대 ~까지'라는 의미로 숫자 앞에 사용하여 최대 범위를 나타내는 (C) up to가 정답이다. (A) far from은 '~에서 멀리', (B) as for는 '~에 대해 말하자면', (D) out of는 '~ 중에서'라는 의미로 문맥상 부자연스럽다.

번역 이 소프트웨어는 컴퓨터 메모리를 효율적으로 사용하여 사용자가 최대 다섯 개의 파일을 동시에 열 수 있도록 해준다.

어휘 efficiently 효율적으로   simultaneously 동시에

123 동사 어휘

해설 명사 way를 수식하는 to부정사 자리에 들어갈 동사 어휘를 고르는 문제이다. your group's activities and events를 목적어로 취해 '여러분 단체의 활동과 행사를 홍보하는 방법'이라는 의미가 되어야 문맥상 자연스러우므로 '홍보하다'를 뜻하는 (D) promote가 정답이다. (A) realize는 '깨닫다', (B) propose는 '제안하다', (C) observe는 '관찰하다'라는 의미이다.

번역 월간 소식지는 여러분 단체의 활동과 행사를 홍보하는 훌륭한 방법입니다.

124 접속사 자리 _ 부사절 접속사

해설 빈칸은 두 개의 완전한 절을 이어주는 접속사 자리이다. 문맥상 '호텔에 식당은 없지만 인근에 식사할 곳이 많다'는 내용이 되어야 적절하므로, '~이긴 하지만'을 뜻하는 부사절 접속사 (A) While이 정답이다. (B) Such as와 (D) Without은 전치사이므로 절을 연결할 수 없고, (C) Unless는 부사절 접속사이지만 '~하지 않는 한'이라는 의미로 문맥에 적합하지 않다.

번역 호텔 내부에 식당은 없지만 인근에 식사할 곳이 많다.

어휘 on site 현장에   dining 식사   nearby 인근에

125 전치사 자리

해설 빈칸은 콤마 뒤의 완전한 절에 빈칸 뒤의 명사구 a slight decline (in revenue from the previous quarter)을 연결하는 자리이므로 전치사가 들어가야 한다. '수익이 약간 감소했음에도 불구하고'라는 의미가 되어야 자연스러우므로 '~에도 불구하고'를 뜻하는 전치사 (B) Despite가 정답이다. (A) Aside와 (D) Often은 부사이므로 빈칸에 들어갈 수 없고, (B) Becoming은 현재분사로 구조상 빈칸에 들어가 현재분사구를 이룰 수는 있으나 문맥상 부적절하다.

번역 지난 분기보다 수익이 약간 감소했음에도 불구하고, 블레이클리 컴포넌츠는 확장 계획을 진행시키고 있다.

어휘 decline 감소   revenue 수익   previous 바로 앞의, 이전의   quarter 분기   move forward 진행하다   expansion 확장

126 전치사 어휘

해설 빈칸 뒤에 기간을 나타내는 명사구 the past ten years가 있고, 문맥상 '지난 10년 동안'이라는 의미가 되어야 자연스러우므로 '~ 동안'을 뜻하는 (A) over가 정답이다. (B) into는 '~ 안으로', (C) since는 '~ 이래로', (D) beside는 '~ 옆에'라는 의미이다.

번역 아벨리아 데어리 컴퍼니는 지난 10년 동안 경영진에 여러 변화를 겪었다.

어휘 undergo 겪다   leadership 지도부

127 명사 자리 _ 동사의 목적어

해설 빈칸은 동사 is holding의 목적어 역할을 하는 명사 자리이므로 명사인 (C) auditions와 (D) audition이 빈칸에 들어갈 수 있다. audition은 가산명사로 단수로 쓰일 경우 한정사 an, the 등이 필요한데 빈칸 앞에 한정사가 보이지 않으므로 복수 명사인 (C) auditions가 정답이다. (A) to audition은 to부정사, (B) auditioned는 동사/과거분사로 빈칸에 들어갈 수 없다.

번역 오팔 시 커뮤니티 극장은 12월 첫 주에 봄 공연 작품을 위한 오디션을 주최한다.

어휘 production 상연 작품, 제작

128 부사 어휘

해설 빈칸은 동사 packed를 수식하는 부사 자리로, so ~ that ...(매우 ~해서 …하다) 구문과 결합하여 '너무 급하게 짐을 싸서 정장과 넥타이 챙기는 것을 깜빡했다'는 내용이 되어야 자연스러우므로 '급히, 서둘러'를 뜻하는 (C) hastily가 정답이다. (A) enormously는 '엄청나게', (B) briefly는 '간단히', (D) mysteriously는 '신비롭게'라는 의미이다.

번역 케인 씨는 오늘 아침 너무 급하게 짐을 싸서 내일 저녁 식사에 입을 정장과 넥타이 챙기는 것을 깜빡했다고 말했다.

129 동사 어형 _ 태 + 시제

해설 빈칸은 주어 Ms. Morris의 동사 자리로, 뒤에 목적어 the schedule이 왔으므로 능동태가 들어가야 한다. 또한 부사절 접속사 before가 이끄는 절의 동사 began이 과거 시제이고, 문맥상 교육 프로그램이 시작된 것보다 이전의 일을 나타내야 하므로 과거보다 앞선 일을 나타내는 과거완료 시제 (C) had revised가 정답이다.

번역 교육 프로그램이 시작되기 훨씬 전에 모리스 씨는 자신의 팀이 참석할 수 있도록 일정을 수정했다.

130 접속사 자리 _ 부사절 접속사

해설 빈칸 뒤에 주어 the interns와 동사 have arrived를 갖춘 완전한 절이 왔으므로 부사절 접속사가 들어가야 한다. 문맥상 '인턴들이 도착하는 대로'라는 내용이 되어야 자연스러우므로 '~하자마자, 일단 ~하면'을 뜻하는 부사절 접속사 (A) once가 정답이다. (B) unlike와 (D) regarding은 전치사이므로 절을 이끌 수 없고, (C) whereas는 접속사이지만 '~한 반면'이라는 뜻으로 의미상 어울리지 않는다.

번역 스완 씨는 인턴들이 도착하는 대로 기획 회의에 복귀할 것이다.

PART 6

131-134 은행 광고

한정된 기간 동안 두 배의 보상을 누리세요!

휴가철 쇼핑을 1월까지 이어가시면 50달러 이상 **131 구매**마다 4달러를 캐시백으로 돌려드립니다. 또한 캐시백 보상은 **132 자동으로** 별도의 아반티 예금 계좌에 입금되며 연 3퍼센트의 이자를 받게 됩니다. 아반티의

휴대전화 또는 컴퓨터 앱에서 두 배 보상 프로그램에 가입하세요. **133 또는**, 아반티 지점에 방문하셔서 도움을 받으세요. **134 두 배 보상 프로모션은 1월 31일에 종료되므로 망설이지 마세요.** 2월 1일 자로 캐시백 보상은 50달러 거래마다 2달러로 돌아갑니다.

> 어휘 take advantage of ~을 이용하다 reward 보상 limited 한정된 stretch 이어지다, 늘이다 spree 흥청망청하기 deposit 입금하다 separate 별도의 savings account 예금 계좌 interest rate 이자율 enroll in ~에 등록하다 transaction 거래

131 명사 자리 _ 전치사의 목적어

해설 빈칸은 전치사 on의 목적어 자리로, 형용사 every의 수식을 받아 '50달러 이상의 모든 구매마다'라는 의미가 되어야 적절하므로 '구매'를 뜻하는 명사 (A) purchase가 정답이다. (B) purchaser는 '구매자'라는 뜻으로 문맥상 적합하지 않고, (C) purchased는 동사/과거분사, (D) purchasing은 명사로 사용할 경우 '구매 업무, 구매 부서'를 뜻하며 불가산 명사로 쓰이기 때문에 every 뒤에 올 수 없다. 동명사로 사용하더라도 purchase가 목적어를 필요로 하는 타동사이기 때문에 뒤에 목적어가 없어서 빈칸에 들어갈 수 없다.

132 부사 자리 _ 동사 수식

해설 미래 시제 수동태 동사구를 이루는 will be와 과거분사 deposited 사이에서 동사를 수식하는 부사 자리이므로 '자동적으로'를 뜻하는 부사 (D) automatically가 정답이다. (A) automate는 동사, (B) automatic은 형용사, (C) automation은 명사이므로 품사상 빈칸에 들어갈 수 없다.

133 접속부사

해설 앞 문장에는 아반티의 휴대전화 또는 컴퓨터 앱에서 두 배 보상 프로그램에 가입하라(Enroll in our double-rewards program on Avanti's mobile or desktop app)고 했고, 빈칸 뒤에는 아반티 지점에 방문해서 도움을 받으라(stop by an Avanti branch for assistance)고 했다. 앱으로 등록하기 어려운 사람들을 위해 지점 방문이라는 다른 방법을 안내하고 있으므로, 대안을 제시할 때 사용하는 '또는, 그렇지 않으면'이라는 뜻의 (A) Alternatively가 정답이다. (B) Likewise는 '마찬가지로', (C) Nevertheless는 '그럼에도 불구하고', (D) Frequently는 '자주'라는 의미이다.

134 문맥에 맞는 문장 고르기

번역 (A) 두 배 보상을 활용하는 것은 은행 업계에서 일반적인 관행입니다.
(B) 두 배 보상 프로모션은 1월 31일에 종료되므로 망설이지 마세요.
(C) 귀하의 신용카드 잔액을 매주 확인해 주십시오.
(D) 최근 거래에 대해 피드백을 제공해 주셔서 감사합니다.

해설 빈칸 앞 내용 전체에 걸쳐 보상 프로그램을 홍보하고 있고 빈칸 뒤 문장에는 2월 1일 자로 캐시백 보상은 원래대로 돌아간다(On February 1, cashback rewards will return to $2 per $50 transaction)고 설명하고 있으므로, 보상 프로그램의 종료일을 안내하는 내용이 들어가는 것이 자연스럽다. 따라서 프로모션이 1월 31일에 종료된다며 참여를 권장하고 있는 (B)가 정답이다.

> 어휘 common 일반적인 practice 관행 balance 잔액

135-138 이메일 ▶동영상 강의

수신: 배송팀
발신: 마르티나 웨스트
날짜: 2월 21일
제목: 기쁜 소식

팀 여러분께,

우리의 오랜 팀장이었던 위니 리우가 새로운 일을 시작한다는 소식을 공유하게 되어 기쁩니다. 다행히도, 그녀가 회사를 떠나는 것은 아닙니다. **135 대신에**, 위니는 우리의 새로운 지역 유통 관리자로 근무하게 됩니다. 우리는 그녀의 **136 승진**이 아주 기쁩니다.

위니가 우리 부서, 특히 우리 팀을 위해 해 온 모든 일에 감사를 표하고 싶습니다. 그녀가 우리와 함께하는 **137 마지막** 날인 2월 28일 오후 3시에 휴게실에서 위니를 위한 파티를 열 예정입니다. **138 함께 커피와 케이크를 드시러 오세요.** 거기서 여러분과 만나기를 기대합니다.

마르티나 웨스트
배송 관리자
크로체 컴퍼니

> 어휘 captain (단체 따위의) 장 move on (새로운 일로) 넘어가다 serve 근무하다 regional 지역의 distribution 유통 thrilled 아주 신이 난 appreciation 감사 break room 휴게실

135 접속부사

해설 빈칸 앞에서 오랜 팀장이었던 위니 리우가 새로운 일을 시작한다(Winnie Liu, our longtime team captain, will be moving on)면서 그녀가 회사를 떠나는 것은 아니라고(she will not be leaving the company) 하고, 빈칸 뒤에서 위니는 우리의 새로운 지역 유통 관리자로 근무하게 된다(Winnie will serve as our new regional distribution manager)고 했다. 서로 대조적인 내용을 연결해야 하므로 내용의 전환이 이루어질 때 사용하는 '대신에'라는 뜻의 (B) Instead가 정답이다. (A) Originally는 '원래', (C) Regardless는 '개의치 않고', (D) Moreover는 '게다가'라는 의미이다.

136 명사 어휘

해설 앞 문장에서 위니는 우리의 새로운 지역 유통 관리자로 근무하게 된다(Winnie will serve as our new regional distribution manager)고 했으므로, 위니가 승진한 일에 대해 기뻐하고 있음을 알 수 있다. 따라서 '승진'을 뜻하는 (B) promotion이 정답이다. (A) availability는 '이용 가능성', (C) cooperation은 '협력', (D) generosity는 '관대함'을 의미한다.

137 형용사 자리 _ 명사 수식

해설 빈칸 앞에 소유격 her, 뒤에 명사 day가 있으므로 명사를 수식하는 형용사 자리이다. '그녀의 마지막 날인 2월 28일'이라는 의미가 되어야 자연스러우므로 '마지막의'라는 뜻의 형용사 (A) final이 정답이다. (B) finalize는 동사, (D) finally는 부사이므로 품사상 빈칸에 들어갈 수 없고, 과거분사 (C) finalized는 형용사 자리에 들어갈 수는 있지만 '완결된, 확정된'이라는 뜻으로 의미상 적합하지 않다.

138 문맥에 맞는 문장 고르기

번역 (A) 우리의 하루는 평소처럼 오전 8시에 시작될 것입니다.
(B) 그녀는 그 직책에 가장 잘 맞는 지원자였습니다.
(C) 함께 커피와 케이크를 드시러 오세요.
(D) 휴게실은 현재 유지 보수를 위해 문을 닫았습니다.

해설 앞 문장에서 위니를 위한 파티가 열리는 시간과 장소를 안내하고 있고(We will be hosting a party for Winnie in the break room at 3:00 P.M. on February 28), 뒤 문장에서 파티에서 만나기를 기대한다(We look forward to seeing you there)고 했으므로 파티에 초대하는 내용이 들어가야 일관성 있는 문맥이 완성된다. 따라서 함께 커피와 케이크를 드시러 오라며 파티 참석을 권하고 있는 (C)가 정답이다.

어휘 candidate 지원자, 후보자   currently 현재   maintenance 유지 보수

139-142 블로그 게시물

> **잠재 투자자에게 당신의 신생 기업을 홍보하는 방법**
>
> 잠재 투자자들을 위한 발표를 준비할 때 그들을 불안한 상태로 두지 마세요. **139 시작부터 회사의 가장 훌륭한 강점을 드러내세요.** 여기에는 투자자들의 주목을 사로잡는 추가적인 이점이 있습니다. 회사의 젊고 역동적인 팀은 가장 큰 자산일 수 있습니다. 한편, 당신의 팀이 오랜 기간 소중한 경험을 함께 했고 이것이 제공하는 제품이나 서비스와 **140 관련이 있다면**, 이 또한 초반에 언급하세요. 마지막으로, 당신의 회사를 차별화시켜주는 **141 것**이 독창적인 비전이라면 그 점을 가장 중요하게 말하세요. 청중들에게 당신 회사의 제품이나 서비스가 성공할 운명이라는 확신을 줄 수 있다면 원하는 **142 자금**을 확보할 수 있을 것입니다.

어휘 pitch 홍보하다   start-up 신생 기업   potential 잠재적인   investor 투자자   in suspense 불안해하는, 초조해하는   benefit 이익   grab 붙잡다   attention 주목   dynamic 역동적인   asset 자산   valuable 소중한   set apart 눈에 띄게 하다   leading 가장 중요한   statement 서술, 진술   convince 확신시키다   audience 청중   destined ~할 운명인   acquire 확보하다, 얻다

139 문맥에 맞는 문장 고르기

번역 (A) 투자자들은 종종 소유 지분을 기대합니다.
(B) 시작부터 회사의 가장 훌륭한 강점을 드러내세요.
(C) 발표 중 인용하는 모든 자료의 출처를 반드시 언급하세요.
(D) 현금의 투입은 성장을 위해 종종 필요합니다.

해설 앞 문장에서 잠재 투자자들을 위한 발표를 준비할 때 그들을 불안한 상태로 두지 말라(When planning a presentation for potential investors, do not keep them in suspense)고 했고 뒤 문장에서 여기에는 투자자들의 주목을 사로잡는 추가적인 이점이 있다(This has the added benefit of grabbing investors' attention)고 했으므로, 발표 초반에 투자자들의 불안감을 해소할 수 있는 확실한 정보를 공개하고 주목을 끌라고 조언하는 내용이 들어가야 자연스럽다. 따라서 시작부터 회사의 강점을 드러내라고 언급하고 있는 (B)가 정답이다.

어휘 share 지분, 몫   ownership 소유(권)   reveal 드러내다   strength 강점   outset 시작   cite 언급하다   source (자료의) 출처   quote 인용하다   infusion 투입

140 형용사 어휘

해설 빈칸 뒤의 전치사 to와 연결될 수 있으면서 적절한 문맥을 완성하는 형용사를 골라야 한다. be relevant to는 '~와 관련이 있는'이라는 뜻으로, '당신의 팀이 오랜 기간 소중한 경험을 함께 했고 이것이 제품이나 서비스와 관련이 있다면'이라고 자연스러운 의미를 나타내므로 (D) relevant가 정답이다. (A) capable은 '유능한', (B) progressive는 '진보적인', (C) first는 '첫 번째의'라는 의미이고, 전치사 to와 어울리지 않는다.

141 명사절 접속사

해설 빈칸에는 동사 is의 주어 역할을 하는 명사절을 이끄는 접속사가 필요한데, 빈칸 뒤에 주어가 빠진 불완전한 절(sets your company apart)이 있으므로 명사절 접속사 (C) what이 정답이다. (A) it과 (D) anything은 대명사이므로 품사상 빈칸에 들어갈 수 없고, 명사절 접속사 (B) that은 뒤에 완전한 절이 와야 한다.

142 명사 어휘

해설 지문의 제목이 잠재 투자자에게 신생 기업을 홍보하는 방법(How to Pitch Your Start-up to a Potential Investor)이고, 지문 전반적으로 잠재 투자자들에게 효과적으로 발표하는 방법에 대해 언급하고 있다. 따라서 빈칸이 있는 문장에서 회사의 성공에 대한 확신을 주어야 하는 청중(audience)은 잠재 투자자들(potential investors)임을 알 수 있고, 신생 기업이 잠재 투자자들로부터 확보하려는 것은 투자금이므로 '자금'을 의미하는 (A) funding이 정답이다. (B) property는 '부동산', (C) materials는 '재료', (D) awards는 '상'이라는 의미이다.

143-146 이메일

> 수신: 보츠와나 마이닝 직원
> 발신: 필다 라모가피, 인사부 이사
> 날짜: 4월 4일
> 제목: 급여 포털 업그레이드
>
> 좋은 아침입니다,

보츠와나 마이닝의 온라인 급여 포털이 소프트웨어 업그레이드로 4월 8일부터 12일까지 이용 불가합니다. 이 5일 동안 **143 시스템**에 접속을 자제해 주시기 바랍니다.

업데이트된 사이트는 사용자가 계좌 입금 설정 및 관리와 세금 문서 열람을 포함한 고급 작업을 수행하는 것을 **144 가능하게 해 줄 것입니다.** 또한 실시간 채팅 기능도 갖추어 사용자가 필요할 때 인사팀 직원에게 직접 연락할 수 있게 됩니다. **145 이 기능은 해당 부서에서 제공하는 서비스를 최적화해 줄 것입니다.**

위에 언급된 기간 **146 중에** 급여 및 복리후생 세부정보를 열람해야 하는 경우, hr@botswanamining.co.bw로 이메일을 보내시거나 우지마 타워 107호 사무실로 방문해 주세요.

필다 라모가피
인사부 이사

어휘 payroll 급여 지급 명세서 refrain 자제하다 advanced 고급의 operation 작업 direct deposit (급여의) 계좌 입금 preference 선호 access 이용하다 feature 포함하다 function 기능 directly 직접 benefits 복리후생 period 기간

143 명사 어휘

해설 앞 문장에서 온라인 급여 포털이 소프트웨어 업그레이드로 이용 불가하다(online payroll portal will be unavailable ~ to allow for a software upgrade)고 했으므로, 앞에서 언급한 포털에 접속하지 말라는 것임을 알 수 있다. 따라서 온라인 급여 포털을 대신할 수 있는 단어로 '시스템'을 뜻하는 (B) system이 정답이다. (A) course는 '강좌', (C) account는 '계좌', (D) plan은 '계획'을 의미한다.

144 동사 어형 _ 시제

해설 주어가 The updated site인 문장에 동사가 보이지 않으므로 빈칸은 동사 자리이다. 앞에서 온라인 급여 포털이 소프트웨어 업그레이드로 4월 8일부터 12일까지 이용 불가할 것(online payroll portal will be unavailable between 8 and 12 April to allow for a software upgrade)이라며 향후 일정을 안내하고 있고, 빈칸이 있는 문장은 '업데이트된 사이트(The updated site)', 즉, 사이트가 업데이트되고 나면 할 수 있는 일을 언급하고 있으므로 미래 시제인 (C) will enable이 정답이다.

145 문맥에 맞는 문장 고르기

번역 (A) 이 모임은 직원들 사이에 혁신을 촉진시켜 줄 것입니다.
(B) 우리 주주들은 이 신제품에 만족할 것입니다.
(C) 다음 달에는 생산성 감소가 발생할 가능성이 있습니다.
(D) 이 기능은 해당 부서에서 제공하는 서비스를 최적화해 줄 것입니다.

해설 앞 문장에서 실시간 채팅 기능을 갖추어 사용자가 필요할 때 인사팀 직원에게 직접 연락할 수 있게 된다(It will also feature a live-chat function so that users can directly contact a human resources team member when needed)고 했

으므로, 실시간 채팅 기능을 This function으로 받아 새로운 기능으로 얻게 되는 효과를 설명하는 내용이 들어가는 것이 자연스럽다. 따라서 이 기능은 그 부서에서 제공하는 서비스를 최적화할 것이라고 언급하는 (D)가 정답이다.

어휘 gathering 모임 promote 촉진하다 innovation 혁신 shareholder 주주 productivity 생산성 reduction 감소 occur 발생하다 optimize 최적화하다

146 전치사 어휘

해설 빈칸 뒤에 기간을 나타내는 명사 the period가 있고, 지문의 첫 문장에서 온라인 급여 포털이 소프트웨어 업그레이드로 4월 8일부터 12일까지 이용 불가하다(online payroll portal will be unavailable between 8 and 12 April to allow for a software upgrade)고 안내한 것으로 보아 '위에 언급된 기간 동안 정보를 열람해야 하는 경우'라는 내용이 되어야 자연스럽다. 따라서 '~ 중에, ~ 동안'을 뜻하는 (C) during이 정답이다. (A) apart from은 '~ 외에', (B) along with는 '~와 함께', (D) toward는 '(시점) ~ 즈음'이라는 의미이다.

PART 7

147-148 광고

섬너 오토 서플라이
서비스 특별 할인

29달러 95센트

포함되는 서비스:

- **147(A)** 일반 오일 교체
- **147(B)** 고급 오일 필터 교체
- **147(C)** 무료 자동차 점검

148 이 할인은 8월 31일까지 스미스빌과 파커타운 지점에서만 유효합니다. 고객은 서비스 이용 시 이 쿠폰을 제시해야 합니다. 고객당 쿠폰 한 장으로 제한됩니다.

어휘 special 특별 할인가 conventional 흔히 있는, 평범한 complimentary 무료 inspection 점검 offer 할인 valid 유효한 present 제시하다 per ~당

147 Not / True

번역 이 특별 할인에 포함되는 서비스가 아닌 것은?
(A) 오일 교체
(B) 필터 교체
(C) 자동차 점검
(D) 세차

해설 지문 중반부에 일반 오일 교체(Conventional oil change)가 있으므로 (A), 고급 오일 필터 교체(Premium oil filter change)가 있으므로 (B), 무료 자동차 점검(Complimentary car inspection)이 있으므로 (C)는 특별 할인에 포함되는 서비스가 맞지만, 세차에 대한 언급은 없으므로 (D)가 정답이다.

148 Not / True

번역 쿠폰에 대해 명시된 것은?
(A) 섬너 오토 서플라이의 전 지점에서 사용할 수 있다.
(B) 첫 방문 고객들만 이용할 수 있다.
(C) 8월 말 이전에 사용해야 한다.
(D) 여러 번 사용할 수 있다.

해설 지문 후반부에서 이 할인은 8월 31일까지 스미스빌과 파커타운 지점에서만 유효하다(This offer is valid only at our Smithville and Parkertown locations through August 31)고 했으므로 (C)가 정답이다.

어휘 multiple 다수의

> **Paraphrasing**
> 지문의 valid only ~ through August 31
> → 정답의 must be used before the end of August

149-150 기사

> **멜버리 데일리 뉴스 요약**
>
> (2월 2일) — **149** 통근자들은 리버 가 기차역이 마침내 개보수된다는 소식에 안도하고 있다. 100년이 된 이 역은 도시에서 가장 붐비는 역 중 하나이며 보수가 절실한 상태이다.
>
> 1월 31일 회의에서 시의회는 새 출입구와 지붕을 포함하여 시 토목 부서가 제출한 개보수 계획안에 최종 승인을 내렸다. **150** 역사 내부 벽을 위한 벽화 또한 계획되어 있다. 지역 예술가들은 3월에 제안서를 제출하라는 의뢰를 받았다.
>
> **149** 공사는 2주 후에 시작되어 완료에 약 8개월이 걸릴 예정이다. 역은 이 기간 내내 계속 운영된다.

어휘 commuter 통근자 relieved 안도하는 renovate 개보수하다 desperate 필사적인 council 의회 approval 승인 municipal 시의 engineering 토목 entrance 출입구 mural 벽화 commission 의뢰하다 approximately 대략

149 주제 / 목적

번역 기사의 주요 목적은?
(A) 기차역의 폐쇄를 보도하려고
(B) 개보수 공사의 시작을 알리려고
(C) 역사적인 건물의 중요성을 설명하려고
(D) 지역 예술가들의 중요한 역할을 강조하려고

해설 첫 단락 첫 문장에서 통근자들은 리버 가 기차역이 마침내 개보수된다는 소식에 안도하고 있다(Commuters are relieved that the River Avenue Railway Station is finally going to be renovated)고 알리고 있고, 마지막 단락 첫 문장에서 공사는 2주 후에 시작되어 완료에 약 8개월이 걸릴 예정(Work will begin in two weeks and take approximately eight months to complete)이라며 지문 전체에 걸쳐 기차역의 개보수 공사 소식 및 일정 등에 대해 설명하고 있으므로 (B)가 정답이다.

어휘 closure 폐쇄 publicize 알리다 describe 설명하다 significance 중요성 emphasize 강조하다

150 세부 사항

번역 기사에 따르면, 3월에 일어날 일은?
(A) 새로운 철도 노선의 운행이 시작된다.
(B) 기차역의 지붕이 교체된다.
(C) 시의회가 리버 가 주차 계획에 대해 투표한다.
(D) 예술가들이 벽 장식 아이디어를 제출한다.

해설 두 번째 단락의 두 번째 문장에서 역사 내부 벽을 위한 벽화 또한 계획되어 있다(Also planned are murals for the station's interior walls)고 했고, 지역 예술가들은 3월에 제안서를 제출하라는 의뢰를 받았다(Local artists have been commissioned to submit proposals in March)고 했다. 따라서 지역 예술가들은 3월에 역사 벽화를 위한 제안서를 제출할 것임을 알 수 있으므로 (D)가 정답이다.

어휘 replace 교체하다

> **Paraphrasing**
> 지문의 murals → 정답의 wall decoration
> 지문의 submit proposals → 정답의 deliver ~ ideas

151-152 이메일

> 수신: 톰 산체스 <tsanchez65@mailcurrent.net>
> 발신: 준 오스만 <josman@oregonartmuseum.org>
> 날짜: 9월 19일
> 제목: 새로운 미술관 별관 개관
>
> 산체스 씨께:
>
> **151** 오리건 미술관의 프로스너 별관 공식 개관식에 참석을 요청드립니다. 행사는 11월 3일 오후 6시에 열릴 예정입니다. 애피타이저와 음료가 제공됩니다. 저희의 첫 초청 작가인 타로 미후네가 함께 자리해 관객들과 교류하며 자신의 전시인 <오리거니언 리플렉션스>에 대해 이야기할 예정입니다.
>
> **152** 이번 비공개 행사는 귀하와 같은 소중한 미술관 회원들에게만 한정됩니다. 행사에는 손님 한 명을 동반할 수 있습니다. 정확한 참석자 수를 파악할 수 있도록 10월 20일까지 회신해 주십시오.
>
> 준 오스만
> 오리건 미술관 관장

어휘 wing 별관 presence 참석 official 공식적인 featured 주연의, 특집의 on hand 자리에 있는 mingle 어울리다 crowd 사람들 invaluable 귀중한 accurate 정확한 attendee 참석자

151 주제 / 목적

번역 이메일의 목적은?
(A) 산체스 씨에게 그림값 지불을 요청하려고
(B) 유명 인사를 행사 사회자로 섭외하려고
(C) 산체스 씨를 행사에 초대하려고
(D) 새로운 미술관 개관을 발표하려고

해설 첫 단락 첫 문장에서 산체스 씨에게 오리건 미술관의 프로스너 별관 공식 개관식에 참석을 요청드린다(Your presence is requested at the official opening of the Oregon Art Museum's Prosner Wing)고 했으므로 산체스 씨를 미술관의 별관 개관 행사에 초대하기 위한 이메일임을 알 수 있다. 따라서 (C)가 정답이다.

어휘 recruit 모집하다   celebrity 유명 인사
master of ceremonies 사회자

152 Not / True

번역 산체스 씨에 대해 명시된 것은?
(A) 미술관 행사에 출장 음식을 공급할 것이다.
(B) 오리건 미술관에서 근무한다.
(C) 오리건 전역에 자신의 작품을 전시한다.
(D) 미술관 회원권을 갖고 있다.

해설 두 번째 단락 첫 문장에서 산체스 씨에게 이번 비공개 행사는 귀하와 같은 소중한 미술관 회원들에게만 한정된다(This private celebration is limited to invaluable museum members like you)고 했으므로, 산체스 씨는 미술관 회원임을 알 수 있다. 따라서 (D)가 정답이다.

어휘 cater 음식을 공급하다

> **Paraphrasing**
> 지문의 museum members like you
> → 정답의 He has a membership at an art museum.

153-154 문자 메시지

아바니 메타 (오전 8시 57분)
안녕하세요, 에드. 지금 창고로 가는 버스를 타고 있어요. 제가 이야기했던 모바일 앱 기억하세요? 153 사용 가능한 보관 장소를 찾아주는 거 말이에요. 지금 그 앱을 사용 중인데, 메이플 가 10번지에 우리에게 맞는 곳을 찾은 것 같아요.

에드 바이거 (오전 8시 59분)
좋네요. 그곳이 단순히 행사 공간이 아닌 게 확실한가요?

아바니 메타 (오전 9시 1분)
153 설명에는 보관 공간이 필요한 소매업자에게 이상적이고 단기 대여 조건을 제공한다고 나와 있어요.

에드 바이거 (오전 9시 2분)
괜찮을 것 같네요. 재고 업무를 끝내고 나서 오늘 중으로 같이 세부 사항을 확인해 봅시다.

아바니 메타 (오전 9시 4분)
좋아요. 우리 밴에는 이미 과잉 재고 물품들이 실려 있어요. 154 당신이 그쪽으로 밴을 몰고 오면 되겠어요. 장소가 적합하다고 확인되면 앱으로 공간을 예약하고 거기서 바로 밴에서 짐을 내리면 돼요.

에드 바이거 (오전 9시 5분)
저도 같은 생각을 하고 있었어요.

아바니 메타 (오전 9시 6분)
훌륭해요. 이따 봐요.

어휘 warehouse 창고   storage 보관   description 설명
ideal 이상적인   retailer 소매업자   temporary 잠시의, 일시적인
term 조건   particular 세부 사항   inventory 재고   load 싣다
overstocked 재고 과잉의, 공급 과잉의   turn out ~으로 드러나다
fit 맞는 것   unload (짐을) 내리다

153 주제 / 목적

번역 메시지 작성자들은 주로 무엇에 대해 논의하고 있는가?
(A) 임시 공간 임대
(B) 계절 근로자 채용
(C) 판매 행사 계획
(D) 모바일 앱 개발

해설 8시 57분에 메타 씨가 사용 가능한 보관 장소를 찾아주는 앱(the one for finding available storage locations)을 언급하며 지금 그 앱을 사용 중인데 메이플 가 10번지에 우리에게 맞는 곳을 찾은 것 같다(I'm using it now, and I think I've found something for us at 10 Maple Street)고 했고, 9시 1분에 보관 공간이 필요한 소매업자에게 이상적이고 단기 대여 조건을 제공한다고 나와 있다(The description says it's ideal for retailers needing storage space, and it offers temporary rental terms)고 했다. 이를 통해 메시지 작성자들은 임시로 대여할 보관 장소를 찾는 일을 상의 중임을 알 수 있으므로 (A)가 정답이다.

어휘 seasonal 계절적인

154 의도 파악

번역 오전 9시 5분에 바이거 씨가 "저도 같은 생각을 하고 있었어요"라고 쓴 의도는?
(A) 메타 씨가 도착할 때쯤 창고에 있을 것이다.
(B) 재고 과잉 물품을 밴에 실을 것이다.
(C) 밴을 그 장소로 운전해 올 생각이다.
(D) 모바일 앱을 다운로드할 것이다.

해설 9시 4분에 메타 씨가 바이거 씨에게 그쪽으로 밴을 몰고 오면 되겠다(You could drive it over)면서 장소가 적합하다고 확인되면 앱으로 공간을 예약하고 거기서 바로 밴에서 짐을 내리면 된다(If the location turns out to be a good fit, we can use the app to book the space and unload the van right there and then)고 제안하자 9시 5분에 바이거 씨가 자신도 같은 생각을 하고 있었다(That's exactly what I was thinking)고 대답한 것이므로, 바이거 씨는 메타 씨가 말하는 장소로 밴을 운전해 가겠다는 의도로 한 말임을 알 수 있다. 따라서 (C)가 정답이다.

155-157 웹페이지

https://www.dannlabrothers.com/about

| 홈 | 소개 | 제품 | 추천글 |

단라 브라더스는 여러분이 스크린 타임을 최대로 활용할 수 있도록 도와드립니다.

컴퓨터는 우리 삶의 중요한 일부이며 특히 노트북은 직장에서 기본형 컴퓨터가 되었습니다. 노트북은 사용자가 집이나 사무실뿐만 아니라 사실상 어디서나 일할 수 있도록 해줍니다. **155 단라 브라더스에는 여러분이 어디서 일하든 스크린 앞에서의 생산성을 극대화할 수 있는 제품들이 있습니다. 저희는 인체 공학적인 노트북 거치대, 편안한 의자, 높이 조절 가능한 입식 책상과 다양한 제품을 제조합니다.**

여러분은 매 근무일마다 하루 종일 저희 제품을 사용하시므로 저희는 디자인 개선을 위해 끊임없이 노력하고 있습니다. 오래 사용할 수 있도록 제작된 저희의 모든 판매 제품은 구성과 마감에 대해 10년 보증이 제공됩니다. **156 저희 추천글 페이지를 방문하셔서 저희 제품에 대한 유명한 비즈니스 및 기술 출판물들의 독자적인 평가를 검토하실 것을 권장합니다.**

저희 제품과 제품 특징을 확인하시려면 제품 페이지를 방문하세요. 150달러 이상의 모든 주문에 대해 무료 일반 배송이 제공됨을 참고하세요. 빠른 배송은 추가 요금으로 이용 가능합니다. 전 직원에게 인체 공학적인 솔루션을 제공하고자 하는 기업 조직을 대표하고 계신다면 상당한 할인 혜택을 제공해 드릴 수 있습니다. **157 대량 주문에 대한 무료 가격 견적을 받으시려면 info@dannlabrothers.com으로 이메일을 보내 주세요.** 24시간 이내에 문의에 답변해 드리겠습니다.

어휘 testimonial 추천글 make the most of ~을 최대한으로 활용하다 in particular 특히 default 기본 enable 가능하게 하다 virtually 사실상 maximize 극대화하다 productivity 생산성 ergonomic 인체 공학적인 adjustable 조절 가능한 constantly 끊임없이 strive 노력하다 back 보증하다 guarantee 보증(서) construction 구성 independent 독자적인 assessment 평가 noted 유명한 feature 특징 expedited 신속한 represent 대표하다 organization 조직 entire 전체의 substantial 상당한 volume 양 quote 견적 bulk 대량

155 세부 사항

번역 단라 브라더스는 어떤 종류의 사업체인가?
(A) 컴퓨터용 가구 제조업체
(B) 인터넷 서비스 공급업체
(C) 중고 컴퓨터 장비 판매업체
(D) 컴퓨터 부품 유통업체

해설 첫 단락의 세 번째 문장에서 단라 브라더스에는 스크린 앞에서의 생산성을 극대화할 수 있는 제품들이 있다(Dannla Brothers has products to maximize your productivity in front of the screen)고 했고, 인체 공학적인 노트북 거치대, 편안한 의자, 높이 조절 가능한 입식 책상과 다양한 제품을 제조한다(We manufacture ergonomic laptop stands, comfortable chairs, and adjustable standing desks, among other products)고 했다. 이를 통해 단라 브라더스는 컴퓨터 사용에 수반되는 가구를 제조하는 업체임을 알 수 있으므로 (A)가 정답이다.

어휘 equipment 장비 distributor 유통업체 component 부품

> **Paraphrasing**
> 지문의 ergonomic laptop stands, comfortable chairs, and adjustable standing desks → 정답의 furniture

156 세부 사항

번역 웹페이지 방문자들은 무엇을 하라고 권장받는가?
(A) 연장 보증 구매
(B) 근무 공간 사진 제출
(C) 기술 세미나 참석
(D) 제품 평가 읽기

해설 두 번째 단락 마지막 문장에서 추천글 페이지를 방문하여 제품에 대한 유명한 비즈니스 및 기술 출판물들의 독자적인 평가를 검토할 것을 권장한다(We invite you to visit our Testimonials page to review independent assessments of our products by noted business and technology publications)고 했으므로 (D)가 정답이다.

어휘 extended 연장된 review 평가

157 세부 사항

번역 웹페이지에 따르면, 이메일을 보내야 하는 이유는?
(A) 시설 견학 일정을 잡기 위해서
(B) 더 빠른 배송 옵션에 대해 알아보기 위해서
(C) 대량 주문에 대한 가격 견적을 받기 위해서
(D) 제품 조립 정보를 받기 위해서

해설 세 번째 단락 다섯 번째 문장에서 대량 주문에 대한 무료 가격 견적을 받으려면 이메일을 보내 달라(To receive a free price quote for a bulk order, please e-mail us at info@dannlabrothers.com)고 했으므로 (C)가 정답이다.

어휘 facility 시설 obtain 얻다 assembly 조립

> **Paraphrasing**
> 지문의 receive a free price quote for a bulk order → 정답의 obtain a price quote for a large order

158-160 회람

회람

수신: 전 직원
발신: 조앤 폴슨, CEO, 오스먼드 마이크로트로닉스 사
날짜: 5월 19일
제목: 후속 공지

158 지난주 회사 전체 회의에서 여러분을 뵐 수 있어 기뻤습니다. 매출 증가와 더불어 신제품 출시를 다시 한번 축하드리며, 이 신제품들은 이미 경쟁사로부터 상당한 시장 점유율을 되찾아오고 있습니다.

몇몇 임원 자리가 채워졌음을 알려드리고자 합니다. 프랭크 그루언이 최고재무책임자, 패트리샤 레스너는 연구개발 부문 부사장으로 근무하게 되며, 라나 에이번은 마케팅 이사, 그리고 159 **제품 디자이너인 루이스 성이 이제 제품 디자인 이사로서 자신의 부서를 감독하게 됩니다.**

한 자리는 공석으로 남았는데 바로 인사 담당 이사 자리입니다. 마커스 브롬리의 임원직은 변경되지 않을 계획이었으나 그가 최근에 은퇴를 결심했습니다. 그의 분석 능력과 밝은 유머 감각이 그리울 것입니다. 160 **브롬리 씨는 6월에 고향인 프리토리아에 영구적으로 정착할 계획입니다.** 우리 모두 그가 행복한 미래를 마땅히 누리기를 바랍니다.

어휘 follow-up 후속 조치 company-wide 회사 전체의 congratulate 축하하다 launch 출시 regain 되찾다 significant 상당한 market share 시장 점유율 competitor 경쟁사 executive 임원 fill 채우다 chief 최고위의 financial 재무의, 재정의 oversee 감독하다 assignment (임명된) 직 retire 은퇴하다 miss 그리워하다 analytical 분석적인 settle 정착하다 permanently 영구적으로 well-deserved 충분한 자격이 있는

158 세부 사항

번역 폴슨 씨가 최근 회의에서 한 일은?
(A) 몇몇 경쟁사들의 합병을 논의했다.
(B) 신제품 마케팅을 위한 향후 계획을 공유했다.
(C) 최신 판매 수치에 대해 직원들을 축하했다.
(D) 새로 채용된 임원 몇 명을 소개했다.

해설 첫 단락 첫 문장에서 폴슨 씨가 직원들에게 지난주 회사 전체 회의에서 여러분을 뵐 수 있어 기뻤다(It was a pleasure to see so many of you at our company-wide meeting last week)면서 매출 증가와 더불어 신제품 출시를 다시 한 번 축하한다(Let me congratulate you again on our sales increase as well as the launch of our newest products)고 했으므로, 폴슨 씨는 지난주 회의에서 판매 증가와 관련해 직원들을 축하했음을 알 수 있다. 따라서 (C)가 정답이다.

어휘 merger 합병 upcoming 다가오는 latest 최신의

159 세부 사항

번역 오스먼드 마이크로트로닉스 사 내부에서 승진한 사람은 누구인가?
(A) 그루언 씨
(B) 레스너 씨
(C) 에이번 씨
(D) 성 씨

해설 두 번째 단락의 두 번째 문장에서 제품 디자이너인 루이스 성이 이제 제품 디자인 이사로서 자신의 부서를 감독하게 된다(product designer Lewis Sung will now oversee his department as director of product design)고 했으므로, 성 씨는 자신이 속해 있던 오스먼드 마이크로트로닉스 사의 제품 디자인 부서 내에서 승진했음을 알 수 있다. 따라서 (D)가 정답이다.

160 세부 사항

번역 폴슨 시가 프리토리아를 언급한 이유는?
(A) 동료가 그곳으로 이사할 계획이다.
(B) 오스먼드 마이크로트로닉스 사가 그곳으로 이전할 예정이다.
(C) 대부분의 경쟁사가 그곳에 본사를 두고 있다.
(D) 회사 제품이 이제 그곳에서 판매된다.

해설 세 번째 단락의 네 번째 문장에서 브롬리 씨는 6월에 고향인 프리토리아에 영구적으로 정착할 계획(Mr. Bromley plans to settle permanently in his native Pretoria in June)이라고 했으므로, 폴슨 씨는 동료인 브롬리 씨의 이사 계획을 알리는 중에 그의 고향인 프리토리아를 언급했다는 것을 알 수 있다. 따라서 (A)가 정답이다.

어휘 relocate 이전하다 headquartered 본사가 있는

> **Paraphrasing**
> 지문의 settle → 정답의 move

161-163 이메일

수신: 헨리 에이블 〈henryable@bormaninstitute.edu〉
발신: 마사 맥그래스 〈mmcgrath@delahuntgreene.com〉
날짜: 12월 2일
제목: 귀하의 발표

에이블 박사님께:

지난주 델라헌트, 그린 앤 어소시에이츠(DGA)에서 직무 능력 개발 세미나를 이끌어 주셔서 감사합니다. 저희는 특히 학계에서 활동하시는 분들의 새로운 관점을 높이 평가합니다. 저희 홍보 직원들은 효과적인 문화 간 소통에 대한 귀하의 통찰력에 깊은 인상을 받았습니다. 특히 163 **국제 커뮤니케이션에 있어 단어 선택의 중요성에 관한 귀하의 연구가 흥미로웠습니다. 귀하의 연구 보고서 전체를 읽어보고 싶습니다.** 163 **참조하신 글의 사본을 저희에게 제공해 주실 수 있을까요?**

161, 162 **DGA는 귀하 또는 보먼 연구소에 계신 다른 연구원분들과 협력할 추가적인 방법을 모색하고 싶습니다.** 향후 함께 일할 수 있는 방법을 논의하기 위해 통화가 가능한 편리한 시간대를 알려주십시오. 그때까지, 귀하의 시간과 의견을 공유해 주신 데 대해 다시 한 번 감사드립니다.

마사 맥그래스, DGA 홍보 이사

어휘 appreciate 높이 평가하다 perspective 관점 individual 개인 academia 학계 public relations 홍보 impressed 감명 받은 cross-cultural 문화 간 intrigue 흥미를 돋우다 reference 참조하다 explore 탐구하다 partner 협력하다 institute 연구소

161 추론 / 암시

번역 에이블 박사에 대해 사실인 것 같은 것은?
(A) 정부 기관을 위해 자문을 해 준다.
(B) 기관에서 연구를 수행한다.
(C) 과거에 DGA의 다른 행사에서 연설한 적이 있다.
(D) 기업 임원으로서 방대한 경험을 했다.

해설 두 번째 단락 첫 문장에서 에이블 박사에게 DGA는 귀하 또는 보먼 연구소의 다른 연구원들과 협력할 추가적인 방법을 모색하고 싶다(DGA would like to explore additional ways we could partner with you or other researchers at the Borman Institute)고 했으므로, 에이블 박사는 보만 연구소에 소속된 연구원 중 한 명임을 알 수 있다. 따라서 (B)가 정답이다.

어휘 government 정부 agency 기관 conduct 수행하다 institution 기관 occasion 행사 vast 방대한 corporate 기업의

162 세부 사항

번역 맥그래스 씨는 앞으로 무엇을 하고 싶다고 명시하는가?
(A) 보만 연구소에서 가르치기
(B) 세미나에서 발표하기
(C) 에이블 박사에게 DGA의 일자리 제안하기
(D) 에이블 박사의 팀과 협력하기

해설 두 번째 단락 첫 문장에서 맥그래스 씨가 에이블 박사에게 DGA는 귀하 또는 보먼 연구소의 다른 연구원들과 협력할 추가적인 방법을 모색하고 싶다(DGA would like to explore additional ways we could partner with you or other researchers at the Borman Institute)며 에이블 박사와 다른 연구원들과 협력하고 싶다고 밝히고 있으므로 (D)가 정답이다.

어휘 collaborate 협력하다

> **Paraphrasing**
> 지문의 partner with → 정답의 Collaborate with

163 문장 삽입

번역 [1], [2], [3], [4]로 표시된 위치 중에서 다음 문장이 들어가기에 가장 적합한 곳은?

"귀하의 연구 보고서 전체를 읽어보고 싶습니다."
(A) [1]
(B) [2]
(C) [3]
(D) [4]

해설 주어진 문장에서 귀하의 연구 보고서 전체(your complete research report)를 읽어보고 싶다고 했으므로, 연구 보고서와 연관 지을 수 있는 내용이 주변에 있어야 한다. [2] 앞에서 국제 커뮤니케이션에 있어 단어 선택의 중요성에 관한 귀하의 연구가 흥미로웠다(We were particularly intrigued by your study on the importance of word choice in international communication)며 연구에 대한 흥미를 나타내고 있고, [2] 뒤에서 참조한 글의 사본을 제공해 줄 수 있는지(Would you mind providing us with a copy of the article you referenced?)를 물으며 연구 자료를 요청하고 있으므로, 이 사이에 연구 보고서에 대한 관심을 표현하는 문장이 들어가야 자연스럽다. 따라서 (B)가 정답이다.

164-167 구인 광고

> 보고서 검토 위원
>
> 네벡 어소시에이츠는 뉴욕 지역 팀에 합류할 보고서 검토 위원을 채용하고자 합니다. **164** 이 직책은 재택근무직이며 **166(A)** 기술 보고서를 검토하고 수정하기 위해 엔지니어들과의 협업이 포함됩니다. **166(B)** 이 정규직의 정규 근무 시간은 월요일부터 금요일까지 오전 9시부터 오후 5시까지입니다. **167** 급여는 경력에 상응하여 결정됩니다. 건강 보험과 퇴직 수당이 포함되어 있습니다.
>
> 직무에는 품질 규격을 충족하고 업계 표준을 따를 수 있도록 엔지니어링 보고서를 편집하는 업무가 포함됩니다. 보고서 검토 위원은 또한 편집 사항을 추적 관리하고 내부 주간 회의에서 작성자들과 피드백 패턴에 대해 논의해야 합니다. **165** 강력한 대인 관계 기술과 회사 부서 간 소통 능력은 필수입니다.
>
> **166(D)** 지원자는 학사 학위와 관련 분야에서 최소 2년의 근무 경력이 있어야 합니다. 기술 서류 작성 관련 공식 교육 경험은 우대 사항입니다. 관심 있는 지원자는 자기소개서와 이력서를 hiringmanager@neveckassociates.com으로 보내야 합니다.

어휘 reviewer 검토자 regional 지역의 collaborate 협업하다 revise 수정하다 regular 정규의 commensurate 상응하는 involve 포함하다 edit 편집하다 specification 규격 comply with ~을 따르다 track 추적하다 author 저자 internal 내부의 interpersonal 대인 관계의 essential 필수적인 applicant 지원자 bachelor's degree 학사 학위 relevant 관련 있는 formal 공식적인 cover letter 자기소개서 résumé 이력서

164 Not / True

번역 채용 중인 직책에 대해 명시된 것은?
(A) 원격 근무직이다.
(B) 관리직이다.
(C) 파트타임직이다.
(D) 수습직이다.

해설 첫 단락 두 번째 문장에서 이 직책은 재택근무직(This is a work-from-home position)이라고 직책에 대해 설명하고 있으므로 (A)가 정답이다.

어휘 remote 원격의 managerial 관리의 trainee 수습 사원

> **Paraphrasing**
> 지문의 work-from-home position → 정답의 remote position

165 세부 사항

번역 직무 요건으로 나열된 것은?
(A) 공학 분야의 배경
(B) 3년의 편집 경력
(C) 훌륭한 의사소통 기술
(D) 네벡 어소시에이츠에서의 이전 근무 경험

해설 두 번째 단락 마지막 문장에서 강력한 대인 관계 기술과 회사 부서 간 소통 능력은 필수(Strong interpersonal skills and the ability to communicate across company departments are essential)라고 했으므로 (C)가 정답이다.

어휘 background (개인의) 배경 editorial 편집의
previous 이전의

> **Paraphrasing**
> 지문의 Strong interpersonal skills and the ability to communicate → 정답의 Good communication skills

166 Not / True

번역 구인 광고에서 언급한 것이 아닌 것은?
(A) 직무 책임
(B) 근무 시간
(C) 시작일
(D) 학력 요건

해설 첫 단락 두 번째 문장에서 기술 보고서를 검토하고 수정하기 위해 엔지니어들과의 협업이 포함된다(involves collaborating with engineers to review and revise their technical reports)고 했으므로 (A), 같은 단락 세 번째 문장에서 이 정규직의 정규 근무 시간은 월요일부터 금요일까지 오전 9시부터 오후 5시까지(The regular work hours for this full-time position are Monday through Friday, 9:00 A.M. to 5:00 P.M.)라고 했으므로 (B), 세 번째 단락 첫 문장에서 지원자는 학사 학위와 관련 분야에서 최소 2년의 근무 경력이 있어야 한다(Applicants must have a bachelor's degree and at least two years of work experience in a relevant area)고 했으므로 (D)는 광고에 언급되어 있다. 근무 시작일에 대한 내용은 없으므로 (C)가 정답이다.

어휘 requirement 요건

167 문장 삽입

번역 [1], [2], [3], [4]로 표시된 위치 중에서 다음 문장이 들어가기에 가장 적합한 곳은?

"건강 보험과 퇴직 수당이 포함되어 있습니다."

(A) [1]
(B) [2]
(C) [3]
(D) [4]

해설 주어진 문장에서 건강 보험(Health insurance)과 퇴직 수당(retirement benefits)이 포함되어 있다며 복리후생을 언급하고 있으므로, 급여는 경력에 상응하여 결정된다(Salary is commensurate with experience)며 직원에게 주어지는 보상에 대해 안내하고 있는 문장 뒤인 [1]에 들어가는 것이 글의 흐름상 자연스럽다. 따라서 (A)가 정답이다.

어휘 insurance 보험 retirement benefits 퇴직 수당

168-171 기사

랙스포드 공원에 곧 새 정원 생긴다

엘바트 시티 (3월 30일) — 지역 공동체 단체 프렌즈 오브 그린 스페이스(FGS)는 랙스포드 공원에 새로운 정원을 조성할 기금을 모으고 있다. 이 단체는 전적으로 기부에 의존하고 있으며, 복원 및 개선 작업에 있어 시 공원 부서와 협력한다. **168 이 단체는 또한 가이드가 이끄는 자연 탐방과 기타 교육 프로그램도 제공한다.**

169 "현 프로젝트의 목표는 지역의 풍부한 조류를 더 많이 유인하기 위한 매력적인 공간을 만드는 것입니다."라고 FGS의 캐롤 레이노소 소장은 말했다.

레이노소 씨는 FGS의 25년차 회원이자 엘바트 시티의 평생 주민이다. 그녀는 이 프로젝트에 특히 열정을 쏟고 있는데 시의 초등학교가 공원과 맞닿아 있기 때문이다. 이는 초등학생들이 매일 정원을 즐길 수 있음을 의미한다.

레이노소 씨는 FGS가 4월 중순에 정원 조성을 시작할 수 있도록 충분한 기금이 이미 확보되었다고 말했다. **170 식물 선정은 엘바트 대학교 교수진에서 맡을 예정이다. 171 FGS 자원봉사자들은 공원 부서 직원들이 정원으로 지정된 부지에 새 표토를 깐 후 나무를 심을 것이다.** 개장 행사는 5월로 계획되어 있다.

어휘 raise (자금 등을) 모으다 fund 기금; 자금을 대다
rely on ~에 의존하다 entirely 전적으로 donation 기부
restoration 복원 enhancement 개선 guided 가이드가 안내하는 draw in ~을 끌어들이다 abundant 풍부한
enthusiastic 열정적인 border ~와 접하다 secure 확보하다
enable 가능하게 하다 selection 선정 faculty 교수진
topsoil 표토 designate 지정하다

168 Not / True

번역 FGS에 대해 언급된 것은?
(A) 10년 전에 설립되었다.
(B) 가이드가 안내하는 산책을 중단했다.
(C) 자연 관련 강좌를 제공한다.
(D) 시 정부에서 자금을 지원한다.

해설 첫 단락의 마지막 문장에서 이 단체는 가이드가 이끄는 자연 탐방과 기타 교육 프로그램도 제공한다(It also offers guided nature tours and other educational programs)고 소개하고 있으므로 (C)가 정답이다.

어휘 establish 설립하다 discontinue 중단하다

> **Paraphrasing**
> 지문의 educational programs → 정답의 courses

169 세부 사항

번역 FGS가 랙스포드 공원에 정원을 조성하고자 하는 이유는?
(A) 지역 자생 꽃을 전시하려고
(B) 학교 급식을 위한 채소를 재배하려고
(C) 야외 자연 실험실을 만들려고
(D) 다양한 새를 유인하려고

해설 두 번째 단락에서 현 프로젝트의 목표는 지역의 풍부한 조류를 더 많이 유인하기 위한 매력적인 공간을 만드는 것이라고 FGS의 캐롤 레이노소 소장은 말했다("The goal of the current project," said FGS director Carol Reynoso, "is to create an attractive space to draw in more of the region's abundant birdlife.")고 했으므로, FGS는 더 많은 새가 지역에서 서식할 공간을 제공하기 위해 정원을 조성하고자 한다는 것을 알 수 있다. 따라서 (D)가 정답이다.

어휘 native 자생의   laboratory 실험실

> **Paraphrasing**
> 지문의 draw in more of ~ abundant birdlife
> → 정답의 attract a wide variety of birds

170 세부 사항

번역 누가 새 정원을 위한 식물을 선정할 것인가?
(A) 레이노소 씨
(B) 지역 주민들
(C) 대학교 교수들
(D) 초등학생들과 선생님들

해설 네 번째 단락의 두 번째 문장에서 식물 선정은 엘바트 대학교 교수진에서 맡을 예정(The selection of plants will be made by Elbart University faculty)이라고 했으므로 (C)가 정답이다.

> **Paraphrasing**
> 지문의 faculty → 정답의 professors

171 세부 사항

번역 엘바트 시티 직원들이 할 일은?
(A) 기금 모금
(B) 개장 행사 준비
(C) 용품 구입
(D) 나무 심기를 위한 땅 준비

해설 네 번째 단락의 세 번째 문장에서 FGS 자원봉사자들은 공원 부서 직원들이 정원으로 지정된 부지에 새 표토를 깐 후 나무를 심을 것(FGS volunteers will do the planting after parks department crews have laid fresh topsoil on the area designated for the garden)이라고 했으므로, 공원 부서 직원들은 부지에 나무를 심을 수 있도록 토양 준비 작업을 할 예정임을 알 수 있다. 따라서 (D)가 정답이다.

어휘 organize 준비하다, 조직하다   supplies 용품

> **Paraphrasing**
> 지문의 have laid fresh topsoil on the area
> → 정답의 Preparing the ground

172-175 온라인 채팅

에바 파킨 (오후 3시)
모두 안녕하세요. 172 다음 주 금요일 이사회 발표를 논의하기 위해 모여 주셔서 감사합니다. 단 몇 분 안에 우리 주장을 설득해야 해서 준비를 해야 합니다.

니자드 나이페 (오후 3시 1분)
이사회가 우리 예산을 증액해 주지 않을 가능성이 있다고 들었어요. 그들이 공격적인 마케팅에 대한 믿음이 있다고 생각했는데요.

에바 파킨 (오후 3시 2분)
그렇긴 한데 우리 제품에 의구심을 갖고 있어요. 최근 매출 하락에 대해 우려하고 있거든요.

니자드 나이페 (오후 3시 3분)
그렇지만 그건 업계 전체의 추세입니다. 173 이맘때는 보통 판매가 둔화되잖아요.

에바 파킨 (오후 3시 4분)
아주 좋은 지적이에요. 174 저에게 관련 데이터를 보내주실 수 있나요?

니자드 나이페 (오후 3시 5분)
지금 제 화면에 세부 정보가 떠 있어요. 잠깐만요.

에바 파킨 (오후 3시 6분)
172, 175 이사회는 왜 우리가 제안한 마케팅 예산안이 신문이나 라디오보다는 소셜 미디어에 초점을 두고 있는지에 대해서도 물을 거예요. 릴리, 이 점에 대해 도와줄 수 있나요?

릴리 투안 (오후 3시 7분)
물론이죠. 제가 무엇에 대해 이야기를 하면 될까요?

에바 파킨 (오후 3시 8분)
175 그들은 우리가 이런 종류의 광고에 충분한 경험이 있는지 궁금해하고 있어요. 이전 직장에서 이게 당신의 전문 분야였으니 여기서 우리가 사용할 수 있는 적절한 전략에 대해서 말해줄 수 있나요?

릴리 투안 (오후 3시 9분)
네, 문제없습니다. 회의에서 몇 가지 전략을 제시할 수 있어요.

어휘 board of directors 이사회   make one's case 주장하다   possibility 가능성   budget 예산   aggressive 공격적인   concerned 우려하는   recent 최근의   downturn 하락   trend 추세   related 관련된   onscreen 화면에   wonder 궁금해하다   specialty 전문 분야   possible 적절한, 그럴듯한   strategy 전략

172 세부 사항

번역 파킨 씨는 이사회가 무엇을 하기를 원하는가?
(A) 팀의 마케팅 예산 증액
(B) 더 공격적인 급여 체계 채택
(C) 새로운 조직 구조 승인
(D) 제품 개발 전략 지지

해설 오후 3시에 파킨 씨가 다음 주 금요일 이사회 발표를 논의하기 위해 모여 주셔서 감사하다(Thanks for meeting to discuss our presentation to the board of directors next Friday)면서 단 몇 분 안에 우리 주장을 설득해야 해서 준비를 해야 한다(We'll only have a few minutes to make our case, so we must be prepared)고 했고, 3시 6분에 이사회는 왜 우리가 제안한 마케팅 예산안이 신문이나 라디오보다는 소셜 미디어에 초점을 두고 있는지에 대해서도 물을 것(The board will also ask why our proposed marketing budget focuses on social media rather than newspapers or radio)이라고 했다. 이를 통해 파킨 씨는 이사회가 팀의 마케팅 예산안을 승인해 주기를 바라고 있음을 알 수 있으므로 (A)가 정답이다.

어휘 adopt 채택하다 pay scale 급여 체계 organizational 조직의 structure 구조 support 지지하다

173 Not / True

번역 메시지 작성자들이 제품에 대해 명시하는 것은?
(A) 업데이트 되어야 한다.
(B) 소매점에서만 판매되고 있다.
(C) 경쟁사의 제품만큼 인기가 없다.
(D) 일 년 중 특정 시기에는 잘 팔리지 않는다.

해설 오후 3시 3분에 나이페 씨가 이맘때는 보통 판매가 둔화된다(Sales usually slow down this time of year)며 연중 특정 시기가 되면 제품의 판매가 감소한다는 것을 언급하고 있으므로 (D)가 정답이다.

어휘 retail 소매 competitor 경쟁자

Paraphrasing
지문의 Sales usually slow down → 정답의 does not sell well

174 의도 파악

번역 오후 3시 5분에 나이페 씨가 "지금 제 화면에 세부 정보가 떠 있어요"라고 쓴 의도는?
(A) 일부 데이터 오류를 수정할 수 있다.
(B) 파킨 씨의 요청을 이행할 수 있다.
(C) 꼼꼼하게 메모를 해 왔다.
(D) 경쟁사의 제품 관련 정보를 공유할 것이다.

해설 3시 4분에 파킨 씨가 관련 데이터를 보내줄 수 있느냐(Could you send me any related data?)고 묻자 3시 5분에 나이페 씨가 지금 자신의 화면에 세부 정보가 떠 있다(I have the details onscreen right now)고 대답한 것이므로, 나이페 씨는 파킨 씨의 요청에 응해 곧바로 데이터를 보내줄 수 있다는 의도로 한 말임을 알 수 있다. 따라서 (B)가 정답이다.

어휘 correct 수정하다 fulfill 이행하다 thorough 꼼꼼한, 철저한

175 세부 사항

번역 투안 씨는 이전 직장에서 어떤 업무를 주력으로 했는가?
(A) 라디오
(B) 텔레비전
(C) 신문
(D) 소셜 미디어

해설 파킨 씨가 3시 6분에 이사회는 왜 우리가 제안한 마케팅 예산안이 신문이나 라디오보다는 소셜 미디어에 초점을 두고 있는지에 대해서도 물을 것(The board will also ask why our proposed marketing budget focuses on social media rather than newspapers or radio)이라고 했고, 3시 8분에 투안 씨에게 그들은 우리가 이런 종류의 광고에 충분한 경험이 있는지 궁금해하고 있다(They wonder whether we have enough experience in this kind of advertising)면서 이전 직장에서 이게 당신의 전문 분야였다(this was your specialty at your last job)고 했다. 따라서 투안 씨는 소셜 미디어 광고가 주 업무였다는 것을 알 수 있으므로 (D)가 정답이다.

176-180 웹페이지 + 온라인 후기

---

https://www.branxleycycles.com.my/about

| 홈 | 소개 | 쇼핑 | 문의 |

제품에 대하여

우리는 상업용과 개인용 3륜 화물 자전거를 만듭니다. **176 당사의 모든 자전거는 쿠알라룸푸르에 있는 생산 시설에서 현지 장인이 만든 부품으로 수작업으로 제작됩니다.** 40년 넘게 우리는 사람과 지구의 건강 모두에 좋은 고품질의 친환경 자전거를 만들어 왔습니다. 우리는 우리 제품을 자랑스럽게 생각하며 **177 고객들에게 브랭슬리 자전거가 작동하고 있는 모습을 사진으로 찍어 소셜 미디어에 이미지를 공유하도록 권합니다.**

업데이트 — 8월 30일

주문이 급격하게 증가했습니다. 물량을 맞추기 위해 직원들이 초과근무를 하고 있는데도 불구하고 고객들이 자전거를 받기까지는 평소보다 더 오래 걸릴 수 있습니다. 현재, **179 8월 15일 이후 주문된 모든 자전거는 10~12주의 배송 기간이 걸릴 것으로 예상됩니다.** 이 문제에 있어 여러분의 이해에 감사드립니다.

어휘 three-wheeled 3륜의 cargo 화물 commercial 상업의 facility 시설 part 부품 craftspeople 장인 eco-friendly 친환경적인 planet 지구 dramatic 극적인 surge 급등 catch up 따라잡다 currently 현재

---

https://www.consumerreviewsplus.com.my

브랭슬리 자전거 후기

저는 거의 평생 자전거 애호가였습니다. 최근에 저는 가게에서 부피가 큰 물건들을 집으로 가져올 자전거가 필요하다고 생각했습니다. 온라인을 검색하고 동네 가게에 문의해 보았지만 어디에도 제가 원하는 것은 없었습니다. **178 동료와 이야기한 뒤 저는 브랭슬리 자전거에 대해 알게 되었습니다.** 이메일로 그 회사에 연락을 했고, 저의 모든 질문은 신속하고 꼼꼼하게 답변을 받았습니다. **179 저는 8월 20일에 3륜 화물 자전거를 주문했고 단 2주만에 배송을 받았습니다.** 브랭슬리 자전거의 화물 자전거는 지역 업체들 사이에서 인기가 높아졌고 이제는 어디서든 그 자전거들을 볼 수 있습니다. 회사가 그 수요를 **180 충족시킬 수 있다**는 것이 믿기 힘들지만, 그들은 그렇게 하고 있습니다. 저는 브랭슬리 자전거를 구입한 것이 매우 만족스러우며, 동네에서 자전거를 타다가 자전거에 대해 말하는 모든 사람들에게 자전거를 추천합니다.

— 제이슨 스튜어트, 9월 20일

어휘 review 후기 enthusiast 애호가 bulky 부피가 큰 search 검색하다 inquire 문의하다 promptly 신속하게 thoroughly 꼼꼼하게 manage 해내다

176 Not / True

번역 웹페이지에 따르면, 브랭슬리 자전거에 대해 사실인 것은?
(A) 새로운 경영진 하에 있다.
(B) 최근 전시장을 열었다.
(C) 지역에서 공급받은 부품으로 제품을 제작한다.
(D) 제품으로 상을 여러 번 받았다.

해설 웹페이지의 첫 단락 두 번째 문장에서 당사의 모든 자전거는 쿠알라룸푸르에 있는 생산 시설에서 현지 장인이 만든 부품으로 수작업으로 제작된다(All our bicycles are made by hand in our production facility in Kuala Lumpur with parts made by local craftspeople)고 했으므로 브랭슬리 자전거는 지역에서 만든 부품으로 완성된다는 것을 알 수 있다. 따라서 (C)가 정답이다.

어휘 showroom 전시장 source (부품 따위를) 공급하다

Paraphrasing
지문의 parts made by local craftspeople
→ 정답의 locally sourced parts

177 세부 사항

번역 브랭슬리 자전거가 고객들에게 하도록 권장하는 것은?
(A) 단체 자전거 타기에 참여
(B) 온라인에 사진 게시
(C) 제조 시설 방문
(D) 세일 행사에 참석

해설 웹페이지의 첫 단락 마지막 문장에서 고객들에게 브랭슬리 자전거가 작동하고 있는 모습을 사진으로 찍어 소셜 미디어에 이미지를 공유하도록 권한다(we invite our customers to take photos of their Branxley bicycles in action and share the images via social media)고 했으므로 (B)가 정답이다.

어휘 participate in ~에 참여하다 post 게시하다

Paraphrasing
지문의 share the images via social media
→ 정답의 Post photos online

178 세부 사항

번역 후기에 따르면, 스튜어트 씨는 어떻게 브랭슬리 자전거에 대해 알게 되었는가?
(A) 직장에서 동료와 이야기함으로써
(B) 지역 상점을 방문함으로써
(C) 온라인으로 검색함으로써
(D) 전국을 여행함으로써

해설 후기의 네 번째 문장에서 스튜어트 씨는 동료와 이야기한 뒤 브랭슬리 자전거에 대해 알게 되었다(After talking with a coworker, I learned about Branxley Cycles)고 했으므로 (A)가 정답이다.

어휘 colleague 동료

Paraphrasing
지문의 coworker → 정답의 colleague

179 연계

번역 후기 작성자에 대해 결론지을 수 있는 것은?
(A) 고향에서 배달원으로 일한다.
(B) 취미로 자전거 만드는 것을 좋아한다.
(C) 자전거 공장을 개인적으로 견학했다.
(D) 예상보다 주문품을 빨리 받았다.

해설 웹페이지의 두 번째 단락 세 번째 문장에서 8월 15일 이후 주문된 모든 자전거는 10~12주의 배송 기간이 걸릴 것으로 예상된다(we are expecting a delivery time of 10 to 12 weeks for all bicycles ordered on or after August 15)고 했고, 후기의 여섯 번째 문장에서 자신은 8월 20일에 3륜 화물 자전거를 주문했고 단 2주만에 배송을 받았다(I ordered a three-wheeled cargo bicycle from them on August 20 that was delivered in only two weeks)고 했다. 따라서 스튜어트 씨는 비록 8월 15일 이후에 자전거를 주문했지만 예상 배송일보다 훨씬 빨리 제품을 받았다는 것을 알 수 있으므로 (D)가 정답이다.

180 동의어 찾기

번역 후기의 첫 단락 8행의 "meet"와 의미가 가장 가까운 것은?
(A) 도달하다
(B) 만족시키다
(C) 마주치다
(D) 연결하다

해설 의미상 회사가 수요를 '충족시킨다'는 뜻으로 쓰였으므로 '만족시키다, 충족시키다'를 뜻하는 (B) satisfy가 정답이다.

181-185 기사 + 후기

에든버러 (7월 2일) — **181 잭슨 밀른은 가족 사업의 일원이 되는 것이 기분 좋다고 말한다.** 그는 자신이 조직에서 최고의 자리에 있다고 농담을 하고, 어떤 면에서는 정말 그렇다. **181, 182 100년 된 기업인 밀른 어소시에이츠는 이곳 에든버러뿐만 아니라 런던과 뉴욕의 극장에도 좌석을 디자인하고 공급한다.** 이 회사는 그의 증조부 앵거스 밀른이 창립했다. 잭슨 밀른은 공장 작업 현장에서부터 임원실까지 회사의 모든 자리에서 일해왔다. 그는 작년에 회사의 디자인 책임자가 되었다.

"이 좌석들을 제작하는 일은 상당히 까다로울 수 있는데, 특히 오래된 건물의 좌석의 경우가 그렇습니다."라고 **185 135년 된 울프 극장의 좌석을 디자인한 밀른 씨**는 말했다. 이곳은 인기 뮤지컬 〈스카이스크래핑〉이 현재 거의 매일 밤 가득 찬 관객석 앞에서 공연되고 있는 곳이다.

60

"우리의 최우선 과제는 기능성이 뛰어나고 주변과 조화를 이루는 작품을 만드는 것입니다."라고 그는 말했다. "우리는 미적 감성, 실용성, 편리함의 균형을 맞추려고 노력합니다."

어휘 prime 최고의 organisation 조직 supply 공급하다 found 창립하다 great-grandfather 증조부 factory floor (공장의) 작업 현장 executive 임원 suite 공간 packed 가득 찬 house 관객석 priority 우선 사항 functional 기능적인 harmony 조화 surroundings (주변) 환경 balance 균형을 맞추다 aesthetics 미적 정서 practicality 실용성 convenience 편리

도시 여행 후기: 볼 거리, 할 거리 모두 풍성한 에든버러

지난주에 에든버러에서 기분 좋은 하루를 보냈습니다. 이 도시에 25년이 넘도록 꽤 오랜 세월 가지 않았는데 정말 많은 것이 바뀌어 있었어요! **183 하루는 모든 것을 보기에 충분하지 않아서 벌써 늦여름에 한 번 더 여행할 계획을 짜고 있습니다.**

제 친구와 저는 기차를 타고 거기에 갔고, 처음 한 일은 가이드가 안내하는 올드 타운 투어였습니다. 환상적이었어요! 우리는 레드 로즈 카페에서 점심을 먹었는데, 합리적인 가격에 맛있는 음식을 먹는 **184 진가를 아는** 사람들에게 적극 추천합니다. 이날의 하이라이트는 〈스카이스크래핑〉 공연을 관람한 것이었습니다. 정말 멋졌어요! 연기, 줄거리, 노래까지 공연의 모든 것이 좋았습니다. **185 울프 극장은 매력적인 역사적 장소입니다.** 시내에서 긴 하루를 보낸 뒤 우리는 극장의 편안한 새 좌석에 감사했습니다.

— 푸남 난디, 7월 15일

어휘 plenty 풍부한 양 delightful 기분 좋은 quite a while 꽤 오랫동안 guided 가이드가 안내하는 marvellous 훌륭한, 멋진 appreciate 진가를 알아보다 reasonable 합리적인 historical 역사적인 venue 장소 grateful 감사하는

181 주제 / 목적

번역 기사의 목적은?
(A) 가족 소유 상점의 개점을 보도하려고
(B) 성공적인 지역 사업체의 프로필을 알려주려고
(C) 좌석 디자인의 변화를 논의하려고
(D) 현재 상연 중인 극장 공연을 홍보하려고

해설 기사의 첫 단락 첫 문장에서 잭슨 밀른은 가족 사업의 일원이 되는 것이 기분 좋다고 말한다(Jackson Milne says being part of a family business feels good)고 했고, 같은 단락 세 번째 문장에서 100년 된 기업인 밀른 어소시에이츠는 에든버러뿐만 아니라 런던과 뉴욕 극장에도 좌석을 디자인하고 공급한다(The century-old company Milne Associates designs and supplies seats to theatres here in Edinburgh as well as in London and New York)면서 이 회사는 그의 증조부 앵거스 밀른이 창립했다(It was founded by his great-grandfather Angus Milne)고 했다. 가족 기업인 밀른 어소시에이츠에 대한 소개와 기업의 역사를 설명하고 있는 것으로 보아, 기업을 소개하기 위한 기사임을 알 수 있으므로 (B)가 정답이다.

어휘 family-owned 가족 소유의 profile 프로필을 알려주다 promote 홍보하다 production 공연

182 Not / True

번역 기사에서 앵거스 밀른에 대해 명시된 것은?
(A) 매년 뉴욕으로 여행을 했다.
(B) 자신의 회사를 런던에서 에든버러로 옮겼다.
(C) 100년 전에 회사를 창립했다.
(D) 인기 있는 뮤지컬을 썼다.

해설 기사의 첫 단락 세 번째 문장에서 100년 된 기업인 밀른 어소시에이츠는 에든버러뿐만 아니라 런던과 뉴욕의 극장에도 좌석을 디자인하고 공급한다(The century-old company Milne Associates designs and supplies seats to theatres here in Edinburgh as well as in London and New York)면서 이 회사는 그의 증조부 앵거스 밀른이 창립했다(It was founded by his great-grandfather Angus Milne)고 했으므로, 앵거스 밀른은 100년 전 밀른 어소시에이츠라는 기업을 창립했음을 알 수 있다. 따라서 (C)가 정답이다.

> **Paraphrasing**
> 지문의 century → 정답의 100 years
> 지문의 founded → 정답의 created

183 Not / True

번역 난디 씨가 자신의 후기에서 언급한 것은?
(A) 7월 초에 가족들과 여행을 갔다.
(B) 에든버러에 다시 가고 싶어 한다.
(C) 〈스카이스크래핑〉을 여러 차례 봤다.
(D) 에든버러의 올드 타운에 살았었다.

해설 후기의 첫 단락 세 번째 문장에서 난디 씨가 하루는 모든 것을 보기에 충분하지 않아서 벌써 늦여름에 한 번 더 여행할 계획을 짜고 있다(One day was not enough to see everything, so I'm already planning another trip for later in the summer)고 했으므로 난디 씨는 올여름 에든버러에 다시 가려 한다는 것을 알 수 있으므로 (B)가 정답이다.

184 동의어 찾기

번역 후기의 두 번째 단락 3행의 "appreciates"와 의미가 가장 가까운 것은?
(A) 소중하게 생각하다
(B) 증가시키다
(C) 이해하다
(D) 알다

해설 의미상 합리적인 가격에 맛있는 음식을 먹는 '진가를 안다'는 뜻으로 쓰였으므로 '소중하게 생각하다, 가치를 두다'를 뜻하는 (A) values가 정답이다.

185 연계

번역 난디 씨에 대해 결론지을 수 있는 것은?
(A) 에든버러 여행을 기대하지 않았다.
(B) 레드 로즈 카페가 너무 비싸다고 생각한다.
(C) 울프 극장에서 자주 공연을 본다.
(D) 밀른 어소시에이츠의 제품과 관련해 좋은 경험을 했다.

해설 기사의 두 번째 단락 첫 문장에서 밀른 씨가 135년 된 울프 극장의 좌석을 디자인했다(Mr. Milne, who designed the seats for the 135-year-old Wolff Theatre)고 했고, 후기의 두 번째 단락 일곱 번째 문장에서 난디 씨는 울프 극장은 매력적인 역사적 장소 (The Wolff Theatre is a lovely historical venue)이며 시내에서 긴 하루를 보낸 뒤 우리는 극장의 편안한 새 좌석에 감사했다 (After our long day around town, we were grateful for the theatre's new, comfortable seating)고 했다. 따라서 난디 씨는 밀른 어소시에이츠의 밀른 씨가 디자인한 울프 극장의 좌석 덕분에 편안하게 공연을 즐겼다는 것을 알 수 있으므로 (D)가 정답이다.

어휘 overpriced 너무 비싼 frequently 자주

186-190 웹페이지 + 이메일 + 이메일

---

https://www.orvalenaturalhistorymuseum.org/upcomingevents

| 홈 | 전시 | 예정된 행사 | 연락처 |

오르베일 자연사 박물관의 월간 강연 시리즈는 10월 18일에 상근 고고학자인 마리아 피알로 박사의 강연으로 계속됩니다. **188 "중부 대초원의 도기 유물"이라는 제목의 이 강연은 박물관 북문 근처의 초비 커뮤니티 룸에서 오후 7시에 열립니다.** 피알로 박사는 지난달에 있었던 중부 대초원 지역에서의 도기 조각 발굴 작업에 대해 논의할 예정으로, 이는 해당 지역에서 도기가 발견된 첫 사례라고 한다. "놀랍게도, **186 그 현장은 자기 땅에서 우물을 파던 농부에 의해 말 그대로 우연히 발견되었습니다.** 감사하게도, 그는 조각들을 발견하자마자 우리 박물관의 연구팀에 알려왔습니다."라고 피알로 박사는 말했다.

190 참석자들은 행사에서 여러 유형의 일상 용품들과 더불어 일부 도기들을 가까이서 보게 됩니다. 하지만 **187 다수의 유물들은 너무 부서지기 쉬운 상태라 이동이 어려워 사진으로 전시될 예정입니다.** 피알로 박사는 이 최근의 발견을 공유할 일이 기대된다고 말합니다. **"190 이 유물들은 800여 년 전 사람들이 어떻게 일상생활을 영위했는지를 엿볼 수 있게 해 줍니다."** 라고 그녀는 말했다.

이 강연은 무료이며 일반 시민에게 개방됩니다.

어휘 upcoming 예정된, 다가오는 resident 상주하는 archaeologist 고고학자 earthenware 도기의 relic 유물 prairie 대초원 take place 열리다 unearth 발굴하다 pottery 도자기 region 지역 literally 말 그대로 stumble upon ~을 우연히 발견하다 dig 파다 well 우물 alert 알리다 spot 발견하다 up close 가까이에서 object 물건 delicate 연약한 latest 최신의 discovery 발견 findings 조사 결과물 glimpse 엿봄

수신: 리처드 최
발신: 데보라 볼
날짜: 10월 11일
제목: 강연 시리즈

안녕하세요, 리처드,

저는 방금 오르베일 대학교 고고학부의 앨런 휘트포드 교수로부터 연락을 받았습니다. 그는 자신의 수업 2개의 학생들을 10월 18일에 있을 피알로 박사의 강연에 데려오고 싶어 합니다. 두 수업 모두 역사 유물을 식별하고 분석하는 방법을 공부하고 있어서 그는 이번 달 우리 강연 주제를 매우 마음에 들어 했습니다. 더욱이 휘트포드 교수는 피알로 박사의 과거 연구 동료입니다. 저는 지지 의사를 보여드리고 싶지만, 참석을 원하는 일반 시민들에 추가로 그가 데려오려고 계획 중인 약 30명의 학생들이 수용 가능한지를 먼저 확인하고 싶습니다.

188 75석 이상이 필요할 것이므로, 강연을 박물관 내 다른 장소로 옮기는 것을 검토해 봅시다. 대체 공간이 몇 군데 있겠죠? 휘트포드 교수에게 가능한 한 빨리 답변을 드리고 싶습니다.

데브

어휘 archaeology 고고학 identify 식별하다 analyze 분석하다 artifact (역사적) 인공물 what's more 더욱이 former 이전의 colleague 동료 inclined ~하고 싶은 indicate 보여 주다 accommodate 수용하다 approximately 대략

수신: 마리아 피알로 <mfiallo@orvalenaturalhistorymuseum.org>
발신: 앨런 휘트포드 <awhitford@orvaleuniversity.edu>
날짜: 10월 19일
제목: 강연

피알로 박사님께,

어제 저녁 유익한 강연에 정말 감사드립니다. **190 제 학생들은 전시 테이블 위 도기들을 가까이서 보게 되어 아주 신났습니다.** 그들은 특히 전시품들 사이에 포함된 석기들에 깊은 감명을 받았습니다. 그 유물들이 그동안 이렇게 가까이 있었다는 사실은 제 학생들이 생각하기에 참으로 놀라운 일이었습니다. 그 유물들이 오르베일 자연사 박물관에 안전하게 있다는 것이 정말 기쁜데요, 그곳이 이러한 보물들을 잘 관리할 수 있는 곳임을 알기 때문입니다.

189 박사님께서 오르베일 대학교의 저희 팀과 함께 저희가 계획 중인 몇 가지 흥미로운 연구 프로젝트에 협업해 주십사하는 저의 제안을 고려해 주시기 바랍니다. 관심 있으실 경우 저에게 알려주시면 제가 세부 사항을 전달해 드리겠습니다.

앨런 휘트포드

어휘 informative 유익한 thrilled 아주 신이 난 impressed 감명받은 stone tool 석기 contemplate 생각하다 steward 관리인 treasure 보물 collaborate 협업하다, 협력하다 forward 전달하다

186 세부 사항

번역 웹페이지에 따르면, 최근 발견을 한 사람은 누구인가?
(A) 농부
(B) 고고학자
(C) 역사학자
(D) 사진작가

해설 웹페이지의 첫 단락 네 번째 문장에서 그 현장은 자기 땅에서 우물을 파던 농부에 의해 말 그대로 우연히 발견되었다(the site was literally stumbled upon by a farmer digging a well on his land)고 했으므로 최근 유적지를 발견한 사람은 농부임을 알 수 있다. 따라서 (A)가 정답이다.

187 세부 사항

번역 강연 도중 일부 물품들은 직접 볼 수 없는 이유는?
(A) 세척 중이다.
(B) 너무 깨지기 쉽다.
(C) 너무 크다.
(D) 다른 장소에 있다.

해설 웹페이지의 두 번째 단락 두 번째 문장에서 다수의 유물들은 너무 부서지기 쉬운 상태라 이동이 어려워 사진으로 전시될 예정(many of the pieces will be shown in photographs, as they are too delicate to be moved around)이라고 했으므로 (B)가 정답이다.

어휘 fragile 깨지기 쉬운

> **Paraphrasing**
> 지문의 delicate → 정답의 fragile

188 연계

번역 초비 커뮤니티 룸에 대해 암시된 것은?
(A) 매일 오후 7시에 문을 연다.
(B) 입장을 위해 특별한 출입증이 필요하다.
(C) 75명 이하만 앉을 수 있다.
(D) 박물관 남문 근처에 있다.

해설 웹페이지의 첫 단락 두 번째 문장에서 "중부 대초원의 도기 유물"이라는 제목의 이 강연은 박물관 북문 근처의 초비 커뮤니티 룸에서 오후 7시에 열린다(The lecture, titled "Earthenware Relics from the Central Prairie," will take place at 7:00 P.M. in the Chovey Community Room near the north entrance of the museum)고 했고, 첫 번째 이메일의 두 번째 단락 첫 문장에서 75석 이상이 필요할 것이므로 강연을 박물관 내 다른 장소로 옮기는 것을 검토해 보자(We will need more than 75 seats, so let's discuss moving the lecture to another location in the museum)고 했다. 따라서 초비 커뮤니티 룸은 75명이 넘는 인원은 수용할 수 없다는 것을 알 수 있으므로 (C)가 정답이다.

어휘 seat 앉히다

189 세부 사항

번역 두 번째 이메일에 따르면, 휘트포드 교수는 피알로 박사가 무엇을 하기를 원하는가?
(A) 박물관에서 그와의 회의를 잡기
(B) 일부 유물을 그의 교실로 가져오기
(C) 대학교에서 그녀의 강연을 다시 하기
(D) 연구 프로젝트에 협력하기

해설 두 번째 이메일의 두 번째 단락 첫 문장에서 휘트포드 교수가 피알로 박사에게 오르베일 대학교의 저희 팀과 함께 저희가 계획 중인 몇 가지 흥미로운 연구 프로젝트에 협업하자는 제안을 고려하기를 바란다(I hope you will consider my invitation to collaborate with my team and me here at Orvale University on some exciting research projects we have planned)고 했으므로 (D)가 정답이다.

190 연계

번역 휘트포드 교수의 학생들이 본 도구에 대해 암시된 것은?
(A) 연구 목적을 위해 대학교에 기증될 것이다.
(B) 진열장 유리 안에 있었다.
(C) 800년 이상 되었다.
(D) 여전히 사용되고 있다.

해설 웹페이지의 두 번째 단락 첫 문장에서 참석자들은 행사에서 여러 유형의 일상 용품들과 더불어 일부 도기들을 가까이서 보게 된다(Audiences will get to see some of the earthenware up close at the event, as well as other types of everyday objects)고 했고, 같은 단락 마지막 문장에서 이 유물들은 800여 년 전 사람들이 어떻게 일상생활을 영위했는지를 엿볼 수 있게 해 준다(The findings give us a glimpse into how people went about their daily lives over 800 years ago)고 했다. 그리고 두 번째 이메일의 첫 단락 두 번째 문장에서 휘트포드 교수의 학생들은 전시 테이블 위 도기들을 가까이서 보게 되어 아주 신났다(My students were thrilled to see some of the pottery up close on the display table)고 했으므로, 휘트포드 교수의 학생들이 강연에서 가까이 본 유물은 800여 년 전에 사용된 도구들임을 알 수 있다. 따라서 (C)가 정답이다.

어휘 donate 기증하다 purpose 목적

191-195 일정표 + 이메일 + 이메일

6월					
	월요일 7	화요일 8	**191** 수요일 9	목요일 10	**194** 금요일 11
오전 9시	사무실에 없음 (보스턴에서 열리는 안경 세미나로부터 이동 중)		**191** 데이터 보안 교육	사무실에 없음 (개인 일정)	주간 계획 및 검토
오전 10시		예산 회의	이메일 검토 및 정리		
오전 11시					
오후 12시					
오후 1시		지원자 면접	인사부 회의	영업 검토 회의	**194** 기술 업데이트
194 오후 2시					
오후 3시					

| 어휘 | eyewear 안경류 security 보안 review 검토 budget 예산 applicant 지원자 |

수신: 신디 위버
발신: 사라 모어랜드
날짜: 6월 7일, 오전 6시 31분
제목: 복귀 지연

안녕하세요, 신디 씨.

돌아가는 항공편이 방금 취소되어서 다음 이용 가능한 항공편은 내일 아침에 있습니다. **191** 데이터 보안 교육 시간에 맞춰 사무실에 들어갈 것으로 예상되지만 **192** 제 일정을 조정하는 데 당신의 도움이 필요합니다.

- **192** 예산 회의는 이번 주에 열려야 하므로 팀에 연락해서 다른 시간을 잡아주세요. 저의 금요일 아침 계획 시간은 사용해도 되지만 목요일 아침의 개인 시간은 안 됩니다.
- 이번 주 후반에 선별된 지원자들의 면접을 보고 싶은데, 후보자들이 가능하다면 아마 금요일 오후가 될 것 같으니 그들에게 전화해서 확인해주세요. 이와 관련해서, **193** 모든 면접이 끝난 후에야 인사부 직원들과 회의를 할 수 있으니 다음 주 초로 회의를 다시 잡아주세요.
- 세미나에서 홍보된 새 안경들에 대해 마케팅 팀에게 전할 중대한 소식이 있습니다. 수요일 오후에 그들이 회의를 할 수 있는지 확인해 주시겠어요?

사라 모어랜드

| 어휘 | delayed 지연된 in time for ~에 시간 맞춰 rearrange 재조정하다 occur 발생하다 selected 선별된 applicant 지원자 candidate 후보자 amenable 잘 받아들이는 in connection with ~와 관련하여 promote 홍보하다 |

수신: 사라 모어랜드
발신: 신디 위버
날짜: 6월 7일, 오후 2시 31분
제목: 회신: 복귀 지연

좋은 오후입니다, 모어랜드 씨,

요청하신 대로 일정표 작업을 하고 있습니다. 금요일 오전 10시로 예산 회의를 옮겼습니다. **194** 에릭 김이 금요일 오후 2시 당신과의 회의에서 공유할 중요한 새 정보가 없다고 하니 그 회의를 연기할 수 있습니다. 다행히도, 모든 지원자들이 금요일 오후에 면접을 보겠다고 동의했고, 인사부 회의를 다음 주 월요일 오전 9시로 옮겼습니다.

195 마케팅 팀 전원에 연락이 닿지 못해 새 안경에 대해 논의하기 위한 회의를 잡지 못했습니다. 계속 시도하겠습니다.

신디

| 어휘 | critical 중요한 postpone 연기하다 get through to ~에 연락하다 |

---

191 연계

번역 모어랜드 씨는 언제 사무실로 복귀할 예정인가?
(A) 화요일
(B) 수요일
(C) 목요일
(D) 금요일

해설 첫 번째 이메일의 첫 단락 두 번째 문장에서 모어랜드 씨는 데이터 보안 교육 시간에 맞춰 사무실에 들어갈 것으로 예상된다(I expect to return to the office just in time for the data security training)고 했고, 일정표 상단에서 수요일(Wednesday)에 데이터 보안 교육(Data security training) 일정이 있음을 확인할 수 있다. 따라서 (B)가 정답이다.

192 추론 / 암시

번역 위버 씨는 누구인 것 같은가?
(A) 여행사 직원
(B) 안경 판매원
(C) 회계사
(D) 임원 비서

해설 첫 번째 이메일의 첫 단락 두 번째 문장에서 모어랜드 씨가 위버 씨에게 일정을 조정하는 데 당신의 도움이 필요하다(I need your help rearranging my calendar)고 하면서, 두 번째 단락 첫 문장에서 예산 회의는 이번 주에 열려야 하므로 팀에 연락해서 다른 시간을 잡아달라(The budget meeting needs to occur this week, so please contact the team to schedule another time)고 요청하고 있다. 모어랜드 씨가 자신의 일정을 조정해달라고 부탁하면서 회의 일정 변경과 팀원 연락 등의 업무를 맡기고 있는 점을 통해 위버 씨는 모어랜드 씨의 비서임을 유추할 수 있으므로 (D)가 정답이다.

어휘 agent 대리인

193 추론 / 암시

번역 첫 번째 이메일에 따르면, 인사부 회의에서 논의될 가능성이 있는 것은?
(A) 면접 결과
(B) 예산 수정 사항
(C) 새로운 일정 소프트웨어의 필요성
(D) 새 안경 모델

해설 첫 번째 이메일의 세 번째 단락 마지막 문장에서 모든 면접이 끝난 후에야 인사부 직원들과 회의를 할 수 있으니 다음 주 초로 회의를 다시 잡아달라(I need to meet with human resources staff only after all the interviews are done; please reschedule that meeting to sometime early next week)고 언급한 부분을 통해 인사부 회의에서는 면접 결과에 대해 논의할 예정임을 짐작할 수 있다. 따라서 (A)가 정답이다.

어휘 result 결과 revision 수정 (사항)

194 연계

번역 모어랜드 씨와 김 씨가 만나는 회의의 주제는?
(A) 인사 정책
(B) 기술 업데이트
(C) 주간 계획
(D) 마케팅 전략

해설 두 번째 이메일의 첫 단락 세 번째 문장에서 에릭 김이 금요일 오후 2시 모어랜드 씨와의 회의에서 공유할 중요한 새 정보가 없다고 한다(Eric Kim says that he has no critical new information to share with you at his 2:00 P.M. meeting with you on Friday)고 했고, 일정표의 금요일(Friday) 오후 2시(2:00 P.M.)에 기술 업데이트(Technology updates) 일정이 잡혀 있음을 확인할 수 있다. 따라서 모어랜드 씨와 김 씨의 금요일 오후 2시 회의 주제는 기술 업데이트이므로 (B)가 정답이다.

어휘 policy 정책

195 세부 사항

번역 위버 씨가 하겠다고 명시하는 것은?
(A) 호텔에 하룻밤 추가 예약
(B) 몇몇 마케팅 팀원들에게 연락 시도
(C) 새 안경 주문
(D) 모어랜드 씨의 사무실이 청소되었는지 확인

해설 두 번째 이메일의 두 번째 단락에서 위버 씨가 마케팅 팀 전원에 연락이 닿지 못해 새 안경에 대해 논의하기 위한 회의를 잡지 못했다(I have been unable to get through to every marketing team member to set up a meeting to discuss the new eyewear)면서 계속 시도하겠다(I will keep trying)고 했다. 따라서 위버 씨는 마케팅 팀 전원에게 연락이 닿을 때까지 계속 연락을 해보겠다는 것이므로 (B)가 정답이다.

어휘 reserve 예약하다 attempt 시도하다

> **Paraphrasing**
> 지문의 get through to → 정답의 contact
> 지문의 trying → 정답의 Attempt

196-200 웹페이지 + 이메일 + 웹페이지 ▶동영상 강의

```
https://www.musiclinkplus.ie/home
```
| 홈 | 구인 목록 | 음악가 프로필 | 자료실 |

뮤직 링크 플러스(MLP)는 음악 업계의 구직자와 채용 담당자를 지원합니다.

구직자들은: 무료 MLP 프로필을 만드는 것으로 시작하세요. 그러면 구인 목록 페이지에서 취업 기회를 모두 열람할 수 있게 됩니다. **200** 자료실 페이지에서는 오디션 준비를 돕기 위한 악보 및 가수들의 녹음 파일을 제공합니다. **200** 이 페이지에는 또한 채용 담당자가 영상 샘플을 요구할 경우 녹화 영상을 제작하고 우리 웹사이트에 업로드하는 방법에 대한 전체적인 지침도 포함되어 있습니다.

198 채용 담당자들은: 300유로의 초기 수수료를 지불하고 계정을 개설하는 것으로 시작하시고, 그 이후에는 매년 150유로가 부과됩니다. 계정에는 무제한으로 구인 목록을 게시할 권한이 주어집니다. 또한 지원자가 연주하기를 원하는 곡을 당사에서 제공하는 폭넓은 목록으로부터 고르실 수 있습니다. 지원자들은 이 웹사이트에 자신의 오디션 영상을 바로 업로드할 수 있습니다.

어휘 support 지원하다 job seeker 구직자 recruiter 채용 담당자 access 접근 employment 취업 opportunity 기회 sheet music 악보 feature 포함하다 instruction 지침 initial 초기의 charge 부과하다 entitle 권한을 주다 perform 연주하다 right 바로

수신: 재니스 트라파니, 합창단 단장
발신: 케빈 엘리스, 총괄 관리자
198 날짜: 7월 7일
제목: 가을 일정 계획

안녕하세요, 재니스,

가을 일정에 영향을 주는 몇 가지 문제에 대해 알려드리고자 합니다.

- 예술 위원회가 우리 그레이디 시티 합창단에 11월에 **196** 그레이디 시티 출신의 제프리 스톨라츠가 작곡한 성가극 〈초원에서〉라는 특별한 곡을 초연해 달라고 요청해 왔습니다. 이 작품을 연주하도록 선정된 것은 크나큰 영광입니다! 이 추가 일정으로 우리 가을 라인업이 완성됩니다.

- **197** 안타깝게도, 8월 리허설이 시작되기 전에 가수 두 명을 교체해야 한다는 사실을 지난주 늦게 알게 되었습니다. 벌써 7월이 일주일이나 지나고 있어서, **198** 모집을 속행할 수 있도록 뮤직 링크 플러스(MLP)에 오늘 아침 계정을 개설했습니다. 내일 그들의 구인 목록 페이지에 우리의 채용 공고를 게시할 계획입니다. 이 웹사이트를 이용하면 수많은 잠재적 지원자들에게 닿을 수 있습니다. 게다가 MLP는 지원자들이 녹화 영상을 제공해 오디션을 볼 수 있는 옵션도 제공합니다. 시간이 제약된 상황이므로 이 같은 방식으로 오디션을 진행하는 것을 고려해야 합니다. 하지만 대면 오디션이 필수적이라고 생각하신다면 오늘까지 저에게 알려주십시오.

케빈

어휘 choir 합창단 general 총괄의 affect 영향을 미치다 commission 위원회 debut 초연하다 oratorio 성가극 meadow 초원 honour 영광 composition 작품 replace 교체하다 rehearsal 리허설 expedite 신속히 처리하다 reach 도달하다 countless 수없이 많은 potential 잠재적인 constraint 제약 in-person 대면의

```
https://www.musiclinkplus.ie/joblistings
```
| 홈 | **구인 목록** | 음악가 프로필 | 자료실 |

가수 직책 (그레이디 시티 합창단)

게시일: 7월 8일

지원 마감일: 7월 21일

그레이디 시티 합창단에서 가을 시즌을 위해 알토와 테너, 두 명의 가수를 구합니다. **199 합격한 지원자는 재니스 트라파니의 지휘 아래 열정적인 우리 합창단에 합류하게 되며 8월 11일 가을 공연 리허설을 위해 노이프리드 강당으로 출석해야 합니다.**

200 지원자는 오디션 영상을 제출해야 합니다. 자료실 페이지의 지침을 따라 주세요. 우리는 지원자들이 부를 곡으로 프랑카 버만의 〈잔잔한 물 칸타타〉 중 일부를 선정했습니다. 채용 결과 통지는 8월 4일에 개인 이메일 주소로 발송됩니다.

> **어휘** vocalist 가수 post 게시하다 application 지원 report to ~으로 출근하다 auditorium 강당 supply 제공하다 portion 부분 still 잔잔한, 고요한 notification 통지

196 Not / True

번역 스톨라츠 씨에 대해 명시된 것은?
(A) 원래 그레이디 시티 출신이다.
(B) 합창 공연을 지휘할 것이다.
(C) 그레이디 시티 합창단에서 노래했었다.
(D) 전임 합창단 지휘자이다.

해설 이메일의 두 번째 단락 첫 문장에서 스톨라츠 씨에 대해 그레이디 시티 출신의 제프리 스톨라츠(Gradey City's own Jeffrey Stolartz)라고 했으므로 (A)가 정답이다.

어휘 originally 원래 former 이전의

> **Paraphrasing**
> 지문의 Gradey City's own Jeffrey Stolartz
> → 정답의 from Gradey City

197 세부 사항

번역 이메일에 따르면, 엘리스 씨가 걱정하는 것은?
(A) 가을 공연 홍보
(B) 짧은 기간에 가수 채용
(C) 〈초원에서〉의 부분 학습
(D) 새로운 합창단 지휘자 훈련

해설 이메일의 세 번째 단락 첫 문장에서 엘리스 씨는 안타깝게도, 8월 리허설이 시작되기 전에 가수 두 명을 교체해야 한다는 사실을 지난주 늦게 알게 되었다(Unfortunately, I learned late last week that two singers need to be replaced before rehearsals begin in August)며 벌써 7월이 일주일이나 지나고 있다(we are already one week into July)고 우려를 표하고 있다. 따라서 엘리스 씨는 짧은 기간 안에 가수 두 명을 채용해야 하는 점을 걱정하고 있으므로 (B)가 정답이다.

198 연계

번역 엘리스 씨가 7월 7일에 한 일 중 한 가지는?
(A) MLP에 할인을 요청했다.
(B) 두 번의 오디션 일정을 잡았다.
(C) MLP에 수수료 300유로를 지불했다.
(D) 스톨라츠 씨에게 연락했다.

해설 이메일의 작성 날짜가 7월 7일(Date: 7 July)이고 세 번째 단락 두 번째 문장에서 엘리스 씨는 모집을 속행할 수 있도록 뮤직 링크 플러스(MLP)에 오늘 아침 계정을 개설했다(I opened an account with Music Link Plus (MLP) this morning to expedite our search)고 했으며, 첫 번째 웹페이지의 세 번째 단락 첫 문장에서 채용 담당자들은 300유로의 초기 수수료를 지불하고 계정을 개설하는 것으로 시작하라(For Recruiters: Begin by opening an account by paying an initial fee of €300)고 나와 있다. 따라서 엘리스 씨는 7월 7일 아침에 MLP에 계정을 개설하면서 초기 수수료 300유로를 지불했다는 것을 알 수 있으므로 (C)가 정답이다.

199 세부 사항

번역 가을 공연을 위한 연습 시간은 언제 시작되는가?
(A) 7월 8일
(B) 7월 21일
(C) 8월 4일
(D) 8월 11일

해설 두 번째 웹페이지의 첫 단락 두 번째 문장에서 합격한 지원자는 8월 11일 가을 공연 리허설을 위해 노이프리드 강당으로 출석해야 한다(Successful candidates ~ will be expected to report to Neufried Auditorium on 11 August for autumn performance rehearsals)고 했으므로 8월 11일에 가을 공연 연습이 시작된다는 것을 알 수 있다. 따라서 (D)가 정답이다.

> **Paraphrasing**
> 지문의 rehearsals → 질문의 practice sessions

200 연계

번역 그레이디 시티 합창단 오디션을 보기 위해 지원자들이 해야 할 일은?
(A) 그레이디 시티 합창단 단원과 함께 선곡된 곡 부르기
(B) 면접 약속 요청하기
(C) 자신이 부르고 싶은 곡 고르기
(D) 자료실 페이지를 방문하여 녹화 영상 업로드하기

해설 두 번째 웹페이지의 두 번째 단락 첫 문장에서 지원자는 오디션 영상을 제출해야 한다(Applicants must supply an audition video)면서 자료실 페이지의 지침을 따라달라(Simply follow the instructions on the Resources page)고 했고, 첫 번째 웹페이지의 두 번째 단락 세 번째 문장에서 자료실 페이지(Our Resources page)를 언급한 뒤, 이 페이지에는 채용 담당자가 영상 샘플을 요구할 경우 녹화 영상을 제작하고 우리 웹사이트에 업로드하는 방법에 대한 전체적인 지침도 포함되어 있다(The page also features complete instructions on how to create and upload a video recording to our Web site if a recruiter requests a video sample from you)고 했다. 따라서 합창단 지원자들은 오디션을 보기 위해 자료실 페이지를 방문하여 그곳에 게시된 지침에 따라 녹화 영상을 제작해 업로드해야 한다는 것을 알 수 있으므로 (D)가 정답이다.

기출 TEST 4

101 (D)	102 (B)	103 (B)	104 (C)	105 (B)
106 (A)	107 (B)	108 (A)	109 (B)	110 (C)
111 (B)	112 (A)	113 (B)	114 (A)	115 (C)
116 (D)	117 (A)	118 (A)	119 (B)	120 (A)
121 (C)	122 (D)	123 (D)	124 (A)	125 (C)
126 (D)	127 (C)	128 (C)	129 (A)	130 (D)
131 (C)	132 (D)	133 (D)	134 (C)	135 (C)
136 (A)	137 (D)	138 (B)	139 (A)	140 (C)
141 (D)	142 (B)	143 (B)	144 (A)	145 (C)
146 (D)	147 (A)	148 (D)	149 (B)	150 (D)
151 (A)	152 (D)	153 (C)	154 (D)	155 (B)
156 (B)	157 (C)	158 (D)	159 (D)	160 (C)
161 (A)	162 (B)	163 (C)	164 (C)	165 (D)
166 (C)	167 (B)	168 (A)	169 (B)	170 (B)
171 (D)	172 (A)	173 (D)	174 (D)	175 (A)
176 (C)	177 (B)	178 (D)	179 (C)	180 (A)
181 (B)	182 (A)	183 (D)	184 (C)	185 (B)
186 (B)	187 (A)	188 (B)	189 (D)	190 (C)
191 (C)	192 (B)	193 (B)	194 (A)	195 (D)
196 (A)	197 (D)	198 (C)	199 (B)	200 (A)

PART 5

101 인칭대명사의 격 _ 주격

해설 빈칸은 접속사 that이 이끄는 명사절에서 동사 is planning의 주어 역할을 하는 자리이므로, 주격 인칭대명사 (D) she가 정답이다. (A) her는 소유격 또는 목적격, 재귀대명사 (C) herself는 주어 자리에 들어갈 수 없고, (B) hers는 소유대명사로 주어 역할을 할 수는 있으나 '그녀의 것'으로 받을만한 대상이 없으므로 답이 될 수 없다.

번역 추 씨는 최근 그녀가 9월에 은퇴할 계획이라고 발표했다.

어휘 retire 은퇴하다

102 전치사 어휘

해설 빈칸 뒤의 시점을 나타내는 명사 the holiday를 목적어로 취해 '휴일 이전에 면접을 볼 것이다'라는 의미가 되어야 자연스러우므로 '~이전에'를 뜻하는 (B) before가 정답이다. (A) above는 '~ 위에', (C) among은 '~ 사이에', (D) along은 '~을 따라'라는 의미이다.

번역 카슈니츠 씨는 휴일 이전에 지원자들과 면접을 볼 것이다.

어휘 applicant 지원자

103 동사 어형 _ 조동사 + 동사원형

해설 앞에 조동사 may가 있으므로 빈칸에는 동사원형이 와야 한다. 따라서 동사원형 (B) provide가 정답이다. (A) providing은 동명사/현재분사, (C) provided는 동사/과거분사, (D) provides는 단수 동사이므로 답이 될 수 없다.

번역 부동산 중개인은 구매자가 요청하면 인근 지역 분석을 제공할 수 있다.

어휘 real estate agent 부동산 중개인 upon request 요청 시

104 명사 어휘

해설 전치사 for의 목적어 역할을 하는 명사 자리로, to plant a community garden의 수식을 받아 적절한 문맥을 이뤄야 한다. '지역 정원을 조성할 장소'라는 내용이 되어야 자연스러우므로 '장소, 위치'를 뜻하는 (C) location이 정답이다. (A) flower는 '꽃', (B) topic은 '주제', (D) show는 '공연'이라는 의미이다.

번역 도시 개발 위원회는 지역 정원을 조성할 장소를 찾고 있다.

어휘 committee 위원회

105 형용사 자리 _ 명사 수식

해설 빈칸 앞에 부정관사 a가 있고, 뒤에 명사 manner가 있으므로 빈칸은 명사를 수식하는 형용사 자리이다. 따라서 '만족스러운'을 뜻하는 형용사 (B) satisfactory가 정답이다. (A) satisfy는 동사, (C) satisfaction은 명사, (D) satisfactorily는 부사이므로 빈칸에 들어갈 수 없다.

번역 저희 고객 서비스 팀이 귀하의 질문에 만족스러운 방식으로 답변을 드렸기를 바랍니다.

어휘 manner 방식

106 부사 어휘

해설 빈칸은 명사 position을 뒤에서 꾸며주는 과거분사 held를 수식하는 부사 자리이다. '아켈로 씨가 이전에 맡았던 직책'이라는 내용이 되어야 자연스러우므로 '이전에'를 뜻하는 (A) previously가 정답이다. (B) slowly는 '천천히', (C) widely는 '널리', (D) loosely는 '느슨하게'라는 의미이다.

번역 한리 씨는 아켈로 씨가 이전에 맡았던 직책에 관심을 표현했다.

107 동사 자리 _ 태

해설 부사절 접속사 Once가 이끄는 절의 동사 자리로, 뒤에 목적어인 명사 the contract가 왔으므로 능동태가 들어가야 한다. 따라서 동사 (B) receives가 정답이다. (A) to receive는 to부정사, (C) was received는 수동태이므로 답이 될 수 없고, (D) receiving은 동명사/현재분사로 동사 자리에 들어갈 수 없다. 참고로, 조건을 나타내는 절에서는 현재시제 동사가 미래를 나타낸다.

번역 정 씨는 일단 계약서를 받고 나면, 거기에 서명하여 알로리 제약 회사로 반납할 것이다.

어휘 contract 계약(서)   pharmaceuticals 제약 회사

108 형용사 어휘

해설 빈칸 뒤의 to부정사구 to approve the proposal의 수식을 받아 '제안을 승인하기에 충분하다'는 의미가 되어야 자연스러우므로 to부정사와 함께 쓰여 '~할 만큼 충분한'을 뜻하는 (A) enough가 정답이다. (B) several은 '몇몇의', (C) most는 '대부분의'라는 의미이고, (D) those는 '저'를 뜻하는 지시형용사로 뒤에 복수 명사가 온다.

번역 10명의 이사가 참석할 계획이며, 이는 제안을 승인하기에 충분하다.

어휘 board member 이사   approve 승인하다
proposal 제안(서)

109 명사 자리 _ 현재분사의 목적어

해설 빈칸은 현재분사 making의 목적어 자리로, 앞에 부정관사 a가 있으므로 명사가 와야 한다. 따라서 명사 (B) delivery가 정답이다. (A) deliver는 동사, (C) delivered는 동사/과거분사, (D) delivering은 동명사/현재분사이므로 품사상 적합하지 않다.

번역 아지즈 씨는 그의 동업자가 배달을 나가는 동안 가게에 종종 혼자 있는다.

110 동사 어휘   ▶동영상 강의

해설 앞의 has been과 함께 수동태를 이루어 적절한 문맥을 만드는 동사 어휘를 고르는 문제이다. to August 31와 결합하여 '8월 31일로 일정이 변경되었다'는 내용이 되어야 자연스러우므로 '일정을 변경하다'라는 뜻의 동사 reschedule의 과거분사 (C) rescheduled가 정답이다. (A)의 cancel은 '취소하다', (B)의 combine은 '결합하다', (D)의 administer는 '관리하다'라는 의미이다.

번역 퍼시픽 코스트 선셋 런은 악천후로 인해 8월 31일로 일정이 변경되었다.

111 상관접속사

해설 pill과 liquid 사이에 and가 있고, 문맥상 '알약과 액상 형태 두 가지로'라는 의미가 되어야 한다. 따라서 and와 상관접속사를 이루어 'A와 B 둘 다'라는 뜻을 나타내는 (B) both가 정답이다.

번역 그레이버의 모발 및 손톱 성장 보충제는 알약과 액상 형태 두 가지로 나온다.

어휘 supplement 보충(제)   pill 알약   liquid 액체   form 형태

112 접속사 자리 _ 부사절 접속사   ▶동영상 강의

해설 빈칸은 두 개의 완전한 절을 이어주는 접속사 자리로, '포스터가 행사 전에 게시될 수 있도록 곧 완성되어야 한다'는 의미가 되어야 자연스럽다. 따라서 '~할 수 있도록'이라는 뜻의 부사절 접속사 (A) so that이 정답이다. (B) despite(~에도 불구하고)는 전치사이므로 품사상 빈칸에 들어갈 수 없고, 부사절 접속사 (C) whenever(~할 때마다)와 (D) as if(마치 ~인 것처럼)는 의미상 답이 될 수 없다.

번역 포스터는 갈라 행사에 앞서 게시될 수 있도록 곧 완성되어야 한다.

어휘 in advance of ~보다 앞서

113 부사 자리 _ 동사 수식

해설 부사절 접속사 even though가 이끄는 절의 주어 he와 동사 disliked 사이에서 동사를 수식하는 부사 자리이므로, '개인적으로'라는 의미의 부사 (B) personally가 정답이다. (A) personal은 형용사, (C) personals와 (D) person은 명사이므로 품사상 답이 될 수 없다.

번역 올리베로 씨는 영화의 미학적 스타일이 개인적으로는 마음에 들지 않았지만, 자신의 논평에서 그 영화를 칭찬했다.

어휘 praise 칭찬하다   aesthetic 미학적인

114 전치사 어휘

해설 빈칸 뒤의 시간을 나타내는 명사 weeks를 목적어로 취해 '기록적인 몇 주간의 폭우 후에'라는 의미가 되어야 자연스러우므로 '~ 후에'를 뜻하며 시간적 순서를 표현하는 전치사 (A) After가 정답이다. (B) Besides는 '~ 외에', (C) Opposite은 '~의 맞은편에', (D) Alongside는 '~ 옆에'라는 의미이다.

번역 기록적인 몇 주간의 폭우 후에, 이번 주말에는 파란 하늘만 기대하세요.

어휘 record-setting 기록적인

115 to부정사 _ 부사적 용법

해설 빈칸 앞에 완전한 절이 있고 빈칸 뒤의 명사구 its stability를 목적어로 취할 수 있어야 하므로 to부정사의 능동태가 와야 한다. 문맥상 '안정성을 확보할 수 있도록'이라는 내용이 되어야 자연스러우므로 '~할 수 있도록, ~하기 위해서'라는 목적의 의미를 나타내는 (C) to ensure가 정답이다.

번역 세레니카 식탁은 평평하지 않은 표면에서 안정성을 확보할 수 있도록 수평계가 딸려 온다.

어휘 leveler 수평계   stability 안정성   uneven 평평하지 않은
surface 표면

116 명사 어휘

해설 동사 can expect의 목적어 역할을 하는 명사 자리로, 회사에 지원하는 지원자들이 3일 이내에 받기를 기대하는 대상이 빈칸에 와야 한다. '일자리에 지원하는 지원자들은 답변을 기대할 수 있다'는 내용이 되어야 자연스러우므로 '답변, 응답'을 뜻하는 (D) response가 정답이다. (A) degree는 '학위', (B) raise는 '인상', (C) change는 '변화'라는 의미이다.

번역 올크레스트 엔지니어링의 모든 일자리에 지원하는 지원자들은 영업일 기준 3일 이내에 답변을 기대할 수 있다.

어휘 applicant 지원자

117 명사절 접속사

해설 빈칸에는 동사 is required의 주어 역할을 하는 명사절을 이끄는 접속사가 필요한데, 빈칸 뒤에 주어가 없는 불완전한 문장이 있고 문맥상 '기록을 작성하는 사람은 누구든지'라는 내용이 되어야 자연스러우므로 '~하는 사람은 누구든'을 뜻하는 명사절 접속사 (A) Whoever가 정답이다. (C) Whose 뒤에는 명사가 와야 하고, (B) Who와 (D) What은 의미상 답이 될 수 없다.

번역 환자의 의료 기록을 작성하는 사람은 누구든지 기밀을 유지해야 한다.

어휘 patient 환자 maintain 유지하다 confidentiality 기밀

118 부사 어휘

해설 빈칸은 동사구 was expanded를 수식하는 부사 자리로, '사무실이 지난해 크게 확장했다'는 의미가 되어야 자연스러우므로 '크게, 상당히'를 뜻하는 (A) significantly가 정답이다. (B) tightly는 '단단히', (C) remotely는 '원격으로', (D) identically는 '동일하게'라는 의미이다.

번역 서비스에 대한 높은 수요 때문에, 우리 사무실은 지난해 크게 확장했다.

어휘 demand 수요 expand 확장하다

119 형용사 자리 _ 명사 수식

해설 빈칸은 전치사 for의 목적어 역할을 하는 명사 architecture를 앞에서 수식하는 형용사 자리이다. 따라서 '지속 가능한'을 뜻하는 형용사 (B) sustainable이 정답이다. (A) sustain과 (D) sustains는 동사로 품사상 답이 될 수 없고, 명사 (C) sustainer(떠받치는 사람)는 architecture와 복합명사를 이루기에 적절하지 않다.

번역 지속 가능한 건축에 주는 테리 호이그 상은 화요일에 헬블론 씨에게 수여되었다.

어휘 architecture 건축

120 동사 어휘 ▶동영상 강의

해설 빈칸 앞의 have been, 뒤의 problems와 함께 '온도 조절기에 문제를 겪고 있다'는 의미가 되어야 자연스러우므로 '경험하다'라는 뜻의 동사 experience의 현재분사 (A) experiencing이 정답이다. (B)의 regard는 '~으로 여기다', (C)의 repurpose는 '용도 변경하다', (D)의 establish는 '설립하다'라는 의미이다.

번역 우리는 창고 서쪽 끝에 있는 온도 조절기에 문제를 겪고 있다.

어휘 thermostat 온도 조절기

121 부사 자리 _ 동사 수식

해설 빈칸 앞에 자동사 worked가 있고, 문맥상 '두 학생이 공동으로 작업했다'는 의미가 되어야 자연스러우므로 '공동으로, 합작하여'라는 뜻으로 동사 worked를 수식하는 부사 (C) collaboratively가 정답이다. (A) collaborate는 동사, (B) collaborative는 형용사, (D) collaborated는 동사/과거분사로 품사상 답이 될 수 없다.

번역 리슬리 대학교 출신의 두 학생은 로스 공원의 새 도서관 설계를 공동으로 작업했다.

122 형용사 어휘 ▶동영상 강의

해설 빈칸은 명사 colors를 수식하는 형용사 자리로, '웹사이트의 이미지들은 예술 작품의 정확한 색상을 반영하지 못할 수도 있다'는 내용이 되어야 자연스러우므로 '정확한'을 뜻하는 (D) exact가 정답이다. (A) loyal은 '충실한', (B) smart는 '똑똑한', (C) close는 '가까운'이라는 의미이다.

번역 우리 갤러리의 웹사이트에 게시된 이미지들은 판매용 예술 작품의 정확한 색상을 반영하지 못할 수도 있습니다.

어휘 reflect 반영하다

123 명사 자리 _ 동사의 목적어

해설 빈칸은 타동사 answer의 목적어 자리이고, 앞에 소유격 customers'가 있으므로 명사가 와야 한다. 문맥상 '고객의 문의에 답변한다'는 내용이 되어야 자연스러우므로 '문의'를 뜻하는 명사 inquiry의 복수형 (D) inquiries가 정답이다. (A)의 inquirer는 '문의자'라는 뜻으로 의미상 적합하지 않고, (B) inquired는 동사/과거분사, (C) to inquire는 to부정사로 품사상 답이 될 수 없다.

번역 뷰티베일 화장품의 직원들은 고객 문의 수령 후 24시간 이내에 답변합니다.

어휘 representative 직원 receipt 수령

124 부사 어휘 ▶동영상 강의

해설 수련회에 참석하고 싶다는 내용을 대조의 의미를 나타내는 but이 연결하고 있으므로, '유감스럽게도 참석할 수 없다'는 내용으로 이어져야 자연스럽다. 따라서 '유감스럽게도'를 뜻하는 (A) regrettably가 정답이다. (B) scarcely는 '거의 ~않다', (C) exceptionally는 '예외적으로', (D) annually는 '매년'이라는 의미이다.

번역 우리는 수련회에 참석하고 싶지만, 유감스럽게도 그 날짜에는 가능하지 않습니다.

어휘 retreat 수련회, 휴양지

125 전치사 자리 / 어휘 ▶동영상 강의

해설 빈칸 뒤에 명사구 the meeting이 있으므로 전치사가 들어가야 한다. the meeting을 목적어로 취해 '회의가 끝난 후에 차와 쿠키가 제공된다'는 내용이 되어야 자연스러우므로 '~ 후에'를 뜻하는 전치사 (C) following이 정답이다. (A) later는 부사/형용사, (B) as soon as는 접속사이므로 품사상 답이 될 수 없고, 전치사 (D) in case of는 '~의 경우에'라는 뜻으로 의미상 적절하지 않다.

번역 쳉 씨의 승진을 축하하여 회의가 끝난 후에 차와 쿠키가 제공될 예정입니다.

어휘 in celebration of ~을 축하하여

126 명사 어휘

해설 빈칸은 동사 will have의 목적어 자리로, of working from home two days per week의 수식을 받아 '직원들은 주 2일 재택근무 옵션을 갖는다'는 내용이 되어야 자연스러우므로 '옵션, 선택권'을 뜻하는 (D) option이 정답이다. (A) place는 '장소', (B) combination은 '조합', (C) range는 '범위'라는 의미이다.

번역 다음 달부터, 사트슨 애널리틱스의 모든 직원에게는 주 2일 재택근무 옵션이 주어진다.

127 형용사 자리 _ 명사 수식 / 현재분사 vs. 과거분사

해설 빈칸에는 정관사와 명사 사이에서 명사 process를 수식하는 형용사 또는 process와 복합명사를 이루는 명사가 들어갈 수 있다. 문맥상 '사무 장비 조달을 위해 선호되는 절차'라는 내용이 되어야 자연스러우므로, '선호되는, 우선 순위의'를 뜻하는 과거분사형 형용사 (C) preferred가 정답이다. 현재분사 (A) preferring은 명사를 수식할 수는 있지만 process는 prefer의 주체가 아닌 대상이므로 답이 될 수 없고, (B) preferably는 부사로 품사상 빈칸에 들어갈 수 없으며, (D) preferability는 '더 나음'이라는 뜻의 명사로 process와 복합명사를 이루기에 적절하지 않다.

번역 회계 부서의 새로운 정책은 사무 장비 조달을 위해 선호되는 절차를 약술한다.

어휘 outline 약술하다   process 절차   procurement 조달

128 동사 어휘

해설 빈칸 뒤 전치사 to와 함께 the company merger를 목적어로 취해 '회사 합병과 관련된 문서'라는 의미가 되어야 자연스러우므로, 전치사 to와 결합하여 '관련되다'를 뜻하는 자동사 pertain의 현재분사 (C) pertaining이 정답이다. (A)의 assign은 '배정하다', (B)의 facilitate는 '용이하게 하다', (D)의 embark는 '착수하다'라는 의미이다.

번역 회사 합병과 관련된 모든 문서는 1년 이내에 대중에게 공개될 예정이다.

어휘 merger 합병

129 명사 자리 _ 전치사의 목적어

해설 빈칸은 전치사 of의 목적어 자리이고, 앞에 소유격 its와 형용사 new가 있으므로 명사가 와야 한다. 문맥상 '간호학교와의 새로운 제휴의 일환'이라는 의미가 되어야 자연스러우므로 '제휴'라는 뜻의 명사 (A) affiliation이 정답이다. (B) affiliated는 동사/과거분사, (C) affiliating은 동명사/현재분사로 품사상 적절하지 않고, (D) affiliates는 동사 이외에 '계열사'를 뜻하는 명사로 쓰일 수는 있으나 의미상 어울리지 않는다.

번역 그랜타 병원은 프리엘 간호학교와의 새로운 제휴의 일환으로 소아과 간호사 여러 명을 직원으로 추가했다.

어휘 pediatric 소아과의

130 상관접속사

해설 「be+able+to부정사」 구문에서 to 뒤의 scan purchased items와 field questions가 병렬 구조로 이어져 있다. 따라서 '질문에 대응할 뿐만 아니라 구매된 제품을 스캔할 수 있어야 한다'는 의미를 만드는 '~뿐만 아니라 …도'라는 뜻의 상관접속사 (D) as well as가 정답이다. (A) but은 '하지만'이라는 대조의 의미를 나타내므로 문맥상 부적절하고, (B) for instance는 '예를 들어'를 뜻하는 접속부사, (C) although는 '비록 ~이지만'을 뜻하는 접속사로 품사상 빈칸에 들어갈 수 없다.

번역 계산하는 동안 출납원들은 고객의 질문에 대응할 뿐만 아니라 구매된 제품을 정확하게 스캔할 수 있어야 한다.

어휘 checkout 계산   cashier 출납원   accurately 정확하게   field (질문 등을) 처리하다

PART 6

131-134 기사

> **새로운 베트남 식당 개점**
>
> 샌프란시스코 (11월 5일) — 유명 셰프인 에릭 황이 자신의 첫 레스토랑인 응온 미엥을 **131 개업했다**. 이 식당은 지난주 노스 비치 지역에 문을 열었다. 응온 미엥은 정통 베트남 요리와 황 셰프가 개발한 몇몇 혁신적인 요리를 제공한다. 식당은 한때 플랜턴즈라는 식당이 있던 자리를 인수했으며, **132 이곳은** 지난해 문을 닫았다.
>
> 황 셰프는 2년 전 리얼리티 TV쇼인 <미국 최고의 셰프>에서 1위를 차지했다. **133 그는 그 대회에서 우승하게 되어 무척 감격했다.** "상을 받고 난 뒤, 식당을 여는 것은 제 꿈이 되었어요."라고 그는 말했다. "제가 창작한 요리를 노스 비치 지역에 선보이게 되어 정말 기쁩니다."
>
> 개업식에서 식당 손님들은 **134 음식**을 향한 황 셰프의 열정에 공감했다. "의심의 여지없이, 제가 먹어본 것 중 최고였습니다."라고 고객인 주디 블랙번은 말했다.

어휘 celebrity 유명 인사   authentic 진짜의, 진정한   cuisine 요리   innovative 혁신적인   take over ~을 인수하다   occupy 차지하다   culinary 요리의   echo (감정 등에) 공감하다   enthusiasm 열정   doubt 의심

131 동사 어형 _ 시제

해설 빈칸 뒤 문장에서 식당이 지난주에 문을 열었다(It opened last week)고 했으므로, 에릭 황이 식당을 개업하여 현재 영업 중인 상태를 나타내는 내용이 되어야 한다. 따라서 현재완료 시제 (C) has launched가 정답이다. (A) will launch는 미래, (B) could launch는 앞으로의 가능성을 나타내므로 부적절하고, (D) was launching은 과거의 특정 순간에 개업 중이었다는 내용이 되므로 문맥상 적합하지 않다.

132 관계대명사 _ 주격

해설 빈칸 이하는 선행사 the restaurant Plantains를 수식하는 관계절로, 빈칸 뒤에 동사가 나오므로 빈칸에는 주어 역할을 하는 관계사가 필요하다. 따라서 주격 관계대명사 (D) which가 정답이다. (A) they와 (B) this는 대명사이므로 빈칸 뒤의 절을 연결할 수 없고, (C) where는 관계부사로 뒤에 완전한 절이 와야 한다.

133 문맥에 맞는 문장 고르기

번역 (A) 샌프란시스코에는 인기 있는 베트남 식당이 많다.
(B) 식당은 내년에 캘리포니아의 다른 도시들로 확장할 수도 있다.
(C) 쇼는 다섯 번째 시즌을 시작하고 있다.
(D) 그는 그 대회에서 우승하게 되어 무척 감격했다.

해설 빈칸 앞에서 황 셰프는 리얼리티 TV쇼에서 1위를 차지했다(Chef Hoang won first place on the reality television show)고 했으므로, 쇼에서 1위를 한 것에 대한 황 셰프의 소감이 들어가야 자연스럽게 연결된다. 따라서 그가 대회에서 우승하고 무척 감격했다고 언급하고 있는 (D)가 정답이다.

어휘 expand 확장하다 thrilled 감격한 competition 대회

134 명사 어휘

해설 빈칸 뒤 문장에서 한 고객이 자신이 먹어본 것 중 최고였다고 했으므로, 빈칸이 있는 문장에서도 요리 또는 먹는 것에 대해 언급해야 연결이 자연스럽다. 따라서 '음식을 향한 황 셰프의 열정'이라는 내용이 되어야 적절하므로 '음식'을 뜻하는 (A) food가 정답이다. (B) event는 '행사', (C) area는 '지역', (D) performance는 '공연'이라는 의미이다.

135-138 공지

> **코넬리 주차장**
>
> 135 참여 매장에서 주차를 인증받지 않을 경우, 주차는 시간당 10달러입니다. 주차를 인증해 줄 수 있는 매장은 레이몬드 백화점, 롤라즈 파인 다이닝, 모니크스 부티크, 그레치 초콜릿 판매점입니다. 이들 매장 중 136 어느 곳이든 입장권을 가져가세요. 137 출납원이 기꺼이 도장을 찍어 드릴 것입니다. 첫 1시간은 무료로 주차하실 수 있습니다. 138 그 후, 요금은 시간당 5달러입니다.

어휘 garage 주차장 validate 인증하다 chocolatier 초콜릿 판매점 entrance 입장 at no charge 무료로

135 형용사 자리 _ 명사 수식 / 현재분사 vs. 과거분사

해설 빈칸에는 부정관사와 명사 사이에서 명사 store를 수식하는 형용사 또는 store와 복합명사를 이루는 명사가 들어갈 수 있다. '참여하는 매장'이라는 의미가 되어야 자연스러우므로 '참여하는'이라는 뜻의 현재분사 (C) participating이 정답이다. (A) participates는 동사로 품사상 빈칸에 들어갈 수 없다. participate는 자동사로 수동의 의미를 나타내는 과거분사형 형용사로 보통 쓰지 않으므로 과거분사 (B) participated는 적절하지 않으며, 명사 (D) participation은 store와 복합명사를 이루기에 적절하지 않다.

136 부정대명사

해설 빈칸은 전치사 to의 목적어 역할을 하며 'of + 복수 명사'의 수식을 받는 자리로, 네 개의 보기가 모두 가능하므로 문맥상 가장 적절한 대명사를 골라야 한다. 앞 문장에서 세 곳의 매장을 제시하고 있고, '이들 매장 중 어느 곳이든 가져가면 된다'는 내용이 되어야 자연스러우므로 '어느 것, 아무 것'을 뜻하는 (A) any가 정답이다. (B) all은 '모든 것', (C) each는 '각각', (D) either는 '둘 중 하나'를 뜻하므로 문맥상 적합하지 않다.

137 문맥에 맞는 문장 고르기

번역 (A) 지정된 자리에만 주차하세요.
(B) 반드시 차량을 잠그세요.
(C) 현재는 현금을 받지 않습니다.
(D) 출납원이 기꺼이 도장을 찍어 드릴 것입니다.

해설 앞에서 주차를 인증해 줄 수 있는 매장(Stores that can validate your parking)을 안내하며 그 매장들로 입장권을 가져가라(bring your entrance ticket)고 안내하고 있다. 따라서 입장권을 가져가면 매장에서 주차 인증을 해줄 것이라는 내용이 연결되어야 자연스러우므로 출납원이 도장을 찍어 줄 것이라고 알려주고 있는 (D)가 정답이다.

어휘 specified 지정된, 명시된 accept 받아들이다
stamp (도장을) 찍다

138 접속부사

해설 빈칸 앞 문장에서 첫 1시간은 무료로 주차할 수 있다고 했는데 뒤 문장에서는 요금이 시간당 5달러라고 안내하고 있으므로, 두 문장은 첫 1시간 이후에는 유료로 전환된다는 시간의 흐름을 나타내는 말로 연결되어야 적절하다. 따라서 '그 후, 그 다음에'를 뜻하는 (B) Then이 정답이다. (A) If not은 '만약 그렇지 않다면', (C) In that case는 '그런 경우에는', (D) Nevertheless는 '그럼에도 불구하고'라는 의미이다.

139-142 공지

로스트 오션 극장은 다음 주에 시내 지점에서 열리는 특별한 공연을 알리게 되어 무척 기쁩니다. 재능 있는 코미디언인 매디 창이 자신의 회고록인 <그게 내가 원하는 전부>를 바탕으로 한 1인극을 **139 공연할 예정입니다.** 재미있고 매력적인 **140 등장인물**로 가득 찬 창 씨의 책은 이 공연을 통해 생생하게 살아납니다. 팬들은 창의 뛰어난 재능을 직접 경험하며 즐기는 한편, 그녀의 작품을 새롭게 접하는 사람들은 그녀의 재미난 세상으로의 **141 유쾌한** 소개를 받게 될 것입니다.

공연 시간은 목요일부터 일요일까지 오후 7시이며, 토요일 오후 1시에 주간 공연이 추가로 있습니다. **142 표를 예약하시려면 704-555-0138로 극장으로 전화 주세요.** 추가 정보는 www.lostoceantheater.com에서 확인할 수 있습니다.

어휘 memoir 회고록 filled with ~로 가득 찬 engaging 매력적인 brilliance 뛰어난 재능 in person 직접 newcomer 신입 matinee 주간 공연

139 동사 자리 _ 시제

해설 빈칸은 주어 The talented comedian Maddy Chang과 목적어 a one-person show 사이의 동사 자리이다. 앞 문장에서 다음 주에 열릴 공연(a unique offering ~ next week)에 대해 알리고 있으므로, 빈칸이 있는 문장도 미래 시제로 '1인극을 공연할 예정이다'라는 내용이 되어야 자연스럽다. 따라서 미래 시제 (A) will perform이 정답이다. (B) to perform은 to부정사, (D) performing은 동명사/현재분사로 품사상 적절하지 않고, (C) performed는 과거 시제로 답이 될 수 없다.

140 명사 어휘

해설 빈칸은 문맥상 책을 구성하는 요소이면서 동시에 공연을 통해 생생하게 살아날 수 있는 대상이어야 한다. 문맥상 '재미있고 매력적인 등장인물로 가득 찬 책'이라는 의미가 되어야 자연스러우므로 '등장인물'을 뜻하는 (C) characters가 정답이다. (A)의 reason은 '이유', (B)의 structure는 '구조', (D)의 sign은 '조짐'이라는 의미이다.

141 형용사 자리 _ 명사 수식

해설 부정관사 a와 명사 introduction 사이에서 명사를 수식하는 형용사 자리이다. 문맥상 '유쾌한 소개'라는 의미가 되어야 자연스러우므로 '유쾌한, 즐거운'을 뜻하는 형용사 (D) delightful이 정답이다. (A) delight와 (B) delights는 명사/동사로 품사상 적합하지 않고, 과거분사 (C) delighted는 수식 받는 명사 introduction이 감정을 느끼는 주체가 될 수 없으므로 답이 될 수 없다.

142 문맥에 맞는 문장 고르기

번역 (A) 극장은 보수 작업을 위해 폐관합니다.
(B) 표를 예약하시려면 704-555-0138로 극장으로 전화 주세요.
(C) 창의 회고록은 온라인과 지역 서점에서 구입할 수 있습니다.
(D) 창은 남부 캘리포니아에서 자랐고 미네소타에서 대학을 다녔습니다.

해설 빈칸 앞에서 공연 시간에 대해 안내하고 있고, 빈칸 뒤에서 추가 정보는 웹사이트에서 확인할 수 있다고 알려주고 있다. 앞뒤 문맥상 빈칸에는 공연 티켓 구입 방법에 대한 안내가 들어가야 연결이 자연스러우므로 표를 예약하려면 극장으로 전화하라는 내용의 (B)가 정답이다.

어휘 renovation 보수 reserve 예약하다 raise 키우다

143-146 이메일

▶동영상 강의

수신: tvargas@sandelleinn.com
발신: moira@petalsaplenty.com
날짜: 11월 2일
제목: 꽃 장식

바르가스 씨께,

저는 오늘 귀하의 접수 담당자에게 무료 꽃꽂이 장식을 맡겼으며, 그분이 저에게 귀하께 직접 연락하라고 제안했습니다. 저는 꽃 디자인을 전문으로 합니다. 저는 귀하를 위해 이 꽃다발을 만들었으며, 호텔 로비에 어울리는 대담한 색상들을 사용하여 제가 작업에 **143 접근하는** 방식을 보여 드릴 수 있도록 했습니다.

귀하께서 현재 장식을 위한 예산은 없다고 말씀하셨습니다. **144 그렇다 하더라도,** 여전히 어떤 방식으로든 협력할 수 있을지도 모릅니다. 귀하께서 소규모 행사를 주최하신다고 알고 있으며 귀하의 웹사이트에는 당신이 추천하는 지역 DJ, 출장 요리업체 및 기타 서비스 제공 업체들에 대한 링크가 있습니다. 귀하의 **145 추천** 목록에 제 회사인 페탈 어플렌티를 포함하는 걸 고려해 주실 수 있을까요? 저는 제 웹사이트에 귀하의 호텔을 홍보함으로써 기꺼이 화답하겠습니다. **146 이 합의가 양측 모두에 유익할 것이라 생각합니다.**

귀하로부터 소식을 듣게 되길 기대합니다.

페탈 어플렌티 대표 모리아 보스

어휘 floral arrangement 꽃꽂이 complimentary 무료 directly 직접적으로 specialize in ~을 전문으로 하다 bouquet 꽃다발 bold 대담한 inn (작은) 호텔 budget 예산 décor 장식 partner 협력하다 caterer 출장 요리업체 reciprocate 화답하다

143 동사 어휘

해설 문장의 앞 부분에서 호텔 로비에 어울리는 대담한 색상들을 사용해 꽃다발을 만들었다며 꽃다발을 제작하면서 고려한 표현 요소에 대해 언급하고 있으므로, '작업에 접근하는 방식'이라는 의미가 되어야 자연스럽다. 따라서 '접근하다'를 뜻하는 (B) approach가 정답이다. (A) document는 '기록하다', (C) schedule은 '일정을 잡다', (D) verify는 '확인하다'라는 의미이다.

144 접속부사

해설 앞 문장에서 현재 장식을 위한 예산이 없는 부정적 상황을 언급한 반면, 뒤 문장에서는 어떤 방식으로든 협력할 수 있을지도 모른다며 긍정적 태도로 제휴를 제안하고 있다. 따라서 '그렇다 하더라도'라는 의미로 앞서 언급된 내용과 상반되는 대안이나 의견을 제시할 때 사용

하는 (A) Even so가 정답이다. (B) For example은 '예를 들어', (C) On the contrary는 '반대로', (D) As you suggested는 '제안하신 대로'라는 의미이다. 참고로, 빈칸 뒤에 예산이 없다는 사실을 정면으로 반박하는 내용이 나온 것이 아니므로 (C) On the contrary는 답이 될 수 없다.

145 명사 자리 _ 전치사의 목적어

해설 빈칸은 전치사 of의 목적어 역할을 하는 명사 자리이므로 '추천, 소개'라는 뜻의 명사 (C) referrals가 정답이다. (A) refers는 동사, (B) referred는 동사/과거분사, (D) referable은 형용사이므로 품사상 답이 될 수 없다.

146 문맥에 맞는 문장 고르기

번역 (A) 추천해 주셔서 다시 한번 감사드리고 싶습니다.
(B) 저는 확실히 유사한 점이 보입니다.
(C) 그것은 단지 오해였던 것 같습니다.
(D) 이 합의가 양측 모두에 유익할 것이라 생각합니다.

해설 빈칸 앞에서 상대방의 업체 추천 목록에 자신의 회사를 포함시켜주면(Would you consider including my company, Petals Aplenty, on your list of referrals?) 자신의 웹사이트에 상대방의 호텔을 홍보하겠다(promoting your inn on my own Web site)며 상호간 거래를 제안하고 있다. 따라서 이 제안에 대해 설득하는 내용이 연결되어야 자연스러우므로 이 합의가 양측 모두에 유익할 것이라고 언급하는 (D)가 정답이다.

어휘 nomination 추천, 임명   resemblance 유사함
misunderstanding 오해   arrangement 합의
benefit 유익하다

PART 7

147-148 채용 공고

직원 구함

제스트풀 퀴진에서 우리 레스토랑 팀과 함께 할 서버를 찾고 있습니다! 우리는 프랑스 요리와 스페인 요리를 전문으로 합니다.

147 이 일자리는 풀타임 또는 파트타임입니다. 주간 근무와 야간 근무가 가능합니다.

지원자는 긍정적인 태도, **148 뛰어난 고객 응대 기술**, 그리고 빠르게 돌아가는 업무 환경에서 여러 작업을 동시에 할 수 있는 능력을 갖고 있어야 합니다.

제스트풀 퀴진은 경력에 따라 경쟁력 있는 급여를 제공합니다. 모든 서버는 각 근무시간 동안 식사 한 끼를 제공받습니다. 우리는 승진 및 임금 인상이 있는 유망한 진로를 제공합니다.

지원서는 우리 웹사이트 www.zestfulcuisine.com에서 이용 가능합니다.

어휘 specialize in ~을 전문으로 하다   candidate 지원자
attitude 태도   multitask 동시에 여러 작업을 하다
fast-paced 빠르게 진행되는   competitive 경쟁력 있는
rate 비율   shift 근무시간   career path 유망한 진로, 출세의 길
application 지원(서)

147 추론 / 암시

번역 제스트풀 퀴진에 대해 암시된 것은?
(A) 직원들에게 유연한 근무시간을 제공한다.
(B) 모든 직원에게 동일한 기본급을 지급한다.
(C) 6개월 후에 승진 기회를 제공한다.
(D) 직원들에게 교육 세션 참석을 요구한다.

해설 두 번째 단락의 첫 문장에서 이 일자리는 풀타임 또는 파트타임(This is a full-time or part-time position)이며 주간 근무와 야간 근무가 가능하다(Days and nights are available)고 했다. 선택할 수 있는 근무시간이 여러 가지인 것으로 보아 제스트풀 퀴진은 직원들에게 유연한 근무시간을 제공하고 있음을 유추할 수 있으므로 (A)가 정답이다.

어휘 flexibility 유연성   salary 급여

148 세부 사항

번역 채용 공고에 따르면, 지원자에게 필수적인 자질은?
(A) 식품 안전 규정 지식
(B) 여러 언어에 대한 유창함
(C) 레스토랑에서의 이전 경력
(D) 고객과의 소통 능력

해설 세 번째 단락에서 지원자가 갖추어야 할 자질 중 하나로 뛰어난 고객 응대 기술(excellent customer service skills)을 꼽고 있으므로 (D)가 정답이다.

어휘 knowledge 지식   regulation 규정   fluency 유창함
previous 이전의

> **Paraphrasing**
> 지문의 customer service skills
> → 정답의 Ability to communicate with customers

149-151 기사

위니펙 (5월 10일) — 매니토바에 본사를 둔 위성 제조업체 **149 알리타 테크놀로지가 기후 데이터 수집에 사용될 비행 감지 기구 개발을 위한 900만 달러의 보조금을 받았다.** 장치는 캐나다 전역에서 적설층의 밀도와 깊이를 계산하도록 설계될 것이다.

알리타 테크놀로지는 이 **150 사업 계획**을 위해 **151 사우섬 대학교의 마이크로웨이브 공학 연구소**와 협력하고 있다. **151 이 연구소의 원격 감지 팀 책임자인 휴 재리스 박사**는 다음 겨울에 데이터를 수집 및 분석함으로써 하나 이상의 시제품을 테스트하는 작업을 이끌 예정이다.

적설층 데이터는 매년 눈의 추세와 변동을 측정하는 데 사용될 뿐 아니라 전국의 주요 지역에서 눈이 녹은 물을 얼마나 사용할 수 있는지 파악하는 데에도 도움을 준다.

어휘 based 본사를 둔 satellite 위성 grant 보조금 airborne 비행 중인, 하늘에 떠있는 sensing 감지 instrument 기구 calculate 계산하다 density 밀도 depth 깊이 snowpack 적설층 collaborate 협력하다 initiative (목적 달성을 위한) 계획 remote 원격의 prototype 시제품 measure 측정하다 year-to-year 매년 fluctuation 변동

149 세부 사항

번역 기사에 따르면, 장치 제작 책임자는 누구인가?
(A) 재리스 박사
(B) 알리타 테크놀로지
(C) 사우섬 대학교의 마이크로웨이브 공학 연구소
(D) 위니펙 정부

해설 첫 단락 첫 문장에서 알리타 테크놀로지가 기후 데이터 수집에 사용될 비행 감지 기구 개발을 위한 900만 달러의 보조금을 받았다(Alita Technology has been awarded a $9 million grant to develop an airborne sensing instrument to be used in the collection of climate data)면서 장치는 캐나다 전역에서 적설층의 밀도와 깊이를 계산하도록 설계될 것(The device will be engineered to calculate the density and depth of snowpack throughout Canada)이라고 설명하고 있으므로 알리타 테크놀로지에서 비행 감지 장치의 설계를 포함한 개발 작업을 맡을 예정임을 알 수 있다. 따라서 (B)가 정답이다.

150 동의어 찾기

번역 두 번째 단락 3행의 "initiative"와 의미가 가장 가까운 단어는?
(A) 동기
(B) 기술
(C) 장점
(D) 계획

해설 의미상 알리타 테크놀로지가 비행 감지 기구 개발 '사업 계획'을 위해 연구소와 협력하고 있다는 뜻으로 쓰였으므로 '계획(된 일), 프로젝트'를 뜻하는 (D) project가 정답이다.

151 Not / True

번역 재리스 박사에 대해 명시된 것은?
(A) 대학교 연구소에 고용된 상태이다.
(B) 장치의 설계 및 개발에 관한 책을 출간했다.
(C) 감지 기구의 시제품을 조립한다.
(D) 알리타 테크놀로지에서 엔지니어로 근무한다.

해설 두 번째 단락의 첫 문장에서 사우섬 대학교의 마이크로웨이브 공학 연구소(the Microwave Engineering Lab at the University of Southam)를 언급했고, 두 번째 문장에서 휴 재리스 박사를 이 연구소의 원격 감지 팀 책임자(Dr. Hugh Jaris, director of the lab's Remote Sensing Unit)라고 소개하고 있으므로 (A)가 정답이다.

어휘 assemble 조립하다

152-153 영수증

스텁 마스터 — 콘서트, 스포츠, 극장용 티켓 공급처

안녕하세요, 사토 씨.

구매해 주셔서 감사합니다! 152 **고객님의 모바일 티켓이 준비되었으며 온라인으로 생성하신 스텁 마스터 계정에서 이용하실 수 있습니다.** 모든 스텁 마스터 티켓은 고유의 바코드가 포함되어 있으며 인쇄, 복사 또는 공유할 수 없습니다. 휴대전화의 스텁 마스터 앱을 이용하여 티켓을 확인하셔서 행사 입장 시 전자상으로 스캔될 수 있도록 해 주세요.

확인 번호:	9035768
날짜:	6월 25일 토요일
시간:	오후 7시
행사:	몬테레이 메달리온스 대 메이빌 다저스의 경기
장소:	알론소 레예스 경기장
153 주문:	티켓 1장, 외야석 – 지붕 없음, 정규 시즌 야구
총액:	25달러 (건물 이용료 3달러 포함 가격)
참고 사항:	현장에서 15달러에 버거와 핫도그 뷔페에 참여하세요. 기업용 티켓 구매는 service@stubmaster.com으로 연락 주세요.

어휘 source 공급처 electronically 전자적으로 entry 입장 venue 장소 bleacher 외야석 participate in ~에 참여하다 on-site 현장에서

152 Not / True

번역 스텁 마스터 티켓에 대해 언급된 것은?
(A) 고객에게 우편으로 발송된다.
(B) 가격에 주차 요금이 포함되어 있다.
(C) 기업 구매 시 할인된다.
(D) 전자적으로 저장된다.

해설 두 번째 문장에서 고객의 모바일 티켓이 준비되었으며 온라인으로 생성한 스텁 마스터 계정에서 이용할 수 있다(Your mobile ticket is ready and available in the Stub Master account you created online)고 했으므로, 티켓이 온라인 상에서 이용할 수 있도록 모바일 티켓의 형태로 저장됨을 알 수 있다. 따라서 (D)가 정답이다.

Paraphrasing
지문의 mobile → 정답의 saved electronically

153 Not / True

번역 사토 씨가 참석할 행사에 대해 사실인 것은?
(A) 6월 7일에 열린다.
(B) 야구 경기이다.
(C) 실내에서 열린다.
(D) 무료 뷔페가 포함되어 있다.

해설 표의 하단에 주문(Order) 항목에서 티켓 1장, 외야석 – 지붕 없음, 정규 시즌 야구(1 ticket; bleachers – uncovered; regular season baseball이라고 나와 있으므로 사토 씨는 야구 경기의 티켓을 구입했다는 것을 알 수 있다. 따라서 (B)가 정답이다.

154-156 보도 자료

즉각 발표용

연락: 나디아 쿠말로, nacia_khumalo@gulfbrookcreations.co.za

케이프타운 (8월 20일) — 걸프브룩 크리에이션스는 오늘 캔디스 마손도 씨를 9월 1일부터 회사의 최고 디자인 책임자(CDO)로 임명한다고 발표했다. 가장 최근에 **155, 156** 마손도 씨는 더반에 본사를 둔 데보라 다이나믹스에서 소재 개발 부서를 이끌었다. 그녀는 10년 동안 이 직책에서 근무했는데, 데보라 다이나믹스가 사업을 시작한지 2년 뒤 입사했었다. **155** 그녀는 남아프리카의 국내 시장에서 독립적인 생활을 향상시키기 위한 접근성 보조 제품을 개발한다는 회사의 사명을 뒷받침하는 주역이었다.

걸프브룩의 사장인 조나단 응고베니 씨는 마손도 씨의 능력과 기지를 인정한다. **154** "30년의 디자인 경력 동안 마손도 씨는 포용성과 자립성을 반영하는 수많은 제품을 설계해왔습니다. 그동안 그녀는 엔지니어, 디자이너 그리고 소비자 간 협력의 중요성을 강조하고 입증해왔습니다. 그녀는 작업에 대해 여러 권위 있는 상을 수상했습니다. 그녀의 성과는 동료들과 제품 사용자들에 대한 그녀의 헌신을 보여줍니다. 우리는 그녀가 팀에 합류하게 되어 정말 기쁩니다."

"걸프브룩의 CDO로 임명된 것은 엄청난 영광이자 특권입니다."라고 마손도 씨는 말했다. "회사의 사명을 발전시키고 업계에서의 입지를 강화하기 위해 최선을 다하겠습니다."

155 걸프브룩 크리에이션스는 요하네스버그에 본사를 두고 있다. 45년 동안 **155** 이 회사는 인체공학적 가구, 시청각 향상 장치, 전동 이동 보조기를 포함한 독립적인 생활을 용이하게 해 주는 장비를 제조해왔다. 이들 제품은 주로 아프리카에서 판매되고 있다.

어휘 immediate 즉각적인 appointment 임명 head 이끌다 material 소재 driving force 주역 mission 사명 accessibility product 접근성 보조 제품 enhance 향상시키다 domestic 국내의 acknowledge 인정하다 resourcefulness 기지 reflect 반영하다 inclusiveness 포용성 self-sufficiency 자립성, 자급자족 emphasize 강조하다 demonstrate 입증하다 collaboration 협력 prestigious 권위 있는 achievement 성과 commitment 헌신 tremendous 엄청난 privilege 특권 strengthen 강화하다 presence 입지 headquarter 본사를 두다 facilitate 용이하게 하다 ergonomic 인체 공학의 motorized 동력을 갖춘 mobility 이동

154 Not / True

번역 마손도 씨에 대해 언급된 것은?
(A) 8월에 몇 개의 상을 수상했다.
(B) 소비자들과 정기적으로 만난다.
(C) 사업차 해외로 자주 나간다.
(D) 30년간 제품 디자이너였다.

해설 두 번째 단락의 두 번째 문장에서 30년의 디자인 경력 동안 마손도 씨는 포용성과 자립성을 반영하는 수많은 제품을 설계해왔다(In her three-decades-long design career, Ms. Masondo has designed numerous products that reflect inclusiveness and self-sufficiency)고 언급하고 있으므로 마손도 씨는 30년 동안 제품 디자이너로 일해 왔음을 알 수 있다. 따라서 (D)가 정답이다.

어휘 regularly 정기적으로 frequently 자주 abroad 해외로

155 세부 사항

번역 걸프브룩 크리에이션스와 데보라 다이나믹스의 공통점은?
(A) 수출 시장
(B) 제품 유형
(C) 사업 기간
(D) 본사 위치

해설 첫 단락의 두 번째 문장에서 마손도 씨는 더반에 본사를 둔 데보라 다이나믹스의 소재 개발 부서를 이끌었다(Ms. Masondo headed the materials development division at Deavora Dynamix, based in Durban)면서 그녀는 남아프리카의 국내 시장에서 독립적인 생활을 향상시키기 위한 접근성 보조 제품을 개발한다는 회사의 사명을 뒷받침하는 주역이었다(She was the driving force behind that company's mission to develop accessibility products to enhance independent living in South Africa's domestic market)고 했고, 마지막 단락의 첫 문장에서 걸프브룩 크리에이션스(Gulfbrook Creations)를 언급하며 이 회사는 인체공학적 가구, 시청각 향상 장치, 전동 이동 보조기를 포함한 독립적인 생활을 용이하게 해 주는 장비를 제조해왔다(the company has been manufacturing equipment that facilitates independent living, including ergonomic furniture, audio- and visual-enhancement devices, and motorized mobility aids)고 했다. 두 회사 모두 독립적인 생활을 도와주는 보조 장비를 생산하고 있으므로 (B)가 정답이다.

어휘 export 수출

156 문장 삽입

번역 [1], [2], [3], [4]로 표시된 위치 중에서 다음 문장이 들어가기에 가장 적합한 곳은?

"그녀는 10년 동안 이 직책에서 근무했는데, 데보라 다이나믹스가 사업을 시작한지 2년 뒤 입사했었다."

(A) [1]
(B) [2]
(C) [3]
(D) [4]

해설 주어진 문장에서 '그녀(She)는 10년 동안 이 직책에서(in that capacity) 근무했으며 데보라 다이나믹스(Deavora Dynamix)가 창업한지 2년 뒤 입사했었다'고 했으므로, 주어진 문장 앞에는 She로 받을 수 있는 여자의 이름과 그녀가 데보라 다이나믹스에서 맡고 있던 직책에 대한 내용이 있어야 한다. 따라서 마손도 씨가 데보라 다이나믹스에서 소재 개발 부서를 이끌었다

(Ms. Masondo headed the materials development division at Deavora Dynamix)며 이름과 직무를 언급하는 내용 뒤인 [2]에 들어가는 것이 글의 흐름상 자연스러우므로 (B)가 정답이다.

어휘 capacity 직책, 지위 operation 사업

157-158 문자 메시지

> **프리야 가오 (오전 7시 52분)**
> 안녕하세요, 루이스. 157 오늘 사무실에서 근무하시나요?
>
> **루이스 푸엔테스 (오전 7시 53분)**
> 지금 집에서 나가는 중이에요.
>
> **프리야 가오 (오전 7시 54분)**
> 다행이네요! 혹시 부탁 하나 드려도 될까 해서요.
>
> **루이스 푸엔테스 (오전 7시 55분)**
> 물론이죠! 뭐가 필요한가요?
>
> **프리야 가오 (오전 7시 56분)**
> 158 오늘 제가 재택근무를 하는데 오전 9시에 지역 관리자들과 전화 회의가 있어요. 그런데 회의에 필요한 노트가 제 책상 위에 있네요. 제 컴퓨터 옆 빨간 폴더 안에요. 보통 사무실에 일찍 출근하시길래 그것들을 스캔해서 이메일로 저에게 보내주실 수 있을까 싶었어요.
>
> **루이스 푸엔테스 (오전 7시 58분)**
> 8시 30분까지는 거기 도착할 거예요. 그것부터 먼저 할게요.
>
> **프리야 가오 (오전 7시 59분)**
> 정말 고맙습니다! 다음에 사무실에 같이 있게 되면 제가 점심을 살게요.
>
> **어휘** wonder 궁금하다 favor 부탁 regional 지역의

157 의도 파악

번역 오전 7시 53분에 푸엔테스 씨가 "지금 집에서 나가는 중이에요"라고 쓴 의도는?
(A) 직장에 늦었다.
(B) 점심 시간에 맞춰 집에 올 것이다.
(C) 사무실로 가는 중이다.
(D) 이미 문서를 스캔했다.

해설 7시 52분에 가오 씨가 오늘 사무실에서 근무하는지(Are you working in the office today?)를 묻는 말에, 7시 53분에 푸엔테스 씨가 지금 집에서 나가는 중(I'm leaving the house now)이라고 대답한 것이므로, 푸엔테스 씨가 출근하는 중이라는 의도로 한 말임을 알 수 있다. 따라서 (C)가 정답이다.

어휘 in time for ~에 시간 맞춰

158 세부 사항

번역 가오 씨는 무슨 문제가 있는가?
(A) 폴더에 라벨을 잘못 붙였다.
(B) 사무실에 중요한 정보를 두고 왔다.
(C) 컴퓨터를 고치는 데 도움이 필요하다.
(D) 전화 회의를 위한 번호를 잊어버렸다.

해설 7시 56분에 가오 씨가 오늘 자신이 재택근무를 하는데 오전 9시에 지역 관리자들과 전화 회의가 있다(I'm working from home today and have a call with the regional managers at 9 A.M.)고 한 뒤, 회의에 필요한 노트가 책상 위에 있다(But the notes I need for the call are on my desk)고 문제점을 말하고 있다. 따라서 가오 씨가 필요한 자료를 사무실에 놓고 왔다는 것을 알 수 있으므로 (B)가 정답이다.

어휘 mislabel 라벨을 잘못 붙이다

> **Paraphrasing**
> 지문의 notes → 정답의 information

159-161 웹페이지

> https://www.morrisville.gov.za/cityplanning/buildingpermits
>
> **건축 허가증 신청하기**
>
> 모리스빌 시 경계 내에서 건설 공사에 착수하기 전에 시에서 발급한 건축 허가증이 필요할 수 있습니다. 배관, 전기 또는 냉난방과 같은 건물 내부 시스템 공사에는 시의 허가증이 요구되지 않습니다. 159 건물을 추가하거나 크기를 확장하는 경우, 건물의 외관을 변경하는 경우, 또는 완전히 새로운 건설 프로젝트의 경우에는 허가증이 필요합니다. 아래는 허가증을 받고 시 정책을 온전히 준수하기 위한 절차입니다.
>
> 1. 건물이 제대로 등록되었는지 확인하세요. 더 많은 정보는 등록 및 토지 이용 페이지를 참고하세요.
>
> 2. 건축 허가증을 위한 신청서를 제출하세요. 160 신청서를 작성하는 데 도움이 필요하시면 도시 계획과의 로널드 아비오예 씨에게 연락하세요.
>
> 3. 귀하는 편지를 받게 되며, 신청서가 승인되었을 경우 공식 건축 허가증이 동봉되어 있을 겁니다. 161 허가서를 받은 다음 공사 현장 주요 출입구의 잘 보이는 곳에 게시하면 공사가 시작될 수 있습니다.

어휘 permit 허가증 issue 발급하다 initiate 착수하다 limit 경계 interior 내부의 plumbing 배관 exterior 외부의 appearance 외관 compliance 준수 appropriately 제대로, 적절하게 register 등록하다 registration 등록 application 신청(서) enclose 동봉하다 commence 시작하다 visible (눈에) 보이는

159 세부 사항

번역 어떤 종류의 프로젝트에 허가증이 필요한가?
(A) 건물의 배관 시스템 개선 작업
(B) 에어컨 시스템 설치 작업
(C) 거주지 내 배선 개선 작업
(D) 사무실 건물 확장 작업

해설 첫 단락 세 번째 문장에서 건물을 추가하거나 크기를 확장하는 경우, 건물의 외관을 변경하는 경우, 또는 완전히 새로운 건설 프로젝트의 경우에는 허가증이 필요하다(A permit will be needed for adding to or expanding the size of a building, for changing the exterior appearance of a building, or for any brand-new construction project)고 했으므로 사무실 건물을 확장하는 데는 허가증이 필요함을 알 수 있다. 따라서 (D)가 정답이다.

어휘 install 설치하다 wiring 배선 residence 거주지 enlarge 확장하다

> **Paraphrasing**
> 지문의 expanding → 정답의 Enlarging

160 세부 사항

번역 웹페이지에 따르면, 왜 아비오예 씨에게 연락해야 하는가?
(A) 계획을 변경하려고
(B) 건물 유지보수 일정을 잡으려고
(C) 양식 작성 시 도움을 받으려고
(D) 신청서의 진행 상황을 확인하려고

해설 세 번째 단락의 두 번째 문장에서 신청서를 작성하는 데 도움이 필요하면 도시 계획과의 로널드 아비오예 씨에게 연락하라(Please contact Ronald Abioye at the City Planning Office if you need assistance completing this application)고 했으므로 (C)가 정답이다.

어휘 maintenance 유지보수 fill out ~을 작성하다 form 양식 status (진행) 상황

> **Paraphrasing**
> 지문의 completing this application
> → 정답의 filling out a form

161 Not / True

번역 웹페이지에 건설 전 단계로 명시된 것은?
(A) 문서가 게시된다.
(B) 공사 현장을 점검 받는다.
(C) 설계도에 엔지니어가 서명한다.
(D) 건물 소유주가 이메일을 받는다.

해설 마지막 단락의 두 번째 문장에서 허가서를 받은 다음 공사 현장 주요 출입구의 잘 보이는 곳에 게시하면 공사가 시작될 수 있다(Work may commence once the permit is received and then posted in an easily visible location at the main entrance of the construction site)고 했다. 따라서 건설 전 단계로 해야 할 일은 허가서를 공사장 출입구에 게시하는 것이므로 (A)가 정답이다.

어휘 inspect 점검하다 plan 설계도

162-163 일정표

밀스버그 여름 축제
밀스버그 연례 여름 축제가 이번 6월 60주년을 맞이합니다!

162 개막 행진
6월 20일, 오전 10시

이것은 여름 축제에서 가장 오래되고 잘 알려진 행사입니다. 행진은 축제의 공식적인 시작을 알리며 화려한 꽃수레와 행진 밴드들이 등장합니다.

162 어린이 놀이 축제 마당
6월 20일-26일, 정오-오후 8시
밀스버그 공원에서 축제 놀이기구와 놀거리

162, 163 야외 콘서트 시리즈
6월 20일-26일, 오후 7시
그린로우 공원에서 포크, 재즈, 클래식을 포함한 라이브 음악
163 장작불로 구운 피자와 다른 간식들을 구입할 수 있습니다.

162 야외 미술 스튜디오
6월 26일, 오후 3시-오후 9시
축제 마지막 날, 현지 화가, 사진작가, 도예가들이 리버사이드 예술 단지 앞 공원에서 열리는 작품 관람에 시민들을 초대합니다.

어휘 parade 행진 official 공식적인 elaborate 화려한 float 꽃수레 fair 축제 마당 carnival 축제 ride 놀이 기구 wood-fired 장작불로 요리한 open-air 야외의 potter 도예가 complex (건물) 단지

162 Not / True

번역 축제에 대해 명시된 것은?
(A) 1년에 여러 번 열린다.
(B) 모든 연령대를 위한 활동이 있다.
(C) 행사는 실내에서 열린다.
(D) 행사는 한 곳에서 열린다.

해설 지문 전체에 나열된 행사 일정이 개막 행진(Opening Parade), 어린이 놀이 축제 마당(Children's Fun Fair), 야외 콘서트 시리즈(Outdoor Concert Series), 야외 미술 스튜디오(Open-Air Art Studio)로, 축제가 어린이에서 어른까지 다양한 연령대를 위한 활동들로 구성되어 있음을 알 수 있다. 따라서 (B)가 정답이다.

어휘 indoors 실내에서

163 세부 사항

번역 방문객들은 어느 행사에서 음식을 구입할 수 있는가?
(A) 개막 행진
(B) 어린이 놀이 축제 마당
(C) 야외 콘서트 시리즈
(D) 야외 미술 스튜디오

해설 세 번째 행사 항목인 야외 콘서트 시리즈(Outdoor Concert Series)에서 장작불로 구운 피자와 다른 간식들을 구입할 수 있다(Wood-fired pizza and other snacks will be available for purchase)고 언급하고 있으므로 (C)가 정답이다.

> **Paraphrasing**
> 지문의 pizza and other snacks → 질문의 food

164-167 정보   ▶동영상 강의

알맞은 가격에 좋아하는 경기를 시청하세요!

164 종합 농구 채널(TBC)의 재미있고 통찰력 넘치는 콘텐츠를 TBC 요금제에 가입하여 스마트폰, 태블릿 또는 스마트 TV로 스트리밍하세요! TBC 앱을 다운로드하시거나 www.totalbasketballchannel.com을 방문하셔서 다음 구독 옵션 중 하나에 가입하세요.

165 TBC 플래티넘 요금제 모든 생중계 경기, 광고 없음	167 TBC 골드 요금제 대부분의 생중계 경기, 광고 없음	166 TBC 실버 요금제 선택한 한 팀의 대부분의 생중계 경기	TBC 코퍼 요금제 TBC 경기 하이라이트
• 모든 경기와 해설 스트리밍 • 최대 3대의 기기에서 시청 • **165** 전국 TV 방송 경기 포함 • 월 29달러 또는 연 149달러	• 모든 팀의 경기 스트리밍 • 최대 3대의 기기에서 시청 • 전국 TV 방송 경기 제외 • **167** 월 19달러 또는 연 99달러	• 좋아하는 TBC 팀의 경기 스트리밍 • 최대 2대의 기기에서 시청 • 광고 포함 • 전국 TV 방송 경기 제외 • 월 9달러 또는 연 49달러	• 경기 하이라이트의 주간 재방송 • 해설 방송 시청 또는 다운로드 • 광고 포함 • 1대의 기기에서 시청 • 월 5달러 또는 연 29달러

어휘 insightful 통찰력 있는 subscribe to ~을 구독하다 plan 요금제 sign up for ~에 가입하다 subscription 구독 commercial 광고 commentary 해설 nationally 전국적으로 televised TV로 방송되는 exclude 제외하다 replay 재방송

164 추론 / 암시

번역 정보는 어디에서 찾아볼 수 있을 것 같은가?
(A) 스포츠 심리학자를 위한 학술지
(B) 농구 규칙 설명서
(C) 스포츠 잡지
(D) 농구 선수의 전기

해설 첫 문장에서 종합 농구 채널(TBC)의 재미있고 통찰력 넘치는 콘텐츠를 TBC 요금제에 가입하여 스마트폰, 태블릿 또는 스마트 TV로 스트리밍하라(Stream exciting, insightful content from the Total Basketball Channel (TBC) on your smartphone, tablet, or smart TV by subscribing to a TBC Plan!)고 스포츠 채널을 홍보하고 있는 것으로 보아 스포츠 잡지에 실린 광고 문임을 유추할 수 있다. 따라서 (C)가 정답이다.

어휘 psychologist 심리학자 journal 학술지 manual 설명서 biography 전기

165 세부 사항

번역 TBC 플래티넘 요금제의 유일한 점은?
(A) 광고가 없다.
(B) 월간 결제 옵션이 없다.
(C) 최대 3대의 기기에서 스트리밍할 수 있게 해 준다.
(D) 전국 TV 방송 경기가 포함된다.

해설 표의 TBC 플래티넘 요금제(TBC Platinum Plan) 항목 하단에 전국 TV 방송 경기 포함(Includes nationally televised games)이라는 특징은 플래티넘 요금제에서만 확인할 수 있으므로 (D)가 정답이다.

166 세부 사항

번역 한 팀에만 관심이 있는 구독자를 위해 고안된 요금제는?
(A) TBC 플래티넘 요금제
(B) TBC 골드 요금제
(C) TBC 실버 요금제
(D) TBC 코퍼 요금제

해설 표의 TBC 실버 요금제(TBC Silver Plan) 항목에서 선택한 한 팀의 대부분의 생중계 경기(Most live games played by a team of your choice)를 시청할 수 있다고 설명하고 있으므로 (C)가 정답이다.

167 세부 사항

번역 TBC 골드 요금제는 얼마인가?
(A) 월 9달러
(B) 월 19달러
(C) 연 29달러
(D) 연 49달러

해설 표의 TBC 골드 요금제(TBC Gold Plan) 항목의 하단에 월 19달러 또는 연 99달러($19 / month or $99 / year)라고 나와 있으므로 (B)가 정답이다.

168-171 블로그 게시글

레지나의 미술 세계 블로그

168 블로그의 정기 독자들은 알다시피 지난 몇 주간 나는 개발업자이자 전직 건축가인 데이비드 그릴리에 의한 브렌틀러 하이츠 해안 지구의 재활성화에 집중해 왔다. 단연코, 이 프로그램의 가장 인상적인 결과는 **170** 팩스턴 가에 있는 옛 산업 건물의 개조이다. 건물의 1층에는 현재 인기 있는 커피숍과 서점이 들어서 있고, 아름답게 조경된 정원에는 색다른 금속 조각들이 있다. **170** 2층은 브렌틀러 하이츠 갤러리가 사용할 것이라는 소식을 전하게 되어 기쁘다.

갤러리는 내가 수년 전 보석 공예 워크숍에서 만났던 브렌틀러 하이츠의 예술가인 **169** 프랜신 스칸다르가 운영할 예정이다. **169** 나는 항상 그녀의 작품에 감탄했으며 내 가게에서 판매하기 위해 그녀의 많은 작품을 구입했다. 그녀가 이 주목받는 갤러리를 운영하게 된다는 것을 알게 되어 매우 기뻤다. 언론 방문 시, 스칸다르 씨는 그릴리 씨가 빈티지한 분위기를 부여하기 위해 팩스턴 가 건물의 본래 특성을 거의 전부 유지했음을 강조했다. 이 덕분에 이 건물은 모든 종류의 예술을 위한 이상적인 배경이 된다.

171 갤러리의 첫 전시에서는 스칸다르 씨의 작품을 전시한다. 장차 스칸다르 씨는 다른 지역 예술가들의 작품들을 선보일 계획이다. 개관식은 6월 8일과 9일 오후 2시부터 오후 7시까지 열릴 예정이다. 자세한 정보는 www.brentlerheightsgallery.org를 방문하면 된다.

— 레지나 응우옌, 5월 2일

어휘 concentrate 집중하다 revitalization 재활성화 waterfront 해안가 district 지구 developer 개발업자 former 이전의 architect 건축가 by far 단연코 industrial 산업의 house 수용하다 landscape 조경하다 sculpture 조각 occupy 사용하다 admire 감탄하다 obtain 얻다 creation 창작품 high-profile 세간의 이목을 끄는 retain 유지하다 feature 특성 ideal 이상적인 backdrop 배경 inaugural 첫 showcase 전시하다

168 주제 / 목적

번역 블로그 게시글에서 어떤 주제를 다루는가?
(A) 도시 지구의 변모
(B) 지역 건축가가 발간한 새 출판물
(C) 브렌틀러 하이츠 갤러리에서 제공하는 미술 수업
(D) 브렌틀러 하이츠 예술가들에게 주어진 보조금

해설 첫 단락 첫 문장에서 블로그의 정기 독자들은 알다시피 지난 몇 주간 개발업자이자 전직 건축가인 데이비드 그릴리에 의한 브렌틀러 하이츠 해안 지구의 재활성화에 집중해 왔다(As regular readers of my blog know, over the past few weeks, I have concentrated on the revitalization of the Brentler Heights waterfront district by developer and former architect David Greeley)고 한 뒤, 지문 전체에 걸쳐 해안 지구가 어떻게 탈바꿈했는지 예를 들어 설명하고 있으므로 (A)가 정답이다.

어휘 transformation 변모 release 발간하다 grant 보조금

Paraphrasing
지문의 revitalization → 정답의 transformation

169 Not / True

번역 스칸다르 씨에 대해 명시된 것은?
(A) 대학교에서 보석 공예 수업을 가르친다.
(B) 응우옌 씨의 사업을 위한 공급업자였다.
(C) 평생 대부분을 브렌틀러 하이츠에서 거주했다.
(D) 정원을 위한 대형 금속 조각을 제작한다.

해설 두 번째 단락의 첫 문장에서 응우옌 씨가 프랜신 스칸다르(Francine Skandar)를 언급하며, 뒤이어 자신이 항상 그녀의 작품에 감탄했으며 가게에서 판매하기 위해 그녀의 많은 작품을 구입했다(I always admired her work, and I obtained many of her creations to sell at my shop)고 했다. 따라서 스칸다르 씨는 응우옌 씨의 가게에 작품을 납품해 왔다는 것을 알 수 있으므로 (B)가 정답이다.

170 Not / True

번역 브렌틀러 하이츠 갤러리에 대해 사실인 것은?
(A) 5년 전에 다른 장소에서 문을 열었다.
(B) 오래되고 새로 단장한 공간에 위치해 있다.
(C) 건물의 두 개 층을 사용한다.
(D) 그릴리 씨가 운영할 예정이다.

해설 첫 단락의 두 번째 문장에서 팩스턴 가에 있는 옛 산업 건물이 개조된 것(the renovation of a former industrial building on Paxton Street)을 언급했고, 같은 단락의 마지막 문장에서 2층은 브렌틀러 하이츠 갤러리가 사용한다는 소식을 전하게 되어 기쁘다(I am pleased to report that the second floor will be occupied by the Brentler Heights Gallery)고 했다. 따라서 브렌틀러 하이츠 갤러리는 오래된 건물의 새롭게 단장된 공간에 입주해 있음을 알 수 있으므로 (B)가 정답이다.

어휘 refurbish 새 단장하다

Paraphrasing
지문의 renovation → 정답의 refurbished

171 문장 삽입

번역 [1], [2], [3], [4]로 표시된 위치 중에서 다음 문장이 들어가기에 가장 적합한 곳은?
"장차 스칸다르 씨는 다른 지역 예술가들의 작품들을 선보일 계획이다."
(A) [1]
(B) [2]
(C) [3]
(D) [4]

해설 주어진 문장에서 장차(In the future) 스칸다르 씨가 선보이려고 계획하는 작품들에 대해 언급하고 있으므로, 주어진 문장 앞에는 스칸다르 씨가 현재 기획 중인 전시에서 소개될 작품에 대한 내용이 있어야 한다. 따라서 갤러리의 첫 전시에는 스칸다르 씨의 작품을 전시한다(The gallery's inaugural exhibit will showcase Ms. Skandar's work)는 내용 뒤인 [4]에 들어가는 것이 글의 흐름상 자연스러우므로 (D)가 정답이다.

172-175 온라인 채팅

리즈 유엔 (오전 8시 58분)
모두들 안녕하세요. 172 그룹 이메일로 보내드린 웹사이트 콘텐츠에 대한 신속한 피드백에 감사드려요. 사진과 거기 딸린 콘텐츠가 달력을 충분히 강하게 마케팅하지 못하는 것 같다는 데 모두가 동의하고 있어요.

헬렌 블랙 (오전 8시 59분)
맞아요. 그런데 우리가 같은 자료를 보고 있는지 확인하려고 하는데, 우리 탁상 달력을 보여주는 사진 몇 장이 있고 각각에는 "스텐멕스 문구점의 달력과 함께하는 새해 다짐"이라는 설명이 있어요.

리즈 유엔 (오전 9시 1분)
맞아요. 하지만 주된 문제는 사진과 거기 딸린 콘텐츠가 더 매력적이고 상호 소통적이어야 한다는 점이에요.

제프 스피나 (오전 9시 2분)
저도 동의해요. 고객들에게 홈 오피스 정리에 도움이 되도록 달력을 어떻게 사용하는지에 대한 의견을 글로 써서 보내달라고 하면 어떨까요? 우리 달력이 포함된 홈 오피스 사진을 우리에게 보낼 수도 있고요.

헬렌 블랙 (오전 9시 4분)
173 제가 재택근무하는 날 중 하루의 제 공간 사진을 기꺼이 공유할게요. 그리고 달력을 사용하는 게 업무 관리에 어떻게 도움이 되는지에 대한 설명도 쓸 수 있어요. 고객들이 따를 수 있는 예시로 그걸 사용할 수 있어요.

리즈 유엔 (오전 9시 5분)
좋은 생각이에요. 그리고 174 웹사이트 기능에 문제가 생긴 건 어떻게 됐죠?

제프 스피나 (오전 9시 6분)
그러면 좋겠네요, 헬렌.

헬렌 블랙 (오전 9시 7분)
저도 봤어요.

제프 스피나 (오전 9시 8분)
175 그 점에 대해서는 려 지와 이야기할게요. 그녀의 팀이 곧 팝업창과 소셜 미디어 링크가 다시 작동하도록 할 수 있을 거예요.

리즈 유엔 (오전 9시 9분)
175 고마워요, 제프. 172 일단 사이트가 기능을 하고 우리 콘텐츠가 마무리되면, 그녀의 팀이 우리가 결정한 것을 홈페이지에 업데이트할 수 있을 거예요.

어휘 prompt 신속한 accompany 딸리다, 동반하다 material 자료 desktop 탁상 caption 설명(문), 표제 engaging 매력적인 interactive 상호 소통적인 organize 정리하다 explanation 설명 keep track of ~을 관리하다 functionality 기능 finalize 마무리하다

172 주제 / 목적

번역 채팅 참가자들은 무엇을 논의하고 있는가?
(A) 웹사이트에 대한 변경 사항
(B) 고객들의 피드백
(C) 새로운 문구류 주문 방법
(D) 어느 마케팅 회사를 선택할지

해설 8시 58분에 유엔 씨가 그룹 이메일로 보낸 웹사이트 콘텐츠에 대한 신속한 피드백에 감사하다(Thank you for your prompt feedback on the Web site content I sent out in the group e-mail)면서 사진과 거기 딸린 콘텐츠가 달력을 충분히 강하게 마케팅하지 못하는 것 같다는 데 모두가 동의하고 있다(Everyone agrees that the photos and the accompanying content do not seem to market the calendars strongly enough)고 논의를 시작했고, 9시 9분에 유엔 씨가 일단 사이트가 기능을 하고 콘텐츠가 마무리되면 결정한 것을 홈페이지에 업데이트할 수 있을 것(Once the site is functional and we have our content finalized, her team can update the home page with what we have decided)이라고 했다. 채팅 전반에 걸쳐 웹사이트 콘텐츠가 충분한 홍보 효과를 내지 못한다는 문제점을 논의하고 그 해결책을 웹사이트에 반영하는 것에 대해 이야기하고 있으므로 (A)가 정답이다.

173 Not / True

번역 블랙 씨에 대해 명시된 것은?
(A) 프리랜서 사진작가이다.
(B) 가끔 재택근무를 한다.
(C) 인기 있는 사무실 달력을 디자인했다.
(D) 최근에 새 사무실 가구를 샀다.

해설 9시 4분에 블랙 씨가 재택근무하는 날 중 하루의 자신의 공간 사진을 기꺼이 공유하겠다(I'd be happy to share a photo of my own setup—from one of the days that I'm working from home)고 했으므로 블랙 씨는 가끔 집에서 근무하는 날이 있음을 알 수 있다. 따라서 (B)가 정답이다.

174 의도 파악

번역 오전 9시 7분에 블랙 씨가 "저도 봤어요"라고 쓴 의도는?
(A) 사진을 몇 장 골랐다.
(B) 유엔 씨의 회의 요청을 수락했다.
(C) 스피나 씨에게 이메일을 여러 개 받았다.
(D) 웹사이트가 제대로 작동하지 않고 있다는 것을 안다.

해설 9시 5분에 유엔 씨가 웹사이트 기능에 문제가 생긴 건 어떻게 됐는지(what about the problems with the functionality of the Web site?)를 묻는 말에 9시 7분에 블랙 씨가 자신도 봤다(I saw those)고 응답한 것이므로, 웹사이트에 문제가 발생한 일을 자신도 알고 있다는 의도로 한 말임을 알 수 있다. 따라서 (D)가 정답이다.

어휘 accept 수락하다

175 세부 사항

번역 유엔 씨는 스피나 씨에게 무엇에 대해 감사하는가?
(A) 동료에게 연락하겠다고 제안한 일
(B) 직원 계약을 마무리 지은 일
(C) 지 씨의 성과를 평가한 일
(D) 작업 공간의 사진을 찍은 일

해설 9시 8분에 스피나 씨가 그 점(웹사이트 기능 문제)에 대해 려 지와 이야기하겠다(I'll speak with Ryeo Jee about that)고 한 것에 대해 9시 9분에 유엔 씨가 고맙다(Thanks)고 한 것이므로, 유엔 씨는 스피나 씨가 동료에게 연락하겠다고 한 일에 감사를 표했음을 알 수 있다. 따라서 (A)가 정답이다.

어휘 review 평가하다 performance 성과

Paraphrasing
지문의 speak with → 정답의 contact

176-180 기사 + 이메일

힐사이드 하우스 영업 준비 완료

오클랜드 (4월 2일) — 힐사이드 하우스는 오클랜드에서 가장 새롭고 호화로운 행사 공간으로 현재 영업 중이다. 이 독특한 장소는 시내 중심부에서 불과 몇 분 거리의 한적한 안식처이다. 176 천장의 여러 창문들이

하늘을 실내 장식의 일부처럼 보이게 하는 한편, 유리 벽은 방문객들에게 초록 정원과 화사한 꽃들의 황홀한 경관을 제공한다.

힐사이드 하우스는 결혼식과 기타 사교 모임뿐만 아니라 기업 행사에도 완벽한 장소이다. **180 주방은 프랭클린 허드 재단상을 두 차례 수상한 바슈 말릭 셰프가 지휘한다.** 말릭 셰프는 행사 주최자가 다채로운 작은 접시 요리, 가족식 정찬, 또는 뷔페식 브런치 등 어떤 것을 선택하든 상관없이 힐사이드 하우스의 메뉴를 감독한다.

"알맞은 장소를 선택하는 것은 성공의 열쇠입니다."라고 힐사이드 하우스의 러셀 이슬리 본부장은 말한다. "저희는 아름다운 장소, 숙련된 직원들, 그리고 훌륭한 음식까지 모든 것을 제공합니다. 저희 행사 진행자는 고객님과 협력하여 고객님의 결혼식 또는 기업 **177 행사**를 기억할 만한 순간으로 만들어 드립니다."

어휘 spectacular 호화로운, 장관의 secluded 한적한 haven 안식처 enchanted 황홀한 setting 장소 gathering 모임 corporate 기업의 direction 지휘 oversee 감독하다 eclectic 다방면의 coordinator 진행자, 조정자 function 행사

수신: 헤일리 콜링 〈hcolling@kitchendesigns.co.nz〉
발신: 레카 타이모나 〈rtaimona@hillsidehouse.co.nz〉
날짜: 5월 10일
제목: 정보
첨부: 🔗 힐사이드 하우스 옵션

콜링 씨께:

178 다가오는 제품 출시와 관련해 힐사이드 하우스에 연락 주셔서 감사합니다! 네, 6월 16일은 이용 가능하며 귀사의 키친 디자인스 기업 행사는 현재 저희 일정에 등록되어 있습니다.

행사를 준비하시면서 저희가 여러 참신한 브랜딩 기회를 제공하고 있다는 점을 참고해 주십시오. 예를 들어, 귀사의 로고를 네온 조명으로 전시하거나 배너를 걸 수 있습니다. **180 말릭 쉐프와 그의 팀이 귀사와 협력하여 음식 품목이나 케이크에 로고가 들어가도록 할 수 있습니다.** **179 메뉴 옵션과 가격에 대한 정보를 첨부합니다.** 저희는 연설과 발표를 위한 최첨단 음향 시스템 및 시청각 장비를 갖추고 있습니다. 행사를 위한 오락거리를 원하신다면 밴드와 음악가 목록 또한 제공해 드릴 수 있습니다.

다른 질문이 있으시면 저에게 알려 주십시오. 저희 힐사이드 하우스는 귀사의 행사를 주최하게 되기를 기대합니다.

레카 타이모나, 행사 담당자
힐사이드 하우스

어휘 reach out 연락하다 launch 출시 opportunity 기회 attach 첨부하다 state-of-the-art 최첨단의 audiovisual 시청각의 entertainment 오락 supply 제공하다

176 Not / True

번역 기사에서 힐사이드 하우스에 대해 명시된 것은?
(A) 오클랜드 시내에서 멀다.
(B) 최근에 개조된 건물에 위치해 있다.
(C) 야외 전망을 특징으로 한다.
(D) 이슬리 씨가 매입할 예정이다.

해설 기사의 첫 단락 마지막 문장에서 천장의 여러 창문들이 하늘을 실내 장식의 일부처럼 보이게 하는 한편 유리 벽은 방문객들에게 초록 정원과 화사한 꽃들의 황홀한 경관을 제공한다(Its glass walls give guests an enchanted view of green gardens and bright flowers, while multiple windows in the ceiling make the sky part of the interior decoration)고 했다. 따라서 힐사이드 하우스는 천장의 유리창과 유리 벽을 통해 바깥 풍경을 감상할 수 있는 점이 특징이라는 것을 알 수 있으므로 (C)가 정답이다.

177 동의어 찾기

번역 기사의 세 번째 단락 7행의 "function"과 의미가 가장 가까운 단어는?
(A) 직업
(B) 사용
(C) 조직
(D) 모임

해설 의미상 결혼식 또는 기업 '행사'라는 뜻으로 쓰였으므로 '모임'을 뜻하는 (D) gathering이 정답이다.

178 주제 / 목적

번역 이메일의 한 가지 목적은?
(A) 서비스 할인을 제공하려고
(B) 메뉴에 대한 피드백을 요청하려고
(C) 마감일을 상기시키려고
(D) 파티 예약을 확인하려고

해설 이메일의 첫 단락 첫 문장에서 다가오는 제품 출시와 관련해 힐사이드 하우스에 연락해 줘서 감사하다(Thank you for reaching out to Hillside House about your upcoming product launch!)고 한 뒤, 6월 16일은 이용 가능하며 귀사의 키친 디자인스 기업 행사가 현재 일정에 등록되어 있다(Yes, 16 June is available; your Kitchen Designs corporate celebration is now on our schedule)며 행사를 위한 예약이 되어 있다는 확인 답신을 보내고 있으므로 (D)가 정답이다.

Paraphrasing
지문의 celebration → 정답의 party

179 세부 사항

번역 타이모나 씨가 이메일과 함께 무엇을 보냈는가?
(A) 장식 이미지
(B) 음악가 목록
(C) 음식 및 비용 관련 세부 정보
(D) 회사 로고 디자인

해설 이메일의 두 번째 단락 네 번째 문장에서 타이모나 씨가 메뉴 옵션과 가격에 대한 정보를 첨부한다(I am attaching information about the menu options and pricing)고 했으므로 (C)가 정답이다.

Paraphrasing
지문의 menu options and pricing → 정답의 food and costs

180 연계

번역 콜링 씨의 기업 행사에 대해 결론지을 수 있는 것은?
(A) 수상 경력이 있는 요리사가 준비한 음식이 포함될 것이다.
(B) 100명이 넘는 사람들이 참석할 것이다.
(C) 키친 디자인스 직원에 대한 시상식과 함께 끝날 것이다.
(D) 라이브 밴드가 연주하는 음악이 포함될 것이다.

해설 기사의 두 번째 단락 두 번째 문장에서 주방은 프랭클린 허드 재단상을 두 차례 수상한 바슈 말릭 쉐프가 지휘한다(The kitchen is under the direction of Chef Bashu Malik, a two-time Franklin Heard Foundation winner)고 했고, 이메일의 두 번째 단락 세 번째 문장에서 콜링 씨에게 말릭 쉐프와 그의 팀이 귀사와 협력하여 음식 품목이나 케이크에 로고가 들어가도록 할 수 있다(Chef Malik and his staff can also work with you to include logos on food items or a cake)고 했다. 따라서 콜링 씨의 기업 행사에는 프랭클린 허드 재단상 수상자인 말릭 쉐프가 준비한 음식이 제공됨을 알 수 있으므로 (A)가 정답이다.

어휘 feature 포함하다 conclude 끝나다, 결론 내리다 presentation 시상식

181-185 이메일 + 이메일

수신: 고객 서비스 〈customerservice@takembootcompany.com〉
발신: 벨라 마이어스 〈b.meyers@leadmail.com〉
날짜: 8월 15일
제목: 13783번 주문

안녕하세요,

183 저는 최근 귀사의 에린 스타일 웨스턴 부츠를 40사이즈, 초콜릿 색상으로 한 켤레 주문했습니다. 부츠는 어제 도착했지만 안타깝게도 **181** 실제 색상이 귀사의 웹사이트 사진에 보이는 색상과 다릅니다. 다음 달 특별한 행사에서 이 부츠를 신고 싶었지만, 예상보다 훨씬 어두운 색상이라 계획하고 있는 의상에 어울리지 않습니다.

183 저는 스타일과 사이즈는 동일하지만 테라코타 색상의 다른 부츠로 교환하기를 원합니다. 어떻게 진행하면 되는지 알려주세요. **182** 저는 과거에 귀사의 부츠를 여러 켤레 구입했고 항상 내구성과 편안함에 만족해 왔습니다.

벨라 마이어스

어휘 match 어울리다 outfit 의상 durability 내구성 comfort 편안함

수신: 벨라 마이어스 〈b.meyers@leadmail.com〉
발신: 고객 서비스 〈customerservice@takembootcompany.com〉
날짜: 8월 16일
제목: 회신: 13783번 주문

마이어스 씨께,

이메일을 보내주셔서 감사합니다. 주문하신 물품에 실망하셨다니 유감입니다. 반품을 원하시는 부츠가 착용되지 않았다면 기꺼이 교환 처리를 해 드리겠습니다.

183 현재 요청하신 사이즈, 스타일, 색상으로는 부츠가 품절되었습니다. 저희는 소규모 회사이기 때문에 재고가 항상 완전히 구비되어 있지는 못합니다. 고객님께서 구매하신 제품 외에, 현재 고객님 사이즈의 에린 부츠는 샌드와 포레스트 색상이 있습니다. 더 연한 색상에 관심이 있으시므로 샌드 색상을 추천합니다. 이 색은 따뜻한 색조로 매우 다양한 스타일에 어울립니다. 또한, **184** 저희의 가장 인기 있는 스타일인 비올라 부츠를 포함하여 고객님께서 선호하시는 색상으로 다른 스타일들도 있습니다.

상기 옵션 중 하나로 부츠를 교환하고 싶으시다면 알려주세요. 그러시면 **185** 귀하께서 댁에서 출력하실 수 있도록 우편 요금 선불 반품 라벨을 이메일로 보내드리겠습니다.

이용해 주셔서 감사합니다. 아직 저희 소식지에 등록하지 않으셨다면 등록을 제안 드립니다. 저희는 단종된 스타일에 할인을 제공합니다.

브렌던 스티븐스, 고객 서비스 담당자
테이켐 부츠 컴퍼니

어휘 arrange 처리하다, 준비하다 out of stock 품절된 inventory 재고 pale 옅은 shade 색조 versatile 다용도의 postage-paid 우편 요금 선불의, 우편 요금 지급필 sign up for ~에 등록하다 discontinued 단종된

181 세부 사항

번역 첫 번째 이메일에서 설명된 문제는?
(A) 주문이 예상보다 늦게 배송되었다.
(B) 웹사이트의 제품 색상이 정확하지 않다.
(C) 일부 부츠가 이전 부츠들만큼 편하지 않았다.
(D) 실수로 제품이 잘못된 사이즈로 주문되었다.

해설 첫 번째 이메일의 첫 단락 두 번째 문장에서 부츠의 실제 색상이 웹사이트 사진에 보이는 색상과 다르다(their actual colour is different from the colour pictured on your Web site)고 설명하고 있으므로 (B)가 정답이다.

어휘 incorrect 부정확한 previous 이전의 accidentally 실수로

182 Not / True

번역 마이어스 씨가 명시하는 것은?
(A) 테이켐 부츠 컴퍼니의 단골 고객이었다.
(B) 아직 행사에 착용할 의상을 사야 한다.
(C) 웹사이트를 찾아내는 데 어려움이 있었다.
(D) 어두운 색상의 부츠를 선호한다.

해설 첫 번째 이메일의 마지막 단락 마지막 문장에서 마이어스 씨가 과거에 이 회사의 부츠를 여러 켤레 구입했고 항상 내구성과 편안함에 만족해 왔다(I have purchased several pairs of boots from your company in the past and have always been pleased with their durability and comfort)고 했으므로 테이켐 부츠 컴퍼니를 애용하는 고객임을 알 수 있다. 따라서 (A)가 정답이다.

어휘 navigate (웹사이트를) 찾다

183 연계

번역 현재 에린 스타일 부츠에서 구입할 수 있는 색상이 아닌 것은?
(A) 샌드
(B) 포레스트
(C) 초콜릿
(D) 테라코타

해설 첫 번째 이메일의 첫 단락 첫 문장에서 마이어스 씨가 최근 에린 스타일 웨스턴 부츠를 40사이즈, 초콜릿 색상으로 한 켤레 주문했다(I recently ordered a pair of your Western boots in style Erin, size 40, in the chocolate colour)고 했고, 두 번째 단락 첫 문장에서 스타일과 사이즈는 동일하지만 테라코타 색상의 다른 부츠로 교환하기를 원한다(I would like to exchange the boots for another pair of the same style and size but in the terracotta colour)고 했다. 그리고 두 번째 이메일의 두 번째 단락 첫 문장에서는 마이어스 씨가 요청한 사이즈, 스타일, 색상으로는 부츠가 현재 품절되었다(At the moment, boots in the size, style, and colour you are requesting are out of stock)고 했다. 따라서 에린 스타일의 테라코타 색상은 현재 품절 상태임을 알 수 있으므로 (D)가 정답이다.

184 추론 / 암시

번역 두 번째 이메일에서 테이켐 부츠 컴퍼니에 대해 암시하는 것은?
(A) 여러 장소에 매장이 있다.
(B) 반품 시 배송비를 청구한다.
(C) 비올라 부츠를 많이 판매한다.
(D) 이 지역에서 가장 인기 있는 부츠 회사이다.

해설 두 번째 이메일의 두 번째 단락 마지막 문장에서 가장 인기 있는 스타일인 비올라 부츠(Viola boots, our most popular style)라고 언급한 것을 통해 비올라 부츠의 판매량이 높다는 것을 짐작할 수 있다. 따라서 (C)가 정답이다.

어휘 charge 청구하다   region 지역

185 세부 사항

번역 스티븐스 씨는 무엇을 하겠다고 제안하는가?
(A) 문서 출력
(B) 배송 라벨의 이메일 발송
(C) 제품 카탈로그 발송
(D) 새 스타일 부츠에 대한 할인 제공

해설 두 번째 이메일의 세 번째 단락 두 번째 문장에서 스티븐스 씨가 마이어스 씨에게 집에서 출력할 수 있도록 우편 요금 선불 반품 라벨을 이메일로 보내겠다(I can send you a postage-paid return label via e-mail for you to print at home)고 제안하고 있으므로 (B)가 정답이다.

186-190 이메일 + 기사 + 웹페이지

수신: 제시카 마폰 〈jmarpone@halecityca.gov〉
발신: 그렉 태너 〈gtanner@halecitynews.com〉
날짜: 7월 1일
제목: 지역 사회 의견

마폰 씨께,

이스트 코어 공원에 대해 제가 작성한 마지막 기사에 꽤 많은 온라인 댓글이 달렸습니다. 댓글들은 블루 트레일의 무성한 잡초와 떨어진 나뭇가지들에 대해 불평하는 주민들로부터 나온 것이었습니다. 그들은 레드 트레일은 상태가 좋지만 186 블루 트레일에는 유지관리 문제가 상당 기간 동안 계속되었다고 말합니다.

시의회의 최신 구성원으로서, 당신은 아직 많은 불만을 듣지 못했을 수도 있습니다. 하지만 186 만약 당신이 이 상황에 관한 브리핑을 받게 된다면, 어떠한 소식이라도 전달해 주시면 감사하겠습니다. 저는 이 사안에 관한 의견을 듣기 위해 187 공원 담당 위원인 오스카 루네스 씨에게 연락했지만 그는 응답하지 않았습니다. 187 그가 은퇴를 준비하느라 바쁠지도 모른다고 누군가 언급했습니다.

그렉 태너
헤일 시티 뉴스

어휘 comment 의견, 댓글   attract 끌다   overgrown (풀, 잡초 등이) 무성한   weed 잡초   branch 나뭇가지   maintenance 유지관리   persist 계속되다   complaint 불만   briefing 브리핑, 요약 보고   pass along ~을 전달하다   reach out 연락하다   commissioner 위원

시 공원 부서, 자원봉사 활동을 시작하다
그렉 태너 작성

헤일 시티 (7월 12일) — 이스트 코어 공원의 산책로 상태에 대한 주민들의 우려에 응하여 헤일 시티 공원 부서는 산책로 유지 계획에 대한 설명 및 개요를 제시한다.

188 "산책로 유지관리는 시 직원들이 수행하던 것에서 전면 자원봉사 모델로 전환 중입니다."라고 187 새로 임명된 공원 담당 위원인 헬렌 얀시가 말했다. "제 전임자가 20년간 시에서 근무한 뒤 사임하기 전에 이 전환 작업을 시작했습니다. 188 그 결과 블루 트레일에 대한 관리가 일시적으로 중단되었습니다."

얀시 씨는 자원봉사 모델이 비용을 절감하고 주민들이 공원 시스템에 더 깊이 참여할 수 있도록 해 줄 것이라고 덧붙였다. 이에 따라, 189 헤일 시티 공원 부서는 첫 자원봉사 청소 행사인 산책로 청소의 날의 일정을 8월 12일 오전 9시부터 오후 2시까지로 정했다. 자원봉사에 관심 있는 사람들은 www.halecityparks.org/events에서 온라인으로 등록할 수 있다.

어휘 launch 시작하다   in response to ~에 응하여   explanation 설명   outline 개요   upkeep 유지   transition 전환하다   appoint 임명하다   predecessor 전임자   step down 사임하다   shift 전환, 변화   temporary 일시적인   suspension 중단   involvement 참여   register 등록하다

헤일 시티 공원 부서

8월 소식

189 8월 8일에 열린 헤일 시티 공원 부서의 첫 산책로 청소의 날은 대성공이었습니다. 열정적인 자원봉사자 단체가 이스트 코어 공원의 블루 트레일에서 쓰레기와 잡초를 치웠고, 맑고 따뜻한 날 정오가 되기 직전 산책로를 깨끗하고 이용할 수 있게 만들었습니다.

다음의 참여자들에게 특별히 감사드립니다.
- 에이미 해리스, 자원봉사 활동을 조직화하고 음료를 가져옴
- **190** 제이슨 스코다, 인근 이스트 하이츠 지역의 주민으로 우리 자원봉사 팀에 전동 트리머, 전지 가위, 갈퀴를 빌려줌

주민 여러분께서는 다가오는 자원봉사 행사에 대해 알 수 있도록 이 페이지를 자주 방문하시기를 권장합니다.

어휘 inaugural 처음의 debris 쓰레기 following 다음의 participant 참여자 coordinate 조직화하다 adjacent 인근의, 인접한 lend 빌려주다 trimmer 트리머(다듬는 기계) pruning shear 전지 가위 rake 갈퀴

186 주제 / 목적

번역 태너 씨가 이메일을 작성한 이유는?
(A) 다가오는 행사에 대해 상관에게 알리려고
(B) 산책로 유지관리에 대한 정보를 요청하려고
(C) 도시 공원 확장을 논의하려고
(D) 새로운 시의회 의원을 축하하려고

해설 이메일의 첫 단락 마지막 문장에서 블루 트레일에는 유지관리 문제가 상당 기간 동안 계속되었다고 한다(maintenance issues have persisted on the Blue Trail for quite some time)고 했고, 두 번째 단락 두 번째 문장에서 만약 당신이 이 상황에 관한 브리핑을 받게 된다면 어떠한 소식이라도 전달해 주면 감사하겠다(if you do get briefings regarding the situation, I would be grateful for any updates you can pass along)고 했다. 따라서, 태너 씨는 마폰 씨에게 블루 트레일의 유지관리 문제에 대한 정보를 요청하려고 글을 썼음을 알 수 있으므로 (B)가 정답이다.

어휘 supervisor 상관

> **Paraphrasing**
> 지문의 updates → 정답의 information

187 연계

번역 얀시 씨에 대해 암시된 것은?
(A) 루네스 씨의 후임자이다.
(B) 이스트 코어 공원 근처에 산다.
(C) 새로운 공원 자원봉사자를 교육한다.
(D) 모금 활동 전문가이다.

해설 이메일의 두 번째 단락 세 번째 문장에서 오스카 루네스 공원 담당 위원(parks commissioner Oscar Lunes)을 언급한 뒤 그 다음 문장에서 그가 은퇴를 준비하느라 바쁠지도 모른다고 누군가 언급했다(Someone mentioned he might be busy preparing for retirement)고 했고, 기사의 두 번째 단락 첫 문장에서 새로 임명된 공원 담당 위원인 헬렌 얀시(newly appointed parks commissioner Helen Yancey)를 언급하고 있다. 따라서, 얀시 씨는 루네스 씨의 후임으로 공원 담당 위원을 맡게 된 사람임을 알 수 있으므로 (A)가 정답이다.

어휘 replacement 후임자 fund-raising 모금

188 세부 사항

번역 무엇이 블루 트레일의 유지관리를 어렵게 했는가?
(A) 레드 트레일의 확장
(B) 부서의 정책 변경
(C) 공원에서 열린 대규모 모임
(D) 길어진 우기

해설 기사의 두 번째 단락 첫 문장에서 산책로 유지관리는 시 직원들이 수행하던 것에서 전면 자원봉사 모델로 전환 중(Trail maintenance is transitioning from being performed by city employees to an all-volunteer model)이며, 같은 단락 마지막 문장에서 그 결과 블루 트레일에 대한 관리가 일시적으로 중단되었다(The result was a temporary suspension of maintenance on the Blue Trail)고 했다. 따라서 블루 트레일에 대한 유지관리가 중단되었던 일은 정책 변경으로 인한 결과임을 알 수 있으므로 (B)가 정답이다.

어휘 expansion 확장 departmental 부서의 gathering 모임 extended 길어진

189 연계

번역 산책로 청소의 날에 대해 사실인 것 같은 것은?
(A) 태너 씨가 처음에 계획했다.
(B) 작업을 완료하는 데 이틀이 걸렸다.
(C) 자원봉사자들은 행사 전에 교육 세션에 참석했다.
(D) 산책로 청소 날짜가 변경되었다.

해설 기사의 세 번째 단락 두 번째 문장에서 헤일 시티 공원 부서는 첫 자원봉사 청소 행사인 산책로 청소의 날의 일정을 8월 12일 오전 9시부터 오후 2시까지로 정했다(the Hale City Parks Department has scheduled its first volunteer cleanup event, Trail Cleanup Day, on August 12, from 9:00 A.M. to 2:00 P.M.)고 했고, 웹페이지의 첫 단락 첫 문장에서 8월 8일에 열린 헤일 시티 공원 부서의 첫 산책로 청소의 날이 대성공이었다(The Hale City Parks Department's inaugural Trail Cleanup Day, held on August 8, was a great success)고 했다. 따라서 산책로 청소의 날은 8월 12일에서 8월 8일로 일정이 변경되었음을 알 수 있으므로 (D)가 정답이다.

어휘 initially 처음에

190 세부 사항

번역 웹페이지에 따르면, 한 인근 주민이 자원봉사자들에게 무엇을 제공했는가?
(A) 아침 식사 음식
(B) 건강을 위한 걷기 조언
(C) 조경 도구
(D) 공원까지의 교통편

해설 웹페이지의 두 번째 단락 마지막 문장에서 제이슨 스코다 씨는 인근 이스트 하이츠 지역의 주민으로 자원봉사 팀에 전동 트리머, 전지 가위, 갈퀴를 빌려줬다(Jason Skoda, resident of the adjacent East Heights neighborhood, for lending his power trimmer, pruning shears, and rakes to our crew of volunteers)고 했으므로 (C)가 정답이다.

어휘 landscaping 조경 transportation 교통

> **Paraphrasing**
> 지문의 power trimmer, pruning shears, and rakes
> → 정답의 Landscaping tools

191-195 이메일 + 차트 + 이메일

수신: 전 직원
발신: 미란다 누난
날짜: 6월 26일
제목: 예술품 경매
첨부: 📎 기부품

직원 여러분께,

191 오군산야 앤 볼든 법률 사무소는 연례 예술품 경매를 주최하며 모든 수익금은 지역 정원 조성에 쓰이게 됩니다. 많은 지역 예술가들이 우리 경매에 작품을 기부할 계획이며, 늘 그랬듯 우리 사무소의 모든 아마추어 예술가들 또한 작품을 기부할 것을 권장합니다. 붓과 연필을 꺼내어 여러분의 창의력을 펼쳐보세요. 전문 예술가들의 작품 옆에 동료들의 미술 작품이 걸려 있는 것을 보는 것은 언제나 특별한 즐거움입니다!

올해의 경매는 7월 27일 금요일 오후 7시에 세븐 게이트 호텔 앤 레스토랑에서 열릴 예정입니다. **192 행사는 호텔 식당에서 열리며 이 식당은 우리의 목적에 맞는 훌륭한 조명을 갖추고 있습니다.**

지금까지 기부된 전문 예술 작품을 나열한 차트를 첨부했습니다. 올해 기부하는 데 관심이 있다면, 제출 작품에 대한 세부 사항을 저에게 이메일로 보내주세요. 사진, 그림, 소묘가 가장 인기 있는 표현 수단임을 기억하세요. 하지만 **193 한 지역 예술가가 대형 조각상을 기부하여 이 작품이 경매의 중심 작품이 될 것입니다.** 이 작품을 제외하고는, 조각품은 50cm 이하만 받을 예정입니다.

미란다 누난, 경매 위원장

어휘 auction 경매 donation 기부(품) proceeds 수익금, 돈 donate 기부하다 unleash 풀어놓다 treat 특별한 것 lighting 조명 purpose 목적 contribute 기부하다 submission 제출 drawing 소묘 medium 표현 수단 sculpture 조각 centerpiece 중심물 apart from ~을 제외하고

오군산야 앤 볼든 미술 경매: 지역 예술가 기부품

이름	작품명 및 표현 수단	크기
브라이언 힐리	〈달의 표면〉 (사진)	45cm x 76cm
193 미카엘라 그린	〈가로등〉 (조각)	90cm
신지 하세가와	〈슈키 - 작가의 개〉 (소묘)	30cm x 45cm
킴 청	**195** 〈옥수수밭의 일출〉 (그림)	40cm x 70cm

어휘 dimension 크기 surface 표면 cornfield 옥수수밭

수신: 미란다 누난
발신: 오모누와 오로우
날짜: 6월 29일
제목: 회신: 예술품 경매

안녕하세요, 누난 씨,

194 저는 올해에도 미술품 하나를 기부할 계획이지만, 작품의 주제가 귀하의 이메일 첨부 파일에 기재된 다른 작품과 매우 비슷하다는 것을 알게 되었습니다. 195 저는 해가 뜰 때 저희 부모님 댁 근처의 과수원이 보이는 모습을 그렸습니다. 제 그림이 그 비슷한 작품과 떨어져 배치되도록 요청드려도 될까요?

오모누와 오로우

어휘 attachment 첨부 파일 orchard 과수원

191 주제 / 목적

번역 첫 번째 이메일의 목적은?
(A) 예술 작품을 의뢰하려고
(B) 지역 정원의 중요성을 강조하려고
(C) 다가오는 행사에 대해 직원들에게 알리려고
(D) 지역 예술가들에 대한 정보를 공유하려고

해설 첫 번째 이메일의 첫 단락 첫 문장에서 오군산야 앤 볼든 법률 사무소는 연례 예술품 경매를 주최하며 모든 수익금은 지역 정원 조성에 쓰이게 된다(Ogunsanya and Bolden Law Firm is hosting our annual art auction, with all proceeds going to building a community garden)며 곧 개최될 경매 행사에 대해 직원들에게 공지하고 있으므로 (C)가 정답이다.

어휘 commission (작품 등을) 의뢰하다 stress 강조하다

192 세부 사항

번역 누난 씨가 행사 장소에 대해 언급한 이유는?
(A) 장소가 너무 붐비지 않을 것임을 직원들에게 안심시키려고
(B) 장소가 행사에 적합한 이유를 설명하려고
(C) 참석자들이 적절한 복장을 하도록 하려고
(D) 사무소에서 돈을 기부하는 이유를 설명하려고

해설 첫 번째 이메일의 두 번째 단락 두 번째 문장에서 행사는 호텔 식당에서 열리며 이 식당은 우리의 목적에 맞는 훌륭한 조명을 갖추고 있다

(Our event will be held in the hotel restaurant, which has excellent lighting for our purposes)고 했다. 따라서, 누난 씨는 호텔 식당이 미술품 경매 행사를 열기에 적합한 이유를 설명하려는 의도로 행사 장소를 언급했다는 것을 알 수 있으므로 (B)가 정답이다.

어휘 reassure 안심시키다 appropriate 적합한 accordingly 적절히

193 연계

번역 경매의 중심작품을 기부한 예술가는?
(A) 브라이언 힐리
(B) 미카엘라 그린
(C) 신지 하세가와
(D) 킴 청

해설 첫 번째 이메일의 세 번째 단락 네 번째 문장에서 한 지역 예술가가 대형 조각상을 기부하여 이 작품이 경매의 중심 작품이 될 것(one local artist donated a large sculpture, which will be the auction's centerpiece)이라고 했고, 차트의 중반부에 미카엘라 그린이 〈가로등〉이라는 조각상을 기부했다(Michaela Green, *Streetlight* (sculpture))고 나와 있다. 따라서, 중심 작품이 될 대형 조각상을 기부한 예술가는 미카엘라 그린이므로 (B)가 정답이다.

194 Not / True

번역 오로우 씨에 대해 명시된 것은?
(A) 과거에 예술 작품을 기부했었다.
(B) 자신의 작품이 입구 근처에 걸리기를 원한다.
(C) 주로 매일 아침 그림을 그린다.
(D) 행사에 부모님을 초대했다.

해설 두 번째 이메일의 첫 문장에서 오로우 씨가 올해에도 미술품 하나를 기부할 계획(I am planning to contribute a piece of art again this year)이라고 했으므로, 그가 이전에 예술 작품을 기부한 경험이 있음을 알 수 있다. 따라서 (A)가 정답이다.

195 연계

번역 오로우 씨의 그림과 주제가 비슷한 작품은?
(A) 〈달의 표면〉
(B) 〈가로등〉
(C) 〈슈키 – 작가의 개〉
(D) 〈옥수수밭의 일출〉

해설 두 번째 이메일의 두 번째 문장에서 오로우 씨가 해가 뜰 때 부모님 댁 근처의 과수원이 보이는 모습을 그렸다(I've painted an orchard near my parents' house as it looks just when the sun is rising above it)고 했고, 차트의 하단에는 〈옥수수밭의 일출〉 (그림)(*Cornfield Sunrise* (painting))이 나와 있다. 두 작품 모두 일출 시간의 자연 경관을 담고 있으므로 (D)가 정답이다.

196-200 이메일 + 이메일 + 표지판

수신: 하루카 마에다 〈hmaeda@frantaexports.co.uk〉
발신: 제롬 레녹스 〈j.lennox@silkmail.co.uk〉
날짜: 5월 7일
제목: 채용 3723번
첨부: 📎 레녹스_이력서

마에다 씨께,

196, 199 저는 제 고향인 이곳 리버풀의 프란타 수출에서 채용 중인 사무 관리자 직책(채용 3723번)에 관하여 글을 씁니다. 저는 사무 관리와 행정에서 8년의 경력을 보유하고 있어, 이 역할에서의 탁월한 수행에 요구되는 기술 및 전문성을 갖추고 있다고 자신합니다. 저는 현재 와일러 인터내셔널에서 사무 관리자로서 예산 편성, 일정 관리, 직원 관리를 포함한 사무 운영의 모든 면을 관리하는 일을 책임지고 있습니다. 제 이력서를 첨부합니다.

저는 저의 기술과 경험을 프란타 수출에 적용해 볼 가능성에 대해 기대하고 있습니다. 귀하로부터 곧 회신이 오기를 기다리겠습니다.

제롬 레녹스

어휘 administration 행정 expertise 전문성 excel 탁월하다 aspect 측면 operation 운영 budgeting 예산 편성

수신: 제롬 레녹스 〈j.lennox@silkmail.co.uk〉
발신: 하루카 마에다 〈hmaeda@frantaexports.co.uk〉
날짜: 5월 23일
제목: 곧 있을 면접

레녹스 씨께,

197 프란타 수출과의 전화 면접에 참여할 의사를 확인할 수 있도록 이 이메일에 회신해 주십시오. 귀하는 5월 28일 오전 11시에 알리샤 스콧과 사무 관리자 직책을 위한 면접이 예정되어 있습니다.

귀하의 1차 면접은 온라인 전화 약속으로 예정되어 있습니다. 귀하는 스마트폰이나 컴퓨터로 전화할 수 있습니다. 하지만 안정적인 인터넷 연결을 확보하도록 해 주십시오. 예정된 면접 시간 30분 전에 추가적인 지침과 함께 문자 메시지를 발송할 예정입니다.

200 온라인 면접 후 2일 이내에, 포츠머스 본사에서 후속 대면 면접 일정을 잡을지 여부에 대해 알려드리겠습니다.

하루카 마에다, 인사부 직원

어휘 verify 확인하다 stable 안정된 further 추가적인 instruction 지침 in-person 대면의 headquarters 본사

---

199 프란타 수출 리버풀 사무소에 오신 것을 환영합니다!

운영 시간: 월요일 ~ 토요일 오전 8시 ~ 오후 4시

199 사무 관리자: 제롬 레녹스

198 프란타 수출은 전 세계에 18개 사무소를 운영하고 있으며, 그 중 영국 내 다섯 곳은 다음의 편리한 위치에 있습니다.

- **200** 파크 가 732번지, 포츠머스 PO5 3QQ (영국 본사)
- 도네갈 레인 10번지, 빌파스트 BT1 3JF
- 리치몬드 가 660번지, 카디프 CF24 2PX
- 처치 가 42번지, 에든버러 EH4 6DU
- 빅토리아 가 9233번지, 리버풀 CH44 6PX

어휘 convenient 편리한

196 주제 / 목적

번역 첫 번째 이메일의 목적은?
(A) 채용 중인 직책에 관심을 표하려고
(B) 사무직에 대한 질문에 답변하려고
(C) 계획된 회의에 대해 알리려고
(D) 다른 사무소로의 전근을 요청하려고

해설 첫 번째 이메일의 첫 단락 첫 문장에서 레녹스 씨가 자신의 고향인 이곳 리버풀의 프란타 수출에서 채용 중인 사무 관리자 직책(채용 3723번)에 관하여 글을 쓴다(I am writing regarding the open office manager position (job 3723) at Franta Exports here in my hometown of Liverpool)고 이메일을 작성하는 목적을 밝히고 있으므로 (A)가 정답이다.

어휘 notice 알림 transfer 전근

197 세부 사항

번역 두 번째 이메일에서 마에다 씨는 레녹스 씨에게 무엇을 요청하는가?
(A) 스콧 씨의 사무실로 방문할 것
(B) 전화 회의 일정을 변경할 것
(C) 온라인 설문조사를 작성할 것
(D) 면접 약속을 확인할 것

해설 두 번째 이메일의 첫 단락 첫 문장에서 프란타 수출과의 전화 면접에 참여할 의사를 확인할 수 있도록 이 이메일에 회신해 달라(Please respond to this e-mail to verify your intention to participate in a telephone interview with Franta Exports)고 요청하고 있으므로 (D)가 정답이다.

198 Not / True

번역 표지판에 명시된 것은?
(A) 프란타 수출의 리버풀 사무소는 일요일에 오후 4시까지 운영된다.
(B) 프란타 수출은 현재 사무 관리자를 채용 중이다.
(C) 프란타 수출은 여러 나라에 사무소를 갖고 있다.
(D) 프란타 수출은 영국에 18개의 사무소를 갖고 있다.

해설 표지판의 중반부에 프란타 수출은 전 세계에 18개 사무소를 운영하고 있다(Franta Exports has eighteen offices worldwide)고 명시되어 있으므로 (C)가 정답이다.

어휘 multiple 여럿의, 다수의

Paraphrasing
지문의 eighteen offices worldwide
→ 정답의 offices in multiple countries

199 연계

번역 레녹스 씨에 대해 결론지을 수 있는 것은?
(A) 카디프에서 관리직 직책을 위한 면접을 봤다.
(B) 그의 고향에 있는 사무소에서 근무하도록 채용되었다.
(C) 영국 전역으로 출장을 다녀야 한다.
(D) 스콧 씨와 같은 장소에서 근무한다.

해설 첫 번째 이메일의 첫 단락 첫 문장에서 레녹스 씨가 자신의 고향인 이곳 리버풀의 프란타 수출에서 채용 중인 사무 관리자 직책(채용 3723번)에 관하여 글을 쓴다(I am writing regarding the open office manager position (job 3723) at Franta Exports here in my hometown of Liverpool)고 했고, 표지판의 상단에는 프란타 수출 리버풀 사무소에 온 것을 환영한다(Welcome to the Franta Exports Liverpool Office!)는 환영 문구가 있으며, 사무 관리자가 제롬 레녹스(Office manager: Jerome Lennox)라고 명시되어 있다. 따라서, 레녹스 씨가 고향인 리버풀의 프란타 수출 사무소에서 사무 관리자로 채용되어 근무 중임을 알 수 있으므로 (B)가 정답이다.

200 연계

번역 레녹스 씨의 후속 면접이 진행된 장소는?
(A) 파크 가 732번지
(B) 도네갈 레인 10번지
(C) 리치몬드 가 660번지
(D) 처치 가 42번지

해설 두 번째 이메일의 마지막 단락에서 레녹스 씨에게 온라인 면접 후 2일 이내에, 포츠머스 본사에서 후속 대면 면접 일정을 잡을지 여부를 알려주겠다(Within two days following your online interview, we will inform you whether we would like to schedule a follow-up in-person appointment at our headquarters in Portsmouth)고 했고, 표지판의 중반부에 파크 가 732번지, 포츠머스 PO5 3QQ (영국 본사)(732 Park Avenue, Portsmouth PO5 3QQ (U.K. Headquarters))라고 본사 주소가 표기되어 있다. 따라서 레녹스 씨의 후속 면접은 포츠머스 본사가 위치한 파크 가 732번지에서 진행되었음을 알 수 있으므로 (A)가 정답이다.

기출 TEST 5

101 (C)	102 (A)	103 (B)	104 (B)	105 (D)
106 (A)	107 (C)	108 (A)	109 (A)	110 (C)
111 (B)	112 (C)	113 (C)	114 (B)	115 (B)
116 (D)	117 (C)	118 (C)	119 (C)	120 (A)
121 (C)	122 (D)	123 (C)	124 (D)	125 (B)
126 (B)	127 (B)	128 (B)	129 (C)	130 (D)
131 (A)	132 (C)	133 (C)	134 (C)	135 (D)
136 (C)	137 (B)	138 (C)	139 (C)	140 (A)
141 (A)	142 (D)	143 (A)	144 (C)	145 (A)
146 (B)	147 (C)	148 (C)	149 (A)	150 (D)
151 (B)	152 (C)	153 (D)	154 (A)	155 (C)
156 (D)	157 (D)	158 (C)	159 (A)	160 (B)
161 (C)	162 (D)	163 (B)	164 (D)	165 (D)
166 (B)	167 (D)	168 (A)	169 (C)	170 (D)
171 (B)	172 (D)	173 (C)	174 (C)	175 (B)
176 (B)	177 (B)	178 (C)	179 (D)	180 (B)
181 (A)	182 (C)	183 (D)	184 (B)	185 (C)
186 (A)	187 (D)	188 (C)	189 (A)	190 (B)
191 (A)	192 (D)	193 (C)	194 (C)	195 (D)
196 (B)	197 (B)	198 (D)	199 (D)	200 (C)

PART 5

101 등위접속사 / 어휘

해설 명사 accountant와 investor를 연결해 줄 등위접속사가 필요하다. '경험 많은 회계사이자 투자자'라는 의미가 되어야 하므로 '~와, 그리고'를 뜻하는 등위접속사 (C) and가 정답이다. (A) but(그러나)과 (D) yet(그렇지만)도 등위접속사이지만 의미상 적합하지 않고, (B) that은 관계대명사 또는 명사절 접속사로 명사를 연결할 수 없다.

번역 최근에 자문 위원회에 합류한 최 씨는 경험 많은 회계사이자 투자자이다.

어휘 advisory board 자문 위원회   accountant 회계사   investor 투자자

102 명사 자리 _ 복합명사

해설 빈칸은 동사 will receive의 목적어 자리로, 부정관사 a와 형용사 complimentary의 수식을 받으면서 빈칸 앞의 명사 water와 함께 복합명사를 만들 수 있는 명사가 들어가야 한다. '무료 물병을 받는다'는 내용이 되어야 자연스러우므로 '병'을 뜻하는 명사 (A) bottle이 정답이다. (B) bottled는 동사/과거분사, (D) to bottle은 to부정사이므로 빈칸에 들어갈 수 없고, (C) bottling은 명사로 쓰일 경우 '병에 채워 넣기'라는 뜻으로 의미상 적합하지 않다.

번역 새 피트니스 파크를 방문하는 첫 150명은 각각 무료 물병을 받게 될 것이다.

어휘 complimentary 무료의

103 부사 자리 _ 동사 수식

해설 빈칸이 없어도 완전한 문장을 이루고 있으므로 빈칸은 부사 자리이다. 동사구 will be e-mailed를 수식하여 '곧 이메일로 발송될 것이다'라는 내용이 되어야 자연스러우므로 '곧'을 뜻하는 (B) shortly가 정답이다. (A) short는 형용사, (C) shorter는 short의 비교급, (D) shortening은 동명사/현재분사이므로 빈칸에 들어갈 수 없다.

번역 프린터 사용 설명서가 곧 직원들에게 이메일로 발송될 것이다.

어휘 operating 조작상의   instructions 사용 설명서

104 형용사 자리 _ 명사 수식

해설 빈칸은 전치사 of의 목적어 역할을 하는 명사 customers를 수식하는 형용사 자리이다. 따라서 '만족한 고객들'이라는 의미를 완성하는 '만족한'이라는 뜻의 형용사 (B) satisfied가 정답이다. (A) satisfy와 (D) satisfies는 동사이므로 빈칸에 들어갈 수 없고, 명사 (C) satisfaction(만족)은 customers와 복합명사를 이루기에 적절하지 않다.

번역 수십 명의 만족한 고객들이 스텔렌보쉬 사이클 워크에 대한 긍정적인 후기를 올렸다.

어휘 dozens of 수십의   post 게시하다   review 후기

105 부사 어휘

해설 동사구 has been praised를 수식하여 '널리 찬사 받아왔다'는 내용이 되어야 자연스러우므로 '널리'를 뜻하는 (D) widely가 정답이다. (A) respectively는 '각각', (B) tightly는 '단단히', (C) unhappily는 '불행하게'라는 의미이다.

번역 임 씨의 베스트셀러 소설은 널리 찬사 받아왔다.

어휘 praise 칭찬하다

106 인칭대명사의 격 _ 소유격

해설 빈칸에는 전치사 following의 목적어 역할을 하는 meeting을 수식하는 인칭대명사가 들어가야 한다. 따라서 명사 앞에 쓰여 한정사 역할을 할 수 있는 소유격 인칭대명사 (A) her가 정답이다.

번역 마케팅 매니저인 아비올라 씨는 부사장과의 회의 후 기자들과 만날 계획이다.

어휘 press 기자들   vice president 부사장

107 형용사 어휘   ▶동영상 강의

해설 복합명사 game night을 수식하여 적절한 문맥을 완성하는 형용사를 고르는 문제이다. '활기찬 게임의 밤을 주최했다'는 내용이 되어야 적절하므로 '활기찬'을 뜻하는 형용사 (C) lively가 정답이다.

(A) removable은 '제거할 수 있는', (B) plentiful은 '풍부한', (D) current는 '현재의'라는 의미이다.

번역 지난 주말에 테리빌 커뮤니티 센터는 지역 어린이들을 위해 활기찬 게임의 밤을 주최했다.

108 명사 자리 _ 동사의 목적어 ▶동영상 강의

해설 빈칸은 동사 will distribute의 목적어 역할을 하는 명사 자리이다. of the workshop agenda와 결합하여 '워크숍 안건의 사본을 배포할 것이다'라는 의미가 되어야 자연스러우므로 '복사(본)'을 뜻하는 copy의 복수 명사 (A) copies가 정답이다. (B) copier(복사기)와 (C) copy는 가산 단수 명사로 한정사 a, the 등이 필요하고, (D) copying은 동명사/현재분사로 빈칸에 들어갈 수 없다.

번역 렌테 씨는 화요일 아침까지 모든 관리자에게 워크숍 안건의 사본을 배포할 것이다.

어휘 distribute 배포하다 agenda 안건

109 접속사 자리 _ 부사절 접속사

해설 빈칸은 두 개의 완전한 절을 이어주는 접속사 자리이다. '5년간 근무한 이후 더 많은 휴가를 받을 수 있다'는 내용이 되어야 자연스러우므로 '~한 후에'를 뜻하는 부사절 접속사 (A) after가 정답이다. 상관접속사 (B) neither는 nor와 함께 쓰여야 절을 연결할 수 있고, 등위접속사 (C) so(그래서)는 의미상 적합하지 않고, (D) thus는 부사이므로 절을 연결할 수 없다.

번역 직원들은 5년 동안 근무한 이후 더 많은 휴가를 받을 수 있다.

어휘 eligible (자격 등이 돼서) ~을 할 수 있는 employ 고용하다

110 형용사 자리 _ 명사 수식

해설 to부정사 to provide의 목적어 역할을 하는 명사 feedback을 수식하는 형용사 자리이다. '건설적인 피드백'이라는 의미가 되어야 자연스러우므로 '건설적인'이라는 뜻의 형용사 (C) constructive가 정답이다. (A) construct는 동사이므로 빈칸에 들어갈 수 없고, 명사인 (B) constructor(건설자)와 (D) construction(건설)은 명사 feedback과 복합명사를 이루기에 문맥상 적절하지 않다.

번역 애프턴 회계의 관리자들은 직원들에게 정기적으로 건설적인 피드백을 제공하라고 권고받는다.

어휘 urge 권고하다 on a regular basis 정기적으로

111 명사 어휘 ▶동영상 강의

해설 빈칸은 전치사 on의 목적어 자리로, 봄에 문을 열고 가을에 문을 닫는다는 문장 내용상 형용사 seasonal의 수식을 받아 '계절적인 기준에 따라 운영된다'는 의미가 되어야 자연스러우므로 '기준'을 뜻하는 (B) basis가 정답이다. (A) topic은 '주제', (C) root는 '뿌리', (D) sum은 '합계'라는 의미이다.

번역 많은 농산물 시장이 계절에 따라 운영되며 봄에 문을 열고 늦가을에 문을 닫는다.

어휘 operate 운영되다 seasonal 계절적인

112 명사 자리 _ 동사의 주어

해설 빈칸은 동사 has continued의 주어 자리이므로 명사가 들어가야 한다. 따라서 in the housing market의 수식을 받아 '주택 시장의 약세'라는 의미가 되어야 적절하므로 '약세'를 뜻하는 명사 (C) Weakness가 정답이다. (A) Weak는 형용사, (B) Weakly는 부사, (D) Weakened는 동사/과거분사이므로 빈칸에 들어갈 수 없다.

번역 주택 시장의 약세는 부동산 수익을 지속적으로 끌어내렸다.

어휘 drag down ~을 끌어내리다 real estate 부동산 profit 수익

113 동사 어휘

해설 빈칸은 주어 The sudden merger와 목적어 most financial analysts 사이의 동사 자리로, '갑작스러운 합병은 대부분의 금융 분석가들을 놀라게 했다'는 의미가 되어야 자연스러우므로 '놀라게 하다'를 뜻하는 동사 surprise의 과거형 (C) surprised가 정답이다. (A)의 enable은 '가능하게 하다', (B)의 arrange는 '마련하다', (D)의 suspect는 '의심하다'라는 의미이다.

번역 앨비 브라더스와 크래포드 엔터프라이즈의 갑작스러운 합병은 대부분의 금융 분석가들을 놀라게 했다.

어휘 sudden 갑작스러운 merger 합병 financial 금융의

114 형용사 자리 _ 최상급 ▶동영상 강의

해설 문장 앞에 Of all the mistakes라며 전체를 비교 대상으로 삼는 구문이 있고, 빈칸 앞에 one of the가 나온 것으로 보아 '가장 ~한 것들 중 하나'를 뜻하는 최상급 표현 「one of the + 최상급 형용사 + (복수 명사)」가 되어야 함을 알 수 있다. 따라서 '가장 흔한 실수 중 하나'라는 의미를 나타내는 형용사 common(흔한)의 최상급인 (B) most common이 정답이다. 명사 (A) commoners(서민)는 의미상 어울리지 않고, (C) in common은 부사 역할을 하는 전치사구, (D) more commonly는 부사의 비교급이므로 빈칸에 들어갈 수 없다.

번역 사람들이 사무실에서 저지르는 모든 실수들 중에서 이메일을 교정하지 않는 것이 가장 흔한 실수 중 하나이다.

어휘 proofread 교정하다

115 형용사 어휘

해설 명사 mission을 수식하여 적절한 문맥을 이루는 형용사를 고르는 문제이다. 적시 운송 및 배달은 '회사의 주요 임무'라는 내용이 되어야 적절하므로 '주요한'을 뜻하는 (B) primary가 정답이다. (A) prompt는 '신속한', (C) bright는 '밝은', (D) nearest는 '가장 가까운'이라는 의미이다.

번역 케이페어 글로벌의 주요 임무는 적시에 고객 물품을 운송하고 배달하는 것입니다.

어휘 mission 임무 transport 운송하다 in a timely manner 적시에, 제 시간에

116 형용사 자리 _ 주격 보어

해설 빈칸은 주어 The department supervisor를 보충 설명하는 주격 보어 자리이고, '부서장은 ~하는 것에 책임이 있다'는 의미가 되어야 적절하므로 전치사 for와 함께 '~에 책임이 있는'을 뜻하는 형용사 (D) responsible이 정답이다. 명사 (A) responsibilities와 (B) responsibility는 주어 The department supervisor와 동격이 아니므로 오답이고, (C) responsibly는 부사이므로 보어 역할을 할 수 없다.

번역 부서장은 근무 종료 시 모든 안전 장비가 제대로 보관되도록 해야 할 책임이 있다.

어휘 supervisor 관리자 gear 장비 stow 집어넣다 properly 제대로 shift 근무 시간

117 명사 어휘 ▶동영상 강의

해설 빈칸 뒤에서 빈칸의 명사를 it으로 받아 대형 화물선 수용이 가능해졌다고 했으므로 '항구가 깊어졌다'는 의미가 되어야 적절하다. 따라서 '항구'를 뜻하는 (C) harbor가 정답이다. (A) tide는 '조수', (B) boat는 '(작은) 배', (D) island는 '섬'이라는 의미이다.

번역 3년간의 프로젝트로 항구가 깊어져 가장 큰 규모의 화물선을 수용하는 것이 가능해졌다.

어휘 deepen 깊게 하다 accommodate 수용하다 cargo ship 화물선

118 부사 자리 _ 형용사 수식

해설 빈칸은 be동사 were와 보어 역할을 하는 형용사 different 사이에서 형용사를 수식하는 부사 자리이다. 따라서 '크게, 매우'를 뜻하는 부사 (C) wildly가 정답이다. (A) wild는 형용사, (B) wildest는 형용사의 최상급, (D) wildness는 명사이므로 빈칸에 들어갈 수 없다.

번역 실험의 초기 결과는 예상했던 것과는 크게 달랐다.

어휘 experiment 실험 initial 초기의

119 전치사 어휘

해설 문맥상 '비판적인 평가에도 불구하고 대성공을 거두었다'는 의미가 되어야 자연스러우므로 '~에도 불구하고'를 뜻하는 (C) Despite가 정답이다. (A) During은 '~ 동안', (B) About은 '~에 관하여', (D) Over는 '~ 위에'라는 의미이다.

번역 비판적인 평가에도 불구하고, 그 영화는 박스 오피스에서 대성공을 거두었다.

어휘 critical 비판적인 review 평가

120 동사 자리

해설 주절의 주어 The spray-on sealant 뒤에 동사가 없으므로 빈칸은 동사 자리이다. 따라서 '작용하다'라는 의미의 동사 act의 단수형 (A) acts가 정답이다. (B) acting은 명사/동명사/현재분사, (C) action은 명사, (D) actively는 부사이므로 빈칸에 들어갈 수 없다.

번역 분무식 밀폐제는 타일이 긁히는 것을 방지해 주는 보호막 역할을 한다.

어휘 spray-on 분무식의 sealant 밀폐제 protective 보호하는 layer 막, 층 scratch 긁다

121 접속사 자리 _ 부사절 접속사

해설 빈칸은 두 개의 완전한 절을 이어주는 접속사 자리로 '모든 입찰서가 제출될 때까지 계약은 체결되지 않을 것이다'라는 의미가 되어야 자연스러우므로 '~까지'를 뜻하는 부사절 접속사 (C) until이 정답이다. 접속사 (A) nor(~도 아니다)는 앞에 부정문이 와야 하고, 뒤에는 주어와 동사가 도치된 절이 와야 한다. (B) next는 형용사/부사이므로 절을 연결할 수 없고, (D) because는 부사절 접속사이지만 의미상 어울리지 않는다.

번역 공원 개보수 계약은 모든 입찰서가 제출될 때까지 체결되지 않을 것이다.

어휘 contract 계약 renovation 보수, 개조

122 명사 자리 _ 복합명사

해설 빈칸은 동사 may have의 목적어 역할을 하는 명사 benefits를 수식하는 형용사 또는 benefits와 복합명사를 이루는 명사가 들어갈 수 있다. 문맥상 '중요한 건강상의 이점'이라는 내용이 되어야 자연스러우므로, '건강상의 이점'이라는 의미의 복합명사를 만들 수 있는 명사 (D) health(건강)가 정답이다. (A) only는 형용사일 때 '유일한'이라는 의미이므로 한정사 some과 어울리지 않고, (B) full은 '가득 찬', (C) legal은 '법적인'이라는 뜻으로 문맥상 적절하지 않다.

번역 최근 연구는 정제 설탕을 메이플 시럽으로 대체하는 것이 중요한 건강상의 이점이 있음을 보여주었다.

어휘 substitute 대체하다 refined 정제된 benefit 이점, 혜택

123 전치사 어휘

해설 빈칸 뒤의 명사 the winners를 목적어로 취해 '마지 펑은 수상자들 중 하나'라는 의미가 되어야 자연스러우므로 '~중 하나로, ~ 사이에'를 뜻하는 (C) among이 정답이다. (A) from은 '~으로부터', (B) upon은 '~에', (D) beyond는 '~을 넘어서'라는 의미이다.

번역 마지 펑은 스터네츠 협회의 미술 대회 수상자들 중 한 명이었다.

어휘 institute 협회 competition 대회

124 to부정사 _ 목적격 보어 / 능동태 vs. 수동태

해설 빈칸은 동사 can cause의 목적격 보어 자리로, cause는 목적격

보어로 to부정사를 취하는 동사이다. 또한, 빈칸 뒤에 목적어가 없으므로 수동형 to부정사인 (D) to be forgotten이 정답이다.

번역 소셜 미디어에 너무 드물게 업데이트를 게시하면 소규모 업체들은 고객들에게 잊혀질 수 있다.

어휘 infrequently 드물게

125 동사 어휘

해설 to부정사의 동사 자리에 들어갈 어휘를 고르는 문제이다. unwanted background noise를 목적어로 취해 '원치 않는 배경 소음을 흡수하도록 설계되었다'는 의미가 되어야 적절하므로 '흡수하다'를 뜻하는 (B) absorb가 정답이다. (A) compete는 '경쟁하다', (C) surpass는 '능가하다', (D) remain은 '~으로 남아 있다'라는 의미이다.

번역 회의실에 최적인 저희 방음 패널은 원치 않는 배경 소음을 흡수하도록 특별히 설계되었습니다.

어휘 ideal 가장 알맞은, 이상적인   soundproof 방음의   panel 패널, 판   background 배경

126 분사구문

해설 빈칸 앞에는 완전한 절이 있고 뒤에는 명사구가 남아 있으므로, 빈칸 이하는 분사구문이 되어야 한다. 따라서 빈칸 뒤에 나온 명사구 the hotel's wireless network를 목적어로 취해 '무선 네트워크를 사용하여'라는 능동의 의미를 나타낼 수 있는 현재분사 (B) using이 정답이다. 과거분사 (A) used는 목적어를 취할 수 없고, (C) use는 동사/명사, (D) had used는 동사이므로 빈칸에 들어갈 수 없다.

번역 사토 씨는 호텔의 무선 네트워크를 사용하여 회의에 참여할 것이다.

어휘 call into ~에 참여하다

127 부사 어휘

해설 동사 worked를 수식하여 적절한 문맥을 완성하는 부사를 고르는 문제이다. '프로젝트에 성실하게 임했다'는 내용이 되어야 적절하므로 '성실하게'를 뜻하는 (B) diligently가 정답이다. (A) accessibly는 '접근할 수 있게', (C) eventfully는 '다사다난하게', (D) completely는 '완전히'라는 의미이다.

번역 오구부 씨는 프로젝트에 성실하게 임했을 뿐만 아니라, 정 씨가 업무를 이어갈 수 있도록 교육시켰다.

128 지시대명사

해설 빈칸은 전치사 for의 목적어 자리이자 who가 이끄는 형용사절의 수식을 받는 명사 자리이다. '~하는 사람들'이라는 의미로, who 뒤의 복수 동사 want와도 수 일치가 되어야 하므로 지시대명사 (B) those가 정답이다. (A) this는 단독으로 선행사 역할을 할 수 없고, (C) somebody와 (D) everyone은 단수를 나타내므로 복수 동사 want와 쓸 수 없다.

번역 벨커 오토는 더 확실히 안심하기를 원하는 사람들을 위해 10년 보증을 제공합니다.

어휘 warranty 보증   peace of mind 마음의 평안

129 동사 어휘

해설 빈칸 뒤에 목적어 없이 전치사 in이 왔으므로 자동사가 들어가야 한다. 따라서 '시작하다'를 뜻하는 자동사 (C) commence가 정답이다. (A) observe(관찰하다), (B) represent(대표하다), (D) access(접근하다)는 모두 타동사로 뒤에 목적어가 와야 한다.

번역 수개월 간의 계획 끝에 랜턴 서점의 학교 독서 프로그램이 마침내 10월에 시작합니다.

130 형용사 어휘

해설 명사 advice를 수식하기에 적절한 형용사를 골라야 한다. 소속된 곳이 없는 독립 컨설턴트에게서 나오는 조언은 '공정한 조언'일 것이므로 '공정한'을 뜻하는 (D) impartial이 정답이다. (A) unfulfilled는 '실현되지 않은', (B) indefinite는 '무기한의', (C) obedient는 '순종적인'이라는 의미이다.

번역 독립 컨설턴트들은 신생 기업가들에게 공정한 조언을 제공할 수 있는 귀중한 원천이 될 수 있다.

어휘 independent 독립적인   valuable 귀중한   source 원천   entrepreneur 기업가

PART 6

131-134 이메일

수신: 크리에이티브 팀
발신: 카밀 파텔
날짜: 12월 9일
제목: 동료 퇴사

팀 여러분께,

많은 분들이 최근에 알게 되셨겠지만, 클라우디아 호프만이 12월 30일 월요일에 아트 디렉터로서의 임기를 마칩니다. 이 **131 역할**을 맡은 지 10년 만에 그녀는 파리에서 새로운 전문적 도전에 임하려고 합니다. **132 그곳에서**, 그녀는 최고의 광고 대행사의 리더십 팀에 합류할 것입니다. 스펜서 디자인 출신인 마르코스 몰리나가 우리의 새로운 아트 디렉터가 될 예정입니다. **133 그는 1월 12일에 우리와 합류합니다.**

저는 호프만 씨의 뛰어난 리더십에 개인적으로 감사드리고 싶습니다. 그녀는 우리 대행사의 성공에 있어 핵심 요소**134 였습니다**. 12월 27일 금요일 퇴근 후 송별 회식에서 그녀의 업적을 기념하는 자리에 함께 해주세요. 자세한 내용은 추후 공지될 것입니다.

카밀 파텔
인사부 담당자

어휘 departure 떠남   tenure 임기   challenge 도전   agency 대행사   tremendous 대단한, 엄청난   factor 요소   achievement 업적   farewell 송별   forthcoming 곧 있을

131 명사 어휘

해설 빈칸 앞 문장에서 클라우디아 호프만이 아트 디렉터로서의 임기를 마친다고 했으므로, 빈칸이 있는 문장에서는 아트 디렉터를 맡은 지 10년 만에 새로운 일에 도전한다는 내용이 되어야 자연스럽다. 따라서 art director를 '이 역할'로 대신하면 적절하므로 '역할'을 뜻하는 (A) role이 정답이다. (B) school은 '학교', (C) production은 '생산', (D) warehouse는 '창고'라는 의미이다.

132 접속부사

해설 빈칸 앞 문장에서 호프만 씨가 파리에서 새로운 직업에 도전한다고 했고, 빈칸 뒤에서 그녀가 광고 대행사 리더십 팀에 합류한다며 파리에서의 새 직장에 대한 구체적인 정보를 제시하고 있다. 따라서 빈칸에는 파리를 대신하는 말이 들어가야 적합하므로 '그곳에서, 거기서'를 뜻하는 (A) There가 정답이다. (B) Instead는 '대신에', (C) Otherwise는 '그렇지 않으면', (D) Afterward는 '그 후에'라는 의미이다.

133 문맥에 맞는 문장 고르기

번역 (A) 지원하기를 원한다면 그에게 알려주세요.
(B) 급여 수준은 더 경쟁력이 있습니다.
(C) 그는 1월 12일에 우리와 합류합니다.
(D) 스펜서 디자인은 지난 2년 동안 수익 손실을 입었습니다.

해설 빈칸 앞에서 마르코스 몰리나가 우리의 새 아트 디렉터가 될 예정(Marcos Molina from Spencer Design will become our new art director)이라며 후임 아트 디렉터로 누가 부임할지를 알리고 있으므로, 새로 오는 디렉터가 언제 업무를 시작하는지 알려주는 내용이 들어가면 연결이 자연스럽다. 따라서 (C)가 정답이다.

어휘 competitive 경쟁력 있는 revenue 수익

134 동사의 시제

해설 앞 문단에서 호프만 씨가 아트 디렉터로서 10년간의 임기를 마치고 회사를 떠난다고 했으므로, 빈칸이 있는 문장은 대행사의 성공에 있어 그녀가 지난 10년 동안 핵심 요소로서 역할을 해왔다는 의미가 되어야 한다. 따라서 과거부터 현재까지 계속된 행위에 대해 이야기할 때 쓰는 현재완료 시제인 (C) has been이 정답이다.

135-138 소책자

> **토미노스 팀 리더십 세미나**
>
> 팀 리더 135 로서 당신의 성공은 팀원들이 최고 수준의 성과를 내도록 지속적으로 고무시키는 역량에 달려 있습니다. 훌륭한 리더들은 직장 내 문제에 대한 실행 가능한 해결책을 찾고 그에 따라 실행하는 방법을 압니다. 136 **그들은 팀과 정기적으로 소통하며 그들에게 정보를 제공합니다.** 어떻게 이러한 기술을 터득할 수 있을까요?
>
> 이 세미나에서는 팀원들의 성과를 조직의 목표와 더 잘 일치시키는 방법을 137 배우게 됩니다. 세미나의 138 참가자들은 오늘날의 빠르게 돌아가는 사업 환경에서 팀을 성공적으로 지휘하기 위한 입증된 도구와 기법들을 습득합니다.

어휘 depend on ~에 달려있다 consistently 지속적으로 inspire 고무하다 viable 실행 가능한 implement 실행하다 accordingly 그에 따라 align 정렬시키다 performance 성과 organization 조직 acquire 습득하다 proven 입증된 fast-paced 빠르게 진행되는

135 전치사 자리 / 어휘

해설 빈칸은 Your success가 주어, depends가 동사인 완전한 문장에서 Your success 뒤에 주어를 수식하는 명사구 a team leader를 연결하는 자리이므로 전치사가 들어가야 한다. '팀 리더로서 당신의 성공'이라는 내용이 되어야 자연스러우므로 '~으로서'를 뜻하는 전치사 (D) as가 정답이다. (A) where는 접속사, (B) therefore는 부사이므로 빈칸에 들어갈 수 없고, 전치사 (C) for는 의미상 적합하지 않다.

136 문맥에 맞는 문장 고르기

번역 (A) 한 가지 흔한 문제는 직원의 지각입니다.
(B) 우리 세미나는 세션당 120파운드입니다.
(C) 그들은 팀과 정기적으로 소통하며 그들에게 정보를 제공합니다.
(D) 지금 등록하고 등록비 10퍼센트 할인 혜택을 받으세요.

해설 빈칸 앞에서 훌륭한 리더는 직장 내 문제에 대한 해결책을 찾고 실행하는 방법을 안다(Good leaders know how to find viable solutions to workplace problems and implement them accordingly)고 했고, 빈칸 뒤에서 어떻게 이러한 기술(these skills)을 확보할 수 있을지를 묻고 있다. 앞뒤 문맥상 훌륭한 리더의 직장 내 문제 해결 기술이 무엇인지를 알려주는 내용이 들어가야 연결이 자연스러우므로 팀과 정기적으로 소통하며 정보를 제공하는 것이라고 언급하는 (C)가 정답이다.

어휘 common 흔한 tardiness 지각 regularly 정기적으로 sign up 등록하다 registration 등록

137 동사의 시제

해설 전체적으로 세미나에 대해 소개하는 안내문이고, 빈칸이 있는 문장은 이 세미나에 참석하면(In this seminar) 배우게 될 것들을 설명하는 내용이므로 미래에 일어날 일을 이야기하는 미래 시제 (B) will learn이 정답이다.

138 명사 어휘

해설 전체적으로 세미나에 대해 소개하는 안내문이고 빈칸 앞 문장에서 세미나에 참석하면 배우게 될 내용에 대해 설명하고 있으므로, 빈칸이 있는 문장에서도 세미나 참가자들이 각종 도구와 기법을 습득하게 된다는 내용이 되어야 자연스럽다. 따라서 '참가자'를 뜻하는 (C) Participants가 정답이다. (A)의 Authority는 '당국', (B)의 Candidate는 '후보자', (D)의 Subscriber는 '구독자'라는 의미이다.

139-142 이메일 ▶동영상 강의

수신: 카나 이노우에 〈kana.inoue@mymail.co.uk〉
발신: 브라이언 할스턴 〈bhalstan@impressionise.co.uk〉
날짜: 5월 9일
제목: 무료 상담 제안

이노우에 씨께,

저는 임프레셔나이즈를 대표하여 이 글을 씁니다. 저희는 대기실, 사무실, 진료실 및 치료실 등의 의료 시설을 전문으로 하는 디자인 회사입니다. 저희 조사에 따르면 귀하께서는 향후 몇 달 139 **이내에** 퀸스 포인트에 물리치료 센터를 개업하실 계획입니다. 틀림없이 귀하께서는 귀하의 시설이 편안하고 차분하면서도 전문성은 강화하고 귀하의 브랜드 이미지에 부합하기를 원하실 것입니다. 140 **저희가 이러한 목표를 이루도록 돕겠습니다.** 귀하께서 자랑스러워하실 만한 매력적인 141 **공간**을 만들기 위해 함께 일하고 싶습니다. www.impressionise.co.uk/portfolio에서 저희의 142 **이전** 프로젝트 사진을 확인하실 수 있습니다. 관심 있으시면 이 이메일에 회신하셔서 무료 상담 일정을 잡으십시오.

브라이언 할스턴, 영업 관리자
임프레셔나이즈

어휘 on behalf of ~을 대표하여 specialise in ~을 전문으로 하다 facility 시설 examination 진찰 therapy 치료 physiotherapy 물리치료 practice (의사·변호사 등의) 영업 장소 no doubt 틀림없이 enhance 강화하다 conform to ~에 부합하다 inviting 매력적인

139 전치사 자리 / 어휘

해설 빈칸 앞에 완전한 문장이 있고, 뒤에 남아있는 명사구 the next few months를 문장에 연결하는 자리이므로 전치사가 필요하다. the next few months는 기간을 나타내는 명사구이고, '향후 몇 달 이내에'라는 의미가 되어야 자연스러우므로 '~ 이내에'를 뜻하는 전치사 (C) within이 정답이다. (A) either는 대명사/형용사/부사, (B) perhaps는 부사이므로 빈칸에 들어갈 수 없고, 전치사 (D) since(~ 이래로)는 의미상 답이 될 수 없다.

140 문맥에 맞는 문장 고르기

번역 (A) 저희가 이러한 목표를 이루도록 돕겠습니다.
(B) 가능한 세금 혜택에 관하여 문의 주십시오.
(C) 저희 소프트웨어는 진료 예약을 쉽게 해 줍니다.
(D) 잘 훈련된 직원은 성공하는 데 필요한 전부입니다.

해설 앞 문장에서 시설이 편안하고 차분하면서도 전문성은 강화하고 브랜드 이미지에 부합하기를 원할 것(you want your facilities to be comfortable and calming while enhancing your professional practice and conforming to your brand image)이라고 했으므로, 앞서 언급한 기대 사항들을 these objectives로 받아 이러한 목표를 이루도록 우리 업체가 돕겠다는 내용이 들어가야 연결이 자연스럽다. 따라서 (A)가 정답이다.

어휘 achieve 달성하다 objective 목표 potential 가능성 있는 advantage 혜택, 이득

141 명사 어휘

해설 지문 초반에 임프레셔나이즈는 대기실, 사무실, 진료실 및 치료실 등의 의료 시설을 전문으로 하는 디자인 회사라고 했으므로, 빈칸이 있는 문장은 '매력적인 공간을 만들기 위해 일하고 싶다'는 의미가 되어야 자연스러우므로 '공간'을 뜻하는 (A) space가 정답이다. (B) event는 '행사', (C) signal은 '신호', (D) moment는 '순간'이라는 의미이다.

142 형용사 어휘

해설 의료 시설을 전문으로 하는 디자인 회사에서 새로 개업하는 병원에 무료 상담을 제안하고 있는 내용의 글이므로, '웹사이트에서 자신들의 이전 프로젝트 사진을 확인하라'는 의미가 되어야 자연스럽다. 따라서 '이전의'를 뜻하는 (D) previous가 정답이다. (A) educational은 '교육의', (B) residential은 '주거의', (C) preventive는 '예방하는'이라는 의미이다.

143-146 정보

〈디지털 시코리〉는 웹 디자이너를 위한 자료와 교육을 제공하는 월간 잡지입니다. 〈디지털 시코리〉는 800자에서 1,200자 분량의 유익하고 잘 작성된 기사를 받습니다. 143 **더 긴 기사들도 때때로 고려됩니다.** 기사에 대한 아이디어가 있으면 writer@digitalchicory.org로 제안서를 보내 주세요. 144 **그렇게 하시기 전에**, 우리 독자층과 일반적인 작문 방식에 대한 이해를 높일 수 있도록 시간을 들여 우리의 출판물을 읽어 주십시오. 145 **우리는** 기사 제안에 신속히 응답하며, 제안서는 단일 페이지 개요로 제출되어야 합니다. 전체 길이의 146 **초안**은 제안 단계에서는 보통 권장되지 않습니다. 그러나 우리 잡지에 기고하는 신규 작가일 경우에는 이전에 출판된 글의 샘플들을 포함시켜 주십시오.

어휘 resource 자료, 재원 tutorial 교육 시간 informative 유익한 general 일반적인 promptly 신속히 outline 개요 discourage 말리다 previously 이전에

143 문맥에 맞는 문장 고르기

번역 (A) 더 긴 기사들도 때때로 고려됩니다.
(B) 편집진은 수많은 상을 수상해 왔습니다.
(C) 지금 구독하시고 무료 토트백을 받으십시오.
(D) 배송을 위해 4주에서 6주를 감안해 주십시오.

해설 앞 문장에서 〈디지털 시코리〉에서 수락하는 기사의 분량(articles of 800 to 1,200 words)에 대해 안내하고 있으므로, 기사 분량에 대한 예외적인 경우에 대한 내용이 들어가면 연결이 자연스럽다. 따라서 가끔 더 긴 기사도 고려 대상이 된다고 언급하는 (A)가 정답이다.

어휘 lengthier 더 긴(lengthy의 비교급) editorial 편집의 subscribe 구독하다

144 접속부사

해설 빈칸 앞 문장에서 기사를 위한 아이디어가 있으면 이메일로 제안서를

보내 달라고 했고, 빈칸 뒤에는 독자층과 작문 방식에 대한 이해를 높일 수 있도록 출판물을 읽어달라고 했다. 출판물의 독자층 및 작문 방식 파악은 제안서를 작성하기 전에 선행되어야 할 일이므로, 빈칸에는 사전 준비사항을 연결하는 말이 들어가야 적합하다. 따라서 '그렇게 하기 전에'를 뜻하는 (C) Before you do가 정답이다. (A) In any event는 '어쨌든', (B) If you cannot은 '만약 그럴 수 없다면', (D) On the contrary는 '그와는 반대로'라는 의미이다.

145 대명사 어휘

해설 빈칸은 동사 respond의 주어 자리이고, 해당 지문은 〈디지털 시코리〉라는 월간 잡지에서 잠재적인 기고 작가를 대상으로 기사 제안서를 요청하는 글이다. 빈칸이 있는 문장에서 기사 제안에 응답하는 주체는 잡지사가 되어야 하고, 마지막 문장에서 글을 작성한 잡지사 측을 our magazine이라고 지칭하고 있으므로 '우리는 기사 제안에 신속히 응답한다'는 내용이 되어야 적절하다. 따라서 (A) We가 정답이다.

146 명사 어휘

해설 빈칸 앞 문장에서 제안서는 단일 페이지 개요로 제출되어야 한다고 했으므로, 빈칸이 있는 문장에서는 전체 길이의 글 초안은 권장되지 않는다는 내용이 되어야 자연스럽다. 따라서 '초안'을 뜻하는 (B) drafts가 정답이다. (A)의 form은 '양식', (C)의 contract는 '계약', (D)의 schedule은 '일정'이라는 의미이다.

PART 7

147-148 정보

> **147 여기에 광고하면 귀하의 사업이 주목받습니다!**
> 최상의 광고 지면이 1/4단에서 전면에 이르기까지 다양한 크기로 이용 가능합니다. **148 〈클리어포인트 타임즈〉는 매주 수천 명의 이웃들에게 전달됩니다.** 〈클리어포인트 타임즈〉를 활용하여 귀하의 사업에 대해 알리세요. 효과가 있습니다! 요금 및 추가 정보는 515-555-0130으로 전화 주세요.

어휘 notice 주목하다 prime 최상의 range from A to B (범위가) A에서 B까지 다양하다 column (인쇄된 페이지의) 세로단 spread 퍼뜨리다 work 효과가 있다

147 주제 / 목적

번역 정보의 주요 목적은?
(A) 신규 업체의 개업을 알리려고
(B) 임대 가능한 보관 공간을 홍보하려고
(C) 사업 홍보를 원하는 사람들을 유치하려고
(D) 사람들에게 신문 구독권 구입을 권하려고

해설 지문의 제목이 여기에 광고하면 귀하의 사업이 주목받는다(Your Business Gets Noticed When You Advertise Here!)인 것으로 보아 이 정보글은 사업을 홍보하고 싶어하는 사람들을 유치하기 위한 광고문임을 알 수 있다. 따라서 (C)가 정답이다.

어휘 publicize 홍보하다 storage 보관 encourage 권장하다 subscription 구독

> **Paraphrasing**
> 지문의 Advertise → 정답의 promote

148 추론 / 암시

번역 〈클리어포인트 타임즈〉에 대해 암시된 것은?
(A) 현재 매물로 나와 있다.
(B) 부동산 잡지이다.
(C) 지역 주간 간행물이다.
(D) 전국 일간 신문이다.

해설 두 번째 문장에서 〈클리어포인트 타임즈〉는 매주 수천 명의 이웃들에게 전달된다(The Clearpoint Times reaches thousands of your neighbors each week)고 한 것을 통해 〈클리어포인트 타임즈〉는 지역 주민들을 대상으로 발행되는 주간 간행물임을 짐작할 수 있다. 따라서 (C)가 정답이다.

어휘 real estate 부동산 national 전국의

> **Paraphrasing**
> 지문의 each week → 정답의 weekly
> 지문의 neighbors → 정답의 local

149-150 이메일

> 수신: 도나 위트 〈d.witt@seemail.net〉;
> 잭 위트 〈j.witt@seemail.net〉
> 발신: 데이비드 팔츠 〈dpaltz@emeraldglen.com〉
> 날짜: 8월 5일
> 제목: 바클리 드라이브 옥외 테라스 프로젝트
>
> 안녕하세요, 도나 그리고 잭,
>
> 다가오는 몇 달간의 저의 일정을 확정 지으면서 확인을 좀 하고자 합니다. **149 귀하의 부지를 재방문하여 조경 프로젝트에 대해 더 상세하게 논의할 시간을 잡고 싶습니다. 150 작업을 시작하기 위해, 두 분께서 프로젝트에 대해 기대하시는 디자인과 전체적인 구상에 관한 아이디어를 내주신다면** 도움이 될 것 같습니다. 두 분의 아이디어는 제가 필요한 자재와 시간을 더 잘 결정하는 데 도움이 될 것입니다. 그런 다음 더 정확한 가격 견적을 제공해 드릴 수 있습니다.
>
> 데이비드 팔츠
> 에메랄드 글렌 조경

어휘 patio 옥외 테라스 property 부동산 landscaping 조경 in detail 상세하게 brainstorm 아이디어를 내다 expectation 기대 overall 전체적인 vision 구상 determine 결정하다 material 자재 accurate 정확한

149 주제 / 목적

번역 이메일의 목적은?
(A) 회의를 요청하려고
(B) 최근 가격 변동을 확인하려고
(C) 일정 지연에 대해 사과하려고
(D) 일부 작업을 위한 추가 직원을 모집하려고

해설 두 번째 문장에서 귀하의 부지를 재방문하여 조경 프로젝트에 대해 더 상세하게 논의할 시간을 잡고 싶다(I would like to schedule a time to revisit your property and discuss your landscaping project in more detail)고 했으므로, 프로젝트 논의를 위한 회의를 요청하려고 이메일을 썼다는 것을 알 수 있다. 따라서 (A)가 정답이다.

어휘 delay 지연   seek 구하다

150 세부 사항

번역 팔츠 씨가 위트 부부에게 하라고 요청하는 것은?
(A) 지불금 납입
(B) 작업 프로젝트 일정 변경
(C) 작업 현장 근처에 주차 자제
(D) 조경 아이디어 제공

해설 세 번째 문장에서 팔츠 씨가 위트 부부에게 작업을 시작하기 위해, 프로젝트에 대해 기대하는 디자인과 전체적인 구상에 관한 아이디어를 내준다면 도움이 될 것 같다(To get started, it would be helpful if the two of you could brainstorm some of your design expectations and overall vision for the project)며 조경 프로젝트에 대한 아이디어를 달라고 요청하고 있으므로 (D)가 정답이다

어휘 reschedule 일정을 변경하다   avoid 피하다   site 현장

151-152 광고

카발리나 호텔
블루 글로브 매거진의 "최고 호텔" 상 수상!

카발리나 호텔은 손님들이 바쁘고 북적거리는 도시 생활에서 벗어날 수 있는 아름다운 안식처입니다. 질 시티 국제공항으로부터 50km 떨어진 곳에 위치한 저희 호텔은 아름다운 씨 마리너 베이를 마주하고 있습니다. **151 윈드서핑, 패들보딩, 그리고 여러 산책로와 자전거 도로가 모두 호텔 입구로부터 짧은 도보 거리에 있습니다. 정보가 풍부한 저희 직원들이 인근 호수 중 한 곳으로 카약 여행이나 낚시 여행을 기꺼이 주선해 드립니다.** 편안한 객실에서 숙면을 취하시고 나면 아침 식사 후 지역을 탐험하시고 싶어질 것입니다!

구내 편의시설: 무료 주차, 수영장, 자전거 대여, 피트니스 센터, 레스토랑 2곳

객실 유형: 싱글룸, 발코니가 있는 투룸 스위트, **152 주방이 있는 투룸 스위트**

어휘   breathtaking 숨 막히게 아름다운   sanctuary 안식처   escape 탈출하다   hectic 정신없이 바쁜   bustle 북적거림   knowledgeable 많이 아는   excursion 여행   property 건물 구내   amenities 편의시설

151 추론 / 암시

번역 광고는 누구를 대상으로 하는 것 같은가?
(A) 질 시티를 관광하고 싶은 사람들
(B) 야외 활동을 즐기는 사람들
(C) 비즈니스 컨퍼런스 주최측
(D) 호텔 업계 전문가들

해설 첫 단락 세 번째 문장에서 윈드서핑, 패들보딩, 그리고 여러 산책로와 자전거 도로가 모두 호텔 입구로부터 짧은 도보 거리에 있다(Windsurfing, paddleboarding, and several hiking and biking trails are all a short walk from our front door)고 했고, 뒤이어 정보가 풍부한 직원들이 인근 호수 중 한 곳으로 카약 여행이나 낚시 여행을 기꺼이 주선한다(Our knowledgeable staff are happy to arrange a kayaking excursion or a fishing trip to one of the nearby lakes)고 했다. 호텔 투숙객들을 위한 즐길 거리로 여러 야외 활동을 나열하고 있는 것으로 보아 광고가 주로 야외 활동을 좋아하는 이들을 대상으로 작성되었다는 것을 알 수 있다. 따라서 (B)가 정답이다.

어휘 organizer 주최측, 조직자   professional 전문가

> **Paraphrasing**
> 지문의 Windsurfing, paddleboarding, hiking and biking / a kayaking excursion or a fishing trip
> → 정답의 outdoor activities

152 추론 / 암시

번역 카발리나 호텔의 일부 객실에 대해 암시된 것은?
(A) 고가구가 있다.
(B) 최근에 개조되었다.
(C) 손님들이 온라인으로 객실을 볼 수 있다.
(D) 손님들이 객실에서 음식을 준비할 수 있다.

해설 세 번째 단락에서 객실 유형에 주방이 있는 투룸 스위트(two-room suite with kitchen)가 있다고 했으므로 호텔의 일부 객실에서는 요리가 가능하다는 것을 알 수 있다. 따라서 (D)가 정답이다.

어휘 contain 들어있다   antique 오래 된, 골동품의

153-154 문자 메시지

폴 조 (오전 9시 47분)
안녕하세요, 마리솔 씨. 제가 야다브 디지털 마케팅의 엘리스 메이어 이사와 이야기했다는 걸 말씀드리고 싶어요. **153 그쪽에 일자리가 하나 있어서 제가 당신에 대해 언급했어요.** 그녀는 당신이 꼭 지원해야 한다고 하네요.

마리솔 로세티 (오전 9시 49분)
정말 좋은 소식이네요! 제 이름을 언급해 주셔서 감사합니다.

폴 조 (오전 9시 50분)
당신이 적임자일 거라는 걸 알아요. **153 당신은 모든 항목을 충족한다고요.**

마리솔 로세티 (오전 9시 51분)
메이어 씨가 제 이력서 외에 자기소개서도 보고 싶어 하실까요?

폴 조 (오전 9시 52분)
안 그래도 될 것 같아요. 154 엘리스와 저는 오랫동안 친구였어요. 이력서가 최신이고 관련 경력을 반영하고 있는지만 확인해 주세요.

마리솔 로세티 (오전 9시 53분)
그럴게요. 정말 고마워요, 폴 씨. 정말 감사합니다!

어휘 fit 꼭 맞는 것 cover letter 자기소개서 bother 신경 쓰다
up to date 최신의 reflect 반영하다 relevant 관련 있는

153 의도 파악

번역 오전 9시 50분에 조 씨가 "당신이 적임자일 거라는 걸 알아요"라고 쓴 의도는?
(A) 로세티 씨를 채용하고 싶어한다.
(B) 야다브 디지털 마케팅에서 오랫동안 근무해 왔다.
(C) 야다브 디지털 마케팅에 새로운 이사가 필요하다고 생각한다.
(D) 로세티 씨가 일자리에 적합한 후보자라고 생각한다.

해설 9시 47분에 조 씨가 로세티 씨에게 그쪽에 일자리가 하나 있어서 당신에 대해 언급했다(There's an open position there, and I mentioned you)고 했고, 9시 50분에 다시 당신이 적임자일 거라는 걸 안다(I know you'd be a great fit)며 당신은 모든 항목을 충족한다(You check all the boxes)고 강조했다. 따라서 조 씨는 자신이 추천한 일자리에 로세티 씨가 딱 맞는 후보자라고 생각한다는 의도로 한 말임을 알 수 있으므로 (D)가 정답이다.

어휘 candidate 후보자

154 Not / True

번역 조 씨에 대해 명시된 것은?
(A) 메이어 씨를 오랫동안 알고 지냈다.
(B) 메이어 씨와 같은 회사에서 근무한다.
(C) 로세티 씨가 자기소개서를 작성하는 것을 도울 것이다.
(D) 마케팅 회사의 이사이다.

해설 9시 52분에 조 씨가 엘리스와 자신은 오랫동안 친구였다(Elise and I have been friends for years)고 언급하고 있으므로 (A)가 정답이다.

> **Paraphrasing**
> 지문의 Elise and I have been friends
> → 정답의 He has known Ms. Mayer
> 지문의 for years → 정답의 for a long time

155-157 기사

제품 출시 연기

155 커버드 브리지 인더스트리즈가 새로운 청량음료인 발미 브리즈의 출시를 연기했다. 이 회사는 여름철 높은 판매 수요를 활용하기 위해 6월에 제품을 공개할 계획이었다. 156 회사는 이번 지연이 음료의 주 성분 중 하나인 망고 추출물의 부족으로 야기되었으며, 이로 인해 8월까지 품질 검사가 연기되었다고 밝혔다.

157 커버드 브리지는 현재 11월까지 모든 품질 검사를 완료하고 그 다음 달에 제품을 출시할 수 있기를 바라고 있다. 판매는 당초 기대보다 부진할 수 있지만 회사는 발미 브리즈를 겨울 휴가철 행사들을 위한 훌륭한 선택으로 홍보할 예정이다.

어휘 launch 출시 delay 연기하다 soft drink 청량음료
release 공개하다 take advantage of ~을 활용하다
demand 수요 shortage 부족 component 성분 extract 추출물 postponement 연기 celebration 기념 행사

155 추론 / 암시

번역 커버드 브리지 인더스트리즈는 어떤 종류의 회사인 것 같은가?
(A) 아이스크림 생산업체
(B) 광고 대행사
(C) 음료 제조업체
(D) 선풍기 제조업체

해설 첫 단락 첫 문장에서 커버드 브리지 인더스트리즈가 새로운 청량음료인 발미 브리즈의 출시를 연기했다(Covered Bridge Industries has delayed the launch of its new Balmy Breeze soft drink)고 한 것을 통해 커버드 브리지 인더스트리즈는 음료를 제조하는 업체임을 짐작할 수 있다. 따라서 (C)가 정답이다.

어휘 agency 대행사 beverage 음료 electric fan 선풍기

> **Paraphrasing**
> 지문의 drink → 정답의 beverage

156 세부 사항

번역 커버드 브리지 인더스트리즈의 지도부가 원래 계획을 따르지 않은 이유는?
(A) 더 유리한 시장 조건을 기다리기를 원했다.
(B) 품질 검사에서 몇 가지 문제가 드러났다.
(C) 광고 캠페인이 제때 준비되지 않았다.
(D) 필수적인 재료를 구할 수 없었다.

해설 첫 단락 세 번째 문장에서 회사는 이번 지연이 음료의 주 성분 중 하나인 망고 추출물의 부족으로 야기되었다(The company said the delay was caused by a shortage of one of the drink's main components, mango extract)고 했으므로 음료에 들어가는 주요 성분을 구할 수 없어 출시가 지연되었음을 알 수 있다. 따라서 (D)가 정답이다.

어휘 favorable 유리한 reveal 드러내다 on time 제때
essential 필수적인 ingredient 재료

> **Paraphrasing**
> 지문의 shortage of one of the drink's main components
> → 정답의 An essential ingredient was unavailable.

157 추론 / 암시

번역 커버드 브리지 인더스트리즈는 어느 달에 신제품을 출시할 것 같은가?
(A) 6월
(B) 8월
(C) 11월
(D) 12월

해설 두 번째 단락의 첫 문장에서 커버드 브리지는 현재 11월까지 모든 품질 검사를 완료하고 그 다음 달에 제품을 출시할 수 있기를 바라고 있다(Covered Bridge now hopes to complete all quality testing by November so that it can launch the product the following month)고 했으므로 12월에 제품을 출시할 계획임을 알 수 있다. 따라서 (D)가 정답이다.

158-160 회람

> **회람**
> 발신: 리아 아첸, 기술 자원 부서장
> 수신: 전 직원
> 날짜: 6월 28일
> 제목: 영상 편집 소프트웨어 변경
>
> 7월 20일부터, **158** 직원들은 동영상 제작을 위해 집비드 앱을 더 이상 이용할 수 없습니다. **158, 160** 대신 우리는 커튼 콜을 사용할 예정으로, 고장 날 가능성이 낮은 좀 더 신뢰할 수 있는 프로그램이 되어 주리라 믿습니다. 그것은 이미 모든 업무용 컴퓨터에 설치되었으므로 즉시 사용하기 시작할 수 있습니다. **159** 집비드에서 사용하던 형식에서 커튼 콜과 호환이 되는 형식으로 영상을 변환해야 하는 직원들은 업무용 컴퓨터에 변환 유틸리티를 설치해야 합니다. 이 유틸리티는 우리 회사의 온라인 소프트웨어 라이브러리에서 찾을 수 있습니다. **159** 이 과정에 도움이 필요하면 기술 지원부의 마누엘 코스타에게 연락하십시오.
>
> **어휘** resource 자원 effective 시행되는 animated 동영상으로 된 prove 드러나다 reliable 신뢰할 수 있는 crash 고장 나다 convert 변환하다 format 형식 compatible 호환이 되는 utility 유틸리티(컴퓨터 이용을 위한 각종 소프트웨어)

158 세부 사항

번역 집비드 앱이 더 이상 사용되지 않는 이유는?
(A) 유사한 프로그램들보다 더 비싸다.
(B) 오직 소수의 직원들만 사용했다.
(C) 너무 자주 오작동 되었다.
(D) 새 컴퓨터와 호환이 되지 않는다.

해설 첫 문장에서 직원들은 동영상 제작을 위해 집비드 앱을 더 이상 이용할 수 없다(employees will no longer have access to the Zipvid app for creating animated videos)면서 다음 문장에서 대신 커튼 콜을 사용할 예정으로 고장 날 가능성이 낮은 좀 더 신뢰할 수 있는 프로그램이 되어 주리라 믿는다(We will instead be using Curtain Call, which we trust will prove to be a more reliable program that is less likely to crash)고 했다. 따라서 집비드 앱은 고장이 잦아 신뢰성이 떨어진다는 이유로 사용을 중단하게 되었음을 알 수 있으므로 (C)가 정답이다.

어휘 malfunction 제대로 작동하지 않다

> **Paraphrasing**
> 지문의 crash → 정답의 malfunctioned

159 세부 사항

번역 회람에 따르면, 코스타 씨는 직원들이 무엇을 하도록 도울 수 있는가?
(A) 영상 변환
(B) 유실된 데이터 복구
(C) 소프트웨어 주문
(D) 양식 작성

해설 네 번째 문장에서 집비드에서 사용하던 형식에서 커튼 콜과 호환이 되는 형식으로 영상을 변환해야 하는 직원들은 업무용 컴퓨터에 변환 유틸리티를 설치해야 한다(Employees who need to convert their videos from the format Zipvid uses to a format compatible with Curtain Call should install the converter utility to their work computers)고 했고, 마지막 문장에서 이 과정에 도움이 필요하면 기술 지원부의 마누엘 코스타에게 연락하라(For assistance with this process, please contact Manuel Costa in Technology Support)고 했다. 따라서 코스타 씨는 직원들이 변환 유틸리티를 설치하여 영상을 변환하는 작업을 도울 것임을 알 수 있으므로 (A)가 정답이다.

어휘 recover 복구하다, 되찾다 complete 작성하다

160 문장 삽입

번역 [1], [2], [3], [4]로 표시된 위치 중에서 다음 문장이 들어가기에 가장 적합한 곳은?

"그것은 이미 모든 업무용 컴퓨터에 설치되었으므로 즉시 사용하기 시작할 수 있습니다."
(A) [1]
(B) [2]
(C) [3]
(D) [4]

해설 주어진 문장에서 그것은 이미 모든 컴퓨터에 설치되었다(It has already been installed on all work computers)고 했으므로, 주어진 문장 앞에는 컴퓨터에 새롭게 설치된 소프트웨어 프로그램에 대한 내용이 있어야 한다. 따라서 기존 프로그램 대신 커튼 콜을 사용할 것(We will instead be using Curtain Call)이라고 언급하고 있는 문장 뒤인 [2]에 들어가는 것이 글의 흐름상 자연스러우므로 (B)가 정답이다.

어휘 immediately 즉시

161-164 기사

> **번창하는 지역 업체들**
>
> 그린우드 (7월 6일) — 특정 업체가 성공하는 이유는 종종 미스터리이지만 몇몇 지역 상점들은 그 비결을 파악한 듯하다. 문을 연 지 2년 만에, 어 사우전드 스토리즈와 로지어 가든 센터는 번성하고 있다.
>
> "**162 처음에는 시행착오가 많았지만 결국 방법을 터득했어요.**"라고 **161 어 사우전드 스토리즈를 산드라 리베라와 함께 소유하고 있는 리즈 오타니**는 말했다. "저는 재고를 관리하고, 산드라는 저자들과의 특별 행사를 포함한 대외적인 부분을 처리합니다."
>
> "우리는 환상적인 팀이에요. 하지만 우리의 가장 강력한 자산은 우리를 지원해 주는 이웃들이라고 생각합니다. **161 이곳 사람들은 책과 독서를 사랑하며 정기적으로 우리 가게를 방문하세요.** 우리는 소셜 미디어에서도 활발하게 활동하고 있는데 그것도 도움이 되고요."라고 리베라 씨는 덧붙였다.
>
> 로지어 가든 센터의 업주인 루이 로지어는 사업을 시작하고 운영하는 데에는 노력과 인내가 필요하다는 데 동의했다.
>
> **162 로지어 씨의 상점은 토종 식물과 꽃을 전문으로 하고 있는데, 그는 가든 센터를 운영하던 첫 해가 힘들었다고 인정했다.** "수익을 **163 거두는** 데 오랜 시간이 걸렸습니다. 때로는 모든 걸 접고 이전 직장으로 돌아갈까도 생각했습니다."라고 그는 회상했다.
>
> 어려운 시작에도 불구하고, 로지어 씨는 굴하지 않고 버텼다. **164 이제 사업이 잘 되고 있어서 그는 다른 가게를 여는 것을 검토 중이다.**
>
> "저는 그린우드 지역 너머의 고객들에게 다가가고 싶습니다."라고 그는 말했다. "현재 모건빌을 둘러보며 그곳이 두 번째 매장을 위한 최적의 장소인지를 가늠하고 있습니다."
>
> **어휘** thrive 번창하다 particular 특정한 flourish 번성하다 trial and error 시행착오 outset 시작, 시초 figure out ~을 알아내다 stock 재고 public-facing 사람들을 대하는 author 저자 asset 자산 supportive 지원하는 regularly 정기적으로 presence 참석 patience 인내 specialize in ~을 전문으로 하다 native 토종의 admit 인정하다 recall 회상하다, 떠올리다 former 이전의 persevere 굴하지 않고 계속하다 now that 이제 ~이므로 explore 탐색하다, 조사하다

161 추론 / 암시

번역 오타니 씨와 리베라 씨는 어떤 종류의 사업체를 운영하는 것 같은가?
(A) 부동산 사무소
(B) 행사 기획 서비스
(C) 서점
(D) 미디어 회사

해설 두 번째 단락의 첫 문장에서 어 사우전드 스토리즈를 산드라 리베라와 함께 소유하고 있는 리즈 오타니(Liz Ohtani, who, together with Sandra Rivera, owns A Thousand Stories)라고 했고, 세 번째 단락의 세 번째 문장에서 리베라 씨가 이곳 사람들은 책과 독서를 사랑하며 정기적으로 우리 가게를 방문한다(People here love books and reading, and they visit us regularly)고 했다. 따라서 두 사람은 서점을 공동 소유하고 있다는 것을 알 수 있으므로 (C)가 정답이다.

162 세부 사항

번역 어 사우전드 스토리즈와 로지어 가든 센터 사이의 한 가지 유사점은?
(A) 두 곳 모두 공동 소유자가 운영한다.
(B) 두 곳 모두 전 세계 고객들에게 서비스를 제공한다.
(C) 두 곳 모두 주로 온라인에서 광고한다.
(D) 두 곳 모두 처음 문을 열었을 때 고군분투했다.

해설 두 번째 단락의 첫 문장에서 처음에는 시행착오가 많았지만 결국 방법을 터득했다고 어 사우전드 스토리즈를 산드라 리베라와 함께 소유하고 있는 리즈 오타니는 말했다("There was a lot of trial and error at the outset, but we finally figured it out," said Liz Ohtani, who, together with Sandra Rivera, owns A Thousand Stories)고 했고, 다섯 번째 단락의 첫 문장에서 로지어 씨의 상점은 토종 식물과 꽃을 전문으로 하고 있는데 그는 가든 센터를 운영하던 첫 해가 힘들었다고 인정했다(Mr. Rosier, whose store specializes in native plants and flowers, admitted that his first year with the garden center was tough)고 했다. 따라서 두 업체 모두 공통적으로 처음 사업을 시작했을 때 힘든 시간을 겪었다는 것을 알 수 있으므로 (D)가 정답이다.

어휘 operate 운영하다 co-owner 공동 소유자 primarily 주로 struggle 고군분투하다, 힘겹게 나아가다

> **Paraphrasing**
> 지문의 There was a lot of trial and error at the outset / his first year with the garden center was tough
> → 정답의 struggled when they first opened

163 동의어 찾기

번역 다섯 번째 단락 4행의 "turn"과 의미가 가장 가까운 단어는?
(A) 가입하다
(B) 얻다
(C) 변경하다
(D) 뒤바꾸다

해설 의미상 수익을 '거두는' 데 오랜 시간이 걸렸다는 뜻으로 쓰였으므로 '(이익을) 얻다'를 뜻하는 (B) gain이 정답이다.

164 추론 / 암시

번역 기사에 따르면, 로지어 씨는 곧 무엇을 할 것 같은가?
(A) 자신의 경험에 관한 책을 쓸 것이다.
(B) 모건빌로 이사 갈 것이다.
(C) 이전 직업으로 돌아갈 것이다.
(D) 다른 가든 센터를 열 것이다.

해설 여섯 번째 단락의 두 번째 문장에서 로지어 씨는 이제 사업이 잘 되고 있어서 다른 가게를 여는 것을 검토 중(Now that the business is doing well, he is exploring opening another store)이라고 했으므로 (D)가 정답이다.

어휘 previous 이전의

165-167 공지

직원 안전 관련 중요 정보

모든 직원은 게시된 안전 수칙뿐 아니라 직원 안내서의 지침을 준수해야 합니다. **165 특정 직무의 경우 직원들은 관리자가 제시하는 추가적인 안전 지침을 따라야 합니다.** 우리는 안전을 중요하게 생각하므로 이러한 규정의 위반을 알게 된 직원은 관리자 또는 안전 담당자에게 연락할 것을 촉구합니다. 또한, 이러한 규정에 관해 우려 사항이 있거나 추가 **166 조치**를 제안하고 싶은 직원은 안전 담당자에게 직접 연락해야 합니다.

더불어, 응급 처치를 교육받은 직원들의 연락처는 직원 안내서에서 찾을 수 있습니다. 무료 응급 처치 교육 및 자격증 교부는 전 직원에게 연 2회 제공됩니다. **167 교육이 진행되는 시기에 관한 더 자세한 정보는 lschneider@rinckindustry.com으로 린 슈나이더에게 연락하세요.**

어휘 guideline 지침 urge 촉구하다 breach 위반 protocol 규약 coordinator 담당자 measure 조치 first aid 응급 처치 certification 증명서 교부

165 Not / True

번역 공지에서 관리자의 책임으로 언급된 것은?
(A) 직원 안내서 배포
(B) 안전 담당자의 업무 감독
(C) 게시된 안전 수칙의 정기적인 업데이트
(D) 특정 직무에 대한 안전 지침 제공

해설 첫 단락 두 번째 문장에서 특정 직무의 경우 직원들은 관리자가 제시하는 추가적인 안전 지침을 따라야 한다(Certain jobs require employees to follow the additional safety guidelines provided by their supervisors)고 했으므로, 관리자의 책임 중에는 직원들에게 특정 직무에 대한 안전 지침을 제공하는 일이 포함되어 있음을 알 수 있다. 따라서 (D)가 정답이다.

어휘 distribute 배포하다 specific 특정한

166 동의어 찾기

번역 첫 번째 단락 6행의 "measures"와 의미가 가장 가까운 단어는?
(A) 양
(B) 절차
(C) 크기
(D) 벌금

해설 의미상 추가 '조치'를 제안한다는 뜻으로 쓰였으므로 '절차, 진행'을 뜻하는 (B) procedures가 정답이다.

167 세부 사항

번역 공지에 따르면, 직원들이 슈나이더 씨에게 연락해야 하는 이유는?
(A) 새로운 직책에 지원하기 위해서
(B) 연락처 정보를 업데이트하기 위해서
(C) 추가적인 안전 수칙을 제안하기 위해서
(D) 교육 일정을 요청하기 위해서

해설 마지막 단락 마지막 문장에서 교육이 진행되는 시기에 관한 더 자세한 정보는 린 슈나이더에게 연락하라(For more information about when trainings are held, please contact Lynn Schneider at lschneider@rinckindustry.com)고 했으므로 (D)가 정답이다.

Paraphrasing
지문의 information about when trainings are held
→ 정답의 training schedule

168-171 직무 설명

도라 카운티 교통과
행정 서비스 부서

도로 관리자

도로 관리자는 도라 카운티 전역의 도로 관련 구조물의 건설 및 유지보수와 관련된 모든 업무를 감독하며, 모든 긴급 프로그램 활동에 대한 작업 목표를 수립하는 것을 포함합니다. **168 주요 책임에는 모든 제설 작업 및 건설 프로젝트의 준비가 포함됩니다.** 그러므로 관리자는 필요시 건설 및 유지보수 작업을 수행할 수 있어야 하며 **170(A) 관련 장비를 조작하는 데 적절한 수준의 기술이 있어야 합니다.**

이 직책은 직원 관리와 관련된 여러 업무를 포함합니다. **171 관리자는 부하 직원의 채용 및 교육을 지원하고 170(B) 부서장들과 협력하여 팀원들의 평가와 연례 인사 고과를 실시합니다.** 결정적으로 관리자는 팀원들에게 안전 절차를 교육하고 진행 중인 작업의 안전을 감독합니다. **169 관리자는 중대한 인사 문제를 부서 책임자에게 알리고 책임자는 모든 경우에 적절한 행동 방침을 권합니다.** 직원들이 제기한 중요한 우려 사항은 관리자에 의해 부서장들의 관심 사안이 되며, 관리자는 팀원들과 행정 서비스 부서 간의 연락 담당자 역할을 합니다.

170(C) 부서의 지정된 예산을 관리하는 것은 이 직책에서 대단히 중요한 부분입니다. 관리자는 매달 예산을 기록 관리할 수 있도록 컴퓨터 사용에 능숙해야 합니다. 관리자는 유지관리 및 보수 활동과 관련된 비용 보고서, 근무 시간 기록표, 통계 및 서술형 보고서를 준비하고, 각 활동에 사용된 총 시간, 직원 수, 자재를 반드시 기록하도록 합니다.

어휘 division 부서 administrative 행정의 highway (고속)도로 oversee 감독하다 maintenance 유지보수 structure 구조물 objective 목표 possess 보유하다 appropriate 적절한 relevant 관련된 subordinate 부하 직원 evaluation 평가 performance review 인사 고과 crucially 결정적으로 instruct 가르치다 procedure 절차 monitor 감시하다 in progress 진행 중인 course of action 행동 방침 instance 경우 significant 중요한 function 기능하다 liaison 연락 담당자 designated 지정된 critical 대단히 중요한 aspect 측면 proficiency 능숙함 keep track of ~을 기록하다 expenditure 비용 time sheet 근무 시간 기록표 statistical 통계의 narrative 서술식의

168 추론 / 암시

번역 도라 카운티에 대해 암시된 것은?
(A) 눈이 내릴 정도로 추워진다.
(B) 인구가 많다.
(C) 지역 판매업체로부터 장비를 구입한다.
(D) 4차선 도로가 많다.

해설 첫 단락 두 번째 문장에서 주요 책무에는 모든 제설 작업 및 건설 프로젝트의 준비가 포함된다(Key responsibilities include the organization of all snow-removal operations and construction projects)고 한 것으로 보아 도라 카운티에 눈이 내리고 쌓일 정도로 날씨가 추워질 수 있음을 알 수 있다. 따라서 (A)가 정답이다.

어휘 population 인구 vendor 판매업체 lane 차선

169 세부 사항

번역 직무 설명에 따르면, 도로 관리자는 팀원에게 심각한 문제가 발생할 경우 무엇을 해야 하는가?
(A) 대체 직원 제안
(B) 해당 팀원의 활동 제한
(C) 부서 책임자에게 해당 문제 통보
(D) 경영진에게 사안을 설명할 연락 담당자 지정

해설 두 번째 단락 네 번째 문장에서 관리자는 중대한 인사 문제를 부서 책임자에게 알린다(The supervisor informs the division director of major personnel problems)고 했으므로 (C)가 정답이다.

어휘 arise 발생하다 replacement 대체 restrict 제한하다 designate 지정하다

> **Paraphrasing**
> 지문의 major personnel problems
> → 질문의 a serious problem with a crew member

170 Not / True

번역 도로 관리자의 책무가 아닌 것은?
(A) 건설 장비 조작
(B) 연간 성과 평가 수행
(C) 월간 예산 관리
(D) 팀원 급여 협상

해설 첫 단락 마지막 문장에서 관리자는 관련 장비를 조작하는 데 적절한 수준의 기술이 있어야 한다(possess an appropriate level of skill in operating the relevant equipment)고 했으므로 (A), 두 번째 단락 두 번째 문장에서 부서장들과 협력하여 팀원들의 평가와 연례 인사 고과를 실시한다(works with division leaders to conduct evaluations and yearly performance reviews of crew members)고 했으므로 (B), 세 번째 단락 첫 문장에서 부서의 지정된 예산을 관리하는 것은 이 직책에서 대단히 중요한 부분(Managing the division's designated budget is a critical aspect of the position)이라고 했으므로 (C)는 관리자의 책무로 언급되었으나, 팀원의 급여 협상에 대한 내용은 없으므로 (D)가 정답이다.

어휘 negotiate 협상하다 salary 급여

171 문장 삽입

번역 [1], [2], [3], [4]로 표시된 위치 중에서 다음 문장이 들어가기에 가장 적합한 곳은?
"이 직책은 직원 관리와 관련된 여러 업무를 포함합니다."
(A) [1]
(B) [2]
(C) [3]
(D) [4]

해설 주어진 문장에서 이 직책에 직원 관리(staff management) 업무가 포함된다고 명시하고 있으므로, 주어진 문장 뒤에는 직원 관리에 대한 구체적인 내용이 나와야 적절하다. 따라서 관리자는 직원 채용과 교육, 평가 및 연례 인사 고과를 실시한다(The supervisor assists in the hiring and training of subordinates ~ to conduct evaluations and yearly performance reviews of crew members)면서 직원 관리 업무를 나열하고 있는 문장 앞인 [2]에 들어가는 것이 글의 흐름상 자연스러우므로 (B)가 정답이다.

172-175 문자 메시지

▶ 동영상 강의

마커스 골란츠 (오후 3시 18분)
172, 173 제니퍼, 내일 오전 7시에 브라운 씨 댁에서 난방 배관을 제거해 줄 수 있나요? 아서의 기초 수리 팀이 집 아래 쪽 좁은 배선 공간에 있는 그 자리에 들어가야 하거든요.

제니퍼 칼루자 (오후 3시 20분)
좋아요, 대략 한 시간 정도 걸릴 거예요. **173** 거기가 레온 드라이브 210번지 맞죠?

마커스 골란츠 (오후 3시 20분)
173 맞아요.

아서 그루이터 (오후 3시 21분)
우리 팀은 내일 오전 8시 직후에 작업을 시작하러 거기로 갈 거예요. **174** 우리 팀의 기초 보수와 방수 작업은 3~4일 정도 걸릴 거예요. 이번 건은 평소와 달리 대형 작업이라서요.

제니퍼 칼루자 (오후 3시 22분)
그럼, 제가 언제 다시 와서 배관을 재설치하면 좋을까요?

마커스 골란츠 (오후 3시 23분)
브라운 씨 부부는 휴가 중이니 금요일 오후가 괜찮을 것 같아요.

제니퍼 칼루자 (오후 3시 23분)
제가 금요일에는 아마디 씨 아파트에서 작업할 예정이라서, **175** 브라운 씨네 배관 작업을 월요일까지 미뤄도 될까요?

마커스 골란츠 (오후 3시 24분)
그럼요. **175** 월요일 일찍이라면 괜찮을 거예요.

제니퍼 칼루자 (오후 3시 25분)
알겠습니다, 마커스.

어휘 furnace 난방로 ductwork 배관 foundation 기초 crew 팀 crawl space (천장의 배선 등을 위한) 좁은 공간 patch (구멍 등을) 때우다 waterproof 방수 처리를 하다 unusually 평소와 달리 reinstall 재설치하다

172 주제 / 목적

번역 대화의 목적은?
(A) 집 주인에게 공사에 대해 알리려고
(B) 수리가 제때 완료될 수 없는 이유를 설명하려고
(C) 공공 행사 일정을 논의하려고
(D) 작업 일정을 조정하려고

해설 3시 18분에 골란츠 씨가 칼루자 씨에게 내일 오전 7시에 브라운 씨 댁에서 난방 배관을 제거해 줄 수 있는지(can you be at the Browns' house at 7:00 A.M. tomorrow to remove the furnace ductwork?)를 물으며 아서의 기초 수리 팀이 집 아래 쪽 좁은 배선 공간에 있는 그 자리에 들어가야 한다(Arthur's foundation-repair crew will need to access that area of the crawl space under the house)고 한 것으로 보아, 팀 간 작업 일정을 조정하기 위해 메시지를 보내고 있음을 알 수 있다. 따라서 (D)가 정답이다.

어휘 coordinate 조정하다

173 추론 / 암시

번역 레온 드라이브 210번지에 대해 결론지을 수 있는 것은?
(A) 개인 주택이다.
(B) 사무실 건물이다.
(C) 아파트 단지이다.
(D) 산업용 창고이다.

해설 3시 18분에 골란츠 씨가 칼루자 씨에게 내일 오전 7시에 브라운 씨 댁에서 난방 배관을 제거해 줄 수 있는지(can you be at the Browns' house at 7:00 A.M. tomorrow to remove the furnace ductwork?)를 묻자, 3시 20분에 칼루자 씨가 거기가 레온 드라이브 210번지가 맞는지(That's 210 Leon Drive, right?)를 되물었고 골란츠 씨가 맞다(That's right)고 확인해 주고 있다. 따라서 레온 드라이브 210번지는 브라운 씨의 개인 주택임을 알 수 있으므로 (A)가 정답이다.

어휘 complex 단지 industrial 산업의

174 추론 / 암시

번역 그루이터 씨의 작업팀에 대해 암시된 것은?
(A) 칼루자 씨를 팀에 영입했다.
(B) 골란츠 씨의 사무실을 수리하고 있다.
(C) 보통 3일보다 짧은 기간 내에 작업을 완료한다.
(D) 아마디 씨의 아파트 작업을 이미 시작했다.

해설 3시 21분에 그루이터 씨가 우리 팀의 기초 보수와 방수 작업은 3~4일 정도 걸릴 것(Our work patching and waterproofing the foundation will likely take three or four days)이라면서 이번 건은 평소와 달리 대형 작업(It's an unusually large job)이라고 했다. 따라서 그루이터 씨의 작업팀은 평소 일반적인 작업을 완료하는 데 3일이 채 걸리지 않는다는 것을 유추할 수 있다. 따라서 (C)가 정답이다.

175 의도 파악

번역 오후 3시 25분에 칼루자 씨가 "알겠습니다"라고 쓴 의도는?
(A) 골란츠 씨가 자신의 말을 이해했는지 확인하기를 원한다.
(B) 월요일 일찍 레온 드라이브 210번지에 있을 것이다.
(C) 그루이터 씨에게 작업 비용 청구서를 보낼 것이다.
(D) 골란츠 씨가 브라운 씨 가족에게 연락하기를 바란다.

해설 3시 23분에 칼루자 씨가 브라운 씨네 배관 작업을 월요일까지 미뤄도 될지(can the Browns' ductwork wait until Monday?) 물었고, 3시 24분에 골란츠 씨가 월요일 일찍이라면 괜찮을 것(Early on Monday would work)이라고 하자 3시 25분에 칼루자 씨가 알겠다(You got it)고 대답한 것으로, 칼루자 씨는 월요일 일찍 브라운 씨네 집이 있는 레온 드라이브 210번지에서 작업을 하겠다는 의도로 한 말임을 알 수 있다. 따라서 (B)가 정답이다.

어휘 bill 청구서

176-180 웹페이지 + 이메일

https://www.jjshomeandgarden.com/cementmixers

JJ 홈 앤 가든 서플라이어즈
시멘트 믹서기

모델	이름	설명	가격
HCC-TX	이지 스타	• 2입방피트, 1마력 • **176 매장 수령만 가능**	189달러
180 CVY-XU	미스터 버디*	• 2입방피트, 5마력 • 배송만 가능, 1~2주 소요	**180** 359달러
PIT-RX	**177** 콘크리타이저	• **177 4입방피트**, 3마력 • 매장 수령 가능, 5일 이내 배송	499달러
HTK-LM	빅 믹스	• 5입방피트, 5마력 • **176 매장 수령만 가능**	629달러
PPP-HT	맥스 포 프로스	• 6입방피트, 7마력 • 배송만 가능, 2~4주 소요	949달러

* 7월 26일까지 재고 없음

어휘 description 설명 cubic feet 입방피트 hp 마력 (horsepower의 약자) in-store 매장 내의 out of stock 재고가 떨어진

수신: 고객 서비스 <customerservice@jjshomeandgarden.com>
발신: 마샬 위버 <mweaver01@gomail.net>
날짜: 6월 25일
제목: 지연된 주문

고객 서비스 담당자께:

177 저는 6월 15일에 JJ 홈 앤 가든 서플라이어즈로부터 저의 4입방피트 시멘트 믹서기가 1주일 전에 배송될 것이라는 확인 이메일을 받았습니다. 저는 작은 업체를 운영하며 장비에 의존하고 있습니다. 저는 아직 제품을 받지 못했으며, 이미 여러 번의 전화 메시지를 남겼지만 답변을 듣지 못했습니다. 오늘까지 제 업체로 시멘트 믹서기가 못 올 경우, 179 내일 오후 작업에 믹서기가 꼭 필요하기 때문에 필요하다면 제가 뉴 그랄렌이나 팔로너 매장에서 직접 받아갈 수 있습니다. 내일까지 제품이 준비되지 않을 경우 제 주문을 취소하고 178 전액 환불해 주실 것을 요청합니다. 180 대신 저는 작은 지역 매장인 얼라이언스 하드웨어 스토어에서 미스터 버디를 구입할 예정이며, 이 곳은 현재 귀사와 동일한 가격에 이 제품을 보유하고 있습니다.

제 주문의 상황을 즉시 알려주십시오. 제가 귀사에 발주한 주문품이 오늘 도착해서 양측 모두에게 추가 조치가 필요하지 않기를 바랍니다.

마샬 위버

어휘 delayed 지연된 dependent 의존하는 unanswered 답변 없는 refund 환불 in stock 재고가 있는 status 상황 immediately 즉시 further 추가의 action 조치

176 Not / True

번역 웹페이지에 명시된 것은?
(A) 빅 믹스는 현재 구입할 수 없다.
(B) 미스터 버디는 가장 많이 팔리는 제품이다.
(C) 일부 품목은 배송될 수 없다.
(D) 모든 시멘트 믹서기의 가격이 할인되었다.

해설 웹페이지의 표에서 HCC-TX와 HTK-LM은 매장 수령만 가능하다(In-store pickup only)고 나와 있으므로 이 두 모델은 배송이 되지 않는다는 것을 알 수 있다. 따라서 (C)가 정답이다.

Paraphrasing
지문의 In-store pickup only → 정답의 cannot be delivered

177 연계

번역 위버 씨는 JJ 홈 앤 가든 서플라이어즈에서 어떤 제품을 주문했는가?
(A) 이지 스타
(B) 콘크리타이저
(C) 빅 믹스
(D) 맥스 포 프로

해설 이메일의 첫 단락 첫 문장에서 위버 씨는 6월 15일에 JJ 홈 앤 가든 서플라이어즈로부터 자신의 4입방피트 시멘트 믹서기가 1주일 전에 배송될 것이라는 확인 이메일을 받았다(I received a confirmation e-mail on June 15 that my 4-cubic-foot cement mixer would be delivered one week ago from JJ's Home and Garden Suppliers)고 했고, 웹페이지의 표 중반부에 4입방피트(4 cubic feet) 제품은 콘크리타이저(Concretizer)라고 나와 있다. 따라서 (B)가 정답이다.

178 동의어 찾기

번역 이메일의 첫 단락 7행의 "full"과 의미가 가장 가까운 단어는?
(A) 공급된
(B) 사용 중인
(C) 완전한
(D) 풍부한

해설 의미상 주문을 취소하고 '전액' 환불해달라, 즉 '전체의'라는 뜻으로 쓰였으므로 '완전한, 전체의'라는 의미의 (C) complete가 정답이다.

179 추론 / 암시

번역 JJ 홈 앤 가든 서플라이어즈에 대해 암시된 것은?
(A) 대형 건설 장비 판매를 전문으로 한다.
(B) 대부분의 제품을 온라인으로 판매한다.
(C) 모든 제품에 무료 배송을 제공한다.
(D) 한 군데보다 많은 지역에 매장이 있다.

해설 이메일의 첫 단락 네 번째 문장에서 위버 씨가 내일 오후 작업에 믹서기가 꼭 필요하기 때문에 필요하다면 뉴 그랄렌이나 팔로너 매장에서 직접 받아갈 수 있다(I can still pick it up at either the New Gralen or the Paloner store if I have to, as I need it for a job tomorrow afternoon)고 한 것을 통해, JJ 홈 앤 가든 서플라이어즈는 적어도 두 곳 이상의 위치에 매장이 있음을 짐작할 수 있다. 따라서 (D)가 정답이다.

어휘 specialize in ~을 전문으로 하다

Paraphrasing
지문의 either the New Gralen or the Paloner store → 정답의 stores in more than one location

180 연계

번역 얼라이언스 하드웨어 스토어에서 시멘트 믹서기 CVY-XU 모델의 가격은 얼마인가?
(A) 189달러
(B) 359달러
(C) 499달러
(D) 629달러

해설 웹페이지의 표 상단에 CVY-XU 모델 미스터 버디(Mr. Buddy)는 359달러($359)이고, 이메일의 첫 단락 마지막 문장에서 작은 지역 매장인 얼라이언스 하드웨어 스토어에서 미스터 버디를 구입할 예정이며 이 곳은 현재 귀사와 동일한 가격에 이 제품을 보유하고 있다(I will instead buy a Mr. Buddy from Alliance Hardware Store, a small, local store where it is currently in stock (and at your same price))고 했다. 따라서 얼라이언스 하드웨어 스토어에서 미스터 버디, 즉 CVY-XU 모델 제품은 JJ 홈 앤 가든 서플라이어즈와 같은 가격인 359달러이므로 (B)가 정답이다.

181-185 웹페이지 + 이메일

---

https://www.collingswoodglobal.com/about

| 홈 | 소개 | 서비스 | 연락처 |

181 국제 무역 사업은 복잡할 수 있으며, 특히 관련 절차와 서류에 익숙하지 않을 경우 더 그렇습니다. **181** 지침은 나라마다 다르고 특별한 면허와 허가증이 필요할 수 있습니다.

콜링스우드 글로벌의 경혐 많은 컨설턴트들이 도와드리겠습니다! 먼저, 귀하의 사업에 대해 짧은 설문지를 작성하시면 됩니다. 일단 귀하의 요구 사항들을 점검하고 나면, 아래에 나열된 저희 팀원 중 한 명과 연결해 드립니다.

- 마가렛 조르다노: 농산물
- **184** 조나 우드로: 가전제품
- 펠리시티 웡: 보석용 원석
- 말리크 파델: 자동차 부품

저희는 시간당 329달러에 1회의 소개 세션을 제공합니다. 귀하의 컨설턴트가 귀하의 요구 사항을 토대로 이후 세션에 대한 요금을 책정할 것입니다. **182** 정기적으로 안내를 받고 싶으시다면 소개 세션 중 협의되는 가격으로 월간 자문료를 지불하시면 됩니다.

어휘 complicated 복잡한 unfamiliar 익숙하지 않은 step 절차 involved 관련된 guideline 지침 vary 다르다 license 면허 permit 허가증 complete 작성하다 questionnaire 설문지 assess 평가하다 match 연결하다 agricultural 농업의 household appliances 가전제품 precious 값싼 automotive 자동차의 introductory 소개의, 도입부의 determine 결정하다 subsequent 그 다음의 guidance 안내 regularly 정기적으로 retainer 자문료 negotiate 협상하다

수신: contact@collingswoodglobal.com
발신: 산지브 야다브 〈sanjeev.yadav@isvaraniltd.com〉
날짜: 12월 12일
제목: 사전 상담 설문지 후속 문의

관계자분께:

183 귀하의 웹페이지에서 설문지를 작성했는데 제 양식이 제대로 보내졌는지 잘 모르겠습니다. 확인 이메일을 받지 못했습니다. 양식에서 언급했다시피 **184** 저희는 고급 세탁기와 건조기를 전문으로 하는 5년 된 회사입니다. 저희는 미국 동부 해안 전역의 상점에 기계를 판매하고 있고, 국내 화물 처리 절차에 대해 잘 알고 있습니다. 하지만 **185** 특히 유럽 전역을 대상으로 국제 무역에 과감히 도전해 보고자 하며 이러한 시도에 지속적인 지원을 받기를 원합니다. 이스바라니 사의 요구 사항에 대해 좀 더 상세히 논의할 수 있도록 저에게 연락해 주십시오.

185 산지브 야다브, 대표, 이스바라니 사

어휘 preconsultation 사전 상담 follow-up 후속 조치 fill out ~을 작성하다 form 양식 high-end 고급의 washer 세탁기 well-informed 잘 아는 domestic 국내의 cargo 화물 procedure 절차 venture 과감히 나아가다 particularly 특히 ongoing 지속적인 support 지원 endeavor 시도

181 Not / True

번역 웹페이지에서 국제 무역을 위한 지침에 대해 명시하는 것은?
(A) 각 나라마다 상이하다.
(B) 종종 여러 목적을 위한 서비스를 제공한다.
(C) 정기적으로 업데이트된다.
(D) 전보다 더 엄격해졌다.

해설 웹페이지의 첫 단락 첫 문장에서 국제 무역 사업은 복잡할 수 있다(The international trade business can be complicated)고 했고, 같은 단락의 두 번째 문장에서 지침은 나라마다 다르다(Guidelines vary from country to country)고 언급했으므로 (A)가 정답이다.

어휘 purpose 목적 regular 정기적인 basis 기준 strict 엄격한

Paraphrasing
지문의 vary from country to country
→ 정답의 different for each country

182 Not / True

번역 웹페이지에서 월간 자문료에 대해 언급하는 것은?
(A) 협의될 수 없다.
(B) 한 달에 329달러이다.
(C) 초기 미팅 중에 정해진다.
(D) 고객의 요구에 따라 면제될 수 있다.

해설 웹페이지의 마지막 단락 마지막 문장에서 정기적으로 안내를 받고 싶다면 소개 세션 중 협의되는 가격으로 월간 자문료를 지불하면 된다(If you would like to receive guidance regularly, you would pay a monthly retainer at a cost to be negotiated during the introductory session)고 했다. 따라서 월간 자문료는 첫 세션 중에 결정된다는 것을 알 수 있으므로 (C)가 정답이다.

어휘 initial 초기의 waive 면제하다

Paraphrasing
지문의 to be negotiated during the introductory session
→ 정답의 set during an initial meeting

183 세부 사항

번역 야다브 씨가 이메일에서 자신의 회사에 대한 정보를 제공하는 이유는?
(A) 예비 동료의 요청에 답변하고 있다.
(B) 양식에 정보를 포함시키는 것을 깜박했다.
(C) 확립된 절차를 따르고 있다.
(D) 자신이 작성한 설문지가 수신되었는지 확신하지 못한다.

해설 이메일의 첫 문장에서 야다브 씨는 웹페이지에서 설문지를 작성했는데 자신의 양식이 제대로 보내졌는지 잘 모르겠다(I filled out the questionnaire on your Web page, but I am not sure that my form went through)면서 확인 이메일을 받지 못했다(I never got a confirmation e-mail)고 언급한 뒤 회사 관련 정보를 나열하고 있다. 따라서 야다브 씨는 설문지가 제대로 접수되었는지를 확인할 수 없어 설문지에 기입한 내용을 이메일로 작성했다는 것을 알 수 있으므로 (D)가 정답이다.

어휘 **prospective** 장래의 **colleague** 동료 **established** 확립된 **process** 절차

> **Paraphrasing**
> 지문의 filled out → 정답의 completed

184 연계

번역 야다브 씨는 누구와 함께 일하게 될 것 같은가?
(A) 조르다노 씨
(B) 우드로 씨
(C) 웡 씨
(D) 파델 씨

해설 이메일의 세 번째 문장에서 야다브 씨의 회사는 고급 세탁기와 건조기를 전문으로 하는 5년 된 회사(we are a five-year-old company specializing in high-end washers and dryers)라고 했고, 웹페이지의 중반부에 조나 우드로가 가전제품 담당자(Jonah Woodrow: household appliances)라고 나와 있다. 따라서 야다브 씨는 우드로 씨를 배정받게 될 것이므로 (B)가 정답이다.

> **Paraphrasing**
> 지문의 washers and dryers → 지문의 household appliances

185 Not / True

번역 이메일에서 이스바라니 사에 대해 언급된 것은?
(A) 공급업체들이 기밀로 남기를 원한다.
(B) 국제 정책을 실수로 위반했다.
(C) 사업을 확장할 계획을 갖고 있다.
(D) 국내 화물 요건에 대한 추가 정보가 필요하다.

해설 이메일의 다섯 번째 문장에서 특히 유럽 전역을 대상으로 국제 무역에 도전해 보고자 한다(we want to venture into international trade, particularly throughout Europe)고 했고, 이메일의 작성자가 이스바라니 사의 대표인 산지브 야다브(Sanjeev Yadav, Owner, Isvarani Ltd.)이므로 이스바라니 사가 해외로 사업을 확장할 계획이 있다는 것을 알 수 있다. 따라서 (C)가 정답이다.

어휘 **confidential** 기밀의 **violate** 위반하다 **by accident** 실수로 **expand** 확장하다 **operation** 사업 **requirement** 요건

> **Paraphrasing**
> 지문의 venture into international trade
> → 정답의 expand its operations

186-190 기사 + 이메일 + 편지

고객 코너

고객 코너는 아프리카 은행 업계에서 고객 중심의 동향을 다루는 〈아틀라스 파이낸셜 리뷰〉(AFR)의 정기 연재 기사이다. 이 연재 기사의 이번 편에서는 손파야 뮤추얼의 사업 이득 예금 계좌(BASA)에 대해 논한다.

손파야 뮤추얼의 BASA는 연 이율이 2.2퍼센트이며, 이는 가장 근접한 경쟁사에서 제공하는 사업 예금 계좌의 이율보다 1.6퍼센트 높은 수치이다. 게다가 **186** 이 상품은 다양한 고객 특전을 제공하는데, 공인 세무사의 연간 세금 정산, 전담 계좌 관리자와의 1대1 상담, 온라인 및 대면 모두 가능한 금융 교육 프로그램이 포함된다. 세금 서류 작업 지원을 제외한 이러한 특전들이 BASA 보유자에게 무료로 제공된다.

BASA를 개설하기 위해서는 최소 10만 르완다 프랑의 예치금이 필요하며, 1,500 르완다 프랑의 월 관리 수수료가 부과된다. **189** BASA의 신규 가입자에게는 첫 6개월간 월간 비용이 면제된다. 자세한 사항은 www.sonfayamutual.com/basa에서 확인할 수 있다.

187 손파야 뮤추얼은 르완다의 키갈리에 본사가 있으며, 탄자니아, 우간다, 잠비아에 지사를 두고 있다. **188** 손파야 뮤추얼의 시초, 성장, 주요 성과에 관한 심도 있는 기사는 〈AFR〉의 1월호에 게재되었다. 이전 호는 www.atlasfinancialreview.com/archives에서 확인할 수 있다. 기록 보관된 내용에 대한 질문은 archivist@atlasfinancialreview.com으로 보내면 된다.

어휘 **recurring** 되풀이하여 발생하는 **feature** 특집 (기사) **installment** (연재물 등의) 1회분 **savings account** 예금 계좌 **yield** 이율 **privilege** 특전 **certified** 인증된 **tax accountant** 세무사 **dedicated** 전담의 **in-person** 대면의 **at no expense** 무료로 **deposit** 예치금 **administration** 관리 **charge** 부과하다 **headquarter** 본사를 두다 **in-depth** 심도 있는 **origin** 기원 **milestone** 이정표 **issue** (간행물의) 호 **previous** 이전의 **archive** 기록 보관소에 보관하다

수신: archivist@atlasfinancialreview.com
발신: ochabinga@mesuradobankofliberia.com.lr
날짜: 11월 1일
제목: 누락된 AFR 호

관계자분께:

188 저는 〈AFR〉 최신 호에서 손파야 뮤추얼의 BASA에 관한 기사를 흥미롭게 읽었습니다. 그 후로, 저는 귀사의 웹사이트를 방문하여 기사에서 언급된 이전 〈AFR〉 호를 찾아보았습니다. 유감스럽게도 저는 아카이브 페이지에서 그것을 찾을 수 없었습니다. 그 지난 호를 구할 수 있는 방법을 알려주십시오.

오데트 차빙가
라이베리아 메수라도 은행, 부행장

어휘 **missing** 빠진 **subsequently** 그 뒤에 **reference** 언급하다, 참조 표시를 하다 **locate** ~의 위치를 찾다 **archival** 기록 보관소의 **obtain** 구하다, 얻다 **vice president** 부사장

11월 23일

줄리엔느 니레레 씨
B.P. 2581
키갈리

니레레 씨께,

손파야 뮤추얼에서 15년 동안 소중한 당좌 예금 계좌 보유자가 되어 주셔서 감사합니다. 게다가 **189 사업 이득 예금 계좌(BASA)를 개설하셔서** 저희와의 관계를 더욱 굳건히 해 주셔서 기쁩니다.

귀하의 당좌 예금 계좌와 예금 계좌는 이제 연결되어, 온라인으로 한 계좌에서 다른 계좌로 이체가 가능합니다. 또한 귀하의 BASA로부터 자금을 인출하시고자 할 경우, 당사의 모든 ATM에서 귀하의 직불카드를 사용하실 수 있습니다.

마지막으로, **190 최근 출시된 저희 온라인 주식 거래 플랫폼이 무료로 제공되며, 투자자가 자신만의 속도로 자산을 관리할 수 있도록 하는데 뛰어납니다.** 자세한 내용은 저희 자산관리 부서로 연락 주십시오.

필버트 아카만지, 수석 계좌 관리자

어휘 furthermore 게다가 strengthen 강화하다 enable 가능하게 하다 transfer 옮기다 withdraw 인출하다 launch 출시하다 at no charge 무료로 investor 투자자 pace 속도

186 Not / True

번역 손파야 뮤추얼의 금융 교육 프로그램에 대해 언급된 것은?
(A) 무료로 제공된다.
(B) 매달 한 번 열린다.
(C) 계좌 관리자들이 진행한다.
(D) 〈AFR〉과 제휴하여 개최된다.

해설 기사의 두 번째 단락 두 번째 문장에서 이 상품은 다양한 고객 특전을 제공하는데 공인 세무사의 연간 세금 정산, 전담 계좌 관리자와의 1대1 상담, 온라인 및 대면 모두 가능한 금융 교육 프로그램이 포함된다(it comes with a range of customer privileges, including yearly tax preparation with a certified tax accountant, one-on-one consultations with a dedicated account manager, and financial education programmes, both in-person and online)고 했고 그 다음 문장에서 세금 서류 작업 지원을 제외한 이러한 특혜들이 BASA 보유자에게 무료로 제공된다(Except for the assistance with tax paperwork, these offerings are provided at no expense to BASA holders)고 했다. 따라서 금융 교육 프로그램이 BASA 보유자에게 무료로 제공된다는 것을 알 수 있으므로 (A)가 정답이다.

어휘 in partnership with ~와 제휴하여

Paraphrasing
지문의 provided at no expense → 정답의 offered for free

187 Not / True

번역 기사에서 손파야 뮤추얼에 대해 명시된 것은?
(A) BASA 개설을 위한 금액을 인상했다.
(B) 고객 특전을 계속해서 추가할 것이다.
(C) 최근에 웹사이트를 업데이트했다.
(D) 국제 기업이다.

해설 기사의 네 번째 단락 첫 문장에서 손파야 뮤추얼은 르완다의 키갈리에 본사가 있으며, 탄자니아, 우간다, 잠비아에 지사를 두고 있다(Sonfaya Mutual is headquartered in Kigali, Rwanda, with offices in the countries of Tanzania, Uganda, and Zambia)고 나와 있으므로 손파야 뮤추얼은 국제 기업임을 알 수 있다. 따라서 (D)가 정답이다.

어휘 raise 올리다

Paraphrasing
지문의 with offices in the countries of Tanzania, Uganda, and Zambia → 정답의 international company

188 연계

번역 차빙가 씨가 〈AFR〉의 지난 호를 찾고 있는 이유는?
(A) 손파야 뮤추얼의 경쟁사의 제공 상품에 대해 알아보기 위해
(B) 현재의 고객 중심 동향에 대해 더 알기 위해
(C) 손파야 뮤추얼의 역사에 대해 알아보기 위해
(D) 손파야 뮤추얼의 BASA에 대해 더 알기 위해

해설 이메일의 첫 문장에서 차빙가 씨는 〈AFR〉 최신 호에서 손파야 뮤추얼의 BASA에 관한 기사를 흥미롭게 읽었고(I read the article on Sonfaya Mutual's BASA in the most recent issue of AFR with interest) 그 후로 웹사이트를 방문하여 기사에 언급된 이전 〈AFR〉 호를 찾아보았다(Subsequently, I visited your Web site, looking for the previous AFR issue referenced in the article)고 했다. 그리고 기사의 네 번째 단락 두 번째 문장에서 손파야 뮤추얼의 시초, 성장, 주요 성과에 관한 심도 있는 기사는 〈AFR〉의 1월호에 게재되었다(An in-depth article about Sonfaya Mutual's origins, growth, and milestones was published in AFR's January issue)면서 이전 호는 www.atlasfinancialreview.com/archives에서 확인할 수 있다(Previous issues are at www.atlasfinancialreview.com/archives)고 했다. 따라서 차빙가 씨는 손파야 뮤추얼의 역사를 다룬 심층 기사를 읽기 위해 〈AFR〉의 1월호를 찾았음을 알 수 있으므로 (C)가 정답이다.

Paraphrasing
지문의 origins, growth, and milestones → 정답의 history

189 연계

번역 니레레 씨에 대해 암시된 것은?
(A) 6개월 동안 BASA의 월간 수수료를 지불할 필요가 없다.
(B) 직불카드를 제때 받지 못했다.
(C) 손파야 뮤추얼의 신규 고객이다.
(D) 최근에 아카만지 씨와 만났다.

해설 편지의 첫 단락 두 번째 문장에서 니레레 씨가 사업 이득 예금 계좌(BASA)를 개설했다(opening a business advantage savings account (BASA))고 했고, 기사의 세 번째 단락 두 번째 문장에서 BASA의 신규 가입자에게는 첫 6개월간 월간 비용이 면제된다(For new BASA holders, the monthly cost is waived for the first six months)고 했다. 따라서 니레레 씨가 BASA를 개설하여 6개월간 월 수수료를 면제받았다는 것을 알 수 있으므로 (A)가 정답이다.

어휘 debit card 직불카드 in a timely fashion 제때, 적시에

> **Paraphrasing**
> 지문의 the monthly cost is waived
> → 정답의 will not have to pay the BASA monthly fee

190 주제 / 목적

번역 편지의 한 가지 목적은?
(A) 투자의 혜택을 설명하려고
(B) 자금 관리를 위한 선택지를 설명하려고
(C) 온라인 주식 거래가 이루어지는 방식을 설명하려고
(D) 부서의 연락처를 제공하려고

해설 편지의 마지막 단락 첫 문장에서 최근 출시된 저희 온라인 주식 거래 플랫폼이 무료로 제공되며 투자자가 자신만의 속도로 자산을 관리할 수 있도록 하는데 뛰어나다(our recently launched online stock-trading platform, available to you at no charge, is excellent for allowing investors to manage their finances at their own pace)고 안내하고 있다. 따라서 고객을 대상으로 새로 출시한 자산 관리 서비스에 대해 알리고자 한다는 것을 알 수 있으므로 (B)가 정답이다.

어휘 benefit 혜택 investing 투자 describe 설명하다 fund 자금 stock 주식 trading 거래

191-195 이메일 + 양식 + 영수증

수신: 밸리 로드 베드 앤 브렉퍼스트 〈info@valleyroadbandb.com〉
발신: 마야 로드리게스 〈m.rodriguez@intermountaingraphics.com〉
날짜: 3월 30일
제목: 조식 일정

안녕하세요,

저는 다음 주에 귀하의 베드 앤 브렉퍼스트에 숙박을 예약했습니다. 조식 시간에 관해 문의드리고 싶습니다. **191 저는 4월 11일 토요일 아침 7시 전에 아이버 호텔 앤 컨퍼런스 센터에서 열리는 컨퍼런스를 위해 출발해야 합니다. 그 전에 조식이 제공되나요?** 그렇지 않다면 컨퍼런스장 근처에 그 시간에 문을 여는 식당을 추천해 주실 수 있을까요?

마야 로드리게스

어휘 reservation 예약 inquire 문의하다

인터마운틴 그래픽스 출장 경비 환급 양식

192 공식적인 회사 업무로 출장을 가는 인터마운틴 그래픽스의 모든 직원들은 당사의 전자 출장비 환급 시스템인 트래블나우에서 출장일로부터 30일 이내에 출장 경비 환급 양식을 작성하고 영수증을 업로드해야 합니다. **194** 모든 양식은 직원의 부서 관리자에 의해 승인 및 서명되어야 합니다.

직원: 마야 로드리게스   날짜: 4월 28일
193 출장 목적: 디지털 그래픽 디자이너 컨퍼런스 참석

날짜	구분	설명	총액
4월 10일	교통	산호세 국제공항 왕복 항공편	230달러
4월 10일	교통	밸리 로드 베드 앤 브렉퍼스트행 택시	31달러
4월 11일	교통	아이버 호텔 앤 컨퍼런스 센터행 택시	22.50달러
4월 11일	식사	**193** 아일린스 다이너에서 아침 식사	23.85달러
4월 11일	기타	컨퍼런스 등록	175달러
4월 11일	식사	안토니오스에서 저녁 식사	48.67달러
4월 12일	숙소	밸리 로드 베드 앤 브렉퍼스트, 2박	299달러
4월 12일	교통	산호세 국제공항행 택시	31달러
		환급될 총 금액	861.02달러

194 승인 *박은*   **194** 서명 *박은*

어휘 expense 경비 reimbursement 환급 form 양식 official 공식적인 fill out ~을 작성하다 electronic 전자의 approve 승인하다 description 설명 transportation 교통 registration 등록 lodging 숙소

---

191 아일린스 다이너
아이버 호텔 앤 컨퍼런스 센터 내 위치

-----

195 20년 넘게 가족이 소유하며 운영 중!
미션 리코 대로 1000번지
193 산타클라라, 캘리포니아 95054
(408) 555-0126

-----

191 4월 11일 토요일 오전 6시 46분

아침 샌드위치	14.99달러
커피	3.50달러
소계	18.49달러
세금	1.11달러
총 결제액:	19.60달러
팁	4.25달러
총 지불액:	**23.85달러**

신용카드: XXXXXXXXXXXX5348
고객명: 마야 로드리게스

고객용 사본

106

어휘 family-owned 가족 소유의   decade 10년
Blvd. 대로(Boulevard의 약자)   subtotal 소계
owed 지불할 의무가 있는

191 연계

번역 밸리 로드 베드 앤 브렉퍼스트에 대해 결론지을 수 있는 것은?
(A) 오전 7시 이전에 조식을 제공하지 않는다.
(B) 공항으로 가는 셔틀 서비스를 제공한다.
(C) 아이버 호텔 앤 컨퍼런스 센터 옆에 위치해 있다.
(D) 4월에는 더 이상 예약을 받지 않고 있다.

해설 이메일의 세 번째 문장에서 로드리게스 씨가 밸리 로드 베드 앤 브렉퍼스트에 4월 11일 토요일 아침 7시 전에 아이버 호텔 앤 컨퍼런스 센터에서 열리는 컨퍼런스를 위해 출발해야 한다(I need to leave before 7 A.M. on Saturday morning, April 11, for my conference at the Ivor Hotel and Conference Center)면서 그 전에 조식이 제공되는지(Will breakfast be available before then?)를 물었고 그렇지 않다면 컨퍼런스장 근처에 그 시간에 문을 여는 식당을 추천해 달라(If not, what restaurants near the conference would you recommend that would be open at that time?)고 요청했다. 영수증 상단에 가게명과 위치(Eileen's Diner, Located in the Ivor Hotel and Conference Center)가 나와 있고, 영수증이 찍힌 날짜와 시간이 4월 11일 토요일 오전 6시 46분(Saturday, April 11, 6:46 A.M.)이라고 표기되어 있다. 따라서 로드리게스 씨가 컨퍼런스 센터에 있는 식당에서 아침 식사를 한 것으로 보아 밸리 로드 베드 앤 브렉퍼스트에서는 오전 7시 이전에 조식을 제공하지 않는다는 것을 유추할 수 있으므로 (A)가 정답이다.

192 세부 사항

번역 양식에 따르면, 직원들은 무엇을 해야 하는가?
(A) 재무 부서로부터 출장 허가를 구하기
(B) 컨퍼런스에서 업무 발표하기
(C) 관리자에게 경비 보고서를 이메일로 보내기
(D) 출장 후 30일 이내에 영수증 제출하기

해설 양식의 첫 문장에서 공식적인 회사 업무로 출장을 가는 인터마운틴 그래픽스의 모든 직원들은 당사의 전자 출장비 환급 시스템인 트래블나우에서 출장일로부터 30일 이내에 출장 경비 환급 양식을 작성하고 영수증을 업로드해야 한다(All Intermountain Graphics employees who travel on official company business must fill out a Travel Expense Reimbursement Form and upload their receipts within 30 days of travel in TravelNow, our electronic travel reimbursement system)고 했으므로 (D)가 정답이다.

어휘 seek (필요한 것을) 구하다   permission 허가
present 발표하다

Paraphrasing
지문의 upload → 정답의 Submit

193 연계

번역 디지털 그래픽 디자이너 컨퍼런스에 대해 사실인 것 같은 것은?
(A) 3일간 계속되었다.
(B) 4월 28일에 시작했다.
(C) 산타클라라에서 열렸다.
(D) 참가자들에게 식사를 제공했다.

해설 양식의 중반부에서 로드리게스 씨의 출장 목적이 디지털 그래픽 디자이너 컨퍼런스 참석(Purpose of Trip: To attend the Digital Graphic Designers Conference)이며 출장 중에 아일린스 다이너에서 아침 식사(Breakfast at Eileen's Diner)를 했다고 나와 있고, 영수증의 중반부에서 아일린스 다이너는 산타클라라(Santa Clara)에 위치해 있음을 확인할 수 있다. 따라서 로드리게스 씨가 참석한 디지털 그래픽 디자이너 컨퍼런스는 산타클라라에서 열렸다는 것을 알 수 있으므로 (C)가 정답이다.

어휘 participant 참가자

194 Not / True

번역 양식에 따르면, 박 씨에 대해 사실인 것은?
(A) 재무 분석가이다.
(B) 컨퍼런스를 조직한다.
(C) 부서 관리자이다.
(D) 베드 앤 브렉퍼스트를 소유하고 있다.

해설 양식의 첫 단락 마지막 문장에서 모든 양식은 직원의 부서 관리자에 의해 승인 및 서명되어야 한다(All forms must be approved and signed by the employee's department manager)고 했고, 하단의 승인(Approved by)과 서명(Signature)란에 박은(Eun Park) 씨의 이름이 기재되어 있으므로 박 씨는 부서 관리자임을 알 수 있다. 따라서 (C)가 정답이다.

어휘 organize 조직하다

195 Not / True

번역 영수증에서 아일린스 다이너에 대해 명시된 것은?
(A) 하루 24시간 운영된다.
(B) 매일 조식 특별 메뉴를 제공한다.
(C) 전국 곳곳에 지점이 있다.
(D) 20년 이상 영업해 왔다.

해설 영수증의 상단에 아일린스 다이너는 20년 넘게 가족이 소유하며 운영 중(Family-owned and operated for over two decades!)이라고 나와 있으므로 (D)가 정답이다.

Paraphrasing
지문의 operated for over two decades
→ 정답의 in business for more than twenty years

196-200 이메일 + 이메일 + 보고서

수신: 남재준
발신: 스테이시 랜던
날짜: 5월 4일
제목: 퀴나 5000

재준,

196, 199 F동에 있는 퀴나 5000이 제대로 작동되지 않고 있어요. 일정한 속도로 작동하지 않아서 라인 작업자들이 지속적으로 주의를 기울여야 해요. 월간 점검 때 검사도 받았고 양호한 평가도 받았어요. 하지만 지금 이것 때문에 F동 전체의 생산이 느려지고 있어요. 곧바로 살펴보지 않으면 완전히 고장 날 수도 있을 것 같아요.

서비스 방문 동안 작동을 중단하는 시간 때문에 생산 일정이 조정되어야 할 테니 **196 가능한 한 빨리 점검할 수 있도록 기술자를 보내주세요.**

스테이시 랜던
생산 관리자

어휘 properly 제대로 steady 변함없는 constant 지속적인 inspection 점검 acceptable 그런대로 괜찮은 rating 평가 adapt 조정하다 downtime (기계가) 작동하지 않는 시간

수신: 스테이시 랜던
참조: 알렉스 나디너
발신: 남재준
날짜: 5월 4일
제목: 회신: 퀴나 5000

스테이시 씨,

안타깝게도 우리 내부 장비 수리 일정이 꽉 차서 다음 주에 새로운 기술자 몇 명을 투입시키려고 해요. 그동안 **197 코너 서비스에서 기술자 한 명을 보내 기계를 점검하고 필요한 수리를 하도록 승인했어요.** 전에도 이 회사를 이용해 본 적이 있는데, 훌륭해요. 그쪽에서 내일 오후 1시에서 2시 사이에 사람을 보낼 거예요. 테스트 때문에 최대 2시간가량 장비가 중단될 수 있다고 하네요. 다음 주에 알트란 모터스로 보내야 하는 대규모 제품 출하가 있다고 알고 있어서 **198 실례를 무릅쓰고 알렉스 나디너를 참조에 포함시켰는데, 그가 지연을 만회하기 위해 일부 라인 작업자들이 초과 근무를 하도록 배정해야 할 수도 있거든요.**

남재준
유지관리 책임

어휘 Cc 참조 수신자(Carbon copy의 약자) internal 내부의 capacity 수용력 authorize 승인하다 inspect 점검하다 due ~하기로 예정된 take the liberty of 실례를 무릅쓰고 ~하다 assign 배정하다 make up for ~을 만회하다 maintenance 유지관리

코너 서비스 점검 및 수리 보고서

----

199 기계: 퀴나 5000
199 장소: 헤이버포드 인더스트리즈, 웨스트 로리 가 837번지, F동
점검일: 5월 5일
인건비 청구: 2.5시간

결과:
테스트 102: 양호
테스트 393: 청소 필요
200 테스트 477: 바움 X33 주요 스위치 결함
테스트 488: 벨트 및 호스 마모
유체 수위: 양호
계기: 양호

의견: 기술자가 기계를 청소했으며 **200 고장 난 스위치를 교체했습니다.** 하지만 벨트와 호스는 곧 교체되어야 하며, 이로 인해 약 4시간 동안 라인 가동을 중단해야 할 것입니다. **198 라인 관리자는 이 수리 기간 동안 직원을 적절히 재배치할 수 있도록 이 상황에 대해 보고를 받았습니다.**

어휘 labor charge 인건비 청구 faulty 결함이 있는 worn 닳은 fluid 유체 gauge 계기 shut down ~을 정지하다 situation 상황 personnel 직원들 accordingly 적절히

196 주제 / 목적

번역 첫 번째 이메일의 목적은?
(A) 장비 주문을 확인하려고
(B) 기계 수리를 요청하려고
(C) 월간 점검에 대해 보고하려고
(D) 생산 증가를 장려하려고

해설 첫 번째 이메일의 첫 단락 첫 문장에서 F동에 있는 퀴나 5000이 제대로 작동되지 않고 있다(The Quinar 5000 in Building F is not working properly)고 기기 고장을 알리며, 두 번째 단락에서 가능한 한 빨리 점검할 수 있도록 기술자를 보내 달라(Please send a technician to check it as soon as possible)고 요청하고 있다. 따라서 고장난 기계에 대한 점검을 요청하기 위해 이 메일을 쓴 것을 알 수 있으므로 (B)가 정답이다.

어휘 verify 확인하다

197 세부 사항

번역 남 씨는 F동의 문제를 해결하기 위해 무엇을 하기로 결정했는가?
(A) 추가 직원 고용
(B) 외부 회사 고용
(C) 새로운 건물 임대
(D) 새로운 기계 구입

해설 두 번째 이메일의 두 번째 문장에서 남 씨는 코너 서비스에서 기술자 한 명을 보내 기계를 점검하고 필요한 수리를 하도록 승인했다(I have authorized Konner Services to send one of their technicians to inspect the machine and make any necessary repairs)고 했으므로, 기기 수리를 위해 외부 업체를 고용하기로 했음을 알 수 있다. 따라서 (B)가 정답이다.

어휘 lease 임대하다

198 연계

번역 나디너 씨는 누구인 것 같은가?
(A) 유지관리 책임자
(B) 수석 기술자
(C) 라인 작업자
(D) 라인 관리자

해설 두 번째 이메일의 마지막 문장에서 실례를 무릅쓰고 알렉스 나디너를 참조에 포함시켰는데 그가 지연을 만회하기 위해 일부 라인 작업자들이 초과 근무를 하도록 배정해야 할 수도 있다(I took the liberty of copying Alex Nadiner, who may need to assign some line workers to put in overtime to make up for the delay)고 했고, 보고서의 마지막 문장에서 라인 관리자는 이 수리 기간 동안 직원을 적절히 재배치할 수 있도록 이 상황에 대해 보고를 받았다(The line manager has been advised of this situation so that personnel can be reassigned accordingly during this repair)고 했다. 따라서 나디너 씨는 라인 작업자들의 근무 배치를 책임지는 라인 관리자임을 알 수 있으므로 (D)가 정답이다.

199 연계

번역 랜던 씨는 어느 회사에서 근무하는 것 같은가?
(A) 퀴나 머신
(B) 알트란 모터스
(C) 코너 서비스
(D) 헤이버포드 인더스트리즈

해설 첫 번째 이메일의 첫 단락 첫 문장에서 랜던 씨가 F동에 있는 퀴나 5000이 제대로 작동되지 않고 있다(The Quinar 5000 in Building F is not working properly)고 했고, 보고서의 상단에 기계명은 퀴나 5000(Machine: Quinar 5000), 서비스 장소는 헤이버포드 인더스트리즈, 웨스트 로리 가 837번지, F동(Location: Haverford Industries, 837 West Lorrie Street, Building F)이라고 나와 있다. 따라서 랜던 씨가 오작동을 보고한 F동의 퀴나 5000은 헤이버포드 인더스트리즈의 기계이며 랜던 씨는 이 회사에서 근무하고 있음을 짐작할 수 있으므로 (D)가 정답이다.

200 세부 사항

번역 보고서에 따르면, 어느 테스트 결과로 기계 부품이 교체되었는가?
(A) 102
(B) 393
(C) 477
(D) 488

해설 보고서의 중반부에 테스트 477를 통해 바움 X33 주요 스위치의 결함(Test 477: Faulty Baum X33 main switch)을 확인했다고 나와 있고, 하단의 의견란 첫 문장에서 고장 난 스위치를 교체했다(replaced the malfunctioning switch)고 언급했다. 따라서 477번 테스트의 결과에 따라 스위치를 교체했다는 것을 알 수 있으므로 (C)가 정답이다.

기출 TEST 6

101 (C)	102 (A)	103 (B)	104 (B)	105 (D)
106 (A)	107 (D)	108 (A)	109 (B)	110 (D)
111 (C)	112 (A)	113 (C)	114 (D)	115 (A)
116 (D)	117 (B)	118 (C)	119 (B)	120 (D)
121 (B)	122 (B)	123 (A)	124 (A)	125 (D)
126 (D)	127 (B)	128 (C)	129 (C)	130 (D)
131 (C)	132 (A)	133 (D)	134 (B)	135 (D)
136 (A)	137 (C)	138 (A)	139 (A)	140 (C)
141 (B)	142 (A)	143 (A)	144 (C)	145 (B)
146 (A)	147 (B)	148 (D)	149 (B)	150 (D)
151 (A)	152 (B)	153 (D)	154 (B)	155 (A)
156 (A)	157 (C)	158 (D)	159 (D)	160 (D)
161 (C)	162 (D)	163 (D)	164 (C)	165 (B)
166 (D)	167 (A)	168 (D)	169 (C)	170 (C)
171 (B)	172 (B)	173 (C)	174 (B)	175 (D)
176 (B)	177 (A)	178 (C)	179 (D)	180 (A)
181 (B)	182 (D)	183 (C)	184 (B)	185 (C)
186 (B)	187 (C)	188 (A)	189 (C)	190 (B)
191 (B)	192 (D)	193 (A)	194 (C)	195 (B)
196 (B)	197 (D)	198 (C)	199 (A)	200 (C)

PART 5

101 동사 어휘

해설 주어 the Edbridge Orchestra의 동사 자리로, '오케스트라는 새로운 작품을 연주할 예정이다'라는 의미가 되어야 적절하므로 '연주하다, 공연하다'를 뜻하는 (C) perform이 정답이다. (A) make는 '만들다', (B) operate는 '운영하다', (D) fulfill은 '(약속 등을) 이행하다'라는 의미이다.

번역 토요일에 에드브릿지 오케스트라는 현지 작곡가 니나 보르스타인의 새로운 작품을 연주할 예정이다.

어휘 composer 작곡가

102 형용사 자리 _ 주격 보어

해설 빈칸에는 가주어 It의 진주어 역할을 하는 to부정사구 to be 뒤에 오기에 적절한 품사를 골라야 한다. to부정사의 동사가 be동사이고 앞에 부사 especially가 있으므로, 빈칸은 be동사의 보어 역할을 하면서 부사의 수식을 받을 수 있는 형용사가 와야 한다. 따라서 '예의 있는'이라는 의미의 형용사 (A) polite가 정답이다. (B) politely는 부사이므로 품사상 빈칸에 들어갈 수 없고, 최상급 형용사 (C) politest는 비교 대상이 없으므로 부적합하며, 명사 (D) politeness는 보어 역할은 할 수 있으나 의미상 어울리지 않고, 부사의 수식도 받지 않는다.

번역 새로운 고객들과 함께 있을 때, 특히 예의를 갖추는 것이 중요하다.

어휘 in the company of ~와 함께   politeness 공손

103 인칭대명사의 격 _ 소유격

해설 빈칸에는 뒤에 온 명사 achievements를 수식하는 인칭대명사가 들어가야 한다. 따라서 명사 앞에 쓰여 한정사 역할을 할 수 있는 소유격 인칭대명사 (B) her가 정답이다.

번역 엔도우 씨는 비록 상을 받지 못했지만, 그녀의 업적은 찬사를 받았다.

어휘 achievement 업적   praise 칭찬하다

104 명사 어휘

해설 to부정사 to achieve의 목적어 역할을 하며 their financial의 수식을 받아 '재정 목표를 달성한다'는 의미가 되어야 자연스러우므로 '목표'를 뜻하는 (B) goals가 정답이다. (A)의 procedure는 '절차', (C)의 season은 '계절', (D)의 bill은 '고지서'라는 의미이다.

번역 연말에는, 기관들이 재정 목표를 달성해야 한다는 압박에 직면한다.

어휘 organization 기관   face 직면하다   pressure 압박   achieve 달성하다

105 형용사 어휘

해설 문맥상 '온라인 주문은 웹사이트에서 이용할 수 있다'는 내용이 되어야 자연스러우므로 '이용할 수 있는'을 뜻하는 (D) available이 정답이다. (A) called는 '~이라고 불리는', (B) printed는 '인쇄된, 출판된', (C) capable은 '(능력상) ~할 수 있는'이라는 의미이다. 참고로, 온라인 주문이 무언가를 '할 수 있는' 능력을 가진 주체가 아니므로 (C)는 답이 될 수 없다.

번역 온라인 주문은 나이토 카페의 웹사이트에서 이용할 수 있습니다.

106 전치사 어휘

해설 빈칸 뒤의 명사구 the televised debate를 목적어로 취해 'TV 토론 이후 만날 계획이다'라는 의미가 되어야 자연스러우므로 '~ 이후에'를 뜻하는 전치사 (A) following이 정답이다. (B) beside는 '~ 옆에', (C) from은 '~으로부터', (D) under는 '~ 아래에'라는 의미이다.

번역 박 시장은 TV 토론 이후 선거운동 단원들과 만날 계획이다.

어휘 campaign (정치적 목적을 위한) 운동   debate 토론

107 형용사 자리 _ 명사 수식

해설 빈칸 앞에 부정관사 a와 비교급을 만들어 주는 부사 more가 있고, 뒤에 명사 copy machine이 있으므로 빈칸은 명사를 수식하는 형용사 자리이다. '더 믿을 만한 복사기'라는 의미가 되어야 자연스러우므로 '믿을 만한, 신뢰할 수 있는'을 뜻하는 형용사 (D) reliable이 정답이다. (A) reliably는 부사로 품사상 답이 될 수 없고, 현재분사 (B) relying은 '의존하고 있는'이라는 능동의 의미이므로 문맥상 어

울리지 않으며, (C) relied는 단독으로 '의지되는'이라는 뜻의 과거분사로 쓰이지 않는다.
- 번역 서 씨는 재무 부서를 위해 더 믿을 만한 복사기를 구매해야 한다고 요청했다.

108 명사 자리 / 어휘

- 해설 빈칸은 전치사 on의 목적어 역할을 하는 명사 자리로, 앞에 있는 the front와 두의 전치사구 of Outward Expansion Magazine과 함께 '잡지의 앞표지'라는 의미가 되어야 적절하므로, '표지'를 뜻하는 명사 (A) cover가 정답이다. (B) coverage도 명사이지만 '보도, 범위'를 뜻하므로 문맥상 어울리지 않고, (C) covered는 동사/과거분사, (D) coverable은 형용사이므로 품사상 답이 될 수 없다.
- 번역 아폰테 씨의 가을 단풍 사진이 <아웃워드 익스팬션 매거진>의 앞표지에 실릴 예정이다.
- 어휘 autumn foliage 가을 단풍   feature 특별히 포함하다

109 전치사 어휘

- 해설 뒤의 명사구 practical and stylish additions를 목적어로 취해 '실용적이고 세련된 추가 정리 공간으로서 역할을 한다'는 의미가 되어야 자연스러우므로, '~으로서'를 뜻하는 전치사 (B) as가 정답이다.
- 번역 핸디 오피스 서플라이즈의 새로운 책상 정리함은 어떤 사무실 작업 공간에도 실용적이고 세련된 추가 정리 공간으로서 역할을 한다.
- 어휘 organizer 정리함, 정리 도구   serve as ~으로서 역할을 하다   practical 실용적인   stylish 세련된   addition 추가물   workstation 작업 공간

110 형용사 어휘

- 해설 빈칸은 전치사 to의 목적어 역할을 하는 명사구 flight delays를 수식하는 형용사 자리고, 문맥상 '더 적은 항공편 지연'이라는 의미가 되어야 자연스러우므로, '더 적은'을 뜻하는 비교급 형용사 (D) fewer가 정답이다. (A) friendlier는 '더 친절한', (B) accurate은 '정확한', (C) previous는 '이전의'라는 의미이다.
- 번역 공항 터미널의 효율적인 재설계는 더 적은 항공편 지연으로 이어졌다.
- 어휘 efficient 효율적인   delay 지연

111 부사 자리 _ 준동사 수식

- 해설 빈칸은 to부정사 to approach를 수식하여 '주제에 객관적으로 접근하는'이라는 의미를 나타내는 부사 자리이므로, '객관적으로'를 뜻하는 부사 (C) objectively가 정답이다. (D) objected는 동사/과거분사이므로 품사상 부적합하고, 명사인 (A) objects와 (B) objectivity는 subject matter와 복합명사를 이루기에 적절하지 않다.
- 번역 오그부 씨의 편집자는 주제에 객관적으로 접근하는 그의 능력을 높이 평가했다.
- 어휘 appreciate 높이 평가하다   approach 접근하다   subject matter 주제

112 전치사 자리 / 어휘

- 해설 빈칸 앞에 완전한 절이 있고 뒤에 동명사구 being new가 있으므로 빈칸은 동명사를 절에 연결해 주는 전치사 자리이다. '회사에 들어온 지 얼마 안 되었음에도 불구하고'라는 의미가 되어야 자연스러우므로 '~에도 불구하고'를 뜻하는 전치사 (A) despite가 정답이다. (B) unless(~하지 않는 한)와 (D) whether(~인지 아닌지)는 접속사이므로 빈칸에 들어갈 수 없고, (C) prior to(~ 전에)는 전치사이지만 의미상 답이 될 수 없다.
- 번역 나카야마 씨는 회사에 들어온 지 얼마 안 되었음에도 불구하고 올해의 직원으로 임명되었다.
- 어휘 name 임명하다

113 형용사 자리 _ 명사 수식

- 해설 빈칸은 전치사 For의 목적어 역할을 하는 명사 selection을 수식하는 형용사 자리이며, 앞에 정관사 the가 있고 '가장 다양한 엄선된 것'이라는 의미가 되어야 적절하므로 wide의 최상급 형용사 (C) widest가 정답이다. (A) widen은 동사, (D) widely는 부사이므로 품사상 빈칸에 들어갈 수 없고, 현재분사 (B) widening(넓어지고 있는)은 형용사 역할을 할 수는 있으나 의미상 어울리지 않는다.
- 번역 어디서든 가장 다양한 엄선된 고급 물감과 미술용품을 찾으신다면, 가장 가까운 페인터스 베스트 매장을 방문하세요.
- 어휘 paint 그림 물감   supplies 용품

114 동사 어휘

- 해설 '~하도록 의도되다'라는 의미의 「be+intended+to부정사」에서 to부정사에 들어갈 적절한 동사 어휘를 고르는 문제이다. employee satisfaction을 목적어로 취해 '직원 만족도를 파악하도록 의도되었다'는 내용이 되어야 자연스러우므로 '파악하다, 알아내다'를 뜻하는 (D) determine이 정답이다. (A) overcome은 '극복하다', (B) prolong은 '연장하다', (C) deserve는 '~할 가치가 있다'라는 의미이다.
- 번역 스톨메인 사의 최신 설문조사는 여러 주요 항목에서 직원 만족도를 파악하도록 의도되었다.
- 어휘 latest 최신의   intend 의도하다   satisfaction 만족   category 항목

115 부사 자리 _ 동사 수식

- 해설 빈칸은 be동사 is와 과거분사 decorated 사이에서 수동태 동사를 수식하는 부사 자리이다. 따라서 '공들여, 정교하게'를 뜻하는 부사 (A) elaborately가 정답이다. (B) elaborating은 동명사/현재분사, (C) elaborates는 동사, (D) elaboration은 명사이므로 품사상 답이 될 수 없다.

번역 가르자스 레스토랑은 남부 멕시코의 그림과 사진들로 공들여 꾸며져 있다.

어휘 decorate 꾸미다, 장식하다

116 명사 자리 _ 동사의 주어

해설 빈칸은 소유격 Mr. Brighton's, 한정사 first의 수식을 받고 있고 동사 was의 주어 자리이므로 명사가 들어가야 한다. 따라서 '배정, 임무'를 뜻하는 명사 (D) assignment가 정답이다. (A) assign은 동사, (B) assigned는 동사/과거분사, (C) assigning은 동명사/현재분사이므로 품사상 답이 될 수 없다.

번역 글린 엔지니어링에서 브라이턴 씨의 첫 업무 배정은 자재 검사 부서에서였다.

어휘 material 자재

117 부사 어휘

해설 빈칸 뒤의 €5,000를 수식하여 '대략 5,000유로'라는 의미가 되어야 자연스러우므로 '대략, 거의'를 뜻하는 부사 (B) roughly가 정답이다. (A) briefly는 '잠시, 간단히', (C) correctly는 '올바르게, 정확히', (D) generously는 '관대하게'라는 의미이다.

번역 헤이버포드 공원 곳곳에 새로운 벤치를 설치하는 작업은 대략 5,000 유로가 들 예정이다.

어휘 installation 설치 cost (비용이) 들다; 비용

118 부정대명사

해설 빈칸은 관계사절(who is ~ stakeholder meeting)의 수식을 받는 선행사이자 단수 동사 is의 주어 자리이다. 따라서 특정하지 않은 사람을 가리키는 단수 대명사인 (C) Anyone이 정답이다. (A) Such는 대명사로 쓰일 경우 '그러한 것, 그러한 상황'을 뜻하며 사람을 나타내지 않으므로 빈칸에 부적합하고, 복합관계대명사 (B) Whichever는 선행사 자리에 올 수 없으며, (D) Those는 뒤에 복수 동사가 와야 한다.

번역 분기별 주주 회의에 참석할 수 없는 사람은 대리인을 지명해도 좋다.

어휘 quarterly 분기별 stakeholder 주주 appoint 지명하다 representative 대리인

119 동사 자리 _ 수 일치

해설 빈칸은 3인칭 단수 주어 Singer Maria Stanley의 동사 자리로, 빈칸 뒤 that절을 목적어로 취해 '월드 투어를 계획하고 있다고 오늘 밝혔다'는 내용이 되어야 하므로 동사 reveal의 과거형 (B) revealed가 정답이다. 단수 동사가 필요하므로 동사원형 (A) reveal은 답이 될 수 없고, (C) to reveal은 to부정사, (D) revealing은 동명사/현재분사이므로 동사 자리에 들어갈 수 없다.

번역 가수 마리아 스탠리는 오늘 월드 투어를 계획하고 있다고 밝혔다.

120 명사 자리 _ 복합명사

해설 빈칸은 전치사 for의 목적어 자리로 앞에 있는 명사 writing과 함께 복합명사를 이루어 '글쓰기 방식'이라는 의미가 되어야 적절하므로 '방식, 스타일'을 뜻하는 명사 (D) style이 정답이다. (A) styleless는 형용사, (B) styled는 동사/과거분사, (C) stylish는 형용사로 품사상 답이 될 수 없다.

번역 전기 작가 앰버 보웬은 독특한 글쓰기 방식으로 인정받아 왔다.

어휘 biographer 전기 작가 recognize 인정하다 distinctive 독특한

121 형용사 어휘   ▶동영상 강의

해설 '~한 특성이 있다, ~한 성질을 가지다'라는 의미를 나타내는 「be of + (형용사) + 명사」 구문에서 명사 quality를 수식해 적절한 문맥을 완성하는 형용사를 고르는 문제이다. '우수한 품질을 지녔다'라는 의미가 되어야 자연스러우므로 '우수한, 뛰어난'을 뜻하는 (B) exceptional이 정답이다. (A) comfortable은 '편안한', (C) hospitable은 '환대하는', (D) ambitious는 '야심 있는'이라는 의미이다.

번역 페이퍼리 디자인즈의 예술가들이 제작한, 상을 받은 문구류는 우수한 품질을 지녔다.

어휘 award-winning 상을 받은 stationery 문구류

122 부사 자리 _ 대명사 수식

해설 빈칸 뒤에 완전한 절이 있고, 주어 역할을 하는 대명사 all을 수식하여 '회사 매출의 거의 전부'라는 내용이 되어야 자연스러우므로 '거의'를 뜻하는 부사 (B) nearly가 정답이다. (C) somewhat은 '다소, 약간'이라는 의미로 all을 수식하기에 적절하지 않고, (A) between과 (D) next to는 전치사이므로 빈칸에 들어갈 수 없다. 참고로, 정도를 나타내는 nearly, only, almost와 같은 부사는 all, every, none 등의 대명사를 수식할 수 있다.

번역 지난 분기 동안, 레나피 테크놀로지 매출의 거의 전부가 한 지역에서 나왔다.

어휘 quarter 분기 region 지역

123 명사 어휘

해설 동사 covers의 목적어 역할을 하며 빈칸 뒤의 과거분사구 (associated with ~ business property)의 수식을 받기에 어울리는 명사를 고르면 된다. '사업체 건물 보수 또는 재건 관련 비용을 보장한다'는 내용이 되어야 자연스러우므로 '비용, 경비'를 뜻하는 (A) expenses가 정답이다. (B)의 symptom은 '증상', (C)의 challenge는 '도전', (D)의 opportunity는 '기회'라는 의미이다.

번역 상업용 부동산 보험은 특정 사건 후 사업체 건물을 보수하거나 재건하는 데 관련된 비용을 보장합니다.

어휘 commercial 상업의 property 부동산 insurance 보험 cover 보장하다 associated 관련된

124 명사 어휘

해설 빈칸은 동사 is recommended의 주어 자리로, 앞에서 수업이 빨리 마감된다고 했으므로 '신속한 등록이 권장된다'는 내용이 되어야 연결이 자연스럽다. 따라서 '등록'을 뜻하는 (A) registration이 정답이다. (B) detection은 '감지', (C) information은 '정보', (D) certification은 '증명서'라는 의미이다.

번역 응급 처치 수업은 보통 빠르게 마감되므로, 신속한 등록이 권장됩니다.

어휘 first-aid 응급 처치 fill up 가득 차다 prompt 신속한

125 동사 어휘 ▶동영상 강의

해설 동사 allows의 목적격 보어 역할을 하는 to부정사 자리에 들어갈 동사 어휘를 고르는 문제이다. every aspect of the production process를 목적어로 취해 '사내 제조가 생산 공정의 모든 측면을 통제할 수 있게 해 준다'는 의미가 되어야 자연스러우므로 '통제하다'를 뜻하는 (D) control이 정답이다. (A) expect는 '기대하다', (B) impress는 '인상을 주다', (C) remain은 '남다'라는 의미이다.

번역 모든 제품을 사내에서 제조함으로써 롱 브리지 스틸 사는 생산 공정의 모든 측면을 통제할 수 있다.

어휘 in-house 사내의 aspect 측면 process 과정

126 전치사 자리 ▶동영상 강의

해설 빈칸은 뒤의 명사구 its use on home-cooking shows를 콤마 뒤의 완전한 절에 연결해야 하므로 전치사가 들어가야 한다. 따라서 '~ 때문에'를 뜻하는 전치사 (D) Because of가 정답이다. (A) Moreover와 (3) For example은 접속부사, (C) Even though는 부사절 접속사이므로 품사상 답이 될 수 없다.

번역 집밥 요리 프로그램에 제품이 사용되면서, 실버샤인 쿡웨어의 소비자 수요가 두 배로 늘었다.

어휘 consumer 소비자 demand 수요

127 부사 자리 _ 동사 수식

해설 빈칸은 동사 work를 수식하는 부사 자리로, with clients와 함께 '고객들과 협력하여 작업한다'는 의미가 되어야 자연스러우므로 '협력하여, 합작으로'라는 의미의 부사 (B) collaboratively가 정답이다. (A) collaborative는 형용사, (C) collaborates는 동사, (D) collaborators는 명사이므로 품사상 답이 될 수 없다.

번역 캐빈 그래픽스의 예술가들은 만족을 보장하기 위하여 디자인의 모든 단계에서 고객들과 협력하며 작업한다.

어휘 ensure 보장하다 satisfaction 만족

128 동사 어형 _ 태

해설 주어 Brile Construction's contract의 동사 자리로, 현재 완료 시제를 나타내는 has been과 결합하여 동사구를 완성해야 한다. 뒤에 목적어가 아닌 전치사 by가 이끄는 전치사구가 왔고, '계약이 검증되었다'라는 수동의 의미가 되어야 하므로 과거분사 (C) verified가 정답이다. (A) verifying은 현재분사/동명사, (B) verifiably는 부사로 빈칸에 들어갈 수 없고, 명사 (D) verification은 be동사의 보어로 쓸 수는 있으나 문맥상 적합하지 않다.

번역 브릴 건설의 쇼핑몰 개발 프로젝트 계약이 마침내 시 감독관에 의해 검증되었다.

어휘 contract 계약 supervisor 감독관

129 부사 어휘

해설 빈칸 뒤의 숫자 4,000을 수식하여 '약 4,000개의 쓰레기 제거 시스템'이라는 의미가 되어야 자연스러우므로 '약, 거의'라는 의미의 (C) Almost가 정답이다. (A) Always는 '항상', (B) Quite은 '꽤', (D) Closely는 '면밀히, 주의하여'라는 의미이다.

번역 약 4,000개의 얼백 쓰레기 제거 시스템이 동부 지역에서 사용되고 있다.

어휘 region 지역

130 접속사 자리 ▶동영상 강의

해설 빈칸 앞의 posted online과 뒤의 mailed to attendees가 병렬 구조를 이루고 있고, '참석자에게 우편 발송되는 대신 온라인에 게시될 것'이라는 두 가지 대안을 비교하는 내용이 되어야 자연스럽다. 따라서 '~ 대신에, ~보다는'을 뜻하며 등위접속사처럼 동등한 요소를 연결하는 접속사 (D) rather than이 정답이다. (A) in order that(~하기 위해), (B) as soon as(~하자마자), (C) in case(~할 경우에 대비해서)는 모두 부사절 접속사로 뒤에 완전한 절이 와야 한다.

번역 회의 일정은 참석자들에게 우편 발송되는 대신 온라인에 게시될 예정이다.

어휘 post 게시하다 attendee 참석자

PART 6

131-134 공지

버스 내 자전거 반입 프로그램

모든 트래블비 버스에는 현재 외부 자전거 거치대가 갖춰져 있습니다. 이 **131 장비**는 우리 승객들이 교통, 운동, 즐거움을 위해 자전거 타기를 생활의 일부로 포함할 수 있도록 장려하기 위해 설치되었습니다. **132 자전거를 반입하는 데에 추가 요금은 부과되지 않습니다.** 하지만 전기 자전거는 **133 허용되지** 않는다는 점을 유의해 주십시오. 당사의 무료 버스 내 자전거 반입 프로그램에 대한 추가 정보는 www.travelbee.com/bicyclesonbuses를 방문해 주십시오. 여기서 당사의 버스 노선에서 이용할 수 있는 훌륭한 자전거 도로에 대해서도 확인하실 **134 수 있습니다.**

어휘 outfit (장비를) 갖추어 주다 exterior 외부의 rack 거치대
install 설치하다 passenger 승객 incorporate 포함하다
transportation 교통 pleasure 즐거움 electric 전기의
complimentary 무료의 access 이용하다

131 명사 어휘

해설 빈칸 앞 문장에서 버스에 외부 자전거 거치대가 갖춰져 있다고 했으므로, 빈칸이 있는 문장에서는 이 자전거 거치대를 가리켜 '이 장비가 설치되었다'는 내용이 되어야 적절하므로 '장비'를 뜻하는 (C) equipment가 정답이다. (A) furniture는 '가구', (B) exhibition은 '전시', (D) application은 '신청, 응용 프로그램'이라는 의미이다.

132 문맥에 맞는 문장 고르기

번역 (A) 자전거를 반입하는 데에 추가 요금은 부과되지 않습니다.
(B) 올바른 버스 정류장에서 내릴 수 있도록 항상 확인하십시오.
(C) 이제 대부분의 고속도로에서 자전거 전용 차선이 보입니다.
(D) 일부 승객은 버스 요금 할인을 받을 수 있습니다.

해설 빈칸 앞 문장에서 자전거 거치대는 버스 승객들이 자전거 타기를 생활의 일부로 포함할 수 있도록 장려하기 위해 설치되었다고 했고, 뒤 문장에서 하지만(however) 전기 자전거는 허용되지 않는다고 했으므로, 빈칸에는 주의 사항을 전달하기에 앞서 자전거 거치대 이용과 관련된 긍정적인 정보를 제시하는 내용이 들어가야 자연스럽다. 따라서 자전거 반입에 추가 요금은 부과되지 않는다고 언급하는 (A)가 정답이다.

어휘 charge 부과하다 lane 차선 highway 고속도로 qualify 자격이 있다 reduced 할인된 fare 요금

133 형용사 어휘

해설 앞에서 모든 버스에 자전거 거치대가 설치되어 있고(All Travelbee buses are now outfitted with exterior bicycle racks) 자전거 반입은 무료(No additional fee)라고 했으나, 빈칸이 있는 문장이 however로 시작하고 있으므로 주의 사항이나 예외 사항이 뒤따라야 적절하다. 따라서 '전기 자전거는 허용되지 않는다'는 내용이 되어야 자연스러우므로 '허용하다'라는 의미의 동사 permit의 과거분사 (D) permitted가 정답이다. (A) efficient는 '효율적인', (B) common은 '흔한', (C) flexible은 '유연한'이라는 의미의 형용사이다.

134 동사 어형 _ 시제

해설 문장의 동사가 현재형이고, 문맥상 '당사의 버스 노선에서 이용할 수 있는 자전거 도로'라는 의미로 현재의 가능성을 나타내는 의미가 되어야 자연스럽다. 따라서 (B) can be가 정답이다. 미래완료 시제는 미래의 특정 시점에 어떤 일이 완료될 것임을 나타내므로 (D) will have been은 답이 될 수 없다.

135-138 기사

기업 교육 소식

다국적 가전제품 제조업체 크리스털 테크놀로지스는 최근 직원들을 위한 혁신적인 교육 프로그램을 135 **시행했다**. 이 프로그램은 '이스케이프 룸즈'라 불리는 것을 사용하여 팀워크와 창의적인 문제 해결 기술을 육성한다. 이러한 목적으로 스코틀랜드 인버네스의 기업 본사 건물에 특별한 시설이 지어졌다. 이 시설은 네 개의 방으로 구성되며, 136 **각각**의 방은 크리스털의 글로벌 사업부에 속한 각기 다른 지리적 지역을 나타내도록 설계되었다. 직원들은 5명으로 이루어진 팀으로 작업하면서, 그 지역에 특정한 사업적 문제를 해결해야 문을 열고 다음 방으로 들어갈 수 있다. 137 **코스는 30분 이내에 완료되어야 한다.** 크리스털은 유럽 외부에 있는 주요 생산 시설에 138 **도** 이스케이프 룸즈를 설치할 계획이다.

어휘 corporate 기업의 multinational 다국적의 appliance 가전제품 innovative 혁신적인 facility 시설 purpose 목적 headquarters 본사 consist of ~으로 구성되다 represent 나타내다 geographic 지리적인 operation 사업(체) particular 특정한 unlock 열다 install 설치하다

135 동사 어휘

해설 뒤 문장에서 이 프로그램은 팀워크와 문제 해결 기술 육성을 위해 특정 방법(escape rooms)을 활용하고 있으며 이를 위해 본사에 특별한 시설까지 지어졌다고 했으므로, 빈칸이 있는 문장은 '이 프로그램을 시행했다'는 내용이 되어야 문맥상 자연스럽게 연결된다. 따라서 '시행하다, 실행하다'를 뜻하는 동사 implement의 과거형 (D) implemented가 정답이다. (A)의 export는 '수출하다', (B)의 change는 '바꾸다', (C)의 consider는 '고려하다'라는 의미이다.

136 대명사 어휘

해설 빈칸 이하의 절은 선행사 four rooms를 「수량표현+of+관계대명사」로 받아 부연 설명하는 문장이다. '이 방들 중 각각은 각기 다른 지리적 지역을 나타내도록 설계되었다'는 내용이 되어야 자연스러우므로 '각각, 각기'를 뜻하는 (A) each가 정답이다. (B) either는 '둘 중 하나', (D) another는 '또 다른 하나'를 뜻하므로 의미상 부적합하며, 소유대명사 (C) theirs는 'of+관계대명사'와 결합하여 쓰지 않는다.

137 문맥에 맞는 문장 고르기

번역 (A) 이스케이프 룸을 짓는 데는 놀라울 정도로 많은 비용이 든다.
(B) 질 낮은 교육은 제조 운영에 있어 문제가 될 수 있다.
(C) 코스는 30분 이내에 완료되어야 한다.
(D) 회사는 전자제품과 주요 가전제품을 생산한다.

해설 앞에서 이스케이프 룸이라는 프로그램이 각 사업부에 속한 지역을 나타내는 네 개의 방으로 구성되어 있고, 직원 5명이 팀이 되어 문제를 해결해야 다음 방으로 갈 수 있다며 직원 훈련 프로그램의 규칙 및 원리를 설명하고 있으므로, 빈칸에도 해당 프로그램의 규칙이나 제한 사항이 추가적으로 이어져야 연결이 자연스럽다. 따라서 30분 이내에 완료되어야 한다며 제한 시간을 언급하는 (C)가 정답이다.

114

어휘 electronics 전자제품 major 주요한

138 부사 어휘

해설 앞에서 스코틀랜드의 기업 본사 건물에 이스케이프 룸이 이미 설치되었다(A special facility has been built ~ within the company's headquarters in Inverness, Scotland)고 했으므로, 빈칸이 있는 문장은 '유럽 외부의 주요 생산 시설에도 또한 이스케이프 룸을 설치할 계획'이라는 내용이 되어야 적절하다. 따라서 문장 끝에 위치하여 '~도 또한'이라는 추가의 의미를 나타내는 (A) as well이 정답이다. (B) again은 '다시', (C) after all은 '결국', (D) at that time은 '그 당시'라는 의미이다.

139-142 이메일

수신: allclients@yardleyriverdentalgroup.com
발신: tliu@yardleyriverdentalgroup.com
날짜: 1월 7일
제목: 주차 구역

고객님께,

야들리 리버 덴탈 그룹은 다음 주에 몇 가지 필요한 보수를 139 **수행하기** 위해 고객 주차 구역을 폐쇄할 예정입니다. 140 **화요일 아침부터 금요일까지 폐쇄됩니다.** 이 기간 동안 고객께서는 평소 주차하시던 구역의 왼쪽에 위치한 직원 주차 구역에 차량을 주차하실 것을 요청드립니다. (직원들은 보수 작업이 이루어지는 동안 특별히 마련된 외부 장소에 주차할 예정입니다.) 직원 주차 구역에서, 건물 측면을 돌아 정문 출입구로 141 **이어지는** 통로를 발견하실 겁니다. 142 **불편**을 드린 점 사과드리며 양해해 주셔서 감사합니다.

티나 리우, 사무실 관리자

어휘 usual 평소의 arrange 마련하다 off-site 외부의 conduct (특정 활동을) 하다 lead 이어지다 entrance 출입구 apologize 사과하다 patience 인내

139 동사 어휘

해설 앞에서 다음 주에 고객 주차 구역을 폐쇄한다(Yardley River Dental Group will be closing our client parking area next week)고 한 것으로 보아 '필요한 보수를 수행하기 위해'라는 내용이 되어야 문맥상 자연스럽다. 따라서 '수행하다'를 뜻하는 (A) carry out이 정답이다. (B) communicate는 '소통하다', (C) bring up은 '(화제 등을) 꺼내다', (D) label은 '라벨을 붙이다'라는 의미이다.

140 문맥에 맞는 문장 고르기

번역 (A) 고객들은 주차 구역의 고르지 못한 포장 상태에 대해 언급할 것입니다.
(B) 저희는 11번과 27번 버스 노선을 따라 위치해 있습니다.
(C) 화요일 아침부터 금요일까지 폐쇄됩니다.
(D) 그룹에서는 최근 새로운 치과 의사들과 위생사들을 맞이했습니다.

해설 빈칸 앞 문장에서 보수 작업을 위해 고객 주차 구역을 폐쇄할 예정(Yardley River Dental Group will be closing our client parking area)이라고 했고, 뒤 문장에서 이 기간 동안(During this time) 직원 주차 구역에 대신 주차하라고 요청하고 있으므로, 빈칸에는 이 기간(this time)에 대해 구체적으로 명시하는 내용이 들어가야 자연스럽다. 따라서 화요일 아침부터 금요일까지라고 폐쇄되는 기간을 구체적으로 제시하는 (C)가 정답이다.

어휘 comment 언급하다 uneven 고르지 않은 pavement 포장 hygienist 위생사

141 동사 자리 _ 시제

해설 빈칸은 선행사 a walkway를 수식하는 관계사절(that ~ to our front entrance)의 동사 자리이다. 또한, 주차장에 있는 통로가 어디로 연결되는지를 설명하는 내용은 현재 시제를 써야 하므로 (B) leads가 정답이다. (A) to lead는 to부정사, (C) leader는 명사이므로 품사상 답이 될 수 없고, 과거 진행형 (D) was leading은 시제가 적합하지 않다.

142 명사 어휘

해설 앞에서 고객들에게 보수를 위해 주차 구역을 폐쇄(closing our client parking area next week)할 것임을 알리며 대신 직원 주차 구역에 주차할 것을 요청(we request that you park your vehicles in the staff parking area)하고 있으므로, 빈칸이 있는 문장은 '불편을 드려 사과한다'며 고객들의 양해를 구하는 내용이 되어야 자연스럽다. 따라서 '불편'을 뜻하는 (A) inconvenience가 정답이다. (B) addition은 '추가', (C) error는 '오류', (D) damage는 '손상'이라는 의미이다.

143-146 공지

랜달-험볼트 전 직원 여러분께 알립니다.

랜달-험볼트는 최근 우편실에 배치된 직원 수가 감소했습니다. 143 **그 결과**, 10월 7일부터 우편물은 더 이상 직원들의 책상으로 배달되지 않습니다. 부서들은 각자의 우편물을 수령하고 배포하는 일을 책임지게 됩니다. 각 부서에서는 우편 업무를 처리할 직원 한 명을 144 **지정해야 합니다.** 이 책임을 어떻게 가장 적절히 배정할지 결정하는 것은 부서장에게 달려 있습니다. 우편물은 매일 오전 10시에 수령할 수 있습니다.

직원들은 원하지 않는 우편물 또는 광고성 우편물의 발송자에게 연락하여 수신 목록에서 삭제해 달라고 요청할 145 **것**이 강력히 권고됩니다. 146 **그렇게 하면 우편물 배포를 간소화하는 데 도움이 될 것입니다.** 이는 또한 쓰레기를 줄임으로써 환경에도 유익할 것입니다.

어휘 reduction 감소 mail-room 우편실 staffing 직원 배치 no longer 더 이상 ~않다 distribute 배포하다 handle 처리하다 determine 결정하다 assign 배정하다 junk mail 광고성 우편 benefit 유익하다

143 접속부사

해설 앞 문장에서 우편실 직원 수가 감소했다(a reduction in mail-room staffing)고 했고, 뒤 문장에는 우편물이 더 이상 직원들의 책상으로 배달되지 않는다(mail will no longer be delivered to employees' desks)고 했다. 두 문장은 직원 감축으로 인해 우편 배달이 중단된다는 인과 관계를 나타내고 있으므로 '그 결과'라는 의미의 (A) As a result가 정답이다. (B) Instead는 '대신에', (C) Nevertheless는 '그럼에도 불구하고', (D) If so는 '만약 그렇다면'이라는 의미이다.

144 동사 어형 _ 조동사 + 동사원형

해설 앞에서 10월 7일부터 우편물이 직원 책상까지 배달되지 않을 것이며, 부서에서 우편물 수령 및 배포를 책임지게 될 것이라며 앞으로 있을 우편물 취급 변동 사항에 대해 안내하고 있다. 빈칸이 있는 문장도 '각 부서에서 우편 담당 직원을 지정해야 한다'며 지침을 전달하는 내용이 되어야 자연스러우므로 '~해야 한다'라는 의미의 「조동사 should + 동사원형」 (C) should designate가 정답이다.

145 명사절 접속사

해설 빈칸에는 가주어 It의 진주어 역할을 하는 명사절을 이끌 수 있는 접속사가 들어가야 한다. 빈칸 뒤에 완전한 절이 있고 '직원들이 ~할 것이 강력히 권고된다'는 내용이 되어야 적절하므로 '~하는 것'을 뜻하는 명사절 접속사 (B) that이 정답이다. 부사절 접속사 (A) since는 It이 대명사로 쓰일 경우 문장 구조상 빈칸에 들어갈 수는 있으나 의미상 부적합하고, (C) such as는 전치사이므로 품사상 답이 될 수 없으며, (D) whoever는 복합관계대명사로 뒤에 불완전한 절이 온다.

146 문맥에 맞는 문장 고르기

번역 (A) 그렇게 하면 우편물 배포를 간소화하는 데 도움이 될 것입니다.
(B) 우편물은 때때로 운송 중에 손상됩니다.
(C) 우편실은 한 번에 네 명 이상의 직원을 수용할 수 없습니다.
(D) 직송 광고 마케팅은 제품을 판매하는 효과적인 방법이 될 수 있습니다.

해설 빈칸 앞에서 필요 없는 우편물을 줄이기 위한 방안을 권고하고 있고, 빈칸 뒤에서는 환경에도 유익하다며 우편물 감소 효과를 추가로 언급하고 있다. 따라서 빈칸에는 우편물 줄이기에 따른 첫 번째 효과가 들어가야 일관성 있는 문맥이 완성되므로, 우편물 배포 업무를 간소화할 수 있다고 언급하고 있는 (A)가 정답이다.

어휘 streamline 간소화하다 distribution 배포 damage 손상시키다 transit 운송 direct mail 직송 광고 effective 효과적인

PART 7

147-148 광고

범블베리 농장
71번가 북서쪽 8715번지, 스탠퍼트, 오리건 주 97074
(971) 555-0144

직접 블루베리를 따세요!

범블베리 농장은 달콤하고 과즙이 풍부한 블루베리로 유명합니다. 저희 블루베리 밭에 오셔서 블루베리를 따며 오후를 즐겨보세요. **147** 저희는 가족단위 손님에 맞춰져 있지만 누구나 환영합니다!

148(A), 148(B) 신선한 블루베리를 건강한 간식으로 즐기시거나 집에서 만든 잼과 구운 음식에 활용해 보세요. **148(C)** 아침에 좋아하시는 시리얼에 넣어 드셔도 훌륭합니다.

올해 수확철은 7월 1일에서 9월 15일까지입니다. 저희 밭은 화요일부터 일요일까지 오전 10시부터 오후 3시까지 운영합니다.

밭 입장료는 1인당 2달러이며, 수확하신 블루베리는 1/2리터당 2.50달러입니다. 단체는 최대 8인까지 환영합니다. 1인당 1리터로 제한됩니다.

자세한 정보는 저희 웹사이트 www.bumbleberryfarm.com으로 방문해 주세요.

어휘 juicy 즙이 풍부한 field 밭 cater to ~에 맞추다, 영합하다 admission 입장료 limit 제한하다

147 Not / True

번역 범블베리 농장에 대해 명시된 것은?
(A) 일주일에 7일 문을 연다.
(B) 가족 친화적이다.
(C) 제과점을 운영한다.
(D) 단체 할인을 제공한다.

해설 첫 단락의 마지막 문장에서 가족단위 손님에 맞춰져 있지만 누구나 환영한다(We cater to families, but everyone is welcome!)고 했으므로 가족 손님을 우대한다는 것을 알 수 있다. 따라서 (B)가 정답이다.

어휘 family-friendly 가족 친화적인

> **Paraphrasing**
> 지문의 cater to families → 정답의 family-friendly

148 Not / True

번역 블루베리를 즐기는 방법으로 언급된 것이 아닌 것은?
(A) 잼
(B) 구운 음식
(C) 아침식사용 시리얼
(D) 아이스크림

해설 두 번째 단락 첫 문장에서 신선한 블루베리를 건강한 간식으로 즐기거나 집에서 만든 잼과 구운 음식에 활용해 보라(Enjoy fresh blueberries as a healthy snack, or use them in homemade jams and baked goods)고 했으므로 (A)와 (B), 아침에 좋아하는 시리얼에 넣어 먹어도 훌륭하다(They are also great for adding to your favorite cereal in the morning)고 했으므로 (C)는 블루베리를 즐기는 방법으로 언급되었지만, 아이스크림에 대한 내용은 없으므로 (D)가 정답이다.

149-151 기사

주석 가격 개선 가능성

런던 (9월 12일) — 8월에 주석 가격이 사상 최고치로 올랐다. 현재 국제 재고는 이례적으로 낮으며, 공급 가능성 문제가 지속되고 있다. **149 가격 상승은 이 금속을 생산하는 국가들의 공급 감소에 150 기인하며**, 부품이 주석 화합물과 결합되는 전자제품에 대한 세계적인 수요 및 제조 증가와도 관련이 있다.
151 주요 생산업체인 칠리언 스멜팅 사는 개선된 장비에 투자하였으며 생산을 늘리는 것을 목표로 하고 있다. 그 결과, 주석 거래업체들은 공급 증가에 따른 약간의 가격 완화를 예측하고 있다.

어휘 tin 주석 record high 사상 최고치 inventory 재고 unusually 이례적으로 persist 지속되다 supply 공급 demand 수요 electronics 전자제품 component 부품 compound 화합물 invest 투자하다 aim 목표하다 trader 거래자 predict 예측하다 moderation 완화, 조정

149 세부 사항

번역 기사에 따르면, 무엇이 주석 수요에 기여하고 있는가?
(A) 주석 생산에 대한 정부 규제
(B) 전자제품의 생산 증가
(C) 채굴 기술의 향상
(D) 통조림 식품 판매의 세계적 증가

해설 첫 단락 세 번째 문장에서 가격 상승은 주석을 생산하는 국가들의 공급 감소에 기인하며, 부품이 주석 화합물과 결합되는 전자제품에 대한 세계적인 수요 및 제조 증가와도 관련이 있다(The price increases are driven by reduced supply in countries that produce the metal, coupled with increasing worldwide demand for and manufacturing of electronics, whose components are joined together with tin compounds)고 했으므로, 전자제품의 수요 및 생산 증가가 주석 수요의 한 요인임을 알 수 있다. 따라서 (B)가 정답이다.

어휘 contribute 기여하다 government 정부 regulation 규제 mining 채굴 canned 통조림으로 된

Paraphrasing
지문의 manufacturing of electronics
→ 정답의 production of electronic goods

150 동의어 찾기

번역 첫 번째 단락 5행의 "driven"과 의미가 가장 가까운 단어는?
(A) 촉구된
(B) 추격된
(C) 운송된
(D) 야기된

해설 의미상 가격 상승은 공급 감소에 '기인한다'는 뜻으로 쓰였으므로 '야기된, 유발된'을 뜻하는 (D) caused가 정답이다.

151 Not / True

번역 칠리언 스멜팅 사에 대해 명시된 것은?
(A) 주석의 선두 공급업체이다.
(B) 최근에 더 많은 직원을 채용했다.
(C) 새로운 투자자를 찾고 있다.
(D) 정기적으로 할인된 가격을 제공한다.

해설 두 번째 단락의 첫 문장에서 주요 생산업체인 칠리언 스멜팅 사(Chilean Smelting, Inc., a major producer)라고 언급하고 있으므로 (A)가 정답이다.

어휘 leading 선두의 supplier 공급업체 investor 투자자 regularly 정기적으로

Paraphrasing
지문의 a major producer → 정답의 a leading supplier

152-153 편지

랑데일 익스테리어 솔루션즈 • 앨더슨 로 39번지 •
하이필드, 셰필드 S2 4UA

9월 17일

아타르브 차터지 씨
크로프트 로 7번지
브리스워스, 로더럼 S60 5AP

안녕하세요, 차터지 씨.

새 집을 구입하신 것을 축하드립니다! **152 저는 랑데일 익스테리어 솔루션즈를 소개해 드리고자 합니다.** 저희는 30년 넘게 셰필드 지역의 고객들과 작업해 왔습니다. **152 노련한 전문가들로 구성된 저희 팀은 저희를 이 지역에서 가장 신뢰받는 조경 회사로 만듭니다.**

저희는 귀하의 야외 공간에 맞는 최적의 솔루션을 합리적인 가격에 찾을 수 있도록 도와드릴 수 있습니다. 저희는 잔디 유지 관리부터 나무 및 관목 관리에 이르는 서비스를 수행합니다. 벽돌로 된 길이나 시골풍의 돌담과 같은 하드스케이프 구성물에 관심이 있으시다면, 귀하의 취향에 맞는 자재와 스타일에 대해 추천을 해드립니다. **153(A), 153(C) 디자인 선택을 도울 수 있도록 샘플도 직접 가져다 드립니다.**

오늘 바로 0114 496 0101로 전화하셔서 **153(B) 무료 첫 상담 일정을 잡으세요.**

타바사 마이어스, 랑데일 익스테리어 솔루션즈 대표

어휘 experienced 노련한, 숙련된 professional 전문가
landscape 조경 optimal 최적의 reasonable 합리적인
maintenance 유지 관리 shrub 관목 hardscape
하드스케이프(조경을 위한 보도, 옹벽 등) brick 벽돌 pathway 길
rustic 시골풍의 material 자재 taste 취향 initial 초기의

152 주제 / 목적

번역 편지의 주요 목적은?
(A) 부동산 매매 서비스를 제공하려고
(B) 조경 업체를 홍보하려고
(C) 원예 제품 라인을 광고하려고
(D) 지역 건설 규정에 관해 조언하려고

해설 첫 단락의 두 번째 문장에서 랑데일 익스테리어 솔루션즈를 소개하고자 한다(I'd like to introduce Langdale Exterior Solutions)고 했고, 같은 단락 마지막 문장에서 노련한 전문가들로 구성된 팀이 회사를 이 지역에서 가장 신뢰받는 조경 회사로 만든다(Our team of experienced professionals makes us the most trusted landscape company in the area)고 했다. 이로 보아 편지는 조경 업체를 홍보하기 위한 글임을 알 수 있으므로 (B)가 정답이다.

어휘 real estate 부동산 gardening 원예 regulation 규정

153 Not / True

번역 랑데일 익스테리어 솔루션즈에 대해 명시되지 않은 것은?
(A) 고객들의 집으로 제품 샘플을 가져간다.
(B) 첫 만남에 대해 비용을 청구하지 않는다.
(C) 고객과 함께 디자인을 결정한다.
(D) 주택 건설을 전문으로 한다.

해설 두 번째 단락의 네 번째 문장에서 디자인 선택을 도울 수 있도록 샘플도 직접 가져다준다(We will even bring samples directly to you to help you make your design selections)고 했으므로 (A)와 (C), 편지의 마지막 문장에서 무료 첫 상담 일정을 잡으라(schedule a free initial consultation)고 했으므로 (B)는 업체에 대해 소개된 내용이 맞지만, 주택 건설에 대한 언급은 없으므로 (D)가 정답이다.

어휘 charge 청구하다 specialize in ~을 전문으로 하다

Paraphrasing
지문의 a free initial consultation
→ 보기 (B)의 do not charge for a first meeting
지문의 design selections → 보기 (C)의 design decisions

154-157 편지

가쓰노리 사누
코튼우드 가 860번지, 아파트 5A호
워커턴, 온타리오 주 N0G 2V0

1월 3일

지젤 발데즈
팔론 드라이브 3758번지
오타와, 온타리오 주 K1Z 7B5

발데즈 씨께,

154 임대 계약에 따라, 이 편지는 임대 계약이 끝나는 날인 2월 28일에 제가 아파트에서 나가겠다는 서면 통지입니다. 저는 토론토에서의 일자리 제안을 수락하였으며 이사할 계획입니다. **154** 보증금을 언제 돌려받을 수 있는지 알려주십시오.

이곳에서 3년간 지내면서 즐거웠습니다. 이 지역에서 임대를 알아보는 누구에게라도 저는 코튼우드 아파트를 기꺼이 추천할 것입니다. **155, 157** 제가 정말 마음에 들었던 한 가지는 세탁실에 기계가 충분히 많아서 세탁기나 건조기 사용을 위해 오래 기다릴 필요가 없었다는 점입니다. 조경이 항상 잘 관리되어 있다는 점도 높이 평가합니다. **157** 하지만 가장 인상 깊었던 점은 귀하의 유지 관리 서비스입니다. **156** 작업팀은 모든 문제를 빠르게 처리해, 연기 감지기를 교체하고, 보일러의 필터를 바꾸고, 추운 계절이 오기 전에 창문에 방수 방풍 작업을 해 주었습니다.

새 주소가 생기는 대로 알려드리겠습니다. 제 휴대전화 613-555-0129로 언제든 연락하셔도 됩니다.

가쓰노리 사누

어휘 per ~에 따라 lease 임대 agreement 계약
constitute ~이 되다 notice 통지 expire 만료되다
relocate 이사하다 security deposit 보증금 laundry 세탁
plenty of 충분한 impressive 인상 깊은 address 처리하다
detector 감지기 furnace 보일러 weatherproof 비바람에 견디게 만들다

154 추론 / 암시

번역 발데즈 씨는 누구인 것 같은가?
(A) 사누 씨의 변호사
(B) 사누 씨의 고용주
(C) 재정 고문
(D) 부동산 관리인

해설 첫 번째 단락 첫 문장에서 발데즈 씨에게 임대 계약에 따라 이 편지는 임대 계약이 끝나는 날인 2월 28일에 아파트에서 나가겠다는 서면 통지(Per my lease agreement, this letter constitutes written notice that I will be moving out of my apartment on February 28, the day my lease expires)라면서, 같은 단락의 세 번째 문장에서 보증금을 언제 돌려받을 수 있는지 알려달라(Please let me know when I can expect the return of my security deposit)고 요청하는 것으로 보아, 발데즈 씨는 건물의 임대를 관리하는 사람임을 알 수 있다. 따라서 (D)가 정답이다.

어휘 employer 고용주 property 부동산, 건물

155 Not / True

번역 편지에서 코튼우드 아파트의 세탁실에 대해 명시하는 것은?
(A) 세탁기와 건조기가 여러 대 있다.

(B) 특대형 세탁기가 있다.
(C) 아침 시간에는 이용할 수 없다.
(D) 비거주자도 요금을 내고 이용할 수 있다.

해설 두 번째 단락의 세 번째 문장에서 정말 마음에 들었던 한 가지는 세탁실에 기계가 충분히 많아서 세탁기나 건조기 사용을 위해 오래 기다릴 필요가 없었다는 점(One thing I have really liked is that I have never had to wait long to use a washer or dryer in the laundry room since there are plenty of machines available)이라고 했으므로 (A)가 정답이다.

어휘 contain 들어 있다 oversized 특대의 nonresident 비거주자

> **Paraphrasing**
> 지문의 plenty of machines
> → 정답의 several washers and dryers

156 Not / True

번역 유지 관리 작업팀에 대해 언급되지 않은 것은?
(A) 주방 가전을 수리했다.
(B) 연기 감지기를 설치했다.
(C) 보일러에 깨끗한 필터를 설치했다.
(D) 아파트를 따뜻하게 유지할 수 있도록 추가 조치를 취했다.

해설 두 번째 단락의 마지막 문장에서 작업팀은 모든 문제를 빠르게 처리해, 연기 감지기를 교체하고, 보일러의 필터를 바꾸고, 추운 계절이 오기 전에 창문에 방수 방풍 작업을 해 주었다(The crew members quickly addressed all issues, replacing smoke detectors, changing filters in my furnace, and weatherproofing windows before the cold season set in)고 했으므로, 작업팀이 한 일로 (B), (C), (D)는 언급되었으나 주방 가전을 수리했다는 내용은 없으므로 (A)가 정답이다.

어휘 appliance 가전 제품

> **Paraphrasing**
> 지문의 weatherproofing windows before the cold season set in → 보기 (D)의 took extra steps to keep the apartments warm

157 문장 삽입

번역 [1], [2], [3], [4]로 표시된 위치 중에서 다음 문장이 들어가기에 가장 적합한 곳은?

"조경이 항상 잘 관리되어 있다는 점도 높이 평가합니다."
(A) [1]
(B) [2]
(C) [3]
(D) [4]

해설 주어진 문장은 '조경이 잘 관리되어 있다는 점도 높이 평가한다'며 아파트의 장점을 들고 있다. 따라서, 세탁실에 기계가 많아 세탁기나 건조기 사용을 위해 오래 기다릴 필요가 없었다(I have never had to wait long to use a washer or dryer in the laundry room since there are plenty of machines available)는 점과 가장 인상 깊었던 점은 유지 관리 서비스(Most impressive, though, is your maintenance service)라는 아파트의 장점을 제시하는 문장들 사이인 [3]에 들어가는 것이 글의 흐름상 자연스러우므로 (C)가 정답이다.

어휘 appreciate 높이 평가하다

158-159 이메일

수신: 사랄 말릭 〈smalik@bristek.co.uk〉
발신: 주나 쉬르머 〈jschirmer@diedrichindustries.de〉
날짜: 5월 11일
제목: 회신: 정보 업데이트
첨부: 🔗 안내 책자

말릭 씨께:

이메일을 보내주셔서 감사합니다. 귀하의 배송품이 현재 운송 중임을 확인드립니다. **158 예상보다 오래 기다리신 점에 사과드립니다. 최근에 저희는 신규 포장 공급업체와 협력하기 시작했는데, 안타깝게도 의사소통에 오류가 있었습니다.** 그 업체에서 귀하의 주문을 처리하기에는 너무 작은 상자를 공급했습니다.

이제 문제가 해결되어 귀하께서는 영업일 기준 향후 5일 이내에 제품을 받으실 수 있을 것입니다. **159 더불어, 저희 신제품 안내 책자와 상세 가격표를 실례를 무릎쓰고 첨부해 드립니다.** 귀하께서 저희의 최신 제품에 관심이 있으실 것이라 생각합니다.

주나 쉬르머
디드리히 인더스트리즈

어휘 brochure 안내 책자 in transit 운송 중인 packaging 포장 supply 공급 miscommunication 의사소통 오류 fulfill 이행하다 take the liberty to 실례를 무릎쓰고 ~하다 attach 첨부하다 latest 최신의

158 주제 / 목적

번역 이메일의 목적은?
(A) 지연의 원인을 설명하려고
(B) 배송에 대해 질문하려고
(C) 지불이 되었음을 확인하려고
(D) 제품에 대한 정보를 요청하려고

해설 첫 단락 세 번째 문장에서 예상보다 오래 기다리신 점에 사과드린다(I apologise for the longer-than-expected wait)면서 최근에 신규 포장 공급업체와 협력하기 시작했는데 안타깝게도 의사소통에 오류가 있었다(We recently started working with a new packaging supply company, and unfortunately, we experienced a miscommunication with them)고 한 것으로 보아, 제품의 배송이 지연된 원인을 설명하고 사과하려는 글임을 알 수 있다. 따라서 (A)가 정답이다.

어휘 cause 원인 delay 지연

> **Paraphrasing**
> 지문의 longer-than-expected wait → 정답의 delay

TEST 6 **119**

159 세부 사항

번역 쉬르머 씨가 이메일에 함께 제공한 것은?
(A) 제품을 제대로 포장하기 위한 점검표
(B) 구매를 위한 신제품 목록
(C) 수정된 상자 사양
(D) 배송 창고에 대한 정보

해설 두 번째 단락의 두 번째 문장에서 쉬르머 씨가 신제품 안내 책자와 상세 가격표를 실례를 무릅쓰고 첨부한다(In addition, I have taken the liberty to attach a brochure of our new products with a detailed price list)고 했으므로 (B)가 정답이다.

어휘 revised 수정된 specification 사양 warehouse 창고

160-161 문자 메시지

> **어빈 포터 (오전 10시 4분)**
> 안녕하세요, 민디. **160** 내일 오크데일 레인 431번지에서 있을 오픈 하우스를 위한 서류를 준비 중이에요. 더 준비해야 할 게 있을까요?
>
> **민디 워너 (오전 10시 6분)**
> 잠재 구매자들에게 제공할 **161** 페이스트리를 사주실 수 있을까요? 물은 이미 몇 병 샀는데 내일 빵집에 들를 시간이 없을 것 같아요.
>
> **어빈 포터 (오전 10시 8분)**
> 그렇게 할게요.
>
> **민디 워너 (오전 10시 9분)**
> 고마워요! 내일 봐요.
>
> **어휘** paperwork 서류 open house 오픈 하우스(주택·아파트를 둘러볼 수 있게 하는 행사) potential 잠재적인 stop by ~에 들르다

160 추론 / 암시

번역 포터 씨와 워너 씨가 종사하는 것 같은 산업은?
(A) 금융
(B) 부동산
(C) 주택 보안
(D) 식품 유통

해설 10시 4분에 포터 씨가 워너 씨에게 내일 오크데일 레인 431번지에서 있을 오픈 하우스를 위한 서류를 준비 중(I'm preparing the paperwork for tomorrow's open house at 431 Oakdale Lane)이라고 업무 보고를 하는 것을 통해, 두 사람은 부동산 분야에서 일하고 있음을 짐작할 수 있다. 따라서 (B)가 정답이다.

어휘 security 보안 distribution 유통

161 의도 파악

번역 오전 10시 8분에 포터 씨가 "그렇게 할게요"라고 쓴 의도는?
(A) 이미 구매자들을 만났다.
(B) 이미 물병을 배달했다.
(C) 제과류 제품을 구입할 것이다.
(D) 서류 작업을 마치는 것을 도울 것이다.

해설 10시 6분에 워너 씨가 페이스트리를 사줄 수 있을지(Could you buy the pastries)를 묻자 10시 8분에 포터 씨가 그렇게 하겠다(Consider it done)고 대답한 것이므로, 포터 씨는 워너 씨의 요청에 따라 빵을 사다 주겠다는 의도로 한 말임을 알 수 있다. 따라서 (C)가 정답이다.

162-164 블로그 게시물

> **게임즈 나우 블로그**
>
> **162** 최근 한 독자가 3D 프린팅의 혁신이 보드게임 산업과 관련이 있는지를 문의했습니다. 이번 달 게시글에서, 몇몇 최신 발전이 보드게임 제작에 흥미로운 가능성을 제공한다는 점을 전하게 되어 기쁩니다. 맞춤 제작이 핵심 이점입니다. 이로 인해 복잡한 디자인의 부품들이 특정 테마에 맞춰 제작이 가능해집니다. **164** 3D 프린터에 탑재할 수 있는 소재의 혁신은 게임 피스들에 전례 없는 질감의 다양성을 제공하여 플레이어의 촉각 경험을 향상시켜줍니다. 기업들은 심지어 생분해성 소재를 선택할 수도 있습니다.
>
> 3D 프린터는 또한 점점 더 빨라지고 있습니다. 이는 특히 보드게임의 소량 생산과 관련이 있습니다. **163** 소량 생산은 한정판 게임과 기존 게임의 새로운 버전에 이상적입니다. 이러한 발전을 활용하는 기업들은 매우 경쟁이 치열한 시장에서 우위를 점할 수 있습니다.
>
> — 살바도르 토레스, 6월 1일

어휘 innovation 혁신 pertinent to ~와 관련 있는 post 게시물 latest 최신의 advance 발전 customization 맞춤 제작 benefit 이점, 혜택 component 부품, 요소 intricate 복잡한 tailor 맞추다 specific 특정한 load 넣다, 끼우다 unprecedented 전례 없는 range 다양성 texture 질감 game piece 게임 피스(보드 게임에 사용되는 말이나 주사위) enhance 향상시키다 tactile 촉각의 particularly 특히 relevant to ~와 관련 있는 small-batch 소규모 ideal 이상적인 existing 기존의 exploit 활용하다 edge 우위 competitive 경쟁을 하는

162 추론 / 암시

번역 토레스 씨에 대해 사실인 것 같은 것은?
(A) 3D 프린터를 만드는 회사에서 일한다.
(B) 비디오 게임 기술에 대한 주간 블로그를 쓴다.
(C) 그래픽 아티스트로 직장 생활을 시작했다.
(D) 3D 프린팅에 관한 질문에 대한 답변을 조사했다.

해설 첫 단락 첫 문장에서 최근 한 독자가 3D 프린팅의 혁신이 보드게임 산업과 관련이 있는지를 문의했다(A reader recently asked whether any innovations in 3-D printing are pertinent to the board game industry)고 했고, 뒤이어 이번 달 게시

글에서 몇몇 최신 발전이 보드게임 제작에 흥미로운 가능성을 제공한다는 점을 전하게 되어 기쁘다(In this month's post, I am happy to report that some of the latest advances do indeed offer exciting possibilities for board game production)고 했다. 따라서 토레스 씨는 독자의 질문에 답하기 위해 조사를 하고, 그에 대한 답변을 제시하고 있음을 알 수 있으므로 (D)가 정답이다.

어휘 research 조사하다

163 Not / True

번역 게임의 소량 생산에 대해 명시된 것은?
(A) 대량 생산보다 더 일반적이다.
(B) 3D 프린팅이 있든 없든 비용은 동일하다.
(C) 아동용 게임을 만드는 데 주로 사용된다.
(D) 게임의 다양한 버전을 만드는 데 유용하다.

해설 두 번째 단락의 세 번째 문장에서 소량 생산은 한정판 게임과 기존 게임의 새로운 버전에 이상적(Small batches are ideal for limited-edition games and new versions of existing games)이라고 했으므로, 소량 생산이 여러 가지 버전의 게임을 제작하는 데 도움이 된다는 것을 알 수 있다. 따라서 (D)가 정답이다.

어휘 common 일반적인 mass 대량의 multiple 다양한

Paraphrasing
지문의 limited-edition games and new versions of existing games → 정답의 multiple versions of a game

164 문장 삽입

번역 [1], [2], [3], [4]로 표시된 위치 중에서 다음 문장이 들어가기에 가장 적합한 곳은?

"기업들은 심지어 생분해성 소재를 선택할 수도 있습니다."
(A) [1]
(B) [2]
(C) [3]
(D) [4]

해설 주어진 문장은 '기업들은 심지어 생분해성 소재를 선택할 수도 있다'며 소재 선택의 폭이 확대되고 있는 점에 대해 언급하고 있으므로, 주어진 문장 앞에는 소재의 다양성과 관련된 내용이 있어야 적절하다. 따라서, 3D 프린터에 탑재할 수 있는 소재의 혁신이 게임 피스들에 질감의 다양성을 제공한다(Innovations in materials that can be loaded into a 3-D printer offer an unprecedented range of textures for game pieces)는 내용 뒤인 [3]에 들어가는 것이 글의 흐름상 자연스러우므로 (C)가 정답이다.

어휘 biodegradable 생분해성의

165-168 공지

멋지게 쉬다 가세요!

QRN 공항은 여행객들이 새로운 리포즈 라운지를 경험해 보도록 초대합니다. 다른 공항의 리포즈 라운지와 마찬가지로, 이곳은 항공편 사이에 경유 시간이 길거나, 비행 시간보다 일찍 도착했거나, 또는 뜻밖의 지연을 겪게 되는 경우 쉴 수 있는 평화롭고 편안한 165 **공간**을 제공합니다. 리포즈 라운지는 매일 오전 5시부터 오후 8시 30분 사이에 운영되며 다음과 같은 편의 시설이 있습니다.

✓ 회의 및 통화를 위한 전용 회의실
✓ 166 **인쇄 및 복사 서비스**
✓ 와이파이 및 충전 스테이션
✓ 167 **음료, 제과류, 간식**
✓ 다양한 최신 신문 및 잡지

리포즈 라운지 이용권은 180달러에 이용하실 수 있으며 구매일로부터 1년간 유효합니다. 리포즈 라운지를 이용하시려면, 정부에서 발급한 사진이 포함된 신분증과 당일 탑승권을 제시하셔야 합니다.

168 **QRN 공항에서의 개점을 기념하여, 3월 15일부터 3월 30일까지 리포즈 라운지 이용권을 반값에 제공해 드립니다.** 이용권을 구입하시거나 예약을 하시려면, www.qrnairport.com/repose로 방문하시거나 B 터미널의 라운지 바로 밖에 있는 서비스 데스크를 방문해 주세요.

어휘 unwind 쉬다 layover 경유 deal with ~을 대하다 unexpected 뜻밖의 delay 지연 feature 포함하다 amenity 편의 시설 charging 충전 beverage 음료 a selection of 다양한 valid 유효한 access 이용하다 present 제시하다 government 정부 issue 발급하다 boarding pass 탑승권

165 동의어 찾기

번역 첫 번째 단락 2행의 "space"와 의미가 가장 가까운 것은?
(A) 거리
(B) 구역
(C) 상태
(D) 공석

해설 의미상 쉴 수 있는 평화롭고 편안한 '공간'이라는 뜻으로 쓰였으므로 '구역, 부분'을 뜻하는 (B) area가 정답이다.

166 Not / True

번역 QRN 공항의 리포즈 라운지에 대해 명시된 것은?
(A) 하루 24시간 운영된다.
(B) 공항 호텔 안에 있다.
(C) 국제선 항공 여행객 전용이다.
(D) 프린터를 이용할 수 있다.

해설 공지 중반부 편의 시설 목록의 두 번째 줄에 인쇄 및 복사 서비스(Printing and copying services)가 나열되어 있으므로 (D)가 정답이다.

167 세부 사항

번역 리포즈 라운지 방문객들에게 제공되는 것은?
(A) 다과
(B) 도서
(C) 영화
(D) 컴퓨터

해설 공지 중반부 편의 시설 목록의 네 번째 줄에 음료, 제과류, 간식(Beverages, baked goods, and snacks)이 라운지에서 제공된다고 나와 있으므로 (A)가 정답이다.

> **Paraphrasing**
> 지문의 Beverages, baked goods, and snacks
> → 정답의 Refreshments

168 세부 사항

번역 공지에 따르면, 3월 15일과 3월 30일 사이에 일어날 일은?
(A) 보수 공사가 완료될 것이다.
(B) 서비스 데스크 직원이 채용될 것이다.
(C) B 터미널이 문을 닫을 것이다.
(D) 할인이 제공될 것이다.

해설 마지막 단락의 첫 문장에서 QRN 공항에서의 개점을 기념하여 3월 15일부터 3월 30일까지 리포즈 라운지 이용권을 반값에 제공한다(To celebrate the grand opening at QRN Airport, we are offering Repose Lounge passes at half price between March 15 and March 30)고 했으므로 (D)가 정답이다.

어휘 representative 직원

> **Paraphrasing**
> 지문의 at half price → 정답의 discount

169-171 기사

> **미스포드의 친환경 의식을 고양하라**
>
> 3월 26일 — 미스포드 마을은 4월에 연례 친환경 의식 주간을 기념할 예정이다. 이 행사는 마을의 녹색 지구 위원회가 주관하며 미스포드를 친환경적이고 깨끗하게 유지하기 위한 장기적인 노력의 일환이다.
>
> **171(C)** 활동은 4월 1일 일요일, 미스포드 하천 산책로 청소와 함께 시작된다. 두 팀의 자원봉사자들이 하천 양쪽에서 쓰레기를 줍고 길에 떨어진 나뭇가지들을 치울 것이다.
>
> **169** 월요일에 주민들은 산책로를 따라 걸으며 사진을 찍도록 권장된다. 녹색 지구 위원회는 디지털 이미지를 제출 받아 최우수 이미지 10장을 선정해 마을 웹사이트에 게시할 예정이다.
>
> 화요일과 수요일에 **171(D)** 마을회관에 오는 주민들은 1회용 비닐봉지를 대체하기 위한 천 가방을 수령할 수 있으며, 비닐봉지 판매는 다음 달부터 우리 지역에서 금지된다.
>
> **170** 목요일에 미스포드 도서관은 에너지를 아끼고 쓰레기를 줄이며 재활용하기 위한 방안에 관해 패널 토론을 주최한다. 이는 마을과 녹색 지구 위원회의 근본적인 지향점이다. 어린이는 어른과 함께 참석할 수 있다.
>
> 마지막으로, 토요일에는 **171(A)** 500그루의 묘목이 주민들에게 무료로 제공된다. 나무는 이 지역 자생종으로, 개인 정원 또는 일부 공공 장소에 심을 수 있다.

> **어휘** green 친환경의 aware 의식이 높은 annual 연례의 awareness 의식 stream 하천, 개울 trail 산책로 rubbish 쓰레기 path 길 branch 나뭇가지 resident 주민 accept 받아 주다 post 게시하다 hall 회관 ban 금지하다 panel 패널 토론 conserve 아끼다 reduce 줄이다 fundamental 근본적인 sapling 묘목 native to ~ 자생의, 토종의

169 세부 사항

번역 미스포드의 웹사이트에 게시될 예정인 것은?
(A) 행사 등록 페이지
(B) 미스포드의 산책로 지도
(C) 지정된 구역의 사진
(D) 새로운 주민을 위한 환경 선물 꾸러미

해설 세 번째 단락의 첫 문장에서 월요일에 주민들은 산책로를 따라 걸으며 사진을 찍도록 권장된다(On Monday, residents are encouraged to walk along the trails and take photographs)고 했고, 녹색 지구 위원회는 디지털 이미지를 제출 받아 최우수 이미지 10장을 선정해 마을 웹사이트에 게시할 예정(The Green Earth Committee is accepting digital images and will select the ten best to post to the village Web site)이라고 했다. 따라서 미스포드의 웹사이트에는 주민들이 산책로에서 찍은 사진이 게시될 것임을 알 수 있으므로 (C)가 정답이다.

어휘 registration 등록 specified 지정된 packet 꾸러미

170 세부 사항

번역 녹색 지구 위원회의 한 가지 목표는?
(A) 어린이들을 감독하려고
(B) 규정을 없애려고
(C) 쓰레기 감소를 장려하려고
(D) 마을 의회 구성원들에게 조언하려고

해설 다섯 번째 단락의 첫 문장에서 목요일에 미스포드 도서관은 에너지를 아끼고 쓰레기를 줄이며 재활용하기 위한 방안에 관해 패널 토론을 주최한다(On Thursday, the Misford Library will host a panel on ways to conserve energy and reduce and recycle waste)고 했고, 이는 마을과 녹색 지구 위원회의 근본적인 지향점(These are fundamental goals of the village and its Green Earth Committee)이라고 했다. 따라서 쓰레기 줄이기는 녹색 지구 위원회의 목표 중 한 가지이므로 (C)가 정답이다.

어휘 supervise 감독하다 eliminate 없애다 regulation 규정 reduction 감소

171 Not / True

번역 친환경 의식 주간 동안 계획된 활동으로 언급되지 않은 것은?
(A) 자생 나무 심기
(B) 산책로에서 자전거 타기
(C) 청소 활동에 참여하기
(D) 천 가방 배포하기

해설 마지막 단락의 첫 문장에서 500그루의 묘목이 주민들에게 무료로 제공된다(500 tree saplings will be offered to residents free of charge)더 나무는 이 지역 자생종으로 개인 정원 또는 일부 공공 장소에 심을 수 있다(The trees are native to the region and can be planted in private gardens or in some public areas)고 했으므로 (A), 두 번째 단락의 첫 문장에서 활동은 4월 1일 일요일, 미스포드 하천 산책로 청소와 함께 시작된다(The activities will start on Sunday, April 1, with a cleanup of the Misford Stream trails)고 했으므로 (C), 네 번째 단락에서 마을회관에 오는 주민들은 1회용 비닐봉지를 대체하기 위한 천 가방을 수령할 수 있다(residents who come to the village hall can pick up cloth bags to replace single-use plastic shopping bags)고 했으므로 (D)는 계획된 활동으로 언급되었다. 자전거 타기에 대한 내용은 없으므로 (B)가 정답이다.

어휘 participate in ~에 참여하다   distribute 배포하다

172-175 온라인 채팅

캐서린 래디스 (오전 9시 12분)
좋은 아침이에요, 지나 그리고 제이. 잠깐 시간 있으세요?

지나 카프 (오전 9시 13분)
그럼요.

캐서린 래디스 (오전 9시 14분)
172, 173, 174 부서 회보가 내일 이메일로 발송될 거예요. 거기에 추가하고 싶은 내용이 있으세요? 이번 달에는 소식이 많지 않네요.

지나 카프 (오전 9시 15분)
얼마나 빨리 필요한가요?

제이 누사푸트라 (오전 9시 16분)
저는 있어요, 캐서린. 휴가 신청 절차를 요약한 간단한 알림 글이에요. 현재로서는 그것 말고는 없어요.

캐서린 래디스 (오전 9시 17분)
오늘 중으로 주실 수 있는 건 무엇이든 필요해요.

지나 카프 (오전 9시 18분)
174 죄송하지만 그렇게 빨리 드릴 수 있는 건 없네요. 오후 내내 있을 인터뷰를 준비하고 있거든요. 174 다음 회보에는 현재 프로젝트에 관한 보고서를 꼭 준비할게요.

제이 누사푸트라 (오전 9시 19분)
175 오늘 오전에는 고객 미팅이 없어서, 끝내려면 한 시간 정도만 있으면 돼요. 점심 전에 알림 글을 보내드릴 수 있어요.

어휘 bulletin 회보   reminder 상기시켜 주는 알림 글   summarize 요약하다   process 절차

172 주제 / 목적

번역 메시지 작성자들은 무엇을 논의하고 있는가?
(A) 면접 요청
(B) 사내 소식지
(C) 프로젝트 평가
(D) 휴가 일정표

해설 9시 14분에 래디스 씨가 부서 회보가 내일 이메일로 발송될 것(The department bulletin is going out tomorrow by e-mail)이라면서 거기에 추가하고 싶은 내용이 있는지(Do you have anything that you would like to add to it?)를 물었고, 그에 대한 답변이 뒤따르고 있다. 따라서 메시지 작성자들은 사내 소식지에 관해 이야기하고 있음을 알 수 있으므로 (B)가 정답이다.

어휘 evaluation 평가   itinerary 일정표

> **Paraphrasing**
> 지문의 department bulletin → 정답의 office newsletter

173 의도 파악

번역 오전 9시 16분에 누사푸트라 씨가 "저는 있어요"라고 쓴 의도는?
(A) 동료의 알림 글을 받았다.
(B) 휴가를 내야만 한다.
(C) 기고할 수 있다.
(D) 주어진 일을 마쳤다.

해설 9시 14분에 래디스 씨가 부서 회보가 내일 이메일로 발송될 것(The department bulletin is going out tomorrow by e-mail)이라면서 거기에 추가하고 싶은 내용이 있는지(Do you have anything that you would like to add to it?)를 물었고, 9시 16분에 누사푸트라 씨가 있다(I do have something)고 대답한 것이므로, 누사푸트라 씨는 회보에 기고할 내용이 있다는 의도로 한 말임을 알 수 있다. 따라서 (C)가 정답이다.

어휘 colleague 동료   take time off 휴가를 내다   contribution 기고

174 추론 / 암시

번역 카프 씨의 보고서는 언제 직원들에게 발송될 것 같은가?
(A) 한 시간 뒤에
(B) 하루 뒤에
(C) 일주일 뒤에
(D) 한 달 뒤에

해설 9시 14분에 래디스 씨가 부서 회보가 내일 이메일로 발송될 것(The department bulletin is going out tomorrow by e-mail)이라면서 거기에 추가하고 싶은 내용이 있는지(Do you have anything that you would like to add to it?)를 물으면서 이번 달에는 소식이 많지 않다(We don't have a lot of news this month)고 했고, 9시 18분에 카프 씨가 죄송하지만 그렇게 빨리 줄 수 있는 건 없다(I'm afraid there's nothing I can get to you that quickly)면서 다음 회보에는 현재 프로젝트에 관한 보고서를 꼭 준비하겠다(I'll be sure to have a report on current projects ready for the next bulletin)고 했다. 따

라서 카프 씨는 다음 달 회보를 위해 보고서를 준비할 계획임을 알 수 있으므로 (D)가 정답이다.

175 세부 사항

번역 누사푸트라 씨가 다음에 할 일은?
(A) 점심 휴식
(B) 고객과 만남
(C) 카프 씨에게 글 작성
(D) 알림 글 작성 마무리

해설 9시 19분에 누사푸트라 씨가 오늘 오전에는 고객 미팅이 없어서 끝내려면 한 시간 정도만 있으면 된다(I'll just need an hour or so to finish it up, as I have no client meetings this morning)면서 점심 전에 알림 글을 보내줄 수 있다(I can send you the reminder before lunch)고 했으므로, 누사푸트라 씨는 곧바로 알림 글을 작성할 계획임을 알 수 있다. 따라서 (D)가 정답이다.

어휘 draft 원고를 작성하다

176-180 이메일 + 이메일

수신: 전 직원
발신: 리자 파쿠라르
제목: 특별 호
날짜: 11월 12일

여러분께,

다시 한 번, 〈베스트 디자인 인사이트〉 잡지의 연례 특별 호 출간 마감일을 맞출 수 있게 도와주신 여러분의 큰 노고에 감사를 표하고 싶습니다. **176 다음은 오늘 회의에서 우리가 논의했던 주안점들을 요약한 것입니다.**

• 카린 쉬가 광고주들이 이번 호에 높은 관심을 보였다고 보고했고, 그에 따라 광고 제출 기한이 일주일 연장됩니다.

• 이번 호는 빠듯한 납기일을 맞추기 위해 대체 인쇄업체인 스클라 프레스를 이용합니다.

• **179 마크 얀스키의 팀이 초과 근무를 하며 특별 레이아웃 요소들, 특히 포토 몽타주에 배열된 여러 사진이 들어간 페이지를 검토할 수 있도록 예산을 증액하라는 승인을 받았습니다.** 이후 마크가 인쇄업체에 맞춤 디자인 요청을 제출할 예정입니다.

• 특별 호의 초안이 우리가 원하는 것보다 깁니다. 그래서, **177 애니메이션 아티스트 브렛 러스크와의 인터뷰 내용을 압축하여 전체 페이지 수를 줄였습니다.**

리자 파쿠라르, 편집장
베스트 디자인 출판

어휘 express 표현하다 gratitude 감사 summary 요약 advertiser 광고주 heightened 높아진 extend 연장하다 alternate 대체의 tight 빠듯한 approval 승인 budget 예산 layout 레이아웃, 배치 component 요소 in particular 특히 photomontage 포토 몽타주(여러 사진을 조합한 이미지) custom 맞춤의 draft 초안 condense 압축하다

수신: 리자 파쿠라르
발신: 카린 쉬
제목: 회신: 특별 호
날짜: 11월 14일

안녕하세요, 리자,

178 작년에 했던 것처럼 우리 잡지의 특별 호를 인쇄하기 위해 스클라 프레스를 이용한다는 계획이 만족스럽습니다. 그들이 우리 출간 마감일을 맞출 수 있을 거라 확신합니다. **179 우리의 맞춤 요청으로 아마도 추가 비용이 발생하겠지만,** 추가된 비용은 광고 수익에서 기대되는 증가분에 의해 상쇄될 것입니다.

180 저의 다음 계획은 구독자들에게 이 특별 호를 기대할 수 있다는 점을 상기시키는 것입니다. 이메일을 통해 알릴 예정입니다.

카린 쉬, 마케팅 담당자
베스트 디자인 출판

어휘 confident 확신하는 incur 발생시키다 expense 비용 offset 상쇄하다 boost 증가 revenue 수익 agenda 계획, 안건 subscriber 구독자 via ~을 통해

176 주제 / 목적

번역 첫 번째 이메일의 목적은?
(A) 새로운 직원을 소개하려고
(B) 회의 요약을 제공하려고
(C) 프로젝트 연기를 제안하려고
(D) 아티스트에게 작업 샘플을 요청하려고

해설 첫 번째 이메일의 첫 단락 두 번째 문장에서 다음은 오늘 회의에서 논의했던 주안점들을 요약한 것(What follows is a summary of the main points we discussed at today's meeting)이라며, 그 뒤로 회의 내용을 요약한 것들을 나열하고 있다. 따라서 이 글은 직원들에게 회의 요약을 제공하기 위한 것이므로 (B)가 정답이다.

어휘 propose 제안하다

177 Not / True

번역 첫 번째 이메일에서, 잡지의 특별 호에 대해 명시된 것은?
(A) 애니메이터와의 인터뷰가 포함될 것이다.
(B) 온라인으로만 제공될 것이다.
(C) 이전 호의 기사들을 재인쇄할 것이다.
(D) 예상보다 적은 광고가 들어갈 것이다.

해설 첫 번째 이메일의 마지막 단락 두 번째 문장에서 애니메이션 아티스트 브렛 러스크와의 인터뷰 내용을 압축하여 전체 페이지 수를 줄였다(we reduced the page total by condensing the text of our interview with animation artist Bret Lusk)고 했으므로, 잡지의 특별 호에 애니메이터와 인터뷰한 내용이 삽입될 예정임을 알 수 있다. 따라서 (A)가 정답이다.

어휘 animator 애니메이터(만화 영화 제작자) reprint 재인쇄하다 previous 이전의

Paraphrasing
지문의 animation artist → 정답의 animator

178 Not / True

번역 두 번째 이메일에서, 스클라 프레스에 대해 언급된 것은?
(A) 대량 주문을 전문으로 한다.
(B) 쉬 씨가 소유했었다.
(C) 과거에 〈베스트 디자인 인사이트〉 잡지를 인쇄한 적이 있다.
(D) 지역에서 가장 오래된 인쇄업체이다.

해설 두 번째 이메일의 첫 단락 첫 문장에서 작년에 했던 것처럼 우리 잡지의 특별 호를 인쇄하기 위해 스클라 프레스를 이용한다는 계획이 만족스럽다(I'm happy with the plan to use Sklarr Press to print our magazine's special issue, just as we did last year)고 했으므로, 스클라 프레스에서 작년에도 〈베스트 디자인 인사이트〉 특별 호를 인쇄했음을 알 수 있다. 따라서 (C)가 정답이다.

어휘 specialize in ~을 전문으로 하다 region 지역

179 연계

번역 올해 특별 호의 인쇄 비용을 증가시킬 것 같은 것은?
(A) 짧아진 마감일
(B) 광고의 증가
(C) 많은 수의 인쇄 페이지
(D) 페이지 속 사진의 배치

해설 첫 이메일의 네 번째 단락에서 마크 얀스키의 팀이 초과 근무를 하며 특별 레이아웃 요소들, 특히 포토 몽타주에 배열된 여러 사진이 들어간 페이지를 검토할 수 있도록 예산을 증액하라는 승인을 받았다(We've gotten approval to increase the budget so that Mark Janskee's team can work overtime to review the pages with special layout components, in particular multiple photographs arranged in a photomontage)고 했고 이후 마크가 인쇄업체에 맞춤 디자인 요청을 제출할 예정(Mark will then submit a custom design request to the printer)이라고 했으며, 두 번째 이메일의 첫 단락 세 번째 문장에서 우리의 맞춤 요청으로 아마도 추가 비용이 발생할 것(Our customization request will probably incur an extra fee)이라고 했다. 따라서 추가 비용을 발생시킬 맞춤 요청이란 페이지 속 구성 요소인 여러 장의 사진 배치와 관련된 것임을 알 수 있으므로 (D)가 정답이다.

어휘 add to ~을 증가시키다 shortened 짧아진, 단축된
placement 배치

180 세부 사항

번역 쉬 씨가 다음에 할 일은?
(A) 구독자들에게 알림 메시지 발송
(B) 일부 기사의 분량 감축
(C) 직원들에게 표지 디자인에 대한 선호도 조사
(D) 그래픽 디자이너 팀과의 만남

해설 두 번째 이메일의 두 번째 단락에서 쉬 씨가 자신의 다음 계획은 구독자들에게 이 특별 호를 기대할 수 있다는 점을 상기시키는 것(Next on my agenda is to remind our subscribers that they have this extra issue to look forward to)이라며 이메일을 통해 알릴 예정(I'll let them know via e-mail)이라고 했다. 따라서 쉬 씨는 구독자들에게 특별 호에 대해 알리는 메시지를 이메일로 발송할 것임을 알 수 있으므로 (A)가 정답이다.

어휘 survey 조사하다 preference 선호(도) cover 표지

181-185 이메일 + 이메일 ▶동영상 강의

수신: 샨 이크발
발신: 매기 로젠
날짜: 7월 12일
제목: 사무실 축하 행사

샨 씨께,

아시다시피, 우리는 7월 28일에 월터 웨버를 축하하기 위한 사무실 파티를 계획했습니다. 제 비서에게서 당신이 참석하신다는 것을 듣고 기뻤고, **181 행사 중에 월터에 대해 몇 마디 해 주실 의향이 있는지 궁금합니다.** 그는 25년 전에 이 회사를 설립했고 항상 회사의 필수적인 존재였습니다. **182 재무 부서에서 그와 밀접하게 일하고 계셔서** 멘토, 직원, 리더로서의 그에 관해 이야기하기에 적절한 위치에 계시다고 생각했습니다. 파티는 오후 6시에 시작될 예정입니다. **185 연설은 오후 7시 30분에 시작해** 약 한 시간 동안 계속될 것입니다. 단지 월터뿐만 아니라 모두가 당신의 이야기를 듣고 싶을 거라고 확신합니다! 가능한 한 빨리 알려주십시오.

매기 로젠
인사부 책임자
웨버 리히터 어소시에이츠

어휘 in honor of ~을 축하하는 be willing to 기꺼이 ~하다
found 설립하다 integral 필수적인 speech 연설

수신: 매기 로젠
발신: 샨 이크발
날짜: 7월 12일
제목: 회신: 사무실 축하 행사

매기 씨께,

저를 생각해 주셔서 감사합니다! 월터의 파티를 정말 기대하고 있고, 그에 관해 이야기하는 것은 저에게 엄청난 영광이 될 것입니다. **183 실제로 15년 전 제가 이 회사에 처음 지원했을 때 월터가 저의 면접관이었습니다.** 수년 동안 그의 지도는 귀중한 것이었습니다.

그 날 오후 5시에 영업팀과 회의가 잡혀 있어 **185 연설이 막 시작될 때 파티에 도착할 것 같다는 점을 184 유념해 주세요.** 후반부 연설 중 하나를 할 수 있게 일정을 잡아 주신다면 문제없을 것 같습니다.

샨 이크발
웨버 리히터 어소시에이츠

어휘 tremendous 엄청난 apply for ~에 지원하다
guidance 지도 invaluable 귀중한

181 주제 / 목적

번역 로젠 씨가 이크발 씨에게 이메일을 보낸 이유는?
(A) 축하 행사에 초대하려고
(B) 파티를 준비하는 데 도움을 요청하려고
(C) 동료의 성과에 대해 알리려고
(D) 행사에서 연설해 달라고 요청하려고

해설 첫 번째 이메일의 두 번째 문장에서 로젠 씨가 이크발 씨에게 행사 중에 월터에 대해 몇 마디 해 주실 의향이 있는지 궁금하다(I was wondering if you would be willing to say a few words about Walter during the event)고 한 것으로 보아 로젠 씨는 이크발 씨에게 행사에서 연설을 해 달라는 요청을 하기 위해 이메일을 썼다는 것을 알 수 있다. 따라서 (D)가 정답이다.

어휘 organize 준비하다 colleague 동료
accomplishment 성취

Paraphrasing
지문의 say a few words → 정답의 give a speech

182 Not / True

번역 이크발 씨에 대해 명시된 것은?
(A) 정기적으로 발표를 한다.
(B) 영업팀과의 회의 일정을 변경할 것이다.
(C) 회사에서 25년간 근무해 왔다.
(D) 재무 부서에서 근무한다.

해설 첫 번째 이메일의 네 번째 문장에서 이크발 씨가 재무 부서에서 월터와 밀접하게 일하고 있다(you work closely with him in the finance department)고 했으므로 (D)가 정답이다.

어휘 regularly 정기적으로

183 Not / True

번역 웨버 씨에 대해 명시된 것은?
(A) 최근에 새 지사를 열었다.
(B) 회사를 매각할 계획이다.
(C) 이크발 씨의 채용에 직접 관여했다.
(D) 7월 28일 파티에 늦게 도착할 것이다.

해설 두 번째 이메일의 첫 단락 세 번째 문장에서 이크발 씨가 실제로 15년 전 이 회사에 처음 지원했을 때 월터가 면접관이었다(Walter actually interviewed me when I first applied for a job with the company fifteen years ago)고 했다. 따라서 월터 웨버 씨는 이크발 씨의 채용 과정에 직접 참여했음을 알 수 있으므로 (C)가 정답이다.

어휘 branch 지사 directly 직접 involved 관련된

184 동의어 찾기

번역 두 번째 이메일의 두 번째 단락 1행의 "note"와 의미가 가장 가까운 것은?
(A) 퍼뜨리다
(B) 주의하다
(C) 보여주다
(D) 언급하다

해설 의미상 연설이 막 시작될 때 파티에 도착할 것 같다는 점을 '유념하라'는 뜻으로 쓰였으므로 '주의하다, 인지하다'를 뜻하는 (B) be aware가 정답이다.

185 연계

번역 이크발 씨는 대략 몇 시쯤 파티에 도착할 계획인가?
(A) 오후 5시
(B) 오후 6시
(C) 오후 7시 30분
(D) 오후 8시 30분

해설 두 번째 이메일의 두 번째 단락 첫 문장에서 이크발 씨는 연설이 막 시작될 때 파티에 도착할 것 같다(I should arrive at the party just as the speeches begin)고 했고, 첫 번째 이메일의 여섯 번째 문장에서 연설은 오후 7시 30분에 시작한다(The speeches will start at 7:30 P.M.)고 했다. 따라서 이크발 씨는 연설이 시작되는 오후 7시 30분쯤 파티에 도착할 수 있다는 것이므로 (C)가 정답이다.

어휘 approximately 대략

186-190 공지 + 이메일 + 웹페이지

알라미토 식물학회

여러분의 집 정원을 7월 3일로 예정된 올해의 고저스 가든 투어의 여러 방문지 중 한 곳이 되도록 신청하세요!

올해의 투어 주제는 날개 달린 천국으로, 작은 황금방울새와 링렛 나비를 포함하여 지역의 새와 나비가 좋아하는 개화 식물에 중점을 두고 있습니다. 186 올해 투어의 입장권 판매에서 나오는 모든 수익금은 프레시디오 카운티 공원의 미루나무 숲에 식물을 새로 심는 데 사용될 예정입니다.

가든 투어를 주최하는 것은 알라미토 식물학회 회원들에게 무료입니다. www.alamitobotanicalsociety.org/gorgeousgardens에서 간단히 양식을 작성하셔서 5월 20일까지 정원의 디지털 사진과 함께 제출해 주세요. 188 투어에 참여하도록 선정된 정원은 프레시디오 카운티 내에 위치해야 하며 지역 자생 식물만 있어야 합니다. 투어 방문지로 참여하는 것에 대해 질문이 있으실 경우, info@alamitobotanicalsociety.org로 이메일을 보내주세요.

어휘 botanical 식물학의 society 학회, 협회 theme 주제
winged 날개 달린 paradise 천국 favor 선호하다
regional 지역의 goldfinch 황금방울새 proceeds 수익금
replant 새로 식물을 심다 cottonwood 미루나무
participate in ~에 참여하다 native 자생의

수신: info@alamitobotanicalsociety.org
발신: rebeccaolton@mailhost.com
날짜: 5월 1일
제목: 가든 투어에 관한 질문

안녕하세요,

저는 지난해 프레시디오 카운티로 이사 온 직후 알라미토 식물학회 회원이 되었습니다. 학회의 웹사이트와 자료, 교육용 강의는 190 **5에이커짜리 제 땅을 새와 다른 동물들을 끌어들일 만한 다양한 자생 식물로 채운다는 저의 야심 찬 프로젝트**에 도움이 되었습니다. 지금까지 약 1.5에이커의 땅이 경작되었습니다.

187 **제 작업을 사람들에게 보여주고 우리 학회 회원들과 마찬가지로 정원을 소중히 여기는 사람들을 더 많이 만나는 것은 큰 영광일 것입니다.** 그래서 저는 고저스 가든 투어에 참여할 수 있을지 문의하고자 글을 씁니다. 188 **이 지역의 자생 식물이 아닌 아름다운 라벤더 덤불이 제가 이곳을 구입하기 전에 이미 부지에서 자라고 있었음을 인정해야겠군요.** 하지만 라벤더는 침입종 목록에 없으며 나비, 벌, 그리고 다른 야생동물들이 그 꽃을 좋아하기 때문에 계속 자라게 두었습니다.

레베카 올턴

어휘 shortly 곧 resource 자료, 자원 educational 교육의 lecture 강의 ambitious 야심 있는 acre 에이커(면적 단위) various 다양한 cultivate 경작하다 so far 지금까지 privilege 영광, 특권 value 소중하게 생각하다 admit 인정하다 bush 덤불 property 부동산 invasive-species 침입종 wildlife 야생동물 bloom 꽃

---

https://www.alamitobotanicalsociety.org/education/lectures

알라미토 식물학회의 지도자들과 회원들은 마르파 커뮤니티 칼리지의 원예학과에서 열리는 교육 강연에 일반 시민 여러분을 정중히 초대합니다. 189 **모든 강연은 매달 세 번째 수요일 저녁 7시에 열립니다.** 사전 등록은 필요하지 않습니다.

2월: 샐러드 일정 짜기 - 채소 심기 일정을 세우고 재배할 맛있는 채소를 선택하기 위한 조언을 얻으세요.

3월: 190 **이웃에 영양 공급하기 - 우리 지역에 자생하는 식물을 이용하여 야생동물에게 매력적인 조경을 하는 방법을 배우세요.**

4월: 해충 방지 - 유해한 곤충이 당신의 과일과 채소를 먹는 것을 방지할 수 있는 천연 무농약 기법을 배우세요.

5월: 꽃가루 옮기기 - 당신의 정원을 찾는 나비나 벌이 없나요? 걱정 마세요. 사람이 간단한 기법을 사용하여 특정 식물을 수분할 수 있어요.

어휘 cordially 정중하게 horticultural 원예의 occur 발생하다 advance 사전의 registration 등록 establish 세우다, 수립하다 nourish 영양분을 공급하다 neighbor 이웃 inviting 매력적인 pest 해충 deterrence 방지 pesticide-free 무농약의 prevent 막다 harmful 유해한 insect 곤충 pollen 꽃가루 pollinate 수분하다

---

186 Not / True

번역 공지에서 고저스 가든 투어에 대해 언급된 것은?
(A) 연못이 있는 정원에 중점을 둘 것이다.
(B) 입장권 판매 수익은 나무 심기에 쓰일 것이다.
(C) 주요 방문지 중 한 곳은 카운티 공원에 있을 것이다.
(D) 5월에 열릴 것이다.

해설 공지의 두 번째 단락 두 번째 문장에서 올해 투어의 입장권 판매에서 나오는 모든 수익금은 프레시디오 카운티 공원의 미루나무 숲에 식물을 새로 심는 데 사용될 예정(All proceeds from ticket sales for this year's tour will go toward replanting the cottonwood forest in Presidio County Park)이라고 했으므로 (B)가 정답이다.

어휘 pond 연못 featured 주요한 take place 열리다

Paraphrasing
지문의 proceeds → 정답의 Profits

187 Not / True

번역 올턴 씨가 이메일에서 언급한 것은?
(A) 알라미토 식물학회에 가입하기를 원한다.
(B) 오락 공간에 필요한 땅을 기부할 계획이다.
(C) 식물에 대한 관심을 공유하는 사람들을 만나고 싶어 한다.
(D) 투어 입장권을 사고 싶어 하는 사람들을 알고 있다.

해설 이메일의 두 번째 단락 첫 문장에서 올턴 씨가 자신의 작업을 사람들에게 보여주고 학회 회원들과 마찬가지로 정원을 소중히 여기는 사람들을 더 많이 만나는 것은 큰 영광일 것(It would be a privilege to show my work to the public and to meet more people who value gardens as we members of the society do)이라며 자신과 같이 정원에 관심 있는 사람들을 만나고 싶다는 것을 언급하고 있으므로 (C)가 정답이다.

어휘 donate 기부하다 recreation 오락

188 연계

번역 올턴 씨의 정원이 투어 방문지로 선정되지 못하게 될 것 같은 이유는?
(A) 다른 지역에서 온 식물이 있다.
(B) 크기 요건을 충족하지 못한다.
(C) 꽃보다는 나무를 특징으로 한다.
(D) 투어 지역 외부에 있다.

해설 공지의 세 번째 단락 세 번째 문장에서 투어에 참여하도록 선정된 정원은 프레시디오 카운티 내에 위치해야 하며 지역 자생 식물만 있어야 한다(Gardens selected to participate in the tour must be within Presidio County and include only plants native to the region)고 했고, 이메일의 두 번째 단락 세 번째 문장에서 올턴 씨는 이 지역의 자생 식물이 아닌 아름다운 라벤더 덤불이 자신이 이곳을 구입하기 전에 이미 부지에서 자라고 있었음을 인정해야겠다(I must admit that beautiful lavender bushes that are not native to the area were already growing on the property before I purchased it)면서 하

지만 라벤더는 침입종 목록에 없으며 나비, 벌, 그리고 다른 야생동물들이 그 꽃을 좋아하기 때문에 계속 자라게 두었다(However, lavender is not on the invasive-species list, and I continue to let them grow because the butterflies, bees, and other wildlife love the blooms)고 했다. 따라서 올턴 씨의 정원에는 지역 자생 식물이 아닌 라벤더가 자라고 있어 투어 방문지 선정 조건에 부합되지 않는다는 것을 알 수 있으므로 (A)가 정답이다.

어휘 meet 충족하다 requirement 요건 feature 특징으로 하다

> **Paraphrasing**
> 지문의 lavender bushes that are not native to the area
> → 정답의 a plant that comes from another region

189 추론 / 암시

번역 웹페이지에서 강연에 대해 암시된 것은?
(A) 알라미토 식물학회 회원 전용이다.
(B) 인쇄된 초대장이 필요하다.
(C) 매달 개최된다.
(D) 다양한 장소에서 제공된다.

해설 웹페이지의 첫 단락 두 번째 문장에서 모든 강연은 매달 세 번째 수요일 저녁 7시에 열린다(All lectures occur on the third Wednesday of the month at 7:00 P.M.)고 공지한 것을 통해 강연이 매달 열리고 있음을 알 수 있다. 따라서 (C)가 정답이다.

어휘 invitation 초대장

> **Paraphrasing**
> 지문의 occur on the third Wednesday of the month
> → 정답의 take place every month

190 연계

번역 올턴 씨가 가장 관심 있을 것 같은 강연은?
(A) 샐러드 일정 짜기
(B) 이웃에 영양 공급하기
(C) 해충 방지
(D) 꽃가루 옮기기

해설 이메일의 첫 단락 두 번째 문장에서 올턴 씨가 자신의 5에이커짜리 땅을 새와 다른 동물들을 끌어들일 만한 다양한 자생 식물로 채운다는 야심 찬 프로젝트(my ambitious project: to cover five acres of my land with various native plants that will attract birds and other animals)에 대해 언급하고 있고, 웹페이지 하단의 강의 목록 두 번째에서 이웃에 영양 공급하기(Nourish the Neighbors)라는 강연에서 우리 지역에 자생하는 식물을 이용하여 야생동물에게 매력적인 조경을 하는 방법을 배운다(Understand how to use plants native to our region to create landscapes that are inviting to wildlife)고 나와 있다. 따라서 올턴 씨는 이웃에 영양 공급하기 강연에 관심이 있을 것임을 알 수 있으므로 (B)가 정답이다.

191-195 광고 + 이메일 + 이메일

토지 소유주들을 위한 기회

191 테라 존츠는 자연 속 하이킹, 농장 민박, 캠핑 여행, 체육 대회 및 기타 기업 수련회를 위한 활동들을 기획합니다. 우리는 행선지 목록을 늘리는 데 도움을 줄 농장 주인과 목장 주인, 그 밖의 토지 소유주를 찾고 있습니다. 테라 존츠는 파트너들에게 주간 부지 사용 대가로 하루 최대 300달러를 지불하며 필요한 모든 또는 대부분의 장비를 제공합니다.

필요한 기준은 다음과 같습니다.

1. **192** 부지는 중대형 도시에서 100km 이내에 있다.
2. 부지에서 매달 하루 또는 이틀간 수련회를 주최할 수 있다.
3. 부지는 승용차 50대 또는 버스 2대를 위한 충분한 주차 공간이 있다.
4. 부지는 최대 75명을 수용할 수 있다.

어휘 opportunity 기회 landowner 토지 소유주 hike 하이킹 athletic 체육의 competition 대회 retreat 수련회 rancher 목장 주인 expand 확장하다 destination 목적지 property 부지 criteria 기준 site 부지, 용지 medium 중간의 adequate 충분한 accommodate 수용하다

수신: 셀리아 뉴섬 〈cnewsom@pinkridgeranch.com〉
발신: 올리버 정 〈ojeong@terrajaunts.com〉
날짜: 4월 19일
제목: 귀하의 신청

뉴섬 씨,

호스트가 되려고 신청해 주셔서 감사합니다. **192** 핑크 리지 목장은 저희가 보통 요구하는 것보다 차량을 위한 공간이 좁기는 하지만, 25명 미만의 소규모 행사에 적합할 것 같습니다. **193** 귀하의 부지에서 야생으로 자라고 있는 모든 자생 꽃과 나무의 삽화 목록을 만들어 주신 점에 감사드리며, 저희 호스트 중 이 같은 것을 제공해 주신 분은 없습니다. 귀하의 식물 목록은 종의 식별 관련 활동에 참여하는 단체들에게 진정한 자산이 될 것입니다.

195 저는 이번 주나 다음 주 중에 저의 동료인 피터 컴벌랜드와 함께 부지 방문을 계획하고 싶습니다. 목요일 또는 금요일 오후 1시 이후가 저희에게 가장 좋긴 하지만, 오전이나 다른 날을 선호하신다면 귀하의 일정에 맞추도록 해보겠습니다.

올리버 정
몬타나 부지 담당자

어휘 application 신청 host (손님을 초대한) 호스트, 주인 normally 보통 ranch 목장 suitable 적합한 appreciate 감사하다 illustrated 삽화를 넣은 native 자생의 asset 자산 engaged in ~에 참여하는 involve 포함하다 identification 식별 species 종 associate 동료

수신: 올리버 정 <ojeong@terrajaunts.com>
발신: 셀리아 뉴섬 <cnewsom@pinkridgeranch.com>
날짜: 5월 1일
제목: 회신: 귀하의 신청

정 씨께:

목요일에 저의 목장을 둘러봐 주셔서 감사합니다. 194 **귀하의 GPS 앱이 작동을 멈추고 나서 저의 복잡한 서면 주행 안내를 따라 목장까지 오가실 수 있어서 다행입니다.** 두 분을 만나 뵙고 구경시켜 드릴 기회를 갖게 되어 무척 좋았습니다.

어제 귀하의 후속 음성 메시지를 받았습니다. 좀 더 숙고한 끝에, 저는 결국 이 기회를 좇지 않기로 결정했습니다. 195 **귀하의 동료께서 지적하신 것처럼 저의 부지에 있는 등산로는 풀이 꽤 무성한 상태입니다.** 유감스럽게도 저에게는 일 년 내내 모든 것이 제대로 손질되도록 할 시간이나 직원이 없습니다. 상황이 바뀐다면 다시 신청하겠습니다.

셀리아 뉴섬, 핑크 리지 목장 주인

어휘 complicated 복잡한 directions 길 안내 follow-up 후속 조치 consideration 고려 pursue 좇다, 추구하다 overgrown (풀 등이) 무성한 properly 제대로 groom 손질하다 situation 상황 reapply 재신청하다

191 Not / True

번역 광고에서 테라 존츠에 대해 언급하는 것은?
(A) 75명을 고용하고 있다.
(B) 기업 고객을 위한 팀워크 구축 여행을 주선한다.
(C) 자사 직원들을 위한 월례 연수를 주최한다.
(D) 버스 회사 두 곳과 서비스 계약을 맺고 있다.

해설 광고의 첫 단락 첫 문장에서 테라 존츠는 자연 속 하이킹, 농장 민박, 캠핑 여행, 체육 대회 및 기타 기업 수련회를 위한 활동들을 기획한다(Terra Jaunts organizes nature hikes, farm stays, camping trips, athletic competitions, and other activities for company retreats)고 했으므로 고객사 직원들의 팀워크를 위한 수련회를 주선한다는 것을 확인할 수 있다. 따라서 (B)가 정답이다.

어휘 employ 고용하다 team-building 팀워크 구축 corporate 기업의

Paraphrasing
지문의 company retreats
→ 정답의 team-building trips for corporate clients

192 연계

번역 핑크 리지 목장에 대해 결론지을 수 있는 것은?
(A) 믿을 만한 무선 네트워크를 갖추고 있다.
(B) 대형 온실을 여러 개 갖고 있다.
(C) 등산객 단체를 유치하여 300달러를 벌었다.
(D) 도시 지역에서 100km 이내에 위치해 있다.

해설 광고의 하단에 나열된 필요한 기준의 첫 항목에서 부지는 중대형 도시에서 100km 이내에 있다(The site is located within 100 kilometers of a medium to large city)는 것을 요건으로 명시하고 있고, 첫 번째 이메일의 첫 단락 두 번째 문장에서 핑크 리지 목장은 차량을 위한 공간이 좁기는 하지만 25명 미만의 소규모 행사에 적합할 것 같다(Even though you have less space for vehicles than we normally require, Pink Ridge Ranch might be suitable for our smaller events with fewer than 25 people)고 언급하고 있다. 따라서 핑크 리지 목장은 도시에서 100km 이내에 있어야 한다는 조건을 충족한다는 것을 알 수 있으므로 (D)가 정답이다.

어휘 reliable 믿을 만한 greenhouse 온실 urban 도시의

193 세부 사항

번역 정 씨에 따르면, 뉴섬 씨를 다른 부지 소유주들과 구별 짓는 점은?
(A) 식물에 대해 제공하는 정보
(B) 재배할 수 있는 꽃의 다양함
(C) 유연한 일정
(D) 예술에 대한 관심

해설 첫 번째 이메일의 첫 단락 세 번째 문장에서 부지에서 야생으로 자라고 있는 모든 자생 꽃과 나무의 삽화 목록을 만들어 준 점에 감사하며, 호스트 중 이 같은 것을 제공해 준 사람은 없다(We appreciate your having created an illustrated list of all the native flowers and trees growing wild on your property; none of our other hosts offers anything like this)고 했다. 따라서 뉴섬 씨가 부지에서 자라는 식물에 대한 자료를 제공한 점이 여타 호스트들과 다르다는 것을 알 수 있으므로 (A)가 정답이다.

어휘 distinguish 구별하다 variety 다양성 flexible 유연한

194 추론 / 암시

번역 핑크 리지 목장에 대해 암시된 것은?
(A) 출입하는 데 입장 코드가 필요하다.
(B) 최근에 소유주가 바뀌었다.
(C) 찾기 어려울 수 있다.
(D) 인기 있는 등산 행선지이다.

해설 두 번째 이메일의 첫 단락 두 번째 문장에서 귀하의 GPS 앱이 작동을 멈추고 나서 복잡한 서면 주행 안내를 따라 목장까지 오갈 수 있어서 다행이다(I am glad you were able to follow my complicated written directions for driving to and from the ranch after your GPS app stopped working)라고 한 것으로 보아 핑크 리지 목장은 가는 길이 복잡하다는 것을 짐작할 수 있다. 따라서 (C)가 정답이다.

어휘 access 입장 ownership 소유(권)

Paraphrasing
지문의 complicated written directions
→ 정답의 difficult to find

195 연계

번역 컴벌랜드 씨에 대해 사실인 것 같은 것은?
(A) 금요일에는 근무하지 않는다.
(B) 일부 등산로에 대해 우려를 표했다.
(C) 몬타나에 유기농 농장을 소유하고 있다.
(D) 4월 22일에 뉴섬 씨에게 음성 메시지를 남겼다.

해설 첫 번째 이메일의 두 번째 단락 첫 문장에서 정 씨가 이번 주나 다음 주 중에 자신의 동료인 피터 컴벌랜드와 함께 부지 방문을 계획하고 싶다(I would like to arrange a site visit with my associate Peter Cumberland either this week or next)고 했고, 두 번째 이메일의 두 번째 단락 세 번째 문장에서 뉴섬 씨가 정 씨의 동료가 지적한 것처럼 자신의 부지에 있는 등산로는 풀이 꽤 무성한 상태(The hiking paths on my property are quite overgrown, as your partner pointed out)라고 했다. 따라서 정 씨의 동료인 컴벌랜드 씨가 뉴섬 씨의 등산로 상태에 대해 우려를 나타냈음을 알 수 있으므로 (B)가 정답이다.

어휘 express 표현하다 concern 우려 trail 등산로, 산길 own 소유하다

Paraphrasing
지문의 hiking paths → 정답의 trails

196-200 이메일 + 일정표 + 이메일

수신: 부서 관리자들 〈managementteam@a-qualityelectronics.com〉
발신: 아일린 렌 〈ewrenn@a-qualityelectronics.com〉
날짜: 10월 7일
제목: 다가오는 켄지 다나카 씨의 방문
첨부: 📎 일정 초안

좋은 아침입니다,

할링턴 씨가 저에게 모든 부서 관리자들에게 우리 일본 자회사 가나자와 전자의 최고운영책임자인 켄지 다나카 씨가 다음 주 기업의 본사를 방문할 예정임을 알리라고 요청하셨습니다. 제가 적절한 준비를 할 수 있도록 **197, 199** 10월 14일에 있을 오후 회의와 저녁 식사에 참석이 가능한지를 가능한 한 빨리 알려 주십시오.

이 이메일에 일정 초안이 첨부되어 있습니다. 다나카 씨는 할링턴 씨가 지난 분기에 우리 기업 문화에 새로운 활기를 불어넣기 위한 노력의 일환으로 작성한 귀빈 방문자 시간표를 따르게 됩니다.

196 부서별 보고는 할링턴 씨와 다나카 씨의 발표가 각각 끝난 뒤 오후 3시 정시에 시작됩니다. 부서 관리자들이 현황 보고에서 발표할 정보에 대한 세부 사항은 곧 공지될 예정입니다.

아일린 렌, 임원 비서

어휘 draft 초안 chief operating officer 최고운영책임자 subsidiary 자회사 corporate 기업의 headquarters 본사 appropriate 적절한 arrangement 준비 attach 첨부하다 distinguished visitor 귀빈, 주요 방문자 reinvigorate 새로운 활기를 불어넣다 promptly 정시에 respectively 각각 details 세부 사항 status 상황 executive 임원

일정표 초안
196 A-퀄리티 전자 분기 회의
10월 14일 월요일

시간	대상	내용
오후 12시 - 1시	전 직원	출장 요리 점심 식사
196 오후 1시 - 2시	사장	회사 목표 및 성과 목표에 대한 논의, 공동 프로젝트의 현황
196 오후 2시 - 3시	귀빈	가나자와 전자 관련 업데이트: **198** 자회사의 3분기 운영 성공 사례 및 직면 과제
오후 3시 - 5시	부서 관리자들	부서별 보고: 안건 추후 결정
200 오후 6시 - 9시	전 직원	메이플턴 시내에 있는 메이플턴 그릴에서 저녁 식사

어휘 quarterly 분기별의 performance 성과 objective 목표 joint 공동의 operational 운영의 challenge 과제 face 직면하다 quarter 분기 departmental 부서의 agenda 안건 determine 결정하다

수신: 아일린 렌 〈ewrenn@a-qualityelectronics.com〉
발신: 데보라 파월 〈dpowell@a-qualityelectronics.com〉
날짜: 10월 7일
제목: 회신: 다가오는 켄지 다나카 씨의 방문

안녕하세요, 아일린

199 저는 켄지 다나카 씨와의 회의에 참석이 가능함을 확인해 드립니다. 저는 3분기 동안 마케팅 팀의 활동에 관해 임원들에게 업데이트를 해 드릴 계획입니다.

질문: 다나카 씨가 저녁 식사 후에 야구 경기를 보러 가고 싶어 할까요? 그는 7월에 2분기 회의에 참석한 후 메이플턴 오스프레이스의 경기를 즐겁게 관람했습니다.

200 한 가지 문제는 10월에는 모든 경기가 저녁 8시에 시작해서, 저녁 식사를 오후 5시경에는 시작해야 한다는 것입니다. 그러면 경기가 시작하기 전에 경기장에 도착할 시간이 충분할 것입니다. 이 요청이 과하다는 점은 알지만, 우리 귀빈이 오스프레이스 경기를 얼마나 즐겼는지와 그가 회사에 얼마나 중요한지를 감안하면 고려해 볼 가치가 있다고 생각합니다.

그가 방문하기 전에 표를 확보할 수 있도록 어떻게 생각하시는지 알려주십시오. 감사합니다!

데보라 파월

어휘 availability 가능성 stadium 경기장 worth 가치가 있는 secure 확보하다

196 연계

번역 할링턴 씨는 누구인 것 같은가?
(A) 가나자와 전자의 창립자
(B) A-퀄리티 전자의 사장
(C) 부서 관리자
(D) 임원 비서

해설 첫 번째 이메일의 세 번째 단락 첫 문장에서 부서별 보고는 할링턴 씨와 다나카 씨의 발표가 각각 끝난 뒤 오후 3시 정시에 시작된다(Departmental reports will begin promptly at 3:00 P.M., following the presentations by Mr. Harlington and Mr. Tanaka, respectively)고 했고, A-퀄리티 전자 분기 회의(A-Quality Electronics Quarterly Meeting) 일정표 중반부에서 오후 3시에 부서별 보고가 시작되기 전 일정이 오후 1시에서 2시에 사장(1:00-2 00 P.M., President), 오후 2시에서 3시에 귀빈(2:00-3:00 P.M., Distinguished visitor) 연설로 나와 있다. 따라서 할링턴 씨는 오후 1시에서 2시에 연설하기로 되어 있는 A-퀄리티 전자의 사장임을 알 수 있으므로 (B)가 정답이다.

어휘 founder 창립자

197 세부 사항

번역 첫 번째 이메일에 따르면, 관리자들이 가능한 한 빨리 해야 할 일은?
(A) 일정표에 대한 의견 제공
(B) 회의를 위한 발표 준비
(C) 점심 식사 날짜 비워두기
(D) 회의 참석 가능성 알리기

해설 첫 번째 이메일의 첫 단락 두 번째 문장에서 부서 관리자들에게 10월 14일에 있을 오후 회의와 저녁 식사에 참석이 가능한지를 가능한 한 빨리 알려 달라(Please let me know as soon as possible whether you will be able to attend the afternoon meeting and dinner on October 14)고 했으므로 (D)가 정답이다.

Paraphrasing
지문의 whether you w ll be able to attend the afternoon meeting → 정답의 availability for a meeting

198 세부 사항

번역 일정표에 따르면, 3분기에 발생한 일은?
(A) 신규 프로젝트가 수익성이 있었다.
(B) 기업 목표가 변경되었다.
(C) 자회사가 몇몇 어려움에 직면했다.
(D) 새로운 운영 직원들이 채용되었다.

해설 일정표의 중반부에서 자회사의 3분기 운영 성공 사례 및 직면 과제(operational successes and challenges faced by the subsidiary in the third quarter)라는 안건 설명을 통해 3분기 동안 자회사가 몇 가지 어려움에 부딪쳤음을 알 수 있다. 따라서 (C)가 정답이다.

어휘 profitable 수익성이 있는

Paraphrasing
지문의 challenges → 정답의 difficulties

199 연계

번역 파월 씨가 10월 14일에 무엇을 할 것 같은가?
(A) 다른 관리자들과 함께 보고서를 발표한다.
(B) 마케팅 부서의 목표를 논의한다.
(C) 야구 경기 표를 구매한다.
(D) 다나카 씨를 점심 식사에 데려간다.

해설 첫 번째 이메일의 첫 단락 두 번째 문장에서 부서 관리자들에게 10월 14일에 있을 오후 회의와 저녁 식사에 참석이 가능한지를 가능한 한 빨리 알려 달라(Please let me know as soon as possible whether you will be able to attend the afternoon meeting and dinner on October 14)고 했고, 두 번째 이메일의 첫 단락 첫 문장에서 파월 씨가 켄지 다나카 씨와의 회의에 참석이 가능함을 확인해 준다(I'm confirming my availability for the meeting with Kenji Tanaka)면서 3분기 동안 마케팅 팀의 활동에 관해 임원들에게 업데이트할 계획(I plan to update the executives on the marketing team's activities for the third quarter)이라고 했다. 따라서 파월 씨는 10월 14일 회의에서 다른 부서 관리자들과 함께 임원 보고를 할 예정임을 알 수 있으므로 (A)가 정답이다.

어휘 deliver (의견 등을) 말하다

200 연계

번역 파월 씨가 요청하는 것은?
(A) 회의 날짜 변경
(B) 다나카 씨에게 마지막 연설 요청
(C) 식사 시간 변경
(D) 경기장에 갈 교통편 마련

해설 두 번째 이메일의 세 번째 단락 첫 문장에서 파월 씨가 한 가지 문제는 10월에는 모든 경기가 저녁 8시에 시작해서 저녁 식사를 오후 5시경에는 시작해야 한다는 것(The only problem is that all games in October begin at 8:00 P.M., so we would need to begin dinner at around 5:00 P.M.)이라고 했고, 일정표의 하단에 오후 6시에 저녁 식사가 예정되어 있다(6:00-9:00 P.M., Dinner at Mapleton Grill, downtown Mapleton)고 되어 있다. 따라서 파월 씨는 경기 시간에 맞춰 저녁 식사 시간을 옮겨달라고 요청하고 있으므로 (C)가 정답이다.

어휘 transportation 교통편

기출 TEST 7

동영상 강의

101 (A)	102 (B)	103 (B)	104 (A)	105 (D)
106 (D)	107 (A)	108 (B)	109 (A)	110 (B)
111 (A)	112 (D)	113 (C)	114 (D)	115 (B)
116 (A)	117 (C)	118 (D)	119 (C)	120 (C)
121 (D)	122 (B)	123 (A)	124 (A)	125 (B)
126 (C)	127 (D)	128 (D)	129 (A)	130 (B)
131 (C)	132 (A)	133 (C)	134 (B)	135 (B)
136 (A)	137 (C)	138 (D)	139 (D)	140 (B)
141 (B)	142 (C)	143 (B)	144 (D)	145 (A)
146 (C)	147 (A)	148 (B)	149 (A)	150 (B)
151 (B)	152 (A)	153 (C)	154 (A)	155 (C)
156 (D)	157 (B)	158 (C)	159 (C)	160 (A)
161 (B)	162 (C)	163 (D)	164 (C)	165 (D)
166 (C)	167 (B)	168 (D)	169 (C)	170 (C)
171 (D)	172 (A)	173 (B)	174 (D)	175 (B)
176 (B)	177 (D)	178 (C)	179 (D)	180 (A)
181 (C)	182 (D)	183 (D)	184 (B)	185 (A)
186 (B)	187 (C)	188 (D)	189 (D)	190 (D)
191 (C)	192 (A)	193 (B)	194 (D)	195 (B)
196 (A)	197 (D)	198 (C)	199 (A)	200 (D)

PART 5

101 인칭대명사의 격 _ 소유격

해설 빈칸에는 뒤에 온 명사 presentation을 수식하는 인칭대명사가 들어가야 한다. 따라서 명사 앞에 쓰여 한정사 역할을 할 수 있는 소유격 인칭대명사 (A) her가 정답이다.

번역 청중들은 타키도 씨가 발표를 마친 후에 질문을 하도록 허락될 것이다.

어휘 audience 청중   permit 허락하다

102 명사 어휘

해설 형용사 free와 전치사구 with every meal의 수식을 받아, 카페에서 식사와 함께 무료로 제공될 수 있는 품목을 골라야 한다. '모든 식사에 무료 음료를 제공한다'라는 의미가 되어야 자연스러우므로 '음료'를 의미하는 (B) drink가 정답이다. (A) table은 '탁자', (C) price는 '가격', (D) menu는 '메뉴'라는 의미이다.

번역 마이크의 카페는 매주 화요일 오전 11시부터 오후 7시까지 모든 식사에 무료 음료를 제공한다.

103 to부정사 _ 동사의 목적어

해설 빈칸은 동사 prefers의 목적어 자리이다. prefer는 to부정사와 동명사 둘 다 목적어로 취할 수 있으나 문맥상 '기차로 출퇴근하는 것을 선호한다'는 평소 습관을 나타내는 내용이므로 (B) to commute가 정답이다. (C) having commuted는 완료형 동명사로 '이미 출근을 마친 것'을 뜻하므로 문맥상 어울리지 않고, (A) commute는 동사/명사이지만 명사일 때 '통근 거리'라는 뜻으로 의미상 적합하지 않으며, (D) is commuting은 동사이므로 빈칸에 들어갈 수 없다.

번역 오자와 씨는 일반적으로 자동차 대신 기차로 출퇴근하는 것을 선호한다.

어휘 generally 일반적으로   commute 출퇴근하다

104 접속사 자리 _ 부사절 접속사

해설 빈칸은 두 개의 완전한 절을 이어주는 접속사 자리이다. 따라서 보기 중에 유일한 접속사로 '~ 때문에'를 뜻하는 (A) Because가 정답이다. (B) Having은 동명사/현재분사, (C) Usually는 부사, (D) Following은 형용사/명사/전치사이므로 절을 연결할 수 없다.

번역 새로운 지점에 인력이 부족했기 때문에 더 많은 직원이 채용되었다.

어휘 branch office 지점   understaffed 인력이 부족한

105 형용사 자리 _ 주격 보어

해설 빈칸은 주어 Dumbbells를 보충 설명하는 주격 보어 자리이고, for keeping fit at home과 결합하여 '집에서 운동하는 데 유용하다'는 의미가 되어야 자연스러우므로 '유용한'이라는 뜻의 형용사 (D) useful이 정답이다. (A) use는 명사로 보어 자리에 들어갈 수 있지만 주어와 동격 관계를 이루지 않으므로 적합하지 않고, (B) using과 (C) to use 또한 be동사 뒤에 올 수는 있지만 능동 형태이므로 목적어가 필요하다.

번역 프리 웨이트라고도 알려진 덤벨은 집에서 운동하는 데 유용하다.

어휘 dumbbell 덤벨   keep fit 건강을 유지하다

106 부사 어휘

해설 동사구 was finished를 수식하여 적절한 문맥을 완성하는 부사를 고르는 문제이다. '예정 완료일은 9월 4일이었지만 실제로 그보다 앞서 끝났다'는 내용이 되어야 자연스러우므로 '실제로'를 뜻하는 (D) actually가 정답이다. (A) additionally는 '추가적으로', (B) rarely는 '드물게', (C) extremely는 '극도로'라는 의미로 문맥상 적절하지 않다.

번역 예정 완료일은 9월 4일이었지만 작업은 실제로 일정보다 2주 앞서 끝났다.

어휘 completion 완료   ahead of schedule 일정보다 앞서

107 명사 자리 _ 전치사의 목적어

해설 빈칸은 전치사 on의 목적어 자리이고 앞에 정관사 the가 있으므

로 명사가 들어가야 한다. 명사 보기인 (A) link(링크)와 (B) linker (연결하는 사람 또는 기계), (D) linkage(관련성) 중에서 인터넷 상에서 '아래의 링크를 클릭하라'는 의미가 되어야 자연스러우므로 (A) link가 정답이다. (C) linking은 동명사/현재분사로 빈칸에 들어갈 수 없다.

번역 아래의 링크를 클릭하여 저희 월간 소식지를 구독하세요.

어휘 subscribe to ~을 구독하다

108 형용사 어휘

해설 명사 understanding을 수식해 신입(entry-level) 직책 지원자에게 요구되는 이해 수준을 나타내기에 적절한 형용사가 들어가야 한다. 따라서 '기본적인'을 뜻하는 (B) basic이 정답이다. (A) proud는 '자랑스러운', (C) short는 '짧은', (D) considerate는 '사려 깊은'이라는 뜻으로 문맥상 어울리지 않는다.

번역 신입 마케팅 직책 지원자들은 소비자 행동에 대한 기본적인 이해가 있어야 한다.

어휘 candidate 지원자 entry-level (직업에서) 신입인, 말단의 consumer 소비자 behavior 행동

109 부사 자리 _ to부정사 수식

해설 빈칸은 형용사 able 뒤에 오는 to부정사 to respond를 수식하는 자리이고, respond는 자동사이므로 목적어를 취하지 않는다. '곧바로 답변할 수 있었다'는 의미가 되어야 자연스러우므로 '곧바로, 직접'을 뜻하는 부사 (A) directly(곧바로, 직접)가 정답이다. (B) direct는 형용사, (C) directions는 명사, (D) directed는 동사/과거분사이므로 빈칸에 들어갈 수 없다.

번역 퍼슨 씨는 자금 조달 계획에 대한 우려에 대해 정부 지도자들에게 곧바로 답변할 수 있었다.

어휘 concern 우려 funding 자금 조달

110 전치사 어휘

해설 빈칸 뒤에 특정 시점을 나타내는 명사구 the age of five가 있고, 문맥상 '다섯 살의 나이에'라는 의미가 되어야 자연스러우므로 '~에'를 뜻하는 시점 전치사 (B) at이 정답이다. (A) on(~에)은 날짜나 요일과 함께 쓰이고, (C) with는 '~와 함께', (D) along은 '~을 따라'라는 뜻으로 의미상 적합하지 않다.

번역 오늘 밤 공연의 특별 솔로 연주자인 리 에인슬리는 다섯 살의 나이에 바이올린 레슨을 받기 시작했다.

어휘 featured 주연의 soloist 독주자 performance 공연

111 부정대명사

해설 빈칸은 동사 must choose의 목적어 자리이다. 앞에서 언급된 명사 candidates의 반복을 피하고, only의 수식을 받아 '오직 한 후보자만 선택해야 한다'는 내용이 되어야 자연스러우므로 '하나'라는 뜻의 (A) one이 정답이다. (B) either는 '(둘 중) 하나', (C) such는 '그러한 것, 그러한 사람'이라는 뜻으로 문맥상 적합하지 않고, (D) other는 형용사로 단독으로는 목적어 역할을 할 수 없다.

번역 관리직 후보자 7명 중에서 채용 위원회는 오직 한 사람만 선택해야 한다.

어휘 committee 위원회

112 부사 어휘

해설 to부정사 to find를 수식하여 자연스러운 문맥을 이루는 부사를 골라야 한다. '다른 곳에서는 찾기 어려운 독특한 제품'이라는 의미가 되어야 적절하므로 '다른 곳에서'라는 뜻의 (D) elsewhere가 정답이다. (A) aside는 '한쪽으로', (B) instead는 '대신에', (C) likewise는 '마찬가지로'라는 의미이다.

번역 GT 인터내셔널 푸드는 다른 곳에서는 찾기 어려운 독특한 제품을 판매한다.

113 접속사 자리 _ 부사절 접속사

해설 빈칸은 주어가 없는 명령문에 빈칸 뒤의 완전한 절을 연결하는 자리이므로 부사절 접속사가 들어가야 한다. 따라서 '만약 ~이라면'을 뜻하는 부사절 접속사 (C) if가 정답이다. (A) moreover(게다가)는 부사, (B) besides(~ 외에, 그 밖에)는 전치사/부사, (D) also(또한)는 부사이므로 절을 연결할 수 없다.

번역 일일 리넨 서비스를 받기 원하시면 호텔 본관 사무실로 연락해 주세요.

114 동사 어휘

해설 빈칸 뒤의 yourself를 목적어로 취하고 전치사 with와 자연스럽게 연결될 수 있는 동사를 골라야 한다. '스스로를 회사의 교육비 환급 정책에 익숙하게 하라'는 의미가 되어야 하므로 familiarize oneself with의 형태로 주로 쓰이는 '~에 익숙하게 하다'라는 뜻의 (D) familiarize가 정답이다. (A) organize는 '정리하다', (B) identify는 '식별하다', (C) consider는 '고려하다'라는 의미이다.

번역 모든 수업에 등록하기 전에 회사의 교육비 환급 정책을 숙지해 주세요.

어휘 tuition 수업료 reimbursement 환급 enroll in ~에 등록하다

115 부사 자리 _ 동사 수식

해설 현재진행 수동태 동사구 is being evaluated 사이에서 동사를 수식하는 부사 자리이므로, '적극적으로'를 뜻하는 부사 (B) actively가 정답이다. (A) active는 형용사, (C) activity는 명사, (D) activate는 동사이므로 품사상 빈칸에 들어갈 수 없다.

번역 제안된 구매 계약은 코를란 테크의 관계자들에 의해 적극적으로 검토되고 있다.

어휘 proposed 제안된 agreement 계약 evaluate 평가하다 official 관계자, 임원

116 형용사 어휘

해설 Another와 함께 명사 option을 수식하여 자연스러운 문맥을 완성하는 형용사를 골라야 한다. 국제선 터미널 지하철역 완공 이후 얻게 되는 이점에 대한 문장이므로 '공항으로 가는 편리한 옵션'이라는 의미가 되어야 적절하다. 따라서 '편리한'을 뜻하는 (A) convenient가 정답이다. (B) receptive는 '수용적인', (C) fortunate은 '운이 좋은', (D) traditional은 '전통적인'이라는 의미이다.

번역 국제선 터미널의 지하철역이 완공되면 공항으로 가는 또 하나의 편리한 옵션이 이용 가능할 것이다.

117 동사 어형 _ 시제

해설 빈칸은 주어 the ceremony의 동사 자리로, 조건 또는 근거를 나타내는 과거분사구 Given the forecast for rain on Saturday에서 향후 일기 예보를 근거로 제시하고 있으므로 '실내에서 열릴 것이다'라는 미래에 대한 내용이 되어야 적절하다. 따라서 미래 시제 (C) will be held가 정답이다.

번역 토요일에 비가 내린다는 예보를 고려하여 기념식은 라힌 갤러리 실내에서 열릴 예정이다.

어휘 given ~을 고려할 때 ceremony 의식 indoors 실내에서

118 전치사 어휘

해설 빈칸 뒤의 명사 the old warehouse를 목적어로 취해 '오래된 창고 뒤에 쌓여 있다'는 의미가 되어야 자연스러우므로 '~ 뒤에'를 뜻하는 (D) behind가 정답이다. (A) between은 '(둘) 사이에'라는 뜻으로 뒤에 복수 명사가 와야 하고, (B) across는 '~을 가로질러', (C) over는 '~ 위에'라는 의미로 문맥상 적합하지 않다.

번역 르자예프 씨께서 요청하신 대로 여분의 나무 운반대는 오래된 창고 뒤에 쌓여 있습니다.

어휘 pallet 화물 운반대 stack 쌓다

119 형용사 자리 _ 명사 수식

해설 빈칸 앞에 부정관사 a, 뒤에 명사 range(범위)가 있으므로 명사를 수식하는 형용사 자리이다. '다양한 범위의 주제'라는 의미를 나타내야 하므로 '다양한'이라는 뜻의 형용사 (C) diverse가 정답이다. (A) diversion(전환)은 range와 복합명사를 이루기에 부적절하고, (B) diversely는 부사, (D) diversify는 동사이므로 품사상 답이 될 수 없다.

번역 맥나마라 교수는 다양한 주제에 대한 책을 출판해 왔다.

120 명사 어휘

해설 빈칸은 동사 was의 주어 역할을 하는 명사 자리로, 주격 보어 자리의 명사절인 프로젝트가 실패한 이유(why the software development project failed)와 동격 관계를 이루려면 '명확한 이정표의 결여'라는 의미가 되어야 적절하다. 따라서 '결여, 부족'을 뜻하는 (C) lack이 정답이다. (A) consent는 '동의', (B) break는 '휴식', (D) complex는 '집합체'라는 의미이다.

번역 명확히 정의된 이정표의 결여가 소프트웨어 개발 프로젝트가 실패한 이유를 가능성이 높다.

어휘 clearly 명확하게 defined 정의된 milestone 이정표

121 형용사 자리

해설 「be said + to부정사(~라고들 한다)」 구문에서 to부정사 to be 뒤에 오기에 적절한 품사를 골라야 한다. to부정사의 동사가 2형식 동사 be이므로 빈칸은 보어 역할을 하는 자리이고, 등위접속사 and가 빈칸 앞의 형용사 well-informed와 뒤의 responsive를 대등하게 연결하고 있으므로 빈칸에도 형용사가 들어가야 한다. 따라서 '친절한, 품위 있는'이라는 의미의 형용사 (D) personable이 정답이다. (A) person은 명사, (B) personably는 부사, (C) personify는 동사이므로 빈칸에 들어갈 수 없다.

번역 로즈몬트 백화점 직원들은 정보를 많이 알고 있고 친절하며 응답이 빠르다고들 한다.

어휘 well-informed 정보를 잘 아는 responsive 바로 응답하는

122 동사 어휘 ▶동영상 강의

해설 빈칸은 delivery drivers를 목적어로 취하여 '보안 요원이 배달 기사들에게 정보를 알려줄 것이다'라는 의미가 되어야 하므로 '(정보를) 알려주다, 지시하다'를 뜻하는 (B) instruct가 정답이다. (A) invite는 '초대하다', (C) provide는 '제공하다', (D) present는 '제시하다'라는 의미이다.

번역 정문에 있는 보안 요원이 배달 기사들에게 어디에 물건을 내려놓을지 알려줄 것이다.

어휘 security 보안 drop off ~을 내려놓다

123 접속사 자리 _ 부사절 접속사

해설 빈칸은 두 개의 완전한 절을 이어주는 접속사 자리이고, 문맥상 '티켓 일부가 구입은 가능하지만 좋은 좌석은 이미 판매되었다'는 의미가 되어야 하므로 '비록 ~이지만'을 뜻하는 부사절 접속사 (A) Although가 정답이다. (B) Except(~을 제외하고)와 (D) After(~ 후에)도 부사절 접속사로 쓰일 수는 있지만 의미상 적합하지 않고, (C) Notice는 동사/명사이므로 절을 연결할 수 없다.

번역 콘서트 티켓 일부가 여전히 구입 가능하지만 가장 좋은 좌석들은 이미 매진되었다.

124 접속사 어휘 ▶동영상 강의

해설 빈칸은 앞의 완전한 절에 Visitors must가 생략된 절을 병렬 관계로 연결하는 등위접속사 자리이다. 지정 구역에 주차해야 한다는 조건이 충족되지 않을 경우 초래될 부정적 결과에 대한 내용이므로, '그렇지 않으면'이라는 의미의 (A) or가 정답이다.

번역 방문객들은 지정된 주차 구역에 주차해야 하며, 그렇지 않으면 차량이 견인될 위험을 감수해야 한다.

어휘 designated 지정된 risk 위험을 감수하다 tow 견인하다

125 명사 자리_동사의 주어

해설 빈칸은 동사 was의 주어 자리이고 앞에 정관사 the가 있으므로 명사가 들어가야 한다. 따라서 '의도'라는 뜻의 명사 (B) intention이 정답이다. (A) intend는 동사, (C) intended는 동사/과거분사, (D) intentional은 형용사이므로 빈칸에 들어갈 수 없다.

번역 리우 씨가 채용되었을 때 그 의도는 그녀를 화학 실험실에서 근무하도록 훈련시키는 것이었다.

어휘 chemistry 화학

126 형용사 어휘 ▶ 동영상 강의

해설 명사 effect를 수식하기에 적절한 형용사를 고르는 문제이다. 일자리가 급격하게 증가했다는 내용으로 보아 '늘어난 관광 수요의 긍정적인 효과'라는 의미가 되어야 자연스럽다. 따라서 '긍정적인, 유리한'을 뜻하는 (C) favorable이 정답이다. (A) tentative는 '임시적인', (B) negotiable은 '협의 가능한', (D) perceptive는 '통찰력 있는'이라는 의미이다.

번역 우리 도시의 늘어난 관광 수요의 긍정적인 효과는 접객 관련 일자리 수가 급격하게 증가한 것이다.

어휘 rapid 빠른 hospitality 접객 related 관련된

127 접속사 자리_부사절 접속사 ▶ 동영상 강의

해설 빈칸은 두 개의 완전한 절을 이어주는 접속사 자리이다. '관리자가 시간표를 수정할 때마다 시스템에서 이메일을 발송할 것이다'라는 의미가 되어야 자연스러우므로 '~할 때마다'를 뜻하는 부사절 접속사 (D) whenever가 정답이다. (A) now that(이제 ~이므로)과 (B) or else(그렇지 않으면)는 접속사이지만 문맥에 어울리지 않고, (C) despite(~에도 불구하고)는 전치사이므로 절을 연결할 수 없다.

번역 새로운 급여 명부 시스템에서는 관리자가 근무 시간표를 수정할 때마다 직원들에게 이메일이 발송될 것이다.

어휘 payroll 급여 명부 edit 수정하다 time sheet 근무 시간표

128 접속사 자리_부사절 접속사

해설 빈칸은 두 개의 완전한 절을 이어주는 접속사 자리로, '첸 씨가 늦을 경우에 대비하여 순서가 변경되었다'는 내용이 되어야 적절하므로 '~할 경우에 대비하여'를 뜻하는 부사절 접속사 (D) in case가 정답이다. (A) so도 접속사이지만 '그래서'라는 뜻으로 so 뒤에는 결과를 나타내는 내용이 나와야 하므로 답이 될 수 없고, (B) as of(~ 일자로)와 (C) during(~ 동안)은 전치사이므로 절을 연결할 수 없다.

번역 첸 씨가 늦게 도착할 경우에 대비하여 발표자 순서가 변경되었다.

129 명사 어휘

해설 '~까지', '최대 ~'라는 뜻으로 양적 한계를 나타내는 up to의 수식을 받기에 잘 어울리는 명사를 고르면 된다. '용기는 최대 10리터까지 담을 수 있다'는 내용이 되어야 자연스러우므로 '최대, 최고'를 뜻하는 (A) maximum이 정답이다. (B) potential은 '잠재력', (C) greatness는 '위대함', (D) collection은 '수집'이라는 뜻으로 의미상 부적절하다.

번역 연료 용기는 최대 10리터까지 담을 수 있지만 제조업체는 9리터만 넣을 것을 권장한다.

어휘 fuel 연료 container 용기 manufacturer 제조업체

130 동사 자리_태 + 시제

해설 빈칸은 주어 it이 이끄는 주절의 동사 자리로, 뒤에 목적어 weekly live music events가 있으므로 능동태가 들어가야 한다. 또한 시간의 부사절 접속사 Ever since(~ 이후로 계속)가 이끄는 절은 과거부터 현재까지 이어지는 기간을 나타내므로 현재완료진행 능동태인 (B) has been hosting이 정답이다. to부정사 (A) to have hosted는 동사 자리에 들어갈 수 없고, (C) was hosted는 수동태, (D) will be hosting은 미래 시제이므로 답이 될 수 없다.

번역 유니사이클 카페는 지난 5월에 개업한 이후로 매주 라이브 음악 공연을 주최해 왔다.

어휘 host 주최하다

PART 6

131-134 광고 ▶ 동영상 강의

친구들과 게임하는 것을 좋아하시나요? 맛있는 차와 간식을 즐기시나요? 그렇다면 셰 투르누아의 게임 나이트를 놓치고 싶지 않으실 겁니다. 매주 금요일 오후 6시부터 10시까지 셰 투르누아는 즐거움과 131 **웃음**이 있는 장소인 킹스턴 브로드 가 44번지로 여러분을 초대합니다. 보드게임, 카드게임, 상식 퀴즈게임 등 저희의 다양한 소장 게임 중에서 골라보세요. 132 **또는 원하실 경우 직접 가져오세요.** 게임을 하는 동안 갓 우려낸 차, 커피, 핫초코133 **뿐만 아니라** 군침 도는 페이스트리도 즐기실 수 있습니다. 셰 투르누아의 게임 나이트는 134 **쉬면서** 사람들과 어울리기에 완벽한 기회입니다. 01555-672212로 전화하시거나 www.cheztournoi.co.uk/gamenight를 방문하셔서 자리를 예약하세요.

어휘 fancy 좋아하다 mate 친구 tasty 맛있는 trivia (퀴즈에 나오는) 일반상식 savour 즐기다 brew 끓이다 mouthwatering 군침 도는 socialise (사람들과) 어울리다 reserve 예약하다 spot 자리 ring 전화하다

131 명사 어휘

해설 빈칸 앞 문장에서 셰 투르누아의 게임 나이트를 놓치지 말라(you won't want to miss Game Night at Chez Tournoi)고 했고, 빈칸이 있는 문장에서도 셰 투르누아의 주소를 알려주며 당

신을 초대한다(welcomes you to its 44 Broad Avenue, Kingston)고 했다. 따라서 for 뒤에는 셰 투르누아의 게임 나이트에 와야 하는 목적 또는 이유가 나와야 적절하고, 빈칸 바로 앞의 등위접속사 and는 비슷한 의미를 병렬 관계로 연결하므로 '즐거움과 웃음'이라는 내용이 되어야 자연스럽다. 따라서 '웃음'을 뜻하는 (C) laughter가 정답이다. (A) cash는 '현금', (B) exercise는 '운동', (D)의 lesson은 '수업'이라는 의미이다.

132 문맥에 맞는 문장 고르기

번역 (A) 또는 원하실 경우 직접 가져오세요.
(B) 가장 좋아하는 코미디언에게 투표하세요.
(C) 가장 인기 있는 음료는 캐러멜 라떼입니다.
(D) 서빙 직원 일자리도 몇 개 있습니다.

해설 앞 문장에서 보드게임, 카드게임, 상식 퀴즈게임 등 다양한 소장 게임 중에서 골라보라(Choose from our collection of board games, card games, trivia games, and more)고 했으므로, 매장 내에 구비된 게임을 즐기는 것 외에 또 다른 선택지에 대한 내용이 들어가는 것이 자연스럽다. 따라서 '원할 경우 직접 게임을 가져오라'고 언급하는 (A)가 정답이다.

어휘 vote 투표하다 opening 일자리, 공석 server 서빙 직원

133 상관접속사

해설 동사 can savour의 독적어인 our freshly brewed tea, coffee, and hot chocolate과 빈칸 뒤에 남아 있는 명사구 our mouthwatering pastries를 연결하며, '갓 우려낸 차, 커피, 핫 초코뿐만 아니라 군침 도는 페이스트리도 즐길 수 있다'는 의미를 만드는 '~뿐만 아니라 …도'라는 뜻의 상관접속사 (D) as well as가 정답이다. 구전치사 (A) in contrast to(~와 대조적으로)도 명사구를 연결할 수는 있으나 의미상 어울리지 않고, (B) furthermore (더욱이)는 부사, (C) so that(~할 수 있도록)은 접속사이므로 빈칸에 들어갈 수 없다.

134 to부정사 _ 형용사적 용법

해설 Game Night가 주어, is가 동사, the perfect opportunity가 보어인 완전한 문장이므로, 빈칸에는 명사 opportunity를 수식하여 '쉴 기회'라는 의미를 나타내는 to부정사 (B) to relax가 정답이다. (A) is relaxing과 (C) relaxes는 동사, (D) relaxation은 명사이므로 품사상 빈칸에 들어갈 수 없다. 참고로, 빈칸 뒤의 socialise는 앞에 to부정사의 to가 생략되었고, to relax와 등위접속사 and로 연결된 상태이다.

135-138 이메일

수신: 패턴 헨리 <p.henry@xmail.com>
발신: 조아나 카나라크 <jkanarak@kanarakrealty.com>
날짜: 12월 29일
제목: 임대차 계약 갱신

헨리 씨께,

제 기록에 따르면 귀하의 임대차 계약은 3월 31일에 만료될 예정입니다. **135 계약**을 갱신하시려면 1월 31일 이전에 알려주세요. 이 이메일에 회신하지 않으시면 **136 저는** 귀하께서 피스터 로 22번지 주택에 계속 거주하기를 원하지 않는다고 간주하겠습니다. **137 그런 경우**, 해당 주택은 4월 1일에 새로운 세입자에게 임대 가능한 매물로 등록될 것입니다. 현재 주택보다 더 크거나 작은 아파트로 이사를 원하실 경우 저에게 알려주세요. **138 카라나크 부동산은 가능한 어떤 방법으로라도 귀하를 기꺼이 돕겠습니다.**

조아나 카나라크, 카나라크 부동산

어휘 lease 임대차 계약 renewal 갱신 due 예정된 expire 만료되다 renew 갱신하다 assume 추정하다 property 건물 rental 임대(물) tenant 세입자 realty 부동산

135 명사 어휘

해설 앞 문장에서 임대차 계약(lease)이 곧 만료될 예정이라고 통지하고 있으므로, 빈칸이 있는 문장에 나오는 갱신(renew)의 대상은 앞 문장에서 언급한 임대차 계약임을 알 수 있다. 따라서 '계약을 갱신하려면'이라는 내용이 되어야 적절하므로 '계약'을 뜻하는 (B) contract가 정답이다. (A) license는 '면허', (C) subscription은 '구독', (D) membership은 '회원 자격'이라는 의미이다.

136 대명사 어휘

해설 빈칸은 동사 will assume의 주어 자리이므로 주격 대명사가 들어가야 한다. 또한 문맥상 부동산 업자인 이메일 발신자(I)와 세입자인 수신자(you) 사이의 임대차 계약에 관련된 내용이고, 앞 문장에서 계약을 갱신하려면 나에게 알려달라(let me know)고 했으므로 이메일에 회신하지 않으면 계약 갱신을 원치 않는다고 간주할 사람도 '나'가 되어야 한다. 따라서 (A) I가 정답이다.

137 접속부사

해설 앞 문장에서 이메일에 회신하지 않으면 주택에 계속 거주하기를 원하지 않는다고 간주하겠다고 했고, 뒤 문장에서는 해당 주택은 새로운 세입자에게 임대 가능한 매물로 등록될 것이라고 했다. 따라서 앞에서 언급한 조건이 실제로 발생했을 경우를 가정할 때 사용하는 '그런 경우에는'이라는 뜻의 (C) In that case가 정답이다. (A) In any event는 '아무튼', (B) As expected는 '예상대로', (D) For instance는 '예를 들면'이라는 의미이다.

138 문맥에 맞는 문장 고르기

번역 (A) 이 사업은 22년 전에 시작되었습니다.
(B) 카라나크 부동산은 가능한 어떤 방법으로라도 귀하를 기꺼이 돕겠습니다.
(C) 귀하는 현재 그 주택에 거의 2년 동안 계셨습니다.
(D) 귀하의 아파트에는 침실 3개와 욕실 2개가 있습니다.

해설 빈칸 앞에서 다른 아파트로 이사하기를 원할 경우 알려 달라(If you want to move to an apartment larger or smaller than your current one, just let me know)고 했으므로, 그럴 경우

에도 기꺼이 서비스를 제공할 수 있다는 내용이 들어가는 것이 자연스럽다. 따라서 부동산에서 어떤 방법으로든 기꺼이 돕겠다고 언급하는 (B)가 정답이다.

어휘 however 어떤 방법으로라도 occupy 사용하다, 거주하다

139-142 안내 책자

> **데베가스의 숙박 시설**
>
> 데베가스 반도는 다양한 139 **숙박** 옵션이 있는 것이 특징입니다. 데베가스 해변을 따라 20곳 이상의 고급 호텔을 찾을 140 **수 있으며**, 데베가스 파크 지역에는 중간 가격대의 호텔도 여러 군데 있습니다. 141 **또한** 다양한 소규모 숙소와 단기 아파트 임대가 지역 곳곳에 분포되어 있습니다. 142 **예산이 한정된 여행객들을 위한 옵션도 있습니다.** 여러 저렴한 캠핑장과 유스호스텔이 연중 이용 가능합니다. 데베가스 반도의 휴양 숙소 및 호텔의 상세한 목록은 이 안내 책자의 뒷면을 참조하세요.
>
> 어휘 peninsula 반도 feature 특징을 이루다 a wide range of 다양한 moderately 중간 정도의 inn 여관 short-term 단기의 scatter 흩어지게 하다 inexpensive 저렴한 campsite 캠핑장

139 명사 어휘

해설 빈칸 뒤에서 20곳 이상의 고급 호텔(More than twenty luxury hotels)과 여러 중간 가격대의 호텔(several moderately priced hotels), 다양한 소규모 숙소와 단기 아파트 임대(a range of small inns and short-term apartment rentals) 등 데베가스에 있는 여러 형태의 숙소에 대해 열거하고 있으므로, 빈칸이 있는 문장은 '데베가스에 다양한 숙박 옵션이 있다'는 내용이 되어야 적절하다. 따라서 '숙박'을 뜻하는 (D) accommodation이 정답이다. (A) dining은 '식사', (B) investment는 '투자', (C) entertainment는 '오락'이라는 의미이다.

140 동사의 시제

해설 앞뒤 문맥에서 데베가스의 다양한 숙박 시설을 현재 시제로 열거하고 있으므로, 중간 가격대의 호텔과 함께 고급 호텔을 '찾을 수 있다'며 현재 시제로 가능성을 표현하는 것이 자연스럽다. 따라서 (B) can be가 정답이다.

141 접속부사

해설 빈칸 앞뒤로 데베가스 지역에 있는 다양한 숙박 시설을 열거하고 있다. 따라서 비슷한 내용을 덧붙일 때 쓰이는 접속부사가 필요하므로 '또한, 추가적으로'라는 의미의 (B) In addition이 정답이다. (A) After all은 '결국', (C) Fortunately는 '다행히도', (D) Nevertheless는 '그럼에도 불구하고'라는 의미이다.

142 문맥에 맞는 문장 고르기

번역 (A) 관광객들은 여름철 동안 이 반도로 몰려듭니다.
(B) 자리가 남아 있을 때 휴가를 계획하세요.
(C) 예산이 한정된 여행객들을 위한 옵션도 있습니다.
(D) 데베가스 반도는 길이가 10km 이상입니다.

해설 앞에서 고급 호텔(luxury hotels) 및 중간 가격대의 호텔(moderately priced hotels) 등 다양한 가격대의 숙소를 열거하다가 빈칸 뒤 문장에서는 여러 저렴한 캠핑장과 유스호스텔이 이용 가능하다(Several inexpensive campsites and youth hostels are available)고 했으므로, 빈칸에는 더 저렴한 숙소를 찾는 여행객을 대상으로 하는 내용이 들어가는 것이 자연스럽다. 따라서 예산이 한정된 여행객들을 위한 옵션도 있다고 언급하는 (C)가 정답이다.

어휘 flock to ~으로 모여들다 space 자리 on a budget 한정된 예산으로

143-146 공지

> **넬사인**
>
> *귀하의 서명이 파일로 저장되었습니다.*
>
> **이 문서는 네 개의 추가 서명을 기다리고 있습니다.**
>
> 모든 당사자가 넬사인 문서에 서명하고 나면 귀하는 이메일로 143 **알림을 받습니다.** 그때 발신자 또한 계약서에 필요한 모든 서명이 확보되었다는 알림을 받게 됩니다. 144 **완료** 즉시 모든 서명자는 문서를 열람하고 저장할 수 있습니다. 넬사인 계정을 갖고 계시다면 이 계약서와 이전에 넬사인으로 전자 서명하신 기타 모든 문서는 귀하의 프로필에 저장됩니다. 145 **계정을 생성해야 하는 분들은 저희 웹사이트를 방문해 주세요.** 서명 절차146 **에 관한** 질문은 inquiries@nelsign.com으로 저희 고객 지원 센터로 연락 주세요.
>
> 어휘 signature 서명 capture (정보를) 캡쳐[파일화]하다 party 당사자 alert 알림, 경보 acquire 획득하다 signer 서명자 previously 이전에 electronically 전자적으로

143 동사 자리 _ 태

해설 앞에 조동사 will이 있으므로 빈칸에는 동사원형이 들어가야 한다. 또한 빈칸 뒤에 목적어가 없으므로 수동태가 들어가야 한다. 따라서 동사원형 수동태인 (B) be notified가 정답이다. (C) notifying은 동명사/현재분사이므로 품사상 적합하지 않고, (A) notify와 (D) have notified는 능동태이므로 답이 될 수 없다.

144 명사 자리 _ 전치사의 목적어

해설 빈칸은 전치사 Upon의 목적어 자리이므로 명사가 들어가야 한다. 따라서 전치사 Upon과 함께 '완료 즉시, 완료하자마자'라는 의미를 나타내는 명사 (D) completion이 정답이다. (A) complete는 형용사/동사, (B) completed는 동사/과거분사, (C) completely는 부사로 품사상 빈칸에 들어갈 수 없다.

145 문맥에 맞는 문장 고르기

번역 (A) 계정을 생성해야 하는 분들은 저희 웹사이트를 방문해 주세요.
(B) 계약서의 효력 발생일은 문서 상단에 표시됩니다.
(C) 개인 정보 보호 조건은 계약서에 첨부되어 있습니다.
(D) 저희 회사는 유타에 있습니다.

해설 앞 문장에서 넬사인 계정을 갖고 있다면 이 계약서와 이전에 넬사인으로 전자 서명한 기타 모든 문서는 프로필에 저장된다(If you have a Nelsign account, this contract and any other documents you have previously signed electronically with Nelsign will be saved in your profile)며 넬사인 계정 소지자를 위한 안내를 하고 있으므로, 빈칸에는 넬사인 계정이 없는 사람을 위한 안내가 들어가야 적절하다. 따라서 계정을 만들어야 하는 사람은 웹사이트를 방문하라고 설명하고 있는 (A)가 정답이다.

어휘 effective 발효[시행]되는 appear 나타나다 privacy 개인 정보 보호 term 조건 attach 첨부하다

146 전치사 자리 / 어휘

해설 뒤의 명사구 the signing process를 목적어로 취해 앞의 명사 any questions를 수식하는 자리이므로 전치사가 들어가야 한다. '서명 절차에 관한 질문'이라는 내용이 되어야 적절하므로 '~에 관한'을 뜻하는 전치사 (C) regarding이 정답이다. (A) around는 '~ 주위에', (B) through는 '~을 통해'라는 뜻으로 의미상 부적절하고, (D) assuming은 접속사 · 형용사이므로 빈칸에 들어갈 수 없다.

PART 7

147-148 쿠폰

쿠폰

트룰리 카페에서 제공하는 맛있는 치즈와 크래커를 좋아하신다면 이제 이 인기 스낵을 집에서도 즐길 수 있습니다! 트룰리 크래커와 치즈가 이제 대형 슈퍼마켓에서 구매 가능합니다.

148 트룰리 치즈 두 팩을 구매하시면 147 트룰리 크래커 한 상자(모든 크기) 구매 시 2달러 할인 혜택을 받을 수 있습니다.

고객당 쿠폰은 한 장으로 제한됩니다. 이 쿠폰은 다른 특별 할인과 결합하여 사용할 수 없습니다.

7월 31일에 만료됩니다.

어휘 limit 제한하다 combine 결합하다 expire 만료되다

---

147 Not / True

번역 트룰리 크래커 상자에 대해 경시된 것은?
(A) 다양한 크기로 나온다.
(B) 여러 맛으로 구입할 수 있다.
(C) 트룰리 카페에서만 독점 판매된다.
(D) 트룰리 치즈 한 팩보다 2달러 더 비싸다.

해설 두 번째 단락에서 트룰리 크래커 한 상자(모든 크기) 구매(on the purchase of ONE box of Truli crackers (any size))라고 언급하였으므로, 크래커 상자가 여러 크기로 나온다는 것을 알 수 있다. 따라서 (A)가 정답이다.

어휘 flavor 맛 exclusively 독점적으로

148 Not / True

번역 쿠폰에 대해 명시된 것은?
(A) 한 번 이상 사용될 수 있다.
(B) 다른 제품의 구매를 요구한다.
(C) 따뜻한 음료 구입에 사용될 수 있다.
(D) 7월 1일 이전에 사용되어야 한다.

해설 두 번째 단락에서 트룰리 치즈 두 팩을 구매하면 트룰리 크래커 한 상자(모든 크기) 구매 시 2달러 할인 혜택을 받을 수 있다(Save $2.00 on the purchase of ONE box of Truli crackers (any size) when you buy any TWO packages of Truli cheese)고 했다. 따라서 치즈 두 팩을 사고 크래커 한 상자를 추가 구입할 때 2달러를 할인받을 수 있는 것이므로 (B)가 정답이다.

149-150 문자 메시지

브라이스 아이스크림 가게

6월 29일, 오후 2시 2분

브라이스 아이스크림 가게의 보상 프로그램에 가입해 주셔서 감사합니다, 네이선 틸렌 님. **150 고객님은 저희 프로그램에 가입하신 것 만으로 첫 포인트를 적립하셨습니다.**

149 저희 아이스크림 매장 중 한 곳에서 1달러를 쓰실 때마다 1포인트를 받게 됩니다. 100포인트를 적립하실 때마다 아이스크림 또는 티셔츠와 토트백을 포함한 매장 상품 구매 시 5달러를 현금처럼 사용하실 수 있습니다. 생일에는 어느 브라이스 아이스크림 가게에서라도 아이스크림 무료 한 스쿱을 받을 자격이 주어집니다.

150 고객님께서 적립하신 포인트는: 20포인트입니다. 다음 보상을 받기까지 80포인트 남았습니다.

어휘 creamery 유제품 판매점 reward 보상 earn 받다 sign up for ~에 가입하다 redeem 현금[상품]으로 교환하다 be entitled to ~할 자격이 있다

---

149 Not / True

번역 문자 메시지에서 브라이스 아이스크림 가게에 대해 명시하는 것은?
(A) 한 곳 이상의 지점이 있다.
(B) 생일 파티를 위한 공간을 대여한다.
(C) 아이스크림 콘을 개당 5달러에 판매한다.
(D) 친구를 추천하면 고객에게 보상을 준다.

해설 두 번째 단락의 첫 문장에서 아이스크림 매장 중 한 곳에서 1달러를 쓸 때마다 1포인트를 받게 된다(For every $1.00 you spend in one of our ice cream shops, you earn 1 point)고 했으므로 매장이 여러 곳임을 알 수 있다. 따라서 (A)가 정답이다.

어휘 reward 보상하다   refer 추천[소개]하다

> **Paraphrasing**
> 지문의 our ice cream shops
> → 정답의 more than one location

150 세부 사항

번역 틸렌 씨가 보상 프로그램에 가입한 것에 대해 받은 것은?
(A) 1포인트
(B) 20포인트
(C) 80포인트
(D) 100포인트

해설 첫 단락의 두 번째 문장에서 틸렌 씨에게 프로그램에 가입한 것 만으로 첫 포인트를 적립했다(You have earned your first points just by signing up for our program)고 했고, 마지막 단락의 첫 문장에서 틸렌 씨가 적립한 포인트는 20포인트(You have earned: 20 points)라고 했으므로 (B)가 정답이다.

151-152 이메일

수신: 찰리 트란 〈Charlie.Tran@mailcrate.com〉
발신: 그레이스 드랜스 〈GDrance@hoppersmedicalcenter.org〉
날짜: 1월 10일
제목: 예약 불이행

트란 씨께,

오늘 호퍼스 메디컬 센터(HMC)에서 오후 1시로 예약하신 연례 건강검진에 오지 않으셔서 연락드립니다. 아시다시피, 환자가 예정된 방문으로부터 최소 24시간 전에 사전 통지하지 않을 경우 예약 불이행에 대해 진료비 전액을 청구하는 것이 저희의 정책입니다.

하지만 저희 센터에 환자로 계신지 15년 만에 처음으로 예약을 놓치셨기 때문에 해당 비용을 면제해 드립니다. **151 예약을 다시 잡기 위해 가능한 한 빨리 사무실로 연락해 주세요.** **152 담당 의사이신 라마나탄 박사님이 2월에 휴가를 가시기 때문에 이번 달에 추가 예약 시간을 내주셨습니다.**

그레이스 드랜스, 일정 관리 담당자

어휘 miss 놓치다   physical exam 건강검진   charge 청구하다   patient 환자   notify 통지하다   in advance 미리   waive 면제하다   physician 의사

151 주제 / 목적

번역 이메일의 한 가지 목적은?
(A) 환자에게 다가오는 진료 예약을 상기시키려고
(B) 예약을 다시 잡을 것을 권하려고
(C) 환자에게 비용이 부과되었음을 알리려고
(D) 환자에게 최근 건강검진 결과를 제공하려고

해설 두 번째 단락의 두 번째 문장에서 예약을 다시 잡기 위해 가능한 한 빨리 사무실로 연락해 달라(Please contact the office as soon as possible to reschedule your appointment)고 한 것으로 보아 예약을 다시 잡으라고 권하기 위해 이메일을 보냈음을 알 수 있다. 따라서 (B)가 정답이다.

어휘 remind 상기시키다   upcoming 다가오는   inform 알리다

152 Not / True

번역 라마나탄 박사에 대해 명시된 것은?
(A) 곧 휴가를 낼 예정이다.
(B) 트란 씨의 오랜 친구이다.
(C) 24년 전에 의학 학위를 받았다.
(D) 2월에 병원을 이전한다.

해설 두 번째 단락의 마지막 문장에서 담당 의사인 라마나탄 박사(Your physician, Dr. Ramanathan)가 2월에 휴가를 간다(he will be on vacation in February)고 했으므로 (A)가 정답이다.

어휘 time off 휴가   degree 학위   practice (의사의) 진료소

> **Paraphrasing**
> 지문의 on vacation → 정답의 taking time off

153-154 문자 메시지

카나에 이케다 (오후 5시 46분)
안녕하세요, 앤더스. **153 혹시 아직 사무실에 있나요?**

앤더스 로크 (오후 5시 48분)
지금 막 정리 중이었어요.

카나에 이케다 (오후 5시 50분)
다행이네요! **154 나오는 길에 사무실 온도 조절기의 온도 설정을 20도로 낮춰 달라는 부탁을 좀 드려도 될까요? 오늘 관리인이 안 계셔서 제가 했어야 하거든요.** 유감스럽게도 제가 주말 동안 지낼 멜버른으로 가는 기차 안이에요.

앤더스 로크 (오후 5시 51분)
지금 바로 할게요. 멜버른에서 좋은 시간 보내요!

카나에 이케다 (오후 5시 52분)
감사해요. 꼭 그렇게요.

어휘 by any chance 혹시라도   pack up (짐을) 챙기다   favour 부탁   adjust 조정하다   thermostat 온도 조절기   custodian 관리인   be supposed to ~하기로 되어 있다

153 의도 파악

번역 오후 5시 48분에 로크 씨가 "지금 막 정리 중이었어요"라고 쓴 의도는?
(A) 여행을 준비하고 있다.
(B) 아직 사무실을 나가지 않았다.
(C) 중요한 문서를 반환해야 한다.
(D) 오늘 저녁에 야근할 계획이다.

해설 5시 46분에 이케다 씨가 혹시 아직 사무실에 있는지(Are you still in the office by any chance?)를 묻자 5시 48분에 로크 씨가 지금 막 정리 중이었다(I was just packing up)고 대답한 것이므로, 로크 씨는 아직 사무실을 나서지 않았다는 의도로 한 말임을 알 수 있다. 따라서 (B)가 정답이다.

154 추론 / 암시

번역 이케다 씨에 대해 사실일 것 같은 것은?
(A) 해야 할 일을 깜빡했다.
(B) 보통 재택근무를 한다.
(C) 정기적으로 멜버른으로 여행을 간다.
(D) 사무실이 너무 춥다고 생각한다.

해설 5시 50분에 이케다 씨가 나오는 길에 사무실 온도 조절기의 온도 설정을 20도로 낮춰 달라는 부탁을 좀 해도 될지(Could you do me a favour and adjust the temperature setting on the office thermostat down to 20° on your way out?)를 물으며 오늘 관리인이 안 계셔서 자신이 했어야 했다(The custodian is out today, and I was supposed to do it)고 한 것으로 보아 이케다 씨가 할 일을 깜빡해 동료에게 대신해 달라고 부탁하는 상황임을 짐작할 수 있다. 따라서 (A)가 정답이다.

어휘 task 일 regularly 정기적으로

155-157 웹페이지

```
https://www.qualitekkresearch.com/aboutus
[홈] [소개] [등록] [후기]
```

수천 개의 대기업들이 사업 개선을 목표로 고객 만족도를 측정하는 설문조사를 활용합니다. 155 퀄리텍 리서치는 설문조사 결과를 분석하고 고객의 선호 사항에 대한 이해를 담은 상세 보고서를 작성하는 서비스를 고객사에 제공합니다. 12년의 운영 기간 동안 퀄리텍 리서치는 가치 있는 데이터를 제공한다는 강력한 명성을 쌓아 왔습니다.

157 매일 소비자들은 수백 가지의 다양한 제품에 대한 피드백을 제공하는 20,000건이 넘는 온라인 설문지를 작성합니다. 이 수치는 온라인 상거래가 증가함에 따라 계속 늘어나고 있습니다. 저희는 소비자들을 그들의 관심을 끌 수 있는 제품에 관한 설문조사와 연결해 줍니다. 저희가 진행하는 설문조사를 제출하는 참여자들은 보상 포인트를 받게 됩니다. 설문조사 5개에 참여한 뒤 포인트는 여러 매장에서 사용 가능한 상품권으로 교환할 수 있습니다.

가입을 원하시면 등록 페이지를 방문해서 회원 프로필 설문을 작성해 주세요. 이 정보는 귀하의 관심사에 맞는 설문조사를 파악하는 데 도움이 됩니다. 그러면 저희가 편한 시간에 작성하실 수 있도록 설문조사의 링크를 보내 드립니다. 156 귀하의 관심사가 바뀔 경우, 프로필을 업데이트해 주세요. 퀄리텍 리서치 설문조사의 모든 응답은 기밀로 유지되며, 귀하는 조사 데이터와 함께 개인적으로 식별되지 않을 것입니다.

어휘 testimonial 후기, 추천 글 measure 측정하다 satisfaction 만족 analyze 분석하다 detailed 상세한 contain 포함하다 insight 이해, 통찰 preference 선호 operation 운영 reputation 명성 valuable 가치 있는 consumer 소비자 complete 작성하다 participant 참여자 facilitate 가능하게 하다 redeem (현금 등으로) 교환하다 register 등록 questionnaire 설문지 identify 알아내다 match 맞추다 at one's leisure 시간 날 때 confidential 기밀의

155 Not / True

번역 퀄리텍 리서치에 대해 명시된 것은?
(A) 최근에 웹사이트를 개편했다.
(B) 서비스 상을 받았다.
(C) 기업들을 위한 보고서를 작성한다.
(D) 20년 동안 사업을 해 왔다.

해설 첫 단락 두 번째 문장에서 퀄리텍 리서치는 설문조사 결과를 분석하고 고객의 선호 사항에 대한 이해를 담은 상세 보고서를 작성하는 서비스를 고객사에 제공한다(Qualitekk Research serves its client companies by analyzing survey results and producing detailed reports containing insights about customers' preferences)고 했으므로 (C)가 정답이다.

어휘 revise 개정하다

156 세부 사항

번역 퀄리텍 리서치의 참여자들은 무엇을 하라고 권장받는가?
(A) 직접 설문조사 질문 작성
(B) 친구들의 등록 설득
(C) 선호하는 제품 사진 제출
(D) 필요할 경우 회원 프로필 업데이트

해설 세 번째 단락의 네 번째 문장에서 귀하의 관심사가 바뀔 경우 프로필을 업데이트해 달라(If your interests change, simply update your profile)고 했으므로 (D)가 정답이다.

어휘 persuade 설득하다 register 등록하다

157 문장 삽입

번역 [1], [2], [3], [4]로 표시된 위치 중에서 다음 문장이 들어가기에 가장 적합한 곳은?

"이 수치는 온라인 상거래가 증가함에 따라 계속 늘어나고 있습니다."
(A) [1]
(B) [2]
(C) [3]
(D) [4]

해설 주어진 문장에서 이 수치(These numbers)는 온라인 상거래가 증가함에 따라 계속 늘고 있다고 했으므로, 주어진 문장 앞에는 온라인 상거래와 연관된 수치가 제시되어야 한다. 따라서 제품 피드백을 제공하는 20,000건이 넘는 온라인 설문지(more than 20,000 online surveys that provide feedback on hundreds of different products)를 언급하는 문장 뒤인 [2]에 들어가는 것이 글의 흐름상 자연스러우므로 (B)가 정답이다.

어휘 commerce 상거래

158-160 회람

회람

수신: 스완지 스포트라이트 극장 직원
발신: 리안 그리퍼드, 최고 경영자
날짜: 9월 7일
제목: 현재 상황

직원 여러분께:

158 저는 머지않은 우리 극장의 재개관에 무척 들떠 있으며 여러분도 같은 마음이길 바랍니다. 긴 과정이었고, 관객들은 커버를 새로 교체한 좌석과 개선된 냉난방 시스템을 포함한 모든 개보수 작업의 진가를 틀림없이 알아봐 줄 것입니다. 극장에서 일하는 우리 모두도 이 변화들을 즐기게 될 것이라고 믿습니다. 다음 주에 새로 단장한 건물에서의 리허설을 매우 기대하고 있다는 것을 압니다.

공간의 개선 사항 중 더 눈에 띄는 한 가지는 **159** 이전의 매점 대신 생긴 대규모 좌석 공간을 갖춘 새 레스토랑 스완지 스포트라이트 비스트로입니다. 이 비스트로는 거리 쪽을 향하고 있으며 공연 일정이 없는 때에도 대중들에게 개방될 예정입니다. 메뉴는 다양한 음료, 간식, 식사로 구성되며 지역에서 구할 수 있는 농산물을 강조할 수 있도록 계절에 따라 바뀔 것입니다.

160 10월 2일, 우리는 웨일스 최고의 배우와 가수들이 출연하는 단 1회의 뮤지컬 특별 공연과 함께 극장의 성대한 재개관을 기념할 예정입니다. 일주일 뒤에는 〈블레이크의 강〉 공연을 시작합니다. 스완지 스포트라이트 극장의 역사에서 새로운 장을 시작하는 이 시기에 여러분의 모든 노고와 인내에 감사드리며 함께할 신나는 미래를 기대합니다.

어휘 chief executive 최고 경영자 thrilled 들뜬, 매우 기쁜 imminent 임박한 process 과정 undoubtedly 틀림없이 appreciate 진가를 알아보다 upholstered (의자 등이) 겉천을 간 eager 간절히 바라는 rehearse 리허설하다 refurbish 재단장하다 visible 눈에 띄는 previous 이전의 concession stand 매점 face 향하다 feature 특징으로 삼다 a selection of 다양한 beverage 음료 showcase 특별 공연 star 출연하다

158 주제 / 목적

번역 회람의 목적은?
(A) 다른 극단과의 협업을 발표하려고
(B) 프로젝트 완료에 대해 직원들에게 알려주려고
(C) 일부 리허설 공간의 일정을 잡으려고
(D) 냉난방 시스템의 문제에 대해 보고하려고

해설 첫 단락의 첫 문장에서 머지않은 우리 극장의 재개관에 무척 들떠 있으며 여러분도 같은 마음이길 바란다(I am thrilled about the imminent reopening of our theatre, and I hope you are too)면서 긴 과정이었고 관객들은 모든 개보수 작업의 진가를 틀림없이 알아봐 줄 것(It has been a long process, and audiences will undoubtedly appreciate all the renovations, ~ the updated heating and air-conditioning system)이라고 했으므로, 극장의 개보수 작업이 완료되어 재개관을 준비하는 상황을 직원들과 공유하기 위한 글임을 알 수 있다. 따라서 (B)가 정답이다.

어휘 collaboration 협업 completion 완료

Paraphrasing
지문의 renovations → 정답의 project

159 Not / True

번역 스완지 스포트라이트 비스트로에 대해 명시된 것은?
(A) 고정 메뉴가 포함될 것이다.
(B) 공연 중에만 문을 열 예정이다.
(C) 매점을 대체한다.
(D) 더 많은 테이블과 의자가 필요하다.

해설 두 번째 단락의 첫 문장에서 이전의 매점 대신 생긴 대규모 좌석 공간을 갖춘 새 레스토랑 스완지 스포트라이트 비스트로(the Swansea Spotlight Bistro, a new restaurant with a large seating area that replaces our previous concession stand)에 대해 언급하고 있다. 비스트로가 매점 대신 생겼다고 했으므로 (C)가 정답이다.

어휘 fixed 고정된

160 Not / True

번역 10월 2일에 대해 언급된 것은?
(A) 단 한 번의 공연이 열린다.
(B) 시 공무원들이 행사에 참석한다.
(C) 〈블레이크의 강〉이 공연을 시작한다.
(D) 다가오는 연극을 위한 새 의상이 배송된다.

해설 세 번째 단락의 첫 문장에서 10월 2일에 웨일스 최고의 배우와 가수들이 출연하는 단 1회의 뮤지컬 특별 공연과 함께 극장의 성대한 재개관을 기념할 예정(On 2 October, we will celebrate the theatre's grand reopening with a one-night musical showcase starring some of the best actors and singers in Wales)이라고 했으므로 (A)가 정답이다.

어휘 take place 열리다 official 공무원 costume 의상 play 연극

Paraphrasing
지문의 one-night musical showcase
→ 정답의 single performance of a show

161-163 회사 웹페이지

▶동영상 강의

빌딩 블록 팀과 함께 하세요

161 빌딩 블록은 밀로스 테크 사에서 가장 최근에 생긴 직원 주도 자원봉사 단체입니다. 자선 모금 행사나 지역 공원 청소를 기획하는 다른 사내 단체들과 달리, 빌딩 블록은 회원들에게 다른 사람들과 전문 지식을 공유하도록 요청합니다. **161, 162** 우리는 랄로타운의 비영리 단체들에게 경영, 홍보, 보조금 신청서 작성, 각종 응용 소프트웨어에 관한 무료 세미나를 제공합니다. 이 단체들에는 청소년 클럽, 지역 스포츠 리그, 랄로타운 자연 센터, 랄로타운 공영 라디오 방송국이 포함됩니다!

163 빌딩 블록 참여에는 일반적으로 밀로스 테크의 다른 자원봉사 단체들이 장려하는 것보다 더 많은 시간이 수반됩니다. 각 세미나는 보통 한 시간 길이이지만 기획과 준비 또한 우리 활동의 일부입니다. 우리와 함께 자원봉사를 하기로 선택하는 이들은 매주 2시간가량을 우리 활동에 할애한다고 예상하면 됩니다.

5월 3일 금요일 오후 12시 30분에 B-2 회의실에서 30분간의 정보 설명회를 개최할 예정입니다. 그동안 질문이 있으시면 변민규 씨에게 byun003@milostek.com으로 연락 주세요.

> 어휘 employee-led 직원 주도의 corporation 회사 organize 조직하다 charity 자선 fund-raiser 모금 행사 expertise 전문 지식 public relations 홍보 grant 보조금 application 응용 nonprofit 비영리 organization 단체 youth 청소년 participation 참여 generally 일반적으로 involve 수반하다 typically 보통 dedicate 할애하다, 바치다

161 추론 / 암시

번역 정보는 누구를 대상으로 작성된 것 같은가?
(A) 비영리 단체에서 일하는 랄로타운 주민
(B) 직업을 바꾸고자 하는 랄로타운 주민
(C) 지역 사회에 도움을 주고자 하는 밀로스 테크 직원
(D) 새로 고용된 직원에게 멘토가 되어 주고자 하는 밀로스 테크 직원

해설 첫 단락의 첫 문장에서 빌딩 블록은 밀로스 테크 사에서 가장 최근에 생긴 직원 주도 자원봉사 단체(Building Blocks is the newest employee-led volunteer group at Milos Tek Corporation)라고 했고 같은 단락의 세 번째 문장에서 우리는 랄로타운의 비영리 단체들에게 경영, 홍보, 보조금 신청서 작성, 각종 응용 소프트웨어에 관한 무료 세미나를 제공한다(We offer free seminars on management, public relations, grant writing, and various types of application software to nonprofit organizations in Lalortown)고 했다. 따라서 이 글은 지역 사회를 위한 자원봉사에 참여하기를 원하는 밀로스 테크 직원을 위한 것임을 알 수 있으므로 (C)가 정답이다.

162 세부 사항

번역 빌딩 블록이 주로 하는 활동은?
(A) 라디오 프로그램 개발
(B) 모금 행사 기획
(C) 정보 설명회 제공
(D) 취업 박람회 조직

해설 첫 단락의 세 번째 문장에서 우리는 랄로타운의 비영리 단체들에게 경영, 홍보, 보조금 신청서 작성, 각종 응용 소프트웨어에 관한 무료 세미나를 제공한다(We offer free seminars on management, public relations, grant writing, and various types of application software to nonprofit organizations in Lalortown)고 했다. 따라서 빌딩 블록은 지역 단체들에 여러 가지 정보 관련 세미나를 제공하는 활동을 주로 하고 있음을 알 수 있으므로 (C)가 정답이다.

> **Paraphrasing**
> 지문의 offer free seminars
> → 정답의 Presenting informational sessions

163 세부 사항

번역 빌딩 블록 회원들에게 요구되는 것은?
(A) 랄로타운의 주민이어야 한다.
(B) 꽤 많은 시간을 들여야 한다.
(C) 고급 학위를 소지해야 한다.
(D) 매달 하루 동안의 세미나에 참석해야 한다.

해설 두 번째 단락의 첫 문장에서 빌딩 블록 참여에는 일반적으로 밀로스 테크의 다른 자원봉사 단체들이 장려하는 것보다 더 많은 시간이 수반된다(Participation in Building Blocks generally involves more time than what is encouraged by other volunteer groups at Milos Tek)고 했으므로 (B)가 정답이다.

> 어휘 fairly 꽤 advanced 고급의 day-long 하루 종일의

164-167 기사

> **164 메한 모터스, 새 CEO 임명**
> 요나스 슐츠 작성
>
> 디트로이트 (1월 2일) — 올해는 메한 모터스에 여러모로 최초의 해가 될 것이다. **164** 35년 역사상 최초로 이 회사는 최고 경영진을 교체한다. 메한은 곧 CEO 직함을 다는 첫 번째 미국인이자 첫 번째 여성을 맞이할 예정이다.
>
> 다나 뢰브는 2월 1일 메한 모터스에서의 임기를 시작한다고 해당 기업이 어제 발표했다. **167** 뢰브 씨는 보스턴의 클로버 공과대학교에서 전기공학 학위를 수료하며 최우수 성적으로 졸업했다. 그녀는 또한 기업 경영 분야의 수료증을 취득했다. **165** 그녀는 결국 디트로이트의 타프츠 모터스에서 전기차(EV) 부서를 이끄는 자리까지 올랐다. 2년 안에 회사는 그녀를 최고운영책임자 직책으로 승진시켰다.
>
> 뢰브 씨는 결국 타프츠 모터스를 떠나 영국 자동차 회사 노라나의 CEO가 되었으며, 이곳에서 **166** 인기 있는 경형 전기차 레이더의 출시를 진두지휘했다. 해당 부문에서 이 차량은 가장 근접한 경쟁 전기차보다 단일 충전으로 20퍼센트나 더 긴 놀라운 주행거리를 달성했다.
>
> 뢰브 씨는 최근 인터뷰에서 메한 자동차를 위한 자신의 비전을 요약했다. "저는 대중 시장에 적당한 가격의 전기차를 만들기 위해 회사의 풍부한 인재를 활용하기를 기대합니다. 자동차는 일반 소비자에게 합리적인 가격에 제공되어야 합니다."

> 어휘 tenure 임기 top honor 1위, 최고의 영예 degree 학위 electrical engineering 전기공학 eventually 결국 division 부서 chief operating officer 최고운영책임자 spearhead 진두지휘하다 subcompact 경차 achieve 달성하다 stunning 깜짝 놀랄 range (차량) 주행거리, 범위 charge 충전 competitor 경쟁자 leverage 활용하다 abundant 풍부한 talent 인재 affordable (가격이) 알맞은 mass 대중적인 reasonable 합리적인 average 일반적인

164 주제 / 목적

번역 기사의 목적은?
(A) 전기차의 미래를 도시하려고
(B) 기업의 새로 부임하는 임원을 소개하려고
(C) 자동차의 판매 가격 동향을 분석하려고
(D) 기업의 결정이 어떻게 내려졌는지 설명하려고

해설 기사의 제목이 메한 모터스, 새 CEO 임명(Mehan Motors Appoints New CEO)이고, 첫 단락 두 번째 문장에서 35년 역사상 최초로 이 회사는 최고 경영진을 교체한다(For the first time in its 35-year history, the company is changing its top leadership)면서 메한은 곧 CEO 직함을 다는 첫 번째 미국인이자 첫 번째 여성을 맞이할 예정(Mehan will soon welcome the first American and the first woman to hold the title of CEO)이라고 했으므로 메한 모터스의 새 CEO 부임을 알리기 위한 글임을 알 수 있다. 따라서 (B)가 정답이다.

어휘 describe 묘사하다 incoming 새로 선출된
automobile 자동차

165 세부 사항

번역 뢰브 씨는 전기차 관련 업무를 어디에서 처음으로 경험했는가?
(A) 메한 자동차
(B) 클로버 공과대학교
(C) 노라나
(D) 타프츠 모터스

해설 두 번째 단락의 네 번째 문장에서 그녀는 결국 디트로이트의 타프츠 모터스에서 전기차(EV) 부서를 이끄는 자리까지 올랐다(She eventually rose to lead the electric vehicle (EV) division at Tafts Motors in Detroit)고 했고, 타프츠 모터스는 뢰브 씨의 전기차 관련 커리어 중 가장 먼저 언급되었으므로 (D)가 정답이다.

166 세부 사항

번역 레이더가 특별한 점은?
(A) 대형 크기
(B) 매력적인 차체 디자인
(C) 긴 배터리 지속 시간
(D) 저렴한 가격

해설 세 번째 단락의 첫 문장에서 뢰브 씨가 인기 있는 경형 전기차 레이더의 출시를 진두지휘했다(she spearheaded the introduction of its popular subcompact EV, the Radar)고 했고, 해당 부문에서 이 차량은 가장 근접한 경쟁 전기차보다 단일 충전으로 20퍼센트나 더 긴 놀라운 주행거리를 달성했다(Within its category, this vehicle achieved a stunning 20% higher range on a single charge than its nearest EV competitor)고 했다. 따라서 레이더는 경쟁 차량에 비해 배터리 지속 시간이 훨씬 길다는 점이 특징임을 알 수 있으므로 (C)가 정답이다.

167 문장 삽입

번역 [1], [2], [3], [4]로 표시된 위치 중에서 다음 문장이 들어가기에 가장 적합한 곳은?
"그녀는 또한 기업 경영 분야의 수료증을 취득했다."
(A) [1]
(B) [2]
(C) [3]
(D) [4]

해설 주어진 문장에서 그녀는 또한(also) 기업 경영 분야의 수료증을 취득했다며 학력상의 추가적인 자격을 소개하고 있으므로, 주어진 문장 앞에는 마찬가지로 학업과 관련된 이력을 다루는 내용이 있어야 한다. 따라서 뢰브 씨는 공과대에서 전기공학 학위를 받았다(Ms. Loeb graduated with top honors from Clover University of Technology in Boston, where she completed a degree in electrical engineering)고 언급하고 있는 문장 뒤인 [2]에 들어가는 것이 글의 흐름상 자연스러우므로 (B)가 정답이다.

어휘 certificate 수료증, 자격증 corporate 기업의

168-171 광고

> **댄 스페셜티 자전거**
> 런던 에버렛 길 60번지 SW11 1AH
> **169** 영업시간: 월요일 ~ 일요일 오전 10시 ~ 오후 6시
>
> **168** 제10회 중고 자전거 연례 세일!
>
> **171(A)** 저희는 고급 경주용 자전거 제품들로 알려져 있지만 매년 한정된 기간 동안 **170** 모든 연령대와 수준을 위한 다양한 중고 산악용, 도로용, 하이브리드 자전거를 제공합니다. 각 자전거는 부드럽고 안전한 주행을 보장하기 위해 **171(B)** 공인 기술자에 의해 재정비되었습니다. 가격은 15파운드에서 50파운드 사이입니다.
>
> 세일 기간은 5월 9일에서 5월 22일까지입니다. **171(C)** 이 광고지를 제시하시거나 언급하시고 중고 또는 새 자전거의 가격에서 10퍼센트를 할인받으세요. 자세한 정보는 www.dansspecialtybicycles.co.uk에서 확인하세요.

어휘 secondhand 중고의 stock 재고(품) high-end 고급의 racing 경주 refurbish 재정비하다 certified 공인된, 증명서를 가진 smooth 부드러운 range from A to B (범위가) A에서 B까지 이르다

168 주제 / 목적

번역 광고의 주요 목적은?
(A) 상점의 개점을 알리려고
(B) 자전거 타는 사람들에게 경주에 참가하라고 권하려고
(C) 연례 행사에 관심을 불러일으키려고
(D) 사람들을 자전거 수리 워크숍에 초대하려고

해설 광고의 제목이 제10회 중고 자전거 연례 세일(Tenth Annual Sale of Secondhand Bicycles!)인 것으로 보아, 해당 광고는 자전거 매장에서 매년 여는 세일에 관심을 끌기 위한 것임을 알 수 있다. 따라서 (C)가 정답이다.

어휘 compete (시합 등에) 참가하다   generate 발생시키다

> **Paraphrasing**
> 지문의 Sale → 정답의 event

169 Not / True

번역 댄 스페셜티 자전거에 대해 명시된 것은?
(A) 내년에 대부분의 자전거 가격을 10퍼센트 인상한다.
(B) 런던에 여러 지점이 있다.
(C) 일주일 내내 영업한다.
(D) 5월에 파티를 개최한다.

해설 지문의 상단에 매장의 영업시간이 월요일부터 일요일까지(Hours: Monday-Sunday)라고 나와 있으므로 댄 스페셜티 자전거는 일주일 내내 영업한다는 것을 알 수 있다. 따라서 (C)가 정답이다.

170 추론 / 암시

번역 중고 자전거에 대해 암시된 것은?
(A) 일 년 내내 판매될 예정이다.
(B) 각 자전거는 헬멧이 함께 제공된다.
(C) 일부는 어린이를 위해 설계되었다.
(D) 일부는 수리가 필요하다.

해설 첫 단락 첫 문장에서 모든 연령대와 수준을 위한 다양한 중고 산악용, 도로용, 하이브리드 자전거를 제공한다(we offer a wide selection of secondhand mountain, road, and hybrid bicycles for all ages and abilities)고 했다. 모든 연령대를 위한 중고 자전거가 있다고 한 것으로 보아 그 중에는 어린이용 자전거도 있음을 유추할 수 있으므로 (C)가 정답이다.

171 Not / True

번역 광고에 포함된 정보가 아닌 것은?
(A) 댄 스페셜티 자전거에서 보통 판매되는 자전거의 종류
(B) 일부 자전거를 정비한 사람들의 자격
(C) 댄 스페셜티 자전거에서 구매 시 돈을 절약하는 방법
(D) 런던 지역에서 자전거 도로를 찾을 수 있는 곳

해설 첫 단락의 첫 문장에서 저희는 고급 경주용 자전거 제품들로 알려져 있다(We are known for our stock of high-end racing bicycles)고 했으므로 (A), 같은 단락 두 번째 문장에서 공인 기술자에 의해 재정비되었다(refurbished by a certified technician)고 했으므로 (B), 두 번째 단락의 두 번째 문장에서 이 광고지를 제시하거나 언급하여 중고 또는 새 자전거의 가격에서 10퍼센트를 할인받으라(Show or mention this advertisement to receive ten percent off the price of any secondhand or new bicycle)고 했으므로 (C)는 광고에서 확인할 수 있으나, 자전거 도로에 관한 정보는 언급되지 않았으므로 (D)가 정답이다.

어휘 credential 자격   trail 길

172-175 온라인 채팅

모턴 탤버트 (오후 7시 32분)
172 뱀 부스터라는 인터넷 기기를 사용해 보신 분 계시나요?

차야 레븐 (오후 7시 37분)
174 과거에는 다른 브랜드를 사용했지만 지금은 뱀 부스터 10을 갖고 있는데 정말 좋아요.

라리아 존스 (오후 7시 38분)
저희 지하실에서는 인터넷 연결이 잘 안 돼요. 173 여러 인터넷 증폭기를 써봤지만 전혀 도움이 안 됐어요. 그것들은 제값을 못 하더라구요.

모턴 탤버트 (오후 7시 40분)
172 설치하기 쉬운 믿을만한 증폭기를 찾는 중이에요.

차야 레븐 (오후 7시 41분)
그게 최고예요.

레너드 켑 (오후 7시 48분)
저는 뱀 부스터 7을 갖고 있어요. 작동도 괜찮고 설치도 쉬웠는데 최신 뱀 부스터 10 모델이 더 좋다고 들었어요.

대니엘 워큰 (오후 7시 52분)
175 저는 지어톡스 시그널 부스터를 가지고 있는데 약간 크고 보기 안 좋아요. 좋은 점은 저렴하고 잘 작동한다는 거예요.

차야 레븐 (오후 7시 58분)
뱀 부스터 10은 훨씬 더 작아요. 하지만 다른 브랜드들보다 가격은 더 높아요.

모턴 탤버트 (오후 8시 2분)
뱀 부스터 모델이 한 개 이상인 줄 몰랐어요. 모두 고맙습니다! 이제 뭘 살지 알겠어요.

어휘 connection 연결   basement 지하실   booster 증폭기   worth ~의 가치가 있는   reliable 믿을만한   somewhat 약간   unsightly 보기 흉한   positive 긍정적인   inexpensive 저렴한   realize 깨닫다

172 주제 / 목적

번역 탤버트 씨가 온라인 채팅 토론을 시작한 이유는?
(A) 제품 구매에 대한 조언을 구하기 위해서
(B) 가전제품에 대한 후기를 제공하기 위해서
(C) 특수 장비를 판매하기 위해서
(D) 지하실에 장비를 설치하는 방법을 묻기 위해서

해설 탤버트 씨가 7시 32분에 뱀 부스터라는 인터넷 기기를 사용해 본 사람이 있는지(Has anyone used the Internet device Bam Booster?) 묻고 있고, 7시 40분에 설치하기 쉬운 믿을만한 증폭기를 찾는 중(I am looking for a reliable booster that's easy to set up)이라고 했다. 따라서 탤버트 씨는 인터넷 기기를 구매하기 전에 사람들로부터 의견을 구하고 있다는 것을 알 수 있으므로 (A)가 정답이다.

어휘 solicit 구하다, 간청하다   review 후기   appliance 가전제품   install 설치하다   equipment 장비

173 세부 사항

번역 여러 제품에 대한 부정적인 경험을 언급한 사람은 누구인가?
(A) 탤버트 씨
(B) 존스 씨
(C) 켑 씨
(D) 워큰 씨

해설 7시 38분에 존스 씨가 여러 인터넷 증폭기를 써봤지만 전혀 도움이 안 됐다(I have tried several Internet boosters, but they haven't helped at all)면서 그것들은 제값을 못 한다(They're just not worth the money)고 했다. 따라서 여러 제품에 대한 부정적인 경험을 언급하는 사람은 존스 씨이므로 (B)가 정답이다.

174 의도 파악

번역 오후 7시 41분에 레븐 씨가 "그게 최고예요"라고 쓴 의도는?
(A) 이전 온라인 채팅 토론의 진가를 인정했다.
(B) 새 제품을 몹시 사용해 보고 싶었다.
(C) 탤버트 씨의 질문이 도움이 됐다고 느꼈다.
(D) 자신이 사용하는 기기에 만족한다.

해설 7시 37분에 레븐 씨가 과거에는 다른 브랜드를 사용했지만 지금은 뱀 부스터 10을 갖고 있는데 정말 좋다(I have used other brands in the past, but now I have the Bam Booster 10, and I love it)고 했고, 7시 41분에 다시 한번 그게 최고(That one is the best)라고 언급하고 있다. 따라서 레븐 씨는 자신이 쓰고 있는 뱀 부스터 10이 매우 만족스럽다는 것을 표현하려는 의도로 한 말임을 알 수 있으므로 (D)가 정답이다.

어휘 appreciate 진가를 인정하다 prior 이전의
eager 간절히 원하는

175 Not / True

번역 지어톡스 시그널 부스터에 대해 명시된 것은?
(A) 너무 비싸다.
(B) 신뢰할 수 없다.
(C) 구 버전보다 낫다.
(D) 비교적 크다.

해설 7시 52분에 워큰 씨가 지어톡스 시그널 부스터를 가지고 있는데 약간 크고 보기 안 좋다(I have the Zeertox Signal Booster and it's somewhat big and unsightly)고 했으므로 (D)가 정답이다.

어휘 comparatively 비교적

> **Paraphrasing**
> 지문의 somewhat big → 정답의 comparatively large

176-180 이메일 + 광고

수신: 마크 슈뢰더
발신: 애슐리 응우옌
날짜: 5월 5일
제목: 계절직 채용

안녕하세요, 마크,

176 올해 우리 여름 직원 채용을 맡아주셨으면 해요. 작년에 낸시 아담스가 〈해안 관찰자〉에 광고를 냈는데 곧바로 지원자들이 있었어요. 이 신문을 다시 이용할 것을 제안 드려요. 177 작년과 동일한 수의 직원을 채용하겠지만 이번에는 네 명 모두 정규직이어야 해요. 새로운 광고를 작성해 주시면 다음 주에 발송하기 전에 함께 검토할 수 있겠네요.

그리고 참, 179 그래블 로 매장 개점 준비 작업을 해 주셔서 감사해요. 다음 달에 그 매장이 운영되면 당신은 훌륭한 매니저가 될 거라는 걸 알아요. 당신의 첫 책무 중 하나는 훌륭한 직원을 모집하는 일이 될 거예요.

애슐리 응우옌, 총괄 매니저
서프 버드 비치웨어

어휘 seasonal 계절적인 shoreline 해안가 observer 관찰자 applicant 지원자 paper 신문 full-time 정규직의 by the way 그나저나 operational 운영되는 terrific 훌륭한

서프 버드 비치웨어에서 여름 직원을 채용합니다!

잭슨 쇼어 최고의 캐주얼 의류 및 해변 용품 매장인 서프 버드 비치웨어에서 4명의 정규직 직원을 채용합니다. 이 계절직 일자리는 6월 초부터 8월 말까지 근무할 수 있습니다. 178 업무에는 판매, 선반에 제품 채우기, 고객 응대, 진열대 세팅이 포함됩니다. 이른 아침과 주말 근무가 일부 요구됩니다. 우리는 경쟁력 있는 급여와 우수한 근무 조건을 제공합니다.

서프 버드 비치웨어는 잭슨 쇼어에 지점이 두 군데 있으며, 180 기존의 펠리컨 인렛 매장과 6월에 문을 여는 그래블 로 신규 매장입니다. 179 모든 면접은 그래블 로 매장에서 진행됩니다. 지원하시려면 www.surfbirdbeachwear.com/jobs를 방문하세요.

어휘 supplies 용품 opening 채용 자리 stock 채우다 competitive 경쟁력 있는 original 원래의 conduct 수행하다

176 주제 / 목적

번역 응우옌 씨가 이메일을 작성한 이유는?
(A) 지원자에게 일자리를 제안하려고
(B) 직원에게 업무를 배정하려고
(C) 매장의 영업시간을 알리려고
(D) 신문 광고에 대해 질문을 하려고

해설 이메일의 첫 단락 첫 문장에서 응우옌 씨가 슈뢰더 씨에게 여름 직원 채용을 맡아주길 바란다(I hope you can take care of our summer hiring this year)고 했으므로 슈뢰더 씨에게 직원 채용 업무를 맡기려고 이메일을 작성했다는 것을 알 수 있다. 따라서 (B)가 정답이다.

어휘 assign 배정하다

177 추론 / 암시

번역 작년에 고용된 직원들에 대해 암시된 것은?
(A) 올해 재고용될 예정이다.
(B) 5월에 근무를 시작할 예정이다.
(C) 잭슨 쇼어 근처에 살았다.
(D) 모두가 풀타임으로 일하지는 않았다.

해설 이메일의 첫 단락 네 번째 문장에서 작년과 동일한 수의 직원을 채용하겠지만 이번에는 네 명 모두 정규직이어야 한다(We should hire the same number of workers as last year, but this time, all four should be full-time)고 한 것으로 보아 작년에 고용되었던 직원 모두가 풀타임으로 근무하지는 않았음을 짐작할 수 있다. 따라서 (D)가 정답이다.

178 Not / True

번역 광고에서 직무로 언급된 것이 아닌 것은?
(A) 선반에 제품 배치
(B) 상품 전시
(C) 배송품 하역
(D) 쇼핑객 돕기

해설 광고의 첫 단락 세 번째 문장에서 업무에는 판매, 선반에 제품 채우기, 고객 응대, 진열대 세팅이 포함된다(Duties include handling sales, stocking shelves, assisting customers, and setting up displays)고 했으므로 (A), (B), (D)는 업무에 포함된다는 것을 알 수 있다. 배송품 하역에 대한 내용은 없으므로 (C)가 정답이다.

어휘 merchandise 상품 unload (짐을) 내리다

> **Paraphrasing**
> 지문의 stocking shelves → 보기 (A)의 Placing items on shelves
> 지문의 setting up displays → 보기 (B)의 Displaying merchandise
> 지문의 assisting customers → 보기 (D)의 Helping shoppers

179 연계

번역 면접에 대해 사실인 것 같은 것은?
(A) 7월에 진행된다.
(B) 펠리컨 인렛 지점에서 진행된다.
(C) 슈뢰더 씨에 의해 진행된다.
(D) 온라인으로 진행된다.

해설 이메일의 두 번째 단락 첫 문장에서 슈뢰더 씨에게 그래블 로 매장 개점 준비 작업을 해 줘서 감사하다(thanks for your work getting the Gravel Road store ready to open)면서 다음 달에 그 매장이 운영되면 당신은 훌륭한 매니저가 될 거라는 걸 안다(I know you will be a great store manager when it is operational next month)고 했고 당신의 첫 책무 중 하나는 훌륭한 직원을 모집하는 일이 될 것(One of your first responsibilities will be to put together a terrific staff)이라고 했다. 또한 광고의 두 번째 단락 두 번째 문장에서 모든 면접은 그래블 로 매장에서 진행된다(All interviews will be conducted at the Gravel Road store)고 했다. 따라서 그래블 로 매장의 직원 채용을 위한 면접은 해당 매장의 매니저 예정자인 슈뢰더 씨가 진행할 예정임을 알 수 있으므로 (C)가 정답이다.

180 동의어 찾기

번역 광고의 두 번째 단락 1행의 "original"과 의미가 가장 가까운 단어는?
(A) 첫 번째의
(B) 유일한
(C) 창의적인
(D) 최고의

해설 의미상 지점 두 군데 중 '기존의' 매장 즉, 처음부터 있던 매장이라는 뜻으로 쓰였으므로 '첫 번째의'라는 의미의 (A) first가 정답이다.

181-185 이메일 + 블로그 게시글

> 수신: 임원진
> 발신: 코타 아다치
> 날짜: 10월 11일
> 제목: 트랙-4 제트기
>
> 팀 여러분께:
>
> 12월 말에 우리는 작년에 주문한 트랙-4 제트기 12대 중 첫 6대를 인수할 예정입니다. **181 남은 제트기들은 내년 한 해 동안 인도될 것입니다.** 저는 이 협체 제트기들이 우리 항공사의 미래를 대변한다고 믿습니다. 이들은 오늘날 시장에서 가장 조용한 제트기일 뿐 아니라, **182 우리가 현재 운항하고 있는 DB90보다 연료 효율이 20퍼센트 더 높습니다.** 이들은 또한 76개의 좌석으로 더 적은 승객을 수용하므로 서비스가 충분히 제공되지 않는 지역 시장에 안성맞춤입니다.
>
> 곧 있을 인도에 대비하여 우리는 새로운 항공기를 어느 노선에서 운항할지 결정해야 합니다. 아마도 당사 전체의 허브 시스템을 다시 생각해야 할 것입니다. 우리는 현재 우리 항공편들이 연결되는 7개의 지역 도심 허브를 가지고 있습니다. 소도시 사이를 비행하는 승객들은 이들 허브 중 한 곳에서 비행기를 갈아타야 합니다. 이들 대형 공항의 착륙 수수료는 매우 높은 경향이 있습니다. **183 우리는 협체 항공기를 주요 도시 중심부에서 떨어져 있는 공항으로 직항 운항함으로써 운영비를 대폭 절감할 수 있습니다.**
>
> 저는 오늘로부터 일주일 뒤 이 안건을 논의하기 위한 회의를 준비하고 있습니다. 우리는 정보에 근거한 결정을 내리기 위해 우리의 현재 노선 각각의 수익성을 분석할 것입니다.
>
> 코타 아다치
> 벤타나 항공 CEO

어휘 possession 소유(권) remaining 남은 narrow-body 폭이 좁은 동체의 represent 대변하다 fuel 연료 efficient 효율적인 passenger 승객 capacity 수용력 ideally 이상적으로 underserved 서비스가 충분하지 못한 regional 지역의 in anticipation of ~을 예상하여 urban 도시의 landing 착륙 drastically 대폭 reduce 줄이다 operating 운영 expense 비용 craft 항공기 profitability 수익성 informed 정보에 근거한

트래블에이더: 어디로, 왜, 어떻게 여행할 것인지에 관한 블로그

켄 오가와 작성

스프링필드 (1월 20일) — 저는 최근 벤타나 항공으로 실버 시티에서 센터빌까지 직항으로 갔습니다. 맞습니다, "직항"이라고 했습니다. **183** 벤타나에서 이제 이 두 소도시 사이에 직항편을 제공해 여행객들이 우리 지역의 유일한 허브인 미드웨스트 국립 공항에서 비행기를 갈아탈 필요가 없습니다. **184** 저는 수많은 다른 승객들을 뚫고 미드웨스트 공항의 터미널 사이를 서둘러 이동하던 것이 절대 그립지 않을 겁니다.

비행 자체에 관해서는 벤타나의 새 제트기는 예전 비행기보다 어마어마하게 개선되었습니다. **182** 가운데 좌석에 갇히게 될 가능성은 더 이상 걱정거리가 아닙니다. 새 항공기는 통로 양쪽에 좌석이 두 개씩만 있어서 모두가 통로 또는 창가 좌석을 차지합니다. 좌석은 대부분의 항공기 좌석보다 더 편안합니다. **185** 제 체격인 사람에게는 다리 공간이 약간 좁았지만 평균 신장인 사람은 다리를 뻗을 공간이 충분할 겁니다.

어휘 a sea of 수많은 fellow 같은 처지의 vast 막대한 stuck 갇힌 legroom 다리 공간 average 평균의 height 신장 plenty of 충분한 stretch out 뻗다

181 세부 사항

번역 이메일에 따르면, 향후 12개월간 어떤 일이 일어날 예정인가?
(A) 소도시로의 여행이 감소할 것이다.
(B) 공항의 착륙 수수료가 인상될 것이다.
(C) 벤타나 항공은 새 항공기를 받을 것이다.
(D) 벤타나 항공은 76명의 추가 직원을 채용할 것이다.

해설 이메일의 첫 단락 두 번째 문장에서 남은 제트기들은 내년 한 해 동안 인도될 것(The remaining jets will be delivered throughout the coming year)이라고 했으므로 (C)가 정답이다.

Paraphrasing
지문의 throughout the coming year
→ 질문의 over the next twelve months

182 연계

번역 트랙-4 제트기는 DB90 항공기와 어떤 점이 비교되는가?
(A) 다리 공간이 더 넓다.
(B) 창문이 더 크다.
(C) 항공편당 더 많은 승객을 수용할 수 있다.
(D) 기내에 가운데 좌석이 없다.

해설 이메일의 첫 단락 네 번째 문장에서 트랙-4 제트기는 우리가 현재 운항하고 있는 DB90보다 연료 효율이 20퍼센트 더 높다(they are 20 percent more fuel efficient than the DB90s that we currently fly)고 했고, 블로그 게시글의 두 번째 단락 두 번째 문장에서 가운데 좌석에 갇히게 될 가능성은 더 이상 걱정거리가 아니며(The possibility of being stuck in the middle seat is no longer a concern) 새 항공기는 통로 양쪽에 좌석이 두 개씩만 있어서 모두가 통로 또는 창가 좌석을 차지한다(The new aircraft have only two seats on each side of the aisle, so everyone gets an aisle or window seat)고 했다. 따라서 기존 항공기인 DB90과는 달리 새로운 트랙-4 제트기는 가운데 좌석이 없다는 것을 알 수 있으므로 (D)가 정답이다.

어휘 accommodate 수용하다 cabin (항공기의) 선실

183 연계

번역 벤타나 항공 임원진에 대해 결론지을 수 있는 것은?
(A) 트랙-4 제트기 이용에 더 이상 관심이 없다.
(B) 다음 회의는 1월 20일에 열린다.
(C) 도심 허브를 건너뛰는 노선을 추가하기로 결정했다.
(D) 수익 목표를 달성하여 상을 받았다.

해설 이메일의 두 번째 단락 마지막 문장에서 벤타나 항공 임원진에게 우리는 협체 항공기를 주요 도시 중심부에서 떨어져 있는 공항으로 직항 운항함으로써 운영비를 대폭 절감할 수 있다(We could drastically reduce our operating expenses by flying narrow-body craft directly to and from airports located away from these major urban centers)고 제의하고 있고, 블로그 게시글의 첫 단락 세 번째 문장에서 벤타나에서 이제 이 두 소도시 사이에 직항편을 제공해 여행객들이 우리 지역의 유일한 허브인 미드웨스트 국립 공항에서 비행기를 갈아탈 필요가 없다(Ventana now offers direct flights between these two small cities with no need for travelers to change planes at Midwest National Airport, our only regional hub)고 했다. 따라서 항공사 임원진이 도심 허브를 거치지 않는 소도시 간 직항 노선을 운영하자는 제안을 수용하였음을 알 수 있으므로 (C)가 정답이다.

어휘 bypass 건너뛰다

184 세부 사항

번역 오가와 씨가 허브 공항에서 환승하는 것에 대해 싫어하는 것은?
(A) 보안 검색대에서 줄을 서서 기다리는 것
(B) 한 터미널에서 다른 터미널로 급히 이동하는 것
(C) 공항에서 빠르게 식사해야 하는 것
(D) 항공기에 타고 내리는 것

해설 블로그 게시글의 첫 단락 마지막 문장에서 오가와 씨가 자신은 수많은 다른 승객들을 뚫고 미드웨스트 공항의 터미널 사이를 서둘러 이동하던 것이 절대 그립지 않을 것(I surely will not miss hurrying between terminals at Midwest through a sea of fellow passengers)이라고 한 말을 통해 오가와 씨는 환승을 위해 인파를 뚫고 터미널 사이를 급하게 오가야 했던 일을 좋아하지 않았음을 알 수 있다. 따라서 (B)가 정답이다.

어휘 security 보안 checkpoint 검색대 rush 서두르다 board 탑승하다 deboard 내리다

Paraphrasing
지문의 hurrying between terminals
→ 정답의 Rushing from one terminal to another

185 추론 / 암시

번역 오가와 씨에 대해 사실인 것 같은 것은?
(A) 비교적 키가 크다.
(B) 상업용 항공기 조종사다.
(C) 센터빌에 산다.
(D) 창가 좌석을 선호한다.

해설 블로그 게시글의 마지막 단락 마지막 문장에서 오가와 씨가 자신의 체격인 사람에게는 다리 공간이 약간 좁았지만 평균 신장인 사람은 다리를 뻗을 공간이 충분할 것(The legroom was a little tight for a person my size, but someone of average height should have plenty of room to stretch out)이라고 한 말을 통해 오가와 씨는 평균 신장보다 키가 더 큰 사람임을 알 수 있으므로 (A)가 정답이다.

어휘 relatively 비교적

186-190 공지 + 이메일 + 일정표

알립니다: 옥스턴 과학 박물관 방문객 여러분

186 박물관의 가트너 관이 현재 폐쇄되었습니다. 불편을 드려 죄송합니다.

186 다음 전시인 〈빛의 힘〉을 위한 공간을 준비하는 동안 기다려 주시기 바랍니다. **188** 사치코 모리시타 큐레이터가 기획한 이 전시는 특히 레이저와 광학 분야에서 미래에 영향을 미칠 혁신들을 탐구합니다. **188** 전시는 8월 15일부터 회원 및 사설 그룹 단체에, 9월 2일부터 일반 대중에 공개됩니다.

어휘 attention (안내 방송에서) 알립니다 inconvenience 불편 patient 인내하는 explore 탐구하다 innovation 혁신 affect 영향을 미치다 particularly 특히 optics 광학

수신: 여름 인턴 〈interns@renmarksolutions.com〉
발신: 문태호 〈thmun@renmarksolutions.com〉
날짜: 7월 7일
제목: 8월 여행

좋은 아침입니다, 팀 여러분,

188 인턴들과 그 멘토들은 8월 19일 금요일에 옥스턴 과학 박물관으로 견학 초대를 받았습니다. **187** 여러분 중 상당수가 이전의 렌마크 솔루션 견학을 다녀오신 경험이 있기 때문에 견학이 항상 교육적이고 흥미롭다는 것을 알고 계십니다. 참가자들은 우리 회사와 고객들을 이끄는 과학과 기술을 둘러보게 됩니다.

우리는 단체 견학의 일부로 〈빛의 힘〉 전시를 관람할 예정입니다. 박물관 내 식당에서 점심 식사를 할 수 있도록 식권이 제공됩니다.

우리 일정은 다음과 같습니다.

오전 9시	회사 로비에서 모임 (버스는 오전 9시 15분에 출발합니다.)
오전 10시 ~ 정오	사설 단체 견학
정오 ~ 오후 1시	박물관 식당에서 점심 식사
189 오후 1시 45분 ~ 오후 2시	203호실에서 모임
오후 3시 15분	렌마크 솔루션 사무실로 돌아가는 버스 출발

문태호
연구개발 관리자

어휘 previous 이전의 educational 교육적인 participant 참가자 drive 이끌다, 움직이다 voucher 상품권

옥스턴 과학 박물관
189 관람실 일정 (203호실) — 8월 19일

시간	행사명	행사 설명
오전 9시 45분	광학 시스템 및 응용 관측	옥스턴 대학교 카오리 오카다 교수의 강의
오전 10시 30분	양자 광학	옥스턴 과학 박물관 큐레이터 윌리스 맥케이브의 발표
오후 1시	레이저 사용의 증가	솔피스 대학교 함지민의 발표
189 오후 1시 45분	〈거울, 렌즈, 그리고 프리즘〉	**189** FK 공과대학의 단편 영화
190 오후 2시 45분	새로운 플랫폼, 새로운 제품	**190** 비감 산업의 제품 시연

어휘 optical 광학의 applied 응용의 observation 관찰 quantum 양자 institute 대학 demonstration 시연

186 주제 / 목적

번역 공지의 한 가지 목적은?
(A) 사람들을 다른 입구로 안내하려고
(B) 방문객들에게 임시 폐쇄에 대해 예고하려고
(C) 기관의 개관을 알리려고
(D) 운영 시간 변경을 설명하려고

해설 공지의 첫 단락 첫 문장에서 박물관의 가트너 관이 현재 폐쇄되었다(The Gartner Wing of the museum is currently closed)고 했고, 두 번째 단락의 첫 문장에서 다음 전시인 〈빛의 힘〉을 위한 공간을 준비하는 동안 기다려 달라(Please be patient as we prepare the space for our next exhibit, The Power of Light)며 박물관의 일부 전시관이 임시 폐쇄됨을 알리고 있으므로 (B)가 정답이다.

어휘 direct 안내하다 entrance 입구 warn 예고하다 temporary 임시의 institution 기관 operating 운영상의

187 Not / True

번역 렌마크 솔루션의 일부 인턴들에 대해 명시된 것은?
(A) 이전에 옥스턴 과학 박물관에서 자원봉사를 했다.
(B) 문 씨를 위해 시청각 장비를 설치했다.
(C) 과거에 렌마크 솔루션 견학에 참가한 적이 있다.
(D) 교육 전시의 설치를 도왔다.

해설 이메일의 첫 단락 두 번째 문장에서 인턴들에게 여러분 중 상당수가 이전의 렌마크 솔루션 견학을 다녀온 경험이 있다(Many of you have been on previous Renmark Solutions trips)고 했으므로 (C)가 정답이다.

어휘 install 설치하다 audiovisual 시청각의 setup 설치

Paraphrasing
지문의 have been on previous Renmark Solutions trips
→ 정답의 have joined Renmark Solutions trips in the past

188 연계

번역 8월 19일 견학에 대해 암시된 것은?
(A) 문 씨가 인솔한다.
(B) 참가자들은 기차로 이동한다.
(C) 모리시타 씨의 전시 관람이 포함되어 있다.
(D) 참가자가 사전에 경비를 지불해야 한다.

해설 공지의 두 번째 단락 두 번째 문장에서 전시가 사치코 모리시타 큐레이터에 의해 기획되었다(Designed by curator Sachiko Morishita)고 했으며, 같은 단락 마지막 문장에서 전시는 8월 15일부터 회원 및 사설 그룹 단체에, 9월 2일부터 일반 대중에 공개된다 (The exhibit will be open to members and private group tours starting August 15 and to the general public starting September 2)고 했다. 또한 이메일의 첫 단락 첫 문장에서 인턴들과 그 멘토들은 8월 19일 금요일에 옥스턴 과학 박물관으로 견학 초대를 받았다(Interns and their mentors are invited to take a trip to the Oxton Science Museum on Friday, August 19)고 했다. 따라서 8월 19일로 예정된 박물관 단체 견학에는 모리시타 씨가 기획한 전시가 포함되어 있음을 알 수 있으므로 (C)가 정답이다.

어휘 in advance 사전에 attendee 참가자

189 연계

번역 인턴들이 203호실로 가야 하는 이유는?
(A) 오카다 씨의 강의에 참석하려고
(B) 맥케이브 씨의 발표를 보려고
(C) 솔피스 대학교의 발표를 보려고
(D) FK 공과대학의 영화를 보려고

해설 이메일의 세 번째 단락에 기재된 일정에서 인턴들은 오후 1시 45분부터 오후 2시까지(1:45 to 2:00 P.M.) 박물관 203호실에서 모인다(Meet in room 203)고 나와 있고, 203호 관람실 일정표 (Viewing Room Schedule (Room 203))의 하단에 오후 1시 45분(1:45 P.M.)에 FK 공과대학의 단편 영화(Short film by FK Institute of Technology)를 상영한다고 나와 있다. 따라서 인턴들은 1시 45분에 203호실에서 FK 공과대학이 제작한 단편 영화를 관람할 예정임을 알 수 있으므로 (D)가 정답이다.

190 세부 사항

번역 일정표에 따르면, 한 회사에서 자사의 상품에 대해 발표하는 시간은 언제인가?

(A) 오전 9시 45분
(B) 오전 10시 30분
(C) 오후 1시
(D) 오후 2시 45분

해설 일정표의 마지막 일정에 오후 2시 45분(2:45 P.M.)에 비감 산업의 제품 시연(Product demonstrations by Bigham Industries)이 예정되어 있다고 표시되어 있으므로 (D)가 정답이다.

Paraphrasing
지문의 Product demonstrations
→ 질문의 give a presentation about its merchandise

191-195 광고 + 가격표 + 후기

프로텍토 우산 포장기

젖은 우산을 들고 건물에 들어와 걸어 다니는 방문객들은 무심결에 바닥을 젖게 하고 미끄럽게 만듭니다. 프로텍토 우산 포장기(PUW 기기)는 이 문제를 해결할 수 있는 간단하고 편리한 방법을 제공합니다. 기계는 건물 입구에 설치하는 것이 가장 좋습니다. 건물에 들어오자마자 방문객들은 젖은 우산을 기계에 넣습니다. 기계가 자동으로 우산을 투명한 비닐봉지로 포장해 주고 나면 방문객들은 우산을 가져갈 수 있습니다. 퇴장할 때는 사용한 봉지를 근처의 쓰레기통에 버리면 됩니다.

PUW 기기는 하나 또는 두 개의 우산 포장 장치가 달린 것으로 구입 가능하며 스테인리스 또는 검정색으로 제공됩니다. 기기는 우산을 1.5초 만에 포장합니다. **191** 스탠드는 이동식이어서 여러 장소로 굴려서 이동시킬 수 있습니다. **193** 11월에 PUW 기기를 구입하시면 저희 회사 로고가 새겨져 있는 경량 우산을 받으실 수 있습니다.

어휘 wrapping 포장 unintentionally 무심결에 slippery 미끄러운 convenient 편리한 address 해결하다 entryway 입구 entry 입장 insert 삽입하다 automatically 자동으로 plastic bag 비닐봉지 discard 버리다 trash can 쓰레기통 device 장치 mobile 이동식의 lightweight 경량의 feature 포함하다

프로텍토 제품 가격표

제품 번호	설명	제품 단가
143	**194** 우산 포장 장치 2개가 달린 PUW 기기. 가격에 비닐봉지 2,000개 포함. 넓고 유동 인구가 많은 장소에 적합. 스테인리스 또는 검정색으로 제공.	**194** 450 달러
144	우산 포장 장치 1개가 달린 PUW 기기. 가격에 비닐봉지 1,000개 포함. 스테인리스 또는 검정색으로 제공.	350달러
192	자사의 모든 제품에 쓸 수 있는 리필용 **192** 비닐봉지 3,000개들이 한 상자. 온라인에서만 구매 가능.	100달러
194	자사의 모든 제품에 쓸 수 있는 리필용 **192** 비닐봉지 1,000개들이 한 상자. 온라인에서만 구매 가능.	35달러

어휘 | unit (상품) 한 개   high-foot-traffic 유동 인구가 많은

---

https://www.setterlyproductreviews.com/officeequipment

사무용 장비 후기: 프로텍토 우산 포장기

저는 새 PUW 기기가 아주 마음에 듭니다! 저는 중간 규모 사무실 건물의 시설 관리자로, 우산을 들고 들어오는 방문객들로 인해 젖게 되는 바닥의 불편함을 종종 처리해야 합니다. **195 전에는 로비에 방문객들이 우산을 둘 수 있는 커다란 우산 꽂이가 있었지만 사용하는 사람이 많지 않았습니다.** 그 후에는 방문객들이 뜯어서 우산을 넣을 수 있는 일회용 비닐봉지가 들어 있는 우산 꽂이를 시도했습니다. 하지만 이 방법은 봉지가 다소 잘 찢어져서 물이 새는 것을 막지 못해 효과적이지 않았습니다.

그래서 **193 11월에 우리는 PUW 기기를 사용해 보기로 결정했습니다.** **194 방문객이 많기 때문에 두 개의 장치가 달린 PUW 기기를 구입했고** 현대적인 로비에 어울리도록 스테인리스 색상으로 주문했습니다.

그 이후로 입구는 더 안전하고 깨끗해졌습니다. 방문객들은 기기가 자동이라는 점을 좋아하고, 로비가 더 이상 우산에서 물이 뚝뚝 떨어지는 것 때문에 젖고 미끄럽지 않은 것에 모두가 감사하고 있습니다!

— 앤드루 바

어휘 | facility 시설   deal with ~을 처리하다   inconvenience 불편   disposable 일회용의   tear off ~을 떼어내다   method 방법   flimsy 잘 찢어지는   prevent 막다   leakage 새어나감   entranceway 입구   dripping 물이 뚝뚝 떨어지는

191 추론 / 암시

번역 | 광고에서 PUW 기기에 대해 암시하는 것은?
(A) 재료가 기기를 비용 효율적이게 해 준다.
(B) 1초 이내에 우산을 포장할 수 있다.
(C) 바퀴가 있어 이리저리 이동시킬 수 있다.
(D) 사용한 봉지를 넣을 수 있는 용기가 포함되어 있다.

해설 | 광고의 두 번째 단락 세 번째 문장에서 스탠드는 이동식이어서 여러 장소로 굴려서 이동시킬 수 있다(The stand is mobile and thus can be rolled around to different locations)고 했으므로 기기에 바퀴가 달려 이동시킬 수 있다는 것을 알 수 있다. 따라서 (C)가 정답이다.

어휘 | cost-efficient 비용 효율적인   receptacle 용기

> **Paraphrasing**
> 지문의 mobile → 정답의 moved around
> 지문의 rolled around → 정답의 wheels

192 Not / True

번역 | 가격표에서 봉지에 대해 명시하는 것은?
(A) 다양한 수량으로 구매할 수 있다.
(B) 모든 브랜드의 우산 포장 기기에 맞는다.
(C) PUW 기기의 가격에 포함되지 않는다.
(D) 소매점에서 판매된다.

해설 | 가격표의 하단에 비닐봉지 3,000개들이 한 상자(Box of 3,000 plastic bags)와 비닐봉지 1,000개들이 한 상자(Box of 1,000 plastic bags)가 기재되어 있는 것으로 보아 비닐봉지 수량을 다르게 구매할 수 있음을 알 수 있다. 따라서 (A)가 정답이다.

어휘 | quantity 수량   fit 맞다   retail 소매

193 연계

번역 | 바 씨에 대해 암시된 것은?
(A) 프로텍토의 장기 고객이다.
(B) 주문 시 우산을 받았다.
(C) 조용한 사무실 건물에서 일한다.
(D) 최근에 직장을 옮겼다.

해설 | 광고의 마지막 단락 마지막 문장에서 11월에 PUW 기기를 구입하면 회사 로고가 새겨져 있는 경량 우산을 받을 수 있다(Purchase a PUW machine throughout November and receive a lightweight umbrella featuring our company logo)고 했고, 후기의 두 번째 단락 첫 문장에서 바 씨는 11월에 우리는 PUW 기기를 사용해 보기로 결정했다(in November, we decided to try a PUW machine)고 했다. 따라서 바 씨는 11월에 PUW 기기를 구입하고 로고가 새겨진 우산을 받았다는 것을 알 수 있으므로 (B)가 정답이다.

194 연계

번역 | 바 씨가 후기를 쓴 제품의 가격은?
(A) 35달러
(B) 100달러
(C) 350달러
(D) 450달러

해설 | 후기의 두 번째 단락 두 번째 문장에서 바 씨는 방문객이 많기 때문에 두 개의 장치가 달린 PUW 기기를 구입했다(Because we have many visitors, we purchased the PUW machine with two devices)고 했고, 가격표의 상단에 우산 포장 장치 2개가 달린 PUW 기기(PUW machine with two umbrella-wrapping devices)는 450달러($450)라고 나와 있다. 따라서 바 씨는 우산 포장 장치 2개가 달린 450달러짜리 기기를 구입했다는 것을 알 수 있으므로 (D)가 정답이다.

195 세부 사항

번역 | 바 씨가 설명하는 문제는?
(A) 프로텍토 제품이 현대적으로 보이지 않는다.
(B) 방문객들이 우산 꽂이를 사용하지 않았다.
(C) 건물의 로비가 깨끗하지 않다.
(D) 일부 일회용 우산 봉지가 너무 작았다.

해설 | 후기의 첫 단락 세 번째 문장에서 바 씨가 전에는 로비에 방문객들이 우산을 둘 수 있는 커다란 우산 꽂이가 있었지만 사용하는 사람이 많지 않았다(We used to have a large umbrella stand in the lobby where visitors could leave umbrellas, but only a few people used it)고 했으므로 (B)가 정답이다.

Paraphrasing
지문의 only a few people used it
→ 정답의 Visitors were not using an umbrella stand.

196-200 웹페이지 + 이메일 + 이메일

https://www.croydonconstruction.co.nz/news

| 홈 | 소식 | 채용 | 연락처 |

12월에 크로이던 건설은 뉴질랜드 남섬에서 사업을 한 지 25주년을 맞이합니다. 우리는 본사가 위치한 이곳 크라이스트처치와 남섬의 동쪽 해안을 따라 여러 장소에서 우리가 건축한 수많은 건물들에 큰 자부심을 느낍니다.

우리는 최근에 몇몇 흥미로운 프로젝트를 진행하느라 바쁘게 지냈습니다. 크라이스트처치에서 **199 우리는 그로브 로에 11월 1일 개원을 목표로 윌로비 메디컬 클리닉을 건설 중이며**, 스프링데일 가의 블레이크필드 주민센터를 확장하고 있습니다. 애쉬버튼에서는 패서린 길의 107세대 아파트 단지를 거의 완공했으며 6번가에 있는 디스머스 학교의 새로운 별관 공사를 시작했습니다. **196 스티브 코글러가 우리의 새로운 현장 수석 엔지니어입니다.**

크로이던 건설에서의 취직에 관심이 있으십니까? 사무실과 작업 현장 직책 두 가지 모두를 채용하고 있습니다. **197 채용 직책을 확인 및 지원하시려면 채용 페이지를 방문하세요.**

어휘 mark 기념하다 take pride in ~에 자부심을 갖다 headquarters 본사 coast 해안 expand 확장하다 unit 구성 단위 complex 단지 break ground 착공하다 wing 부속 건물 site 현장 employment 고용 apply 지원하다

수신: 사나 라히자 <srahija@wilmawindows.co.nz>
발신: 잭 마코아레 <zmakoare@croydonconstruction.co.nz>
날짜: 8월 15일
제목: 배송 지연

라히자 씨께:

47992번 주문의 상태를 확인하고자 글을 쓰고 있으며, 이 주문은 7월 31일까지 여기 도착해야 하는데 지금 2주나 지연되었습니다. 우리는 매우 우려하고 있습니다. 건물의 완공일은 연기될 수 없습니다. 창문이 언제 도착할 수 있는지 알려주십시오. **200 물품을 받을 때까지 잔금 지급은 보류하겠습니다.** 윌마 윈도우는 수년간 자사의 공급업체였으며 이러한 문제가 발생한 것은 이번이 처음입니다.

이 문제에 즉각적인 관심을 가져주시기 바랍니다.

잭 마코아레
크로이던 건설, 건설 관리자

어휘 overdue 늦어진 status 상태 postpone 연기하다 withhold 보류하다 balance 잔금 supplier 공급업체 occur 발생하다 prompt 즉각적인 attention 관심

수신: 잭 마코아레 <zmakoare@croydonconstruction.co.nz>
발신: 사나 라히자 <srahija@wilmawindows.co.nz>
날짜: 8월 16일
제목: 회신: 발송 지연

마코아레 씨께:

199 47992번 주문의 지연에 대해 사과를 받아 주시기 바랍니다. 198 저희 공장의 기계 한 대가 오작동되어 창문 유리에 결함이 발생했습니다. 해당 기계는 수리되었으며 공장은 평상시의 생산 일정으로 복귀했습니다. 귀사의 주문을 신속히 처리하여 내일 발송하겠습니다. **199, 200 물품은 8월 20일에 귀사의 메디컬 클리닉 건설 현장에 도착할 예정입니다.** 선의의 표시로 배송비 전체를 환불해 드리겠습니다.

사나 라히자

어휘 accept 받아들이다 apology 사과 malfunction 오작동하다 flaw 결함 expedite 신속히 처리하다 goodwill 선의 gesture 표시 entire 전체의

196 추론 / 암시

번역 웹페이지에서 크로이던 건설에 대해 암시된 것은?
(A) 최근에 코글러 씨를 채용했다.
(B) 사업을 한 지 얼마 되지 않았다.
(C) 본사를 크라이스트처치로 옮길 계획이다.
(D) 뉴질랜드 외 다른 나라에서도 프로젝트를 완수한다.

해설 웹페이지의 두 번째 단락 마지막 문장에서 스티브 코글러가 우리의 새로운 현장 수석 엔지니어(Steve Kogler is our new chief site engineer)라고 한 것을 통해 크로이던 건설에서 최근에 코글러 씨를 영입했음을 알 수 있으므로 (A)가 정답이다.

197 세부 사항

번역 웹페이지에 따르면, 구직자들은 무엇을 해야 하는가?
(A) 회사 본사 직접 방문
(B) 취업 박람회 참석
(C) 이메일로 채용 담당자에게 연락
(D) 온라인으로 지원서 제출

해설 웹페이지의 마지막 단락 마지막 문장에서 채용 직책을 확인 및 지원하려면 채용 페이지를 방문하라(Go to our Jobs page to view open positions and to apply)고 했으므로 구직자들은 온라인으로 지원해야 한다는 것을 알 수 있다. 따라서 (D)가 정답이다.

어휘 application 지원(서)

Paraphrasing
지문의 Jobs page → 정답의 online
지문의 apply → 정답의 Submit an application

198 세부 사항

번역 두 번째 이메일에서, 라히자 씨가 설명하는 문제는?
(A) 잘못된 제품이 생산되었다.
(B) 공장에 인력이 부족했다.
(C) 일부 장비가 제대로 작동하지 않았다.
(D) 주문 제품 중 일부가 운송 중 파손되었다.

해설 두 번째 이메일의 두 번째 문장에서 라히자 씨가 공장의 기계 한 대가 오작동되어 창문 유리에 결함이 발생했다(A machine in our factory malfunctioned, creating flaws in the window glass)고 설명하고 있으므로 (C)가 정답이다.

어휘 manufacture 생산하다 understaffed 인원이 부족한
operate 작동하다 properly 제대로 transport 운송

> **Paraphrasing**
> 지문의 malfunctioned → 정답의 did not operate properly

199 연계

번역 47992번 주문은 어디로 배송될 것 같은가?
(A) 그로브 로
(B) 스프링데일 가
(C) 패서린 길
(D) 6번가

해설 웹페이지의 두 번째 단락 두 번째 문장에서 그로브 로에 11월 1일 개원을 목표로 윌로비 메디컬 클리닉을 건설 중(we are building the Willoughby Medical Clinic on Grove Road, with a grand opening date of 1 November)이라고 했고, 두 번째 이메일의 첫 문장에서 47992번 주문(order 47992)에 대해 언급하면서 다섯 번째 문장에서 물품은 귀사의 메디컬 클리닉 건설 현장에 도착할 예정(It will arrive at your medical clinic construction site)이라고 했다. 따라서 47992번 주문품은 메디컬 클리닉의 건설 현장이 있는 그로브 로에 배송될 것임을 알 수 있으므로 (A)가 정답이다.

200 연계

번역 마코아레 씨에 대해 결론지을 수 있는 것은?
(A) 11월 1일에 은퇴할 계획이다.
(B) 자신의 주문을 더 좋은 종류의 유리창으로 변경하기를 원한다.
(C) 아마 건물의 완공일을 연기해야 할 것이다.
(D) 곧 공급업체에 전액을 지급할 것이다.

해설 8월 15일에 작성한 첫 번째 이메일의 다섯 번째 문장에서 마코아레 씨는 물품을 받을 때까지 잔금 지급은 보류하겠다(We shall withhold the balance of payment until the items have been received)고 했고, 두 번째 이메일의 다섯 번째 문장에서 물품은 8월 20일에 귀사의 메디컬 클리닉 건설 현장에 도착할 예정(It will arrive at your medical clinic construction site on 20 August)이라고 했다. 따라서 마코아레 씨는 8월 20일에 물품을 받고 나면 공급업체에 잔금을 지급할 것임을 알 수 있으므로 (D)가 정답이다.

기출 TEST 8

101 (B)	102 (A)	103 (B)	104 (A)	105 (C)
106 (B)	107 (B)	108 (C)	109 (D)	110 (A)
111 (C)	112 (B)	113 (D)	114 (B)	115 (D)
116 (B)	117 (A)	118 (C)	119 (C)	120 (D)
121 (A)	122 (D)	123 (C)	124 (A)	125 (C)
126 (C)	127 (D)	128 (A)	129 (B)	130 (B)
131 (B)	132 (A)	133 (D)	134 (A)	135 (C)
136 (B)	137 (D)	138 (A)	139 (D)	140 (B)
141 (C)	142 (B)	143 (B)	144 (A)	145 (C)
146 (A)	147 (C)	148 (B)	149 (A)	150 (D)
151 (C)	152 (B)	153 (B)	154 (C)	155 (C)
156 (A)	157 (C)	158 (C)	159 (A)	160 (B)
161 (A)	162 (B)	163 (B)	164 (C)	165 (B)
166 (C)	167 (A)	168 (C)	169 (D)	170 (A)
171 (D)	172 (A)	173 (A)	174 (D)	175 (C)
176 (D)	177 (B)	178 (A)	179 (C)	180 (A)
181 (B)	182 (A)	183 (B)	184 (C)	185 (D)
186 (D)	187 (B)	188 (C)	189 (C)	190 (B)
191 (A)	192 (B)	193 (C)	194 (B)	195 (D)
196 (D)	197 (B)	198 (B)	199 (C)	200 (D)

PART 5

101 형용사 자리 _ 명사 수식

해설 빈칸은 전치사 of의 목적어 역할을 하는 명사 visitors를 수식하는 형용사 자리이다. '들떠 있는 방문객들'이라는 의미가 되어야 자연스러우므로, '들뜬, 신이 난'을 뜻하는 형용사 (B) excited가 정답이다. (A) excite와 (C) excites는 동사이고, 명사 (D) excitement는 visitors와 복합명사를 이루기에 적절하지 않으므로 답이 될 수 없다.

번역 시드니 패션 위크는 지난주 수천 명의 들떠 있는 방문객들을 도시로 끌어들였다.

어휘 draw 끌다

102 인칭대명사의 격 _ 주격

해설 빈칸은 접속사 that이 이끄는 명사절에서 동사 is의 주어 자리이고, Ms. Choi를 대신하므로 주격인 (A) she가 정답이다. (B) her와 (D) herself는 목적어 역할을 하므로 주어 자리에 들어갈 수 없고, 소유대명사인 (C) hers는 '그녀의 것'을 의미하므로 문맥상 빈칸에 적합하지 않다.

번역 최 씨는 자신이 기술 대회의 결선 진출자라는 것을 알게 되어 기뻤다.

어휘 finalist 결선 진출자 competition 대회

103 명사 자리 _ 동사의 목적어

해설 빈칸은 동사 should use의 목적어 자리이고 앞에 정관사 the가 있으므로 명사가 들어가야 한다. 따라서 '출입구'를 뜻하는 명사 (B) entrance가 정답이다. (A) enter는 동사, (C) entering은 현재분사/동명사, (D) entered는 동사/과거분사이므로 품사상 답이 될 수 없다.

번역 공장의 모든 방문객들은 건물의 북쪽에 있는 출입구를 사용해야 한다.

104 형용사 어휘

해설 명사 time을 수식하여 '정확한 배송 시간'이라는 의미가 되어야 자연스러우므로 '정확한'이라는 뜻의 (A) exact가 정답이다. (B) obvious는 '(눈으로 보거나 이해하기에) 분명한', (C) absent는 '부재한', (D) inspirational은 '영감을 주는'이라는 의미이다.

번역 유감스럽게도, 저희는 새 노트북 컴퓨터의 정확한 배송 시간을 알려드릴 수 없습니다.

105 to부정사 _ 목적격 보어

해설 ask는 목적격 보어로 to부정사를 취하는 동사로, 주어진 문장은 「ask + 목적어 + to부정사」가 수동태로 된 문장이다. 따라서 「be asked + to부정사」 형태가 되어야 하므로 (C) to respect가 정답이다. (A) respects는 동사/명사, (B) have respected와 (D) will respect는 동사이므로 품사상 답이 될 수 없다.

번역 스타 아일랜드를 방문하는 관광객들은 주민들의 사생활을 존중해 달라고 요청 받는다.

어휘 privacy 사생활

106 부사 어휘

해설 빈칸은 숫자 표현인 11 million kilograms를 강조하는 부사 자리이다. '약 1,100만 킬로그램'이라는 의미가 되어야 자연스러우므로 '대략, 거의'를 뜻하는 부사 (B) nearly가 정답이다. (A) firmly는 '단호히', (C) closely는 '자세히', (D) freely는 '자유롭게'라는 의미이다.

번역 리블린 주식회사는 지난 10년간 약 1,100만 킬로그램의 종이 폐기물을 재활용해 왔다.

어휘 decade 10년

107 명사 어휘

해설 새로운 도르베일 500 운동 기구와 비교 대상이 될 수 있는 명사가 필요하다. previous의 수식을 받아 '이전 모델'이라는 의미가 되어야 자연스러우므로 '모델, 기종'이라는 뜻의 (B) model이 정답이다. (A) time은 '시간', (C) weight는 '무게', (D) class는 '수업'이라는 의미이다.

번역 새로운 도르베일 500 운동 기구는 이전 모델보다 훨씬 더 무겁고 견고하다.

어휘 significantly 훨씬, 상당히　sturdy 견고한　previous 이전의

108 동사 어휘

해설 명사 place를 수식하는 to부정사 자리에 들어갈 동사 어휘를 고르는 문제이다. 빈칸 뒤의 an event를 목적어로 취해 '행사를 개최하기에 완벽한 장소'라는 의미가 되어야 자연스러우므로 '개최하다'를 뜻하는 (C) host가 정답이다. (A) entertain은 '즐겁게 하다', (B) gather는 '모으다', (D) stay는 '머무르다'라는 의미이다.

번역 비치사이드 인은 기업 고객을 위한 행사를 개최하기에 완벽한 장소이다.

어휘 corporate 기업의

109 명사 자리 _ 동사의 주어 / 수 일치

해설 문장의 동사가 복수 동사 have transformed이므로, 빈칸에는 복수 명사인 주어가 들어가야 한다. 따라서 '발전, 진보'를 뜻하는 복수 명사인 (D) Advancements가 정답이다. (A) Advance와 (C) Advancement는 단수 명사이고, (B) Advancing은 동명사일 경우 단수 취급하므로 답이 될 수 없다.

번역 클라우드 컴퓨팅의 발전은 여러 방식으로 게임 산업을 탈바꿈시켰다.

어휘 transform 탈바꿈시키다, 변형시키다

110 전치사 어휘

해설 빈칸 뒤의 명사구 your recent dental appointment를 목적어로 취해 '최근 치과 진료에 대한 의견'이라는 의미가 되어야 자연스러우므로 '~에 대한'을 뜻하는 (A) about이 정답이다. (B) below는 '~ 아래에', (C) near는 '~에서 가까이', (D) onto는 '~ 위로'라는 의미이다.

번역 최근 치과 진료에 대한 의견을 제공하시려면 이 간단한 설문조사에 응해 주십시오.

어휘 appointment (병원·미장원 따위의) 예약　brief 간단한

111 부사 자리 _ 형용사 수식

해설 빈칸은 주격 보어 역할을 하는 형용사 functional을 수식하는 부사 자리이므로 '완전히'라는 뜻의 부사 (C) completely가 정답이다. (A) complete는 동사/형용사, (B) completed는 동사/과거분사, (D) completing은 동명사/현재분사이므로 품사상 답이 될 수 없다.

번역 회사 컴퓨터가 완전히 작동하지 않을 경우, 내선번호 12번으로 IT 부서에 전화하세요.

어휘 functional 작동하는　extension 내선번호

112 명사 어휘　▶ 동영상 강의

해설 주어 역할을 하는 명사 자리로, 전치사구 of electric buses의 수식을 받고 그 뒤의 전치사 to와 잘 어우러져 '기존 차량에 전기 버스를 추가한 것'이라는 내용이 되어야 적절하므로 '추가'를 뜻하는 명사 (B) addition이 정답이다. (A) replacement는 '교체', (C) substitution은 '대체', (D) building은 '건물'을 의미한다.

번역 우리의 기존 차량에 전기 버스를 추가한 것이 통근을 훨씬 더 쾌적하게 만들었다.

어휘 fleet 운행 중인 차량 등의 집합　commuting 통근

113 부사 자리 _ 준동사 수식

해설 빈칸이 없어도 완전한 문장을 이루고 있으므로 빈칸은 부사 자리이다. 앞에 나온 to부정사구 to cool your workspace를 수식하여 '작업 공간을 빠르게 식히기 위해'라는 의미가 되어야 자연스러우므로 '빠르게'라는 뜻의 부사 (D) quickly가 정답이다. (A) quickness는 명사, (B) quicken과 (C) quickens는 동사이므로 품사상 답이 될 수 없다.

번역 즈윕 에어 웨이브는 작업 공간을 빠르게 식히기 위해 강력한 바람을 발생시킨다.

어휘 generate 발생시키다　blast 강한 바람

114 형용사 어휘

해설 뒤에 나온 limited-time exhibits가 기간 한정 전시를 언급하고 있으므로, 빈칸에는 이에 상응하는 '상설 전시'라는 의미를 완성하는 형용사가 와야 한다. 따라서 '상설의, 영구적인'을 뜻하는 (B) permanent가 정답이다. (A) previous는 '이전의', (C) inevitable은 '불가피한', (D) entire는 '전체의'라는 의미이다.

번역 오크힐 미술관은 여러 상설 전시와 일련의 기간 한정 전시들을 제공한다.

115 동사 어휘

해설 주어 Any remote employees와 목적어 Ms. Suzuki 사이의 동사 자리로, '원격 근무 직원은 스즈키 씨에게 알려야 한다'는 의미가 되어야 자연스러우므로 사람을 목적어로 취해 '알리다, 통지하다'를 뜻하는 (D) notify가 정답이다. (A) participate는 '참여하다', (B) activate는 '활성화하다', (C) convene은 '소집하다'라는 의미이다.

번역 추가 컴퓨터 모니터를 원하는 원격 근무 직원은 스즈키 씨에게 알려야 한다.

어휘 remote 원격의

116 형용사 자리 _ 주격 보어

해설 빈칸은 주어 Customer loyalty programs를 보충 설명하는 주격 보어 자리이다. '고객 충성도 프로그램은 이익이 된다'라는 내용이 되어야 자연스러우므로 '이익이 되는, 유익한'을 뜻하는 형용사 (B) profitable이 정답이다. be동사와 결합하여 수동의 의미를 나타내는 과거분사 (A) profited는 고객 충성도 프로그램이 수익의 대상이 아니므로 의미상 적절하지 않고, 부사 (C) profitably는 보어 역할

을 할 수 없으며, 명사 (D) profitability는 고객 충성도 프로그램과 동격을 이루지 않으므로 답이 될 수 없다.

번역 고객 충성도 프로그램은 많은 소매업체들에 이익이 된다.

어휘 loyalty 충성   profit 이득을 주다

117 전치사 어휘

해설 빈칸 뒤의 명사구 the accounts department를 목적어로 취해 '회계 부서에 영수증을 제출하는 것'이라는 의미가 되어야 자연스러우므로 '~에게, ~으로'를 뜻하는 (A) to가 정답이다. (B) as는 '~으로서', (C) on은 '~ 위에', (D) up은 '~ 위로'라는 의미이다.

번역 회계 부서에 출장 증빙 서류를 신속히 제출하면 환급이 더 빨리 처리됩니다.

어휘 prompt 신속한   submission 제출   voucher 증빙 서류   accounts 회계, 계좌   expedite 신속히 처리하다

118 동명사 _ 전치사의 목적어

해설 빈칸은 전치사 After의 목적어 자리로, 부사 extensively의 수식을 받고 있으며 뒤에 목적어 our hiring policies가 있으므로 동명사 (C) reviewing이 정답이다. (A) be reviewing은 동사, (B) reviewed는 동사/과거분사, (D) reviews는 동사/명사이므로 답이 될 수 없다.

번역 채용 정책을 광범위하게 검토한 후, 자문 위원은 더 간단한 절차를 권고했다.

어휘 extensively 광범위하게   process 절차

119 명사 어휘

해설 빈칸은 of Ms. Kenu와 함께 '케누 씨의 지휘'라는 의미가 되어야 자연스러우므로 '지휘, 감독'을 뜻하는 (C) direction이 정답이다. (A) cover는 '덮개', (B) field는 '분야', (D) summary는 '요약'이라는 의미이다. 참고로, under the direction of는 '~의 지휘 아래'라는 의미의 관용표현이다.

번역 케누 씨의 지휘 하에, 올해 역사 학회의 모금 행사는 매우 성공적이었다.

어휘 fund-raiser 모금 행사

120 부사 자리 _ 준동사 수식   ▶ 동영상 강의

해설 동사 decided의 목적어 역할을 하는 to부정사 to proceed 뒤에 빈칸이 있고, proceed는 전치사 with와 함께 '~을 진행하다'라는 의미를 나타내는 자동사로 이미 완전한 문장에 빈칸이 있으므로 부사가 들어가면 된다. 따라서 '신중하게, 조심스럽게'를 뜻하는 부사 (D) cautiously가 정답이다. (A) caution은 동사/명사, (B) cautionary와 (C) cautious는 형용사이므로 답이 될 수 없다.

번역 회사는 새로운 영업 지역으로 확장하려는 계획을 신중하게 진행하기로 결정했다.

어휘 proceed 진행하다   expand 확장하다   territory 지역

121 to부정사 _ 부사적 용법

해설 콤마 뒤에 명령문 형태의 완전한 절이 있고, 빈칸 뒤의 '동사원형+목적어'로 이루어진 구를 연결할 수 있어야 하므로 to부정사가 와야 한다. '건물에 출입하려면'이라는 의미가 되어야 자연스러우므로 '~하기 위해서'라는 목적의 의미를 나타내는 (A) In order to가 정답이다. (B) For instance는 부사 역할을 하는 전치사구, (C) Due to와 (D) As a result of는 전치사이므로 동사를 연결할 수 없다.

번역 건물에 출입하시려면 세입자 안내서에 기재된 코드를 입력하세요.

어휘 tenant 세입자   directory 안내서

122 전치사 자리 / 어휘

해설 Mr. Davis가 주어, will attend가 동사, Monday's meeting이 목적어인 완전한 절이 왔으므로, 빈칸에는 명사구 the marketing department를 목적어로 취해 Mr. Davis를 수식하는 전치사가 들어가야 한다. 문맥상 '마케팅 부서의 데이비스 씨'라는 의미가 되어야 자연스러우므로 '~ 출신의'라는 뜻으로 출신 또는 출처를 나타내는 전치사 (D) from이 정답이다. (A) when은 부사절 접속사, (C) so는 절을 연결하는 등위접속사이고, 전치사 (B) into는 '~ 안으로'라는 의미이므로 답이 될 수 없다.

번역 마케팅 부서의 데이비스 씨는 월요일에 있을 고객과의 미팅에 참석할 예정이다.

123 형용사 어휘

해설 한정사 Several과 명사 reviews 사이에서 reviews를 수식하여 적절한 문맥을 이루는 형용사를 골라야 한다. 소설이 베스트셀러가 되는 데 도움이 되려면 '호평, 좋은 평가'라는 의미가 되어야 자연스러우므로 '좋은, 우수한'을 뜻하는 (C) outstanding이 정답이다. (A) pending은 '미정인', (B) resolved는 '해결된', (D) equivalent는 '동등한'이라는 의미이다.

번역 여러 호평이 그 데뷔 소설을 베스트셀러로 만드는 데 도움이 되었다.

어휘 debut 데뷔, 첫 등장

124 동사 자리 _ 명령문의 동사원형

해설 주어가 생략된 채 Please로 시작하는 명령문에서 동사가 보이지 않으므로 빈칸은 동사 자리이다. 따라서 동사원형 (A) join이 정답이다.

번역 항공 우주 산업에서의 10년 경력을 갖고 새로운 직책에 오르는 시토 박사를 환영하는 데 함께해 주세요.

어휘 aerospace 항공 우주

125 동사 어휘   ▶ 동영상 강의

해설 from most to least important라는 평가 척도에 대한 단서가 있으므로 features를 목적어로 취해 '기능에 대한 순위를 매기다'라는 의미가 되어야 자연스러우므로 '(순위를) 매기다'를 뜻하는 (C) rank가 정답이다. (A) opt는 '선택하다'라는 뜻의 자동사로 목적어

를 취하지 않으며, (B) turn은 '돌리다', (D) guide는 '안내하다'라는 의미로 문맥상 적합하지 않다.

번역 신차 구매자 대상의 설문조사는 중요도가 가장 높은 것에서 가장 낮은 것의 순서로 기능에 대한 순위를 매겨달라고 요청했다.

어휘 feature 기능 in order 순서대로

126 명사 자리 _ 동사의 목적어

해설 빈칸은 동사 oversaw의 목적어 자리이고 앞에 정관사 the가 있으므로 명사가 들어가야 한다. 따라서 '인수, 취득'을 뜻하는 명사 (C) acquisition이 정답이다. (A) acquires는 동사, (B) acquired는 동사/과거분사, (D) acquisitional은 형용사이므로 품사상 답이 될 수 없다.

번역 포엘즈 미술관의 관장으로서, 아후자 씨는 여러 중요한 미술 작품의 인수를 감독했다.

어휘 oversee 감독하다 significant 중요한

127 접속사 자리 _ 부사절 접속사 ▶동영상 강의

해설 빈칸 뒤에 주어 they와 동사 go를 갖춘 완전한 절이 왔으므로 부사절 접속사가 들어가야 한다. '다음 달에 그것들이 시행되기 전에'라는 의미가 되어야 자연스러우므로 '~ 전에'를 뜻하는 부사절 접속사 (D) before가 정답이다. (A) rather than은 '~ 보다는', (B) as well as는 '~뿐만 아니라'라는 의미이고, (D) despite는 '~에도 불구하고'라는 뜻의 전치사이므로 절을 연결할 수 없다.

번역 우리는 다음 달 규약의 변경사항이 시행되기 전에, 오늘 중으로 이를 논의하기 위한 회의를 열 것이다.

어휘 protocol 규약 go into effect 시행되다

128 전치사 자리 / 어휘

해설 빈칸 앞에 완전한 절이 있으므로 calling 800-555-0121은 분사구문 또는 전치사의 목적어 역할을 하는 동명사구로 볼 수 있다. 문맥상 '800-555-0121번으로 전화함으로써'라는 의미가 되어야 자연스러우므로, 동명사구를 목적어로 취해 '~함으로써'라는 뜻으로 수단이나 방법을 나타내는 전치사 (A) by가 정답이다. (B) because는 부사절 접속사, (C) ever는 부사이고, 전치사 (D) at은 의미상 적합하지 않다.

번역 고객 서비스 담당자에게 오전 8시부터 오후 4시 사이에 800-555-0121번으로 전화하여 연락하실 수 있습니다.

129 부사 어휘

해설 동사구 is challenging 사이에서 동사를 수식하는 부사 자리로, 문맥상 '협업은 종종 쉽지 않지만 우리의 컨설팅이 그 과정을 단순화할 수 있다'는 내용이 되어야 자연스러우므로 '종종'을 뜻하는 (B) often이 정답이다. (A) well은 '잘', (C) deliberately는 '고의로', (D) finally는 '마침내'라는 의미이다.

번역 여러 대행사 간의 협업은 종종 쉽지 않은 일이지만, 저희의 프로젝트 기반 컨설팅은 그 과정을 단순화시켜 드릴 수 있습니다.

어휘 collaboration 협업, 협력 simplify 단순화하다 process 과정

130 지시대명사 ▶동영상 강의

해설 빈칸은 「as+원급+as」 뒤의 목적어 자리로, Giovanni's Bistro의 디저트와 비교되는 대상이 와야 한다. 앞서 언급된 복수 명사 The desserts를 반복해서 사용하는 것을 피하기 위해 지시대명사가 오는 것이 자연스러우므로 (B) those가 정답이다. 정확히 동일한 대상을 지칭할 때 쓰는 인칭대명사 (D) them은 답이 될 수 없다. 참고로, 대명사 those는 뒤에 수식어가 붙을 수 있다.

번역 지오반니스 비스트로에서 우리가 먹었던 디저트는 몬테베르디즈 타베르나에서 즐겼던 것들만큼 맛있지 않았다.

PART 6

131-134 길 안내

캐릴 연구소로 오시는 길

보우먼 가 3017번지에 있는 정문으로 들어오셔서 **131 보안** 요원에게 서명을 남겨 주세요. 엘리베이터를 타고 2층으로 올라가세요. **132 아니면**, 엘리베이터 왼쪽에 있는 계단을 이용하셔도 됩니다. 2층에 도착하시면 **133 바로** 왼쪽으로 돌아서 이중문이 나올 때까지 계속 직진하세요. 문을 통과하시고 방문객 라운지를 지나세요. **134 연구소는 오른쪽에 있는 다음 문입니다.**

어휘 directions 길 안내 laboratory 연구소, 실험실 sign in 서명하고 들어가다 proceed 나아가다

131 명사 자리 _ 복합명사

해설 전치사 with의 목적어 역할을 하는 명사 guard와 그 앞의 정관사 the 사이에 빈칸이 있으므로 형용사 또는 복합명사를 이루는 명사가 들어가야 한다. '보안 요원에게 서명을 남겨 달라'는 내용이 되어야 자연스러우므로, '보안'이라는 뜻으로 guard와 복합명사를 이루는 명사 (B) security가 정답이다. 형용사 (A) secure는 '안심하는, 안전한', 현재분사 (D) securing은 '확보하는'이라는 뜻으로 의미상 어울리지 않고, (C) securely는 부사이므로 품사상 답이 될 수 없다.

132 접속부사

해설 앞 문장에서 엘리베이터를 타고 2층으로 가라(Take the elevator to the second floor)며 2층에 갈 수 있는 하나의 방법을 알려주고 있고, 뒤 문장에서 엘리베이터 왼쪽의 계단을 이용해도 된다(you may use the stairs to the left of the elevator)며 2층으로 가는 다른 방법을 추가적으로 제시하고 있다. 따라서 '아니면, 그 대신에'라는 뜻으로 대안을 소개할 때 사용하는 (A) Alternatively가 정답이다. (B) Consequently는 '결과적으로', (C) Furthermore는 '게다가', (D) Nevertheless는 '그렇기는 하지만'이라는 의미이다.

133 부사 어휘

해설 이동 경로를 안내하는 문장으로, 각 경로가 끝날 때마다 즉각적으로 다음 경로에 대한 지침이 수행되어야 한다. '도착하면 바로 왼쪽으로 돌아라'는 의미가 되어야 자연스러우므로 '바로, 즉시'를 뜻하는 (D) immediately가 정답이다. (A) temporarily는 '일시적으로', (B) responsibly는 '책임감 있게', (C) patiently는 '참을성 있게'라는 의미이다.

134 문맥에 맞는 문장 고르기

번역 (A) 연구소는 오른쪽에 있는 다음 문입니다.
(B) 방문객 주차장은 평일에는 보통 만차입니다.
(C) 연구소의 연사 시리즈는 일반인들에게 공개됩니다.
(D) 올해는 연구소의 35주년을 기념합니다.

해설 지문 전체에 걸쳐 연구소로 오는 길을 안내하고 있고, 바로 앞 문장에서도 문을 통과하고 방문객 라운지를 지나라(Proceed through the doors and pass the visitors' lounge)며 경로 안내를 계속하고 있으므로, 이 안내문의 마지막 문장으로는 연구소의 위치를 최종적으로 알려주는 내용이 적합하다. 따라서 연구소는 오른쪽에 있는 다음 문으로 가야 한다고 언급하는 (A)가 정답이다.

어휘 mark 기념하다 anniversary 기념일

135-138 공지

메이플글렌 대학교

경영학 석사

메이플글렌 대학교는 12월이 학부생들에게 일 년 중 **135 바쁜** 시기임을 알고 있습니다. 그래서 여러분에게 경영학 석사(MBA) 과정에 지원서를 제출할 수 있는 추가 시간을 드리고자 합니다. 우리는 원래 마감일을 12월 31일로 연장했습니다. 3월 학기 입학에 **136 고려되기 위해서는**, 우리가 동일 날짜까지 여러분의 공식 학부 성적 증명서를 받아볼 수 있도록 해 주십시오. MBA 과정의 요건**137 에 관한** 질문이 있을 경우, apply@mapleglen.ecu로 입학처에 연락하십시오. **138 여러분의 지원서를 읽게 되기를 기대합니다.**

어휘 master 석사 business administration 경영학 undergraduate 학부생 application 지원서 extend 연장하다 admission 입학 semester 학기 official 공식적인 transcript 성적 증명서 requirement 요건

135 형용사 어휘

해설 뒤 문장에서 경영학 석사 과정 지원서 제출을 위한 추가 시간을 주기 위해 마감일을 연장했다고 했으므로, '12월은 바쁜 시기'라는 내용이 되어야 추가 시간을 주는 합당한 이유가 제시된다. 따라서 '바쁜'을 뜻하는 (C) busy가 정답이다. (A) cold는 '추운', (B) long은 '긴', (D) sure는 '확신하는'이라는 의미이다.

136 to부정사 _ 부사적 용법

해설 콤마 뒤에 명령문 형태의 완전한 절이 있으므로, 빈칸에는 전치사구 for admission to the March semester를 뒤의 절에 적절히 연결할 수 있는 to부정사 또는 분사구문이 들어가야 한다. 문맥상 '3월 학기 입학에 고려되기 위해서는'라는 의미가 되어야 자연스러우므로 '~하기 위해서, ~할 수 있도록'이라는 뜻으로 목적의 의미를 나타내는 to부정사 (B) To be considered가 정답이다. (A) Being considered와 (C) Having been considered는 의미상 적합하지 않고, (D) Considering은 뒤에 목적어가 와야 한다.

137 전치사 어휘

해설 빈칸 뒤의 명사구 the MBA program requirements를 목적어로 취해 빈칸 앞의 명사구 any questions를 수식하기에 적절한 전치사를 고르는 문제이다. 'MBA 과정 요건에 관한 질문'이라는 의미가 되어야 자연스러우므로 '~에 관하여'를 뜻하는 (D) regarding이 정답이다. (A) between은 '~ 사이에', (B) after는 '~ 후에', (C) except는 '~을 제외하고'라는 의미이다.

138 문맥에 맞는 문장 고르기

번역 (A) 여러분의 지원서를 읽게 되기를 기대합니다.
(B) 학부 과정은 종종 자기소개서를 요구합니다.
(C) 공중 위생학에 과정을 추가했습니다.
(D) 기록적인 수의 예비 학생들이 지원했습니다.

해설 앞 문장에서 MBA 과정 요건에 관한 질문이 있을 시 연락할 수 있는 입학처의 이메일 주소(Please contact our admissions department at apply@mapleglen.edu)를 알려주고 있으므로, 빈칸에는 마지막으로 MBA 지원을 독려하는 내용이 들어가야 자연스럽다. 따라서 지원서를 읽게 되기를 기대한다고 언급하는 (A)가 정답이다.

어휘 frequently 종종, 자주 personal statement 자기소개서 record 기록적인 prospective 예비의, 장래의 apply 지원하다

139-142 이메일

수신: 고위 임원진
발신: 강 석
날짜: 9월 15일
제목: 앱 업데이트
첨부: 앱 사양; 보도 자료

모두 아시다시피, 레스토랑의 다가오는 신 메뉴 출시에 맞춰 우리 모바일 앱에 몇 가지를 변경했습니다. **139 가장 중요한 점으로**, 우리는 이전 버전의 여러 문제를 바로잡았습니다. **140 이 문제들 중에는 화면이 정지되는 경향이 있었습니다.** 저는 포커스 그룹의 구성원들이 재설계된 앱에 훌륭한 평가를 내렸다는 것을 보고하게 되어 아주 기쁩니다. 특히, **141 그들은** 다양한 기능을 사용하기가 얼마나 간단한지에 대해 언급했습니다. 앱의 사양 설명서와 보도 자료 초안을 이 이메일에 첨부했습니다. 문의 사항이나 제안 사항이 있으실 경우, 9월 17일까지 알려주십시오. 앱과 메뉴의 공식 출시는 9월 25일 목요일에 **142 발표될 예정입니다.**

> 어휘 senior 고위의, 상급의   executive 임원   specs 사양
> press release 보도 자료   coincide with ~에 맞추다,
> ~와 동시에 일어나다   launch 출시   previous 이전의
> delighted 아주 기쁜   in particular 특히   feature 기능
> specifications 사양 설명서   draft 초안

139 접속부사

해설 빈칸 앞 문장에서 신 메뉴 출시에 맞춰 모바일 앱에 몇 가지를 변경했다고 했고, 빈칸 뒤에서 이전 버전의 여러 문제를 바로잡았다며 변경 사항 중 일부 내용을 언급하고 있다. 몇 가지 변경 사항 중 문제에 대한 수정을 가장 먼저 언급하고 있으므로 여러 사안 중 핵심적 항목을 강조할 때 사용하는 '가장 중요하게, 특히'라는 뜻의 (D) Most significantly가 정답이다. (A) After all은 '결국', (B) In any case는 '어쨌든', (C) On the contrary는 '그와는 반대로'라는 의미이다.

140 문맥에 맞는 문장 고르기

번역 (A) 새 지점에 관하여 곧 업데이트 받기를 바랍니다.
(B) 이 문제들 중에는 화면이 정지되는 경향이 있었습니다.
(C) 이제 많은 레스토랑 앱에 온라인 주문이 포함되어 있습니다.
(D) 새로운 항목들이 다음 달에 메뉴에 추가될 예정입니다.

해설 앞 문장에서 이전 버전의 여러 문제를 바로잡았다(we have corrected several issues with the previous version)고 했다. 문맥상 앞에서 언급한 문제가 어떠한 문제였는지를 설명하는 내용이 들어가야 자연스러우므로 (B)가 정답이다.

어휘 tendency 경향   freeze 정지하다

141 인칭대명사의 격 _ 주격

해설 빈칸은 동사 commented의 주어 자리이므로 주격 대명사가 들어가야 한다. 또한 앞 문장에서 언급된 포커스 그룹의 구성원들이 내린 평가 중 일부 내용을 언급하고 있으므로 포커스 그룹의 구성원들(our focus group members)을 지칭하는 주격 인칭대명사 (C) they가 정답이다.

142 동사 자리 _ 시제

해설 빈칸은 주어 The official launch의 동사 자리이다. 이메일의 작성 날짜가 9월 15일(15 September)이고, 빈칸이 있는 문장에서는 9월 25일(25 September)에 있을 앱과 메뉴의 공식 출시에 대해 언급하고 있으므로 미래 시제가 들어가야 한다. 따라서 (B) will be announced가 정답이다.

143-146 제품 후기 ▶동영상 강의

이 게시글의 대가로 팁티 PX200 디지털 카메라를 무료로 받았음을 미리 밝힙니다. 143 **하지만** 무료 카메라와 장비를 받을 때조차, 저는 솔직한 의견을 공유하기를 결코 망설이지 않습니다. 144 **저는 제품을 평가할 때 항상 정직합니다.** 팁티 PX200은 영상 블로거들과 온라인 콘텐츠 제작자들을 위해 기획되었지만 더 다양한 기능이 필요한 영화 제작자들에게는 적합하지 않습니다. 이는 중요한 145 **차이점**입니다. 짧은 영상을 온라인에 게시하는 작업을 146 **쉽게** 해주는 소형 카메라를 찾고 있다면 이 제품은 가격 대비 훌륭한 선택입니다.

— 손야 스탠베리

> 어휘 disclose 밝히다   up front 미리, 먼저   receive 받다
> in exchange for ~의 대가로   post 게시글   hesitate 망설이다
> candid 솔직한   unsuitable 적합하지 않은   a range of 다양한
> feature 기능   compact 소형의

143 접속부사

해설 빈칸 앞 문장에서 게시글의 대가로 무료 카메라를 받았음을 밝힌다고 했고, 빈칸 뒤에서 솔직한 의견 공유를 망설이지 않는다고 했다. 따라서 '제품은 무료로 받았지만 솔직한 의견을 낸다'며 대조적인 의미로 연결되어야 자연스러우므로 '하지만, 그러나'라는 뜻의 (B) However가 정답이다. (A) In fact는 '사실은', (C) Therefore는 '그러므로', (D) To the contrary는 '그와는 반대로'라는 의미이다.

144 문맥에 맞는 문장 고르기

번역 (A) 저는 제품을 평가할 때 항상 정직합니다.
(B) 저는 비슷한 크기의 다른 카메라가 궁금합니다.
(C) 많은 사람들이 휴대전화로 사진을 찍습니다.
(D) 출판사들도 평론가들에게 무료 책을 정기적으로 제공합니다.

해설 앞 문장에서 무료 제품을 받을 때조차 솔직한 의견을 공유한다(share my candid opinion)고 했으므로, 빈칸에는 제품에 대한 솔직한 평가를 강조하는 내용이 들어가야 자연스럽다. 따라서 제품을 평가할 때 항상 정직하다고 언급하는 (A)가 정답이다.

어휘 curious 궁금한   regularly 정기적으로   reviewer 평론가

145 명사 어휘

해설 앞 문장에서 팁티 PX200이 영상 블로거들과 온라인 콘텐츠 제작자들을 위해 기획되었지만 영화 제작자들에게는 적합하지 않다는 차이점에 대해 언급하고 있고, 빈칸이 있는 문장에서 This는 앞 문장에서 언급된 차이를 가리키므로 '이는 중요한 차이점이다'라는 내용이 되어야 자연스럽다. 따라서 '차이, 구분'을 뜻하는 (D) distinction이 정답이다. (A) event는 '행사', (B) policy는 '정책', (C) credential은 '자격(증)'을 의미한다.

146 형용사 자리 _ 목적격 보어

해설 빈칸은 a compact camera를 수식하는 관계사절의 동사 makes의 목적격 보어 자리로 it이 가목적어, to post 이하가 진목적어 역할을 하는 「make + it + 형용사 + to부정사」 구문으로 이루어져 있다. 따라서 빈칸에는 형용사가 들어가야 하므로 (A) easy가 정답이다. (B) ease는 동사/명사, (C) easing은 동명사/현재분사, (D) to ease는 to부정사이므로 빈칸에 들어갈 수 없다.

PART 7

147-148 이메일

수신: 전 직원
발신: 카리나 리박, 마케팅 부서
날짜: 2월 2일
제목: 정보

여러분 중 일부는 아시다시피, 박선이 씨가 우리 서울 지사로 전근을 갑니다. **147** 그녀의 송별회가 2월 21일 오후 3시에 2층 회의실에서 열립니다. **148** 참석하실 계획이라면 2월 16일까지 이 이메일로 회신하셔서 저에게 알려주세요. 회사에서 피자와 케이크를 제공할 예정이며, 모두를 위해 충분한 음식이 있도록 하고자 합니다. 선이 씨를 축하하는 자리에서 여러분을 볼 수 있기를 바랍니다!

어휘 transfer 전근 가다; 전근

147 주제 / 목적

번역 이메일의 목적은?
(A) 회의 계획에 도움을 요청하려고
(B) 새로운 직원을 소개하려고
(C) 사교 행사에 직원을 초대하려고
(D) 서울 지사가 문을 여는 것을 알리려고

해설 두 번째 문장에서 박선이 씨의 송별회가 2월 21일 오후 3시에 2층 회의실에서 열린다(Her going-away party will take place at 3:00 P.M. on 21 February in the second-floor conference room)는 것을 알리고 있으므로 직원들을 송별회에 초대하려고 작성한 이메일임을 알 수 있다. 따라서 (C)가 정답이다.

어휘 social 사교상의

Paraphrasing
지문의 going-away party → 정답의 social event

148 세부 사항

번역 이메일에 따르면, 2월 16일까지 직원들은 무엇을 해야 하는가?
(A) 전근 요청
(B) 리박 씨에게 이메일 발송
(C) 카드 서명
(D) 출장 음식 주문 제출

해설 세 번째 문장에서 리박 씨가 직원들에게 참석할 계획이라면 2월 16일까지 이 이메일로 회신해서 알려달라(Please reply to this e-mail by 16 February to let me know if you plan to attend)고 요청하고 있으므로 (B)가 정답이다.

어휘 submit 제출하다

149-150 전단

149 요한의 고압 청소
149 메도우브룩 지역에 25년 넘게 서비스를 제공해왔습니다!

고압 청소는 여러분의 집을 아름답게 해주고
건물의 온전한 상태를 유지하는 데 도움을 줍니다!

150(B) 저희가 제공하는 서비스는 다음과 같습니다:
• 건물 외장재, 현관, 데크 등의 고압 청소
• 배수로 청소 및 광택 작업
• 콘크리트 청소 및 보호막 처리
• 창문 청소

요한 G. 마티
150(C) 506-555-0193
150(A) www.johanspowerwashing.ca

무료 견적을 원하시거나 청소 일정을 잡으시려면 지금 바로 전화 주세요.

어휘 beautify 아름답게 하다 maintain 유지하다
integrity 온전함 structure 건축물 siding 건물 외장재
porch 현관 gutter 배수로 scrub (솔로) 문질러 씻다
seal (보호막 등을) 바르다 estimate 견적

149 주제 / 목적

번역 전단의 목적은?
(A) 지역 업체를 광고하려고
(B) 지역 회의를 공지하려고
(C) 회사 서비스에 대한 의견을 요청하려고
(D) 주민들에게 주택 유지관리 규정을 알리려고

해설 광고 상단에 요한의 고압 청소(Johan's Power Washing)라는 업체 이름과 메도우브룩 지역에 25년 넘게 서비스를 제공해왔다(Serving the Meadowbrook community for over 25 years!)는 문구가 있는 것으로 보아 메도우브룩 지역의 청소 업체를 광고하는 글임을 알 수 있다. 따라서 (A)가 정답이다.

어휘 maintenance 유지관리 regulation 규정

150 Not / True

번역 전단에 포함된 정보가 아닌 것은?
(A) 웹 주소
(B) 서비스 목록
(C) 전화번호
(D) 우편 주소

해설 전단의 중반부에서 제공하는 서비스는 다음과 같다(The services we offer include)며 서비스 목록을 나열하고 있으므로 (B), 전단의 하단에 506-555-0193과 www.johanspowerwashing.ca라고 전화번호와 웹사이트 주소가 나와 있으므로 (C)와 (A)는 지문에 명확히 언급되어 있다. 우편 주소에 대한 내용은 없으므로 (D)가 정답이다.

151-152 문자 메시지

메이 킴 (오전 10시 2분)
안녕하세요, 스탠. 점심 약속 있으세요?

스탠 스나이더 (오전 10시 5분)
회사 카페에서 샌드위치를 사다 책상에서 먹으려고요. 왜 물어보시나요?

메이 킴 (오전 10시 6분)
152 써니 아울 레스토랑에서 같이 식사하는 건 어떠세요? 오늘 오후에 고객과 만나기 전에 맥밀런 프로젝트에 대해 이야기하고 싶어요.

스탠 스나이더 (오전 10시 9분)
좋은 생각이에요. 151 저도 프로젝트 예산에 대해 질문이 좀 있거든요. 151, 152 아무래도 마리아 트루히요 씨도 함께 하자고 물어보는 게 좋을까요?

메이 킴 (오전 10시 10분)
제가 할게요. 11시 45분에 로비에서 만날까요?

스탠 스나이더 (오전 10시 11분)
완벽해요. 그때 봐요.

어휘 budget 예산 handle 처리하다

151 추론 / 암시

번역 트루히요 씨에 대해 사실일 것 같은 것은?
(A) 스나이더 씨와 킴 씨의 상사이다.
(B) 회사 카페에서 정기적으로 점심을 먹는다.
(C) 프로젝트 예산에 대한 정보를 가지고 있다.
(D) 오후에 고객과 만날 수 없다.

해설 10시 9분에 스나이더 씨가 프로젝트 예산에 대해 질문이 좀 있다(I have some questions too—about the project's budget)면서 마리아 트루히요 씨도 함께 하자고 물어보는 게 좋을지(Maybe we should ask Maria Trujillo to join us as well?)를 묻는 것으로 보아, 트루히요 씨가 프로젝트 예산에 관한 정보를 가지고 있음을 유추할 수 있다. 따라서 (C)가 정답이다.

어휘 supervisor 상사 regularly 정기적으로

152 의도 파악

번역 오전 10시 10분에 킴 씨가 "제가 할게요"라고 쓴 의도는?
(A) 고객의 사무실로 가는 길이다.
(B) 동료를 점심 식사에 초대할 것이다.
(C) 써니 아울 레스토랑에 음식을 배달해 달라고 요청할 것이다.
(D) 고객 미팅에 가져가야 할 것을 기억했다.

해설 10시 6분에 킴 씨가 써니 아울 레스토랑에서 같이 식사하는 게 어떨지(How about joining me at the Sunny Owl Restaurant?)를 제안하자, 10시 9분에 스나이더 씨가 마리아 트루히요 씨도 함께 하자고 물어보는 게 좋을지(Maybe we should ask Maria Trujillo to join us as well?)를 추가적으로 제안하고 있다. 이에 대해 킴 씨가 자신이 하겠다(I'll handle it)고 답한 것은 자신이 트루히요 씨를 점심 식사에 초대하겠다는 의도임을 알 수 있다. 따라서 (B)가 정답이다.

153-154 공지

웨스트오버 동물원에 오신 것을 환영합니다!

- 153(A) 유아를 포함한 모든 방문객에게 입장권이 요구됩니다. 153(D) 티켓은 인쇄하거나 전자상으로 제시하실 수 있습니다.

- 티켓은 명시된 날짜에만 유효합니다. 교환은 티켓에 기재된 날짜로부터 24시간 전까지 요청할 수 있습니다. 교환 및 기타 정보는 153(C) 저희 웹사이트 westoverzoo.org로 방문하세요.

- 154 주차장은 무료이나 빠르게 만차가 됩니다. 방문객들은 대중교통을 이용하실 것을 권장합니다. 오렌지와 블루 노선의 버스는 모두 동물원 입구에 정차합니다. 여름철에는 방문객들을 수용하기 위해 해당 노선에 추가 버스가 운행됩니다.

어휘 admission 입장 infant 유아 present 제시하다 electronically 전자적으로 good 유효한 fill 채워지다 public transportation 대중교통 entrance 입구 extra 추가의, 여분의 accommodate 수용하다

153 Not / True

번역 웨스트오버 동물원에 대해 명시되지 않은 것은?
(A) 동물원을 방문하는 어린이들은 티켓이 있어야 한다.
(B) 동물원은 여름철에만 운영된다.
(C) 동물원은 웹사이트가 있다.
(D) 동물원 방문객들은 종이 또는 전자 티켓을 사용할 수 있다.

해설 첫 단락 첫 문장에서 유아를 포함한 모든 방문객에게 입장권이 요구된다(Admission tickets are required for all visitors, including infants)고 했으므로 (A), 같은 단락 두 번째 문장에서 티켓은 인쇄하거나 전자상으로 제시할 수 있다(Tickets may be printed or presented electronically)고 했으므로 (D), 두 번째 단락 마지막 문장에서 웹사이트 westoverzoo.org로 방문하라(visit our Web site, westoverzoo.org)고 했으므로 (C)는 모두 언급된 사실이다. 여름철에만 운영된다는 내용은 없으므로 (B)가 정답이다.

Paraphrasing
지문의 Tickets may be printed or presented electronically
→ 보기 (D)의 paper or electronic tickets

154 Not / True

번역 공지에서 교통편에 대해 언급된 것은?
(A) 방문객은 동물원에 주차하기 위해 추가 요금을 지불해야 한다.
(B) 방문객은 무료로 공영 버스를 탈 수 있다.
(C) 방문객이 이용할 수 있는 주차 공간이 한정적이다.
(D) 동물원 입구에 방문객을 위한 택시 승차장이 있다.

해설 세 번째 단락의 첫 문장에서 주차장은 무료이나 빠르게 만차가 된다(Our parking area is free but fills quickly)고 했으므로 방문객은 주차 공간을 이용할 수는 있으나 공간이 한정적임을 알 수 있다. 따라서 (C)가 정답이다.

어휘 taxi stand 택시 승차장

155-157 기사

건설 프로젝트 계획

힐스데일 (7월 7일) — 155 힐스데일의 계속 증가하는 인구를 수용하기 위해, 시의회는 두 가지 주요 건설 프로젝트가 계획되어 있다고 목요일에 발표했다.

첫 번째 프로젝트는 도시 남쪽 끝에 새로운 상업 지역을 건설하는 것이며, 이는 도심 상업 지구가 확장할 공간이 없기 때문이다. 이 지역의 한 구역은 오로지 음식점과 소규모 상점 전용인 반면 다른 한 구역은 사무실 공간으로 마련될 것이다.

155, 157 두 번째 프로젝트로는 남쪽 끝의 대규모 부지에 주거용 주택을 건설할 예정이다. 이 지역에는 아파트뿐만 아니라 단독 주택도 포함될 것이다. 156 새로운 주거 지역과 새로운 상업 지역은 포장 보도가 있는 공원으로 연결된다.

도시 계획자들은 두 프로젝트 모두 다음 달 이내에 시작되어, 내년 말에는 업체와 주민들이 입주하기를 바라고 있다.

어휘 accommodate 수용하다 ever-growing 계속 증가하는 population 인구 commercial 상업의 district 지구 expand 확장하다 dedicated ~ 전용의 exclusively 오로지 residential 주거의 housing 주택 lot 부지 paved 포장된 pathway 보도, 좁은 길

155 추론 / 암시

번역 힐스데일 시에 대해 암시된 것은?
(A) 도심에 식당이 없다.
(B) 남쪽으로 큰 공원과 접해 있다.
(C) 더 많은 주택이 필요하다.
(D) 최근 몇 년간 많은 공사를 겪었다.

해설 첫 단락 첫 문장에서 힐스데일의 계속 증가하는 인구를 수용하기 위해 시의회는 두 가지 주요 건설 프로젝트가 계획되어 있다고 목요일에 발표했다(To accommodate Hillsdale's ever-growing population, the town council announced on Thursday that two major construction projects are planned)고 했고, 세 번째 단락의 첫 문장에서 두 번째 프로젝트로는 남쪽 끝의 대규모 부지에 주거용 주택을 건설할 예정(The second project will build residential housing on a large empty lot at the south end)이라고 했다. 이를 통해 힐스데일의 인구가 증가함에 따라 주택에 대한 수요 또한 증가하여 주택 건설이 추진되고 있음을 추론할 수 있다. 따라서 (C)가 정답이다.

어휘 border (경계를) 접하다 undergo 겪다

156 Not / True

번역 계획된 상업 지역에 대해 명시된 것은?
(A) 새 주택으로부터 도보 거리 이내에 있을 것이다.
(B) 새로운 주거 지역보다 건설 비용이 덜 들 것이다.
(C) 새 주택이 완공된 후에 건설될 것이다.
(D) 현재 공원으로 사용되는 땅에 건설될 것이다.

해설 세 번째 단락의 세 번째 문장에서 새로운 주거 지역과 새로운 상업 지역은 포장 보도가 있는 공원으로 연결된다(The new residential area and the new commercial area will be connected by a park with paved pathways)고 했으므로 상업 지역은 새 주택과 도보 거리 이내에 있다는 것을 알 수 있다. 따라서 (A)가 정답이다.

어휘 distance 거리

157 문장 삽입

번역 [1], [2], [3], [4]로 표시된 위치 중에서 다음 문장이 들어가기에 가장 적합한 곳은?

"이 지역에는 아파트뿐만 아니라 단독 주택도 포함될 것이다."

(A) [1]
(B) [2]
(C) [3]
(D) [4]

해설 주어진 문장에서 이 지역(This area)에는 아파트와 단독 주택(apartments as well as single-family homes)도 포함될 것이라고 했으므로, 주어진 문장 앞에는 주거 지역 건설 계획에 대한 내용이 있어야 한다. 따라서 남쪽 끝의 대규모 부지에 주거지를 구성한다는 계획을 언급하는 문장 뒤인 [3]에 들어가는 것이 글의 흐름상 자연스러우므로 (C)가 정답이다.

158-160 정보

미레이 헤어 케어

158 칼린데 글로벌 화장품의 일본 자회사

158 미레이 헤어 케어를 위한 투자 옵션

옵션	예상 비용	주요 이점
1. 더 큰 생산 시설 건설	4억 1천8백만 엔	160(A) 더 큰 생산 능력
159 2. 광고 예산 증액	2억 1천만 엔	159 브랜드 인지도 향상
3. 선두 경쟁사 인수	1억 8천만 엔	경쟁 감소
4. 유통 확장	1억 4천8백만 엔	160(D) 판매 증가
5. 포장 재설계	1억 2천9백만 엔	160(C) 제품당 비용 감소

어휘 subsidiary 자회사 investment 투자 estimated 예상의 benefit 이점 facility 시설 capacity 능력 budget 예산 awareness 인지도 competitor 경쟁자 reduced 감소한 competition 경쟁 expand 확장하다 distribution 유통 packaging 포장 lower 낮추다

158 추론 / 암시

번역 누구를 대상으로 하는 정보인 것 같은가?
(A) 헤어 케어 산업에 투자하는 개인
(B) 화장품을 개발하는 연구자
(C) 국제 기업을 이끄는 임원
(D) 미레이 헤어 케어 제품을 구매하는 고객

해설 지문의 상단에 미레이 헤어 케어가 칼린데 글로벌 화장품의 일본 자회사(a Japanese subsidiary of Khalinde Global

Cosmetics, Inc.)라고 나와 있고 미레이 헤어 케어를 위한 투자 옵션(Investment Options for Mirei Hair Care)이라는 제목의 표가 있는 것으로 보아, 글로벌 기업의 지도부에서 향후 투자 방안을 논의하는 데 필요한 정보 자료임을 알 수 있다. 따라서 (C)가 정답이다.

어휘 individual 개인 researcher 연구자 executive 임원

> **Paraphrasing**
> 지문의 Global → 정답의 international

159 세부 사항

번역 회사를 대중에게 더 널리 알리기 위해 제안된 전략은?
(A) 옵션 2
(B) 옵션 3
(C) 옵션 4
(D) 옵션 5

해설 표의 두 번째 항목에서 광고 예산 증액(2. Increase advertising budget)의 주요 이점은 브랜드 인지도 향상(Better brand awareness)이라고 했으므로, 두 번째 옵션은 브랜드를 대중에게 널리 홍보하기 위한 전략임을 알 수 있다. 따라서 (A)가 정답이다.

어휘 strategy 전략

> **Paraphrasing**
> 지문의 Better brand awareness → 질문의 make the company more widely known by the public

160 Not / True

번역 잠재적 이점으로 나열된 것이 아닌 것은?
(A) 생산 능력 제고
(B) 공석 감소
(C) 비용 절감
(D) 매출 증대

해설 표의 주요 이점을 나열한 항목 중 첫 번째는 더 큰 생산 능력(Larger production capacity)이므로 (A), 네 번째는 판매 증가(Increased sales)이므로 (D), 다섯 번째는 제품당 비용 감소(Lower per-item cost)이므로 (C)는 언급되었으나, 일자리에 관한 내용은 없으므로 (B)가 정답이다.

어휘 potential 잠재적인 capability 능력 vacancy 공석

161-163 정책

https://www.barbadosairlines.com/baggage

바베이도스 항공 수하물 정책

모든 바베이도스 항공 승객들은 161 **개인 소지품(예를 들어, 핸드백이나 노트북 가방)** 하나를 기내에 가지고 들어갈 수 있습니다. 개인 물품은 좌석 아래에 들어가야 하므로 45x35x20센티미터보다 커서는 안 됩니다. 아동용 안전 시트는 승객의 개인 물품 허용 범주에 포함되지 않습니다.

20유로의 수수료에 승객은 여행 가방이나 더플백과 같은 기내용 수하물을 기내에 가지고 갈 수 있습니다. 좌석 상단의 수하물 칸에 맞도록 162 **기내용 물품은 손잡이, 끈, 바퀴를 포함해 56x36x23센티미터를 초과해서는 안 됩니다.** 이 치수보다 큰 기내용 물품은 위탁 수하물로 처리되며 50유로의 수수료가 발생됩니다.

163 **특별 허가가 있으면 스포츠 장비와 악기 같은 대형 물품도 기내용 물품처럼 기내에 반입될 수 있습니다.** 이 같은 대형 물품은 기내에 가지고 가기 전에 고객 서비스 담당자에게 연락해 주십시오.

어휘 baggage 수하물 passenger 승객 cabin 기내 child safety seat 아동용 안전 시트 count toward ~에 포함되다 allowance 허용량 carry-on 기내용 compartment 칸 exceed 초과하다 strap 끈 dimension 치수 baggage hold 화물 칸 incur 발생시키다 permission 허가

161 세부 사항

번역 정책에 따르면, 개인 소지품으로 간주되는 것은?
(A) 핸드백
(B) 기타
(C) 큰 여행 가방
(D) 아동용 시트

해설 첫 단락 첫 번째 문장에서 개인 소지품의 예로 핸드백이나 노트북 가방(personal item (for example, a handbag or laptop bag))을 언급하고 있으므로 (A)가 정답이다.

> **Paraphrasing**
> 지문의 handbag → 정답의 purse

162 Not / True

번역 기내용 수하물에 대해 명시된 것은?
(A) 모든 승객들에게 무료이다.
(B) 최대 허용 크기가 있다.
(C) 바퀴가 있으면 안 된다.
(D) 스포츠 장비는 포함되지 않는다.

해설 두 번째 단락 두 번째 문장에서 기내용 물품은 손잡이, 끈, 바퀴를 포함해 56×36×23센티미터를 초과해서는 안 된다(carry-on items must not exceed 56×36×23 centimetres, including handles, straps, and wheels)고 크기 제한을 두고 있으므로 (B)가 정답이다.

어휘 allowable 허용되는

> **Paraphrasing**
> 지문의 must not exceed 56×36×23 centimetres → 정답의 have a maximum allowable size

163 문장 삽입

번역 [1], [2], [3], [4]로 표시된 위치 중에서 다음 문장이 들어가기에 가장 적합한 곳은?

"이 같은 대형 물품은 기내에 가지고 가기 전에 고객 서비스 담당자에게 연락해 주십시오."
(A) [1]
(B) [2]
(C) [3]
(D) [4]

해설 주어진 문장에서 이 같은 대형 물품(large items like these)은 기내에 반입하기 전에 연락해 달라고 했으므로, 주어진 문장 앞에는 대형 물품에 대한 내용이 있어야 한다. 따라서 스포츠 장비와 악기 같은 대형 물품(oversized items like sporting equipment and musical instruments)의 기내 반입 허용 조건에 대해 설명하고 있는 문장 뒤인 [4]에 들어가는 것이 글의 흐름상 자연스러우므로 (D)가 정답이다.

164-167 초대장

> **164 매드슨 인더스트리얼 서플라이 가상 직원 행사**
>
> **164 4월 11일 오후 7시~10시**
>
> 매드슨 인더스트리얼 서플라이 직원 여러분께 알립니다! 올해의 직원 모임에는 대중문화, 스포츠, 연예에 대한 여러분의 지식을 테스트하는 온라인 상식 퀴즈 대회가 새롭게 도입됩니다. 회사 전반의 협력을 증진하기 위해 **167 런던과 글래스고 지점에서 근무하는 직원들은 집에서 Z-하이프 룸에 접속하여 이 친목 대회를 위한 가상의 팀으로 편성됩니다.**
>
> 온라인 상식 퀴즈의 밤은 대략 2시간 동안 진행됩니다. **165 우승팀에게는 맨체스터의 굿 스터프 테마파크 1일 입장권이 수여됩니다.** 상식 퀴즈 대회가 끝나고 난 후, 한 시간 동안 직원들이 어울릴 수 있도록 Z-하이프 룸을 열어둘 예정입니다.
>
> 상식 퀴즈 대회 외에도, **166 인기 있는 기존의 두 대회인 최고의 축제 의상을 입은 직원상과 가장 창의적인 Z-하이프 가상 배경상** 또한 행사로 구성할 수 있어 기쁩니다. 가상 해변에서 근무하는 직원들은 많이 봐 왔지만 유명한 세계 문화유산이나 외계 우주라면 어떨까요? **166 작년에 제러드 백스터가 토성의 고리에서 전화를 걸면서 하얀 턱시도를 자랑스럽게 입고 있던 모습을 기억하시나요?** 여러분의 상상력을 이용해 예상치 못한 무언가를 생각해 내 보세요! **165 각 수상자는 손드라즈 그릴에서 식사할 수 있는 상품권을 받게 됩니다.**
>
> 이 즐거움에 함께 하실 계획이라면 3월 28일까지 회사 웹사이트의 설문지를 작성해 주세요. 친구와 가족들의 참여도 환영합니다. 여러분과 그곳에서 만나기를 기대합니다!
>
> **어휘** virtual 가상의 twist 전환 trivia (퀴즈의) 일반상식 competition 대회 foster 촉진하다 collaboration 협력 roughly 대략 mingle 어울리다 World Heritage site 세계 문화유산 extraterrestrial 외계의 sport 자랑스럽게 입다 Saturn 토성 unexpected 예상치 못한 participate 참여하다

164 Not / True

번역 직원 행사에 대해 명시된 것은?
(A) 1시간 동안 진행된다.
(B) 런던 지점에서 개최된다.
(C) 직원들에게만 공개된다.
(D) 4월 11일에 열린다.

해설 초대장의 상단에 매드슨 인더스트리얼 서플라이 가상 직원 행사(Madson Industrial Supply Virtual Staff Event)가 4월 11일(11 April)에 열린다고 나와 있으므로 (D)가 정답이다.

165 세부 사항

번역 행사의 세 가지 대회가 가진 공통점은?
(A) 참가자는 팀에 합류해야 한다.
(B) 우승자에게 상을 준다.
(C) 상식 퀴즈 문제에 답하는 것이 포함된다.
(D) 이전 직원 행사에서 했던 적이 있다.

해설 두 번째 단락의 두 번째 문장에서 상식 퀴즈 대회의 우승 팀에게는 맨체스터의 굿 스터프 테마파크 1일 입장권이 수여된다(Day passes to Good Stuff Theme Park in Manchester will be awarded to the winning team)고 했고, 세 번째 단락의 마지막 문장에서 나머지 두 대회의 각 수상자는 손드라즈 그릴에서 식사할 수 있는 상품권을 받게 된다(Each prize winner will receive a gift card for a meal at Sondra's Grill)고 했다. 따라서 세 가지 대회 모두 우승자에게 상품이 수여되므로 (B)가 정답이다.

어휘 participant 참가자 involve 포함하다 previous 이전의

166 세부 사항

번역 초대장에서 백스터 씨를 언급하는 이유는?
(A) 새로운 지도자를 소개하려고
(B) 참석자의 우려를 해결하려고
(C) 과거에 사람들이 어떻게 참여했는지 예로 들려고
(D) 장기근속 직원의 승진을 발표하려고

해설 세 번째 단락의 첫 문장에서 인기 있는 기존의 두 대회인 최고의 축제 의상을 입은 직원상과 가장 창의적인 Z-하이프 가상 배경상(two contests that are old favourites: an award for the employee wearing the finest festive attire and an award for the most creative Z-Hype virtual background)에 대해 언급하면서, 같은 단락 세 번째 문장에서 작년에 제러드 백스터가 토성의 고리에서 전화를 걸면서 하얀 턱시도를 자랑스럽게 입고 있던 모습을 기억하는지(Remember last year when Gerard Baxter sported a white tuxedo while phoning in from the rings of Saturn?)를 묻고 있다. 따라서 과거 대회 참가자의 사례를 들기 위해 백스터 씨를 언급했음을 알 수 있으므로 (C)가 정답이다.

어휘 address 해결하다 attendee 참석자

167 추론 / 암시

번역 Z-하이프는 무엇일 것 같은가?
(A) 화상 회의 플랫폼
(B) 놀이공원
(C) 이메일 서비스
(D) 온라인 설문 조사 회사

해설 첫 번째 단락의 세 번째 문장에서 런던과 글래스고 지점에서 근무하는 직원들은 집에서 Z-하이프 룸에 접속하여 이 친목 대회를 위한 가상의 팀으로 편성된다(employees based in the London and Glasgow offices will sign into the Z-Hype room from their homes and be combined into virtual teams for this friendly competition)고 했다. 따라서 Z-하이프 룸은 여러 직원이 동시에 접속할 수 있는 온라인 가상 공간임을 알 수 있으므로 (A)가 정답이다.

168-171 계약서

그로텔 사

행사 연사 계약

168 본 계약은 그로텔 사와 잭 콜먼(행사 연사) 사이의 것이다. 당사자들은 행사 연사가 다음의 행사를 위해 60분간 연설하는 데 합의한다.

168 행사명: 연례 직원 표창 및 시상
일시: 9월 12일 오후 7~8시
장소: 밀러 컨퍼런스 홀

1. **보상 및 비용.** 계약 이행 시, 그로텔 사는 행사 연사에게 1,250달러의 사례비를 지급하기로 합의한다. **169** 그로텔 사는 행사 연사에게 최대 500달러의 숙박 및 교통비를 환급할 예정이며, 원본 영수증 제출을 조건으로 한다.

2. **장비.** **170** 그로텔 사는 행사 연사에게 다음의 장비를 제공한다: 프로젝터, 대형 스크린, 인터넷 연결, 마이크.(상세 정보는 첨부 문서 참조)

3. **취소.** **171** 행사일로부터 최소 30일 전에 취소 의사를 서면 통보하는 한, 당사자 중 어느 한 쪽이든 상대방에게 임의대로 계약을 취소할 수 있다.

행사 연사 서명: 잭 콜먼	그로텔 사 대표: 에즈라 탄
날짜: 6월 2일	날짜: 6월 4일

어휘 agreement 계약 party 당사자 recognition 표창 honor 상 fulfillment 이행 lodging 숙박 transportation 교통편 provided that ~을 조건으로 accompanying 첨부한 specific 구체적인 cancellation 취소 without obligation 임의대로, 의무 없이 intent 의사

---

168 추론 / 암시

번역 콜먼 씨는 어떤 종류의 행사에 고용된 것 같은가?
(A) 학술 회의
(B) 산업 박람회
(C) 시상식
(D) 기업 연수 워크숍

해설 계약서 상단에서 본 계약은 그로텔 사와 잭 콜먼(행사 연사) 사이의 것(This agreement is between Grotel Corporation and Jack Kolman (Event Speaker))이며 당사자들은 행사 연사가 다음의 행사를 위해 60분간 연설하는 데 합의한다(The parties agree that the Event Speaker shall deliver a speech lasting 60 minutes for the following)고 했고, 행사명이 연례 직원 표창 및 시상(Name: Annual Employee Recognition and Honors)이라고 나와 있다. 따라서 콜먼 씨는 그로텔 사의 직원을 위한 시상식에서 연설하도록 고용되었음을 알 수 있으므로 (C)가 정답이다.

> **Paraphrasing**
> 지문의 Recognition and Honors → 정답의 awards

169 Not / True

번역 콜먼 씨가 받게 될 지불금에 대해 명시된 것은?
(A) 은행으로 바로 입금될 것이다.
(B) 사전에 지급될 것이다.
(C) 행사가 한 시간이 넘을 경우 증액될 수 있다.
(D) 교통비가 포함될 수 있다.

해설 1번 계약 조항의 마지막 문장에서 그로텔 사는 행사 연사에게 최대 500달러의 숙박 및 교통비를 환급할 예정이며 원본 영수증 제출을 조건으로 한다(Grotel Corporation will reimburse the Event Speaker for lodging and transportation up to $500, provided that original receipts are submitted)고 했으므로, 행사 연사인 콜먼 씨는 숙박 및 교통비 명목으로 일정 금액을 환급받게 될 것임을 알 수 있다. 따라서 (D)가 정답이다.

어휘 deposit 입금하다 directly 바로 issue 지급하다 in advance 사전에

170 세부 사항

번역 계약서에 포함된 정보는?
(A) 제공될 장비에 대한 세부 사항
(B) 원본 영수증 제출을 위한 지침
(C) 행사장까지의 운전 길 안내
(D) 행사 의제

해설 2번 계약 조항에서 그로텔 사는 행사 연사에게 프로젝터, 대형 스크린, 인터넷 연결, 마이크의 장비를 제공한다(상세 정보는 첨부 문서 참조)(Grotel Corporation will provide the Event Speaker with the following equipment: projector, large screen, Internet connection, microphone. (Please see accompanying document for specific information))라고 했다. 따라서 계약서에는 연사에게 제공되는 장비에 대한 세부 정보가 포함되어 있음을 알 수 있으므로 (A)가 정답이다.

어휘 details 세부 사항 instructions 지침 directions 길 안내 venue (행사) 장소 agenda 의제

171 Not / True

번역 행사 취소에 대해 명시된 것은?
(A) 행정 수수료가 발생할 수 있다.
(B) 전화로 통지될 수 있다.
(C) 타당한 이유가 없으면 인정되지 않는다.
(D) 행사 시점이 2주 남아 있는 경우에는 허용되지 않는다.

해설 3번 계약 조항에서 행사일로부터 최소 30일 전에 취소 의사를 서면 통보하는 한 당사자 중 어느 한 쪽이든 상대방에게 임의로 계약을 취소할 수 있다(Either party may cancel the agreement without obligation to the other as long as written notice of intent to cancel is provided at least 30 days before the date of the event)고 했으므로, 행사일로부터 30일이 채 남지 않은 시점에는 행사를 취소할 수 없음을 추론할 수 있다. 따라서 (D)가 정답이다.

어휘 administrative 행정의 accept 받아들이다 valid 타당한 permit 허용하다

172-175 온라인 채팅

> **브렛 테니슨 (오전 8시 16분)**
> 안녕하세요, 리앤 그리고 슈루티. 두 분 어제 제가 보낸 이메일 받으셨나요?
>
> **리앤 개먼 (오전 8시 17분)**
> 당신이 만들고 싶어하는 회사 영상에 대한 거요?
>
> **브렛 테니슨 (오전 8시 18분)**
> 네. 사람들은 함께 일하는 회사와 개인적인 유대감을 느끼고 싶어 해요. 172영상은 잠재 고객들이 우리 팀에 더 쉽게 공감하고 거래를 만들어내는 데 도움을 줄 수 있어요.
>
> **슈루티 메타 (오전 8시 19분)**
> 173답장 이메일 초안을 작성하긴 했는데 아직 보내지는 않았어요. 공유하기 전에 머릿속으로 검토하고 싶었거든요.
>
> **리앤 개먼 (오전 8시 20분)**
> 아이디어는 좋아요. 그렇지만 사람들의 관심을 얻으려면 참신해야 하겠네요.
>
> **슈루티 메타 (오전 8시 21분)**
> 174우리에 관한 영상이 좋은 생각이라는 확신이 서지는 않아요. 저는 온종일 컴퓨터로 일만 해요. 174누가 그걸 보고 싶겠어요?
>
> **브렛 테니슨 (오전 8시 22분)**
> 그래서 제가 의견을 요청한 거예요. 영상에서 우리가 하는 일이 무엇인지는 물론이고 우리의 개성도 보여줘야 할 거예요. 편집을 위해 전문가를 고용할 수 있어요. 하지만 먼저 영상을 어떻게 구성할지를 결정한 다음, 직접 녹화해 봅시다.
>
> **리앤 개먼 (오전 8시 23분)**
> 175다양한 시청자에게 도달할 수 있도록 몇 개를 만들어 보는 게 어떨까요? 유료 광고로 사용할 짧은 영상이랑 우리 웹사이트에 올릴 긴 영상이 어떠세요?

어휘 connection 연결 potential 잠재적인 relate 마음이 통하다 draft 초안을 작성하다 go over ~을 검토하다 convinced 확신하는 input 의견 personality 개성 structure 구성하다, 조직하다 audience 시청자

172 세부 사항

번역 테니슨 씨가 영상을 만들고 싶어 하는 이유는?
(A) 새로운 거래를 만들어내려고
(B) 혁신적인 제품을 강조하려고
(C) 직원들에게 새로운 절차를 교육하려고
(D) 지도부의 변화를 발표하려고

해설 8시 18분에 테니슨 씨가 영상은 잠재 고객들이 우리 팀에 더 쉽게 공감하고 거래를 만들어내는 데 도움을 줄 수 있다(A video could help potential clients relate better to our team and generate business)며 영상을 제작함으로써 얻게 되는 이점을 설명하고 있다. 따라서 거래 기회를 만들어내기 위해 영상을 만들고 싶어한다는 것을 알 수 있으므로 (A)가 정답이다.

어휘 innovative 혁신적인 process 절차

173 세부 사항

번역 메타 씨가 이메일에 응답하지 않은 이유는?
(A) 그것에 대해 생각할 시간이 더 필요했다.
(B) 다른 일로 너무 바빴다.
(C) 자신의 의견이 필요 없다고 생각했다.
(D) 이메일의 내용을 이해하지 못했다.

해설 8시 19분에 메타 씨가 답장 이메일 초안을 작성하긴 했는데 아직 보내지는 않았다(I drafted an e-mail in response, but I haven't sent it yet)면서 공유하기 전에 머릿속으로 검토하고 싶었다(I wanted to go over it in my mind before sharing)고 했다. 따라서 메타 씨는 사안에 대해 생각할 시간이 더 필요했음을 알 수 있으므로 (A)가 정답이다.

> **Paraphrasing**
> 지문의 go over it in my mind → 정답의 think about it

174 의도 파악

번역 오전 8시 21분에 메타 씨가 "저는 온종일 컴퓨터로 일만 해요"라고 쓴 의도는?
(A) 자신의 직업에 만족하지 않는다.
(B) 잠재 고객을 도울 자격이 없다.
(C) 업무 책임이 매우 적다.
(D) 자신의 일에 대한 영상이 지루할 것이라고 생각한다.

해설 8시 21분에 메타 씨가 우리에 관한 영상이 좋은 생각이라는 확신이 서지 않는다(I'm not convinced that a video about us is a good idea)면서 자신은 온종일 컴퓨터로 일만 한다(I just work at my computer all day)고 했고, 뒤이어 누가 그걸 보

고 싶겠냐(Who would want to watch that?)고 했다. 따라서 메타 씨는 컴퓨터 앞에서 일만 하는 모습이 담긴 영상이 지루할 것 같아서 그 효과에 대해 확신할 수 없다는 의도로 한 말임을 알 수 있으므로 (D)가 정답이다.

어휘 qualified 자격이 있는

175 세부 사항

번역 개먼 씨가 영상에 대해 메시지 작성자들에게 제안하는 것은?
(A) 사무실에서 편집
(B) 원곡 음악 추가
(C) 여러 버전으로 제작
(D) 회사 연혁 삽입

해설 8시 23분에 개먼 씨가 다양한 시청자에게 도달할 수 있도록 몇 개를 만들어 보는 게 어떨지(Why don't we make a few—so that we can reach different audiences?)를 제안하고 있으므로 (C)가 정답이다.

176-180 광고 + 후기

메리디언 프레스에서 곧 출간합니다!
〈환한 조명 속 삶: 이브라 말림의 진짜 이야기〉
헬레나 매케이 글

〈환한 조명 속 삶〉은 영화에서 가장 기억에 남는 몇몇 캐릭터들을 연기한 이브라 말림의 첫 전기입니다. 정치인과 신문 기자의 아들인 말림 씨는 원래 고고학자가 될 계획이었습니다. 그는 대학생이었을 때 니나 첸 감독과 우연히 만났고, 그녀는 자신의 영화 〈소렌토의 바람〉의 작은 역할에 말림 씨를 캐스팅했습니다. 그는 빠르게 유명해졌습니다. 그 후 30년 동안 **176 말림 씨는 영국과 미국의 영화에 자주 출연하며 누구나 아는 이름이 되었습니다.**

177 매케이 씨는 그녀의 수많은 전기 속 인물에 대해 균형 있고 객관적인 시각을 부여하는 것으로 알려져 있으며, 〈환한 조명 속 삶〉도 예외는 아닙니다. **179 그녀는 말림 씨의 오랜 매니저와의 광범위한 인터뷰를 통해 수집한, 말림 씨의 삶에서 이전에 알려지지 않았던 세부적인 것들을 조명합니다.** 수상 경력이 있는 작가의 솔직하고 **178 이해하기 쉬운** 문체로 쓰인 이 책은 말림 씨의 삶을 인도에서의 유년 시절부터 들여다봅니다. 이 책은 그의 모든 팬들에게 유익한 정보와 재미를 선사할 것입니다.

어휘 spotlight 환한 조명 biography 전기 memorable 기억에 남는 politician 정치인 archaeologist 고고학자 chance 우연한 encounter 만남 cast 캐스팅하다 household name 누구나 아는 이름 motion picture 영화 objective 객관적인 numerous 수많은 subject (논의의) 대상 exception 예외 shed light on ~에 조명하다, 빛을 비추다 previously 이전에 extensive 광범위한 agent (연예인 등의) 매니저 straightforward 솔직한 accessible 이해하기 쉬운 prose 산문(체)

★★★★☆ 말림 팬들이 꼭 읽어야 할 책!

이브라 말림의 오랜 팬으로서 저는 〈환한 조명 속 삶〉을 무척 읽고 싶었습니다. 실망하지 않았습니다. 매케이 씨는 이 수수께끼 같은 인물을 매력적인 초상화로 그려냅니다. **179 그의 무대 위와 무대 밖의 삶에 대한 흥미로운 일화가 수십 가지 있는데, 대부분은 말림 씨를 잘 알고 있는 알리디아 루고와의 인터뷰에서 매케이 씨가 들은 것들입니다.** 매케이 씨는 말림 씨의 강점과 약점을 드러내며 책에 신뢰감을 더합니다. 불만은 두 가지뿐입니다. 책은 그의 어린 시절이나 리즈 대학교 동문과의 관계에 대해서는 거의 언급하지 않습니다. 그리고 **180 사진이 두 장보다는 더 있었으면 좋겠는데,** 특히 말림 씨의 명성이 그의 사진 속 모습에 얼마나 많이 근거하고 있는지를 고려한다면 말이죠.

— 살바도르 게레로

어휘 fascinating 매력적인 portrait 초상화 enigmatic 수수께끼 같은 figure 인물 dozens of 수십의 anecdote 일화 reveal 드러내다 strength 강점 shortcoming 단점 credible 신뢰할 수 있는 complaint 불만 fellow 동료의 reputation 명성 photogenic 사진이 잘 받는

176 세부 사항

번역 말림 씨는 무엇으로 가장 유명한가?
(A) 고고학적 발견을 한 것
(B) 소설을 쓴 것
(C) 정치인이 된 것
(D) 영화에서 연기한 것

해설 광고의 첫 단락 마지막 문장에서 말림 씨는 영국과 미국의 영화에 자주 출연하며 누구나 아는 이름이 되었다(Mr. Maalim became a household name, regularly appearing in motion pictures in Britain and the United States)고 했으므로 말림은 유명한 영화배우임을 알 수 있다. 따라서 (D)가 정답이다.

어휘 archaeological 고고학적인 discovery 발견 fictional 소설의 politician 정치인

Paraphrasing
지문의 motion pictures → 정답의 films

177 Not / True

번역 광고에서 매케이 씨에 대해 명시하는 것은?
(A) 말림 씨를 여러 번 인터뷰했다.
(B) 많은 전기를 썼다.
(C) 신문 기자로 근무했다.
(D) 첸 씨와 프로젝트에서 협업했다.

해설 광고의 두 번째 단락 첫 문장에서 매케이 씨는 그녀의 수많은 전기 속 인물에 대해 균형 있고 객관적인 시각을 부여하는 것으로 알려져 있다(Ms. Mackay is known for giving balanced, objective views of her numerous biographical subjects)고 언급했으므로 (B)가 정답이다.

어휘 collaborate 협업하다

178 동의어 찾기

번역 광고의 두 번째 단락 4행의 "accessible"과 의미가 가장 가까운 단어는?
(A) 이해할 수 있는
(B) 열린
(C) 인기 있는
(D) 유행하는

해설 의미상 솔직하고 '이해하기 쉬운' 문체로 쓰인 책이라는 뜻으로 쓰였으므로 '이해할 수 있는'을 뜻하는 (A) understandable이 정답이다.

179 연계

번역 루고 씨는 말림 씨를 어떻게 알고 있었을 것 같은가?
(A) 대학 동기였다.
(B) 어린 시절 친구였다.
(C) 매니저였다.
(D) 가장 좋아하는 감독이었다.

해설 광고의 두 번째 단락 두 번째 문장에서 말림 씨의 오랜 매니저와의 광범위한 인터뷰를 통해 수집한, 말림 씨의 삶에서 이전에 알려지지 않았던 세부적인 것들을 조명한다(She sheds light on previously unknown details of Mr. Maalim's life, gathered from extensive interviews with his longtime agent)고 했고, 후기의 네 번째 문장에서 말림 씨의 무대 위와 무대 밖의 삶에 대한 흥미로운 일화가 수십 가지 있는데 대부분은 말림 씨를 잘 알고 있는 알리디아 루고와의 인터뷰에서 매케이 씨가 들은 것들(There are dozens of interesting anecdotes about his life on and off set, most of which were told to Mackay in interviews with Alidia Lugo, who knew Maalim well)이라고 했다. 따라서 매케이 씨가 책을 위해 인터뷰했던 말림 씨의 매니저가 루고 씨임을 알 수 있으므로 (C)가 정답이다.

180 세부 사항

번역 후기에 따르면, 〈환한 조명 속 삶〉의 문제점 한 가지는?
(A) 사진이 충분히 없다.
(B) 어떠한 상도 수상하지 않았다.
(C) 너무 비싸다.
(D) 너무 많은 유명한 일화가 반복된다.

해설 후기의 마지막 문장에서 두 가지 불만 중 하나로 사진이 두 장보다는 더 있었으면 좋겠다(I also wish there were more than two photographs)고 했으므로 (A)가 정답이다.

181-185 광고 + 후기

빅 스트라이크 레인즈
글래스고 포춘 로 20번지, 우편번호 G41 4LM
(0141) 496 0184

빅 스트라이크 레인즈에서는 즐거움이 가득합니다! **181 가족과 친구들을 데려와 볼링도 치고, 비디오 게임도 하고, 신기한 가상 현실 기기도 체험하고, 우리 식당에서 맛있는 식사도 즐기세요.** 18개의 볼링 레인, 최첨단 게임기, 수상 경력이 있는 음식이 있는 빅 스트라이크 레인즈에는 모두를 위한 즐길거리가 있습니다.

182 오늘 오셔서 저희 할인 프로그램 중 하나를 즐겨보세요. 5월 31일 이후에는 이용하실 수 없습니다!

골드 프로그램	184 플래티넘 프로그램
볼링 1시간과 25파운드 상당의 게임 크레딧을 즐기세요. 단 30파운드로 40파운드의 가치를 즐기세요!	볼링 2시간과 184 가상 현실 체험 2회를 즐기세요. 184 단 40파운드로 50파운드의 가치를 즐기세요!

어휘 virtual-reality 가상 현실 savour (맛을) 즐기다 state-of-the-art 최첨단의 deal 할인 value (가격 대비) 가치

빅 스트라이크 레인즈: 풍성한 즐길거리

5월 16일

183 작년에 프리사이드 볼링이 문을 닫았을 때 정말 슬펐습니다. 소박하고 예스럽고 한 가족이 3대에 걸쳐 운영해 온 이곳은 오래된 장소만이 풍길 수 있는 그런 종류의 매력이 있었습니다. 그곳에서 좋은 시간을 보낸 행복한 추억이 많습니다.

그러더니 빅 스트라이크 레인즈가 몇 달 전에 문을 열었고, 그곳과 어떻게 다를지 궁금했습니다. **184 친구들 몇 명과 방문해서 판촉 할인을 이용해 보기로 했는데**, 우리의 경험은 기대했던 것보다 더 좋았다고 말하게 되어 기쁩니다. 볼링은 재미있었고, 전에 해 본 적이 없었던 **184 가상 현실도 정말 재미있었습니다.**

식당에서 서빙 직원들은 친절했고 음식은 맛있었습니다. 이 장소에 대한 유일한 비판거리는 위치입니다. 빅 스트라이크 레인즈는 번잡한 고속도로 옆의 대형 쇼핑센터에 **185 위치해** 있어서 주변 환경이 그다지 매력적이지는 않습니다.

— 소피 쇼

어휘 plenty 풍성함 rustic 소박한 quaint 예스러운 charm 매력 take advantage of ~을 이용하다 offer (짧은 기간의) 할인 criticism 비판 motorway 고속도로 surrounding 주변 환경 inviting 매력적인

181 세부 사항

번역 빅 스트라이크 레인에서 손님들이 할 수 있는 것은?
(A) 영화 구매
(B) 장소 내 식사
(C) 볼링 수업
(D) 파티 장소 예약

해설 광고의 첫 단락 두 번째 문장에서 가족과 친구들을 데려와 볼링도 치고, 비디오 게임도 하고, 신기한 가상 현실 기기도 체험하고, 식당에서 맛있는 식사도 즐기라(Bring your family and friends to bowl, play video games, try out our unique virtual-reality station, and savour delicious meals at our own restaurant)고 했으므로 손님들은 빅 스트라이크 레인즈 안에서 식사를 할 수 있음을 알 수 있다. 따라서 (B)가 정답이다.

어휘 on-site 현장의 reserve 예약하다 site 장소

> **Paraphrasing**
> 지문의 savour delicious meals → 정답의 Eat

182 세부 사항

번역 광고에 따르면, 5월 31일에 일어날 일은?
(A) 가격 할인이 종료된다.
(B) 후기가 온라인에 게시된다.
(C) 특별 메뉴가 이용 가능해진다.
(D) 게임 아케이드가 문을 연다.

해설 광고의 두 번째 단락에서 오늘 와서 할인 프로그램 중 하나를 즐기라(Visit us for one of our deals today)면서 5월 31일 이후에는 이용할 수 없다(they will not be available after 31 May!)고 했다. 따라서 할인 행사는 5월 31일까지만 진행된다는 것을 알 수 있으므로 (A)가 정답이다.

어휘 reduction 할인, 감소 post 게시하다 arcade 아케이드(지붕이 있는 상가)

> **Paraphrasing**
> 지문의 deals → 정답의 price reduction

183 추론 / 암시

번역 쇼 씨가 후기에서 암시하는 것은?
(A) 이전에 가상 현실을 체험해 본 적이 있다.
(B) 오래된 건물보다 현대식 건물을 선호한다.
(C) 오락 시설이 폐업한 것을 아쉬워한다.
(D) 식당에서 서빙 직원으로 일한 적이 있다.

해설 후기의 첫 단락 첫 문장에서 쇼 씨가 작년에 프리사이드 볼링이 문을 닫았을 때 정말 슬펐다(I was very sad when Freeside Bowling shut its doors last year)면서 그곳의 분위기와 추억에 대해 언급한 것으로 보아 볼링장이 폐업해 아쉬워하고 있음을 짐작할 수 있다. 따라서 (C)가 정답이다.

어휘 participate in ~에 참여하다 regret 유감이다

> **Paraphrasing**
> 지문의 shut its doors → 정답의 closed

184 연계

번역 쇼 씨가 오락 활동에 지불한 금액은 얼마인가?
(A) 25파운드
(B) 30파운드
(C) 40파운드
(D) 50파운드

해설 후기의 두 번째 단락의 두 번째 문장에서 친구들 몇 명과 방문해서 판촉 할인을 이용해 보기로 했다(A few friends and I decided to visit and take advantage of a promotional offer)고 한 후, 세 번째 문장에서 가상 현실도 정말 재미있었다(I really enjoyed the virtual reality)고 했다. 광고의 하단에 기재된 할인 프로그램 중 플래티넘 프로그램(Platinum Deal)에 가상 현실 체험(virtual-reality experiences)이 포함되어 있으며 40파운드에 50파운드의 가치(A £50 value for only £40!)를 즐길 수 있다고 했으므로, 쇼 씨는 40파운드를 지불하고 플래티넘 프로그램을 즐겼음을 알 수 있다. 따라서 (C)가 정답이다.

185 동의어 찾기

번역 후기의 세 번째 단락 2행의 "situated"와 의미가 가장 가까운 단어는?
(A) 설립된
(B) 정리된
(C) 주차된
(D) 위치한

해설 의미상 대형 쇼핑센터에 '위치해' 있다는 의미로 쓰였으므로 '위치한, 자리 잡은'을 뜻하는 (D) positioned가 정답이다.

186-190 회의록 + 기사 + 이메일

알포드 시의회 특별 회의 회의록
1월 14일

1. 회의 시작
트렘블레이 시장이 오후 6시 30분에 회의를 시작했습니다. 모든 의원이 참석했습니다.

2. 결의안 2023-167B번에 대한 표결
의회는 알포드 지역 공항에 윙라이트 항공 서비스가 들어서는 것과 관련된 비용으로 150만 달러를 배정하기 위한 결의안을 승인했습니다. 공항 운영 기금 조정을 승인하는 이 결의안은 7대 0의 표결로 통과되었습니다. **186 윙라이트 항공과 시는 일부 비용을 동등하게 부담합니다. 분담되어야 할 비용에는 추가 보안 및 응급 서비스 직원의 모집 및 교육이 포함됩니다.** 기타 비용은 알포드 시가 100퍼센트 부담합니다. 이 중 가장 중요한 것은 예상되는 공항 교통 증가분을 수용하기 위해 항공 대로에 추가 도로를 건설하는 것입니다. **188 대로 관련 공사는 항공사가 서비스를 시작하기 전에 완료되도록 즉시 시작될 것입니다.**

3. 폐회
회의는 오후 7시 25분에 폐회되었습니다.

어휘 minutes 회의록 council 의회 call ~ to order (회의 등의) 시작을 알리다 vote 표결 resolution 결의안 earmark 배정하다 establish 설립하다 regional 지역의 authorize 승인하다 adjustment 조정 operating 운영 fund 기금 bear 감당하다 split 나누다 recruitment 모집 security 보안 expense 비용 chief 가장 중요한 aviation 항공 boulevard 대로 accommodate 수용하다 immediately 즉시 adjournment 폐회

윙라이트 항공, 알포드 지역 공항에서 서비스 개시

알포드 (3월 18일) — 디-윈에 본사를 둔 항공사인 윙라이트 항공은 알포드 지역 공항과 크랜턴 간 일일 직항 항공편을 개시한다는 계획을 발표했다. **187** 윙라이트 항공은 주요 항공사들이 서비스를 제공하지 않는 호주의 소규모 시장으로의 운항을 전문으로 하는 최근 신생 기업들 중 하나이다. "우리는 지역 주민들에게 크랜턴으로 가는 저렴하고 편리한 서비스를 제공하게 되기를 기대하고 있습니다."라고 윙라이트 항공의 홍보 책임자인 사비타 그레왈이 말했다.

그레왈 씨에 따르면, **188** 항공사는 알포드 지역 공항에서 출발하는 첫 항공편을 8월 1일로 예정하고 있다. 처음에 **190** 윙라이트는 크랜턴행 일일 항공편 두 편을 제공할 예정이다. 아이더 베이와 웨스트 린포트를 포함한 추가 목적지들도 향후 서비스를 위해 고려되고 있다. 추가 노선에 관한 결정은 12월 31일까지 내려질 것으로 예상된다.

어휘 specialise in ~을 전문으로 하다 affordable 저렴한 convenient 편리한 state 말하다 public relations 홍보 inaugural 첫, 개시의 initially 처음에 destination 목적지

수신: oliverp01@roommateroundup.com
발신: sgirard@emailcloud.com
날짜: 7월 15일
제목: 알포드 도심의 숙소

안녕하세요, 올리버,

당신이 룸메이트 라운드업 웹사이트에 올린 아파트를 공유하는 데 관심이 있습니다. 개인 욕실이 있고 가구가 완비된 공간을 찾고 있으며, 귀하의 아파트는 이 모든 것에 더해 지정 주차 공간이라는 덤까지 있다고 보았습니다. **189** 공과금을 포함한 월세가 850달러로 저의 예산에 딱 들어옵니다. 요구하신 보증금으로 한 달 치 월세를 미리 드리는 데 동의합니다.

저는 조용하고 느긋하며 꽤 깔끔합니다. 저는 윙라이트 항공의 승무원으로 일하고 있습니다. **190** 다음 달에 시작되는 항공사의 알포드발 신규 노선에 배정받았습니다. 저는 알포드에 일주일의 절반 정도만 있고 나머지는 목적지 공항 근처의 호텔에서 지낼 것입니다. 이는 대부분의 시간 동안 아파트에서 귀하 혼자 지내게 된다는 의미입니다.

저는 현재 아이더 베이에 있지만 다음 주에 돌아올 예정입니다. 귀하를 만나서 아파트를 둘러볼 수 있는 시간을 정할 수 있을까요?

스튜어트 지라드

어휘 fully 완전히 furnished 가구가 비치된 reserved 지정의 utilities 공금 security deposit 보증금 in advance 미리 easygoing 느긋한 reasonably 꽤 neat 깔끔한 flight attendant 승무원 assign 배정하다

186 세부 사항

번역 윙라이트 항공과 알포드 시가 비용을 분담할 활동은?
(A) 활주로 연장
(B) 공항 이용에 대한 데이터 수집
(C) 공항 인근 도로 개선
(D) 추가 보안 직원을 위한 비용 지불

해설 회의록의 두 번째 단락 세 번째 문장에서 윙라이트 항공과 시는 일부 비용을 동등하게 부담한다(Winglite Airlines and the city will bear some costs equally)면서 분담되어야 할 비용에는 추가 보안 및 응급 서비스 직원의 모집 및 교육이 포함된다(Costs to be split include recruitment and training of additional security and emergency services workers)고 했다. 따라서 (D)가 정답이다.

어휘 extend 연장하다 runway 활주로 usage 이용 personnel 직원

187 Not / True

번역 기사에서 윙라이트 항공에 대해 명시하는 것은?
(A) 그레왈 씨가 이끈다.
(B) 인기가 덜한 공항으로 운항한다.
(C) 수십 년간 운영되어 왔다.
(D) 현재 알포드로부터 여러 목적지로 항공편을 제공한다.

해설 기사의 첫 단락 두 번째 문장에서 윙라이트 항공은 주요 항공사들이 서비스를 제공하지 않는 호주의 소규모 시장으로의 운항을 전문으로 하는 최근 신생 기업들 중 하나(Winglite Airlines is one of several recent start-ups specialising in flying to smaller markets in Australia that are not served by the main airlines)라고 언급했다. 따라서 윙라이트 항공은 상대적으로 수요가 적은 공항 위주로 운항하는 항공사임을 알 수 있으므로 (B)가 정답이다.

어휘 head 이끌다 operation 운영 decade 10년

188 연계

번역 항공 대로 공사는 언제까지 완료되어야 하는가?
(A) 1월 14일까지
(B) 3월 18일까지
(C) 8월 1일까지
(D) 12월 31일까지

해설 회의록의 두 번째 단락 마지막 문장에서 대로 관련 공사는 항공사가 서비스를 시작하기 전에 완료되도록 즉시 시작될 것(Work on the boulevard will start immediately so that it will be finished before the airline begins its service)이라고 했고, 기사의 두 번째 단락 첫 문장에서 항공사는 알포드 지역 공항에서

출발하는 첫 항공편을 8월 1일로 예정하고 있다(the airline has scheduled its inaugural flight from Arlford Regional Airport for 1 August)고 했다. 따라서, 항공 대여 공사는 항공사가 첫 운항 서비스를 시작하기로 예정된 8월 1일까지는 완료되어야 하므로 (C)가 정답이다.

189 세부 사항

번역 이메일에 따르면, 지라드 씨가 아파트로 이사하게 될 경우 무엇을 할 것인가?
(A) 노상 주차
(B) 자기 소유의 가구 제공
(C) 보증금 850달러 지불
(D) 욕실 공유

해설 이메일의 첫 단락 세 번째 문장에서 지라드 씨가 공과금을 포함한 월세가 850달러로 자신의 예산에 딱 들어온다(At $850, including utilities, the monthly rent is just within my budget)며, 요구한 보증금으로 한 달 치 월세를 미리 주는 것에 동의한다(I agree to give you the required security deposit of one month's rent in advance)고 했다. 따라서 지라드 씨는 이사하기로 계약할 경우, 350달러의 보증금을 선불할 예정이므로 (C)가 정답이다.

190 연계

번역 지라드 씨는 알포드에 없을 때 보통 어디서 머물 예정인가?
(A) 다윈
(B) 크랜턴
(C) 아이더 베이
(D) 웨스트 린포트

해설 기사의 두 번째 단락 두 번째 문장에서 윙라이트는 크랜턴행 일일 항공편 두 편을 제공할 예정(Winglite will offer two daily flights to Cranton)이라고 했고, 이메일의 두 번째 단락 세 번째 문장에서 지라드 씨는 다음 달에 시작되는 항공사의 알포드발 신규 노선에 배정받았다(I have been assigned to the airline's new route out of Arlford that begins next month)면서 알포드에 일주일의 절반 정도만 있고 나머지는 목적지 공항 근처의 호텔에서 지낼 것(I will be in Arlford only half the time and will stay in a hotel near my destination airport for the rest of the week)이라고 했다. 따라서, 지라드 씨는 신규 노선의 목적지인 크랜턴에서 일주일의 절반을 지낼 예정임을 알 수 있으므로 (B)가 정답이다.

191-195 웹페이지 + 웹페이지 + 온라인 후기

https://forklifttrainingacademy.com/certification

| 소개 | 자격증 | 등록 | 학생 로그인 | 연락처 |

지게차 운전 교육 및 자격증

지게차 교육 아카데미의 1일 과정은 캐나다와 미국의 모든 자격 증명 요건을 충족합니다. 우리는 초급 자격증이 필요한 초보자를 위한 과정과 자격증 갱신이 필요한 경력 운전자를 위한 과정을 제공합니다. 자격증을 받으려면 최종 시험에서 합격 점수가 필요합니다. 자격증은 3년간 유효합니다.

191 우리는 최근에 대면 수업에서 휴대기기, 태블릿 또는 컴퓨터에서 이용 가능한 온라인 수업 전용으로 전환했습니다.

192 자세한 정보나 등록을 원하시면 등록 페이지를 방문하세요. 모든 예약은 선택된 수업일로부터 최소 3일 전에 선행되고 결제되어야 합니다.

어휘 certification 자격증, 자격 증명 forklift 지게차 operation 운전 satisfy 만족시키다 initial 처음의 operator 운전자 recertification 자격증 갱신 examination 시험 valid 유효한 transition 전환하다 in-person 대면의, 직접 registration 등록 reservation 예약 in advance 미리

https://forklifttrainingacademy.com/registration

| 소개 | 자격증 | 등록 | 학생 로그인 | 연락처 |

192 등록 양식
192 성함: 필립 듀랑
이메일: philippe.durand@silkmail.com

선호하는 수업일을 선택하세요:
• 자격증 — 강사: 해리스 씨 / 4월 4일, 오전 8시 – 오후 4시 ☐
• 자격증 갱신 — **194** 강사: 고흐 씨 / 4월 7일, 오전 8시 30분 – 오후 2시 30분 ☐
• 자격증 — 강사: 볼드윈 씨 / 4월 10일, 오전 8시 – 오후 4시 ☒
• 자격증 갱신 — **193** 강사: 볼드윈 씨 / 4월 14일, 오전 8시 30분 – 오후 2시 30분 ☐
• 자격증 — 강사: 마이노스 씨 / 4월 21일, 오전 8시 – 오후 4시 ☐

어휘 form 양식 instructor 강사

후기: 지게차 교육 과정
줄리 다이 작성
5월 18일
★★★★☆

저는 지난달에 에이블 인더스트리즈에서의 업무를 위해 **195** 자격증 갱신용 지게차 교육 과정을 수강했습니다. 저는 온라인으로 수업을 듣는 것에 대해 걱정했지만, **195** 수업은 제가 기존 자격증을 위해 받았던 현장 교육의 모든 내용을 다루었으며 그 이상이었습니다. 또한 수업을 듣기 위해 이동할 필요가 없었다는 것과 바로 같은 날 자격증 갱신을 받았다는 점도 좋았습니다! **194** 강사인 고흐 씨는 훌륭했습니다. 그녀는 저의 모든 질문에 답변해 주셨고, 지게차 기사들이 직면하는 어려움에도 동조해 주셨습니다. 제가 지게차 교육 아카데미에 제안하고 싶은 유일한 점은 수업일과 시간을 좀 더 다양하게 제공해 주는 것입니다.

어휘 cover 다루다 material 내용 on-site 현장의 attune 동조하다, 맞추다 variety 다양성

191 Not / True

번역 지게차 교육 아카데미 과정에 대해 명시된 것은?
(A) 온라인으로 진행된다.
(B) 하루 이상 걸린다.
(C) 대면 시험을 봐야 한다.
(D) 통과하기 어렵다.

해설 첫 번째 웹페이지의 두 번째 단락에서 지게차 교육 아카데미가 최근에 대면 수업에서 휴대기기, 태블릿 또는 컴퓨터에서 이용 가능한 온라인 수업 전용으로 전환했다(We have recently transitioned from in-person to online courses only, available on mobile devices, tablets, or computers)고 했다. 따라서 (A)가 정답이다.

192 연계

번역 듀랑 씨에 대해 암시된 것은?
(A) 승진을 위해 수업을 들었다.
(B) 최소한 3일 전에 미리 수업료를 지불했다.
(C) 시험 점수가 온라인에 게시되었다.
(D) 자격증이 만료될 예정이었다.

해설 두 번째 웹페이지 상단의 등록 양식(Registration Form)에 신청하는 사람의 이름이 필립 듀랑(Name: Philippe Durand)이라고 나와 있고, 첫 번째 웹페이지의 세 번째 단락에서 자세한 정보나 등록을 원하면 등록 페이지를 방문하라(Visit our registration page for more information or to sign up)면서 모든 예약은 선택된 수업일로부터 최소 3일 전에 선행되고 결제되어야 한다(All reservations must be booked and paid for at least three days in advance of the selected course date)고 했다. 듀랑 씨가 등록 페이지에서 수업을 예약한 것으로 보아, 최소 3일 전에 수업료를 미리 결제했음을 알 수 있으므로 (B)가 정답이다.

193 세부 사항

번역 4월 14일에 누가 수업을 가르쳤는가?
(A) 해리스 씨
(B) 고흐 씨
(C) 볼드윈 씨
(D) 마이노스 씨

해설 두 번째 웹페이지에 나열된 수업 목록 하단에 강사 볼드윈 씨가 4월 14일(Instructor: Ms. Baldwin / April 14)에 수업을 진행한다고 나와 있으므로 (C)가 정답이다.

194 연계

번역 다이 씨는 언제 수업을 들었는가?
(A) 4월 4일
(B) 4월 7일
(C) 4월 10일
(D) 4월 21일

해설 후기의 네 번째 문장에서 다이 씨가 강사인 고흐 씨는 훌륭했다(The trainer, Ms. Gogh, was excellent)고 했고, 두 번째 웹페이지에 나열된 수업 목록 중반부에 강사 고흐 씨는 4월 7일(Instructor: Ms. Gogh / April 7)에 수업을 진행한다고 나와 있다. 따라서, 다이 씨는 고흐 씨가 진행한 4월 7일 수업에 참석했다는 것을 알 수 있으므로 (B)가 정답이다.

195 추론 / 암시

번역 다이 씨에 대해 결론지을 수 있는 것은?
(A) 교육이 불만족스러웠다.
(B) 온라인 수업을 가르쳤다.
(C) 생계를 위해 후기를 쓴다.
(D) 경력이 있는 지게차 기사이다.

해설 후기의 첫 문장에서 다이 씨가 자격증 갱신용 지게차 교육 과정을 수강했다(I took the forklift training class for recertification)고 했고, 두 번째 문장에서 수업은 자신이 기존 자격증을 위해 받았던 현장 교육의 모든 내용을 다루었으며 그 이상이었다(it covered all the material from the on-site training that I had for my original certification—and more)고 한 것으로 보아 다이 씨는 이미 지게차 기사로서 경력을 보유하고 있음을 짐작할 수 있다. 따라서 (D)가 정답이다.

196-200 이메일 + 차트 + 이메일 ▶동영상 강의

수신: 재니스 블레드스톤 〈jbledstone@nickbeatsband.com〉
발신: 마이클 청 〈mcheung@stickersbeyours.com〉
날짜: 6월 13일
제목: 닉 비츠 홍보용 스티커

블레드스톤 씨께:

닉 비츠 밴드 관리에 엄청난 성공을 거두신 점 축하드립니다. 저에게 귀하를 위한 제안이 하나 있습니다. 그룹의 로고를 범퍼 스티커나 롤 스티커, 종이 스티커, 또는 비닐 스티커로 제작해 보시는 게 어떨까요?

스티커나 데칼은 밴드를 홍보할 수 있는 훌륭한 방법입니다. 이것들은 관객들에게 판매할 수 있는 아주 저렴한 상품입니다. 공연 후에는 이것들을 무료로 나눠줄 수도 있습니다. 스티커를 사은품으로 사용하시든 추가적인 수입원으로 이용하시든 스티커스 비 유어스가 대신 처리해 드립니다. **196 스티커는 방수가 되며** 색 바램에 강합니다. 스티커는 오래 가며 어떠한 표면에도 잘 붙습니다. 수백 개의 템플릿에서 고르시거나 자체 이미지를 업로드하실 수 있습니다. 자세한 정보는 863-555-0128로 저에게 전화 주시거나 저희 웹사이트 stickersbeyours.com을 방문해 주세요.

참고로, **197 저는 개인적으로 맷 그림의 팬입니다. 사실 저는 밴드에서 직접 연주를 하는데 그의 연주 스타일을 본받으려고 노력합니다.** 저희와 함께 거래를 하는 것과 상관없이 그에게 안부를 전해주세요.

마이클 청

어휘 vinyl 비닐 decal 데칼(판박이 스티커) give away ~을 나눠주다 cover 대신하다 waterproof 방수의 resist 잘 견디다 fade 바래다 adhere 붙다

	닉 비츠 비닐 스티커		
품목 번호	스티커 이름	설명	소매 가격
1022	사인 드럼 세트	**197 맷 그림의 드럼 세트와 사인**	1.99달러
1028	인물 사진	다섯 명의 밴드 멤버를 모두 보여주는 콜라주	2.25달러
1035	투어 버스	**198 그룹의 유명한 줄무늬 버스**	**198** 2.99달러
1042	앨범 커버	〈토렐 인 러브〉의 커버 이미지	3.45달러
200 1056	닉 비츠 밴드	현란한 색상의 그룹 로고와 이름	**200** 4.99달러

어휘 striped 줄무늬의 cover 표지 flaming 현란한

수신: 마이클 청 〈mcheung@stickersbeyours.com〉
발신: 재니스 블레드스톤 〈jbledstone@nickbeatsband.com〉
날짜: 8월 4일
제목: 재주문

청 씨께,

닉 비츠를 위해 멋진 작업을 해 주셔서 다시 한 번 감사드립니다. 맷 그림과 다른 밴드 멤버들이 스티커를 좋아하며 판매도 잘 되고 있습니다. **199 그룹 콜라주에 대해 가장 많은 호응을 받았습니다. 이미지가 정말 아름답게 나왔고 199 그 작업에 도움을 주셔서 감사드립니다.** 원본 사진을 촬영했던 로레인 파리나가 당신이 그래픽 아트로 제2의 커리어를 가져도 되겠다고 생각하더군요!

아직 첫 주문에서 남은 분량이 충분히 있지만 **200 1056번 품목이 500개 더 필요합니다.**

재니스 블레드스톤

어휘 outstanding 뛰어난 comment 의견 plenty 충분한 양

196 추론 / 암시

번역 첫 번째 이메일에서 스티커스 비 유어스가 제작한 제품에 대해 암시된 것은?
(A) 주로 어린이들을 대상으로 한다.
(B) 벽돌이나 콘크리트로 만들어진 표면에는 사용할 수 없다.
(C) 광고 목적으로만 의도된다.
(D) 비 오는 날씨에도 접착력이 유지된다.

해설 첫 번째 이메일의 두 번째 단락 다섯 번째 문장에서 스티커는 방수가 된다(Our stickers are waterproof)고 했으므로 비 오는 날에도 접착력이 유지될 수 있음을 알 수 있다. 따라서 (D)가 정답이다.

197 연계

번역 청 씨에 대해 사실일 것 같은 것은?
(A) 드럼을 연주한다.
(B) 밴드를 관리한다.
(C) 그림 씨와 같은 학교에 다녔다.
(D) 닉 비츠 공연에서 블레드스톤 씨를 만났다.

해설 첫 번째 이메일의 세 번째 단락 첫 문장에서 청 씨가 맷 그림의 팬(I am a personal fan of Matt Grimm)이라면서 밴드에서 직접 연주를 하는데 그의 연주 스타일을 본받으려고 노력한다(I play in a band myself, and I try to model my style of playing after his)고 했고, 차트의 상단에 맷 그림의 드럼 세트와 사인(Matt Grimm's drum set and signature)이라고 나와 있다. 따라서 맷 그림은 드럼 연주자이고, 청 씨 또한 드러머임을 알 수 있으므로 (A)가 정답이다.

198 세부 사항

번역 차량이 등장하는 스티커는 얼마인가?
(A) 2.25달러
(B) 2.99달러
(C) 3.45달러
(D) 4.99달러

해설 차트의 중반부에 그룹의 유명한 줄무늬 버스(The group's famous striped bus)를 표현한 스티커는 2.99달러($2.99)라고 나와 있으므로 (B)가 정답이다.

199 추론 / 암시

번역 닉 비츠의 가장 인기 있는 스티커에 대해 결론지을 수 있는 것은?
(A) 닉 비츠 콘서트에서 관객들에게 무료로 배포된다.
(B) 그림 씨의 이미지를 더 크게 바꿀 것이다.
(C) 청 씨의 도움을 받아 디자인되었다.
(D) 파리나 씨의 사인이 포함되어 있다.

해설 두 번째 이메일의 세 번째 문장에서 스티커 중에서 그룹 콜라주에 대해 가장 많은 호응을 받았다(They received the most comments on the group collage)고 했고, 그 작업에 도움을 줘서 감사하다(we appreciate your help with it)며 원본 사진을 촬영했던 로레인 파리나는 청 씨가 그래픽 아트로 제2의 커리어를 가져도 되겠다고 생각한다(Lorraine Farina, who did the original photography, thinks you could have a second career in graphic art!)고 했다. 따라서 청 씨는 닉 비츠의 가장 인기 있는 그룹 콜라주의 이미지 작업에 직접 참여했다는 것을 짐작할 수 있으므로 (C)가 정답이다.

200 연계

번역 블레드스톤 씨가 주문한 스티커에 대해 명시된 것은?
(A) 다른 스티커보다 작다.
(B) 앨범 표지를 바탕으로 제작되었다.
(C) 이전에 재주문된 적이 있다.
(D) 판매되는 스티커 중 가장 비싸다.

해설 두 번째 이메일의 마지막 단락에서 블레드스톤 씨는 1056번 품목이 500개 더 필요하다(I do need 500 more of item 1056)며 스티커를 주문하고 있고, 차트의 하단에 따르면 1056번 품목은 4.99달러($4.99)로 닉 비츠 스티커 중 가장 가격이 높다. 따라서 (D)가 정답이다.

기출 TEST 9

101 (A)	102 (B)	103 (B)	104 (C)	105 (A)
106 (A)	107 (C)	108 (A)	109 (B)	110 (D)
111 (C)	112 (A)	113 (C)	114 (B)	115 (D)
116 (A)	117 (C)	118 (B)	119 (D)	120 (D)
121 (D)	122 (B)	123 (C)	124 (C)	125 (A)
126 (B)	127 (B)	128 (B)	129 (D)	130 (A)
131 (B)	132 (D)	133 (A)	134 (C)	135 (D)
136 (B)	137 (A)	138 (B)	139 (C)	140 (D)
141 (A)	142 (D)	143 (C)	144 (C)	145 (A)
146 (A)	147 (D)	148 (A)	149 (D)	150 (B)
151 (C)	152 (D)	153 (B)	154 (D)	155 (A)
156 (B)	157 (B)	158 (D)	159 (C)	160 (B)
161 (A)	162 (C)	163 (D)	164 (C)	165 (B)
166 (C)	167 (D)	168 (C)	169 (A)	170 (B)
171 (C)	172 (A)	173 (B)	174 (C)	175 (D)
176 (D)	177 (D)	178 (A)	179 (B)	180 (C)
181 (C)	182 (A)	183 (D)	184 (C)	185 (B)
186 (B)	187 (A)	188 (D)	189 (C)	190 (D)
191 (C)	192 (D)	193 (C)	194 (A)	195 (B)
196 (A)	197 (C)	198 (A)	199 (C)	200 (B)

PART 5

101 명사 자리 _ 동사의 주어 / 수 일치

해설 빈칸은 앞에 소유격 대명사 Our가 있고 복수 동사 indicate의 주어 자리이므로 복수 명사가 들어가야 한다. 따라서 '기록'을 뜻하는 복수 명사 (A) records가 정답이다. (B) recording(녹음, 기록)도 명사이지만 단수 명사이므로 답이 될 수 없고, (C) recorded는 동사/과거분사, (D) recordable은 형용사이므로 품사상 적합하지 않다.

번역 저희 기록에 따르면 귀사의 차량은 다음 달에 정기 점검을 받기로 되어 있습니다.

어휘 indicate 나타내다   due 예정된

102 형용사 어휘

해설 사무실 건물의 출입구(entrance)를 수식하기에 적절한 형용사가 들어가야 한다. '주 출입구'라는 의미가 되어야 하므로 '주요한'을 뜻하는 (B) main이 정답이다. (A) next(다음의)는 기준이 되는 대상이 제시되어 있지 않으므로 의미가 모호하여 적절하지 않고, (C) sure는 '확실한', (D) early는 '이른'이라는 뜻으로 의미상 부적절하다.

번역 우리 사무실 건물의 주 출입구는 공사로 인해 화요일에 폐쇄될 예정이다.

어휘 entrance 출입구

103 부사 자리 _ 동사 수식

해설 빈칸은 등위접속사 and로 연결된 동사구 must be handled and stored를 수식하는 부사 자리이므로 (B) carefully(신중하게, 주의하여)가 정답이다. (A) careful과 (D) more careful은 형용사, (C) carefulness는 명사이므로 빈칸에 들어갈 수 없다.

번역 "기밀"이라고 표시된 문서는 신중하게 다뤄지고 보관되어야 한다.

어휘 mark 표시하다   confidential 기밀의   store 보관하다

104 동사 어휘

해설 빈칸 뒤에 명사 trains와 to부정사 to switch가 있는 것으로 보아 「allow + 목적어 + 목적격 보어(to부정사)」 형태로 '~가 …하는 것을 가능하게 해 준다'는 의미를 나타내는 동사 (C) allows가 정답이다. (A)의 ride는 '타다', (B)의 form은 '형성하다', (D)의 conduct는 '수행하다'라는 의미이다.

번역 신기술은 기차가 전기 모드와 디젤 모드 사이에서 신속하게 전환할 수 있게 해 준다.

어휘 switch 전환하다

105 명사 자리 _ to부정사의 목적어 / 수 일치

해설 빈칸은 to부정사 to open의 목적어 역할을 하는 명사 자리이고, 앞에 28이라는 수사의 수식을 받고 있으므로 복수 명사가 들어가야 한다. 따라서 복수 명사 (A) stores가 정답이다. 동명사 (B) storing은 뒤에 목적어가 필요하며, (C) store는 단수 명사, (D) storage는 불가산명사이므로 답이 될 수 없다.

번역 초코본느 사는 향후 3년간 28개의 신규 매장을 개점할 계획이라고 한다.

106 동사 어휘

해설 빈칸은 new tenants를 목적어로 취하는 타동사 자리로, 빈칸 앞의 be동사 is와 함께 '새로운 세입자를 찾고 있다'는 내용이 되어야 자연스러우므로 동사 seek(찾다, 구하다)의 현재분사형 (A) seeking이 정답이다. (B)의 grow는 '키우다', (C)의 face는 '직면하다', (D)의 relate는 '관련시키다'라는 의미이다.

번역 로프스트롬 쇼핑센터는 비어 있는 소매 공간을 임대할 새로운 세입자를 찾고 있다.

어휘 tenant 세입자   vacant 비어 있는   retail 소매의

107 인칭대명사의 격 _ 소유격

해설 빈칸에는 뒤에 온 명사구 distinctive style을 수식하는 인칭대명사가 들어가야 한다. 따라서 명사 앞에 쓰여 한정사 역할을 할 수 있는 소유격 인칭대명사 (C) her가 정답이다.

번역 화가 마리온 세티미는 인도네시아에서 거주한 몇 년 동안 그녀만의 독특한 스타일을 개발했다.

어휘 distinctive 독특한

108 전치사 어휘

해설 뒤의 시간 명사구 4:00 P.M.을 목적어로 취해 '오후 4시경에'라는 의미가 되어야 자연스러우므로 '약, ~쯤'을 뜻하는 (A) around가 정답이다. (B) until은 '~까지', (C) outside는 '~ 밖에서'라는 뜻이고, (D) within은 '~ 이내에'라는 의미로 기간 명사를 목적어로 취한다.

번역 플로럴 공원에서 열리는 회사 야유회는 토요일 정오에 시작해서 오후 4시경에 끝납니다.

109 동사 어형 _ 시제

해설 빈칸은 주어 the department의 동사 자리로, 앞에 과거를 나타내는 시간 부사구 Last Monday가 있으므로 과거 시제인 (B) celebrated가 정답이다.

번역 지난 월요일에 부서는 오카다 씨의 최근 관리자 승진을 축하했다.

어휘 recent 최근의 promotion 승진

110 명사 어휘

해설 빈칸에 들어갈 명사는 회사의 에너지 소비 절감을 위해 쉬안 씨가 한 것이면서 동시에 고려할 가치가 있는 대상이어야 하므로 '쉬안 씨의 제안'이라는 내용이 되어야 적절하다. 따라서 '제안'을 뜻하는 (D) proposal이 정답이다. (A) revision은 '수정', (B) attention은 '주목', (C) meaning은 '의미'라는 의미이다.

번역 회사의 에너지 소비 절감을 위한 쉬안 씨의 제안은 고려할 가치가 있다.

어휘 reduce 줄이다 consumption 소비 worth ~할 가치가 있는

111 부사 자리 _ 동사 수식

해설 빈칸은 주어 Dr. Grayston과 동사 accepted 사이에서 동사를 수식하는 부사 자리이다. 따라서 '의욕적으로, 열정적으로'를 뜻하는 부사 (C) enthusiastically가 정답이다. (A) enthusiast와 (D) enthusiasm은 명사, (B) enthusiastic은 형용사이므로 품사상 빈칸에 들어갈 수 없다.

번역 그레이스턴 박사는 학교장 직책을 의욕적으로 받아들였다.

어휘 accept 받아들이다 superintendent 관리자

112 전치사 어휘

해설 빈칸 뒤의 명사구 the Verdigris Bistro를 목적어로 취해 '버디그리스 비스트로 맞은편에'라는 의미가 되어야 자연스러우므로 '~ 맞은편에'를 뜻하는 (A) opposite이 정답이다. (B) except는 '~을 제외하고', (C) across는 '가로질러', (D) plus는 '~도 또한'이라는 의미이다. 참고로, (C) across는 across from의 형태로 '~ 맞은편에'를 뜻한다.

번역 오스티나 갤러리는 아치 가의 북쪽 끝, 버디그리스 비스트로 맞은편에 위치해 있다.

113 to부정사 _ 동사의 목적어

해설 빈칸은 동사 promised의 목적어 자리이다. 동사 promise는 to부정사를 목적어로 취해 '~할 것을 약속하다'라는 의미를 나타내므로 to부정사 (C) to become이 정답이다. (A) became과 (D) had become은 동사, (B) becoming은 동명사/현재분사이므로 빈칸에 들어갈 수 없다.

번역 가르시아 씨는 은퇴 후 윈스턴 씨의 멘토가 되겠다고 약속했다.

114 부사 어휘

해설 형용사 available을 수식하여 적절한 문맥을 완성하는 부사를 고르는 문제이다. '재활용 소재로 제작된 신발은 널리 구할 수 있다'는 내용이 되어야 자연스러우므로 '널리'를 뜻하는 (B) widely가 정답이다. (A) upward는 '위쪽으로', (D) closely는 '면밀히'라는 의미로 문맥상 적절하지 않고, (C) enough는 형용사를 뒤에서 수식하므로 빈칸의 위치상 답이 될 수 없다.

번역 한때 특제품으로 여겨지던 재활용 소재로 제작된 신발은 이제 널리 구할 수 있다.

어휘 specialty 특제품 material 재료

115 명사 자리 _ 동사의 목적어

해설 빈칸은 동사 has formed의 목적어 역할을 하는 명사 자리로, '제휴 관계를 맺었다'는 의미가 되어야 하므로 '제휴 (관계), 협력'을 뜻하는 (D) partnerships가 정답이다. (A) partner와 (B) partners는 '동업자'라는 뜻이므로 의미상 적절하지 않고, 특히 (A) partner는 가산 단수 명사로 한정사 없이 단독으로 쓸 수 없으며, (C) partnering은 동명사로 뒤에 목적어가 필요하다.

번역 유핑 대학교는 학생들에게 인턴십 기회를 만들어 주기 위해 지역 업체들과 제휴를 맺었다.

어휘 form 형성하다 opportunity 기회

116 명사 어휘

해설 빈칸에 들어갈 명사는 구매자의 입장에서 제품에 대해 갖고 있는 것이어야 하고, 전문적인 정보를 찾는다고 한 것으로 보아 '제품에 대한 지식이 제한적인 구매자'라는 의미가 되어야 적절하다. 따라서 '지식'을 뜻하는 (A) knowledge가 정답이다. (B) approval은 '승인', (C) perception은 '인식', (D) consideration은 '고려'라는 의미이다.

번역 우리의 시장 조사는 제품에 대해 제한된 지식을 갖고 있는 구매자들이 종종 전문적인 출처에서 정보를 찾는다는 것을 보여준다.

어휘 limited 제한된 expert 전문적인; 전문가

117 부정대명사

해설 빈칸은 동사 is preventing의 주어 자리이다. 문장의 동사가 단수형인 is이므로 단수 동사와 수가 일치하는 부정대명사 (C) Something이 정답이다. (A) Many는 뒤에 복수 동사가 와야 하

고, (B) Other는 형용사로 단독으로는 주어 역할을 할 수 없고, (D) Whoever는 접속사이므로 품사상 답이 될 수 없다.

번역 무엇인가가 그래픽 아티스트들이 주요 데이터베이스에서 이미지 파일에 접근하는 것을 막고 있다.

어휘 prevent 막다   access 접근하다

118 전치사 자리 / 어휘

해설 빈칸은 뒤에 있는 명사구 a delay를 콤마 뒤의 완전한 절에 연결하는 자리이므로 전치사가 들어가야 한다. '지연에도 불구하고'라는 의미가 되어야 자연스러우므로 '~에도 불구하고'를 뜻하는 전치사 (B) Despite가 정답이다. (C) According to(~에 따르면)는 의미상 어울리지 않고, (A) Although(비록 ~하지만)는 부사절 접속사, (D) However(하지만)는 부사이므로 품사상 적합하지 않다.

번역 지연에도 불구하고, 타인테크는 창고 개조를 목표일인 4월 7일 이전에 완료했다.

어휘 renovation 개조   warehouse 창고   target 목표

119 부사 자리 _ 형용사 수식

해설 be동사 is와 형용사 closed(닫힌, 휴업한) 사이에서 형용사를 수식하는 부사 자리이므로 '사실상'이라는 의미의 부사 (D) effectively가 정답이다. (A) effect는 명사/동사, (B) effecting은 동명사/현재분사, (C) effective는 형용사이므로 품사상 빈칸에 들어갈 수 없다.

번역 신용카드 시스템이 오프라인 상태인 동안 렉슬러 백화점은 사실상 영업을 중단했다.

120 전치사 어휘

해설 빈칸 뒤의 명사구 the last two years를 목적어로 취해 '지난 2년 동안'이라는 의미가 되어야 자연스러우므로, 기간 명사 앞에서 '~ 동안'을 뜻하는 (D) over가 정답이다. (A) onto는 '~ 위로', (B) under는 '~ 아래에', (C) against는 '~에 반대하여'라는 의미이다.

번역 조사된 장난감 제조업체의 거의 절반이 지난 2년 동안 증가한 매출을 보고했다.

어휘 nearly 거의   manufacturer 제조업체

121 동사 자리 _ 수 일치 ▶동영상 강의

해설 빈칸은 주어 Nonprofit groups의 동사 자리로, 주어가 복수 명사이므로 복수 동사가 들어가야 한다. 조동사 may는 주어의 수에 상관없이 쓸 수 있고, 문맥상 '비영리 단체들은 최대 세 개의 신청서를 제출할 수 있다'는 의미가 되면 자연스러우므로 (D) may submit이 정답이다. (A) be submitted는 동사원형으로 시작하고, (C) submits는 단수 동사이므로 빈칸에 들어갈 수 없고, (B) submitting은 동명사·/현재분사이므로 품사상 적합하지 않다.

번역 비영리 단체들은 재정 지원 심사를 위해 어느 특정 연도 내에서든 최대 세 개의 신청서를 제출할 수 있다.

어휘 nonprofit 비영리적인   application 신청(서)   funding 재정 지원   consideration 심사, 고려   given 특정한

122 부사 어휘 ▶동영상 강의

해설 동사 reacted를 수식하여 적절한 문맥을 완성하는 부사를 고르는 문제이다. 콤마 뒤에서 무대 디자인과 안무를 호평했다(praising)고 한 것으로 보아 '새 뮤지컬에 호의적으로 반응했다'는 내용이 되어야 자연스러우므로 '호의적으로'라는 뜻의 (B) favorably가 정답이다. (A) intentionally는 '의도적으로', (C) uncertainly는 '불확실하게', (D) continuously는 '지속적으로'라는 의미이다.

번역 비평가들은 새 뮤지컬에 호의적으로 반응하며 흥미로운 무대 디자인과 인상적인 안무를 호평했다.

어휘 critic 비평가   react 반응하다   praise 칭찬하다   impressive 인상적인   choreography 안무

123 전치사 자리 ▶동영상 강의

해설 빈칸은 앞의 완전한 절에 명사구 writers and publishers를 연결하는 자리이므로 전치사가 들어가야 한다. '작가와 출판업자들 사이에서'라는 의미가 되어야 자연스러우므로 '(여럿) 사이에'를 뜻하는 전치사 (C) among이 정답이다. (A) owed to는 「동사 owe+목적어+전치사 to」의 수동형으로 be owed to(~ 때문이다)의 형태로 사용되며, (B) because는 부사절 접속사이고, (D) in between은 두 개의 대상(A and B) 사이에 있을 때만 사용 가능하며 셋 이상 사이를 표현할 때는 쓰지 않으므로 답이 될 수 없다.

번역 〈클라우젠의 노트〉는 작가와 출판업자들 사이에서 심층적인 도서 비평으로 유명하다.

어휘 well-known 유명한   in-depth 심층적인   review 비평

124 동사 어휘

해설 5형식 동사 has caused의 목적격 보어 역할을 하는 to부정사 자리에 들어갈 동사 어휘를 고르는 문제이다. '목재 부족으로 가격이 치솟았다'는 내용이 되어야 자연스러우므로 '치솟다, 급등하다'라는 뜻의 (C) soar가 정답이다. (A) drain은 '배수하다', (B) loop는 '고리 모양으로 움직이다', (D) fling은 '내던지다'라는 의미이다.

번역 단단한 목재의 지속적인 부족으로 인해 특정 가구 품목의 가격이 치솟았다.

어휘 ongoing 지속적인   shortage 부족   hardwood 단단한 목재

125 형용사 자리 _ 명사 수식

해설 빈칸에는 정관사와 명사 사이에서 명사 tray를 수식하는 형용사 또는 tray와 복합명사를 이루는 명사가 들어갈 수 있다. 문맥상 '자성을 띤 트레이'라는 의미를 나타내야 하므로 '자석의, 자성을 띤'을 뜻하는 형용사 (A) magnetic이 정답이다. (B) magnetize는 동사, (D) magnetically는 부사로 품사상 답이 될 수 없고, (C) magnets는 다른 명사 앞에 위치해 복합명사를 이룰 수 없으므로 오답이다.

번역 가정용 또는 자동차 공구를 쉽게 보관하고 이용할 수 있도록 자석 트레이를 평평한 강철 표면에 부착해 주세요.

어휘 attach 부착하다 tray 트레이, 쟁반 steel 강철 surface 표면 storage 보관 household 가정용의 automotive 자동차의

126 동사 어휘 ▶동영상 강의

해설 빈칸 뒤에 to부정사 to buy가 있고 문맥상 '그 고객은 연장 보증을 구매하지 않았다'는 내용이 되어야 자연스러우므로, to부정사를 목적어로 취해 '(해야 할 일을) 하지 않다'를 뜻하는 neglect의 과거형 (B) neglected가 정답이다. (A)의 reject(거절하다)와 (D)의 dismiss(해고하다)는 보통 to부정사를 목적어로 취하지 않으며, (C) omit(생략하다) 또한 법률 문서와 같은 특정 문맥을 제외하고는 to부정사보다는 동명사를 주로 목적어로 취한다.

번역 그 고객은 식기세척기에 대한 연장 보증을 구매하지 않았으므로 무상 수리 대상이 아니다.

어휘 extended 연장된 warranty 보증 eligible 자격이 있는

127 형용사 자리 ▶동영상 강의

해설 빈칸에는 동사 appeared의 목적어 역할을 하는 to부정사 to remain 뒤에 오기에 적절한 품사를 골라야 한다. to부정사의 동사가 2형식 동사 remain이므로 빈칸은 remain의 보어 역할을 할 수 있는 형용사 또는 명사 자리이다. 문맥상 '청중이 집중하는 듯 보였다'는 내용이 되어야 자연스러우므로 '집중한, 열중한'을 뜻하는 과거분사 형태의 형용사 (B) engaged가 정답이다. (A) engage는 동사, (C) engagingly는 부사이므로 품사상 빈칸에 들어갈 수 없고, 명사 (D) engagement는 주어 audience와 동격 관계를 이루지 않으므로 답이 될 수 없다.

번역 비록 자료의 많은 부분이 기술적인 성격을 띠었지만 청중은 샤르마 씨의 발표 내내 집중하는 듯 보였다.

어휘 audience 청중 appear ~인 것처럼 보이다

128 전치사 어휘

해설 뒤의 명사구 fresh fruit and vegetables를 목적어로 취해 '신선한 과일과 채소뿐만 아니라'라는 의미가 되어야 자연스러우므로 '~뿐만 아니라, ~에 더하여'를 뜻하는 전치사 (B) In addition to가 정답이다. (A) Compared with는 '~와 비교하여', (C) Rather than은 '~이라기보다는', (D) As a result of는 '~의 결과로'라는 의미이다.

번역 신선한 과일과 채소뿐만 아니라 와트빌 농산물 시장의 판매자들은 다양한 수제품도 판매한다.

어휘 vendor 판매업자 various 다양한

129 복합관계대명사 ▶동영상 강의

해설 빈칸 뒤의 주어와 동사가 있는 절을 콤마 뒤의 완전한 절에 연결해야 하므로 부사절 접속사가 필요하다. 따라서 빈칸 뒤의 명사 route를 수식하면서 부사절을 이끌어 '어느 경로를 택하든'이라는 의미를 나타내는 복합관계대명사 (D) Whichever(어느 것이든지 간에)가 정답이다. (A) What은 명사절 접속사, (B) Some은 한정사/대명사, (C) Somewhere는 대명사/부사이므로 부사절을 이끌 수 없다. 참고로, whichever는 보통 명사절을 이끌지만, 부사절도 이끌 수 있다.

번역 어느 경로를 택하든 관리팀이 앙티브에 있는 호텔까지 운전해 가는 데 약 4시간이 걸릴 것이다.

어휘 approximately 대략

130 형용사 어휘

해설 명사 inspections를 수식하기에 적합한 형용사가 필요하고, 결함이 없음을 보장하기 위한(to ensure they are free of defects) 검사라고 했으므로 '엄격한 검사'라는 의미가 되어야 적절하다. 따라서 '엄격한'을 뜻하는 (A) rigorous가 정답이다. (B) negotiated는 '협상된', (C) returnable은 '반품할 수 있는', (D) portable은 '휴대 가능한'이라는 의미이다.

번역 바라안텍 사의 모든 수공구는 결함이 없음을 보장하기 위해 엄격한 검사를 거친다.

어휘 undergo 겪다 inspection 검사 defect 결함

PART 6

131-134 광고

> 레트로 크래프터스는 1950년대부터 1970년대까지의 가구 디자인에 집중합니다. 우리 제품은 천연 **131 목재**의 아름다움이 돋보이도록 공들여 제작됩니다. 우리에게 나무의 작은 옹이, 미세한 흠집, 그리고 색상의 변형은 결함이 아닙니다. **132 이것들은 각각의 제품을 독특하게 만들어 주는 것입니다.** 우리의 최신 컬렉션은 폭이 좁은 레일이 있는 벽걸이형 오크 선반 시스템이 포함되어 있습니다. 이 레일은 선반, 캐비닛, 서랍, 심지어 데스크톱 컴퓨터까지 지탱할 수 있어서 맞춤형 시스템을 만들 수 있습니다. **133 게다가**, 벽걸이형 디자인은 바닥 공간을 확보해 줍니다. 우리 제품은 전국 여러 도심지의 가구 **134 소매점**에서 판매됩니다. 우리 제품을 판매하는 데 관심이 있으신 가구점은 영업 이사 니아 페르노에게 연락하시면 됩니다.

> 어휘 craft 공들여 만들다 knot (나무의) 옹이 tiny 아주 작은 nick 흠집 variation 변형 imperfection 결함 feature 포함하다 wall-mounted 벽에 고정된 narrow 좁은 drawer 서랍 customizable 맞춤형의 free up ~을 확보하다

131 명사 어휘

해설 앞 문장에서 가구 디자인(furniture designs)을, 뒤 문장에서 나무의 작은 옹이, 미세한 흠집, 색상의 변형(small knots, tiny nicks, and color variations)에 대해 언급했다. 문맥상 가구 제품과 그 재료인 나무에 대해 언급하는 문장이므로, '천연 목재의 아름다움이 돋보이도록 제작된다'는 내용이 되어야 자연스럽다. 따라서 '목재'를 뜻하는 (B) wood가 정답이다. (A)의 textile은 '직물', (C) environment는 '환경', (D) light는 '조명'을 뜻하며, 가구의 재료를 의미하기에 적절하지 않다.

132 문맥에 맞는 문장 고르기

번역 (A) 이것들은 쉽게 페인트로 덮일 수 있습니다.
(B) 이것들은 형편없는 유지관리의 결과입니다.
(C) 이것들은 제품의 가치를 떨어뜨릴 수 있습니다.
(D) 이것들은 각각의 제품을 독특하게 만들어 주는 것입니다.

해설 빈칸 앞에서 나무의 작은 옹이, 미세한 흠집, 색상의 변화는 결함이 아니라(small knots, tiny nicks, and color variations are not imperfections)고 했으므로, 이것들이 결함이 아닌 대신 어떤 의미를 갖는지 또는 어떤 역할을 하는지에 대해 설명하는 내용이 들어가는 것이 자연스럽다. 따라서 각각의 제품을 독특하게 만들어 주는 것이라고 언급하는 (D)가 정답이다.

어휘 maintenance 유지관리 reduce 줄이다

133 접속부사

해설 빈칸 앞부분에는 벽걸이형 선반 시스템에 딸린 레일의 장점을 언급하고 있고, 빈칸 뒤에서는 벽걸이형 디자인이 바닥 공간을 확보해 준다는 장점을 추가로 제시하고 있다. 따라서 '게다가, 더욱이'라는 뜻으로 추가적인 내용을 덧붙일 때 사용하는 (A) Moreover가 정답이다. (B) Nevertheless는 '그럼에도 불구하고', (C) On the contrary는 '그와는 반대로', (D) Regardless는 '상관없이'라는 의미이다.

134 명사 자리 _ 복합명사

해설 빈칸은 전치사 by의 목적어 자리로, 앞에 있는 명사 furniture와 함께 복합명사를 만들 수 있는 명사가 들어가야 한다. '제품이 전국 여러 도시의 가구 소매점에서 판매된다'는 내용이 되어야 자연스러우므로 '소매업체'를 뜻하는 (C) retailers가 정답이다. (A) retail은 '소매', (B) retailing은 '소매업'으로 furniture와 복합명사를 이룰 수는 있으나 문맥상 적절하지 않고, (D) retailed는 동사/과거분사로 품사상 빈칸에 들어갈 수 없다.

135-138 설명

밥솥 관리

밥솥을 청소하기 전에 전기 콘센트에서 전원 코드를 분리하세요. 모든 **135 부품**이 완전히 식었는지 확인하세요. 다음으로 분리 가능한 솥을 제거하고 뚜껑 및 주걱과 함께 따뜻한 비눗물에 손으로 세척하세요. 솥은 식기세척기에서 세척할 수 없다는 점을 유의하세요. 또한 솥의 코팅된 표면이 연마제에 의해 손상 **136 될 수 있다**는 점을 유의하세요. 단단한 잔여물을 긁어내기보다는 따뜻한 비눗물에 10분 동안 솥을 담가 두세요. **137 그런 다음, 부드러운 솔이나 스펀지를 사용해 세척을 마무리하세요.** 밥솥의 외부는 물에 담가서는 절대 안 됩니다. **138 대신**, 적신 천으로 부드럽게 닦으세요.

어휘 rice cooker 밥솥 detach 분리하다 outlet 콘센트 pot 솥 soapy 비눗기가 있는 rice paddle 주걱 dishwasher safe 식기세척기에서 세척할 수 있는 nonstick 코팅된, 들러붙지 않는 abrasive 연마제의 scrape off ~을 긁어내다 residue 잔여물 soak 담그다 exterior 외부 submerge 물 속에 넣다 gently 부드럽게 damp 축축한

135 명사 어휘

해설 앞 문장에서 밥솥을 청소하기 전에 전기 콘센트에서 전원 코드를 분리하라(Before cleaning your rice cooker, detach the power cord from the electrical outlet)고 했고, 뒤 문장에서 다음으로 솥(pot)을 제거하고 뚜껑 및 주걱(the lid and rice paddle)과 함께 세척하라고 했다. 따라서 빈칸이 있는 문장에서 식었는지 확인하라는 것은 솥, 뚜껑, 주걱과 같은 밥솥의 구성물임을 알 수 있으므로 '부품, 요소'를 뜻하는 (D) components가 정답이다. (A)의 vehicle은 '차량', (B)의 appliance는 '가전제품', (C)의 ingredient는 '재료'를 의미한다.

136 동사 어형 _ 시제

해설 지문 전체에 걸쳐 밥솥 세척 시 유의해야 할 사항을 설명하고 있으므로 빈칸이 있는 문장도 이미 일어났거나 현재 일어나고 있는 일이 아니라 '연마제에 의해 손상될 수 있다'고 가능성에 대해 언급하는 내용이 되어야 자연스러우므로 (B) can be가 정답이다.

137 문맥에 맞는 문장 고르기

번역 (A) 그런 다음, 부드러운 솔이나 스펀지를 사용해 세척을 마무리하세요.
(B) 세척 도구는 별도로 구매해야 합니다.
(C) 마지막으로, 밥솥을 상자 안에 다시 넣으세요.
(D) 밥이 다 되면 조명이 켜질 것입니다.

해설 앞에서 단단한 잔여물을 긁어내기보다는 따뜻한 비눗물에 10분 동안 솥을 담가 두라(Rather than scrape off any tough residue, soak the pot in warm, soapy water for ten minutes)고 했다. 문맥상 단단한 잔여물을 제거하기 위해 그 다음에 할 일을 설명하는 내용이 들어가야 적절하므로 그런 다음 부드러운 솔이나 스펀지로 세척을 마무리하라고 언급하는 (A)가 정답이다.

어휘 utensil 도구 separately 별도로

138 접속부사

해설 앞 문장에서 밥솥의 외부는 물에 담가서는 절대 안 된다고 당부하고 있고, 뒤 문장에서는 적신 천으로 부드럽게 닦으라며 물에 담그는 대신에 할 수 있는 세척 방법에 대해 알려주고 있다. 따라서 앞서 언급된 내용에 대한 대안을 제시할 때 사용하는 '대신에'라는 뜻의 (B) Instead가 정답이다. (A) If not은 '그렇지 않으면', (C) Meanwhile은 '그동안', (D) In that case는 '그 경우에는'이라는 의미이다.

139-142 이메일

수신: 브리타 게링 〈bgehring@gehringaccounting.com〉
발신: 미켈 주비온도 〈mikel@zubiondodesign.com〉
날짜: 12월 12일
제목: 로고 스케치
첨부: 게링_스케치

게링 씨께,

귀하의 업체를 위한 로고 디자인 을 저에게 맡겨 주셔서 감사합니다. 지난 주 회의 동안 139 **상세한** 메모를 했으며 로고를 통해 전달하려는 업체의 가치를 이해했다고 생각합니다. 귀하를 위한 5개의 스케치를 첨부했습니다. 140 **각 스케치**는 귀하의 업체를 약간 다른 방식으로 표현합니다. 2개는 고전적이면서 시대를 초월한 느낌인 반면, 나머지는 미니멀하고 현대적입니다. 141 **그럼에도 불구하고, 스케치들은 모두 신뢰할 수 있고 정확하다는 인상을 줍니다.**

스케치를 검토하시고 나서 어느 것이 마음에 드시는지 그리고 혹시 변경할 사항이 있다면 무엇을 바꿔야 하는지를 알려 주세요. 귀하와 함께 디자인을 142 **마무리할** 수 있기를 기대합니다.

미켈 주비온도
주비온도 디자인

어휘 entrust 맡기다 value 가치 convey 전달하다 attach 첨부하다 represent 표현하다 timeless 시대를 초월한 minimalist 미니멀리즘의

139 형용사 자리 _ 명사 수식

해설 빈칸은 명사 notes를 수식하는 형용사 자리이고, '상세한 메모를 했다'는 의미가 되어야 적합하므로 '광범위한, 대규모의'를 뜻하는 형용사 (C) extensive가 정답이다. 명사 (A) extents(규모)는 notes와 복합명사를 이루기에 부적절하고, 현재분사 (B) extending은 '연장하는'이라는 뜻으로 의미상 어울리지 않으며, (D) extensively는 부사이므로 빈칸에 들어갈 수 없다.

140 대명사 어휘

해설 빈칸은 단수 동사 represents의 주어 자리이고, 해당 문장은 앞 문장에서 언급한 5개의 스케치(five sketches)의 특성을 설명하는 내용이다. '각 스케치는 다른 방식으로 업체를 표현한다'는 내용이 되어야 자연스러우므로 five sketches를 '각각'이라는 단수의 의미로 지칭할 수 있는 대명사 (D) Each가 정답이다.

141 문맥에 맞는 문장 고르기

번역 (A) 그럼에도 불구하고, 스케치들은 모두 신뢰할 수 있고 정확하다는 인상을 줍니다.
(B) 그 회사들은 매우 기억에 남는 로고를 가지고 있습니다.
(C) 그렇다 하더라도, 로고를 디자인하는 것은 비용이 많이 드는 과정일 수 있습니다.
(D) 저는 처음에 요청된 것보다 적은 색상을 사용하시기를 추천드립니다.

해설 앞에서 5개의 스케치(five sketches)를 언급하면서 그 중 2개는 고전적이고 시대를 초월한 느낌인 반면 나머지는 미니멀하고 현대적이라며 각각의 상반된 디자인 특성에 대해 설명하고 있다. 따라서 이 스케치들을 they all로 받아 각기 다른 느낌에도 불구하고 모두 신뢰할 수 있고 정확하다는 인상을 준다는 공통적인 특성을 강조하는 내용이 들어가는 것이 자연스러우므로 (A)가 정답이다.

어휘 nonetheless 그럼에도 불구하고 impression 인상 trustworthiness 신뢰성 precision 정확성 memorable 기억할 만한 even so 그렇다 하더라도 costly 비용이 많이 드는 process 과정 initially 처음에

142 동사 어휘

해설 앞 문장에서 스케치를 검토한 뒤 마음에 드는 것과 필요한 변경 사항을 알려달라고 했으므로, 빈칸이 있는 문장은 '디자인을 마무리할 수 있기를 기대한다'는 내용이 되어야 문맥상 자연스럽다. 따라서 '마무리하다'를 뜻하는 동사 finalize의 동명사형 (D) finalizing이 정답이다. (A)의 research는 '조사하다, 연구하다', (B)의 publicize는 '홍보하다', (C)의 demonstrate는 '시연하다'라는 의미이다.

143-146 기사 ▶동영상 강의

런던 (6월 2일) — 퍼스비 구두와 운동화의 소유주인 록 앤 지브스는 오늘 143 **비공개** 금액으로 시플리 디자인의 인수를 발표했다. 시플리의 재정상 어려움에 대해 한동안 추측해 온 신발 업계 내부자들에게 이번 144 **인수**는 전혀 놀라운 일이 아니다. 이곳 런던에 있는 대표 매장을 포함하여 시플리 매장 여섯 개 중 다섯 곳은 록 앤 지브스의 이번 거래에 포함될 예정이다. 145 **리즈에 있는 매장의 운명은 아직 알려지지 않고 있다.**

록 앤 지브스의 CEO인 자카리 테인은 이번 거래에 대해 열의를 표했다. "시플리는 상징적인 디자인 회사로 확고하게 전통성을 지켜온 신발 분야에서 록 앤 지브스의 포트폴리오에 많은 것을 146 **더해 줄 것입니다.**"라고 테인 씨는 말했다.

어휘 athletic 운동의 acquisition 인수 insider 내부자 speculate 추측하다 challenge 어려움 deal 거래 flagship store 대표 매장 enthusiasm 열의 iconic 상징적인 reliably 확실히 traditional 전통의

143 형용사 어휘

해설 빈칸 뒤의 명사 amount를 수식하기에 적절한 형용사를 고르는 문제이다. '비공개 금액'이라는 의미가 되어야 자연스러우므로 '비공개의, 공개되지 않은'을 뜻하는 (D) undisclosed가 정답이다. (A) external은 '외부의', (B) arbitrary는 '독단적인', (C) indivisible은 '불가분의'라는 뜻으로 amount(금액)를 수식하기에 부적절하다.

144 명사 어휘

해설 앞 문장에서 록 앤 지브스는 시플리 디자인의 인수(acquisition)를 발표했다고 했고, 빈칸이 있는 문장은 인수 발표에 대한 업계 관계자

들의 반응을 언급하는 것이 자연스럽다. 따라서 빈칸에는 인수를 대신할 수 있는 '구매, 매입'이라는 의미의 (C) purchase가 정답이다. (A) trade는 '교역', (B) closure는 '폐쇄', (D) appointment는 '약속'을 의미한다.

145 문맥에 맞는 문장 고르기

번역 (A) 리즈에 있는 매장의 운명은 아직 알려지지 않고 있다.
(B) 시플리 디자인은 약 90년 전에 설립되었다.
(C) 고객들은 이제 좋은 거래를 할 수 있다.
(D) 모든 런던 지점은 주 7일 운영된다.

해설 앞에서 런던의 대표 매장을 포함하여 시플리 매장 여섯 개 중 다섯 곳이 거래에 포함될 것(Five of the six Shipley stores will be part of the Locke and Jeeves deal)이라고 했으므로, 언급되지 않은 나머지 한 매장에 대한 내용이 들어가는 것이 자연스럽다. 따라서 '리즈 매장의 운명은 아직 알려지지 않고 있다'고 언급하는 (A)가 정답이다.

어휘 fate 운명 found 설립하다 take advantage of ~을 이용하다

146 동사 어형 _ 시제

해설 앞에서 시플리 디자인에 대한 인수 결정을 발표하며 앞으로의 절차에 대해 설명하고 있다. 따라서 빈칸이 있는 문장은 시플리를 인수함으로써 앞으로 기대되는 이점을 언급하는 내용이 되어야 자연스러우므로 미래 시제 (A) will be adding이 정답이다.

PART 7

147-148 초대장

러셋 캐피탈

148 동료들과 함께 페이스트리와 커피를 즐기며
147 최고 재무 책임자 이미선 씨를 환영해 주세요.

9월 5일 화요일
오후 3시 – 오후 4시
2100호 회의실

사장실 주관

어휘 pastry 페이스트리, 빵류 Chief Financial Officer 최고 재무 책임자

147 주제 / 목적

번역 행사의 목적은?
(A) 경영직 후보자를 인터뷰하려고
(B) 직원의 은퇴를 축하하려고
(C) 회의 참가자들이 서로 교류할 수 있도록 하려고
(D) 직원들에게 새로운 회사 임원을 소개하려고

해설 초대장 상단에서 최고 재무 책임자 이미선 씨를 환영해 달라(welcome Ms. Misun Lee as Chief Financial Officer)고 했으므로 행사는 새로 영입한 임원을 소개하기 위한 자리임을 알 수 있다. 따라서 (D)가 정답이다.

어휘 candidate 후보자 retirement 은퇴 participant 참가자 network 교류하다 executive 임원

> **Paraphrasing**
> 지문의 Chief Financial Officer → 정답의 company executive

148 세부 사항

번역 초대장에 따르면, 행사에서 일어날 일은?
(A) 다과가 제공된다.
(B) 사장이 연설을 한다.
(C) 재무 보고서가 배부된다.
(D) 최고 재무 책임자가 상을 받는다.

해설 초대장 상단에서 동료들과 함께 페이스트리와 커피를 즐기라(Join your colleagues for pastries and coffee)고 했으므로 행사에서 즐길 수 있는 음식이 제공된다는 것을 알 수 있다. 따라서 (A)가 정답이다.

어휘 refreshments 다과 distribute 배부하다

> **Paraphrasing**
> 지문의 pastries and coffee → 정답의 Refreshments

149-150 이메일

수신: 마이클 홍 〈mhong73@mailcrate.co.uk〉
발신: 고객 지원팀 〈support@toppmanagement.co.uk〉
날짜: 6월 20일
제목: 귀하의 계정 접근
첨부: 톱 매니지먼트 사용자 지침

홍 씨께:

149 귀하께서 최근에 톱 매니지먼트 온라인 앱에 로그인하시지 않은 것으로 보입니다. 6개월 동안 활동이 없을 경우 사용자 계정이 자동으로 휴면 상태가 됩니다. **150** 7월 20일에 계정이 비활성화되는 것을 방지하시려면 해당 날짜 이전에 앱에 로그인만 하시면 됩니다. 비밀번호를 잊으셨거나 계정을 이용하시는 데 어려움이 있을 경우, 첨부된 톱 매니지먼트 사용자 지침을 확인해 주세요.

수천 명이 프로젝트 업무 진행을 관리하는 데 수상 경력이 있는 저희 톱 매니지먼트 앱을 사용하고 있습니다. 귀하께서 계속 소중한 사용자로 남아주실 거라 믿습니다. 귀하께 도움이 될 수 있는 방법이 있다면 언제든지 고객 지원팀으로 연락 주세요.

톱 매니지먼트 고객 지원팀

어휘 attachment 첨부 guideline 지침 inactivity 비활동 deactivation 비활성화 workflow 작업 흐름 valued 소중한

149 추론 / 암시

번역 홍 씨의 계정에 대해 사실인 것 같은 것은?
(A) 새 비밀번호가 필요하다.
(B) 6월 20일에 생성되었다.
(C) 그의 동료가 업데이트했다.
(D) 몇 달간 사용되지 않았다.

해설 첫 단락 첫 번째 문장에서 홍 씨에게 최근에 톱 매니지먼트 온라인 앱에 로그인하지 않은 것으로 보인다(It appears you have not logged in to your Topp Management online app recently)면서 6개월 동안 활동이 없을 경우 사용자 계정이 자동으로 휴면 상태가 된다(After six months of inactivity, user accounts are automatically closed)고 안내하고 있다. 따라서 홍 씨는 지난 몇 달간 계정을 이용하지 않았다는 것을 알 수 있으므로 (D)가 정답이다.

어휘 colleague 동료

150 세부 사항

번역 홍 씨가 계정 이용을 유지하기 위해 해야 하는 일은?
(A) 이메일 회신
(B) 7월 20일 전에 로그인
(C) 연간 멤버십 갱신
(D) 고객 서비스 직원과의 상담

해설 첫 단락 세 번째 문장에서 홍 씨에게 7월 20일에 계정이 비활성화되는 것을 방지하려면 해당 날짜 이전에 앱에 로그인만 하면 된다(To avoid account deactivation on 20 July, simply sign in to the app before that date)고 했으므로 (B)가 정답이다.

어휘 renew 갱신하다

151-152 온라인 채팅

존 데이커스 (오전 9시 30분)
안녕하세요. 151 제가 오늘 아침에 보일러 서비스 예약이 되어 있어요. 기사님께서 저희 집으로 오고 계신가요?

HVAC 고객 서비스 (오전 9시 31분)
확인해 드리겠습니다.

HVAC 고객 서비스 (오전 9시 32분)
저희 시스템에는 오늘 오후 3시에서 5시 사이에 방문 드릴 예정이라고 나오네요.

존 데이커스 (오전 9시 33분)
제 기록에는 오늘 오전 9시에서 11시 사이라고 되어 있어요. 근무도 쉬었는데요.

HVAC 고객 서비스 (오전 9시 34분)
소통에 혼선이 있어 죄송합니다. 152 기술자가 오늘 오후에 방문 드릴 거예요.

존 데이커스 (오전 9시 36분)
하지만 저는 곧 사무실로 가야 해요.

HVAC 고객 서비스 (오전 9시 37분)
죄송합니다, 데이커스 씨. 일정을 변경할 수 있는지 확인해 보겠습니다.

HVAC 고객 서비스 (오전 9시 42분)
좋은 소식입니다. 기술자와 연락이 됐어요. 지금 작업을 마무리 중이라 한 시간 내에 거기 도착할 수 있답니다.

존 데이커스 (오전 9시 43분)
정말 감사합니다. 고맙습니다.

어휘 furnace 보일러   miscommunication 소통 오류

151 주제 / 목적

번역 데이커스 씨가 HVAC 고객 서비스에 연락한 이유는?
(A) 작업의 품질에 대해 불만을 표현하기 위해서
(B) 근무가 가능함을 확인하기 위해서
(C) 계획된 대로 서비스가 제공되는지 확인하기 위해서
(D) 더 이상 필요하지 않은 서비스를 취소하기 위해서

해설 9시 30분에 데이커스 씨가 오늘 아침에 보일러 서비스 예약이 되어 있다(I have a furnace service appointment scheduled this morning)면서 기사가 집으로 오고 있는지(Is a technician on the way to my house yet?)를 묻고 있다. 따라서 데이커스 씨는 예약 일정대로 서비스를 받을 수 있는지 확인하기 위해 연락했다는 것을 알 수 있으므로 (C)가 정답이다.

어휘 displeasure 불만

152 의도 파악

번역 오전 9시 36분에 데이커스 씨가 "하지만 저는 곧 사무실로 가야 해요"라고 쓴 의도는?
(A) 상관에게 질문이 있다.
(B) 사무실에서 먼 곳에 산다.
(C) 기술자가 데이커스 씨의 직장으로 가야 한다.
(D) 오후 예약은 받아들일 수 없다.

해설 9시 34분에 HVAC 고객 서비스에서 기술자가 오늘 오후에 방문할 것(A technician will be there later today)이라고 한 데 대해 9시 36분에 데이커스 씨가 하지만 곧 사무실로 가야 한다(But I need to get to the office soon)고 대답했다. 따라서 데이커스 씨는 곧 출근해야 해서 오후 일정은 수용할 수 없다는 의도로 한 말임을 알 수 있으므로 (D)가 정답이다.

어휘 supervisor 상관   unacceptable 받아들일 수 없는

153-155 회람

회람

수신: 전 직원
발신: 로레타 히라노, 인사 책임자
날짜: 4월 7일 금요일 오전 9시 3분
제목: 여름 근무 준비

동료 여러분께,

아시다시피, 6월 1일부터 8월 31일까지의 기간은 153 **보통** 우리가 가장 바쁜 시기입니다. 올여름은 작년 이맘때보다 업무가 15퍼센트 증가했기 때문에 평년보다 훨씬 더 바쁠 것 같습니다.

경영진도 여름이 많은 직원들이 직장에서 휴가를 내고 싶어 하는 때라는 것을 잘 알고 있습니다. 그렇지만 154 **우리는 최고 품질의 서비스를 제공하기 위해 충분한 직원이 자리에 있어야 하며, 이 정책으로 인해 벨러슨 파이낸셜은 고객들로부터 높은 평가를 받고 있습니다.**

따라서 6월 1일부터 8월 31일 사이에 휴가를 계획하고 계시다면 155 **4월 28일 금요일까지 요청서를 제출해 주십시오.** 가능한 한 빨리, 늦어도 5월 8일 월요일까지는 답변을 받게 될 것입니다.

협조해 주셔서 감사합니다.

어휘 arrangement 준비 ordinarily 보통 promise ~일 것 같다 still 그런데도 sufficient 충분한 on hand 준비된 regard 평가하다, 간주하다 response 대답 no later than 늦어도 ~까지는 assistance 도움, 지원

153 동의어 찾기

번역 첫 번째 단락 1행의 "ordinarily"와 의미가 가장 가까운 단어는?
(A) 지루하게
(B) 일반적으로
(C) 받아들일 수 있게
(D) 최소한으로

해설 의미상 여름은 '보통' 가장 바쁜 시기라는 뜻으로 쓰였으므로 '보통, 일반적으로'를 뜻하는 (B) typically가 정답이다.

154 Not / True

번역 벨러슨 파이낸셜에 대해 명시된 것은?
(A) 최근에 히라노 씨를 인사 책임자로 승진시켰다.
(B) 최근 몇 달간 재정적 어려움을 겪었다.
(C) 6월과 8월 사이에 연장된 서비스 시간을 제공한다.
(D) 우수한 서비스로 고객들 사이에서 평판을 쌓았다.

해설 두 번째 단락의 두 번째 문장에서 우리는 최고 품질의 서비스를 제공하기 위해 충분한 직원이 자리에 있어야 하며 이 정책으로 인해 벨러슨 파이낸셜은 고객들로부터 높은 평가를 받고 있다(we must have sufficient staff on hand to deliver service of the highest quality, a policy for which Bellerson Financial is highly regarded by its customers)고 했다. 따라서 벨러슨 파이낸셜은 고품질의 서비스로 고객들 사이에서 평판이 좋다는 것을 알 수 있으므로 (D)가 정답이다.

어휘 extended 연장된 reputation 평판

> **Paraphrasing**
> 지문의 highly regarded by its customers
> → 정답의 built a reputation among customers

155 세부 사항

번역 휴가 신청 마감일은 언제인가?
(A) 4월 28일
(B) 5월 8일
(C) 6월 1일
(D) 8월 31일

해설 세 번째 단락의 첫 문장에서 4월 28일 금요일까지 요청서를 제출해 달라(submit your request by Friday, April 28)고 했으므로 휴가 신청 마감일은 4월 28일이다. 따라서 (A)가 정답이다.

156-158 기사

텔레테크닉, 새 휴대전화 모델 공개

시드니 (3월 21일) — 전자제품 대기업 텔레테크닉은 자사의 인기 스마트폰인 스트라토, 알토, 시로의 새로운 모델을 출시한다고 발표했다. 물리적 크기와 데이터 저장 면에서 스트라토가 가장 작은 모델이고, 알토는 중간, 시로는 가장 큰 모델이다. 156 **시로 모델에는 화면에 글을 쓰거나 그림을 그릴 수 있는 전자 펜도 포함되어 있다.**

157 **텔레테크닉의 이전 휴대전화 모델과의 차이는 대부분 사소하다. 그러나 사용자들은 카메라의 상당한 개선에 감명받을 것이다.** 모든 새로운 모델에는 고급 줌 기능과 자동 초점 기능을 갖춘 업그레이드된 카메라가 내장되어 있다. 또한 조도가 낮은 환경에서도 사용자가 더 나은 사진을 찍을 수 있게 해준다. 또 다른 개선점은 배터리인데, 최신 휴대전화는 배터리 수명이 더 길고 더 빨리 충전된다.

소비자들은 회사 웹사이트 www.teleteknic.com.au에 게시된 홍보 영상에서 휴대전화를 엿볼 수 있고, 또는 다음 달에 있을 기술 산업 박람회에서 직접 모델을 확인할 수 있다. 158 **텔레테크닉의 온라인 매장에서 현재 사전 주문을 받고 있다.** 새 휴대전화는 11월에 매장 진열대에 오를 것으로 예상된다.

어휘 unveil 공개하다 giant 거대 기업 launch 출시하다 in terms of ~ 면에서 physical 물리적인 dimension 크기 stylus (컴퓨터나 스마트폰의) 펜 minor 사소한 impressed 감명을 받은 significant 상당한 advanced 고급의 advancement 발전 charge 충전되다 consumer 소비자 glimpse 잠깐 봄 in person 직접 preorder 사전 주문

156 세부 사항

번역 시로 모델은 다른 새 휴대전화 모델들과 어떤 차이가 있는가?
(A) 개발하는 데 가장 오랜 시간이 걸렸다.
(B) 추가적인 도구가 함께 제공된다.
(C) 확장 가능한 메모리가 들어있다.
(D) 앞면과 뒷면에 화면이 있다.

해설 첫 단락의 마지막 문장에서 시로 모델에는 화면에 글을 쓰거나 그림을 그릴 수 있는 전자 펜도 포함되어 있다(The Cirro model also includes an electronic stylus for writing or drawing on the screen)고 했다. 시로 모델에만 전자 펜이 포함되어 있다고 언급하고 있으므로 (B)가 정답이다.

어휘 expandable 확장 가능한

> **Paraphrasing**
> 지문의 includes an electronic stylus
> → 정답의 comes with an additional tool

157 세부 사항

번역 휴대폰의 어떤 기능이 가장 크게 개선되었는가?
(A) 운영 시스템
(B) 카메라
(C) 화면
(D) 스피커

해설 두 번째 단락의 첫 문장에서 텔레테크닉의 이전 휴대전화 모델과의 차이는 대부분 사소하다(Most of the changes from Teleteknic's previous phone models are minor)고 했고 그러나 사용자들은 카메라의 상당한 개선에 감명받을 것(However, users will be impressed by a significant improvement to the camera)이라고 했다. 따라서 카메라 기능이 가장 크게 개선되었다는 것을 알 수 있으므로 (B)가 정답이다.

158 세부 사항

번역 고객들은 현재 어디에서 새로운 휴대폰을 주문할 수 있는가?
(A) 전자제품 매장
(B) 백화점
(C) 기술 산업 박람회
(D) 회사의 온라인 매장

해설 세 번째 단락의 두 번째 문장에서 텔레테크닉의 온라인 매장에서 현재 사전 주문을 받고 있다(Preorders are now being accepted at Teleteknic's online shop)고 했으므로 (D)가 정답이다.

159-160 온라인 게시물

토튼턴 커뮤니티 온라인 게시판 > 일반

9월 14일 목요일 오전 11시 41분에 탈리아 핀리가 게시함:

159 저는 다큐멘터리 영화 제작자로서 어떻게 토튼턴이 쇠퇴한 공업 도시에서 환경적으로 책임 있는 건축 사업과 지속 가능한 건축 디자인의 중심지로 변모했는지에 대한 이야기를 전하기 위해 작업을 하고 있습니다. **160** 저는 변화의 시기에 이곳에 살았고 그 시기가 어땠는지 말씀해 주실 수 있는 최소 50세 이상인 토튼턴 주민을 찾고 있습니다. 참여에 관심 있으시면 020 7946 0532로 저에게 전화 주세요. 그러면 제가 작성하실 개인 출연 동의서를 보내드리고, 30~45분가량의 인터뷰 일정을 잡을 수 있습니다.

어휘 message board 게시판 general 일반적인 evolve (점진적으로) 변화하다 decay 쇠퇴하다 hub 중심지 initiative 계획, 사업 sustainable 지속 가능한 architectural 건축의 transition 전환 participate 참여하다 release 공개 form 양식 fill out ~을 작성하다 arrange 마련하다

159 세부 사항

번역 핀리 씨의 영화 프로젝트는 무엇에 관한 것인가?
(A) 유명 인사의 삶
(B) 역사적 명소의 복원
(C) 일정 기간 동안의 도시의 변화
(D) 제조 회사의 획기적인 정책들

해설 첫 문장에서 핀리 씨가 자신은 다큐멘터리 영화 제작자로서 어떻게 토튼턴이 쇠퇴한 공업 도시에서 환경적으로 책임 있는 건축 사업과 지속 가능한 건축 디자인의 중심지로 변모했는지에 대한 이야기를 전하기 위해 작업을 하고 있다(I am a documentary filmmaker working to tell the story of how Tottenton evolved from a decaying industrial town into a hub for environmentally responsible building initiatives and sustainable architectural design)고 했다. 따라서 핀리 씨의 영화 프로젝트는 토튼턴이라는 도시가 변화하는 과정에 관한 것이므로 (C)가 정답이다.

어휘 figure 인물 restoration 복원 transformation 변화 innovative 획기적인

160 세부 사항

번역 핀리 씨는 사람들이 무엇을 해주기를 원하는가?
(A) 영화 상영회 참석
(B) 추억 공유
(C) 건설적인 비판 제공
(D) 촬영 중인 구역으로의 접근 자제

해설 두 번째 문장에서 핀리 씨가 변화의 시기에 이곳에 살았고 그 시기가 어땠는지 말해 줄 수 있는 최소 50세 이상인 토튼턴 주민을 찾고 있다(I am seeking Tottenton residents at least 50 years of age who lived here during the period of transition and can tell me what it was like)고 했으므로 핀리 씨는 지역 주민이 지역에 대한 추억을 이야기해주기를 바라고 있다는 것을 알 수 있다. 따라서 (B)가 정답이다.

어휘 screening 상영(회) constructive 건설적인 criticism 비판

> **Paraphrasing**
> 지문의 tell me what it was like
> → 정답의 Share their memories

161-164 설명

자기소개서

161 자기소개서는 구직자의 가장 주목할 만한 재능, 성취, 자질을 보여주는 짧은 글입니다. **162(B)** 자기소개서는 제공하는 사실 및 세부내용뿐 아니라 글쓴이가 그 정보를 전달하는 방식에 대해서도 평가받습니다. 그러므로 자기소개서를 작성할 때는 단어 선택과 어조 같은 문제에 대해 신중해야 한다는 점이 중요합니다.

자기소개서에 정해진 길이는 없지만 고용주는 때때로 지침을 제공합니다. **162(A)** 고용주가 단어 수를 명시하지 않은 경우, 300~500단어를 목표로 정하세요. 일반적으로 한 페이지가 최대 길이로 간주됩니다.

162(D) 자기소개서를 작성할 때는 당신만의 고유한 자질에 의존해야 했던 경우에 대해 구체적인 예시를 제시하세요. 이는 장래의 고용주에게 어려움을 극복하는 당신의 능력을 보여주는 효과적인 방법일 수 있습니다. **164** 다른 사람들과 어떻게 협력하는지 또는 다른 사람들로부터 어떻게 배우는지에 대한 예를 드는 것 또한 좋은 생각입니다. 예를 들어, 존경하는 사람이 어떤 식으로 당신의 삶에 긍정적인 영향을 주었는지를 설명할 수 있습니다.

당신이 지원하는 특정 직무를 언급하고 당신이 적임자인 이유를 설명하는 것을 잊지 마세요. **163** 지원하는 직책마다 이 문단을 별도의 버전으로 작성할 수 있기 때문에 마지막 문단은 이 정보를 넣기에 이상적인 위치입니다. 마지막으로, 제출하기 전에 소개서를 꼼꼼하게 교정했는지 확인하세요.

어휘 statement 진술(서) brief 짧은 showcase 보여주다 applicant 지원자 notable 주목할 만한 talent 재능 accomplishment 성취 evaluate 평가하다 convey 전달하다 thoughtful 신중한 tone 어조 length 길이 aim 목표로 삼다 generally 일반적으로 concrete 구체적인 demonstrate 보여주다 prospective 장래의 overcome 극복하다 challenge 어려움 specific 특정한 fit 꼭 맞는 것[사람] ideal 이상적인 separate 별도의 paragraph 문단 proofread 교정하다

161 추론 / 암시

번역 설명은 누구를 대상으로 하는 것 같은가?
(A) 구직자
(B) 경영팀 구성원
(C) 전문 작가
(D) 인사부 직원

해설 첫 단락의 첫 문장에서 자기소개서는 구직자의 가장 주목할 만한 재능, 성취, 자질을 보여주는 짧은 글(Personal statements are brief pieces of writing that showcase a job applicant's most notable talents, accomplishments, and qualities)이라고 한 것으로 보아 구직자를 대상으로 자기소개서 작성법을 설명하는 글임을 알 수 있다. 따라서 (A)가 정답이다.

162 Not / True

번역 자기소개서를 작성할 때 고려되어야 할 요소로 언급되지 않은 것은?
(A) 총 단어 수
(B) 작문의 질
(C) 작성자의 교육에 대한 세부 사항
(D) 과거의 도전 사례

해설 두 번째 단락의 두 번째 문장에서 고용주가 단어 수를 명시하지 않은 경우 300~500단어를 목표로 정하라(If the employer does not provide a word count, aim for between 300 and 500 words)고 했으므로 (A), 첫 단락의 두 번째 문장에서 자기소개서는 제공하는 사실 및 세부내용뿐 아니라 글쓴이가 그 정보를 전달하는 방식에 대해서도 평가받는다(Personal statements are evaluated both for the facts and details they offer and for the way the writer conveys this information)고 했으므로 (B), 세 번째 단락의 첫 문장에서 자기소개서를 작성할 때는 자신만의 고유한 자질에 의존해야 했던 경우에 대해 구체적인 예시를 제시하라(When crafting a personal statement, provide concrete examples of times when you had to rely on your unique qualities)고 했으므로 (D)는 자기소개서 작성 시 고려해야 할 요소로 꼽힌 반면, 학력에 대한 내용은 언급되어 있지 않으므로 (C)가 정답이다.

Paraphrasing
지문의 word count → 보기 (A)의 total number of words
지문의 the way the writer conveys this information → 보기 (B)의 quality of the writing

163 추론 / 암시

번역 자기소개서의 마지막 문단에 대해 결론지을 수 있는 것은?
(A) 사실과 세부 사항의 요약을 배치하기 이상적이다.
(B) 꼼꼼한 교정이 필요하지 않은 유일한 문단이다.
(C) 두 번째 페이지에 나와야 한다.
(D) 쉽게 변경해 쓸 수 있어야 한다.

해설 네 번째 단락의 두 번째 문장에서 지원하는 직책마다 이 문단을 별도의 버전으로 작성할 수 있다(you can create a separate version of this paragraph for each position you apply for)고 한 것으로 보아 지원하는 일자리에 맞게 내용을 바꿔 쓸 수 있어야 한다는 것을 알 수 있다. 따라서 (D)가 정답이다.

어휘 customizable 맞춤 제작할 수 있는

Paraphrasing
지문의 can create a separate version of this paragraph for each position → 정답의 customizable

164 문장 삽입

번역 [1], [2], [3], [4]로 표시된 위치 중에서 다음 문장이 들어가기에 가장 적합한 곳은?
"예를 들어, 존경하는 사람이 어떤 식으로 당신의 삶에 긍정적인 영향을 주었는지를 설명할 수 있습니다."
(A) [1]
(B) [2]
(C) [3]
(D) [4]

해설 주어진 문장은 '예를 들어 존경하는 사람이 어떤 식으로 긍정적인 영향을 주었는지 설명할 수 있다'며 다른 사람으로부터 좋은 점을 배우게 된 방식에 대해서 쓰라고 예시를 들고 있다. 따라서 다른 사람들과 어떻게 협력하는지 또는 다른 사람들로부터 어떻게 배우는지에 대한 예를 드는 게 좋다(It is also a good idea to give examples of how you work with or learn from others)고 제안하고 있는 문장 뒤인 [3]에 들어가는 것이 글의 흐름상 자연스러우므로 (C)가 정답이다.

어휘 respect 존경하다 positive 긍정적인 impact 영향

165-168 문자 메시지

전지민 (오전 8시 4분)
칼, 165, 166 저는 지금 크로슬리 다리 현장에 있어요.

칼 숄츠 (오전 8시 6분)
어떤 것 같으세요?

전지민 (오전 8시 8분)
165 확실히 정기적인 유지보수가 필요하고 일부 추가 작업을 계획해야 할 수도 있겠네요.

칼 숄츠 (오전 8시 9분)
우리 작업팀이 할 수 있는 건가요, 아니면 외주를 줘야 할까요?

전지민 (오전 8시 13분)
아직 모르겠어요. 아직 사진도 찍고 정기 점검도 마쳐야 해요. 심각해 보이는 건 없지만 연식을 고려해 볼 때 예방을 위한 작업이 필요할 것으로 생각해요. 어쨌든 다음 정밀 점검 날짜를 앞당기는 것을 고려해 보시기를 권해드려요.

아나 베가 (오전 8시 14분)
안녕하세요, 지민. 168 12시 30분 점심 회의를 위해 여기로 돌아오실 수 있을까요? 갑작스럽다는 것은 알지만 오늘 오후에 제가 진행할 9번가 다리 점검에 대해 몇 가지 질문이 있어요. 그 다리의 수리 작업으로 이어졌던 당신의 예전 정밀 보고서가 훌륭했잖아요.

칼 숄츠 (오전 8시 15분)
167 지민, 다른 다리를 검사하러 렌톡스 카운티로 가시라고 지시했다는 건 알지만 그 일은 오늘 오후에 하셔도 됩니다.

전지민 (오전 8시 18분)
감사합니다, 아나. 168 여기 일을 마무리하고 12시 30분까지 가겠습니다.

아나 베가 (오전 8시 19분)
좋습니다.

어휘 on-site 현장의 definitely 확실히 routine 정기적인 maintenance 유지보수 contract out 외주를 주다 inspection 점검 critical 위태로운 preventive 예방을 위한 move up (날짜를) 앞당기다 in-depth 정밀한 conduct 실시하다 previous 이전의 lead to ~으로 이어지다

165 주제 / 목적

번역 문자 메시지의 주요 목적은?
(A) 직원이 현재 업무가 가능한지 파악하려고
(B) 다리에 대한 업데이트를 제공하려고
(C) 도급업자가 필요한지 논의하려고
(D) 정밀 보고서에 대해 동료에게 감사를 표현하려고

해설 8시 4분에 전 씨가 지금 크로슬리 다리 현장에 있다(I am on-site at the Crosley Bridge now)고 했고, 8시 8분에 확실히 정기적인 유지보수가 필요하고 일부 추가 작업을 계획해야 할 수도 있겠다(It definitely needs routine maintenance, and we may have to plan some additional work)고 했다. 따라서 문자 메시지를 통해 크로슬리 다리에 대한 점검 결과를 동료들과 공유하기 위한 것임을 알 수 있으므로 (B)가 정답이다.

어휘 determine 알아내다 contractor 도급업자 coworker 동료

166 세부 사항

번역 문자 메시지가 오간 시점에 전 씨가 있던 장소는?
(A) 구내식당
(B) 자신의 사무실
(C) 크로슬리 다리
(D) 렌톡스 카운티의 현장

해설 8시 4분에 전 씨가 지금 크로슬리 다리 현장에 있다(I am on-site at the Crosley Bridge now)고 했으므로 (C)가 정답이다.

167 추론 / 암시

번역 숄츠 씨에 대해 결론지을 수 있는 것은?
(A) 베가 씨의 조수이다.
(B) 베가 씨와 점심 식사를 할 계획이다.
(C) 최근에 전 씨를 고용했다.
(D) 전 씨의 업무를 지시한다.

해설 8시 15분에 숄츠 씨가 전 씨에게 다른 다리를 검사하러 렌톡스 카운티로 가라고 지시했지만 그 일은 오늘 오후에 해도 된다(I know I asked you to go to Lentox County to check out another bridge, but you can do that later this afternoon)고 한 것으로 보아 숄츠 씨는 전 씨에게 업무를 지시하는 상관임을 짐작할 수 있다. 따라서 (D)가 정답이다.

어휘 direct 지시하다

168 의도 파악

번역 오전 8시 18분에 전 씨가 "12시 30분까지 가겠습니다"라고 쓴 의도는?
(A) 지금 현장을 떠나고 있다.
(B) 다른 다리를 점검해야 한다.
(C) 회의에 참석하려고 한다.
(D) 점심시간 이후에 도착할 것이다.

해설 8시 14분에 베가 씨가 전 씨에게 12시 30분 점심 회의를 위해 여기로 돌아올 수 있는지(Would it be possible for you to be back here for a 12:30 lunch meeting?)를 물은 데 대해, 8시 18분에 전 씨가 여기 일을 마무리하고 12시 30분까지 가겠다(I'll be there by 12:30, after I finish up here)고 대답했다. 따라서 전 씨는 베가 씨가 요청한 점심 회의에 참석하겠다는 의도로 한 말임을 알 수 있으므로 (C)가 정답이다.

어휘 inspect 점검하다 intend to ~할 작정이다

169-171 이메일

수신: 존 후키야마 〈john.fukiyama6775@xmail.ca〉
발신: 스테파니 애크로 〈sacro@salvadorfashionassociates.ca〉
날짜: 11월 18일
제목: 선발 위원회
첨부: 📎 기밀 유지 계약서

후키야마 씨께:

169, 170 저는 지금 이곳 살바도르 패션 어소시에이츠에서 새로 공석이 된 그래픽 디자인 수석 책임자 자리를 위한 선발 위원회의 일원이 되시는 데 관심이 있으신지 알아보고자 글을 씁니다. 들으셨겠지만 제이크 해리스가 지난달 우리 회사를 떠나 자신의 사업을 시작했고, 우리 그래픽 디자인 부서를 이끌 사람이 없는 상황입니다. **170** 4년 전 은퇴하시기 전에 이 역할을 맡으셨던 분으로서 이 직책에 어떤 지식과 기술이 필요한지를 정확히 알고 계시니 우리 선발 위원회에 이상적인 후보자이십니다. 마케팅 전무인 실라 멘데즈와 저 또한 이번 선발을 수행할 위원회에 참여할 예정입니다.

위원회의 일원이 되는 데 동의하신다면 첨부된 기밀 유지 계약서에 서명하고 회신해 주십시오. 그 시점에 **171** 지원서와 각 지원서에 딸린 이력서, 채용 일정표를 보내드리겠습니다. 귀하의 시간과 노력에 대해 외부 자문 위원에 해당하는 표준 요율로 보상해 드릴 예정입니다. 가능한 한 빨리 답변을 알려주십시오. 다시 함께 일할 수 있다면 좋겠습니다.

스테파니 애크로
인사부 책임자
살바도르 패션 어소시에이츠, 토론토

> **어휘** committee 위원회 confidentiality 기밀성 gauge 알아내다, 판단하다 vacated 공석이 된 senior 수석의, 상급의 ideal 이상적인 executive director 전무, 상무 application 지원서 respective 각각의 résumé 이력서 compensate 보상하다 rate 요율 external 외부의

169 주제 / 목적

번역 이메일의 목적은?
(A) 자문 기회를 제안하기 위해서
(B) 부서 회의 일정을 잡기 위해서
(C) 곧 생길 공석을 알리기 위해서
(D) 최근 고용된 직원을 환영하기 위해서

해설 첫 단락 첫 문장에서 살바도르 패션 어소시에이츠에서 새로 공석이 된 그래픽 디자인 수석 책임자 자리를 위한 선발 위원회의 일원이 되는 데 관심이 있는지 알아보고자 글을 쓴다(I am writing to gauge your interest in becoming a part of a search committee for the newly vacated Senior Director of Graphic Design position here at Salvador Fashion Associates)고 했으므로 임원 채용을 위한 선발 위원회의 위원으로 참여할 기회를 제안하고자 쓴 글임을 알 수 있다. 따라서 (A)가 정답이다.

어휘 present 제시하다 upcoming 곧 있을 job opening 공석

> **Paraphrasing**
> 지문의 becoming a part of a search committee
> → 정답의 consulting opportunity

170 Not / True

번역 후키야마 씨에 대해 명시된 것은?
(A) 애크로 씨와 정기적으로 만난다.
(B) 고위 임원이었다.
(C) 자신의 패션 사업을 운영한다.
(D) 선발 위원회로 자주 일한다.

해설 첫 단락 첫 문장에서 애크로 씨가 후키야마 씨에게 이곳 살바도르 패션 어소시에이츠에서 새로 공석이 된 그래픽 디자인 수석 책임자 자리를 위한 선발 위원회의 일원이 되는 데 관심이 있는지 알아보고자 글을 쓴다(I am writing to gauge your interest in becoming a part of a search committee for the newly vacated Senior Director of Graphic Design position here at Salvador Fashion Associates)고 했고, 같은 단락 세 번째 문장에서 4년 전 은퇴하기 전에 이 역할을 맡았던 분으로서(As someone who held this role prior to your retirement four years ago)라고 언급하고 있다. 따라서 후키야마 씨는 은퇴하기 전에 그래픽 디자인 수석 책임자 직책에 있었다는 것을 알 수 있으므로 (B)가 정답이다.

어휘 regularly 정기적으로 operate 운영하다
serve on ~으로 역할을 하다

> **Paraphrasing**
> 지문의 Senior Director → 정답의 senior executive

171 세부 사항

번역 애크로 씨는 후키야마 씨에게 무엇을 보내겠다고 제안하는가?
(A) 지불 일정표
(B) 필요한 기술 목록
(C) 이력서 모음
(D) 수정된 회의 안건

해설 두 번째 단락의 두 번째 문장에서 애크로 씨가 후키야마 씨에게 지원서와 각 지원서에 딸린 이력서, 채용 일정표를 보내주겠다(I will send you the applications with their respective résumés and a timeline for the hiring process)고 했으므로 (C)가 정답이다.

어휘 collection 모음, 더미 revised 수정된 agenda 안건

172-175 기사

> **지역 박물관, 대화형으로 바뀌다**
>
> 데리 (4월 7일) — **172** 지역 역사 박물관(RHM)은 대화형 기술을 도입할 수 있도록 많은 전시물을 업그레이드했다. 향상된 전시는 예정된 완료일보다 한 주 일찍 월요일에 문을 열었다. 박물관은 설치 기간 동안 계속 운영되었지만 업그레이드가 진행되는 동안 일부 전시는 이용할 수 없었다. 이번 개선 작업은 지역의 주요 산업 회사인 안스비 금속 제조사에서 자금을 지원받았다.
>
> RHM의 관장인 앤 워트에 따르면, 대화형 기술은 전시물이 정보를 제시하고 이용객들이 다양한 음성 및 시각 매체를 통해 참여하도록 한다. "방문객들은 이제 몰입형 방식으로 지역의 역사를 배울 수 있습니다."라고 워트 씨는 말했다.

관장의 끈질긴 노력은 프로젝트의 우선순위를 결정하는 데 도움이 되었다. 173 "박물관 로비에서 매주 이용객들을 인터뷰하고 그들의 의견을 기록합니다."라고 워트 씨는 말했다. "이 변화는 그들의 바람과 아이디어를 반영한 것입니다."

175 향상된 RHM 전시는 이용객에게 체험에 대한 통제권 또한 부여한다. 방문객들은 이제 더 알아보고 싶은 주제를 선택할 수 있게 될 것이다. 터치스크린은 방문객들이 전시물 고유의 데이터베이스와 전자상으로 대화하고 자신의 관심사에 맞출 수 있게 해 준다. 박물관은 이제 음성해설과 유익한 영상을 재생하는 대화형 전시물 26개를 선보이고 있다.

174 워트 씨는 방문객들에게 박물관을 관람하고 나서 도시 인근의 문화유산 지구를 산책하며 고전적인 건축물을 감상할 것을 제안한다. 해당 지구의 안내 지도는 박물관 로비에서 구할 수 있다.

> 어휘 interactive 대화형의 regional 지역의 enhance 향상시키다 completion 완료 offering 제공된 것 unavailable 이용할 수 없는 industrial 산업의 engage 참여시키다 immersive 몰입형의 persistent 끈질긴 determine 결정하다 priority 우선순위 patron 고객 reflect 반영하다 feature 포함하다 narrative 설명, 이야기 stroll 산책하다 adjoining 인접한 heritage 유산 district 지구 admire 감탄하며 바라보다 vintage 고전적인

172 Not / True

번역 전시물 업그레이드에 대해 기사에 명시된 것은?
(A) 예정보다 일찍 완료되었다.
(B) 안스비 금속 제조사가 설계했다.
(C) 기자 회견에서 시연되었다.
(D) 입장료 인상으로 이어졌다.

해설 첫 단락 첫 문장에서 지역 역사 박물관(RHM)은 대화형 기술을 도입할 수 있도록 많은 전시물을 업그레이드했다(The Regional History Museum (RHM) has upgraded many of its exhibits to include interactive technologies)고 했고, 향상된 전시는 예정된 완료일보다 한 주 일찍 월요일에 문을 열었다(The enhanced exhibitions opened on Monday, one week before the scheduled completion date)고 했으므로 전시물 업그레이드가 예정보다 한 주 일찍 완료되었음을 알 수 있다. 따라서 (A)가 정답이다.

어휘 demonstrate 시연하다 press conference 기자 회견

> **Paraphrasing**
> 지문의 one week before the scheduled completion date
> → 정답의 ahead of schedule

173 추론 / 암시

번역 워트 씨에 대해 암시된 것은?
(A) 최근에 박물관장으로 임명되었다.
(B) 박물관 방문객들을 직접 만난다.
(C) 박물관의 초기 전시물 일부를 디자인했다.
(D) 이전에 기술 회사에서 근무했다.

해설 세 번째 단락의 두 번째 문장에서 박물관 로비에서 매주 이용객들을 인터뷰하고 그들의 의견을 기록한다고 워트 씨는 말했다("Every week in the museum lobby, I interview patrons and record their opinions," said Ms. Wert)고 한 것으로 보아 워트 씨는 박물관 로비에서 직접 이용객들을 만나 의견을 듣는다는 것을 짐작할 수 있다. 따라서 (B)가 정답이다.

어휘 name 임명하다 original 최초의 previously 이전에

> **Paraphrasing**
> 지문의 patrons → 정답의 museum visitors

174 세부 사항

번역 워트 씨는 박물관 방문객들에게 무엇을 권장하는가?
(A) 기념품점에서 제품 구입
(B) 박물관 회원 가입
(C) 인근의 역사 지구 방문
(D) 소셜 미디어에 방문 사진 게시

해설 다섯 번째 단락의 첫 문장에서 워트 씨는 방문객들에게 박물관을 관람하고 나서 도시 인근의 문화유산 지구를 산책하며 고전적인 건축물을 감상할 것을 제안한다(Ms. Wert suggests that guests stroll around the city's adjoining heritage district and admire its vintage architecture after they visit the museum)고 했으므로 (C)가 정답이다.

어휘 sign up for ~에 가입하다 post 게시하다

> **Paraphrasing**
> 지문의 adjoining heritage district
> → 정답의 nearby historic neighborhood

175 문장 삽입

번역 [1], [2], [3], [4]로 표시된 위치 중에서 다음 문장이 들어가기에 가장 적합한 곳은?

"방문객들은 이제 더 알아보고 싶은 주제를 선택할 수 있게 될 것이다."
(A) [1]
(B) [2]
(C) [3]
(D) [4]

해설 주어진 문장은 '방문객들은 원하는 주제를 선택할 수 있게 된다'며 방문객에게 직접 주제를 선택할 수 있는 권한이 부여되는 점에 대해 언급하고 있다. 따라서 향상된 전시는 이용객에게 체험에 대한 통제권을 부여한다(The improved RHM exhibits also give the user control over the experience)는 문장 뒤인 [4]에 들어가는 것이 글의 흐름상 자연스러우므로 (D)가 정답이다.

176-180 차트 + 이메일

	제6회 연례 예술 공예 축제	
	180 스프링데일 브로드 가 소머빌 공원	
판매업체	부스	설명
그레이트 우즈 크래프츠	**176** 101	**176** 우아한 샐러드 그릇, 서빙 도구, 도마, 정화시킨 재활용 목재로 정성껏 깎아 만든 관련 제품들
폴딩 디자인	**179** 102	**179** 장신구, 연하장, 책갈피, 벽걸이 장식 등의 멋진 종이 예술품
페어리 더스트 포터리	**176** 103	기발하면서도 실용적인 **176** 도자기 머그잔, 그릇, 접시, 물주전자
177 프래니즈 센세이셔널 센츠	104	다양한 색상, 향기, 질감의 천연 유기농 비누, **177** 전부 직접 가꾼 정원에서 채취한 허브와 꽃으로 향을 입힘
참드 글래스	105	독특한 수제 귀걸이, 목걸이, 핀 및 유리로 만든 기타 착용 가능한 예술품

어휘 craft 공예 vendor 판매업자 description 설명
elegant 우아한 utensil (가정용) 도구 lovingly 정성껏
carve 깎아서 만들다 salvage (재활용을 위해 폐품을) 이용하다
purified 정화된 stunning 멋진 jewelry 장신구, 보석
bookmark 책갈피 whimsical 기발한 functional 실용적인
pitcher 주전자 scent 향기 texture 질감 infuse 불어넣다
harvest 수확하다 wearable 착용 가능한

수신: cho@mailcurrert.com
발신: k.mcfarlan@magentamail.com
날짜: 7월 14일
제목: 질문 있습니다.
첨부: 📎 사진

안녕하세요, 조 씨,

지난달 소머빌 공원에서 열린 공예 축제에서 당신과 대화하게 되어 즐거웠습니다. **179** 당신이 판매한 아름다운 펜던트를 착용할 때마다 그것을 본 사람들에게 펜던트가 책의 한 페이지를 예술적으로 접은 것이라고 말하면 몹시 놀랍니다.

안타깝게도, **178** 제품의 일부가 망가졌는데 저에게는 그것을 고칠 도구가 없습니다. 명함을 주셨을 때 문제가 생기면 연락하라고 말씀하셨습니다. 이 이메일에 제품 사진을 첨부했습니다. **180** 저는 스프링데일에서 근무하는데, 사실 소머빌 공원에서 북쪽으로 불과 3km 떨어져 있고, 축제가 열렸던 바로 그 거리에 있습니다. 그 지역에 살고 계시다면 제가 직접 제품을 가져갈 수도 있고, 아니면 우편으로 보낼 수도 있습니다. 제품을 수리받으려면 어떻게 해야 하는지 알려주세요.

켈리 맥팔런

어휘 admirer 감탄하는 사람 stunned 놀란 fold 접다
proceed 진행하다

---

176 세부 사항

번역 101번과 103번 부스의 판매업체들의 공통점은?
(A) 재활용된 재료만을 사용한다.
(B) 스프링데일에 소매점이 있다.
(C) 벽걸이 장식을 만든다.
(D) 주방용품을 판매한다.

해설 차트에서 101번 부스에서는 우아한 샐러드 그릇, 서빙 도구, 도마(Elegant salad bowls, serving utensils, cutting boards)를, 103번 부스에서는 도자기 머그잔, 그릇, 접시, 물주전자(ceramic mugs, bowls, plates, and water pitchers)를 판매한다고 나와 있다. 따라서 두 부스의 판매업체는 모두 주방용품을 판매하는 곳임을 알 수 있으므로 (D)가 정답이다.

어휘 material 재료 exclusively 오로지 retail 소매

177 Not / True

번역 프래니즈 센세이셔널 센츠에 대해 언급된 것은?
(A) 향초를 판매한다.
(B) 매년 공예 축제에서 부스를 연다.
(C) 제품이 온라인에서도 판매된다.
(D) 식물 성분이 제품에 들어 있다.

해설 차트 하단에 프래니즈 센세이셔널 센츠(Franny's Sensational Scents)는 전부 직접 가꾼 정원에서 채취한 허브와 꽃으로 향을 입힌(all infused with herbs and flowers harvested from our own garden) 제품을 판매한다고 나와 있으므로 (D)가 정답이다.

어휘 contain ~이 들어 있다

> **Paraphrasing**
> 지문의 herbs and flowers → 정답의 plants

178 주제 / 목록

번역 맥팔런 씨가 조 씨에게 이메일을 보낸 이유는?
(A) 제공받은 서비스에 대해 후속 조치를 하려고
(B) 주문을 하려고
(C) 마케팅 전략을 설명하려고
(D) 협력을 제안하려고

해설 이메일의 두 번째 단락 첫 문장에서 맥팔런 씨가 조 씨에게 제품의 일부가 망가졌는데 그것을 고칠 도구가 없다(a piece of the item has broken, and I do not have the tools to repair it)면서 명함을 주었을 때 문제가 생기면 연락하라고 말했다(When you gave me your business card, you told me to contact you if I had any problems)고 했다. 따라서 맥팔런 씨는 조 씨에게서 구입한 제품을 수리받기 위해 이메일을 보낸 것이므로 (A)가 정답이다.

어휘 follow up 후속 조치하다 outline 개요를 설명하다

179 연계

번역 맥팔런 씨는 축제에서 어느 부스의 제품을 구입했을 것 같은가?
(A) 101번 부스
(B) 102번 부스
(C) 104번 부스
(D) 105번 부스

해설 이메일의 첫 단락 두 번째 문장에서 맥팔런 씨가 당신이 판매한 아름다운 펜던트를 착용할 때마다 그것을 본 사람들에게 펜던트가 책의 한 페이지를 예술적으로 접은 것이라고 말하면 몹시 놀란다(Anytime I wear the beautiful pendant you sold me, admirers are stunned when I tell them it is an artistically folded page from a book)고 했고, 차트의 중반부에 102번 부스에서 장신구, 연하장, 책갈피, 벽걸이 장식 등의 멋진 종이 예술품(Stunning paper art items, such as jewelry, greeting cards, bookmarks, and wall hangings)을 판매한다고 나와 있다. 따라서 맥팔런 씨는 종이를 접어 만든 펜던트를 종이 예술품을 판매하는 102번 부스에서 구입했다는 것을 알 수 있으므로 (B)가 정답이다.

180 연계

번역 맥팔런 씨의 직장에 대해 암시된 것은?
(A) 예술 공예 작업실이다.
(B) 조 씨의 집 근처이다.
(C) 브로드 가에 있다.
(D) 출판사이다.

해설 이메일의 두 번째 단락 네 번째 문장에서 맥팔런 씨가 자신은 스프링데일에서 근무하는데, 소머빌 공원에서 북쪽으로 불과 3km 떨어져 있고, 축제가 열렸던 바로 그 거리에 있다(I work in Springdale, just 3 kilometers north of Somerville Park, on the same street where the festival took place, in fact)고 했고, 차트의 상단에 축제 주소는 스프링데일 브로드 가 소머빌 공원(Somerville Park, Broad Avenue, Springdale)이라고 나와 있다. 따라서 맥팔런 씨의 직장은 축제가 열렸던 브로드 가에 있다는 것을 알 수 있으므로 (C)가 정답이다.

어휘 studio 작업실

181-185 웹페이지 + 온라인 후기 ▶동영상 강의

https://www.superracleaning.com/specialservices

수페라 클리닝 — 특별 서비스

수페라 클리닝은 엘름우드 밸리 지역에서 주거 청소 서비스를 제공하는 선두업체입니다. 181 저희는 철저한 주간, 격주, 월간 주택 청소 패키지를 통해 명성을 쌓아왔습니다. 하지만 고객들은 저희의 집중 특별 청소 서비스에 대해서는 잘 모르실 수 있습니다. 이 서비스는 장기 계약이 필요하지 않으며 가격도 적당합니다. 다음은 저희가 제공하는 서비스 목록과 모든 고객이 이용할 수 있는 새로운 특징입니다.

• 행사 후 청소: 182 청소팀 2명과 감독자가 특별 행사가 끝난 뒤 귀하가 도착하기 전까지 공간이 사용하기 전 상태처럼 보이도록 청소합니다.

• 184 1회 주택 청소: 손님을 초대하지만 사전에 청소할 시간이 없는 분들을 위한 이상적인 서비스입니다. 182, 184 감독자가 3명의 청소팀을 감독하며 집이 반짝거릴 만큼 깨끗하게 해드립니다.

• 이사 청소: 아파트나 주택에서 나가는 세입자를 위한 완벽한 서비스로, 이사에만 신경 쓰실 수 있도록 저희가 청소를 해드립니다. 182 감독자의 지휘 하에 2인의 팀이 필요한 모든 먼지 제거와 닦는 작업을 처리합니다.

• 무료 청소 팁: 183 지난 두 달 동안 저희는 기발한 청소 팁이 담겨 있는 동영상 강의를 게시했습니다. 동영상이 유용하기를 바랍니다.

각 특별 서비스의 가격은 공간의 규모에 따라 다릅니다. 가격 견적을 요청하시려면 (616) 555-0189로 연락하세요.

어휘 residential 주거의 region 지역 reputation 명성 thorough 철저한 biweekly 격주의 familiar 잘 아는 long-term 장기적인 affordably 알맞게 feature 특징 supervisor 감독자 ideal 이상적인 tidy up 정리하다 beforehand 사전에 sparkling 반짝이는 tenant 세입자 vacate 비우다 guidance 지휘 dusting 먼지 제거 scrubbing 문지르기 tutorial 강의 vary 다르다 quote 견적

5월 24일 케네스 싱 게시

저는 최근에 수페라 클리닝의 특별 서비스 중 하나가 필요한 상황에 처했습니다. 184 갑작스럽게 친구가 다음 날 방문하겠다고 연락했는데 저는 집 청소가 밀려 있었습니다. 전문 청소 서비스를 이용해야 했던 건 처음이었는데 수페라를 선택해서 다행입니다. 청소팀은 제때 도착했고 오후 내내 열심히 일했습니다. 그들은 촉박한 통보도 개의치 않았습니다. 청소팀은 저희 집 내부를 청소한 뒤 현관 앞마당까지 쓸어주었습니다.

수페라는 여름철에 상당히 분주할 수 있다는 점에 유의하세요. 알고 보니 제가 185 딱 알맞은 시간에 연락을 했던 것이었습니다. 운 좋게도, 다른 고객이 제가 전화하기 한 시간쯤 전에 청소 예약을 취소했는데, 그렇지 않았더라면 수페라는 한주 내내 예약이 꽉 차 있었을 겁니다.

어휘 situation 상황 fall behind 뒤처지다 mind 신경 쓰다 sweep off ~을 쓸어내다 porch 현관 manage to 간신히 ~하다 or so ~쯤 otherwise 그렇지 않으면 booked up 예약이 꽉 찬

181 추론 / 암시

번역 수페라 클리닝에 대해 암시된 것은?
(A) 환경친화적인 청소 재료를 사용한다.
(B) 경쟁사와 합병했다.
(C) 정기 서비스 패키지로 가장 유명하다.
(D) 서비스 가격을 낮추었다.

해설 웹페이지의 첫 단락 두 번째 문장에서 철저한 주간, 격주, 월간 주택 청소 패키지를 통해 명성을 쌓아왔다(We have built our reputation on our thorough weekly, biweekly, and monthly house cleaning packages)고 강조하는 것으로 보아 수페라 클리닝은 정기 주택 청소 패키지 서비스로 유명하다는 것을 알 수 있으므로 (C)가 정답이다.

어휘 environmentally friendly 환경친화적인   merge 합병하다
compete 경쟁하다   lower 낮추다

> **Paraphrasing**
> 지문의 weekly, biweekly, and monthly → 정답의 regular

182 세부 사항

번역 웹페이지에 따르면, 특별 서비스의 공통점은?
(A) 감독자가 있는 작업팀
(B) 저렴한 장기 계약
(C) 주말 서비스 옵션
(D) 첫 이용 고객을 위한 할인

해설 웹페이지의 중반에 열거된 특별 서비스의 각 항목에 순서대로 청소팀 2명과 감독자(A two-person cleaning crew, plus a supervisor), 감독자가 3명의 청소팀을 감독(A supervisor will oversee a three-person cleaning team), 감독자의 지휘 하에 2인의 팀(Under the guidance of a supervisor, a two-person team)을 언급하고 있다. 따라서 모든 서비스에서 감독자가 있는 팀을 명시하고 있으므로 (A)가 정답이다.

어휘 supervised 감독을 받는   affordable 가격이 적당한

183 세부 사항

번역 수페라 클리닝이 최근 한 일은?
(A) 고객 설문조사 결과를 발표했다.
(B) 회사 기념일을 축하했다.
(C) 추가 직원을 고용했다.
(D) 교육용 콘텐츠를 게시했다.

해설 웹페이지의 다섯 번째 단락 첫 문장에서 지난 두 달 동안 기발한 청소 팁이 담겨 있는 동영상 강의를 게시했다(Over the past two months, we have posted video tutorials featuring clever cleaning tips)고 했으므로 (D)가 정답이다.

어휘 release 발표하다   anniversary 기념일   instructional 교육용의

> **Paraphrasing**
> 지문의 posted video tutorials
> → 정답의 published instructional content

184 연계

번역 싱 씨에 대해 사실인 것 같은 것은?
(A) 자신의 청소 도구를 팀에 제공했다.
(B) 청소 서비스 예약을 취소해야 했다.
(C) 세 명의 청소팀이 방문했다.
(D) 수페라 클리닝의 정기 이용 고객이다.

해설 후기의 첫 단락 두 번째 문장에서 싱 씨가 갑작스럽게 친구가 다음 날 방문하겠다고 연락했는데 집 청소가 밀려 있었다(At the last minute, a friend informed me that he would be visiting the next day, and I had fallen behind on my house cleaning)면서 전문 청소 서비스를 이용해야 했던 건 처음이었는데 수페라를 선택해서 다행(It was the first time that I had to use a professional cleaning service, and I am glad I chose Superra)이라고 했다. 그리고 웹페이지의 세 번째 단락에서 1회 주택 청소는 손님을 초대하지만 사전에 청소할 시간이 없는 분들을 위한 이상적인 서비스(One-time house cleaning: The ideal service for anyone who hosts guests but does not have time to tidy up beforehand)이며 감독자가 3명의 청소팀을 감독한다(A supervisor will oversee a three-person cleaning team)고 했다. 따라서 싱 씨는 갑작스러운 손님의 방문에 대비하여 수페라의 3인의 청소팀이 제공되는 1회 주택 청소를 이용했음을 알 수 있으므로 (C)가 정답이다.

185 동의어 찾기

번역 온라인 후기의 두 번째 단락 2행의 "just"와 의미가 가장 가까운 단어는?
(A) 직접
(B) 정확히
(C) 간단히
(D) 아마

해설 의미상 '딱' 알맞은 시간이라는 뜻으로 쓰였으므로 '정확히'를 뜻하는 (B) exactly가 정답이다.

186-190 웹페이지 + 이메일 + 표지판

---

https://www.beachsideusedbooks.co.uk

| 홈 | 소개 | 도서 목록 | 도서 교환 |

186 비치사이드 중고책은 헌 책에 대해 가게 적립금을 드립니다!

저희는 가게 적립금과 교환할 중고 양장본 책을 환영합니다. **188 20년 이상 전에 출판된 책과 초판이 선호됩니다.** **186 재판매를 위해 책을 받아들이는 기준은 다음과 같습니다.**

- 어떤 페이지에도 얼룩 또는 물에 의한 손상이 없어야 합니다.
- 구김, 찢어짐 또는 빠진 페이지가 없어야 합니다.
- 교과서, 백과사전 또는 기타 참고서는 받지 않습니다.
- **187 이안 우와 같은 유명 요리사의 책을 제외한 요리책은 받지 않습니다.**
- 아동용 그림책은 받지 않습니다.

어휘 exchange 교환   credit 적립금   secondhand 중고의
hardback 양장본   favour 선호하다   stain 얼룩   crease 주름지다   tear 찢다   missing 빠진   encyclopaedia 백과사전
reference 참고   celebrity 유명인

수신: info@beachsideusedbooks.co.uk
발신: rhys.townsend@walemail.com
날짜: 1월 3일 목요일 오전 11시 3분
제목: 문의

안녕하세요,

저는 이 지역에 새로 왔고 이웃 주민께서 귀하의 가게에 대해 말씀해 주셨어요. 저의 헌 책 일부를 가져가서 가게 적립금을 이용해 여섯 살짜리 아들을 위한 책을 사고 싶어요. 아이가 흥미를 잃은 그림책 외에도 상태가 좋은 최신 공상 과학 문고본 몇 권과 **188 증조할머니께 물려받은 초판 고전 소설 2권, 189 제가 운영하는 자선단체** 회원들이 내어 준 조리법으로 가득한 요리책 3권도 갖고 있어요. **190 다음 주 화요일이나 수요일에 들러도 될까요?** 만약 가능하지 않다면 **토요일이나 일요일 오전 9시 이전에 갈 수도 있습니다.**

리스 타운센드

어휘 enquiry 문의 outgrow (나이가 들어서) ~에 흥미를 잃다 paperback 문고본(종이 표지 책) inherit 상속받다 great-grandmother 증조할머니 charity 자선단체

비치사이드 중고책
운영 시간

월요일: 휴무
190 화요일: 휴무
190 수요일: 오전 9시 ~ 오후 8시
목요일: 오전 9시 ~ 오후 8시
금요일: 오전 9시 ~ 오후 8시
190 토요일: 오전 10시 ~ 오후 5시
190 일요일: 정오 ~ 오후 5시

어휘 operation 운영

186 주제 / 목적

번역 웹페이지의 목적은?
(A) 상점의 할인 행사를 알리려고
(B) 상점의 정책을 설명하려고
(C) 사람들을 독서 모임에 초대하려고
(D) 기부용 중고 책을 수집하려고

해설 웹페이지의 제목에서 비치사이드 중고책은 헌 책에 대해 가게 적립금을 준다(Beachside Used Books will give you store credit for your old books!)고 했고, 세 번째 문장에서 재판매를 위해 책을 받아들이는 기준은 다음과 같다(Our standards for accepting a book for resale are as follows)며 헌 책을 받는 기준에 대해 설명하고 있다. 따라서 웹페이지는 중고책 서점에서 중고 서적을 받고 가게 적립금으로 교환해 주는 매장의 정책과 기준에 대해 설명하는 글을 담고 있으므로 (B)가 정답이다.

어휘 donation 기부

187 추론 / 암시

번역 웹페이지에서 우 씨에 대해 암시하는 것은?
(A) 유명인이다.
(B) 식당 주인이다.
(C) 손상된 책을 수리한다.
(D) 비치사이드 중고책의 단골이다.

해설 웹페이지의 헌 책을 받는 기준의 네 번째 항목에서 이안 우와 같은 유명 요리사(a celebrity chef such as Ian Wu)라고 한 것으로 보아 우 씨는 유명한 요리사임을 알 수 있다. 따라서 (A)가 정답이다.

Paraphrasing
지문의 celebrity → 정답의 famous person

188 연계

번역 타운센드 씨가 제공한 물건 중 비치사이드 중고책에서 받아줄 것 같은 것은?
(A) 그림책
(B) 공상 과학 소설
(C) 고전 소설
(D) 요리책

해설 이메일의 세 번째 문장에서 타운센드 씨가 증조할머니께 물려받은 초판 고전 소설 2권(two first-edition classic novels inherited from my great-grandmother)을 갖고 있다고 했고, 웹페이지의 두 번째 문장에서 20년 이상 전에 출판된 책과 초판이 선호된다(Books published twenty or more years ago and first editions are favoured)고 했다. 따라서 비치사이드 중고책에서는 타운센드 씨의 책 중 초판 고전 소설 2권을 받아 주리라는 것을 알 수 있으므로 (C)가 정답이다.

189 Not / True

번역 타운센드 씨가 이메일에서 명시한 것은?
(A) 할머니로부터 요리법을 배웠다.
(B) 친구에게 비치사이드 중고책을 추천했다.
(C) 아들을 도서관에 자주 데리고 간다.
(D) 자선단체를 관리한다.

해설 이메일의 세 번째 문장에서 타운센드 씨가 자신이 운영하는 자선단체(a charity I run)에 대해 언급하고 있으므로 (D)가 정답이다.

어휘 oversee 감독하다 organization 단체

190 연계

번역 타운센드 씨는 언제 비치사이드 중고책을 방문할 것 같은가?
(A) 화요일
(B) 수요일
(C) 토요일
(D) 일요일

해설 이메일의 네 번째 문장에서 타운센드 씨가 다음 주 화요일이나 수요일에 들러도 될지(May I stop in next Tuesday or Wednesday?)를 물었고 가능하지 않다면 토요일이나 일요일 오

전 9시 이전에 갈 수도 있다(If that's not possible, I could come on Saturday or Sunday before 9:00 A.M.)고 했다. 표지판의 운영 시간은 화요일은 휴무(Tuesday: CLOSED), 수요일은 오전 9시 ~ 오후 8시(Wednesday: 9:00 A.M. to 8:00 P.M.), 토요일은 오전 10시 ~ 오후 5시(Saturday: 10:00 A.M. to 5:00 P.M.), 일요일은 정오 ~ 오후 5시(Sunday: Noon to 5:00 P.M.)라고 나와 있다. 타운센드 씨가 언급한 요일을 표지판의 영업 시간에서 확인한 결과 수요일에만 방문이 가능하므로 (B)가 정답이다.

어휘 extension 내선 번호 retail 소매

191-195 이메일 + 연락처 목록 + 일정표

192 수신: 맥스 오리넨 〈maurinen@edwildurables.com〉
발신: 제시카 승 〈jseung@edwildurables.com〉
날짜: 4월 21일
제목: 그림자 실습 일정

안녕하세요, 맥스,

191 5월 6일에 신입 직원으로 첫 출근하는 데이비드 라인 씨를 맞이할 예정입니다. 라인 씨는 노스버그 대학교를 졸업했고 젤레호스트 사와 도르팍스 인더스트리즈에서 근무했습니다. **193** 라인 씨는 당사의 대형 가전 부서에서 부 생산감독 역할을 수행하게 됩니다. **192** 그의 초기 입사 서류를 준비해 주시고 에드윌 듀러블스 사에서의 첫 2주간을 위한 일정을 잡아 주십시오.

191 새로운 직책을 위한 교육의 일환으로 그가 며칠 동안 여러 부서의 팀장들과 함께하며 배우도록 합시다. 이렇게 하면 그가 결국 함께 일하게 될 다양한 부서에 대해 더 많이 배울 수 있을 겁니다. 또한, **195** 아모스 힐먼 씨가 태국에서의 휴가로부터 예정된 날짜에 돌아온다면 라인 씨가 제품 실험실에서 시제품이 어떻게 개발되는지 배우도록 일정을 잡아 주세요.

제시카 승, 인사 책임

어휘 shadow (배우기 위해) 함께 하다 graduate 졸업생 fulfill 수행하다 supervisor 감독관 appliance 가전제품 division 부서 initial 초기의 onboarding 입사 절차 arrange ~의 예정을 세우다, 준비하다 various 다양한 eventually 결국 interact 소통하다 assuming 만약 ~이라면 prototype 시제품

에드윌 듀러블스 사
부서장 연락처 목록

이름	직함 및 부서	건물 및 사무실	내선 번호
셰인 파라치	책임, 정보 시스템	**194** 아드모어, 210호	022
마저리 가즈다	수석 책임, 소매	아드모어, 323호	023
파트리샤 네스빗	책임, 소형 가전	**194** 윈스턴 웨스트, 07호	333
193 라티샤 레이크	**193** 책임, 대형 가전	**194** 윈스턴 이스트, 102호	145
오빌 마틴	수석 책임, 전자	**194** 마이즈너, 410호	254

데이비드 라인 입사 기간 일정표

서류 작업 및 오리엔테이션

5월 6일	오전 9시 ~ 정오	서류 작성, 복리후생 설명, 입사 등록
	정오 ~ 오후 1시	점심 식사
	오후 1시 ~ 오후 3시	배정된 부서 책임자와 만남
	오후 3시 ~ 오후 5시	노트북 컴퓨터 및 프로필 설정을 위한 정보 시스템 부서 직원과 만남

그림자 실습

5월 7일	오전 9시 ~ 오후 5시	라티샤 레이크
5월 8일	오전 9시 ~ 오후 5시	오빌 마틴
195 5월 9일	오전 9시 ~ 오후 5시	아모스 힐먼
5월 10일	오전 9시 ~ 오후 5시	마저리 가즈다

어휘 documentation 서류 benefits 복리후생 enrollment 등록 assigned 배정된

191 주제 / 목적

번역 승 씨가 이메일을 작성한 이유는?
(A) 구직자를 추천하기 위해서
(B) 고객 문의에 응답하기 위해서
(C) 신입 사원을 위한 계획을 설명하기 위해서
(D) 직원의 휴가를 승인하기 위해서

해설 이메일의 첫 단락 첫 문장에서 5월 6일에 신입 직원으로 첫 출근하는 데이비드 라인 씨를 맞이할 예정(On May 6, we will welcome Mr. David Rein for his first day as a new employee)이라고 했고, 두 번째 단락의 첫 문장에서 새로운 직책을 위한 교육의 일환으로 그가 며칠 동안 여러 부서의 팀장들과 함께하며 배우도록 하자(As part of his training for his new position, let's have him shadow our team leaders in several areas for a couple of days)고 했다. 이메일 전체에 걸쳐 신입 사원에 대한 소개와 입사 적응 일정에 관해 논의하고 있으므로 (C)가 정답이다.

어휘 inquiry 문의 outline 개요를 설명하다 approve 승인하다

Paraphrasing
지문의 employee → 정답의 staff member

192 추론 / 암시

번역 오리넨 씨는 누구인 것 같은가?
(A) 노스버그 대학교 학생
(B) 젤레호스트 사의 영업 사원
(C) 도르팍스 인더스트리즈의 고객
(D) 에드윌 듀러블스 사의 행정 보조 직원

해설 이메일의 수신자가 맥스 오리넨(To: Max Aurinen)이고, 첫 단락의 마지막 문장에서 오리넨 씨에게 신입 직원의 초기 입사 서류를 준비해 주고 에드윌 듀러블스 사에서의 첫 2주간을 위한 일정을 잡아 달라(Please prepare his initial onboarding paperwork and arrange a schedule for his first two weeks with Edwil Durables, Inc)고 업무 지시를 내리고 있는 것으로 보아 오리넨 씨는 에드윌 듀러블스 사의 행정 직원임을 짐작할 수 있다. 따라서 (D)가 정답이다.

어휘 administrative 행정의

193 연계

번역 라인 씨의 상사는 누구인가?
(A) 파라치 씨
(B) 가즈다 씨
(C) 레이크 씨
(D) 마틴 씨

해설 이메일의 첫 단락 세 번째 문장에서 라인 씨는 당사의 대형 가전 부서에서 부 생산감독 역할을 수행하게 된다(Mr. Rein will fulfill the role of an assistant manufacturing supervisor in our Large Appliance Division)고 했고, 연락처 목록의 하단에 라티샤 레이크 씨(Latisha Lake)가 대형 가전 책임(Director, Large Appliance Division)이라고 나와 있으므로 레이크 씨는 라인 씨의 상사라는 것을 알 수 있다. 따라서 (C)가 정답이다.

194 추론 / 암시

번역 연락처 목록에서 암시된 것은?
(A) 회사에 여러 건물이 있다.
(B) 전화 교환원이 각 수신 전화를 연결한다.
(C) 책임 한 명이 부서 두 개를 관리한다.
(D) 일부 책임들은 사무실을 공유한다.

해설 연락처 목록의 건물 항목에 아드모어(Ardmore), 윈스턴 웨스트(Winston West), 윈스턴 이스트(Winston East), 마이즈너(Meisner)라는 각기 다른 건물 이름이 명시되어 있는 것으로 보아 회사에 건물이 여러 채라는 것을 짐작할 수 있다. 따라서 (A)가 정답이다.

어휘 operator 전화 교환원 incoming 들어오는 direct (편지 등을) ~에게 보내다

195 연계

번역 힐먼 씨에 대해 암시된 것은?
(A) 새로운 팀원이다.
(B) 제때 여행에서 돌아와서 라인 씨를 만나게 되었다.
(C) 최근 승진했다.
(D) 인사부에서 근무한다.

해설 이메일의 두 번째 단락 마지막 문장에서 아모스 힐먼 씨가 태국에서의 휴가로부터 예정된 날짜에 돌아온다면 라인 씨가 제품 실험실에서 시제품이 어떻게 개발되는지 배우도록 일정을 잡아 달라(assuming Amos Hillman returns on the expected date from his vacation in Thailand, please schedule a day for Mr. Rein to learn how prototypes are developed in the product labs)고 했고, 일정표 하단에서 5월 9일에 아모스 힐먼 씨(May 9, 9 A.M. to 5 P.M., Amos Hillman)와의 일정이 잡혀 있음을 확인할 수 있다. 따라서 힐먼 씨는 휴가로부터 예정일에 돌아와 라인 씨와 만나게 되었음을 알 수 있으므로 (B)가 정답이다.

> **Paraphrasing**
> 지문의 vacation → 정답의 trip
> 지문의 on the expected date → 정답의 in time

196-200 기사 + 웹페이지 + 작업 주문서

영상 회사, 새로운 차원에 달하다

프리토리아 (3월 22일) — 산업용 영상 제작사인 블루 라피스는 오늘 고객들에게 항공 영상 촬영 서비스를 제공하기 위해 2명의 드론 조종사와 계약을 체결한다고 발표했다.

"우리는 다양한 산업을 위해 훌륭한 영상 이미지를 담아내는 데 항상 뛰어났지만 이제 새로운 관점에서도 그 일이 가능해졌습니다."라고 블루 라피스의 CEO 유누스 마세코 씨는 말했다. "**196 마케팅, 진행 사항 보고, 교육 또는 그 밖의 어떤 것을 위한 목적이든, 우리는 하늘에서 촬영한 고해상도 영상을 고객에게 제공합니다.** 사실, 콴두마 부동산 회사를 위한 첫 항공 영상 작업을 최근 완료했으며 모두 결과에 매우 만족했습니다."

항공 영상 촬영 가격은 세션 당 15,000랜드에서 45,000랜드 사이이다. 가격에는 블루 라피스 스튜디오에서의 기본 편집 작업이 포함된다. **200 광범위한 편집 또는 특수 효과가 필요한 경우에는 시간당 추가 요금이 청구된다.** 자세한 정보는 www.bluelapis.co.za를 방문하라.

어휘 reach 도달하다 height 높이 industrial 산업의 aerial 공중의 videography 영상 촬영 excel 뛰어나다 capture 포착하다 breathtaking 숨 막히게 훌륭한 imagery 이미지 perspective 관점 progress 진행, 진전 high-resolution 고해상도 realty 부동산 range from A to B A에서 B까지 이르다 charge 청구하다 extensive 광범위한

```
https://www.rfa.web.za/certification
```

| 소개 | 소식 | **자격증** | 자료실 |

원격 비행 협회(RFA)는 무인 항공기 조종 자격증을 취득할 수 있는 교육을 제공합니다.

상업적 용도의 드론 조종은 자격증을 고용의 전제 조건으로 요구합니다. 자격증 카드 취득에는 다음 사항이 수반됩니다:

- 무인 항공기 비행 규정 과정 수료하기
- 온라인 신청서 제출하기
- **199 적절한 민간 항공 당국에 장비 등록하기**
- **197 공역 규정 지식을 입증하기 위해 비행 시험관과 면접보기**

모든 필수 절차를 성공적으로 마치고 난 후, 비행 시험관이 처리를 위해 결과를 제출하게 됩니다. 자격증 카드는 영업일 기준 10일 이내에 받게 됩니다.

자격증 과정의 전체적인 개요가 필요하시면 설명서를 다운로드하세요.

어휘 certification 자격증 resources 자원 remote 원격의 operation 운전, 작동 unmanned 무인의 aircraft 항공기 commercial 상업적인 precondition 전제 조건 obtain 얻다 involve 수반하다 regulation 규정 file 제출하다 application 신청서 register 등록하다 appropriate 적절한 civil 민간의 aviation 항공 authority 당국 examiner 시험관 demonstrate 입증하다 airspace 공역 processing 처리 manual 설명서 outline 개요

블루 라피스
드론 영상 작업 주문

고객: 런스클립 건설

사무실 주소: 샌드 리버 가 220번지, 프리토리아, 0048

담당자: 토코질레 샤방구, 전화번호 012 555 0175

작업 요청일: 4월 12일 금요일

199 드론 계약자: 올리비아 롤리, 카드 번호 01562

영상 촬영: 고객은 투자자에게 보여줄 영상을 원합니다. 고객은 고속도로 전 구간을 드론 비행하여 프로젝트 규모를 보여주고, 현재 공사 중인 구역 위에서는 정지 비행하여, 공사 작업 장면을 포착할 수 있도록 확대 촬영할 것을 요청합니다. **198 목표는 고속도로 공사가 어떻게 진행되고 있는지를 보여주고 지금까지 완료된 작업을 강조하는 것입니다.** 샤방구 씨에게 연락하여 비행 계획을 검토하고 고속도로의 기타 집중 촬영 구간을 논의하세요.

주의 사항: 200 특수 효과나 추가 편집은 원하지 않습니다. 제목 크레디트에 고객사 이름, 프로젝트명, 비행 영상이 촬영된 날짜를 포함시켜 주세요. 런스클립 건설은 기대 수준이 높은 장기 고객입니다. 촬영 및 편집 과정 전반에 걸쳐 샤방구 씨와 상의하세요.

어휘 investor 투자자 length 길이 demonstrate 보여주다 hover 정지 비행하다 zoon in 확대하다 objective 목표 proceed 진행하다 highlight 강조하다 thus far 지금까지 expectation 기대

196 Not / True

번역 기사에서 블루 라피스에 대해 언급된 것은?
(A) 작업이 다양한 사업 목적에 기여할 수 있다.
(B) 가격이 경쟁사보다 저렴하다.
(C) 새로운 최고 경영 책임자가 왔다.
(D) 여러 영상 편집자를 채용하고 있다.

해설 기사의 두 번째 단락 두 번째 문장에서 마케팅, 진행 사항 보고, 교육 또는 그 밖의 어떤 것을 위한 목적이든 우리는 하늘에서 촬영한 고해상도 영상을 고객에게 제공한다(Whether for marketing, progress reporting, training, or something else, we offer our clients high-resolution videos from the sky)고 했으므로 블루 라피스의 영상 서비스가 사업에 다용도로 활용됨을 알 수 있다. 따라서 (A)가 정답이다.

어휘 serve 기여하다 competitor 경쟁사

Paraphrasing
지문의 for marketing, progress reporting, training, or something else → 정답의 many business purposes

197 세부 사항

번역 웹페이지에 따르면, 드론 조종사가 되기를 바라는 사람이 해야 할 한가지는?
(A) 협회 사무실로 전화
(B) 온라인 시험 응시
(C) 면접 참여
(D) 전문 추천서 제출

해설 웹페이지의 세 번째 단락 마지막 항목에서 드론 조종 자격증 취득 요건으로 공역 규정 지식을 입증하기 위해 비행 시험관과 면접보기(completing an interview with a flight examiner to demonstrate knowledge of airspace regulations)를 명시하고 있으므로 (C)가 정답이다.

어휘 association 협회 participate in ~에 참여하다 reference 추천서

Paraphrasing
지문의 completing an interview
→ 정답의 Participate in an interview

198 세부 사항

번역 작업 주문서에 따르면, 런스클립 건설이 영상을 요청한 이유는?
(A) 프로젝트의 진행 상황을 보여주려고
(B) 안전 검사를 수행하려고
(C) 고속도로의 최적 경로를 찾으려고
(D) 지역의 지형을 지도로 제작하려고

해설 작업 주문서의 영상 촬영 항목 세 번째 문장에서 목표는 고속도로 공사가 어떻게 진행되고 있는지를 보여주고 지금까지 완료된 작업을 강조하는 것(The objective is to present how the highway project is proceeding and highlight what has been completed thus far)이라고 런스클립 건설을 위한 영상 촬영의 목표를 제시하고 있으므로 (A)가 정답이다.

어휘 conduct 수행하다   inspection 검사   map 지도를 만들다
land feature 지형, 지세

> **Paraphrasing**
> 지문의 present how the highway project is proceeding
> → 정답의 show progress on a project

199 연계

번역 롤리 씨에 대해 결론지을 수 있는 것은?
(A) 샤방구 씨와 수년간 함께 일했다.
(B) 런스클립 건설의 공사 감독관이다.
(C) 항공 당국에 장비를 등록했다.
(D) 비행 시험관이다.

해설 작업 주문서의 드론 계약자 항목에 올리비아 롤리, 카드 번호 01562(Drone contractor: Olivia Rowley, Card No. 01562)라고 나와 있고, 웹페이지의 세 번째 단락 세 번째 항목에서 드론 자격증 카드 취득 요건으로 적절한 민간 항공 당국에 장비 등록하기(registering your equipment with the appropriate civil aviation authority)가 명시되어 있다. 롤리 씨는 드론 카드 번호를 취득한 자격증 보유자이므로 항공 당국에 장비를 등록했다는 것을 알 수 있다. 따라서 (C)가 정답이다.

어휘 supervisor 감독관   examiner 시험관

200 연계

번역 런스클립 건설에 대해 사실인 것 같은 것은?
(A) 영상을 위한 계획을 제시하지 않았다.
(B) 시간당 추가 요금을 지불할 필요가 없다.
(C) 콴두마 부동산 회사와 제휴 관계이다.
(D) 블루 라피스의 신규 고객이다.

해설 작업 주문서의 주의 사항 항목의 첫 문장에서 런스클립에서 특수 효과나 추가 편집은 원하지 않는다(No special effects or extra editing is wanted)고 했고, 기사의 세 번째 단락 세 번째 문장에서 광범위한 편집 또는 특수 효과가 필요한 경우에는 시간당 추가 요금이 청구된다(An additional hourly fee is charged if extensive editing or special effects are required)고 했다. 따라서 런스클립 건설은 추가 편집이나 특수 효과에 대한 추가 요금을 지불할 필요가 없으므로 (B)가 정답이다.

어휘 additional 추가의   partnership 제휴 관계

기출 TEST 10

101 (A)	102 (D)	103 (B)	104 (A)	105 (D)
106 (B)	107 (A)	108 (B)	109 (D)	110 (B)
111 (B)	112 (A)	113 (B)	114 (D)	115 (C)
116 (B)	117 (C)	118 (A)	119 (B)	120 (A)
121 (C)	122 (D)	123 (B)	124 (D)	125 (A)
126 (A)	127 (D)	128 (D)	129 (C)	130 (B)
131 (D)	132 (C)	133 (B)	134 (A)	135 (D)
136 (B)	137 (C)	138 (B)	139 (C)	140 (A)
141 (B)	142 (D)	143 (C)	144 (D)	145 (B)
146 (D)	147 (D)	148 (B)	149 (B)	150 (D)
151 (A)	152 (D)	153 (C)	154 (C)	155 (C)
156 (C)	157 (C)	158 (C)	159 (C)	160 (D)
161 (B)	162 (D)	163 (A)	164 (C)	165 (D)
166 (A)	167 (B)	168 (A)	169 (C)	170 (B)
171 (C)	172 (C)	173 (B)	174 (A)	175 (C)
176 (B)	177 (A)	178 (B)	179 (C)	180 (C)
181 (B)	182 (A)	183 (C)	184 (D)	185 (C)
186 (A)	187 (C)	188 (D)	189 (D)	190 (B)
191 (B)	192 (B)	193 (C)	194 (D)	195 (A)
196 (B)	197 (A)	198 (B)	199 (C)	200 (B)

PART 5

101 인칭대명사의 격 _ 소유격

해설 빈칸 뒤에 온 명사 work를 수식하는 인칭대명사가 들어가야 한다. 따라서 명사 앞에 쓰여 한정사 역할을 할 수 있는 소유격 인칭대명사 (A) her가 정답이다.

번역 소피아 홀링거는 칼라 고객사에 관한 업무로 칭찬받았다.

어휘 commend 칭찬하다   account 고객, 거래

102 동사 어휘

해설 주어가 jazz musician Jay Deswani이므로 문맥상 '무대에서 공연했다'는 의미가 되어야 자연스럽다. 따라서 '공연하다'라는 의미의 동사 perform의 과거형 (D) performed가 정답이다. (A)의 locate는 '위치를 찾아내다', (B)의 request는 '요청하다', (C)의 supply는 '공급하다'라는 의미이다.

번역 지난 여름, 재즈 음악가 제이 데스와니는 워터프런트 공원의 메인 콘서트 무대에서 공연했다.

103 형용사 자리 _ 명사 수식 / 형용사 vs. 현재분사

해설 빈칸 앞에 수사 six가 있고, 뒤에 명사 cases가 있으므로 빈칸은 명사를 수식하는 형용사 자리이다. 따라서 '추가의'를 뜻하는 형용사 (B) additional이 정답이다. (A) add(추가하다)는 동사, (C) additionally(추가로)는 부사이므로 품사상 빈칸에 들어갈 수 없고, cases는 add의 주체가 아닌 대상이므로 현재분사 (D) adding (추가하는)은 답이 될 수 없다.

번역 구매 부서는 잉크 토너 여섯 상자를 추가로 주문했다.

어휘 purchasing 구매

104 부사 어휘

해설 to help의 목적격 보어로 쓰인 원형부정사 understand를 수식하며, '더 잘 알 수 있도록'이라는 의미가 되어야 자연스러우므로 '더 잘'을 뜻하는 비교급 부사 (A) better가 정답이다. (B) more는 '더 (많이)', (C) very는 '매우'라는 뜻으로 주로 형용사나 부사를 수식하고 단독으로 동사를 수식하지 않는다. (D) surely는 '분명히'라는 뜻으로 말하는 사람의 확신을 나타내므로, 이해의 정도를 나타내야 하는 문맥에는 어울리지 않는다.

번역 귀하가 관심이 있는 금융 서비스를 저희 팀에서 더 잘 알 수 있도록 설문지를 작성해 주십시오.

어휘 questionnaire 설문지

105 명사 자리 _ 동사의 주어 / 어휘

해설 빈칸은 동사 will begin의 주어 자리이므로 명사가 들어가야 한다. of the garments의 수식을 받아 '의류 생산이 시작될 것이다'라는 의미가 되어야 자연스러우므로 '생산'을 뜻하는 명사 (D) Production이 정답이다. (A) Product(제품)는 가산 단수 명사로 앞에 관사나 한정사가 와야 하고, (B) Produce(농산물)는 불가산명사로 한정사는 필요 없지만 의미상 적절하지 않다. (C) Produced는 동사/과거분사로 품사상 답이 될 수 없다.

번역 의류 생산은 계약이 체결된 2주 후에 시작될 것이다.

어휘 garment 의류   contract 계약

106 형용사 어휘

해설 빈칸 앞의 only three와 결합하여 명사 errors를 수식해 '단 세 개의 사소한 오류'라는 의미가 되어야 자연스러우므로 '사소한'을 뜻하는 (B) minor가 정답이다. (A) junior는 '하급의', (C) soft는 '부드러운', (D) light는 '(무게가) 가벼운'이라는 뜻이다.

번역 지난주 이사회 회의록에는 단 세 개의 사소한 오류가 있었다.

어휘 minutes 회의록   board 이사회

107 접속사 자리 _ 부사절 접속사

해설 빈칸 앞뒤로 완전한 절이 왔으므로 빈칸은 부사절 접속사 자리이다. 문맥상 '공연이 시작될 때'라는 의미가 되어야 자연스러우므로, '~할

때'라는 의미의 부사절 접속사 (A) when이 정답이다. (B) which, (C) what, (D) why는 명사절 접속사로 빈칸에 들어갈 수 없다.

번역 이용객들은 공연이 시작될 때 전화기를 무음으로 해달라는 요청을 받는다.

어휘 patron 이용객   silence 조용하게 하다

108 전치사 어휘

해설 빈칸 뒤의 교통수단을 나타내는 명사 train을 목적어로 취해 '기차로 출퇴근한다'는 의미가 되어야 자연스러우므로, 수단을 나타내는 전치사 (B) by가 정답이다. (A) on은 '~ (위)에', (C) in은 '~ (안)에', (D) from은 '~으로부터'라는 의미로 문맥상 어울리지 않는다.

번역 그 회사 직원 대부분은 기차로 출퇴근한다.

어휘 majority 대부분   commute 출퇴근하다

109 부사 자리 _ 형용사 수식   ▶동영상 강의

해설 빈칸 앞의 최상급 표현 the oldest와 빈칸 뒤의 현재분사 operating이 복합명사 bus line을 수식하고 있고, 빈칸은 operating을 수식하는 부사 자리이다. 따라서 '지속적으로'라는 의미의 부사 (D) continuously가 정답이다. (A) continues는 동사, (B) continued는 동사/과거분사, (C) continuous는 형용사이므로 답이 될 수 없다.

번역 73번 노선은 레모 시의 역사상 가장 오래 지속적으로 운행하고 있는 버스 노선이다.

어휘 operating 작동하고 있는, 가동하는

110 명사 어휘

해설 빈칸은 be동사 is의 보어 자리로, 주어 This message와 동격을 이루는 명사가 들어가야 한다. 문맥상 '이 메시지는 우체국에서 소포를 수령해 가라는 알림이다'라는 의미가 되어야 자연스러우므로 '알림, 상기시키는 것'을 뜻하는 (B) reminder가 정답이다. (A) promotion은 '승진, 홍보', (C) process는 '과정', (D) report는 '보고서'라는 의미이다.

번역 이 메시지는 지역 우체국에서 가능한 한 빨리 귀하의 소포를 수령하라는 알림입니다.

어휘 package 소포

111 관계대명사 _ 주격

해설 빈칸은 뒤에 있는 동사 want의 주어 역할을 하면서, 선행사이자 문장의 본동사 can opt의 주어인 Pet Orbit customers를 수식하는 관계대명사 자리로 주격 관계대명사 (B) who가 정답이다. (A) whose는 뒤에 명사가 와야 하고, (C) those는 대명사, (D) whoever는 복합관계대명사로 빈칸에 들어갈 수 없다.

번역 이메일로 영수증을 받기를 원하는 펫 오빗 고객들은 이 서비스를 선택할 수 있다.

어휘 opt for ~을 선택하다

112 접속사 자리 / 어휘

해설 빈칸은 두 개의 절을 이어주는 접속사 자리이므로 등위접속사인 (A) but과 (B) or 중 하나를 선택해야 한다. 타카지안 씨가 말단 직원인 것과 솔선한다는 것은 서로 상반되는 상황이므로 역접의 의미를 나타내는 (A) but이 정답이다. (B) or는 '또는'이라는 뜻으로 의미상 적절하지 않고, (C) equally(동일하게)와 (D) accordingly(그에 따라)는 부사이므로 품사상 빈칸에 들어갈 수 없다.

번역 타카지안 씨는 말단 사원일지도 모르지만, 솔선하는 것을 망설이지 않는다.

어휘 entry-level 말단의, 초급의   hesitate 망설이다
take initiative 솔선하다, 주도권을 잡다

113 to부정사 / 능동태 vs. 수동태

해설 빈칸은 「allow+목적어+목적격 보어(to부정사)」 구조에서 목적격 보어에 해당하는 자리이므로 to부정사가 들어가야 한다. 빈칸 뒤에 to부정사의 목적어 items가 있으므로 능동태인 (B) to place가 정답이다. 수동태 (D) to be placed는 목적어를 취할 수 없고, (A) place는 동사/명사, (C) placing은 현재분사/동명사이므로 답이 될 수 없다.

번역 카터 백화점은 고객들이 최대 24시간 동안 상품을 보류할 수 있도록 해 준다.

어휘 on hold 보류된

114 형용사 어휘

해설 집의 스타일을 수식하기에 적절한 형용사가 들어가야 한다. '세련된 분위기'라는 의미가 되어야 자연스러우므로 '세련된'을 뜻하는 (D) fashionable이 정답이다. (A) brief는 '짧은, 간단한', (B) dependent는 '의존적인', (C) motivational은 '동기를 부여하는'이라는 의미이다.

번역 매미즈 인테리어의 실내 장식 전문가들은 독특한 색상과 스타일을 사용하여, 집에 세련된 분위기를 불어넣는다.

어휘 decor (실내) 장식   expert 전문가

115 전치사 자리 / 어휘   ▶동영상 강의

해설 빈칸은 뒤에 있는 명사구 efficient project management를 콤마 뒤의 완전한 절에 연결하는 자리이므로 전치사가 들어가야 한다. '효율적인 프로젝트 관리 때문에'라는 의미가 되어야 자연스러우므로 '~ 때문에'를 뜻하는 전치사 (C) Because of가 정답이다. (A) Along with(~와 함께)와 (B) Regarding(~에 관하여)은 전치사이지만 의미상 적절하지 않고, (D) Subsequent(그 다음의)는 형용사이므로 빈칸에 들어갈 수 없다.

번역 효율적인 프로젝트 관리 때문에, 스팍스웨어의 최신 소프트웨어 프로그램은 제때 공개되었다.

어휘 efficient 효율적인   latest 최신의   release 공개하다
on time 제때

116 전치사 어휘

해설 빈칸 뒤에 장소를 나타내는 명사구 select stores가 있고, 문맥상 '일부 매장에서 이용 가능하다'는 내용이 되어야 자연스러우므로 '~에서'라는 뜻의 전치사 (B) at이 정답이다. (A) until은 '~까지', (C) over는 '~ 위에', (D) before는 '~ 전에'라는 의미로 문맥상 어울리지 않는다.

번역 여름용 야외 가구 라인은 이르면 2월에 일부 매장에서 이용 가능할 예정입니다.

어휘 outdoor 야외의 available 이용 가능한 select 선택된

117 형용사 자리 _ 명사 수식 / 형용사 vs. 현재분사

해설 빈칸 앞에 부정관사 a가 있고, 뒤에 명사 decrease가 있으므로 빈칸은 명사를 수식하는 형용사 자리이다. 따라서 '눈에 띄는'을 뜻하는 형용사 (C) noticeable이 정답이다. (A) notice는 '공지'라는 뜻의 명사로 쓰일 수 있지만 decrease와 복합명사를 이루기에 적절하지 않고, (D) noticeably는 부사로 품사상 빈칸에 들어갈 수 없다. 또한 decrease는 notice의 주체가 아닌 대상이므로 능동의 의미를 나타내는 현재분사 (B) noticing은 답이 될 수 없다.

번역 이번 분기에 고객 지원 요청이 눈에 띄게 감소했다.

어휘 decrease 감소 support 지원 quarter 분기

118 접속사 자리 / 어휘

해설 빈칸은 두 개의 완전한 절을 이어주는 접속사 자리이다. 빈칸 앞에서 비나 달은 항상 외교관이 되기를 원했다고 했고, 뒤에서 대학교에서 국제 관계론을 공부했다며 원인과 결과의 관계를 언급하고 있다. 따라서 '그래서'라는 의미의 (A) so가 정답이다. 부사절 접속사인 (B) once(~하자마자)와 (D) whereas(반면에)는 의미상 적합하지 않고, (C) overall은 명사/형용사/부사로 품사상 빈칸에 들어갈 수 없다.

번역 비나 달은 항상 외교관이 되기를 원해서, 대학교에서 국제 관계론을 공부했다.

어휘 diplomat 외교관 international relations 국제 관계론

119 부사 자리 _ 준동사 수식

해설 빈칸은 동명사 responding을 수식하는 부사 자리이므로 부사 (B) promptly(신속하게)가 정답이다. (A) prompt가 부사로 쓰일 때는 시간 표현 뒤에서 '(~시) 정각에'를 뜻하므로 의미상 적절하지 않고, (C) prompted는 동사/과거분사, (D) prompts는 동사/명사이므로 품사상 빈칸에 들어갈 수 없다.

번역 티맥스 400 프린터와 스캐너에 관한 정보로 신속하게 응대해 주셔서 감사합니다.

어휘 respond 응대하다, 대답하다

120 동사 어휘

해설 to부정사 자리에 들어갈 동사 어휘를 고르는 문제이다. your appointment를 목적어로 취해 '예약 일정을 변경해야 한다'는 의미가 되어야 자연스러우므로, '일정을 변경하다'라는 뜻의 (A) reschedule이 정답이다. (B) borrow는 '빌리다', (C) contain은 '포함하다', (D) reconstruct는 '재구성하다'라는 의미이다.

번역 날씨 때문에, 저희는 귀하의 수목 제거 서비스 예약 일정을 변경해야 합니다.

어휘 owing to ~ 때문에 appointment (만날) 예약, 약속 removal 제거

121 형용사 자리 _ 명사 수식 / 과거분사 vs. 형용사

해설 빈칸은 명사 effort를 수식하는 형용사 자리로 문맥상 '협력된 노력'이라는 의미가 되어야 자연스러우므로, '협력된, 조화된'이라는 수동의 의미를 나타내는 과거분사 (C) coordinated가 정답이다. (A) coordinate는 형용사로 쓸 수 있지만 '(관계가) 동등한, 동격의'라는 의미로 문맥상 적절하지 않고, (B) coordinates는 명사로 쓰면 '좌표'라는 의미로 복합명사를 이루기에 적절하지 않으며, (D) coordination(조화) 또한 의미상 복합명사를 이루기에 부적절하다.

번역 철도선을 완성하기 위해서는, 두 국가간 협력된 노력이 필요할 것이다.

어휘 effort 노력 complete 완성하다 railway line 철도선

122 명사 어휘

해설 빈칸은 전치사 According to(~에 따르면)의 목적어 역할을 하는 명사 자리이다. 빈칸 앞 the restaurant's와 결합하여 손님은 직원의 안내를 기다려야 한다는 식당 규정의 기준이 될 수 있는 말이 들어가야 적절하므로, '정책, 방침'을 뜻하는 (D) policy가 정답이다. (A)의 offering은 '제공된 것', (B)의 fund는 '자금', (C) bill은 '계산서'라는 의미이다.

번역 식당 정책에 따르면, 손님들은 안내 직원이 자리로 안내하기를 기다려야 한다.

어휘 seat 앉히다 front-of-house 손님 안내

123 동사 자리 _ 시제

해설 빈칸은 비교급 접속사 than이 이끄는 절에서 주어 organizers의 동사 자리이다. 주절에서 티켓이 매진되었다(sold out)는 과거 사실을 언급하고 있고 '주최측이 예상한 것'은 그보다 먼저 일어난 일이므로 과거완료 시제를 써야 한다. 따라서 (B) had anticipated가 정답이다. 동명사/현재분사인 (C) anticipating과 to부정사인 (D) to anticipate는 품사상 적절하지 않다.

번역 토요일 풋볼 경기의 티켓이 주최측에서 예상했던 것보다 훨씬 빠르게 목요일에 매진되었다.

어휘 organizer 주최자 anticipate 예상하다

124 접속사 자리 ▶동영상 강의

해설 빈칸은 동명사구 Renewing your auto registration online과 (renewing your auto registration) at the motor vehicle office를 연결하는 자리이며, 두 대상을 비교하여 '자동차 등록증을 차량 관리 사무소 대신 온라인으로 갱신하다'라는 의미를 나타내야 적절하다. 따라서 '~ 대신, ~보다는'을 뜻하며 등위접속사처럼 동등한 요소를 연결하는 접속사 (D) rather than이 정답이다. (A) just는 부사, (B) neither는 한정사/대명사/부사, '어쨌든'이라는 의미의 (C) at any rate는 부사구로 품사상 적합하지 않다.

번역 자동차 등록증을 차량 관리 사무소 대신 온라인으로 갱신하면 시간을 절약할 수 있다.

어휘 renew 갱신하다 registration 등록

125 전치사 자리 / 어휘

해설 빈칸은 뒤에 있는 명사구 Latoya Model Management's sound reputation을 콤마 뒤의 완전한 절에 연결하는 전치사 자리이다. '견실한 명성을 고려할 때'라는 의미가 되어야 자연스러우므로 '~을 고려해 볼 때'를 뜻하는 전치사 (A) Given이 정답이다. (B) Ahead of는 전치사이지만 '~ 앞에'라는 뜻으로 의미상 적합하지 않고, (C) Preferably(가급적이면)는 부사, (D) Provided that(만약 ~이라면)은 접속사이므로 품사상 빈칸에 들어갈 수 없다.

번역 라토야 모델 매니지먼트의 견실한 명성을 고려할 때, 모델 지망생들은 성공적인 출세를 기대할 수 있다.

어휘 sound 견실한 reputation 명성 aspiring 장차 ~이 되려는 flourishing 번영하는 career 출세, 성공

126 접속사 자리 _ 부사절 접속사

해설 빈칸은 두 개의 절을 연결하는 접속사 자리이다. 문맥상 '직원 명부가 마무리될 수 있도록'이라는 의미가 되어야 자연스러우므로 '~하도록'을 뜻하는 부사절 접속사 (A) so that이 정답이다. (B) as though도 부사절 접속사이지만 '마치 ~인 것처럼'이라는 뜻으로 의미상 적합하지 않고, (C) namely(즉)와 (D) likewise(마찬가지로)는 부사로 품사상 빈칸에 들어갈 수 없다.

번역 직원 명부가 마무리될 수 있도록 직원들은 연락처를 업데이트해 달라는 요청을 받는다.

어휘 contact 연락 directory 명부 finalize 마무리짓다, 완성하다

127 명사 자리

해설 빈칸은 to부정사 to buy의 목적어 역할을 하는 명사 자리로, 빈칸 앞의 형용사 inferior와 뒤의 전치사구 of its adjustable desks의 수식을 받는다. 문맥상 '조절형 책상의 하급 모조품'이라는 의미가 되어야 자연스러우므로 '모조품'을 뜻하는 명사 (D) imitations가 정답이다. (A) imitates는 동사, (B) imitative는 형용사, (C) imitated는 동사/과거분사로 품사상 적합하지 않다.

번역 글리스톤포드 제조사는 소비자들에게 자사의 높낮이 조절형 책상의 하급 모조품을 구입하지 말라고 경고한다.

어휘 manufacturing 제조(업) caution 경고하다 consumer 소비자 inferior 하급의 adjustable 조절 가능한

128 전치사 어휘

해설 빈칸은 동격절(that ~ widespread)의 수식을 받고 있는 명사구 the fact를 콤마 뒤의 완전한 절에 연결하는 전치사 자리이다. '소셜 미디어 사용이 널리 퍼져 있다는 사실에도 불구하고'라는 의미가 되어야 자연스러우므로 '~에도 불구하고'를 뜻하는 전치사 (D) Despite가 정답이다. (A) Opposite은 '~ 건너편에', (B) Without은 '~ 없이', (C) Unlike는 '~와 달리'라는 의미이다.

번역 소셜 미디어 사용이 널리 퍼져 있다는 사실에도 불구하고, 많은 사람들이 확실한 정보를 위해 여전히 신문에 의존하고 있다.

어휘 widespread 널리 퍼진 rely on ~에 의존하다 fact-checked 사실 확인된

129 형용사 어휘

해설 명사 arguments를 수식하여 '설득력 있는 주장'이라는 의미가 되어야 자연스러우므로 '설득력 있는'을 뜻하는 (C) convincing이 정답이다. (A) absent는 '부재한', (B) affordable은 '저렴한', (D) intrigued는 '흥미로워 하는'이라는 의미이다.

번역 발표자는 에너지 효율성과 비용 절감을 들며, 태양광 패널 설치에 대한 몇 가지 설득력 있는 주장을 펼쳤다.

어휘 cite (예나 이유를) 들다 efficiency 효율성 reduction 감소 presenter 발표자 argument 주장 install 설치하다 solar 태양의

130 동사 어휘 ▶동영상 강의

해설 빈칸 뒤에 목적격 보어 Director of the Nanboro Youth Farming Program이 있고, '프로그램의 책임자로 임명되었다'는 의미가 되어야 적절하므로 '임명하다'라는 뜻의 동사 name의 과거분사 (B) named가 정답이다. 「name + 목적어 + 목적격 보어」의 구조에서 목적어 Dr. Beasly가 주어 자리로 가면서 수동태 문장이 된 형태이다. (A)의 hire는 '고용하다', (C)의 admit은 '인정하다', (D)의 establish는 '설립하다'라는 의미이다. 참고로, (A) hired가 답이 되려면 뒤에 전치사 as가 와야 한다.

번역 공식적인 정부 직책에서 물러난 후, 비즐리 박사는 난보로 청년 농업 프로그램의 책임자로 임명되었다.

PART 6

131-134 회람

수신: 모든 창고 직원
발신: 폴 완다이, 창고 관리자
날짜: 3월 15일
제목: 새로운 상자 입고

4월 1일부터 윈드퀘스트 농장은 과일과 채소 운송에 플렉스머지 상자를 사용합니다. 이 131 **용기**는 작업을 단순화하고 운영비를 줄여 줄 것입니다.

플렉스머지 상자는 접이식으로, 쌓기 쉽고 공간을 절약할 수 있다는 것을 의미합니다. 132 **따라서, 비어 있을 때 그것들을 더 많이 트럭에 실을 수 있습니다.** 또한 내구성이 아주 뛰어납니다. 이 특징은 상자의 잦은 교체 133 **에 대한** 필요성을 최소화해 줍니다. 마지막으로, 이것들은 인체 공학적으로 설계되어 있고, 그로 인해 부상의 위험을 134 **줄여 줍니다.** 윈드퀘스트 농장에서는 안전이 최우선입니다.

> 어휘 crate 상자 simplify 단순화하다 shrink 줄이다 operational 운영의 collapsible 접을 수 있는 stack 쌓다 durable 내구성이 있는 frequent 잦은 replacement 교체 ergonomic 인체 공학의 thereby 그로 인해 injury 부상 priority 우선순위

131 명사 어휘

해설 앞 문장에서 4월 1일부터 플렉스머지 상자를 사용한다(Beginning 1 April, Windquest Farms will use Flexmerge crates)고 했으므로, 빈칸에는 상자를 대신할 수 있는 '용기'라는 의미의 (D) containers가 정답이다. (A)의 desk는 '책상', (B)의 program은 '프로그램', (C)의 agency는 '대행사'라는 의미이다.

132 문맥에 맞는 문장 고르기

번역 (A) 우리는 앞으로 몇 달간 그것들이 더 많이 필요할 것입니다.
(B) 농부들과 도매업자들이 그것들을 더 많이 구입했습니다.
(C) 따라서, 비어 있을 때 그것들을 더 많이 트럭에 실을 수 있습니다.
(D) 곧 우리 웹사이트에서 그것들을 더 많이 구매할 수 있을 겁니다.

해설 앞 문장에서 상자가 접이식이라서 쌓기 쉽고 공간을 절약할 수 있다(Flexmerge crates are collapsible, which means they are easy to stack and they save space)고 강조하고 있으므로, 접이식 특성으로 인한 이점을 구체적인 실례로 제시하는 내용이 들어가야 연결이 자연스럽다. 따라서 (C)가 정답이다.

어휘 ahead 앞으로 wholesaler 도매업자 accordingly 따라서 load 싣다

133 전치사 어휘

해설 빈칸 앞의 명사 need는 전치사 for와 주로 결합하여 '~에 대한 필요(성)'이라는 의미를 나타낸다. 빈칸 뒤의 명사구 frequent replacement를 목적어로 취해 '잦은 교체에 대한 필요성'이라는 내용이 되어야 적절하므로 (B) for가 정답이다. need는 to부정사와도 자주 결합하지만 빈칸 뒤에 명사가 왔으므로 전치사 (A) to(~으로)는 답이 될 수 없고, (C) among(~ 중에서)과 (D) besides (~ 외에) 또한 의미상 어울리지 않는다.

134 분사구문 _ 현재분사 vs. 과거분사

해설 앞에 완전한 절(they are designed with ergonomic features)과 콤마가 있으므로, thereby 이하는 분사구문이다. 빈칸 뒤의 명사구 the risk of injuries를 목적어로 취해 '부상의 위험을 줄여 준다'는 의미가 되어야 자연스러우므로 능동의 의미를 나타내는 현재분사 (A) reducing이 정답이다. 동사 (B) reduces와 명사 (D) reducer는 품사상 적합하지 않고, 과거분사 (C) reduced는 목적어를 취할 수 없다.

135-138 기사

> 인기 TV쇼, 3번째 시즌으로 돌아온다
>
> 수상 경력에 빛나는 TV 시리즈 〈킹 오브 더 미어〉의 세 번째 시즌이 일요일에 시작된다. 이 정치 스릴러는 노리아키 아리시마의 책 〈속삭이는 환상〉을 135 **기반으로 한다.**
>
> 이 TV 시리즈의 일부 평론가들은 세 번째 시즌이 이전 시즌보다 훨씬 더 좋을 것이라고 생각한다. 136 **그에 반해,** 다른 평론가들은 너무 많은 새로운 캐릭터들이 등장하면서 이 시리즈가 매력을 잃고, 복잡하고 혼란스러운 줄거리로 귀결될 수 있다고 주장한다.
>
> 앰버 랜돌프 감독은 이 137 **비판**에 응답했다. "새로운 캐릭터들이 많아지면 이야기를 따라오기가 어려워질 수 있습니다."라고 그녀는 말했다. "138 **하지만 그들은 이야기에 훨씬 더 깊이를 더해줍니다.** 이 쇼의 팬들이 어떻게 생각하는지 알게 될 것입니다."

> 어휘 award-winning 상을 받은 political 정치적인 whisper 속삭이다 illusion 환상 reviewer 평론가 previous 이전의 argue 주장하다 appeal 매력 result in 그 결과 ~이 되다 complicated 복잡한 confusing 혼란스러운 plotline 줄거리 abundance 풍부 challenging 어려운

135 동사 자리 _ 시제

해설 빈칸은 주어 This political thriller의 동사 자리이다. 또한 곧 방영될 TV 시리즈에 대한 사실을 설명하는 내용이므로 현재 시제를 써야 한다. 따라서 (D) is based가 정답이다. (A) basing은 현재분사/동명사이므로 품사상 답이 될 수 없고, (B) will be based와 (C) was based는 시제가 적합하지 않다.

136 접속부사

해설 앞 문장에서 TV 시리즈에 대한 일부 평론가들의 긍정적인 반응에 대해 언급하고 있고, 빈칸 뒤에는 다른 평론가들의 부정적인 반응에 대해 언급하고 있다. 따라서 빈칸에는 서로 상반되는 상황을 연결하는 접속부사가 들어가야 자연스러우므로 '그에 반해'라는 뜻의 (B) In contrast가 정답이다. (A) From here on은 '지금부터', (C) To be specific은 '구체적으로 말하면', (D) To sum up은 '요약하자면'이라는 의미이다.

137 명사 어휘

해설 앞 문장에서 너무 많은 캐릭터 때문에 시리즈가 매력을 잃고, 복잡하고 혼란스러운 줄거리가 될 수 있다(the series might lose its appeal with the introduction of so many new characters, resulting in a complicated and confusing plotline)는 일부 평론가들의 부정적인 비평에 대해 언급했으므로, 빈칸에는 이를 대신할 수 있는 '비판'이라는 의미의 (C) criticism이 정답이다. (A) advertisement는 '광고', (B) treatment는 '치료', (D) need는 '필요'라는 의미이다.

138 문맥에 맞는 문장 고르기

번역 (A) 하지만 그들은 많은 어려움에도 불구하고 성공했습니다.
(B) 하지만 그들은 이야기에 훨씬 더 깊이를 더해줍니다.
(C) 하지만 그것은 유용한 학습 경험이 될 것입니다.
(D) 하지만 그것은 그들을 더 가깝게 해 주었습니다.

해설 앞 문장에서 랜돌프 감독이 새로운 캐릭터들이 많아지면 이야기를 따라오기가 어려워질 수 있다(The abundance of new characters can make the story challenging to follow)고 했으므로, 서로 상반되는 의미를 연결하는 등위접속사 But 뒤에는 그와 반대로 새로운 캐릭터들이 이야기에 불러올 장점을 언급하는 내용이 들어가야 자연스럽다. 따라서 (B)가 정답이다.

어휘 depth 깊이 narrative 이야기 useful 유용한

139-142 이메일

수신: 지와 조 〈cho8876@sunmail.com〉
발신: 켄 벨판트 〈kenbelfant@fluffytimeindustries.com〉
날짜: 4월 6일
제목: 조리법 대회

조 씨께,

저희의 저지방, 무설탕 플러피 타임 휘핑 토핑을 사용한 흥미로운 조리법을 139 **공유해** 주셔서 감사합니다. 140 **그 조리법은** 곧 있을 저희 대회에 등록되었습니다. 우승한 조리법은 저희 제품의 포장지에 실릴 예정입니다. 141 **대회 우승자들은 6월에 통보를 받게 됩니다.** 그동안 142 **곧** 받게 될 별도의 이메일을 통해, 향후 어떤 플러피 타임 제품을 구매하더라도 25퍼센트를 할인 받을 수 있는 쿠폰을 보내 드리겠습니다.

저희 제품을 좋아해 주셔서 매우 기쁩니다. 대회에서 행운이 따르길 바랍니다!

감사합니다.

켄 벨판트, 홍보 담당자
플러피 타임 인더스트리즈

어휘 recipe 조리법 upcoming 곧 있을, 다가오는 appear 나타나다 packaging 포장 in the meantime 그동안 via ~을 통해 separate 별도의 gratitude 감사

139 동명사 _ 전치사의 목적어

해설 빈칸은 전치사 for의 목적어 자리로, your interesting recipe를 목적어로 취할 수 있는 동명사 (C) sharing이 정답이다. (B) shared는 동사/과거분사로 품사상 빈칸에 들어갈 수 없고, (A) share와 (D) shares는 명사로 쓰일 경우 전치사의 목적어 역할을 할 수는 있지만 뒤에 목적어를 취할 수는 없다.

140 대명사 어휘

해설 빈칸은 동사 has been entered의 주어 자리로, 해당 문장은 앞 문장에서 언급된 조 씨의 조리법(your interesting recipe)이 대회에 등록되었음을 알리는 내용이다. 따라서 빈칸에는 your interesting recipe를 지칭하는 대명사 (A) It이 정답이다. (B) One은 '(불특정한) 하나'를 의미하고, (C) Each는 복수 명사 중 '각각'을 의미하므로 빈칸에 들어갈 수 없고, (D) Theirs는 '그들의 것'이라는 소유대명사로 답이 될 수 없다.

141 문맥에 맞는 문장 고르기

번역 (A) 플러피 타임은 어디에서나 어린이들이 가장 좋아하는 제품입니다.
(B) 대회 우승자들은 6월에 통보를 받게 됩니다.
(C) 실망하셨다니 유감입니다.
(D) 저희 초콜릿 크림 조리법을 시도해 보고 싶으실 수도 있습니다.

해설 앞 문장에서 우승 조리법은 제품의 포장지에 실릴 예정(The winning recipes will appear on our product's packaging)이라며 우승 조리법이 누리게 될 특전에 대해 설명하고 있으므로, 대회 우승과 관련된 정보가 뒤이어 들어가야 연결이 자연스럽다. 따라서 우승자 발표 일정을 안내하고 있는 (B)가 정답이다.

어휘 notify 통보하다

142 부사 어휘

해설 동사구 should receive를 수식하여 적절한 문맥을 완성하는 부사를 고르는 문제이다. 앞으로 할 일에 대해 언급하는 문맥상 '곧 받게 될 별도의 이메일'이라는 내용이 되어야 자연스러우므로 '곧'이라는 뜻의 (D) shortly가 정답이다. (A) briefly는 '짧게, 간략하게', (B) concisely는 '간결하게', (C) temporarily는 '일시적으로'라는 의미이다.

143-146 안내 책자

▶ 동영상 강의

빙고 임프린트는 공책, 냉장고 자석, 의류와 같은 홍보용 제품의 디자인을 제작합니다. 저희는 고객이 디자인 과정에 관여하는 수준을 결정할 수 있도록 합니다. 143 **그 결과,** 어떤 고객들은 디자인의 상세한 스케치를 제출합니다. 다른 고객들은 디자인의 개발 및 제작을 저희 그래픽 아티스트들에게 기꺼이 144 **전적으로** 맡깁니다. 일단 고안물이 완성되고 나면, 승인을 받기 위해 고객과 공유합니다. 145 **이 단계는 제품이 기대에 충족하도록 보장해 줍니다.** 저희는 모든 작업이 주문이 이루어지고 영업일 5일 이내에 완료됨을 보장합니다.

독창적인 디자인, 경쟁력 있는 가격, 적시 납품을 원하신다면 빙고 임프린트를 146 **믿으시면** 됩니다.

어휘 promotional 홍보의 magnet 자석 apparel 의류 determine 결정하다 involvement 관여 be content to 기꺼이 ~하다 invention 고안물, 발명품 finalize 완성하다 approval 승인 guarantee 보장하다 competitive 경쟁력 있는 timely 적시의 delivery 납품, 배송

143 접속부사

해설 앞 문장에서 고객이 디자인 과정에 관여하는 수준을 결정할 수 있도록 한다고 했고, 빈칸 뒤에는 어떤 고객들은 디자인의 상세 스케치를 제출한다며 그에 따른 예시를 들고 있다. 두 문장이 인과관계를 나타내고 있으므로 '그 결과'라는 뜻의 (C) As a result가 정답이다. (A) Similarly는 '유사하게', (B) However는 '하지만', (D) In the meantime은 '그 동안에'라는 의미이다.

144 부사 자리 _ 형용사 수식

해설 be동사와 형용사 content 사이에서 형용사를 수식하는 부사 자리이므로, '전적으로, 완전히'를 뜻하는 부사 (D) perfectly가 정답이다. (A) perfect는 동사/형용사, (B) perfected는 동사/과거분사, (C) perfection은 명사이므로 품사상 적합하지 않다.

145 문맥에 맞는 문장 고르기

번역 (A) 이 단계는 직원 간 의사소통을 원활하게 해 줍니다.
(B) 이 단계는 제품이 기대에 충족하도록 보장해 줍니다.
(C) 고객들은 회사에서 제안한 대안의 진가를 알아봅니다.
(D) 고객들은 크게 우려하며 이번 조치를 받아들였습니다.

해설 앞 문장에서 고안물이 완성되고 나면 승인을 받기 위해 고객과 공유한다(Once the invention has been finalized, it will be shared with the client for approval)고 했으므로, 빈칸에는 이 단계에서 고객의 승인을 받기 위해 고객과 최종 시안을 확인하는 이유가 들어가야 연결이 자연스럽다. 따라서 (B)가 정답이다.

어휘 facilitate 원활하게 하다 ensure 보장하다 expectation 기대 appreciate 진가를 알아보다 alternative 대안 greet 맞이하다 measure 조치 concern 우려

146 전치사 어휘

해설 빈칸 앞의 동사 count는 전치사 on과 결합해 '~을 믿다, 기대하다'라는 의미를 나타낸다. 뒤의 Bingo Imprint를 목적어로 취해 '빙고 임프린트를 믿으면 된다'는 내용이 되어야 자연스러우므로 (D) on이 정답이다. (A) along은 '~을 따라', (B) down은 '~ 아래로', (C) off는 '(~에서) 떨어져서'라는 의미이다.

PART 7

147-148 양식

크리스탈 브라더스
만족도 조사

귀하의 건물을 청소하는 데 크리스탈 브라더스를 고용해 주셔서 감사합니다. 5 '우수'에서 1 '불량'까지 적절한 숫자에 동그라미를 쳐 주세요. **147 청소된 장소에 있지 않은 유형의 방에 대해서는 'NP'에 동그라미를 쳐 주세요.**

고객: 제럴딘 황   날짜: 2월 22일

147 청소 서비스					
거실	5	④	3	2	1	NP
부엌	⑤	4	3	2	1	NP
식당	5	④	3	2	1	NP
침실	⑤	4	3	2	1	NP
로비	5	4	3	2	1	㊉
회의실	5	4	3	2	1	㊉
기타 정보						
148 예약이 쉬웠나요?	5	4	3	2	①
직원이 귀하의 특정 지시를 따랐나요?	⑤	4	3	2	1
방문 전에 직원이 정보를 제공했나요?	5	④	3	2	1
서비스 비용이 예상한 정도였나요?	⑤	4	3	2	1

어휘 circle 동그라미를 치다 appropriate 적절한 range (범위가 ~에서 …에) 이르다 appointment (방문) 예약, 약속 specific 특정한 instruction 지시

147 세부 사항

번역 크리스탈 브라더스가 청소한 건물의 유형은?
(A) 호텔
(B) 창고
(C) 사무실 건물
(D) 주택

해설 세 번째 문장에서 청소된 장소에 있지 않은 유형의 방에 대해서는 'NP'에 동그라미를 치라(Circle "NP" for a type of room that is not present in the location that was cleaned)고 했고, 중반부에 있는 청소 서비스(Cleaning Services) 표의 항목에서 거실(Living room), 부엌(Kitchen), 식당(Dining room), 침실(Bedroom(s))에 대해서는 평가가 되어 있는데 반해, 로비(Lobby)와 회의실(Conference room(s))에는 NP에 동그라미가 쳐 있다. 따라서 크리스탈 브라더스가 청소한 장소는 일반 주택임을 짐작할 수 있다. 따라서 (D)가 정답이다.

148 세부 사항

번역 황 씨가 가장 만족하지 못한 청소 서비스 부분은?
(A) 가격
(B) 일정 잡기
(C) 맞춤 서비스
(D) 직원의 시간 엄수

해설 지문 하단의 기타 정보 표에서 예약이 쉬웠는지(Was it easy to make an appointment?)를 묻는 첫 항목에 대해 황 씨가 가장 낮은 점수인 1점을 준 것으로 보아 (B)가 정답이다.

어휘 customize 맞춤 제작하다 punctuality 시간 엄수

Paraphrasing
지문의 make an appointment → 정답의 scheduling

149-150 웹페이지

https://www.hamptonlandscaping.com/productdelivery

제품 배송

햄프턴 조경은 고객들에게 거주지나 사업장으로 조경 제품을 배송해 드리는 옵션을 제공합니다. 여기에는 표토, 퇴비, 자갈, 나무껍질 가루, 장작 및 식재 혼합물이 포함됩니다. 고객님의 편의를 위해 149 **저희는 월요일부터 토요일까지 대량 및 소량 배송을 제공합니다.** 배송비는 용량, 제품, 지역에 따라 다릅니다. 자세한 가격 정보에 대해서는 904-555-0132로 전화 주세요. 배송을 위해 집에 계실 필요는 없습니다. 150 **요청된 배송 지역은 저희 트럭이 접근할 수 있어야 한다는 점을 유념해 주세요. 이 요건이 충족되지 않을 경우, 50달러의 재입고 비용이 부과됩니다.**

어휘 landscaping 조경 residence 거주지 topsoil 표토 compost 퇴비 gravel 자갈 bark 나무껍질 dust 가루, 먼지 firewood 장작 volume 용량 rate 요금 vary 다르다 accessible 접근 가능한 restocking 재입고 charge 청구하다

149 Not / True

번역 햄프턴 조경에 대해 사실인 것은?
(A) 개인 거주지에만 서비스를 제공한다.
(B) 다양한 규모의 주문을 배송한다.
(C) 하나의 표준 배송 요금을 청구한다.
(D) 일주일 내내 배송을 한다.

해설 세 번째 문장에서 월요일부터 토요일까지 대량 및 소량 배송을 제공한다(we offer large- and small-volume deliveries Monday through Saturday)고 했으므로 (B)가 정답이다.

어휘 varying 다양한

> **Paraphrasing**
> 지문의 large- and small-volume → 정답의 varying sizes

150 세부 사항

번역 어떤 상황에서 고객은 50달러를 청구 받게 되는가?
(A) 배송될 제품이 특정 무게를 초과할 때
(B) 고객이 주문품을 받으러 나타나지 않을 때
(C) 배송 주소가 도시권에 있지 않을 때
(D) 배송 기사가 하차 장소에 접근할 수 없을 때

해설 일곱 번째 문장에서 요청된 배송 지역은 회사 트럭이 접근할 수 있어야 한다는 점을 유념해 달라(Please note that the requested delivery area must be accessible for our trucks)면서 이 요건이 충족되지 않을 경우 50달러의 재입고 비용이 부과된다(In the event that this requirement is not met, a $50 restocking fee will be charged)고 했다. 따라서 (D)가 정답이다.

어휘 bill 청구하다 exceed 초과하다 drop-off 내려주는 곳

> **Paraphrasing**
> 지문의 the requested delivery area
> → 정답의 a drop-off location

151-152 문자 메시지

한나 피스크 (오후 1시 18분)
안녕하세요, 프랭크. 151, 152 **제가 작업 중인 예산 보고서를 오늘 오후 늦게 회계 부서에 제출하기 전에 점검해 주실 수 있을지 궁금해요.** 제가 계산한 추정치에 이상 없는지 확인하고 싶어요.

프랭크 걸린 (오후 1시 20분)
45분 정도 시간을 주실 수 있을까요? 151 **제 월간 실적 업데이트를 하는 중이거든요.** 예상했던 것보다 조금 오래 걸리고 있네요.

한나 피스크 (오후 1시 22분)
아, 괜찮아요! 152 **그동안 비용 데이터를 다시 점검하면 돼요.**

프랭크 걸린 (오후 1시 24분)
좋은 생각이에요. 그 추정치는 까다로울 수 있거든요!

한나 피스크 (오후 1시 25분)
2시 30분에 사무실에 들르면 될까요?

프랭크 걸린 (오후 1시 26분)
좋아요. 그때 봐요.

어휘 budget 예산 estimate 추정(치) sound 이상 없는 performance 실적, 성과 in the meantime 그동안 tricky 까다로운 stop by ~에 들르다

151 의도 파악

번역 오후 1시 20분에 걸린 씨가 "45분 정도 시간을 주실 수 있을까요?"라고 쓴 의도는?
(A) 이따가 피스크 씨를 기꺼이 도울 것이다.
(B) 그의 실적 업데이트는 어제 마감이었다.
(C) 비용 추정치를 집계하는 데 한 시간이 걸리지 않을 것이다.
(D) 예산 보고서를 직접 작성할 것이다.

해설 1시 18분에 피스크 씨가 작업 중인 예산 보고서를 점검해 줄 수 있는지(I was wondering if you could check the budget report I've been working on before I submit it to Accounting later this afternoon) 묻자, 1시 20분에 걸린 씨가 45분 정도 시간을 줄 수 있는지(Can you give me 45 minutes or so?)를 되물으며 월간 실적 업데이트를 하는 중(I'm in the middle of my monthly performance update)이라고 대답했다. 따라서 걸린 씨는 자신이 지금 하고 있는 업무를 끝내고 나서 피스크 씨를 돕겠다는 의도로 한 말임을 알 수 있으므로 (A)가 정답이다.

어휘 be willing to 기꺼이 ~하다 compile 집계하다

152 추론 / 암시

번역 피스크 씨는 다음에 무엇을 할 것 같은가?
(A) 자신의 월간 실적 업데이트 작업을 할 것이다.
(B) 회계 부서에 마감 기한 연장을 요청할 것이다.
(C) 다른 동료에게 조언을 구하러 연락할 것이다.
(D) 예산 보고서의 일부를 검토할 것이다.

해설 피스크 씨가 1시 13분에 자신이 작업 중인 예산 보고서(the budget report I've been working on)를 언급했고, 1시 22분에 걸린 씨를 기다리는 동안 비용 데이터를 다시 점검하겠다(I'll double-check the cost data in the meantime)고 했다. 따라서 피스크 씨는 예산 보고서의 데이터를 다시 검토할 것임을 알 수 있으므로 (D)가 정답이다.

어휘 extend 연장하다 colleague 동료 portion 부분

153-154 이메일

수신: 장서윤 〈s_jang@lazulinamail.com〉
발신: 트래블 투데이 〈team@traveltoday.com〉
날짜: 3월 18일
153 제목: 가격 알림

안녕하세요, 트래블 투데이 구독자님,

고객님께서는 최근 항공료 알림을 신청하셨습니다. **153** 선호하시는 여행의 가격 할인에 대해 아래 정보를 확인하세요. 항공사는 보통 한정된 수량의 최저 운임을 제공하므로, 이 가격을 활용하시려면 예약을 서두르시기 바랍니다.

문의사항이 있으시거나 예약하는 데 도움이 필요하실 경우, 210-555-0137로 연락 주세요.

감사합니다,
트래블 투데이 팀

여행 1: 시애틀에서 시카고로 7월 28일 편도, 성인 1인, 이코노미석		여행 2: 로스앤젤레스에서 뉴욕으로 8월 15일 편도, 성인 1인, 컴포트 플러스석	
154 노마타 항공 1회 경유(덴버) 오후 2시 42분 – 오후 11시 05분	평균가: 401달러 현재가: 315달러	**154** 노마타 항공 1회 경유(휴스턴) 오전 6시 – 오후 5시 32분	평균가: 465달러 현재가: 385달러
154 블루 레인지 항공 직항 오후 4시 40분 – 오후 10시 40분	평균가: 439달러 현재가: 373달러	**154** 블루 레인지 항공 직항 오전 11시 30분 – 오후 8시	평균가: 518달러 현재가: 436달러

어휘 airfare 항공료 notification 알림, 통지 fare 운임, 요금 take advantage of ~을 활용하다 nonstop 직항의

153 주제 / 목적

번역 이메일의 목적은?
(A) 구매를 확인하려고
(B) 가격 정보를 제공하려고
(C) 좌석 업그레이드를 요청하려고
(D) 예약을 취소하려고

해설 이메일의 제목이 가격 알림(Subject: Price alert)이고, 첫 단락 두 번째 문장에서 선호하는 여행의 가격 할인에 대해 아래 정보를 확인하라(Please see the information below for price cuts on your preferred trips)고 했으므로 구독자들에게 가격 할인 정보를 알리려는 글임을 알 수 있다. 따라서 (B)가 정답이다.

154 세부 사항

번역 두 여행이 갖고 있는 공통점은?
(A) 출발 날짜
(B) 목적 도시
(C) 항공사 선택지
(D) 좌석 유형

해설 지문 하단의 표 양쪽에 기재된 항공사가 노마타 항공(Nomata Airlines)과 블루 레인지 항공(Blue Range Airways)으로 동일하므로 (C)가 정답이다.

어휘 departure 출발 destination 목적지

155-157 이메일

수신: rogelio.garza@gerimail.net
발신: sasha_lombardo@onyxmail.com
날짜: 1월 18일
제목: 저의 요리책
첨부: 📎 초안 원고

로헬리오,

이것은 제가 자가 출판할 요리책의 최신 초안이에요. **155** 제 조리법이 따라하기 쉬운지 확인하기 위해 검토해 주셔서 감사합니다. 당신의 의견에 정말 감사드려요. 이 프로젝트에 지난 몇 년 동안 많은 에너지를 쏟았는데, 마침내 완성되고 있어 매우 신이 나네요.

이미 다른 몇몇 사람들로부터 피드백을 받았는데 몇몇 부분의 설명이 혼란스럽게 쓰였다고 들었어요. 당신도 그렇게 생각하는지 알고 싶어요. **157** 한 가지 요청이 있는데, 답변 주실 때 당신의 의견 모두가 이 문서 하나에 들어갈 수 있도록 여백에다 의견을 남겨 주실 수 있을까요? 그렇지 않으면 모든 변경 사항을 기록하기가 어려워요.

그리고 **156** 몇몇 페이지에 빨간색으로 크게 X가 표시된 특별한 네모가 있는 것을 보게 될 거예요. 그것들은 무시하시면 돼요. **156** 특정 단계의 사진을 잘 못 찍어서, X는 나중에 더 나은 사진을 삽입하라고 알려주는 거예요.

다시 한번 감사드려요!

사샤

어휘 attachment 첨부 draft 초안 manuscript 원고 input 의견 thrilled 신이 난 instruction 설명 confusingly 혼란스럽게 word 말을 쓰다 comment 의견 margin 여백 mark 표시하다 ignore 무시하다 certain 특정한 reminder 알려주는 것, 상기시키는 것 insert 삽입하다

155 세부 사항

번역 롬바르도 씨는 가르자 씨에게 무엇을 하라고 요청하는가?
(A) 조리법이 명확한지 확인
(B) 모든 재료의 색인 제작
(C) 책을 출판할 가능성이 있는 출판사 추천
(D) 최종 원고의 서식화 작업 도움

해설 첫 단락 두 번째 문장에서 롬바르도 씨가 가르자 씨에게 조리법이 따라하기 쉬운지 확인하기 위해 검토해 줘서 감사하다(Thank you for reviewing my recipes to ensure they are easy to follow)고 했으므로 (A)가 정답이다.

어휘 index 색인 ingredient 재료 format 서식을 만들다

> **Paraphrasing**
> 지문의 easy to follow → 정답의 clear

156 세부 사항

번역 빨간 X로 표시된 네모는 무엇을 나타내는가?
(A) 서식 설정 변경을 위한 아이디어
(B) 페이지 나누기를 삽입하기 위한 제안
(C) 교체되어야 하는 이미지
(D) 정의되어야 하는 용어

해설 세 번째 단락의 첫 문장에서 몇몇 페이지에 빨간색으로 크게 X가 표시된 특별한 네모가 있다(some pages have special boxes marked with a big red X)고 했고, 같은 단락 세 번째 문장에서 특정 단계의 사진을 잘 못 찍어서 X는 나중에 더 나은 사진을 삽입하라고 알려주는 것(I did not take great pictures of certain steps, so the Xs are reminders to take better ones to insert later)이라고 언급하고 있다. 따라서 (C)가 정답이다.

어휘 formatting 서식 설정 modification 변경 insert 삽입하다 replace 교체하다 term 용어 define 정의하다

> **Paraphrasing**
> 지문의 to take better ones to insert later
> → 정답의 to be replaced

157 문장 삽입

번역 [1], [2], [3], [4]로 표시된 위치 중에서 다음 문장이 들어가기에 가장 적합한 곳은?

"그렇지 않으면 모든 변경 사항을 기록하기가 어려워요."

(A) [1]
(B) [2]
(C) [3]
(D) [4]

해설 주어진 문장에서 '그렇지 않으면 모든 변경 사항을 기록하기가 어렵다'고 했으므로, 변경 사항 기록과 관련된 요청이 앞에 있어야 적절하다. 따라서 여백에다 의견을 남겨 모든 사항이 문서 하나에 들어갈 수 있도록 해달라는 요청 뒤인 [4]에 들어가는 것이 글의 흐름상 자연스러우므로 (D)가 정답이다.

어휘 otherwise 그렇지 않으면 keep track of ~을 기록하다

158-160 편지

프리실라 야마구치
팔켄베그 19번지
10719 베를린

3월 23일

야마구치 씨께,

저는 아쿠아 보야지 크루즈 라인즈가 올해 7월에 선단을 확대할 예정이라는 기쁜 소식을 공유하고자 편지를 씁니다. 저희 계획의 일환으로, 귀하와의 제휴 기회를 환영합니다.

158 귀하께서는 레스토랑 체인인 샤프란 문의 159 견고한 명성을 쌓아 오셨습니다. 158 유럽 전역의 고객들에게 참신하고 맛있는 메뉴를 제공하고자 하는 귀하의 헌신은 크루즈 승객들에게 차별화된 레스토랑 옵션을 제공하려는 저희의 비전과 일치합니다.

저희와 제휴를 맺으면 여러 이점이 있습니다. 160(C) 저희 크루즈 여행에는 다양한 사람들이 오기 때문에, 훨씬 더 많은 사람들이 귀하의 레스토랑 체인을 알게 될 것입니다. 160(A) 아쿠아 보야지 크루즈 라인즈는 귀하의 가장 인기 있는 체인을 저희 안내 책자에서 다루고 웹사이트에 올릴 것입니다. 160(B) 저희의 공급업체망을 통해 조리법의 재료 및 레스토랑 장비와 관련해 매우 낮은 가격을 협상하는 데 도움을 드릴 수 있으며, 이로 인해 귀하의 비용을 절감할 수 있습니다.

이 제의를 진행시키는 데 관심이 있고 세부 사항을 논의하고 싶을 경우 kbasrawi@aquavoyagecruiselines.de로 연락하시거나 30-23125 032로 전화하시면 됩니다.

칼리드 바스라위, 기업 개발 부사장
아쿠아 보야지 크루즈 라인즈

어휘 expand 확대하다 fleet 선단 opportunity 기회 form 형성하다 partnership 제휴 관계 establish 수립하다 commitment 헌신, 전념 align 나란하다 passenger 승객 distinct 차별화된, 전혀 다른 benefit 이점 excursion 여행 diverse 다양한 top-rated 가장 인기 있는 supplier 공급업체 negotiate 협상하다 exceptionally 매우 ingredient 재료 reduce 줄이다 expense 비용

158 추론 / 암시

번역 야마구치 씨에 대해 암시된 것은?
(A) 여러 비즈니스 상을 수상했다.
(B) 7월에 크루즈 휴가를 예약했다.
(C) 유럽 여러 지역에 레스토랑을 운영한다.
(D) 자신의 레스토랑 체인의 메뉴를 변경할 계획이다.

해설 두 번째 단락의 첫 문장에서 야마구치 씨가 레스토랑 체인인 샤프란 문의 견고한 명성을 쌓아 왔다(You have established a solid reputation regarding your restaurant chain, Saffron Moon)면서 유럽 전역의 고객들에게 참신하고 맛있는 메뉴를 제공하고자 하는 그녀의 헌신(Your commitment to offering your customers across Europe unique and delicious menu items)에 대해 언급하고 있는 것으로 보아, 야마구치 씨가 유럽 곳곳에서 레스토랑 체인을 운영하고 있다는 것을 알 수 있다. 따라서 (C)가 정답이다.

어휘 operate 운영하다 multiple 여럿의, 다수의 revise 변경하다

Paraphrasing
지문의 across Europe
→ 정답의 in multiple European locations

159 동의어 찾기

번역 두 번째 단락 1행의 "solid"와 의미가 가장 가까운 단어는?
(A) 정확한
(B) 믿을 수 있는
(C) 소형의
(D) 철저한

해설 의미상 레스토랑의 '견고한' 명성을 쌓아 왔다는 뜻으로 쓰였으므로 '믿을 수 있는'을 뜻하는 (B) reliable이 정답이다.

160 Not / True

번역 제안된 제휴의 이점으로 언급되지 않은 것은?
(A) 증가된 광고 기회
(B) 음식 준비 물품의 비용 절감
(C) 새로운 고객층에 대한 노출
(D) 고급 교육 프로그램

해설 세 번째 단락에서 크루즈 여행에는 다양한 사람들이 오기 때문에 훨씬 더 많은 사람들이 레스토랑 체인을 알게 될 것(Since our cruise excursions attract a diverse group of people, an even more extensive group will become familiar with your restaurant chain)이라고 했으므로 (C), 아쿠아 보야지 크루즈 라인즈는 야마구치 씨의 가장 인기 있는 체인을 안내 책자와 웹사이트에 올릴 것(Aqua Voyage Cruise Lines will mention your top-rated chain in our brochures and feature it on our Web site)이라고 했으므로 (A), 공급업체망을 통해 조리법의 재료 및 레스토랑 장비와 관련해 매우 낮은 가격을 협상하는 데 도움을 줄 수 있으며 이로 인해 비용을 절감할 수 있다(Through our network of suppliers, we can help negotiate exceptionally low rates for recipe ingredients and restaurant equipment, thereby reducing your expenses)고 했으므로 (B)를 제휴의 이점으로 꼽고 있다. 교육 프로그램에 대해서는 언급되지 않았으므로 (D)가 정답이다.

어휘 preparation 준비 exposure 노출 quality 고급의, 양질의

Paraphrasing
지문의 an even more extensive group will become familiar → 보기 (C)의 Exposure to a new customer base

지문의 will mention your top-rated chain in our brochures and feature it on our Web site
→ 보기 (A)의 Increased advertising opportunities

지문의 reducing your expenses → 보기 (B)의 Lower cost

161-163 기사

KMC 중대한 승리를 거두다

웨스턴 오스트레일리아 (6월 21일) — 6월 19일, 161 웨스턴 오스트레일리아의 카리냐 메디컬 센터(KMC)는 호주 병원이 받을 수 있는 가장 높은 명예 중 하나로 여겨지는 발로케어 재단의 스텔라 서비스 공로상을 수상했다. 162(B) 이 상을 받기 위해서, 병원들은 적시의 치료 제공, 우수한 의료 성과, 광범위한 직원 교육, 뛰어난 환자 만족도를 포함한 일련의 기준을 충족해야 한다.

"KMC의 이사회, 경영진, 그리고 직원들에게 축하를 드립니다."라고 발로케어 재단의 회장인 리 신더는 말했다. "이 센터는 한결같이 고품질 진료에 대한 헌신을 보여주었습니다. 따라서, 올해 이 센터를 국가의 뛰어난 의료 시설 중 하나로 공인하게 되어 기쁩니다."

162(C) 지난 3월에 KMC의 CEO가 된 린 응우옌 박사는 "KMC가 발로케어 재단에서 인정하는 국내 7대 병원으로 꼽힌다는 사실이 매우 자랑스럽습니다. 이 상은 환자의 건강을 우리가 하는 모든 일의 중심에 두겠다는 우리의 전념을 163 반영합니다. KMC가 문을 연 이후로, 우리는 높은 환자 진료 기준을 설정해 왔으며 매년 이 목표를 유지하고자 노력하고 있습니다. 162(A) 지금까지 47년 동안 이 노력이 상당히 성공적이었다고 믿습니다."라고 말했다.

어휘 score (성공 등을) 거두다, 점수를 올리다 triumph 승리 foundation 재단 merit 공로 regard 여기다 criteria 기준 superior 우수한 outcome 결과 extensive 광범위한 exceptional 뛰어난, 우수한 satisfaction 만족 consistently 한결같이, 지속적으로 demonstrate 보여주다 dedication 헌신 recognise 인정하다 outstanding 뛰어난 facility 시설 extremely 대단히, 극도로 reflect 반영하다 commitment 전념 forefront 중심 strive 노력하다 maintain 유지하다 endeavour 노력

161 주제 / 목적

번역 기사의 한 가지 목적은?
(A) 병원 합병을 발표하려고
(B) 기관에 대한 찬사를 전달하려고
(C) 지도부 교체에 대한 이유를 설명하려고
(D) 고품질 진료에 대한 필요성을 강조하려고

해설 첫 단락 첫 문장에서 웨스턴 오스트레일리아의 카리냐 메디컬 센터(KMC)는 호주 병원이 받을 수 있는 가장 높은 명예 중 하나로 여겨지는 발로케어 재단의 스텔라 서비스 공로상을 수상했다(Western Australia's Karinya Medical Centre (KMC) was awarded the Valorcare Foundation's Stellar Service Merit, regarded as one of the highest honours an Australian hospital can receive)고 KMC의 수상 소식을 전하며, 병원이 그간 기울여 온 노력 및 성과에 대해 기사 전체에 걸쳐 언급하고 있으므로 (B)가 정답이다.

어휘 merger 합병 praise 찬사 organization 기관 emphasize 강조하다

162 Not / True

번역 KMC에 대해 명시되지 않은 것은?
(A) 40년 이상 운영되었다.
(B) 환자의 만족도가 높다.
(C) 최근 새로운 지도자를 임명했다.
(D) 여러 해 동안 많은 상을 받았다.

해설 마지막 단락의 마지막 문장에서 지금까지 47년 동안 이 노력이 상당히 성공적이었다고 믿는다(For 47 years now, I believe we have been quite successful in this endeavour)고 했으므로 (A), 첫 단락 두 번째 문장에서 상을 받기 위해서 병원들은 뛰어난 환자 만족도를 포함한 일련의 기준을 충족해야 한다(To qualify for the award, hospitals must meet a set of criteria, including ~ exceptional patient satisfaction)고 했으므로 (B), 세 번째 단락의 첫 문장에서 지난 3월에 KMC의 CEO가 된 린 응우옌 박사(Dr. Linh Nguyen, who became CEO of KMC last March)라고 했으므로 (C)가 명시되어 있지만, 많은 상을 받았다는 내용은 없으므로 (D)가 정답이다.

어휘 operation 운영 decade 10년 appoint 임명하다

163 동의어 찾기

번역 세 번째 단락 5행의 "reflects"와 의미가 가장 가까운 단어는?
(A) 보여주다
(B) 알아차리다
(C) 모방하다
(D) 추천하다

해설 의미상 이 상이 환자의 건강을 모든 일의 중심에 두겠다는 KMC의 전념을 '반영한다'는 뜻으로 쓰였으므로 '보여주다'를 뜻하는 (A) shows가 정답이다.

164-167 온라인 채팅

> **알렉사 발로그 (오후 4시 2분)**
> 저는 오늘 로즈무어 공원에서 안전 요원 근무 중이에요. 제이미 커가 저에게 대신 근무해 달라고 부탁했거든요. 날씨가 나빠서 수영장을 여러 번 닫아야 했다는 점을 알려드려요.
>
> **맥스웰 디에고 (오후 4시 3분)**
> 지금 날씨가 안 좋은가요?
>
> **알렉사 발로그 (오후 4시 3분)**
> 아니요, 하지만 약 20분 전에는 비가 심하게 내렸어요.
>
> **맥스웰 디에고 (오후 4시 4분)**
> 그러면 다시 열기 전에 10분 더 기다리셔야 해요. 164 아시다시피 풀 가디언 안전 요원의 규정은 악천후가 지나고 30분간 기다리는 것입니다.
>
> **알렉사 발로그 (오후 4시 6분)**
> 네, 알겠습니다. 하지만 165 2시 30분 이후로 여기에 아무도 없었어요. 지금 수영장을 닫아도 될까요?
>
> **맥스웰 디에고 (오후 4시 7분)**
> 그래도 되겠네요. 그에 관한 우리의 방침은 무엇인가요, 놀란 씨?
>
> **웨이드 놀란 (오후 4시 8분)**
> 안타깝지만 그럴 수 없어요. 166 당사 계약에 따르면 목요일마다 오후 5시까지 로즈무어 공원에 안전 요원을 제공해야 해요. 따라서 알렉사가 남아 있어야 해요.
>
> **알렉사 발로그 (오후 4시 9분)**
> 알겠습니다. 167 저는 지금 장비 창고에 있어요. 여기를 청소하고 수영장 용품을 정리정돈하고 있어요.
>
> **웨이드 놀란 (오후 4시 10분)**
> 하지만 4시 30분 이후에 다시 비가 많이 내릴 경우에는 그냥 수영장을 닫도록 하세요, 알렉사.
>
> **맥스웰 디에고 (오후 4시 10분)**
> 167 이제 거기가 아주 말끔하겠네요.
>
> **알렉사 발로그 (오후 4시 11분)**
> 이렇게 좋아 보인 적이 없었어요. 그리고 감사합니다, 놀란 씨.

어휘 lifeguard 안전 요원 on duty 근무 중인 fill in for ~을 대신하다 shed 창고 straighten up ~을 깨끗이 정리하다 supplies 용품 spotless 티끌 하나 없는

164 추론 / 암시

번역 발로그 씨에 대해 결론 내릴 수 있는 것은?
(A) 폭우를 두려워한다.
(B) 수영장을 청소하기 위해 고용되었다.
(C) 풀 가디언의 직원이다.
(D) 매주 목요일 로즈무어 공원에서 근무한다.

해설 4시 4분에 디에고 씨가 발로그 씨에게 풀 가디언 안전 요원의 규정은 악천후가 지나고 30분간 기다리는 것(As you know, the rule for Pool Guardian lifeguards is to wait for 30 minutes after bad weather passes)이라고 설명하는 것으로 보아, 발로그 씨가 풀 가디언의 안전 요원이라는 것을 짐작할 수 있다. 따라서 (C)가 정답이다.

165 세부 사항

번역 발로그 씨가 수영장을 일찍 닫고 싶어 하는 이유는?
(A) 모든 업무를 완료했기 때문에
(B) 커 씨가 도착하지 않았기 때문에
(C) 수영을 할 수 없기 때문에
(D) 현재 수영장을 이용하는 손님이 없기 때문에

해설 4시 6분에 발로그 씨가 2시 30분 이후로 여기에 아무도 없었다(no one has been here since 2:30)면서 지금 수영장을 닫아도 될지(Can I close the pool now?)를 묻고 있으므로 (D)가 정답이다.

어휘 currently 현재

166 추론 / 암시

번역 로즈무어 공원에 대해 암시된 것은?
(A) 안전 요원을 제공하는 회사와 계약을 맺고 있다.
(B) 수영장이 일주일 내내 문을 닫았다.
(C) 수영장이 형편없이 관리되고 있다.
(D) 발로그 씨를 정규직으로 고용하고 싶어 한다.

해설 4시 8분에 놀란 씨가 당사 계약에 따르면 목요일마다 오후 5시까지 로즈무어 공원에 안전 요원을 제공해야 한다(Our contract says we must supply Rosemoor Park with a lifeguard until 5 P.M. on Thursdays)고 언급한 것으로 보아, 로즈무어 공원은 안전 요원을 제공하는 회사와 계약을 맺고 있다는 것을 알 수 있다. 따라서 (A)가 정답이다.

어휘 provide 제공하다

167 의도 파악

번역 오후 4시 11분에 발로그 씨가 "이렇게 좋아 보인 적이 없었어요"라고 쓴 의도는?
(A) 수영장 데크를 청소했다.
(B) 장비 창고 정리를 잘 했다.
(C) 마침내 비가 그쳤다.
(D) 수영장의 물이 매우 맑다.

해설 4시 9분에 발로그 씨가 지금 장비 창고에 있으며(I'm in the equipment shed) 여기를 청소하고 수영장 용품을 정리정돈하고 있다(I've been cleaning it up and straightening up the pool supplies here)고 했고, 4시 10분에 디에고 씨가 이제 거기가 아주 말끔하겠다(It must be spotless now)고 하자, 4시 11분에 발로그 씨가 이렇게 좋아 보인 적이 없었다(It has never looked so good)고 대답한 것이므로, 발로그 씨는 장비 창고가 깨끗하게 정리되었음을 알려 주려는 의도로 한 말임을 알 수 있다. 따라서 (B)가 정답이다.

어휘 organize 정리하다

168-171 웹페이지

https://www.sagemontservices.com

| 홈 | 소개 | IT 서비스 | 고객 추천글 |

168 세이지몬트 서비스에서는 다양한 산업의 고객들에게 맞춤형 정보 기술 해결책을 제공합니다. 20년보다 더 전에 설립된 세이지몬트 서비스는 경쟁으로 가득한 분야에서 대기업들과 경쟁하는 신생 업체로 시작했습니다. 그 후 우리는 업계의 선두 주자가 되었습니다. 우리의 전문 직원들은 우리 서비스의 모든 측면에서 다방면으로 훈련받고 있습니다.

169 우리는 지난 몇 달 동안 여러 기업들이 마감 기한이 빠듯한 기술 프로젝트를 완수하는 것을 도왔습니다. 예를 들어, **170** 온라인 소매업체인 클로딩 디스카운터스가 빠르게 사업을 확장하는 동안, 우리는 이 회사의 콜센터 역량을 높이도록 도왔습니다. 구체적으로, **171** 단 이틀 만에 우리는 새로 채용된 고객 서비스 직원들이 재택으로 전화를 처리할 수 있도록 모든 장비와 연결을 이 회사에 제공했습니다. 이 해결책은 사업에 방해가 되는 가능성을 제거해 주었습니다.

우리가 고객들의 요구를 어떻게 충족하는지에 대해 더 알아보시려면, 고객 추천글 페이지를 방문해 주세요.

어휘 testimonial 추천글 custom-tailored 맞춤형의 various 다양한 found 설립하다 start-up 신생 업체 compete 경쟁하다 field 분야 subsequently 그 후 expert 전문적인 cross-train 다방면으로 훈련하다 aspect 측면 retailer 소매업체 rapidly 빠르게 expand 확장하다 capability 역량 connection 연결

168 세부 사항

번역 세이지몬트 서비스는 어떤 종류의 사업체인가?
(A) 기술 컨설팅 회사
(B) 전화 서비스 제공업체
(C) 컴퓨터 소프트웨어 공급업체
(D) 임원 채용 서비스 업체

해설 첫 단락 첫 문장에서 세이지몬트 서비스에서는 다양한 산업의 고객들에게 맞춤형 정보 기술 해결책을 제공한다(At Sagemont Services, we offer custom-tailored information technology solutions to clients in various industries)고 했으므로 (A)가 정답이다.

어휘 executive 임원 recruit 채용하다, 모집하다

169 세부 사항

번역 웹페이지에 따르면, 세이지몬트 서비스가 최근에 한 일은?
(A) 일련의 온라인 워크숍을 개발했다.
(B) 추가 직원을 고용했다.
(C) 본사 내 일부 공간을 업데이트했다.
(D) 짧은 기간 내에 프로젝트를 완료했다.

해설 두 번째 단락 첫 문장에서 지난 몇 달 동안 여러 기업들이 마감 기한이 빠듯한 기술 프로젝트를 완수하는 것을 도왔다(We have helped several businesses complete technology projects on tight deadlines in the past few months)고 했으므로 (D)가 정답이다.

Paraphrasing
지문의 on tight deadlines
→ 정답의 within a short time period

170 Not / True

번역 클로딩 디스카운터스에 대해 명시된 것은?
(A) 상을 받았다.
(B) 빠르게 성장하고 있다.
(C) 1년이 안 된 업체이다.
(D) 오프라인 매장을 열 계획이다.

해설 두 번째 단락의 두 번째 문장에서 온라인 소매업체인 클로딩 디스카운터스가 빠르게 사업을 확장하는 동안(with the online retailer Clothing Discounters rapidly expanding)이라고 언급하고 있으므로 (B)가 정답이다.

어휘 win an award 상을 받다

Paraphrasing
지문의 rapidly expanding → 정답의 growing quickly

171 문장 삽입

번역 [1], [2], [3], [4]로 표시된 위치 중에서 다음 문장이 들어가기에 가장 적합한 곳은?

"이 해결책은 사업에 방해가 되는 가능성을 제거해 주었습니다."
(A) [1]
(B) [2]
(C) [3]
(D) [4]

해설 주어진 문장에서 이 해결책(This solution)은 사업에 방해가 되는 가능성을 제거해 주었다고 했으므로, 주어진 문장 앞에는 이 해결책에 대한 내용이 있어야 한다. 따라서 짧은 기간 내에 신입 직원들이 재택으로 업무를 처리할 수 있도록 장비와 서비스를 제공했다며, 세이지몬트 서비스에서 제공한 해결책 뒤인 [3]에 들어가는 것이 글의 흐름상 자연스러우므로 (C)가 정답이다.

어휘 eliminate 제거하다   disruption 방해

172-175 기사

▶ 동영상 강의

MCAC, 알론소 작품 전시한다

모렐리 시 (8월 29일) — 재활용 재료를 사용하는 작업이 예술가들에게 인기를 얻고 있고, 지역 조각가인 아이다 알론소도 이 트렌드를 기꺼이 받아들였다. 모렐리 시 미술관(MCAC)에서 174 **그녀의 새로운 전시 <폐물에서 보물로>가 오늘부터 11월 4일까지 열린다.** 172 알론소 씨는 <전문 조경 건축가 저널>에서 재활용 플라스틱을 공원 벤치로 만드는 것에 대해 읽던 도중 프로젝트에 대한 아이디어를 떠올렸다. 그 후 그녀는 오래된 플라스틱 병과 종이 택배 상자를 수집하기 시작했고, 이를 상업적으로 제작된 재활용 건축 자재와 획기적으로 결합시켰다.

전시를 위해 알론소 씨는 재생 재료로 만든 칸막이 공간 및 파티션이 있는 실물 크기의 상업용 사무실 모형을 제작했다. "인공 사무 공간을 이용해서, 저는 낡고 필요 없는 물건이 새로운 용도를 가질 수 있다는 아이디어를 강조하고 싶어요."라고 알론소 씨는 말했다. 173 **전시회에 참석한 관람객들은 재활용 가능한 플라스틱 용품을 가져와서 전시실 주변에 설치된 대형 수거 가방에 넣을 기회를 갖게 된다.** 알론소 씨는 또한 전시가 진행되면서 더 많은 재활용 재료를 자신의 설치물에 추가할 계획이다.

MCAC가 알론소 씨의 유일한 전시 장소이기는 하지만 전시는 다른 방식으로 옮겨갈 것으로 예상된다. 174 **전시의 마지막 날, 작품들은 해체될 예정이며 방문객이 가져온 용품을 포함한 모든 재활용 재료는 플라이너 인더스트리즈 시설로 운반되어 잘게 잘려서 방수 커튼 재료로 변형될 것이다.**

MCAC는 매일 오전 10시부터 오후 5시까지 운영된다. 미술관 입장은 무료이다. 알론소 씨의 전시 외에도 175 **여러 지역 미술 학생들의 작품이 MCAC의 메인 갤러리에서 전시될 예정이다.**

어휘 material 재료   sculptor 조각가   embrace 받아들이다   throwaway 버리는 물건   treasure 보물   landscape 조경   architect 건축가   cardboard 판지   innovatively 혁신적으로   combine 결합하다   commercially 상업적으로   life-size 실물 크기의   cubicle (칸막이 해 만든) 좁은 공간   by means of ~을 이용해서, ~에 의하여   synthetic 인공의   take on (특정 특징이나 태도를) 띠다, 갖추다   purpose 용도   perimeter 주변   installation 설치   progress 진행되다   venue 장소   dismantle 해체하다   shred 잘게 자르다   transform 변형시키다   admission 입장(료)

172 Not / True

번역 알론소 씨에 대해 명시된 것은?
(A) 자신이 소유한 미술 갤러리를 운영한다.
(B) 이전에 배송 회사에서 근무했다.
(C) 업계 간행물의 기사에서 영감을 받았다.
(D) 인테리어 디자이너로 시간제 근무를 한다.

해설 첫 단락의 세 번째 문장에서 알론소 씨는 <전문 조경 건축가 저널>에서 재활용 플라스틱을 공원 벤치로 만드는 것에 대해 읽던 도중 프로젝트에 대한 아이디어를 떠올렸다(Ms. Alonso had the idea for the project while reading about recycled plastic being made into park benches in the Journal for Professional Landscape Architects)고 했으므로 (C)가 정답이다.

어휘 previously 이전에   inspire 영감을 주다

Paraphrasing
지문의 had the idea → 정답의 was inspired
지문의 Journal → 정답의 publication

173 세부 사항

번역 기사에 따르면, 알론소 씨의 전시 방문객들은 무엇을 할 수 있는가?
(A) 지역 예술가들을 직접 만나기
(B) 재활용 가능한 플라스틱을 가져다 놓기
(C) 특수 사무 장비 조작
(D) 재활용된 종이 제품 구매

해설 두 번째 단락의 세 번째 문장에서 전시회에 참석한 관람객들은 재활용 가능한 플라스틱 용품을 가져와서 전시실 주변에 설치된 대형 수거 가방에 넣을 기회를 갖게 된다(Guests who attend the art show will have the opportunity to bring in their own recyclable plastic items and place them in large collection bags set up around the perimeter of the exhibition room)고 했으므로 (B)가 정답이다.

어휘 in person 직접   drop off ~을 내려놓다   operate 조작하다   specialized 특수한   repurpose 다른 용도로 고치다

174 세부 사항

번역 11월 4일에 발생할 일은?
(A) 전시 구성물이 산업 공장으로 옮겨질 것이다.
(B) 재활용에 관한 영화 몇 편이 상영될 것이다.
(C) 슬로건 공모전의 수상자가 발표될 것이다.
(D) 미술관이 보수 공사를 위해 폐관할 것이다.

해설 첫 단락의 두 번째 문장에서 알론소 씨의 새로운 전시 〈폐물에서 보물로〉가 오늘부터 11월 4일까지 열린다(Her new exhibition, Throwaways into Treasure, runs from today until November 4)고 했고, 세 번째 단락의 두 번째 문장에서 전시의 마지막 날 작품들은 해체될 예정이며 방문객이 가져온 용품을 포함한 모든 재활용 재료는 플라이너 인더스트리즈 시설로 운반된다(On the exhibition's final day, the works will be dismantled, and all the recyclable materials, including the items brought by visitors, will be transported to a Flyner Industries facility)고 했다. 따라서 전시 마지막 날인 11월 4일에는 전시물이 해체되어 공장으로 보내질 예정이므로 (A)가 정답이다.

어휘 renovation 보수

> **Paraphrasing**
> 지문의 transported to a Flyner Industries facility
> → 정답의 taken to an industrial plant

175 Not / True

번역 MCAC에 대해 명시된 것은?
(A) 방문하려면 예약이 필요하다.
(B) 입장료를 부과한다.
(C) 미술 학생들의 작품을 전시한다.
(D) 자체적인 미술 워크숍을 후원한다.

해설 마지막 단락 마지막 문장에서 여러 지역 미술 학생들의 작품이 MCAC의 메인 갤러리에서 전시될 예정(works by several local art students will be on view in MCAC's main gallery)이라고 했으므로 (C)가 정답이다.

어휘 sponsor 후원하다

> **Paraphrasing**
> 지문의 be on view → 정답의 displays

176-180 표 + 기사

슈퍼브 호텔 — 리스본
176 고객 설문조사 결과 / 6월

주요점	만족도	176 5월 대비 변화
객실	91퍼센트	+8퍼센트 ↑
조식	82퍼센트	+10퍼센트 ↑
접수처	80퍼센트	-5퍼센트 ↓
176 전반적인 경험	87퍼센트	176 +7퍼센트 ↑

177 수집 및 분석: 179 나오미 아크데미르, 고객 지원 부서, 엑셀레이트 사

어휘 satisfaction 만족 overall 전반적인 analyse 분석하다

엑셀레이트 사, 본사 이전하다

토론토 (179 7월 3일) — 소비자 분석 대기업 엑셀레이트가 곧 토론토에 새로운 본사 건축을 시작할 예정이다. 많은 유명 기업들이 고객의 경험을 정확하게 이해하기 위해 엑셀레이트의 서비스를 이용하고 있다. 이 기업의 북미 시장 진입은 향후 예상되는 성장의 유망한 신호이다. 179 최근 승진한 개발 부사장 로사 마틴은 이번 달 말, 프랑크푸르트에 있는 엑셀레이트의 현재 본사에서 고객 지원 팀을 운영하는 업무를 마무리하는 대로 이번 확장을 178 총괄할 예정이다.

180 새로운 사무실 건물은 프랑크 츠다마가 설계했으며, 그의 최근 프로젝트에는 서울의 미래파적인 글로벌 무역 센터가 포함되어 있다. 엑셀레이트의 건물에는 대중이 이용할 수 있는 좌석 구역이 딸린 1층 마당이 포함될 예정이며, 이는 지역사회로의 편입을 상징한다. 엑셀레이트와 같은 기업의 설립은 데이터 및 경영 컨설팅의 중심지로서 토론토의 명성을 공고히 하는 데 도움이 될 것이다.

어휘 relocate 이전하다 giant 대기업 headquarters 본사 obtain 얻다 accurate 정확한 promising 유망한 direct 총괄하다 expansion 확장 wrap up ~을 마무리하다 involve 포함하다 futurist 미래파 ground-level 1층 courtyard 마당 symbolise 상징하다 insertion 편입 establishment 설립 cement 공고히 하다, 굳히다 fame 명성

176 Not / True

번역 표에서 전반적인 경험에 관한 고객들의 만족도에 대해 명시하는 것은?
(A) 마케팅 자료에서 언급된다.
(B) 이전 달보다 더 좋다.
(C) 분기별로 보고된다.
(D) 6월에 5퍼센트 감소했다.

해설 표의 상단에 6월 고객 설문조사 결과(Customer Survey Results / June)라고 나와 있고, 표의 전반적인 경험(Overall experience) 항목이 5월 대비 변화(Change from May) 수치에서 7퍼센트 올랐다고 표기되어 있으므로 이전 달보다 향상되었음을 알 수 있다. 따라서 (B)가 정답이다.

어휘 material 자료 previous 이전의 quarterly 분기의

177 추론 / 암시

번역 엑셀레이트에 대해 암시된 것은?
(A) 데이터를 수집하고 분석한다.
(B) 호텔 체인이다.
(C) 산업용 건물을 개조한다.
(D) 토론토에서 설립되었다.

해설 표의 하단에 엑셀레이트 사 고객 지원 부서의 나오미 아크데미르가 설문조사 결과를 수집하고 분석(Collected and analysed by Naomi Akdemir, Customer Solutions, Exelrate)한 것으로 나와 있으므로 엑셀레이트는 고객에게 필요한 데이터를 수집 및

분석하는 서비스를 제공한다는 것을 짐작할 수 있다. 따라서 (A)가 정답이다.

어휘 renovate 개조하다 industrial 산업의

178 동의어 찾기

번역 기사의 첫 번째 단락 10행의 "directing"과 의미가 가장 가까운 단어는?
(A) 목표로 하다
(B) 지휘하다
(C) 자금을 조달하다
(D) 해결하다

해설 최근 승진한 개발 부사장이 확장 프로젝트를 '총괄한다'는 뜻으로 쓰였으므로 '지휘하다'를 뜻하는 (B) leading이 정답이다.

179 연계

번역 7월에 아크데미르 씨의 상관은 어디에서 근무했는가?
(A) 토론토
(B) 리스본
(C) 프랑크푸르트
(D) 서울

해설 기사의 작성일이 7월 3일(3 July)이고, 첫 단락 마지막 문장에서 최근 승진한 개발 부사장 로사 마틴은 이번 달 말에 프랑크푸르트에 있는 엑셀레이트의 현재 본사에서 고객 지원 팀을 운영하는 업무를 마무리하는 대로 이번 확장을 총괄할 예정(The recently promoted vice president of development, Rosa Martin, will be directing this expansion once she wraps up her work running the Customer Solutions Team at Exelrate's current headquarters in Frankfurt at the end of this month)이라고 했다. 표의 하단에 나오미 아크데미르는 엑셀레이트 사의 고객 지원 부서(Naomi Akdemir, Customer Solutions, Exelrate) 소속이라고 나와 있다. 따라서 아크데미르가 있는 고객 지원 팀의 관리자 마틴 씨는 7월 현재 프랑크푸르트의 본사에서 근무하고 있으므로 (C)가 정답이다.

180 세부 사항

번역 츠다마 씨의 전문 분야는 무엇인가?
(A) 경영 컨설팅
(B) 관광
(C) 건축
(D) 접객

해설 기사의 두 번째 단락 첫 문장에서 새로운 사무실 건물은 프랭크 츠다마가 설계했으며, 그의 최근 프로젝트에는 서울의 미래파적인 글로벌 무역 센터가 포함되어 있다(The new office building was designed by Frank Tsudama, whose latest project involved Seoul's futurist Global Trade Centre)고 했으므로 (C)가 정답이다.

어휘 architecture 건축 hospitality 접객

181-185 공지 + 후기

리치몬드 슈퍼마켓에 오신 것을 환영합니다!
알고 계셨나요?

181 리치몬드 슈퍼마켓은 이제 저희의 최신식 주방에서 요리 수업을 제공하며, 이 주방은 저희 조리 식품 부서에서 맛있는 수프와 샐러드, 메인 요리를 만드는 바로 그 주방입니다. 매주 월요일 저녁 7시부터 8시 30분까지 리치몬드의 여러 훌륭한 식당 중 한 곳에서 온 초청 요리사에게 저희 주방을 맡깁니다. 참가자들은 매주 다른 요리를 조리하는 것을 배웁니다. 집으로 가져갈 수 있는 새로운 기술을 배워서 당신의 친구와 가족을 즐겁게 해주세요! 모든 수업에서는 바로 이 매장에서 구할 수 있는 재료를 사용합니다.

이번 달 수업은 다음과 같습니다:

182	8월 2일	버터 치킨 (인도)
182	8월 9일	팟타이 (태국)
182, 183	8월 16일	피시 타코 (멕시코)
182	8월 23일	구운 야채 라자냐 (이탈리아)

각 수업의 수강료는 55달러입니다. 등록하시려면 604-555-0175로 전화 주시거나 www.richmondsupermarket.ca를 방문해 주세요. 각 수업당 학생은 15명으로 제한됩니다. 수업이 빠르게 마감되므로 오늘 당신의 자리를 예약하세요.

어휘 state-of-the-art 최신식의 flavourful 맛있는 entrée 메인 요리 participant 참가자 delight 즐겁게 하다 ingredient 재료 roast 구운 register 등록하다 reserve 예약하다 spot 자리

https://www.richmondsupermarket.ca/reviews

| 온라인 쇼핑 | 문의처 | 후기 | 요리 수업 |

리치몬드 슈퍼마켓의 새로운 요리 수업 덕분에, 지역 주민들은 이 지역 최고의 요리사들로부터 수업을 들을 수 있습니다. 지난주에 저는 베르날즈 레스토랑의 수석 주방장인 마테오 베르날과 함께 183 **피시 타코를 조리하는 법을 배웠습니다. 184 옥수수 또띠아, 구운 틸라피아, 토마틸로 살사를 포함해 타코의 모든 요소를 처음부터 만들었습니다.** 떠나기 전에, 각 참가자는 그날 우리가 만든 조리법뿐만 아니라 베르날 씨가 아끼는 다른 조리법 몇 가지가 들어 있는 작은 노트를 받았습니다. 185 **저는 월요일 저녁마다 일정을 비워서 다시 계속해서 가려고 합니다!**

– 아스트리드 클라인

어휘 component 요소 from scratch 맨 처음부터 grilled 구운 attendee 참가자 contain 포함하다

181 추론 / 암시

번역 공지는 누구를 대상으로 하는 것 같은가?
(A) 주방 직원
(B) 매장 고객
(C) 식당 요리사
(D) 요리책 작가

해설 공지의 첫 단락 첫 문장에서 리치몬드 슈퍼마켓이 이제 최신식 주방에서 요리 수업을 제공하며, 이 주방은 조리 식품 부서에서 맛있는 수프와 샐러드, 메인 요리를 만드는 바로 그 주방(Richmond Supermarket is now offering cooking classes in our own state-of-the-art kitchen, the same kitchen where we create flavourful soups, salads, and entrées for our prepared foods department)이라고 한 것으로 보아, 공지는 리치몬드 슈퍼마켓의 매장 이용객들을 대상으로 요리 수업을 홍보하기 위한 것임을 알 수 있다. 따라서 (B)가 정답이다.

어휘 author 작가

182 Not / True

번역 공지에서 리치몬드 슈퍼마켓의 8월 요리 수업에 대해 명시하는 것은?
(A) 여러 나라의 요리를 포함한다.
(B) 한 주의 다른 날에 열린다.
(C) 슈퍼마켓 직원들이 가르친다.
(D) 학생들이 직접 등록해야 한다.

해설 공지의 중반부에 이번 달 수업이 8월 2일에는 인도의 버터 치킨(2 August, Butter Chicken (India)), 8월 9일에는 태국의 팟타이(9 August, Pad Thai (Thailand)), 8월 16일에는 멕시코의 피시 타코(16 August, Fish Tacos (Mexico)), 8월 23일에는 이탈리아의 구운 야채 라자냐(23 August, Roast Vegetable Lasagna (Italy))라고 열거되어 있으므로 8월에는 여러 나라의 요리를 다룬다는 것을 알 수 있다. 따라서 (A)가 정답이다.

어휘 feature 포함하다 in person 직접, 대면으로

183 연계

번역 클라인 씨는 언제 리치몬드 슈퍼마켓 요리 수업에 참여했을 것 같은가?
(A) 8월 2일
(B) 8월 9일
(C) 8월 16일
(D) 8월 23일

해설 후기의 두 번째 문장에서 클라인 씨가 피시 타코를 조리하는 법을 배웠다(I learned how to prepare fish tacos)고 했고, 공지의 중반부에 8월 16일에는 멕시코의 피시 타코(16 August, Fish Tacos (Mexico)) 수업을 한다고 나와 있다. 따라서 클라인 씨는 8월 16일 수업에 참석했다는 것을 알 수 있으므로 (C)가 정답이다.

184 Not / True

번역 후기에서 언급된 재료가 아닌 것은?
(A) 옥수수 또띠아
(B) 구운 틸라피아
(C) 토마틸로 살사
(D) 채 썬 양배추

해설 후기의 세 번째 문장에서 옥수수 또띠아, 구운 틸라피아, 토마틸로 살사를 포함해 타코의 모든 요소를 처음부터 만들었다(We made every component of the tacos from scratch, including the corn tortillas, grilled tilapia, and tomatillo salsa)며 (A), (B), (C)를 모두 언급했고, 양배추에 대한 내용은 없으므로 (D)가 정답이다.

어휘 shred 채를 썰다

185 세부 사항

번역 클라인 씨는 무엇을 할 계획이라고 말하는가?
(A) 멕시코로 여행 가기
(B) 베르날즈 레스토랑에서 식사하기
(C) 더 많은 요리 수업에 참석하기
(D) 노트에 조리법 모으기

해설 후기의 마지막 문장에서 클라인 씨가 월요일 저녁마다 일정을 비워서 다시 계속해서 가려고 한다(I'm going to clear my Monday evenings so I can go back again and again!)고 했으므로 클라인 씨는 앞으로도 계속 요리 수업에 참석할 계획임을 알 수 있다. 따라서 (C)가 정답이다.

186-190 기사 + 일정표 + 이메일

연구소에 새로운 학장이 임명되다

요크 (1월 17일) — 186 캘러드 안과 연구소는 화요일에 제니퍼 로빈스 의학 박사가 즉시 발효되는 학장직을 수락했다고 발표했다.

로빈스 박사는 요크에서 자라, 라바토 의과 대학에서 의학 학위를 취득했으며 187 피터슨 메디컬 센터에서 박사 후 레지던트 과정을 마쳤다. 연구소에 오기 전, 로빈스 박사는 모스빌 병원의 안과 병동의 설립자이자 책임자였다. 안과 질환 치료에 있어 그녀의 혁신은 전 세계적으로 수천 명의 환자들에게 혜택을 주었다.

188 4월 17일에 로빈스 박사는 국제 시력 증진 센터의 올해 컨퍼런스에서 크라머 우수 의학 메달을 받기 위해 베를린에 머물 예정이다.

어휘 dean 학장 appoint 임명하다 institute 연구소 M.D. 의학 박사 accept 수락하다 effective 발효되는, 시행되는 immediately 즉시 degree 학위 postdoctoral 박사 후의 residency 레지던트 과정 founder 설립자 ophthalmology 안과학 innovation 혁신 treat 치료하다 disease 질환, 질병 benefit 혜택을 주다 vision 시력

국제 시력 증진 센터(ICVA) 컨퍼런스
JT 페퍼 컨벤션 홀 (4월 17일 – 19일)
로젠탈러 가 65번지, 베를린, 독일 25627

첫 날 일정: 4월 17일 월요일

오전 8시 – 10시	조식	마이발트 라운지
190 오전 10시 – 11시	환영 및 기조 연설	얀 컨퍼런스 홀
오전 11시 15분 – 오후 1시 15분	세션 1: 신기술	배정된 소회의실
오후 1시 30분 – 3시 30분	중식 그룹 세미나	에드워즈 룸
오후 3시 45분 – 5시 45분	세션 2: 양질의 안과 치료	배정된 소회의실

오후 6시 – 7시 30분	자유 시간	–
오후 7시 30분 – 9시	석식	리갈 볼룸
오후 9시 – 9시 30분	**188** 디저트 및 시상식	**188** 리갈 볼룸

> **어휘** keynote address 기조 연설 breakout room 소회의실
> assign 배정하다 quality 양질의, 고품질의

수신: 손대호
발신: 폴리나 라스킨
제목: 귀하의 발표
날짜: 4월 22일

손 박사님께,

189 지난주 베를린에서 열린 ICVA 컨퍼런스에서 연설을 해 주신 데 대해 다시 한번 감사드리고 싶었습니다. **190** 컨퍼런스의 하이라이트는 박사님의 기조 연설이었다고 말하는 사람이 저 혼자는 아닐 거라고 확신합니다. 안과 수술 기법의 최근 진보에 대한 박사님의 통찰력은 회의장의 모든 이들의 관심을 사로잡았습니다. 저희와 함께해 주신 데 감사드리며, ICVA 이사회 구성원으로 활동하시면서 그동안 제공해 주신 모든 지원과 지도에 더욱더 감사드립니다.

폴리나 라스킨
국제 시력 증진 센터 회장

> **어휘** insight 통찰력 surgery 수술 capture 사로잡다
> grateful 감사하는 appreciative 감사하는 guidance 지도

186 Not / True

번역 기사에서 로빈스 박사에 대해 명시된 것은?
(A) 새로운 일을 시작하고 있다.
(B) 요크에 집을 갖고 있다.
(C) 안경 디자인을 전문으로 한다.
(D) 베를린에서 수업을 가르친 적이 있다.

해설 기사의 첫 단락 첫 문장에서 캘러드 안과 연구소는 화요일에 제니퍼 로빈스 의학 박사가 즉시 발효되는 학장직을 수락했다고 발표했다(The Callard Eye Institute announced on Tuesday that Jennifer Robbins, M.D., has accepted the position of dean, effective immediately)고 했으므로 (A)가 정답이다.

어휘 specialize in ~을 전문으로 하다

> **Paraphrasing**
> 지문의 has accepted the position
> → 정답의 starting a new job

187 세부 사항

번역 로빈스 박사는 박사 후 레지던트 과정을 어디에서 수료했는가?
(A) 캘러드 안과 연구소
(B) 라바토 의과 대학
(C) 피터슨 메디컬 센터
(D) 모스빌 병원

해설 기사의 두 번째 단락 첫 문장에서 로빈스 박사는 피터슨 메디컬 센터에서 박사 후 레지던트 과정을 마쳤다(completed a postdoctoral residency at Petersen Medical Center)고 했으므로 (C)가 정답이다.

188 연계

번역 로빈스 박사는 크라머 메달을 어디에서 받았을 것 같은가?
(A) 마이발트 라운지
(B) 얀 컨퍼런스 홀
(C) 에드워즈 룸
(D) 리갈 볼룸

해설 기사의 마지막 단락에서 4월 17일에 로빈스 박사는 국제 시력 증진 센터의 올해 컨퍼런스에서 크라머 우수 의학 메달을 받기 위해 베를린에 머물 예정(On April 17, Dr. Robbins will be in Berlin to receive the Kramer Medal for Medical Excellence at this year's conference of the International Center for Vision Advancement)이라고 했고, 일정표 하단에 시상식은 리갈 볼룸에서 열린다(Dessert and awards ceremony, Regal Ballroom)고 나와 있다. 따라서 로빈스 박사는 리갈 볼룸에서 메달을 받을 예정임을 알 수 있으므로 (D)가 정답이다.

189 주제 / 목적

번역 라스킨 씨가 손 박사에게 이메일을 보낸 이유는?
(A) ICVA 이사회에 가입해 줄 것을 요청하려고
(B) 컨퍼런스에서 연설하도록 초대하려고
(C) 수술 기법에 대해 정보를 요청하려고
(D) 행사 참여에 대한 감사를 표하려고

해설 이메일의 첫 문장에서 라스킨 씨가 손 박사에게 지난주 베를린에서 열린 ICVA 컨퍼런스에서 연설해 준 것에 대해 다시 한번 감사드리고 싶었다(I just wanted to thank you again for speaking at the ICVA conference in Berlin last week)고 했으므로 (D)가 정답이다.

어휘 surgical 수술의 gratitude 감사 participation 참여

190 연계

번역 손 박사는 4월 17일에 언제 연설을 했을 것 같은가?
(A) 오전 8시
(B) 오전 10시
(C) 오전 11시 15분
(D) 오후 3시 45분

해설 이메일의 두 번째 문장에서 라스킨 씨가 손 박사에게 컨퍼런스의 하이라이트는 박사의 기조 연설이었다(the highlight of the conference was your keynote address)고 했고, 일정표의 상단에 기조 연설은 오전 10시에 시작한다(10:00-11:00 A.M., Welcome and keynote address)고 나와 있다. 따라서 (B)가 정답이다.

191-195 웹페이지 + 이메일 + 이메일

https://www.freewheeoasis.com/trade-in-and-consignment

| 홈 | 서비스 및 수리 | 보상 및 위탁 판매 | 부대용품 |

프리휠 오아시스는 자전거 판매를 더 쉽게 해주는 두 가지 프로그램인 보상 판매와 위탁 판매를 제공합니다. 보상 판매 프로그램을 선택하실 경우, 고객님의 자전거를 저희에게 주시고 그 대가로 저희는 새 자전거 구매 시 사용할 수 있는 적립금을 드립니다. 위탁 판매 프로그램을 선택하실 경우, 저희가 고객님 대신 자전거를 판매해 드립니다.

어느 옵션이든 이용하시려면 **195** programs@freewheeloasis.com으로 이메일을 보내 예약을 잡으세요. 이메일에 자전거를 보상 판매할 것인지 위탁 판매할 것인지도 명시해야 합니다. **195 고객님께서는 저희 고객 서비스 관리자로부터 응답을 받게 됩니다.** 저희는 월요일부터 토요일, 오전 9시부터 오후 5시까지, 정규 영업시간 동안 예약을 받습니다.

191 예약에 맞춰 방문하시면, 기술자가 고객님의 자전거 상태를 평가하고 영업 사원이 현재 가치를 결정할 것입니다. 제시된 가치가 만족스러우시고 자전거를 보상 판매하기를 원하실 경우, 저희는 새 자전거의 구매 가격에서 해당 금액을 차감해 드립니다. 고객님께서 위탁 판매 방식을 선호하실 경우, 저희는 합의된 금액으로 고객님의 자전거를 판매해 드립니다. 참고로, **193 고객님의 자전거가 판매되면 그 금액의 15퍼센트에 상응하는 서비스 수수료를 제하고 나머지 수익금은 고객님께 송금된다는 점에 유의하십시오.**

어휘 trade-in 보상 판매 consignment 위탁 판매 accessories 부대용품 in exchange 그 대가로 credit 적립금 opt for ~을 선택하다 take advantage of ~을 이용하다 indicate 명시하다 response 응답 assess 평가하다 sales associate 영업 사원 determine 결정하다 current 현재의 value 가치 deduct 차감하다 arrangement (처리) 방식 withhold 공제하다, 원천징수하다

수신: programs@freewheeloasis.com
발신: 니콜라 존슨 <njohnson92@rapidonet.com>
날짜: 11월 2일
제목: 예약 요청

안녕하세요,

192 저는 현재 6년 된 산악자전거를 가지고 있습니다. 하지만 처음 3년 동안만 사용했습니다. 직접 팔려고 해 봤지만 성공하지 못하여, **193 귀사의 위탁 판매를 이용하고 싶습니다.** 따라서 예약을 잡기를 원합니다.

그리고, 저는 최근 쿠웨이트의 일자리를 수락해서 11월 30일에 떠날 예정입니다. 그때까지 자전거가 팔릴 것으로 예상하시나요? 그렇지 않다면 판매 가격 중 제 몫은 어떻게 받을 수 있나요?

니콜라 존슨

어휘 accept 수락하다 portion 몫, 부분

수신: 니콜라 존슨 <njohnson92@rapidonet.com>
발신: programs@freewheeloasis.com
날짜: 11월 2일
제목: 회신: 예약 요청

안녕하세요, 니콜라 씨,

프리휠 오아시스의 위탁 판매에 자전거를 맡기는 데 관심 가져 주셔서 감사합니다. 귀하의 예약은 11월 4일 금요일 오후 3시로 예정되었습니다. 이 일정이 괜찮은지 알려주세요.

194 저희 위탁 판매 정책에서는 자전거 판매가 마무리되는 즉시, 고객님께 지급되어야 할 금액은 고객님의 은행 계좌로 입금되어야 한다고 규정하고 있습니다. 프리휠 오아시스는 자전거 소유자가 명시한 날짜까지 자전거 판매를 보장할 수 없음을 유의해 주세요.

고객님의 새로운 시도에 행운이 따르기를 빕니다!

195 피터 모란

어휘 stipulate 규정하다 owed 지불해야 하는 guarantee 보장하다 specify 명시하다 endeavor 시도

191 추론 / 암시

번역 웹페이지에 따르면, 프리휠 오아시스에 대해 암시된 것은?
(A) 현재 중고 자전거 할인 행사를 하고 있다.
(B) 특정 자전거에 대해 검사를 수행한다.
(C) 최근 인기가 증가했다.
(D) 매일 영업한다.

해설 웹페이지의 세 번째 단락 첫 문장에서 예약에 맞춰 방문하면 기술자가 고객의 자전거 상태를 평가하고 영업 사원이 현재 가치를 결정할 것(When you come in for your appointment, a technician will assess the condition of your bicycle, and a sales associate will determine its current value)이라고 한 것을 통해, 프리휠 오아시스에서는 고객이 가져온 자전거에 대해 가치 평가를 위한 검사를 진행한다는 것을 알 수 있으므로 (B)가 정답이다.

192 Not / True

번역 존슨 씨는 그녀의 이메일에서 무엇을 명시하는가?
(A) 정기적으로 해외 여행을 한다.
(B) 6년 전에 자전거를 구입했다.
(C) 11월 30일 예약을 선호한다.
(D) 자전거를 직접 수리했다.

해설 첫 번째 이메일의 첫 단락 첫 문장에서 존슨 씨가 현재 6년 된 산악자전거를 가지고 있다(I have a mountain bicycle that is now six years old)고 했으므로 (B)가 정답이다.

Paraphrasing
지문의 have a mountain bicycle that is now six years old
→ 정답의 got her bicycle six years ago

TEST 10 213

193 연계

번역 존슨 씨에 대해 결론지을 수 있는 것은?
(A) 현재 쿠웨이트에서 근무 중이다.
(B) 이전에 프리휠 오아시스와 거래를 한 적이 있다.
(C) 프리휠 오아시스가 서비스 수수료를 부과하는 것에 동의했다.
(D) 프리휠 오아시스에서 자전거를 구입할 계획이다.

해설 웹페이지의 마지막 단락 마지막 문장에서 프리휠 오아시스는 고객의 자전거가 판매되면 그 금액의 15퍼센트에 상응하는 서비스 수수료를 제하고 나머지 수익금을 고객에게 송금한다(Note that we will withhold a service fee equal to 15 percent of this amount at the time your bicycle is sold, while the rest of the earnings will be sent to you)고 안내하고 있고, 첫 번째 이메일의 첫 단락 세 번째 문장에서 존슨 씨가 프리휠 오아시스의 위탁 판매를 이용하고 싶다(I would like to place it on consignment with you)고 했다. 존슨 씨가 프리휠 오아시스의 자전거 위탁 판매 서비스를 이용하기로 결정한 것으로 보아, 수수료를 지불하는 데 동의했다는 것을 알 수 있으므로 (C)가 정답이다.

어휘 currently 현재 charge 부과하다

194 주제 / 목적

번역 모란 씨가 쓴 이메일의 한 가지 목적은?
(A) 서비스 요청에 대한 추가 정보를 요청하려고
(B) 예약 변경을 요청하려고
(C) 서비스 완료일을 알리려고
(D) 회사 규정을 명시하려고

해설 두 번째 이메일의 두 번째 단락에서 위탁 판매 정책에서는 자전거 판매가 마무리되는 즉시, 고객에게 지급되어야 할 금액은 고객의 은행 계좌로 입금되어야 한다고 규정하고 있으며(Our consignment policy stipulates that once the sale of a bicycle has been finalized, the money owed to the customer must be paid into the person's bank account), 프리휠 오아시스는 자전거 소유자가 명시한 날짜까지 자전거 판매를 보장할 수 없음을 유의해 달라(Please note that Freewheel Oasis cannot guarantee the sale of a bicycle by a date specified by the bicycle owner)고 회사의 규정에 대해 설명하고 있다. 따라서 (D)가 정답이다.

어휘 completion 완료 state 명시하다

195 연계

번역 모란 씨는 누구인 것 같은가?
(A) 고객 서비스 관리자
(B) 은행 회계사
(C) 영업 사원
(D) 자전거 수리 기사

해설 웹페이지의 두 번째 단락 첫 문장에서 programs@freewheeloasis.com으로 이메일을 보내서 예약을 잡으라(e-mail us at programs@freewheeloasis.com to schedule an appointment)고 한 뒤, 같은 단락의 세 번째 문장에서 고객은 고객 서비스 관리자로부터 응답을 받게 된다(You will receive a response from our customer service manager)고 했다.

두 번째 이메일의 하단에 작성자가 피터 모란(Peter Moran)이라고 나와 있으므로, 모란 씨가 고객의 예약 요청 이메일에 응대하는 고객 서비스 관리자임을 알 수 있으므로 (A)가 정답이다.

196-200 이메일 + 점검 목록 + 이메일

수신: y.kuroda@coralmail.com
발신: simoncady@techsolve.com
197 날짜: 5월 12일, 오후 1시 30분
제목: 서류 작업
첨부: 📎 점검 목록

구로다 씨께,

196 귀하의 직원 파일에는 아직 몇 가지가 필요합니다. **196, 197** 오늘 아침 신입 사원 교육에서 파일에 필요한 서류의 점검 목록을 드렸습니다. 참고하시도록 이 이메일에 점검 목록의 스캔본을 첨부했습니다.

먼저, 우리 보안 사무실에서는 귀하의 신원에 대한 증명이 필요합니다. 직원들은 보통 운전면허증(앞면) 또는 여권의 개인 정보 페이지의 사본을 제출하지만, 공식적인 정부 발급 신분증은 어떤 것이든 가능합니다. 또한 귀하의 계좌로 급여가 전자 이체되도록 설정하기 위해 은행 정보가 필요합니다.

198 목록의 마지막 항목은 회사 소프트볼 팀에 가입할 경우에만 필요합니다. 소프트볼을 하시나요? 우리 회사 팀은 리그에 참가하고 있으며, 이는 함께 근무할 사람들과 관계를 형성하기 위한 훌륭한 방법입니다. 시즌이 막 시작되고 있습니다. 관심 있으시면 제가 자세한 내용을 보내드릴 수 있습니다.

마지막으로, 항상 5월 셋째 주 금요일에 브라이어우드 공원에서 열리는 회사 야유회에 참석하시기를 권장합니다. 이는 편안하고 업무에서 벗어난 환경에서 동료들과 교류할 수 있는 기회입니다. 늘 참석자가 많습니다.

질문이 있을 경우, 저에게 연락 주시면 대화 일정을 잡을 수 있습니다.

사이먼 케이디, 인사 부서
테크솔브 주식회사

어휘 personnel 직원 new hire 신입 사원 reference 참고 security 보안 proof 증명 identity 신원 official 공식적인 government 정부 identification 신분증 transfer 이체 participate in ~에 참가하다 rapport (친밀한) 관계 alongside 함께 encourage 권장하다 interact 교류하다 informal 편안한, 격식에 얽매이지 않는 nonworking 업무가 아닌

신입 직원 서류 점검 목록

이름: 유미코 구로다
부서: 데이터 입력
시작일: 5월 15일

____ 1. 신원 증명(운전면허증, 여권 또는 기타 공식 신분증 사본)
✓ 2. 개인 정보 양식
✓ 3. 세금 원천징수 양식
200 ____ 4. 은행 계좌 정보 양식
✓ 5. 보험 선택 양식
____ **198** 6. 책임 면제 양식(필요한 경우)

어휘	entry 입력 form 양식 withholding 원천징수 insurance 보험 selection 선택 liability 책임

수신: simoncady@techsolve.com
발신: y.kuroda@coralmail.com
날짜: 5월 12일, 오후 3시 21분
제목: 회신: 서류 작업

안녕하세요 케이디 씨,

이메일을 보내주셔서 감사합니다. 근무를 시작하기를 기대하고 있습니다. 그리고 오리엔테이션 때 받은 점검 목록의 사본을 보내주신 점도 감사드립니다. 저는 운전을 하지 않아 운전면허증은 없지만 제 여권의 사본을 드릴 수 있습니다. **200 목록의 네 번째 항목에 필요한 정보를 막 확보하려고 하고 있습니다.** 월요일에 전부 사무실로 가져가겠습니다.

회사 소프트볼 팀에 가입할지에 대해서는 생각해 봐야 할 것 같습니다. 시간을 얼마나 할애해야 하나요? 저는 대학에서 소프트볼을 했습니다. 잘 하지는 못했지만 하는 걸 좋아했습니다.

199 회사 야유회는 재미있을 것 같습니다. 저는 브라이어우드 공원을 좋아하고 동료들을 더 잘 알 수 있는 기회가 기대됩니다. 직원들이 야유회에 음식을 가져온다면, 저도 기꺼이 뭔가를 만들어 가겠습니다. 아니면 출장 요리 업체에서 음식을 제공하나요?

도움을 주셔서 다시 한번 감사드립니다.

유미코 구로다

어휘	be about to 막 ~하려고 하다 caterer 출장 요리 업체

196 주제 / 목적

번역 첫 번째 이메일의 주요 목적은?
(A) 구로다 씨에게 일자리를 제안하려고
(B) 몇몇 서류를 요청하려고
(C) 구로다 씨에게 구기 종목 경기를 보라고 초대하려고
(D) 약속을 잡으려고

해설 첫 번째 이메일의 첫 단락 첫 문장에서 귀하의 직원 파일에는 아직 몇 가지가 필요하다(We still need a few things for your personnel file)면서 오늘 아침 신입 사원 교육에서 파일에 필요한 서류의 점검 목록을 줬다(At the training for new hires this morning, we provided you with a checklist of the documents that we need to have on file)고 했다. 따라서 서류 제출을 요청하려는 이메일임을 알 수 있으므로 (B)가 정답이다.

197 추론 / 암시

번역 구로다 씨는 5월 12일 아침에 어디에 있었을 것 같은가?
(A) 신입 사원 교육
(B) 취업 면접
(C) 보안 사무실
(D) 대학 동창회

해설 첫 번째 이메일을 작성한 날짜가 5월 12일(Date: May 12)이고, 첫 단락 두 번째 문장에서 오늘 아침 신입 사원 교육에서 서류의 점검 목록을 줬다(At the training for new hires this morning, we provided you with a checklist of the documents)고 한 것을 통해 구로다 씨는 5월 12일 아침에 신입 사원 교육에 참석했다는 것을 알 수 있다. 따라서 (A)가 정답이다.

198 연계

번역 구로다 씨는 왜 면제 양식을 제출해야 할 수도 있는가?
(A) 돈을 빌릴 경우
(B) 스포츠 팀에서 경기할 경우
(C) 사교 행사에 참석할 경우
(D) 승진할 경우

해설 첫 번째 이메일의 세 번째 단락 첫 문장에서 목록의 마지막 항목은 회사 소프트볼 팀에 가입할 경우에만 필요하다(The final item on the list will only be needed if you join the company softball team)고 했고, 점검 목록의 마지막 항목은 6. 책임 면제 양식(필요한 경우)(6. Release of liability form (if required))이라고 나와 있다. 따라서 소프트볼 팀에서 운동을 할 경우에만 면제 양식을 제출해야 하므로 (B)가 정답이다.

199 Not / True

번역 구로다 씨가 회사 야유회에 대해 명시하는 것은?
(A) 어디에서 열리는지 모른다.
(B) 참석할 수 있을지 모른다.
(C) 거기서 동료들을 만나기를 간절히 바란다.
(D) 야유회를 위한 출장 요리 준비를 기꺼이 하겠다.

해설 두 번째 이메일의 세 번째 단락 첫 문장에서 구로다 씨가 회사 야유회는 재미있을 것 같다(The company picnic sounds like fun)고 한 뒤, 브라이어우드 공원을 좋아하고 동료들을 더 잘 알 수 있는 기회가 기대된다(I love Briarwood Park and look forward to the opportunity to get to know my coworkers better)고 했으므로 (C)가 정답이다.

200 연계

번역 구로다 씨는 다음에 무엇을 할 것 같은가?
(A) 동료들과 점심 식사하기
(B) 은행 계좌의 세부 정보 찾기
(C) 케이디 씨에게 목록을 이메일로 보내기
(D) 케이디 씨에게 여권 신청에 대해 문의하기

해설 두 번째 이메일의 첫 단락 다섯 번째 문장에서 구로다 씨가 목록의 네 번째 항목에 필요한 정보를 막 확보하려고 하고 있다(I am about to gather the necessary information for the fourth item on the list)고 했고, 점검 목록의 네 번째 항목은 은행 계좌 정보 양식(4. Bank account information form)이라고 나와 있다. 따라서 구로다 씨는 곧이어 은행 계좌 정보를 수집하려고 하고 있음을 알 수 있으므로 (B)가 정답이다.

어휘 apply for ~을 신청하다